Student Solutions Manual

to accompany

College Algebra

Ninth Edition

Raymond Barnett
Merritt College

Michael Ziegler
Marquette University

Karl Byleen
Marquette University

David Sobecki
Miami University

Prepared by
Fred Safier

Mc Graw Hill

Connect Learn Succeed™

The McGraw-Hill Companies

Student Solutions Manual to accompany
COLLEGE ALGEBRA, NINTH EDITION
RAYMOND BARNETT, MICHAEL ZIEGLER, KARL BYLEEN, AND DAVID SOBECKI

Published by McGraw-Hill Higher Education, an imprint of The McGraw-Hill Companies, Inc., 1221 Avenue of the Americas, New York, NY 10020. Copyright © 2011, 2008, 2001 by The McGraw-Hill Companies, Inc. All rights reserved.

 This book is printed on recycled, acid-free paper containing 10% post consumer waste.

1 2 3 4 5 6 7 8 9 0 WDQ/WDQ 10 9 8 7 6 5 4 3 2 1 0

ISBN: 978–0–07–729718–3
MHID: 0–07–729718–0

www.mhhe.com

TABLE OF CONTENTS

CHAPTER R

Section R-1

1. $\dfrac{1}{3} + \dfrac{1}{5} = \dfrac{1 \cdot 5 + 1 \cdot 3}{15} = \dfrac{8}{15}$

3. $\dfrac{3}{4} - \dfrac{4}{3} = \dfrac{3 \cdot 3 - 4 \cdot 4}{12} = -\dfrac{7}{12}$

5. $\dfrac{2}{3} \cdot \dfrac{4}{7} = \dfrac{8}{21}$

7. $\dfrac{11}{5} \div \dfrac{1}{3} = \dfrac{11}{5} \cdot \dfrac{3}{1} = \dfrac{33}{5}$

9. Division by zero is not defined. Undefined.

11. $\left(-\dfrac{3}{5}\right)\left(-\dfrac{5}{3}\right) = \dfrac{15}{15} = 1$

13. $\dfrac{17}{8} \cdot \dfrac{2}{7} = \dfrac{34}{56} = \dfrac{17}{28}$

15. $\left(\dfrac{3}{8}\right)^{-1} + 2^{-1} = \dfrac{8}{3} + \dfrac{1}{2} = \dfrac{16 + 3}{6} = \dfrac{19}{6}$

17. Commutative ($\cdot$)

19. Distributive

21. Inverse ($\cdot$)

23. Inverse (+)

25. Identity (+)

27. Negatives (Theorem 1)

29. Yes. This restates Zero Property (2). (Theorem 2, Part 2)

31. (A) True

    (B) False; $\dfrac{2}{3}$ is an example of a real number that is not rational.

    (C) True.

33. $\dfrac{3}{5}$ and -1.43 are two examples of infinitely many.

35. (A) $\left\{1, \sqrt{144}\right\}$

    (B) $\left\{-3, 0, 1, \sqrt{144}\right\}$

    (C) $\left\{-3, -\dfrac{2}{3}, 0, 1, \dfrac{9}{5}, \sqrt{144}\right\}$

    (D) $\left\{\sqrt{3}\right\}$

37. (A) 0.888 888…; repeating; repeated digit: 8
    (B) 0.272 727…; repeating; repeated digits: 27
    (C) 2.236 067 977…; nonrepeating and nonterminating
    (D) 1.375; terminating

39. (A) True; commutative property for addition.
    (B) False; for example: $3 - 5 \neq 5 - 3$.
    (C) True; commutative property for multiplication.
    (D) False; for example $9 \div 3 \neq 3 \div 9$.

41. F; $3 - 8 = -5$ is one of many counterexamples.

43. T

45. F; $\sqrt{2} \cdot \dfrac{\sqrt{2}}{2} = 1$ is one of many counterexamples.

47. T

49. Let $c = 0.090909\ldots$
    Then $100c = 9.0909\ldots$
    $100c - c = 9.0909\ldots - 0.090909\ldots$
    $99c = 9$
    $c = \dfrac{9}{99} = \dfrac{1}{11}$

Section R-2

1. 2187

3. $\left(\dfrac{1}{2}\right)^8 = \dfrac{1^8}{2^8} = \dfrac{1}{256}$

5. $6^{-3} = \dfrac{1}{6^3} = \dfrac{1}{216}$

7. 625

9. $(-3)^{-1} = \dfrac{1}{-3} = -\dfrac{1}{3}$

11. $-7^{-2} = -\dfrac{1}{7^2} = -\dfrac{1}{49}$

13. 1

15. $58{,}620{,}000 = 5.862 \times 10^7$

17. $0.027 = 2.7 \times 10^{-2}$

19. $0.000000064 = 6.4 \times 10^{-8}$

21. 0.004

23. 299,000

25. 0.00000031

27. $\sqrt[5]{32}$

29. $4x^{-1/2} = 4\sqrt{x^{-1}}$ or $\dfrac{4}{\sqrt{x}}$

31. $\sqrt[3]{x} - \sqrt[3]{y}$

33. $361^{1/2}$

35. $4xy^{3/5}$

37. $\left(x^2 + y^2\right)^{1/3}$

39. 10

41. 11

43. 5

45. -3

47. Undefined (not a real number)

49. $9^{-3/2} = \dfrac{1}{9^{3/2}} = \dfrac{1}{\left(9^{1/2}\right)^3} = \dfrac{1}{3^3} = \dfrac{1}{27}$

51. $x^5 x^{-2} = x^{5+(-2)} = x^3$

53. $(2y)\left(3y^2\right)\left(5y^4\right) = 2\cdot 3\cdot 5\, yy^2 y^4$
$= 30y^{1+2+4}$
$= 30y^7$

55. $\left(a^2 b^3\right)^5 = \left(a^2\right)^5 \left(b^3\right)^5 = a^{10} b^{15}$

57. $u^{1/3} u^{5/3} = u^{1/3+5/3} = u^{6/3} = u^2$

59. $\left(x^{-3}\right)^{1/6} = x^{-3/6} = x^{-1/2} = \dfrac{1}{x^{1/2}}$

61. $\left(\dfrac{m^{-2} n^3}{m^4 n^{-1}}\right)^2 = \left(\dfrac{n^3 n}{m^4 m^2}\right) = \left(\dfrac{n^4}{m^6}\right)^2 = \dfrac{n^8}{m^{12}}$

63. $\left(\dfrac{w^4}{9x^{-2}}\right)^{-1/2} = \dfrac{w^{4(-1/2)}}{9^{-1/2}\left(x^{-2}\right)^{(-1/2)}}$

$= \dfrac{w^{-2}}{\dfrac{1}{9^{1/2}} x} = \dfrac{\dfrac{1}{w^2}}{\dfrac{x}{3}} = \dfrac{1}{w^2}\cdot\dfrac{3}{x} = \dfrac{3}{xw^2}$

65. $-\sqrt{128} = -\sqrt{64\cdot 2} = -8\sqrt{2}$

67. $\sqrt{27} - 5\sqrt{3} = \sqrt{9\cdot 3} - 5\sqrt{3}$
$= \sqrt{3^2 \cdot 3} - 5\sqrt{3}$
$= \sqrt{3^2}\,\sqrt{3} - 5\sqrt{3}$
$= 3\sqrt{3} - 5\sqrt{3} = -2\sqrt{3}$

69. $\sqrt[3]{5} - \sqrt[3]{25} + \sqrt[3]{625} = \sqrt[3]{5} - \sqrt[3]{25} + \sqrt[3]{125 \cdot 5}$

$\qquad = \sqrt[3]{5} - \sqrt[3]{25} + \sqrt[3]{5^3 \cdot 5}$

$\qquad = \sqrt[3]{5} - \sqrt[3]{25} + \sqrt[3]{5^3}\sqrt[3]{5}$

$\qquad = \sqrt[3]{5} - \sqrt[3]{25} + 5\sqrt[3]{5}$

$\qquad = 6\sqrt[3]{5} - \sqrt[3]{25}$

71. $\sqrt[3]{25}\sqrt[3]{10} = \sqrt[3]{250}$

$\qquad = \sqrt[3]{125 \cdot 2}$

$\qquad = \sqrt[3]{5^3 \cdot 2}$

$\qquad = \sqrt[3]{5^3}\sqrt[3]{2} = 5\sqrt[3]{2}$

73. $\sqrt{16m^4 y^8} = \sqrt{16}\sqrt{m^4}\sqrt{y^8} = 4m^2 y^4$

75. $\dfrac{1}{2\sqrt{5}} = \dfrac{1}{2\sqrt{5}} \cdot \dfrac{\sqrt{5}}{\sqrt{5}} = \dfrac{\sqrt{5}}{2 \cdot 5} = \dfrac{\sqrt{5}}{10}$

77. $\dfrac{3}{\sqrt[3]{54}} = \dfrac{3}{\sqrt[3]{3^3 \cdot 2}}$

$\qquad = \dfrac{3}{\sqrt[3]{3^3 \cdot 2}} \cdot \dfrac{\sqrt[3]{2^2}}{\sqrt[3]{2^2}} = \dfrac{3\sqrt[3]{4}}{3\sqrt[3]{2^3}} = \dfrac{\sqrt[3]{4}}{2}$

79. $\dfrac{4}{\sqrt{6}-2} = \dfrac{4}{(\sqrt{6}-2)} \cdot \dfrac{(\sqrt{6}+2)}{(\sqrt{6}+2)}$

$\qquad = \dfrac{4(\sqrt{6}+2)}{6-4}$

$\qquad = \dfrac{4(\sqrt{6}+2)}{2}$

$\qquad = 2(\sqrt{6}+2)$

$\qquad = 2\sqrt{6}+4$

81. $x\sqrt[5]{3^6 x^7 y^{11}} = x\sqrt[5]{(3^5 x^5 y^{10})(3x^2 y)}$

$\qquad = x\sqrt[5]{3^5 x^5 y^{10}}\sqrt[5]{3x^2 y}$

$\qquad = x(3xy^2)\sqrt[5]{3x^2 y}$

$\qquad = 3x^2 y^2 \sqrt[5]{3x^2 y}$

83. $\dfrac{\sqrt{2m}\sqrt{5}}{\sqrt{20m}} = \dfrac{\sqrt{10m}}{\sqrt{20m}}$

$\qquad = \sqrt{\dfrac{10m}{20m}}$

$\qquad = \sqrt{\dfrac{1}{2}}$

$\qquad = \sqrt{\dfrac{1}{2} \cdot \dfrac{2}{2}} = \sqrt{\dfrac{2}{4}} = \dfrac{\sqrt{2}}{2}$ or $\dfrac{1}{2}\sqrt{2}$

85. $\dfrac{2\sqrt{5}+3\sqrt{2}}{5\sqrt{5}+2\sqrt{2}}$

$\qquad = \dfrac{(2\sqrt{5}+3\sqrt{2})}{(5\sqrt{5}+2\sqrt{2})} \cdot \dfrac{(5\sqrt{5}-2\sqrt{2})}{(5\sqrt{5}-2\sqrt{2})}$

$\qquad = \dfrac{2\sqrt{5}\cdot 5\sqrt{5} - 2\sqrt{5}\cdot 2\sqrt{2} + 3\sqrt{2}\cdot 5\sqrt{5} - 3\sqrt{2}\cdot 2\sqrt{2}}{(5\sqrt{5})^2 - (2\sqrt{2})^2}$

$\qquad = \dfrac{10\cdot 5 - 4\sqrt{10} + 15\sqrt{10} - 6\cdot 2}{25\cdot 5 - 4\cdot 2}$

$\qquad = \dfrac{50 + 11\sqrt{10} - 12}{125 - 8}$

$\qquad = \dfrac{38 + 11\sqrt{10}}{117}$

87. $2^{3^2} = 64$ on the assumption that 2^3^2 is entered, without parentheses.

89. One person's share of national debt
= amount of national debt ÷ no. of persons
= 8,868,000,000,000 ÷ 301,000,000
= $8.868 \times 10^{12} \div 3.01 \times 10^8$
= 2.95×10^4 or \$29,500 per person to three significant digits

91. We are to calculate $N = 10x^{3/4}y^{1/4}$ given $x = 256$ units of labor and $y = 81$ units of capital.

$\qquad N = 10(256)^{3/4}(81)^{1/4}$

$\qquad = 10\left(\sqrt[4]{256}\right)^3\left(\sqrt[4]{81}\right)$

$\qquad = 10\left(4^3\right)(3)$

$\qquad = 1,920$ units of finished product.

93. We are to calculate $d = 0.0212v^{7/3}$ given $v = 70$ miles/hour.

$$d = 0.0212(70)^{7/3}$$
$$= 0.0212(70)^{(7 \div 3)}$$
$$= 428 \text{ feet (to the nearest foot)}$$

95. $\dfrac{M_0}{\sqrt{1 - \dfrac{v^2}{c^2}}} = M_0 \div \sqrt{1 - \dfrac{v^2}{c^2}}$

$$= M_0 \div \sqrt{\dfrac{c^2 - v^2}{c^2}}$$

$$= M_0 \div \dfrac{\sqrt{c^2 - v^2}}{c}$$

$$= M_0 \cdot \dfrac{c}{\sqrt{c^2 - v^2}}$$

Now rationalize the denominator

$$= M_0 \cdot \dfrac{c}{\sqrt{c^2 - v^2}} \cdot \dfrac{\sqrt{c^2 - v^2}}{\sqrt{c^2 - v^2}}$$

$$= \dfrac{M_0 c \sqrt{c^2 - v^2}}{c^2 - v^2}$$

Section R-3

1. 2

3. $(x^2 + 1) + (x^4 - 2x + 1)$
$$= x^2 + 1 + x^4 - 2x + 1$$
$$= x^4 + x^2 - 2x + 2$$
This polynomial has degree 4.

5. $(x^2 + 1)(x^4 - 2x + 1)$
$$= x^6 - 2x^3 + x^2 + x^4 - 2x + 1$$
$$= x^6 + x^4 - 2x^3 + x^2 - 2x + 1$$

7. (a) − (b) $= (x^2 + 1) - (x^4 - 2x + 1)$
$$= x^2 + 1 - x^4 + 2x - 1$$
$$= -x^4 + x^2 + 2x$$

9. Yes; 2

11. No

13. Yes; 5

15. $2(x - 1) + 3(2x - 3) - (4x - 5)$
$$= 2x - 2 + 6x - 9 - 4x + 5$$
$$= 4x - 6$$

17. $m^2 - n^2$

19. $(3x + 2y)(x - 3y) = 3x^2 - 9xy + 2xy - 6y^2$
$$= 3x^2 - 7xy - 6y^2$$

21. $(a + b)(a^2 - ab + b^2)$
$$= a^3 - a^2b + ab^2 + a^2b - ab^2 + b^3$$
$$= a^3 + b^3$$

23. $2x^2(3x^2 - 4x - 1)$

25. $xy(x + 2y + xy)$

27. $(2w - x)(y - 2z)$

29. $x^2 + 4x + x + 4 = (x^2 + 4x) + (x + 4)$
$$= x(x + 4) + (x + 4)$$
$$= (x + 4)(x + 1)$$

31. $x^2 - xy + 3xy - 3y^2$
$$= (x^2 - xy) + (3xy - 3y^2)$$
$$= x(x - y) + 3y(x - y)$$
$$= (x - y)(x + 3y)$$

33. $8ac + 3bd - 6bc - 4ad$
$= 8ac - 4ad - 6bc + 3bd$
$= (8ac - 4ad) - (6bc - 3bd)$
$= 4a(2c - d) - 3b(2c - d)$
$= (2c - d)(4a - 3b)$

35. $2x - 3\{x + 2[x - (x + 5)] + 1\}$
$= 2x - 3\{x + 2[x - x - 5] + 1\}$
$= 2x - 3\{x + 2(-5) + 1\}$
$= 2x - 3(x - 9)$
$= 2x - 3x + 27$
$= -x + 27$

37. $(2x^2 - 3x + 1)(x^2 + x - 2)$
$= 2x^4 + 2x^3 - 4x^2 - 3x^3 - 3x^2$
$\qquad\qquad\qquad + 6x + x^2 + x - 2$
$= 2x^4 - x^3 - 6x^2 + 7x - 2$

39. $(3u - 2v)^2 - (2u - 3v)(2u + 3v)$
$= (9u^2 - 12uv + 4v^2) - (4u^2 - 9v^2)$
$= 9u^2 - 12uv + 4v^2 - 4u^2 + 9v^2$
$= 5u^2 - 12uv + 13v^2$

41. $(2m - n)^3$
$= (2m - n)^2(2m - n)$
$= (4m^2 - 4mn + n^2)(2m - n)$
$= 8m^3 - 4m^2n - 8m^2n + 4mn^2 + 2mn^2 - n^3$
$= 8m^3 - 12m^2n + 6mn^2 - n^3$

43. $(2x + 3)(x - 1)$

45. $(x + 7y)(x - 2y)$

47. $4x^2 - 20x + 25 = (2x)^2 - 2(2x)(5) + 5^2$
$\qquad\qquad\qquad\quad = (2x - 5)^2$

49. Prime

51. Prime

53. $6x^2 + 48x + 72 = 6(x^2 + 8x + 12)$
$\qquad\qquad\qquad\quad = 6(x + 2)(x + 6)$

55. $2x^4 - 24x^3 + 40x^2 = 2x^2(x^2 - 12x + 20)$
$\qquad\qquad\qquad\qquad\quad = 2x^2(x - 10)(x - 2)$

57. $(3m + 4n)(2m - 3n)$

59. $3m(m^2 - 2m + 5)$

61. $(m + n)(m^2 - mn + n^2)$

63. $3(x + h) - 7 - (3x - 7)$
$= 3x + 3h - 7 - 3x + 7$
$= 3h$

65. $2(x + h)^2 - 3(x + h) - (2x^2 - 3x)$
$= 2(x^2 + 2xh + h^2) - 3x - 3h - 2x^2 + 3x$
$= 2x^2 + 4xh + 2h^2 - 3x - 3h - 2x^2 + 3x$
$= 4xh + 2h^2 - 3h$

67. $(x + h)^3 - 2(x + h)^2 - (x^3 - 2x^2)$
$= (x + h)^2(x + h) - 2(x + h)^2 - (x^3 - 2x^2)$
$= (x^2 + 2xh + h^2)(x + h) - 2(x^2 + 2xh + h^2)$
$\qquad\qquad\qquad\qquad\qquad\quad - x^3 + 2x^2$
$= x^3 + hx^2 + 2x^2h + 2h^2x + h^2x + h^3$
$\qquad\qquad - 2x^2 - 4xh - 2h^2 - x^3 + 2x^2$
$= 3hx^2 - 4hx + 3h^2x - 2h^2 + h^3$

69. $2x(x + 1)^4 + 4x^2(x + 1)^3$
$= 2x(x + 1)^3[(x + 1) + 2x]$
$= 2x(x + 1)^3(3x + 1)$

71. $6(3x - 5)(2x - 3)^2 + 4(3x - 5)^2(2x - 3)$
$= 2(3x - 5)(2x - 3)[3(2x - 3) + 2(3x - 5)]$
$= 2(3x - 5)(2x - 3)(6x - 9 + 6x - 10)$
$= 2(3x - 5)(2x - 3)(12x - 19)$

73. $5x^4(9 - x)^4 - 4x^5(9 - x)^3$
$= x^4(9 - x)^3[5(9 - x) - 4x]$
$= x^4(9 - x)^3(45 - 5x - 4x)$
$= x^4(9 - x)^3(45 - 9x)$
$= 9x^4(9 - x)^3(5 - x)$

75. $(a-b)^2 - 4(c-d)^2$
$= (a-b)^2 - [2(c-d)]^2$
$= [(a-b) - 2(c-d)][(a-b) + 2(c-d)]$

77. $2am - 3an + 2bm - 3bn$
$= (2am - 3an) + (2bm - 3bn)$
$= a(2m - 3n) + b(2m - 3n)$
$= (2m - 3n)(a + b)$

79. Prime

81. $x^3 - 3x^2 - 9x + 27$
$= (x^3 - 3x^2) - (9x - 27)$
$= x^2(x - 3) - 9(x - 3)$
$= (x - 3)(x^2 - 9)$
$= (x - 3)(x - 3)(x + 3)$
$= (x - 3)^2(x + 3)$

83. Prime

85. $m^4 - n^4 = \left(m^2\right)^2 - \left(n^2\right)^2$
$= (m^2 - n^2)(m^2 + n^2)$
$= (m - n)(m + n)(m^2 + n^2)$

87. One example is given by choosing $a = 1$ and $b = 1$. Then $(a+b)^2 = (1+1)^2 = 2^2 = 4$ but $a^2 + b^2 = 1^2 + 1^2 = 1 + 1 = 2$. Thus, in general $(a+b)^2 \neq a^2 + b^2$. In fact, since $(a+b)^2 = a^2 + 2ab + b^2$, this quantity can only equal $a^2 + b^2$ if $2ab = 0$. By the properties of 0, either $a = 0$ or $b = 0$. In these cases $(a+b)^2$ would equal $a^2 + b^2$, but only in these .

89. (A) If $\sqrt{2} = \dfrac{a}{b}$, then $2 = \dfrac{a^2}{b^2}$ and $a^2 = 2b^2$.

(B) Any factor of a must appear in the factorization of a^2 twice for each time it appears in the factorization of a. This means that it appears an even number of times (possibly 0 times).

(C) Any factor of b^2 appears an even number of times by the reasoning of (B). Then the number of times 2 appears must be 1 more than this even number, that is, an odd number of times.

(D) To have two different numbers of appearances of a factor contradicts the uniqueness of a prime factorization.

91. There are three quantities in this problem, perimeter, length, and width. They are related by the perimeter formula $P = 2l + 2w$. Since $x =$ length of the rectangle, and the width is 5 meters less than the length, $x - 5 =$ width of the rectangle. So $P = 2x + 2(x - 5)$ represents the perimeter of the rectangle. Simplifying: $P = 2x + 2x - 10 = 4x - 10$ (meters).

93. There are several quantities involved in this problem. It is important to keep them distinct by using enough words. We write:
$$x = \text{number of nickels}$$
$$x - 5 = \text{number of dimes}$$
$$(x - 5) + 2 = \text{number of quarters}$$
This follows because there are five fewer dimes than nickels ($x - 5$) and 2 more quarters than dimes (2 more than $x - 5$). Each nickel is worth 5 cents, each dime worth 10 cents, and each quarter worth 25 cents. Hence the value of the nickels is 5 times the number of nickels, the value of the dimes is 10 times the number of dimes, and the value of the quarters is 25 times the number of quarters.
value of nickels $= 5x$
value of dimes $= 10(x - 5)$
value of quarters $= 25[(x - 5) + 2]$
Value of the pile
$=$ (value of nickels) + (value of dimes)
$\qquad\qquad\qquad$ + (value of quarters)
$= 5x + 10(x - 5) + 25[(x - 5) + 2]$
Simplifying this expression, we get:
The value of the pile
$= 5x + 10x - 50 + 25[x - 5 + 2]$
$= 5x + 10x - 50 + 25[x - 3]$
$= 5x + 10x - 50 + 25x - 75$
$= 40x - 125$ (cents)

95. The volume of the plastic shell is equal to the volume of the larger sphere $\left(V = \dfrac{4}{3}\pi r^3\right)$ minus the volume of the hole. Since the radius of the hole is x cm and the plastic is 0.3 cm thick, the radius of the larger sphere is $x + 0.3$ cm. Thus, we have

$$\begin{pmatrix}\text{Volume} \\ \text{of Shell}\end{pmatrix} = \begin{pmatrix}\text{Volume of} \\ \text{larger sphere}\end{pmatrix} - \begin{pmatrix}\text{Volume of} \\ \text{hole}\end{pmatrix}$$

Volume

$$= \frac{4}{3}\pi(x+0.3)^3 - \frac{4}{3}\pi x^3$$

$$= \frac{4}{3}\pi(x+0.3)(x+0.3)^2 - \frac{4}{3}\pi x^3$$

$$= \frac{4}{3}\pi(x+0.3)(x^2+0.6x+0.09) - \frac{4}{3}\pi x^3$$

$$= \frac{4}{3}\pi(x^3+0.6x^2+0.09x+0.3x^2$$

$$\qquad\qquad +0.18x+0.027) - \frac{4}{3}\pi x^3$$

$$= \frac{4}{3}\pi(x^3+0.9x^2+0.27x+0.027) - \frac{4}{3}\pi x^3$$

$$= \frac{4}{3}\pi x^3 +1.2\pi x^2+0.36\pi x+0.036\pi - \frac{4}{3}\pi x^3$$

$$= 1.2\pi x^2+0.36\pi x+0.036\pi \ \ (\text{cm}^3)$$

97. (A) The area of the cardboard can be written as (Original area) – (removed area), where the original area = $20^2 = 400$ and the removed area consists of 4 squares of area x^2 each; thus,

(Orig. area) – (Removed area)

$= 400 - 4x^2$ in expanded form

$= 4(100 - x^2)$

$= 4(10 - x)(10 + x)$ in factored form

(B) See figure.

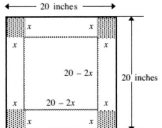

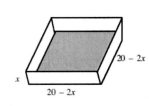

Volume of box $= lwh$

$$= x(20 - 2x)(20 - 2x)$$

$$= 4x(10 - x)(10 - x)$$

in factored form.

In expanded form,

$$4x(10-x)(10-x) = 4x[10^2 - 2(10)x + x^2]$$

$$= 4x[100 - 20x + x^2]$$

$$= 400x - 80x^2 + 4x^3$$

Section R-4

1. $\dfrac{17}{85} = \dfrac{17 \cdot 1}{17 \cdot 5} = \dfrac{1}{5}$

3. $\dfrac{360}{288} = \dfrac{72 \cdot 5}{72 \cdot 4} = \dfrac{5}{4}$

5. $\dfrac{x+1}{x^2+3x+2} = \dfrac{\overset{1}{\cancel{x+1}}}{\underset{1}{\cancel{(x+1)}}(x+2)} = \dfrac{1}{x+2}$

7. $\dfrac{x^2-9}{x^2+3x-18} = \dfrac{\overset{1}{\cancel{(x-3)}}(x+3)}{(x+6)\underset{1}{\cancel{(x-3)}}} = \dfrac{x+3}{x+6}$

9. $\dfrac{3x^2y^3}{x^4y} = \dfrac{\cancel{x^2}y \cdot 3y^2}{\cancel{x^2}y \cdot x^2} = \dfrac{3y^2}{x^2}$

11. $\dfrac{5}{6} + \dfrac{11}{15} = \dfrac{25}{30} + \dfrac{22}{30} = \dfrac{47}{30}$

13. $\dfrac{1}{8} - \dfrac{1}{9} = \dfrac{9}{72} - \dfrac{8}{72} = \dfrac{1}{72}$

15. $\dfrac{1}{n} - \dfrac{1}{m} = \dfrac{m}{mn} - \dfrac{n}{mn} = \dfrac{m-n}{mn}$

17. $\dfrac{5}{12} \div \dfrac{3}{4} = \dfrac{5}{\underset{3}{\cancel{12}}} \cdot \dfrac{\overset{1}{\cancel{4}}}{3} = \dfrac{5}{3} \cdot \dfrac{1}{3} = \dfrac{5}{9}$

19. $\left(\dfrac{25}{8} \div \dfrac{5}{16}\right) \cdot \dfrac{4}{15} = \left(\dfrac{\overset{5}{\cancel{25}}}{\cancel{8}} \cdot \dfrac{\overset{2}{\cancel{16}}}{\cancel{5}}\right) \cdot \dfrac{4}{15}$

$\qquad = \dfrac{\cancel{5} \cdot 2}{1} \cdot \dfrac{4}{\underset{3}{\cancel{15}}}$

$\qquad = \dfrac{8}{3}$

21. $\left(\dfrac{b^2}{2a} \div \dfrac{b}{a^2}\right) \cdot \dfrac{a}{3b} = \left(\dfrac{b^2}{2a} \cdot \dfrac{a^2}{b}\right) \cdot \dfrac{a}{3b} = \left(\dfrac{\overset{b}{\cancel{b^2}}}{2\underset{1}{\cancel{a}}} \cdot \dfrac{\overset{a}{\cancel{a^2}}}{\underset{1}{\cancel{b}}}\right) \cdot \dfrac{a}{3b}$

$\qquad = \dfrac{ab}{2} \cdot \dfrac{a}{3b}$

$\qquad = \dfrac{a^2}{6}$

23. $\dfrac{x^2-1}{x+2} \div \dfrac{x+1}{x^2-4}$

$\qquad = \dfrac{x^2-1}{x+2} \cdot \dfrac{x^2-4}{x+1}$

$\qquad = \dfrac{(x-1)\overset{1}{\cancel{(x+1)}}}{\underset{1}{\cancel{x+2}}} \cdot \dfrac{(x-2)\overset{1}{\cancel{(x+2)}}}{\underset{1}{\cancel{x+1}}}$

$\qquad = (x-1)(x-2)$

25. $\dfrac{1}{c} + \dfrac{1}{b} + \dfrac{1}{a} = \dfrac{ab}{abc} + \dfrac{ac}{abc} + \dfrac{bc}{abc}$

$\qquad = \dfrac{ab+ac+bc}{abc}$

27. $\dfrac{2a-b}{a^2-b^2} - \dfrac{2a+3b}{a^2+2ab+b^2}$

$\qquad = \dfrac{2a-b}{(a-b)(a+b)} - \dfrac{2a+3b}{(a+b)(a+b)}$

$\qquad = \dfrac{(2a-b)(a+b)}{(a+b)(a+b)(a-b)} - \dfrac{(2a+3b)(a-b)}{(a+b)(a+b)(a-b)}$

$\qquad = \dfrac{(2a-b)(a+b) - (2a+3b)(a-b)}{(a+b)^2(a-b)}$

$\qquad = \dfrac{2a^2+ab-b^2 - (2a^2+ab-3b^2)}{(a-b)(a+b)^2}$

$\qquad = \dfrac{2a^2+ab-b^2 - 2a^2-ab+3b^2}{(a-b)(a+b)^2}$

$\qquad = \dfrac{2b^2}{(a-b)(a+b)^2}$

29. $m+2 - \dfrac{m-2}{m-1} = \dfrac{(m+2)(m-1)}{m-1} - \dfrac{m-2}{m-1}$

$\qquad = \dfrac{(m^2+m-2) - (m-2)}{m-1}$

$\qquad = \dfrac{m^2+m-2-m+2}{m-1}$

$\qquad = \dfrac{m^2}{m-1}$

31. $\dfrac{3}{x-2} - \dfrac{2}{2-x} = \dfrac{3}{x-2} - \dfrac{-2}{x-2}$

$\qquad = \dfrac{3+2}{x-2}$

$\qquad = \dfrac{5}{x-2}$

33. $\dfrac{3}{y+2} + \dfrac{2}{y-2} - \dfrac{4y}{y^2-4}$

$= \dfrac{3(y-2)}{(y+2)(y-2)} + \dfrac{2(y+2)}{(y-2)(y+2)} - \dfrac{4y}{(y-2)(y+2)}$

$= \dfrac{3(y-2) + 2(y+2) - 4y}{(y+2)(y-2)}$

$= \dfrac{3y-6+2y+4-4y}{(y+2)(y-2)}$

$= \dfrac{\overset{1}{\cancel{y-2}}}{(y+2)\underset{1}{\cancel{(y-2)}}} = \dfrac{1}{y+2}$

35. $\dfrac{\dfrac{x^2}{y^2}-1}{\dfrac{x}{y}+1} = \dfrac{y^2\left(\dfrac{x^2}{y^2}-1\right)}{y^2\left(\dfrac{x}{y}+1\right)}$

$\qquad = \dfrac{x^2-y^2}{xy+y^2} = \dfrac{(x-y)\overset{1}{\cancel{(x+y)}}}{y\underset{1}{\cancel{(x+y)}}} = \dfrac{x-y}{y}$

37. $\dfrac{6x^3(x^2+2)^2 - 2x(x^2+2)^3}{x^4}$

$= \dfrac{2x(x^2+2)^2[3x^2-(x^2+2)]}{x^4}$

$= \dfrac{2x(x^2+2)^2[3x^2-x^2-2]}{x^4}$

$= \dfrac{2\,\overset{1}{\cancel{x}}(x^2+2)^2(2x^2-2)}{\underset{x^3}{\cancel{x^4}}}$

$= \dfrac{2(x^2+2)^2\cdot(2x^2-2)}{x^3}$

$= \dfrac{2(x^2+2)^2\cdot 2(x^2-1)}{x^3}$

$= \dfrac{4(x^2+2)^2(x+1)(x-1)}{x^3}$

39. $\dfrac{2x(1-3x)^3 + 9x^2(1-3x)^2}{(1-3x)^6}$

$= \dfrac{x(1-3x)^2[2(1-3x)+9x]}{(1-3x)^6}$

$= \dfrac{x(1-3x)^2(2-6x+9x)}{(1-3x)^6}$

$= \dfrac{x\,\overset{1}{\cancel{(1-3x)^2}}\,(2+3x)}{\underset{(1-3x)^4}{\cancel{(1-3x)^6}}}$

$= \dfrac{x(2+3x)}{(1-3x)^4}$

41. $\dfrac{-2x(x+4)^3 - 3(3-x^2)(x+4)^2}{(x+4)^6}$

$= \dfrac{(x+4)^2[-2x(x+4)-3(3-x^2)]}{(x+4)^6}$

$= \dfrac{(x+4)^2(-2x^2-8x-9+3x^2)}{(x+4)^6}$

$= \dfrac{\overset{1}{\cancel{(x+4)^2}}\,(x^2-8x-9)}{\underset{(x+4)^4}{\cancel{(x+4)^6}}}$

$= \dfrac{(x+1)(x-9)}{(x+4)^4}$

43. $\dfrac{y}{y^2-2y-8} - \dfrac{2}{y^2-5y+4} + \dfrac{1}{y^2+y-2}$

$= \dfrac{y}{(y+2)(y-4)} - \dfrac{2}{(y-4)(y-1)} + \dfrac{1}{(y+2)(y-1)}$

$= \dfrac{y(y-1)}{(y+2)(y-4)(y-1)} - \dfrac{2(y+2)}{(y-4)(y-1)(y+2)}$
$\qquad\qquad + \dfrac{1(y-4)}{(y+2)(y-1)(y-4)}$

$= \dfrac{y(y-1)-2(y+2)+(y-4)}{(y+2)(y-4)(y-1)}$

$= \dfrac{y^2-y-2y-4+y-4}{(y+2)(y-4)(y-1)}$

$= \dfrac{y^2-2y-8}{(y+2)(y-4)(y-1)}$

$= \dfrac{\overset{1}{\cancel{(y+2)}}\,\overset{1}{\cancel{(y-4)}}}{\underset{1}{\cancel{(y+2)}}\,\underset{1}{\cancel{(y-4)}}(y-1)}$

$= \dfrac{1}{y-1}$

45. $\dfrac{16-m^2}{m^2+3m-4}\cdot\dfrac{m-1}{m-4}$

$= \dfrac{\overset{-1}{\cancel{(4-m)}}\,\overset{1}{\cancel{(4+m)}}}{\underset{1}{\cancel{(m+4)}}\,\underset{1}{\cancel{(m-1)}}}\cdot\dfrac{\overset{1}{\cancel{(m-1)}}}{\underset{1}{\cancel{m-4}}}$

$= \dfrac{-1}{1} = -1$

47. $\dfrac{x+7}{ax-bx} + \dfrac{y+9}{by-ay} = \dfrac{x+7}{x(a-b)} + \dfrac{y+9}{y(b-a)}$

$= \dfrac{y(x+7)}{xy(a-b)} + \dfrac{-x(y+9)}{xy(a-b)}$

$= \dfrac{xy+7y-xy-9x}{xy(a-b)}$

$= \dfrac{7y-9x}{xy(a-b)}$

49.

$$\frac{x^2-16}{2x^2+10x+8}\div\frac{x^2-13x+36}{x^3+1}$$

$$=\frac{x^2-16}{2x^2+10x+8}\cdot\frac{x^3+1}{x^2-13x+36}$$

$$=\frac{(x+4)\,(x-4)}{2\,(x+4)\,(x+1)}\cdot\frac{(x+1)(x^2-x+1)}{(x-4)(x-9)}$$

$$=\frac{x^2-x+1}{2(x-9)}$$

51.

$$\left(\frac{x}{x^2-16}-\frac{1}{x+4}\right)\div\frac{4}{x+4}$$

$$=\left(\frac{x}{(x-4)(x+4)}-\frac{1}{x+4}\right)\div\frac{4}{x+4}$$

$$=\left(\frac{x}{(x-4)(x+4)}-\frac{x-4}{(x-4)(x+4)}\right)\div\frac{4}{x+4}$$

$$=\frac{x-(x-4)}{(x-4)(x+4)}\div\frac{4}{x+4}=\frac{x-x+4}{(x-4)(x+4)}\div\frac{4}{x+4}$$

$$=\frac{4}{(x-4)(x+4)}\cdot\frac{x+4}{4}=\frac{1}{x-4}$$

53.

$$\frac{1+\dfrac{2}{x}-\dfrac{15}{x^2}}{1+\dfrac{4}{x}-\dfrac{5}{x^2}}=\frac{x^2\left(1+\dfrac{2}{x}-\dfrac{15}{x^2}\right)}{x^2\left(1+\dfrac{4}{x}-\dfrac{5}{x^2}\right)}$$

$$=\frac{x^2+2x-15}{x^2+4x-5}$$

$$=\frac{(x+5)(x-3)}{(x+5)(x-1)}=\frac{x-3}{x-1}$$

55.

$$\frac{\dfrac{1}{x+h}-\dfrac{1}{x}}{h}=\frac{\dfrac{x}{x(x+h)}-\dfrac{x+h}{x(x+h)}}{h}$$

$$=\frac{\dfrac{x-x-h}{x(x+h)}}{h}$$

$$=\frac{\dfrac{-h}{x(x+h)}}{h}=-\frac{h}{x(x+h)}\div\frac{h}{1}$$

$$=\frac{-h}{x(x+h)}\cdot\frac{1}{h}=\frac{-1}{x(x+h)}$$

57.

$$\frac{\dfrac{(x+h)^2}{x+h+2}-\dfrac{x^2}{x+2}}{h}=\frac{\dfrac{(x+h)^2(x+2)}{(x+h+2)(x+2)}-\dfrac{x^2(x+h+2)}{(x+h+2)(x+2)}}{h}$$

$$=\frac{\dfrac{(x+h)^2(x+2)-x^2(x+h+2)}{(x+h+2)(x+2)}}{h}$$

$$=\frac{\dfrac{(x^2+2xh+h^2)(x+2)-x^3-x^2h-2x^2}{(x+h+2)(x+2)}}{h}$$

$$=\frac{\dfrac{x^3+2x^2h+h^2x+2x^2+4xh+2h^2-x^3-x^2h-2x^2}{(x+h+2)(x+2)}}{h}$$

$$=\frac{\dfrac{x^2h+h^2x+4xh+2h^2}{(x+h+2)(x+2)}}{h}=\frac{x^2h+h^2x+4xh+2h^2}{(x+h+2)(x+2)}\div h$$

$$=\frac{x^2h+h^2x+4xh+2h^2}{(x+h+2)(x+2)}\div\frac{h}{1}=\frac{h(x^2+hx+4x+2h)}{(x+h+2)(x+2)}\cdot\frac{1}{h}$$

$$=\frac{x^2+hx+4x+2h}{(x+h+2)(x+2)}$$

59.

$$\frac{y-\dfrac{y^2}{y-x}}{1+\dfrac{x^2}{y^2-x^2}}$$

$$=\frac{(y^2-x^2)\left[y-\dfrac{y^2}{y-x}\right]}{(y^2-x^2)\left[1+\dfrac{x^2}{y^2-x^2}\right]}$$

$$=\frac{(y^2-x^2)y-(y^2-x^2)\dfrac{y^2}{y-x}}{y^2-x^2+(y^2-x^2)\dfrac{x^2}{y^2-x^2}}$$

$$=\frac{y^3-x^2y-y^3-xy^2}{y^2-x^2+x^2}$$

$$=\frac{-x^2y-xy^2}{y^2}=\frac{-xy(x+y)}{y^2}=\frac{-x(x+y)}{y}$$

61.

$$2 - \cfrac{1}{1 - \cfrac{2}{a+2}} = 2 - \cfrac{(a+2)\cdot 1}{(a+2)\left[1 - \cfrac{2}{a+2}\right]}$$

$$= 2 - \cfrac{a+2}{a+2 - (a+2)\cfrac{2}{a+2}}$$

$$= 2 - \cfrac{a+2}{a+2-2}$$

$$= 2 - \frac{a+2}{a} = \frac{2}{1} - \frac{a+2}{a}$$

$$= \frac{2a}{a} - \frac{(a+2)}{a}$$

$$= \frac{2a-a-2}{a} = \frac{a-2}{a}$$

Chapter R Review

1. $\dfrac{5}{6} + \dfrac{3}{4} = \dfrac{10}{12} + \dfrac{9}{12} = \dfrac{19}{12}$ *(R-1)*

2. $\dfrac{2}{3} - \dfrac{4}{9} = \dfrac{6}{9} - \dfrac{4}{9} = \dfrac{2}{9}$ *(R-1)*

3. $7^{-1}9^{-1} = \dfrac{1}{7} \cdot \dfrac{1}{9} = \dfrac{1}{63}$ *(R-1)*

4. $\left(-\dfrac{10}{3}\right)\left(-\dfrac{6}{5}\right) = \dfrac{10}{3} \cdot \dfrac{6}{5} = \dfrac{2}{1} \cdot \dfrac{2}{1} = 4$ *(R-1)*

5. $\dfrac{5}{7} \div \left(\dfrac{1}{3} - 3^{-1}\right) = \dfrac{5}{7} \div \left(\dfrac{1}{3} - \dfrac{1}{3}\right) = \dfrac{5}{7} \div 0$;

This is undefined   *(R-1)*

6. $\dfrac{11}{12} \div \left(-\dfrac{3}{4}\right) = \dfrac{11}{12} \cdot \left(-\dfrac{4}{3}\right) = \dfrac{11}{3}\left(-\dfrac{1}{3}\right) = -\dfrac{11}{9}$

     (R-1)

7. 4   *(R-3)*

8. 4   *(R-3)*

9. $(a) + (b) = (x^4 + 3x^2 + 1) + (4 - x^4)$
$$= x^4 + 3x^2 + 1 + 4 - x^4$$
$$= 3x^2 + 5$$
This polynomial has degree 2.   *(R-3)*

63. One example is given by choosing $a=1$ and $b=2$. Then $\dfrac{a+b}{b} = \dfrac{1+2}{2} = \dfrac{3}{2}$, but $a + 1 = 1 + 1 = 2$. Thus, in general, $\dfrac{a+b}{b} \neq a+1$. In fact, since

$$a + 1 = \frac{(a+1)b}{b} = \frac{ab+b}{b},$$ this quantity can

only equal $\dfrac{a+b}{b}$ if $ab = a$, that is, if $ab - a = a(b-1) = 0$. By the properties of 0, either $a = 0$ or $b = 1$. In these cases $\dfrac{a+b}{b} = a+1$, but only in these.

10. $(x^4 + 3x^2 + 1)(4 - x^4)$
$$= 4x^4 + 12x^2 + 4 - x^8 - 3x^6 - x^4$$
$$= -x^8 - 3x^6 + 3x^4 + 12x^2 + 4$$
This polynomial has degree 8.   *(R-3)*

11. See problem 10: $-x^8 - 3x^6 + 3x^4 + 12x^2 + 4$
     (R-3)

12. See problem 9: $3x^2 + 5$ *(R-3)*

13. 17   *(R-2)*

14. 6   *(R-2)*

15. $8^{-2/3} = \dfrac{1}{8^{2/3}} = \dfrac{1}{(8^{1/3})^2} = \dfrac{1}{(2)^2} = \dfrac{1}{4}$ *(R-2)*

16. $(-64)^{5/3} = \left[(-64)^{1/3}\right]^5 = (-4)^5 = -1024$
     (R-2)

17. $\left(\dfrac{9}{16}\right)^{-1/2} = 1 \div \left(\dfrac{9}{16}\right)^{1/2} = 1 \div \dfrac{3}{4} = 1 \cdot \dfrac{4}{3} = \dfrac{4}{3}$
     (R-2)

18. $(121^{1/2} + 25^{1/2})^{-3/4} = (11 + 5)^{-3/4}$
$$= 16^{-3/4}$$
$$= \frac{1}{16^{3/4}}$$
$$= \frac{1}{(16^{1/4})^3}$$
$$= \frac{1}{(2)^3} = \frac{1}{8} \qquad (R\text{-}2)$$

19. $5x^2 - 3x[4 - 3(x - 2)]$
$$= 5x^2 - 3x(4 - 3x + 6)$$
$$= 5x^2 - 3x(10 - 3x)$$
$$= 5x^2 - 30x + 9x^2$$
$$= 14x^2 - 30x \qquad (R\text{-}3)$$

20. $9m^2 - 25n^2 \qquad (R\text{-}3)$

21. $(2x + y)(3x - 4y) = 6x^2 - 8xy + 3xy - 4y^2$
$$= 6x^2 - 5xy - 4y^2$$
$$\qquad (R\text{-}3)$$

22. $(2a - 3b)^2 = (2a)^2 - 2(2a)(3b) + (3b)^2$
$$= 4a^2 - 12ab + 9b^2$$
$$\qquad (R\text{-}3)$$

23. $(3x - 2)^2 \qquad (R\text{-}3)$

24. Prime $\qquad (R\text{-}3)$

25. $6n^3 - 9n^2 - 15n = 3n(2n^2 - 3n - 5)$
$$= 3n(2n - 5)(n + 1) \quad (R\text{-}3)$$

26. $\dfrac{2}{5b} - \dfrac{4}{3a^3} - \dfrac{1}{6a^2b^2}$
$$= \frac{12a^3b}{30a^3b^2} - \frac{40b^2}{30a^3b^2} - \frac{5a}{30a^3b^2}$$
$$= \frac{12a^3b - 40b^2 - 5a}{30a^3b^2} \qquad (R\text{-}4)$$

27.
$$\frac{3x}{3x^2 - 12x} + \frac{1}{6x} = \frac{3x}{3x(x - 4)} + \frac{1}{6x}$$
$$= \frac{2 \cdot 3x}{2 \cdot 3x(x - 4)} + \frac{1 \cdot (x - 4)}{6x \cdot (x - 4)}$$
$$= \frac{6x + (x - 4)}{6x(x - 4)}$$
$$= \frac{7x - 4}{6x(x - 4)} \qquad (R\text{-}4)$$

28. $\dfrac{y - 2}{y^2 - 4y + 4} \div \dfrac{y^2 + 2y}{y^2 + 4y + 4}$
$$= \frac{y - 2}{y^2 - 4y + 4} \cdot \frac{y^2 + 4y + 4}{y^2 + 2y}$$
$$= \frac{\cancel{y - 2}}{(y - 2)\cancel{(y - 2)}} \cdot \frac{(y + 2)\cancel{(y + 2)}}{y\cancel{(y + 2)}}$$
$$= \frac{y + 2}{y(y - 2)} \qquad (R\text{-}4)$$

29. $\dfrac{u - \dfrac{1}{u}}{1 - \dfrac{1}{u^2}} = \dfrac{u^2\left(u - \dfrac{1}{u}\right)}{u^2\left(1 - \dfrac{1}{u^2}\right)}$
$$= \frac{u^3 - u}{u^2 - 1}$$
$$= \frac{u\cancel{(u^2 - 1)}}{\cancel{u^2 - 1}} = u \qquad (R\text{-}4)$$

30. $6(xy^3)^5 = 6x^5(y^3)^5 = 6x^5y^{15} \qquad (R\text{-}2)$

31. $\dfrac{9u^8v^6}{3u^4v^8} = \dfrac{3u^4}{v^2} \qquad (R\text{-}2)$

32. $(2 \times 10^5)(3 \times 10^{-3}) = (2 \cdot 3) \times 10^{5 + (-3)}$
$$= 6 \times 10^2 \qquad (R\text{-}2)$$

33. $(x^{-3}y^2)^{-2} = (x^{-3})^{-2}(y^2)^{-2} = x^6y^{-4} = \dfrac{x^6}{y^4}$
$$\qquad (R\text{-}2)$$

34. $u^{5/3}u^{2/3} = u^{5/3 + 2/3} = u^{7/3} \qquad (R\text{-}2)$

35. $(9a^4b^{-2})^{1/2} = 9^{1/2}(a^4)^{1/2}(b^{-2})^{1/2}$
$= 3a^2b^{-1}$
$= \dfrac{3a^2}{b}$ *(R-2)*

36. $3\sqrt[5]{x^2}$ *(R-2)*

37. $-3(xy)^{2/3}$ *(R-2)*

38. $3x\sqrt[3]{x^5y^4} = 3x\sqrt[3]{x^3y^3 \cdot x^2y}$
$= 3x\sqrt[3]{x^3y^3}\sqrt[3]{x^2y}$
$= 3x(xy)\sqrt[3]{x^2y}$
$= 3x^2y\sqrt[3]{x^2y}$ *(R-2)*

39. $\sqrt{2x^2y^5}\sqrt{18x^3y^2} = \sqrt{(2x^2y^5)(18x^3y^2)}$
$= \sqrt{36x^5y^7}$
$= \sqrt{36x^4y^6 \cdot xy}$
$= \sqrt{36x^4y^6}\sqrt{xy}$
$= 6x^2y^3\sqrt{xy}$ *(R-2)*

40. $\dfrac{6ab}{\sqrt{3a}} = \dfrac{6ab}{\sqrt{3a}} \cdot \dfrac{\sqrt{3a}}{\sqrt{3a}} = \dfrac{\cancel{6}^2\,\cancel{a}b\sqrt{3a}}{\cancel{3}\,\cancel{a}} = 2b\sqrt{3a}$
     (R-2)

41. $\dfrac{\sqrt{5}}{3-\sqrt{5}} = \dfrac{\sqrt{5}}{(3-\sqrt{5})} \cdot \dfrac{(3+\sqrt{5})}{(3+\sqrt{5})}$
$= \dfrac{\sqrt{5}(3+\sqrt{5})}{3^2 - (\sqrt{5})^2} = \dfrac{\sqrt{5}(3+\sqrt{5})}{9-5}$
$= \dfrac{\sqrt{5}(3+\sqrt{5})}{4} = \dfrac{3\sqrt{5}+5}{4}$ *(R-2)*

42. $\sqrt[8]{y^6} = \sqrt[2\cdot4]{y^{2\cdot3}} = \sqrt[4]{y^3}$ *(R-2)*

43. Subtraction   *(R-1)*

44. Commutative (+)   *(R-1)*

45. Distributive   *(R-1)*

46. Associative (·)   *(R-1)*

47. Negatives   *(R-1)*

48. Identity (+)   *(R-1)*

49. (A) T
(B) F   *(R-1)*

50. 0 and –3 are two examples of infinitely many.   *(R-1)*

51. (A) (a) and (d)
(B) None   *(R-3)*

52. $(2x-y)(2x+y) - (2x-y)^2$
$= (4x^2 - y^2) - (4x^2 - 4xy + y^2)$
$= 4x^2 - y^2 - 4x^2 + 4xy - y^2$
$= 4xy - 2y^2$ *(R-3)*

53. This can be simplified directly using the distributive property or:
$(m^2 + 2mn - n^2)(m^2 - 2mn - n^2)$
$= \left[(m^2 - n^2) + 2mn\right]\left[(m^2 - n^2) - 2mn\right]$
$= (m^2 - n^2)^2 - (2mn)^2$
$= m^4 - 2m^2n^2 + n^4 - 4m^2n^2$
$= m^4 - 6m^2n^2 + n^4$ *(R-3)*

54. $5(x+h)^2 - 7(x+h) - (5x^2 - 7x)$
$= 5(x^2 + 2xh + h^2) - 7(x+h) - (5x^2 - 7x)$
$= 5x^2 + 10xh + 5h^2 - 7x - 7h - 5x^2 + 7x$
$= 10xh + 5h^2 - 7h$ *(R-3)*

55. $-2x\left\{(x^2+2)(x-3) - x[x - x(3-x)]\right\}$
$= -2x\left\{(x^2+2)(x-3) - x[x - 3x + x^2]\right\}$
$= -2x\left\{x^3 - 3x^2 + 2x - 6 - x(-2x + x^2)\right\}$
$= -2x(x^3 - 3x^2 + 2x - 6 + 2x^2 - x^3)$
$= -2x(-x^2 + 2x - 6)$
$= 2x^3 - 4x^2 + 12x$ *(R-3)*

56. $(4x-y)^2 - 9x^2$
$= (4x-y)^2 - (3x)^2$
$= [(4x-y) - 3x][(4x-y) + 3x]$
$= (x-y)(7x-y)$ *(R-3)*

57. Prime   *(R-3)*

58. $3xy(2x^2 + 4xy - 5y^2)$ *(R-3)*

59. $(y-b)^2 - y + b$
$= (y-b)(y-b) - 1(y-b)$
$= (y-b)[(y-b)-1]$
$= (y-b)(y-b-1)$ *(R-3)*

60. $y^3 + 2y^2 - 4y - 8$
$= y^2(y+2) - 4(y+2)$
$= (y+2)(y^2-4)$
$= (y+2)(y+2)(y-2)$
$= (y-2)(y+2)^2$ *(R-3)*

61. $2x(x-4)^3 + 3x^2(x-4)^2$
$= x(x-4)^2[2(x-4)+3x]$
$= x(x-4)^2(2x-8+3x)$
$= x(x-4)^2(5x-8)$ *(R-3)*

62. $\dfrac{3x^2(x+2)^2 - 2x(x+2)^3}{x^4}$
$= \dfrac{x(x+2)^2[3x-2(x+2)]}{x^4}$
$= \dfrac{\cancel{x}(x+2)^2(3x-2x-4)}{\cancel{x}\,x^3}$
$= \dfrac{(x+2)^2(x-4)}{x^3}$ *(R-4)*

63. $\dfrac{m-1}{m^2-4m+4} + \dfrac{m+3}{m^2-4} + \dfrac{2}{2-m}$
$= \dfrac{m-1}{(m-2)(m-2)} + \dfrac{m+3}{(m-2)(m+2)} + \dfrac{-2}{m-2}$
$= \dfrac{(m-1)(m+2)}{(m-2)^2(m+2)} + \dfrac{(m+3)(m-2)}{(m-2)^2(m+2)}$
$\qquad + \dfrac{-2(m-2)(m+2)}{(m-2)(m-2)(m+2)}$
$= \dfrac{(m-1)(m+2)+(m+3)(m-2)-2(m-2)(m+2)}{(m-2)^2(m+2)}$
$= \dfrac{m^2+m-2+m^2+m-6-2(m^2-4)}{(m-2)^2(m+2)}$
$= \dfrac{2m^2+2m-8-2m^2+8}{(m-2)^2(m+2)}$
$= \dfrac{2m}{(m-2)^2(m+2)}$ *(R-4)*

64. $\dfrac{y}{x^2} \div \left(\dfrac{x^2+3x}{2x^2+5x-3} \div \dfrac{x^3y-x^2y}{2x^2-3x+1} \right)$
$= \dfrac{y}{x^2} \div \left(\dfrac{x^2+3x}{2x^2+5x-3} \cdot \dfrac{2x^2-3x+1}{x^3y-x^2y} \right)$
$= \dfrac{y}{x^2} \div \left(\dfrac{\cancel{x}(x+3)}{(2x-1)(x+3)} \cdot \dfrac{(2x-1)(x-1)}{x\,\cancel{x}\,y(x-1)} \right)$
$= \dfrac{y}{x^2} \div \dfrac{1}{xy} = \dfrac{y}{x^2} \cdot \dfrac{xy}{1} = \dfrac{y^2}{x}$ *(R-4)*

65.
$\dfrac{1 - \dfrac{1}{1+\frac{x}{y}}}{1 - \dfrac{1}{1-\frac{x}{y}}} = \dfrac{1 - \dfrac{y\cdot 1}{y\left(1+\frac{x}{y}\right)}}{1 - \dfrac{y\cdot 1}{y\left(1-\frac{x}{y}\right)}}$

$= \dfrac{1 - \dfrac{y}{y+x}}{1 - \dfrac{y}{y-x}}$

$= \dfrac{\dfrac{y+x}{y+x} - \dfrac{y}{y+x}}{\dfrac{y-x}{y-x} - \dfrac{y}{y-x}}$

$= \dfrac{\dfrac{x}{y+x}}{\dfrac{-x}{y-x}} = \dfrac{x}{y+x} \div \dfrac{-x}{y-x}$

$= \dfrac{\cancel{x}^{-1}}{y+x} \cdot \dfrac{y-x}{\cancel{x}_1}$

$= \dfrac{-1(y-x)}{y+x} = \dfrac{x-y}{x+y}$ *(R-4)*

66. $\dfrac{0.00000000052}{(1,300)(0.000002)} = \dfrac{5.2\times10^{-10}}{(1.3\times10^3)(2\times10^{-6})}$
$= \dfrac{\overset{2}{\cancel{5.2}}\times10^{-10}}{\underset{}{\cancel{2.6}}\times10^{-3}}$
$= 2\times10^{-10-(-3)}$
$= 2\times10^{-7}$ *(R-2)*

67. $-2x\sqrt[5]{3^6 x^7 y^{11}} = -2x\sqrt[5]{3^5 x^5 y^{10} \cdot 3x^2 y}$

$\qquad = -2x\sqrt[5]{3^5 x^5 y^{10}} \sqrt[5]{3x^2 y}$

$\qquad = -2x \cdot 3xy^2 \sqrt[5]{3x^2 y}$

$\qquad = -6x^2 y^2 \sqrt[5]{3x^2 y} \qquad (R\text{-}2)$

68. $\dfrac{2x^2}{\sqrt[3]{4x}} = \dfrac{2x^2}{\sqrt[3]{4x}} \cdot \dfrac{\sqrt[3]{2x^2}}{\sqrt[3]{2x^2}}$

$\qquad = \dfrac{2x^2 \sqrt[3]{2x^2}}{\sqrt[3]{8x^3}}$

$\qquad = \dfrac{\overset{x}{\cancel{2x^2}} \sqrt[3]{2x^2}}{\cancel{2x}} = x\sqrt[3]{2x^2} \qquad (R\text{-}2)$

69. $\sqrt[5]{\dfrac{3y^2}{8x^2}} = \sqrt[5]{\dfrac{3y^2}{8x^2} \cdot \dfrac{4x^3}{4x^3}}$

$\qquad = \sqrt[5]{\dfrac{12x^3 y^2}{32x^5}}$

$\qquad = \dfrac{\sqrt[5]{12x^3 y^2}}{\sqrt[5]{32x^5}} = \dfrac{\sqrt[5]{12x^3 y^2}}{2x} \qquad (R\text{-}2)$

70. $\sqrt[9]{8x^6 y^{12}} = \sqrt[9]{2^3 x^6 y^{12}}$

$\qquad = \sqrt[3\cdot 3]{2^{3\cdot 1} x^{3\cdot 2} y^{3\cdot 4}}$

$\qquad = \sqrt[3]{2x^2 y^4}$

$\qquad = \sqrt[3]{y^3 \cdot 2x^2 y}$

$\qquad = \sqrt[3]{y^3} \sqrt[3]{2x^2 y} = y\sqrt[3]{2x^2 y} \qquad (R\text{-}2)$

71. $\sqrt{\sqrt[3]{4x^4}} = \sqrt[2\cdot 3]{2^{2\cdot 1} x^{2\cdot 2}} = \sqrt[3]{2x^2} \qquad (R\text{-}2)$

72. $\left(2\sqrt{x} - 5\sqrt{y}\right)\left(\sqrt{x} + \sqrt{y}\right)$

$\qquad = 2\sqrt{x}\sqrt{x} + 2\sqrt{x}\sqrt{y} - 5\sqrt{x}\sqrt{y} - 5\sqrt{y}\sqrt{y}$

$\qquad = 2x - 3\sqrt{x}\sqrt{y} - 5y$

$\qquad = 2x - 3\sqrt{xy} - 5y \qquad (R\text{-}2)$

73.

$\dfrac{3\sqrt{x}}{2\sqrt{x} - \sqrt{y}} = \dfrac{3\sqrt{x}}{\left(2\sqrt{x} - \sqrt{y}\right)} \cdot \dfrac{2\sqrt{x} + \sqrt{y}}{2\sqrt{x} + \sqrt{y}}$

$\qquad = \dfrac{3\sqrt{x}\left(2\sqrt{x} + \sqrt{y}\right)}{\left(2\sqrt{x}\right)^2 - \left(\sqrt{y}\right)^2}$

$\qquad = \dfrac{3\sqrt{x}\left(2\sqrt{x} + \sqrt{y}\right)}{4x - y}$

$\qquad = \dfrac{6x + 3\sqrt{xy}}{4x - y}$

74.

$\dfrac{2\sqrt{u} - 3\sqrt{v}}{2\sqrt{u} + 3\sqrt{v}}$

$\qquad = \dfrac{\left(2\sqrt{u} - 3\sqrt{v}\right)}{\left(2\sqrt{u} + 3\sqrt{v}\right)} \cdot \dfrac{\left(2\sqrt{u} - 3\sqrt{v}\right)}{\left(2\sqrt{u} - 3\sqrt{v}\right)}$

$\qquad = \dfrac{\left(2\sqrt{u}\right)^2 - 2\left(2\sqrt{u}\right)\left(3\sqrt{v}\right) + \left(3\sqrt{v}\right)^2}{\left(2\sqrt{u}\right)^2 - \left(3\sqrt{v}\right)^2}$

$\qquad = \dfrac{4u - 12\sqrt{uv} + 9v}{4u - 9v} \qquad (R\text{-}2)$

75. $\dfrac{y^2}{\sqrt{y^2 + 4} - 2}$

$\qquad = \dfrac{y^2}{\left(\sqrt{y^2 + 4} - 2\right)} \cdot \dfrac{\left(\sqrt{y^2 + 4} + 2\right)}{\left(\sqrt{y^2 + 4} + 2\right)}$

$\qquad = \dfrac{y^2\left(\sqrt{y^2 + 4} + 2\right)}{\left(\sqrt{y^2 + 4}\right)^2 - (2)^2}$

$\qquad = \dfrac{y^2\left(\sqrt{y^2 + 4} + 2\right)}{y^2 + 4 - 4}$

$\qquad = \dfrac{y^2\left(\sqrt{y^2 + 4} + 2\right)}{y^2} = \sqrt{y^2 + 4} + 2 \qquad (R\text{-}2)$

76. The volume of the concrete wall is equal to the volume of the outer cylinder $\left(V = \pi r^2 h\right)$ minus the volume of the basin. Since the radius of the basin is x ft and the concrete is 2 ft thick, the radius of the outer cylinder is $x + 2$ ft. Thus, we have

$$\begin{pmatrix} \text{Volume} \\ \text{of Concrete Wall} \end{pmatrix} = \begin{pmatrix} \text{Volume of} \\ \text{Outer Cylinder} \end{pmatrix} - \begin{pmatrix} \text{Volume of} \\ \text{Basin} \end{pmatrix}$$

$$\begin{aligned} \text{Volume} &= \pi(x+2)^2(3) - \pi x^2(3) \\ &= 3\pi(x^2 + 4x + 4) - 3\pi x^2 \\ &= 3\pi x^2 + 12\pi x + 12\pi - 3\pi x^2 \\ &= 12\pi x + 12\pi \quad (\text{ft}^3) \qquad (R\text{-}3) \end{aligned}$$

77. Average personal income
$$\begin{aligned} &= \text{Total personal income} \div \text{no. of persons} \\ &= 11{,}580{,}000{,}000{,}000 \div 301{,}000{,}000 \\ &= 1.158 \times 10^{13} \div 3.01 \times 10^8 \\ &= 3.85 \times 10^4 \end{aligned}$$
or \$38,500 to three significant digits   (R-2)

78. (A) We are to estimate
$N = 20x^{1/2}y^{1/2}$ given $x = 1{,}600$ units of capital and $y = 900$ units of labor.
$$\begin{aligned} N &= 20(1{,}600)^{1/2}(900)^{1/2} \\ &= 20(40)(30) \\ &= 24{,}000 \text{ units produced.} \end{aligned}$$

(B) Given $x = 3{,}200$ units of capital and $y = 1{,}800$ units of labor, then
$$\begin{aligned} N &= 20(3{,}200)^{1/2}(1{,}800)^{1/2} \\ &= 20(2 \cdot 1{,}600)^{1/2}(2 \cdot 900)^{1/2} \\ &= 20 \cdot 2^{1/2}(1{,}600)^{1/2} \cdot 2^{1/2}(900)^{1/2} \\ &= 20 \cdot 2^{1/2}(40) \cdot 2^{1/2}(30) \\ &= 20(40)(30) \cdot 2^{1/2} \cdot 2^{1/2} \\ &= 24{,}000 \cdot 2^1 \\ &= 48{,}000 \text{ units produced} \end{aligned}$$

(C) The effect of raising x to $2x$ and y to $2y$ is to replace N by
$$\begin{aligned} &= 20(2x)^{1/2}(2y)^{1/2} \\ &= 20 \cdot 2^{1/2}x^{1/2} \cdot 2^{1/2}y^{1/2} \\ &= 20 \cdot 2^{1/2} \cdot 2^{1/2} \cdot x^{1/2} \cdot y^{1/2} \\ &= 2^1 \cdot 20x^{1/2}y^{1/2} \\ &= 2N \end{aligned}$$
Thus, the production is doubled at any production level.   (R-2)

79.
$$\cfrac{1}{\dfrac{1}{R_1} + \dfrac{1}{R_2} + \dfrac{1}{R_3}}$$

$$= \cfrac{R_1 R_2 R_3 \cdot 1}{R_1 R_2 R_3 \cdot \left(\dfrac{1}{R_1} + \dfrac{1}{R_2} + \dfrac{1}{R_3}\right)}$$

$$= \frac{R_1 R_2 R_3}{R_2 R_3 + R_1 R_3 + R_1 R_2} \qquad (R\text{-}4)$$

80. (A) The area of the cardboard can be written as Area = (Original area) − (Removed area), where the original area = $16 \times 30 = 480$ and the removed area consists of 6 squares of area x^2 each; thus
(Original area) − (Removed area)
$= 480 - 6x^2$ in expanded form. In factored form, $= 480 - 6x^2 = 6(80 - x^2)$.

(B) See figure.

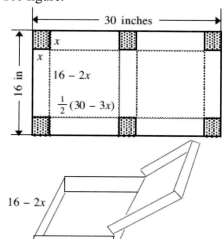

$$\begin{aligned} \text{Volume} &= lwh \\ &= x(16 - 2x) \cdot \tfrac{1}{2}(30 - 3x) \\ &= x(16 - 2x)(15 - 1.5x) \\ \text{or } & 3x(8 - x)(10 - x) \end{aligned}$$
in factored form. In expanded form,
$$\begin{aligned} V &= 3x(8 - x)(10 - x) \\ &= 3x(80 - 18x + x^2) \\ &= 3x^3 - 54x^2 + 240x \qquad (R\text{-}3) \end{aligned}$$

CHAPTER 1

Section 1-1

1. To solve an equation is to find the solution set, that is, to find the set of all elements in the domain of the variable that make the equation true.

3. An equation is linear if it can be written, through simplification, in the form $ax + b = 0$, $a \neq 0$.

5. To check a solution, substitute the value obtained into the original equation to see whether a true statement is obtained.

7. If an equation, like $P = 2\ell + 2w$, contains more than one variable, it only makes sense to solve it if the variable to be solved for is specified.

9.
$$10x - 7 = 4x - 25$$
$$6x - 7 = -25$$
$$6x = -18$$
$$x = -3$$

11.
$$3(x + 2) = 5(x - 6)$$
$$3x + 6 = 5x - 30$$
$$-2x + 6 = -30$$
$$-2x = -36$$
$$x = 18$$

13.
$$5 + 4(t - 2) = 2(t + 7) + 1$$
$$5 + 4t - 8 = 2t + 14 + 1$$
$$4t - 3 = 2t + 15$$
$$2t - 3 = 15$$
$$2t = 18$$
$$t = 9$$

15.
$$5 - \frac{3a - 4}{5} = \frac{7 - 2a}{2} \quad \text{LCD} = 10$$
$$10 \cdot 5 - 10 \cdot \frac{(3a - 4)}{5} = 10 \cdot \frac{(7 - 2a)}{2}$$
$$50 - 2(3a - 4) = 5(7 - 2a)$$
$$50 - 6a + 8 = 35 - 10a$$
$$-6a + 58 = 35 - 10a$$
$$4a = -23$$
$$a = -\frac{23}{4}$$

Common Error:
After line 2, students often write
$$50 - \cancel{10} \; \overset{2}{\underset{\;}{\cancel{5}}} \frac{3a - 4}{\cancel{5}} = \cdots$$
$$50 - 6a - 4 = \cdots$$
forgetting to distribute the –2.
Put compound numerators in parentheses to avoid this.

17.
$$\frac{x + 3}{4} - \frac{x - 4}{2} = \frac{3}{8} \quad \text{LCD} = 8$$
$$8 \cdot \frac{(x + 3)}{4} - 8 \cdot \frac{(x - 4)}{2} = 8 \cdot \frac{3}{8}$$
$$2(x + 3) - 4(x - 4) = 3$$
$$2x + 6 - 4x + 16 = 3$$
$$-2x + 22 = 3$$
$$-2x = -19$$
$$x = \frac{19}{2}$$

19.
$$0.1(t + 0.5) + 0.2t = 0.3(t - 0.4)$$
$$0.1t + 0.05 + 0.2t = 0.3t - 0.12$$
$$0.3t + 0.05 = 0.3t - 0.12$$
$$0.05 = -0.12$$
No solution

21.
$$0.35(s + 0.34) + 0.15s = 0.2s - 1.66$$
$$0.35s + 0.119 + 0.15s = 0.2s - 1.66$$
$$0.5s + 0.119 = 0.2s - 1.66$$
$$0.3s = -1.779$$
$$s = -5.93$$
Solution: –5.93

23. $\dfrac{2}{y} + \dfrac{5}{2} = 4 - \dfrac{2}{3y}$

Excluded value: $y \neq 0$ LCD $= 6y$

$$6y \cdot \dfrac{2}{y} + 6y \cdot \dfrac{5}{2} = 6y(4) - 6y \cdot \dfrac{2}{3y}$$

$$12 + 15y = 24y - 4$$
$$-9y = -16$$
$$y = \dfrac{16}{9}$$

25. $\dfrac{z}{z-1} = \dfrac{1}{z-1} + 2$

Excluded value: $z \neq 1$ LCD $= z - 1$

$$(z-1)\dfrac{z}{z-1} = (z-1)\dfrac{1}{z-1} + 2(z-1)$$

$$z = 1 + 2z - 2$$
$$-z = -1$$
$$z = 1$$

No solution: 1 is excluded

27. $\dfrac{y}{3} + \dfrac{y-10}{5} = \dfrac{2y-2}{4} - 3$ LCD $= 60$

$$60 \cdot \dfrac{y}{3} + 60 \cdot \dfrac{(y-10)}{5} = 60 \cdot \dfrac{(2y-2)}{4} - 60 \cdot 3$$

$$20y + 12(y - 10) = 15(2y - 2) - 180$$
$$20y + 12y - 120 = 30y - 30 - 180$$
$$32y - 120 = 30y - 210$$
$$2y - 120 = -210$$
$$2y = -90$$
$$y = -45$$

29. $1 - \dfrac{x-3}{x-2} = \dfrac{2x-3}{x-2}$

Excluded value: $x \neq 2$ LCD $= x - 2$

$$(x-2)1 - (x-2)\dfrac{(x-3)}{x-2} = (x-2)\dfrac{(2x-3)}{x-2}$$

$$x - 2 - (x - 3) = 2x - 3$$
$$x - 2 - x + 3 = 2x - 3$$
$$1 = 2x - 3$$
$$4 = 2x$$
$$2 = x$$

No solution: 2 is excluded

31. $\dfrac{6}{y+4} + 1 = \dfrac{5}{2y+8}$

Excluded value: $y \neq -4$ LCD $2(y+4)$

$$2(y+4)\dfrac{6}{y+4} + 2(y+4)1 = 2(y+4)\dfrac{5}{2(y+4)}$$

$$12 + 2y + 8 = 5$$
$$2y + 20 = 5$$
$$2y = -15$$
$$y = -\dfrac{15}{2}$$

33. $\dfrac{3a-1}{a^2+4a+4} - \dfrac{3}{a^2+2a} = \dfrac{3}{a}$

$\dfrac{3a-1}{(a+2)^2} - \dfrac{3}{a(a+2)} = \dfrac{3}{a}$ Excluded values: $a \neq 0, -2$

$$a(a+2)^2 \dfrac{(3a-1)}{(a+2)^2} - a(a+2)^2 \dfrac{3}{a(a+2)} = a(a+2)^2 \dfrac{3}{a}$$

$$a(3a - 1) - (a + 2)3 = (a + 2)^2 3$$
$$3a^2 - a - 3a - 6 = 3(a^2 + 4a + 4)$$
$$3a^2 - 4a - 6 = 3a^2 + 12a + 12$$
$$-16a = 18$$
$$a = -\dfrac{9}{8}$$

35.
$$3.142x - 0.4835(x - 4) = 6.795$$
$$3.142x - 0.4835x + 1.934 = 6.795$$
$$2.6585x + 1.934 = 6.795$$
$$2.6585x = 4.861$$
$$x = \frac{4.861}{2.6585}$$
$$x = 1.83$$
to 3 significant digits

37. $\dfrac{2.32x}{x-2} - \dfrac{3.76}{x} = 2.32$

Excluded values: $x \neq 0, 2$ LCD $= x(x - 2)$
$$x(x-2)\frac{2.32x}{x-2} - x(x-2)\frac{3.76}{x} = 2.32x(x-2)$$
$$2.32x^2 - 3.76(x-2) = 2.32x(x-2)$$
$$2.32x^2 - 3.76x + 7.52 = 2.32x^2 - 4.64x$$
$$-3.76x + 7.52 = -4.64x$$
$$7.52 = -0.88x$$
$$x = -8.55$$

39.
$$a_n = a_1 + (n-1)d$$
$$a_1 + (n-1)d = a_n$$
$$(n-1)d = a_n - a_1$$
$$d = \frac{a_n - a_1}{n-1}$$

41. $\dfrac{1}{f} = \dfrac{1}{d_1} + \dfrac{1}{d_2}$ LCD $= d_1 d_2 f$
$$d_1 d_2 f\frac{1}{f} = d_1 d_2 f\frac{1}{d_1} + d_1 d_2 f\frac{1}{d_2}$$
$$d_1 d_2 = d_2 f + d_1 f$$
$$d_2 f + d_1 f = d_1 d_2$$
$$(d_2 + d_1)f = d_1 d_2$$
$$f = \frac{d_1 d_2}{d_2 + d_1}$$

43.
$$A = 2ab + 2ac + 2bc$$
$$2ab + 2ac + 2bc = A$$
$$2ab + 2ac = A - 2bc$$
$$a(2b + 2c) = A - 2bc$$
$$a = \frac{A - 2bc}{2b + 2c}$$

45.
$$y = \frac{2x - 3}{3x + 5}$$
$$(3x + 5)y = 2x - 3$$
$$3xy + 5y = 2x - 3$$
$$5y + 3 = 2x - 3xy$$
$$5y + 3 = x(2 - 3y)$$
$$\frac{5y + 3}{2 - 3y} = x$$
$$x = \frac{5y + 3}{2 - 3y}$$

47.   The "solution" is incorrect. Although 3 is a solution of the two last equations, they are not equivalent to the first equation because both sides have been multiplied by $x - 3$, which is zero when $x = 3$. It is not permitted to multiply both sides of an equation by zero. When $x = 3$, the first equation involves division by zero. Since 3, the only possible solution, is not a solution, the given (first) equation has no solution.

49.

$$\frac{x-\frac{1}{x}}{1+\frac{1}{x}} = 3 \text{ Excl. val.: } x \neq 0$$

$$\frac{x\left(x-\frac{1}{x}\right)}{x\left(1+\frac{1}{x}\right)} = 3$$

$$\frac{x^2-1}{x+1} = 3 \text{ Excl. val.: } x \neq -1$$

$$\frac{(x-1)\;\overset{1}{\cancel{(x+1)}}}{\underset{1}{\cancel{x+1}}} = 3$$

$$x - 1 = 3$$
$$x = 4$$

51.

$$\frac{x+1-\frac{2}{x}}{1-\frac{1}{x}} = x+2 \text{ Excl. val.: } x \neq 0$$

$$\frac{x\left(x+1-\frac{2}{x}\right)}{x\left(1-\frac{1}{x}\right)} = x+2$$

$$\frac{x^2+x-2}{x-1} = x+2 \text{ Excl. val.: } x \neq 1$$

$$\frac{\overset{1}{\cancel{(x-1)}}(x+2)}{\underset{1}{\cancel{x-1}}} = x+2$$

$$x+2 = x+2$$

Solution: All real numbers except the excluded numbers 0 and 1.

53.

$$y = \frac{a}{1+\frac{b}{x+c}}$$

$$y = \frac{a(x+c)}{(x+c)\left(1+\frac{b}{x+c}\right)}$$

$$y = \frac{a(x+c)}{x+c+b}$$

$$y = \frac{ax+ac}{x+c+b}$$

$$y(x+c+b) = ax+ac$$
$$xy+cy+by = ax+ac$$
$$cy+by-ac = ax-xy$$
$$cy+by-ac = x(a-y)$$
$$\frac{cy+by-ac}{a-y} = x$$

$$x = \frac{cy+by-ac}{a-y}$$

55. Let x = the number,
Then 10 less than two thirds the number is one fourth the number.

$$\frac{2}{3}x - 10 = \frac{1}{4}x$$

$$\frac{2}{3}x - 10 = \frac{1}{4}x$$

$$12\left(\frac{2}{3}x\right) - 12(10) = 12\left(\frac{1}{4}x\right)$$

$$8x - 120 = 3x$$
$$-120 = -5x$$
$$x = 24$$

The number is 24.

57. Let x = first of the consecutive even numbers
$x + 2$ = second of the numbers
$x + 4$ = third of the numbers
$x + 6$ = fourth of the numbers
first + second + third = 2 more than twice fourth

$$x + x + 2 + x + 4 = 2 + 2(x + 6)$$
$$3x + 6 = 2 + 2x + 12$$
$$3x + 6 = 2x + 14$$
$$x = 8$$

The four consecutive numbers are 8, 10, 12, 14.

59. Let P = perimeter of triangle, 16 = length of one side, $\frac{2}{7}P$ = length of second side, $\frac{1}{3}P$ = length of third side.

We use the perimeter formula
$$P = a + b + c$$

$$P = 16 + \frac{2}{7}P + \frac{1}{3}P$$

$$21P = 21(16) + 21\left(\frac{2}{7}P\right) + 21\left(\frac{1}{3}P\right)$$

$$21P = 336 + 6P + 7P$$
$$21P = 336 + 13P$$
$$8P = 336$$
$$P = 42 \text{ feet}$$

60. Let w = width of rectangle
$2w - 3$ = length of rectangle
We use the perimeter formula
$P = 2a + 2b.$
$54 = 2w + 2(2w - 3)$
$54 = 2w + 4w - 6$
$54 = 6w - 6$
$60 = 6w$
$10 = w$
$17 = 2w - 3$
dimensions: 17 meters × 10 meters

63. Let P = price before discount

$0.30P$ = 30 percent discount on P
Then price before discount – discount = price after discount
$$P - 0.30P = 140$$
$$0.7P = 140$$
$$P = \frac{140}{0.7}$$
$$P = \$200$$

65. Let x = sales of employee

Then $x - 7,000$ = sales on which 8% commission is paid
$0.08(x - 7,000)$ = (rate of commission) × (sales) = (amount of commission)
$2,150 + 0.08(x - 7,000)$ = (base salary) + (amount of commission) = earnings
Earnings = 3,170
$2,150 + 0.08(x - 7,000) = 3,170$
$2,150 + 0.08x - 560 = 3,170$
$0.08x + 1,590 = 3,170$
$0.08x = 1,580$
$$x = \frac{1,580}{0.08}$$
$$x = \$19,750$$

67. (A) We note: The temperature increased 2.5°C for each additional 100 meters of depth. Hence, the temperature increased 25 degrees for each additional kilometer of depth.

Let x = the depth (in kilometers), then $x - 3$ = the depth beyond 3 kilometers.
$25(x - 3)$ = the temperature increase for $x - 3$ kilometers of depth.
T = temperature at 3 kilometers + temperature increase.
$T = 30 + 25(x - 3)$

(B) We are to find T when $x = 12$. We use the above relationship as a formula
$T = 30 + 25(12 - 3)$
$= 255°C$

(C) We are to find x when $T = 200$. We use the above relationship as an equation.
$200 = 30 + 25(x - 3)$
$200 = 30 + 25x - 75$
$200 = -45 + 25x$
$245 = 25x$
$x = 9.8$ kilometers

69. Let x = total population
Using the assumption given for the ratios, we have

$$\frac{\text{number tagged in second sample}}{\text{number in second sample}} = \frac{\text{total number tagged}}{\text{total population}}$$

$$\frac{22}{80} = \frac{80}{x} \quad \text{LCD: } 80x$$

$$80x\left(\frac{22}{80}\right) = 80x\left(\frac{80}{x}\right)$$

$$22x = 6{,}400$$

$$x = \frac{6{,}400}{22} \approx 291$$

$$x = 291 \text{ kangaroo rats total (approximately)}$$

71. Let x = amount of distilled water
$\quad 50$ = amount of 30% solution
Then $50 + x$ = amount of 25% solution
acid in 30% solution + acid in distilled water = acid in 25% solution

$$0.3(50) + 0 = 0.25(50 + x)$$
$$0.3(50) = 0.25(50 + x)$$
$$15 = 12.5 + 0.25x$$

$$2.5 = 0.25x$$

$$x = 10 \text{ gallons}$$

73. Let x = amount of 50% solution
$\quad 5$ = amount of distilled water
Then $x - 5$ = amount of 90% solution
acid in 90% solution + acid in distilled water = acid in 50% solution

$$0.9(x - 5) + 0 = 0.5x$$
$$0.9x - 4.5 = 0.5x$$
$$-4.5 = -0.4x$$
$$x = 11.25 \text{ liters}$$

75. Let t = time for both computers to finish the job
Then $t + 1$ = time worked by old computer
$\quad t$ = time worked by new computer
Since the old computer can do 1 job in 5 hours, it works at a rate

$$(1 \text{ job}) \div (5 \text{ hours}) = \frac{1}{5} \text{ job per hour}$$

Similarly the new computer works at a rate of $\frac{1}{3}$ job per hour.

Part of job completed by old computer in $t + 1$ hours	+	Part of job completed by new computer in t hours	= 1 whole job.
(Rate of old)(time of old)	+	(Rate of new)(Time of new)	= 1
$\frac{1}{5}(t + 1)$	+	$\frac{1}{3}(t)$	= 1

$$15\left(\frac{1}{5}\right)(t+1) + 15\left(\frac{1}{3}t\right) = 15$$

$$3(t + 1) + 5t = 15$$
$$3t + 3 + 5t = 15$$
$$8t + 3 = 15$$
$$8t = 12$$
$$t = 1.5 \text{ hours}$$

77. Let d = distance flown north

(A) Using $t = \dfrac{d}{r}$, we note:

$$\text{rate flying north} = 150 - 30 = 120 \text{ miles per hour}$$
$$\text{rate flying south} = 150 + 30 = 180 \text{ miles per hour}$$
$$\text{time flying north} + \text{time flying south} = 3 \text{ hours}$$

$$\frac{d}{120} + \frac{d}{180} = 3$$

$$360\frac{d}{120} + 360\frac{d}{180} = 3(360)$$

$$3d + 2d = 1080$$
$$5d = 1080$$
$$d = 216 \text{ miles}$$

(B) We still use the above ideas, except that rate flying north
= rate flying south = 150 miles per hour.

$$\frac{d}{150} + \frac{d}{150} = 3$$

$$\frac{2d}{150} = 3$$

$$\frac{d}{75} = 3$$

$$d = 225 \text{ miles}$$

79. Let x = the speed of the current.

$$\begin{array}{ll} \text{Then distance upstream} = 1{,}000 & \text{rate upstream} = 3 - x \\ \text{distance downstream} = 1{,}200 & \text{rate downstream} = 3 + x \end{array}$$

We can use the formula $d = r \cdot t$ to find an expression for each time:

$$1{,}000 = (3 - x) \cdot (\text{time upstream}); \text{ time upstream} = \frac{1{,}000}{3 - x}$$

$$1{,}200 = (3 + x) \cdot (\text{time downstream}); \text{ time downstream} = \frac{1{,}200}{3 + x}$$

The problem tells us that these two times are equal, so we set them equal to each other and solve.

$$\frac{1{,}000}{3 - x} = \frac{1{,}200}{3 + x} \quad \text{LCD: } (3 + x)(3 - x)$$

$$(3 + x)(3 - x)\frac{1{,}000}{3 - x} = (3 + x)(3 - x)\frac{1{,}200}{3 + x}$$

$$(3 + x)1{,}000 = (3 - x)1{,}200$$

$$3{,}000 + 1{,}000x = 3{,}600 - 1{,}200x$$

$$2{,}200x = 600$$

$$x = \frac{600}{2{,}200} \approx 0.27$$

The speed of the current is about 0.27 meters per second.

81. Let x = frequency of second note

y = frequency of third note

$$\frac{264}{4} = \frac{x}{5} = \frac{y}{6}$$

$$\frac{264}{4} = \frac{x}{5} \qquad \frac{264}{4} = \frac{y}{6}$$

$$66 = \frac{x}{5} \qquad 66 = \frac{y}{6}$$

$$x = 330 \text{ hertz} \quad y = 396 \text{ hertz}$$

83. We are to find d when $p = 40$.

$$40 = -\frac{1}{5}d + 70$$

$$5(40) = 5\left(-\frac{1}{5}d\right) + 5(70)$$

$$200 = -d + 350$$

$$-150 = -d$$

$$d = 150 \text{ centimeters}$$

Section 1-2

1. To solve an inequality is to find the solution set, that is, to find the set of all values of the variables that make the inequality a true statement.

3. The sense of an inequality reverses if we multiply or divide both sides by a negative number. There is no corresponding distinction in solving an equation.

5. $-8 \leq x \leq 7$

7. $-6 \leq x < 6$

9. $x \geq -6$

11. $(-2, 6]$

13. $(-7, 8)$

15. $(-\infty, -2]$

17. $[-7, 2); -7 \leq x < 2$

19. $(-\infty, 0]; x \leq 0$

21. $12 > 6, 12 + 5 > 6 + 5$

23. $-6 > -8, -6 - 3 > -8 - 3$

25. $2 > -1, -2(2) < -2(-1)$

27. $2 < 6, \dfrac{2}{2} < \dfrac{6}{2}$

29. $7x - 8 < 4x + 7$

$3x < 15$

$x < 5$ or $(-\infty, 5)$

31. $12 - y \geq 2(9 - 2y)$

$12 - y \geq 18 - 4y$

$12 + 3y \geq 18$

$3y \geq 6$

$y \geq 2$

or $[2, \infty)$

33. $\dfrac{N}{-2} > 4$

$N < -8$ or $(-\infty, -8)$

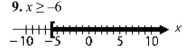

35. $-5t < -10$

$t > 2$ or $(2, \infty)$

37. $3 - m < 4(m - 3)$

$3 - m < 4m - 12$

$-5m < -15$

$m > 3$ or $(3, \infty)$

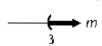

Common Error:

Neglecting to reverse the order after division by -5

39. $-2 - \dfrac{B}{4} \leq \dfrac{1 + B}{3}$

41. $-4 < 5t + 6 \leq 21$

$-10 < 5t \leq 15$

$-2 < t \leq 3$ or $(-2, 3]$

$$12\left(-2 - \frac{B}{4}\right) \le 12\,\frac{(1+B)}{3}$$

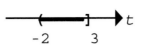

$$-24 - 3B \le 4(1 + B)$$
$$-24 - 3B \le 4 + 4B$$
$$-7B \le 28$$
$$B \ge -4 \quad \text{or} \quad [-4, \infty)$$

43.

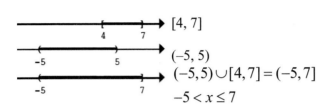

$$[4, 7]$$
$$(-5, 5)$$
$$(-5, 5) \cup [4, 7] = (-5, 7]$$
$$-5 < x \le 7$$

45.

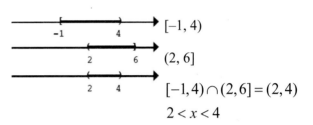

$$[-1, 4)$$
$$(2, 6]$$
$$[-1, 4) \cap (2, 6] = (2, 4)$$
$$2 < x < 4$$

47.

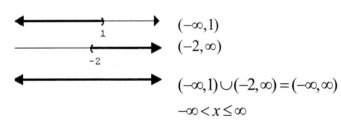

$$(-\infty, 1)$$
$$(-2, \infty)$$
$$(-\infty, 1) \cup (-2, \infty) = (-\infty, \infty)$$
$$-\infty < x \le \infty$$

49.

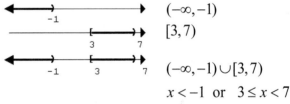

$$(-\infty, -1)$$
$$[3, 7)$$
$$(-\infty, -1) \cup [3, 7)$$
$$x < -1 \quad \text{or} \quad 3 \le x < 7$$

51.

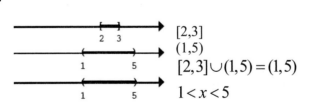

$$[2, 3]$$
$$(1, 5)$$
$$[2, 3] \cup (1, 5) = (1, 5)$$
$$1 < x < 5$$

53.

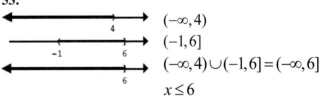

$$(-\infty, 4)$$
$$(-1, 6]$$
$$(-\infty, 4) \cup (-1, 6] = (-\infty, 6]$$
$$x \le 6$$

55.
$$\frac{q}{7} - 3 > \frac{q-4}{3} + 1$$
$$21\left(\frac{q}{7} - 3\right) > 21\left(\frac{(q-4)}{3} + 1\right)$$
$$3q - 63 > 7(q - 4) + 21$$
$$3q - 63 > 7q - 28 + 21$$
$$3q - 63 > 7q - 7$$
$$-4q > 56$$
$$q < -14 \quad \text{or} \quad (-\infty, -14)$$

57.
$$\frac{2x}{5} - \frac{1}{2}(x-3) \le \frac{2x}{3} - \frac{3}{10}(x+2) \qquad \text{LCD} = 30$$
$$12x - 15(x - 3) \le 20x - 9(x + 2)$$
$$12x - 15x + 45 \le 20x - 9x - 18$$
$$-3x + 45 \le 11x - 18$$
$$-14x \le -63$$
$$x \ge 4.5 \quad \text{or} \quad [4.5, \infty)$$

59.

$$-4 \le \frac{9}{5}x + 32 \le 68$$

$$-36 \le \frac{9}{5}x \le 36$$

$$\frac{5}{9}(-36) \le x \le \frac{5}{9}(36)$$

$$-20 \le x \le 20 \text{ or } [-20, 20]$$

61.

$$-20 < \frac{5}{2}(4 - x) < -5$$

$$\frac{2}{5}(-20) < 4 - x < \frac{2}{5}(-5)$$

$$-8 < 4 - x < -2$$

$$-12 < -x < -6$$

$$6 < x < 12 \text{ or } (6, 12)$$

63.

$$16 < 7 - 3x \le 31$$

$$9 < -3x \le 24$$

$$-3 > x \ge -8$$

$$-8 \le x < -3 \text{ or } [-8, -3)$$

65.

$$-8 \le -\frac{1}{4}(2 - x) + 3 < 10$$

$$(-4)(-8) \ge (-4)\left(-\frac{1}{4}\right)(2 - x) + (-4)3 > -4(10)$$

$$32 \ge 2 - x - 12 > -40$$

$$32 \ge -x - 10 > -40$$

$$42 \ge -x > -30$$

$$-42 \le x < 30 \text{ or } [-42, 30)$$

67.

$$0.1(x - 7) < 0.8 - 0.05x$$

$$0.1x - 0.7 < 0.8 - 0.05x$$

$$0.1x + 0.05x - 0.7 < 0.8$$

$$0.15x - 0.7 < 0.8$$

$$0.15x < 0.8 + 0.7$$

$$0.15x < 1.5$$

$$x < 10 \text{ or } (-\infty, 10)$$

69.

$$0.3x - 2.04 \ge 0.04(x + 1)$$

$$0.3x - 2.04 \ge 0.04x + 0.04$$

$$0.3x - 0.04x - 2.04 \ge 0.04$$

$$0.26x - 2.04 \ge 0.04$$

$$0.26x \ge 0.04 + 2.04$$

$$0.26x \ge 2.08$$

$$x \ge 8 \text{ or } [8, \infty)$$

71. $\sqrt{1 - x}$ represents a real number exactly when $1 - x$ is positive or zero. We can write this as an inequality statement and solve for x.

$$1 - x \ge 0$$

$$-x \ge -1$$

$$x \le 1$$

73. $\sqrt{3x + 5}$ represents a real number exactly when $3x + 5$ is positive or zero. We can write this as an inequality statement and solve for x.

$$3x + 5 \ge 0$$

$$3x \ge -5$$

$$x \ge -\frac{5}{3}$$

75. $\dfrac{1}{\sqrt[4]{2x + 3}}$ represents a real number exactly when $2x + 3$ is positive. (*not* zero).

We can write this as an inequality statement and solve for x.

$$2x + 3 > 0$$

$$2x > -3$$

$$x > -\frac{3}{2}$$

77. (A) For $ab > 0$, ab must be positive, hence a and b must have the same sign. Either
    1. $a > 0$ and $b > 0$ or
    2. $a < 0$ and $b < 0$
(B) For $ab < 0$, ab must be negative, hence a and b must have opposite signs. Either
    1. $a > 0$ and $b < 0$ or
    2. $a < 0$ and $b > 0$

(C) For $\dfrac{a}{b} > 0$, $\dfrac{a}{b}$ must be positive, hence a and b must have the same sign. Answer as in (A).

(D) For $\dfrac{a}{b} < 0$, $\dfrac{a}{b}$ must be negative, hence a and b must have opposite signs. Answer as in (B).

79. (A) If $a - b = 1$, then $a = b + 1$. Therefore, a is greater than b. >

(B) If $u - v = -2$, then $v = u + 2$. Therefore, u is less than v. <

81. If $\dfrac{b}{a}$ is greater than 1

$$\frac{b}{a} > 1$$

$$a \cdot \frac{b}{a} < a \cdot 1. \text{ (since } a \text{ is negative.)}$$

$$b < a$$
$$0 < a - b$$
$$a - b \text{ is positive}$$

83. (A) F (B) T (C) T

85. If $a < b$, then by definition of $<$, there exists a positive number p such that $a + p = b$. Then, adding c to both sides, we obtain $(a + c) + p = b + c$, where p is positive. Hence, by definition of $<$, we have
$$a + c < b + c$$

87. (A) If $a < b$, then by definition of $<$, there exists a positive number p such that $a + p = b$. If we multiply both sides of this by the positive number c, we obtain $(a + p)c = bc$, or $ac + pc = bc$, where pc is positive. Hence, by definition of $<$, we have $ac < bc$.

(B) If $a < b$, then by definition of $<$, there exists a positive number p such that $a + p = b$. If we multiply both sides of this by the negative number c, we obtain $(a + p)c = bc$, or $ac + pc = bc$, where pc is negative. Hence, by definition of $<$, we have $ac > bc$.

89.
$$150 \leq T \leq 250$$
$$150 \leq 30 + 25(x - 3) \leq 250$$
$$150 \leq 30 + 25x - 75 \leq 250$$
$$150 \leq 25x - 45 \leq 250$$
$$195 \leq 25x \leq 295$$
$$7.8 \leq x \leq 11.8$$
Depth from 7.8 km to 11.8 km.

91. Let x = number of calculators sold

Then Revenue = (price per calculator) $\times$ (number of calculators sold) = $63x$
    Cost = fixed cost + variable cost
        = 650,000 + (Cost per calculator) $\times$ (number sold)
        = $650,000 + 47x$

(A) We want Revenue > Cost
$$63x > 650,000 + 47x$$
$$16x > 650,000$$
$$x > 40,625$$
More than 40,625 calculators must be sold for the company to make a profit.

(B) We want

$$\text{Revenue} = \text{Cost}$$
$$63x = 650,000 + 47x$$
$$16x = 650,000$$
$$x = 40,625$$

(C) 40,625 calculators sold represents the break-even point, the boundary between profit and loss.

93. (A) The company might try to increase sales and keep the price the same (see part B). It might try to increase the price and keep the sales the same (see part C). Either of these strategies would need further analysis and implementation that are out of place in a discussion here.

(B) Here the cost has been changed to $650,000 + 50.5x$, but the revenue is still $63x$.

$$\text{Revenue} > \text{Cost}$$
$$63x > 650,000 + 50.5x$$
$$12.5x > 650,000$$
$$x > 52,000 \text{ calculators}$$

(C) Let $p =$ the new price. Here the cost is still $650,000 + 50.5x$ as in part (B) where x is now known to be 40,625. Thus, cost $= 650,000 + 50.5(40,625)$.

The revenue is (price per calculator) $\times$ (number of calculators) $= p(40,625)$.

$$\text{Revenue} > \text{Cost}$$
$$p(40,625) > 650,000 + 50.5(40,625)$$
$$p > \frac{650,000 + 50.5(40,625)}{40,625}$$
$$p > 66.50$$

The price could be raised by \$3.50 to \$66.50.

95. We want $220 \leq W \leq 2,750$. We are given $W = 110I$. Substituting, we must solve
$$220 \leq 110I \leq 2,750$$
$$2 \leq I \leq 25 \text{ or } [2, 25].$$

Section 1-3

1. The absolute value of a positive number is equal to the number. The absolute value of 0 is 0. If the number is negative, find its absolute value by changing its sign. This is Definition 1 in words.

3. The equation $|x - 5| = 10$ states that the distance of x from 5 is 10. Then either $x = 5 + 10$, thus $x = 15$, or $x = 5 - 10$, thus $x = -5$.

5. The $\sqrt{}$ symbol denotes the nonnegative square root. Thus the left side of this statement is nonnegative, while the right side need not be.

7. $\sqrt{5}$

9. $|(-6) - (-2)| = |-4| = 4$

11. $|5 - \sqrt{5}| = 5 - \sqrt{5}$ since $5 - \sqrt{5}$ is positive.

13. $|\sqrt{5} - 5| = -(\sqrt{5} - 5) = 5 - \sqrt{5}$ since $\sqrt{5} - 5$ is negative.

15. $d(B,O) = |0 - (-4)|$
$= |4|$
$= 4$

17. $d(O,B) = |-4 - 0|$
$= |-4|$
$= 4$

19. $d(B,C) = |5 - (-4)|$
$= |9|$
$= 9$

21. The distance between x and 3 is equal to 4.
$|x - 3| = 4$

23. The distance between m and -2 is equal to 5.
$|m - (-2)| = 5$
$|m + 2| = 5$

25. The distance between x and 3 is less than 5.
$|x - 3| < 5$

27. The distance between p and -2 is more than 6.
$|p - (-2)| > 6$
$|p + 2| > 6$

29. The distance between q and 1 is not less than 2.
$|q - 1| \geq 2$

31. y is 3 units from 5.

33. y is less than 3 units from 5.

35. y is more than 3 units from 5.

$|y - 5| = 3$
$y - 5 = \pm 3$
$y = 5 \pm 3$
$y = 2, 8$

$|y - 5| < 3$
$-3 < y - 5 < 3$
$2 < y < 8$
$(2, 8)$

$|y - 5| > 3$
$y - 5 < -3 \text{ or } y - 5 > 3$
$y < 2 \text{ or } y > 8$
$(-\infty, 2) \cup (8, \infty)$

37. $|u - (-8)| = 3$
u is 3 units from -8.
$|u + 8| = 3$
$u + 8 = \pm 3$
$u = -8 \pm 3$
$u = -11 \text{ or } -5$

39. $|u - (-8)| \le 3$
u is no more than 3 units from -8.
$|u + 8| \le 3$
$-3 \le u + 8 \le 3$
$-11 \le u \le -5$
$[-11, -5]$

41. $|u - (-8)| \ge 3$
u is at least 3 units from -8.
$|u + 8| \ge 3$
$u + 8 \le -3 \text{ or } u + 8 \ge 3$
$u \le -11 \text{ or } u \ge -5$
$(-\infty, -11] \cup [-5, \infty)$

43. $|2x - 11| \le 13$
$-13 \le 2x - 11 \le 13$
$-2 \le 2x \le 24$
$-1 \le x \le 12$
$[-1, 12]$

45. $|100 - 40t| > 60$
$100 - 40t > 60 \quad \text{ or } \quad 100 - 40t < -60$
$-40t > -40 \quad \text{ or } \quad -40t < -160$
$t < 1 \quad \text{ or } \quad t > 4$
$(-\infty, -1) \cup (4, \infty)$

47. $|4x - 7| = 13$
$4x - 7 = 13 \text{ or } 4x - 7 = -13$
$4x = 20 \text{ or } \quad 4x = -6$
$x = 5 \quad \text{ or } \quad x = -\dfrac{3}{2}$

49. $\left|\dfrac{1}{2}w - \dfrac{3}{4}\right| < 2$

$-2 < \dfrac{1}{2}w - \dfrac{3}{4} < 2$

$-8 < 2w - 3 \quad < 8$
$-5 < 2w \quad < 11$
$-\dfrac{5}{2} < w \quad < \dfrac{11}{2}$
$-2.5 < w \quad < 5.5$
$(-2.5, 5.5)$

51. $|0.2u + 1.7| \ge 0.5$
$0.2u + 1.7 \ge 0.5 \text{ or } 0.2u + 1.7 \le -0.5$
$0.2u \ge -1.2 \text{ or } \quad 0.2u \le -2.2$
$u \ge -6 \text{ or } \quad u \le -11$
$(-\infty, -11] \cup [-6, \infty)$

53. $\left|\dfrac{9}{5}C + 32\right| < 31$

$-31 < \dfrac{9}{5}C + 32 < 31$

$-63 < \dfrac{9}{5}C < -1$

$-35 < C < -\dfrac{5}{9}$

$\left(-35, -\dfrac{5}{9}\right)$

55. $\sqrt{x^2} < 2$
$|x| < 2$
$-2 < x < 2$
$(-2, 2)$

57. $\sqrt{(1 - 3t)^2} \le 2$
$|1 - 3t| \le 2$
$-2 \le 1 - 3t \le 2$
$-3 \le -3t \le 1$
$1 \ge t \ge -\dfrac{1}{3}$

$-\dfrac{1}{3} \le t \le 1$

$\left[-\dfrac{1}{3}, 1\right]$

59. $\sqrt{(2t - 3)^2} > 3$
$|2t - 3| > 3$
$2t - 3 < -3 \text{ or } 2t - 3 > 3$
$2t < 0 \quad 2t > 6$
$t < 0 \quad t > 3$
$(-\infty, 0) \cup (3, \infty)$

61. $|2.25 - 1.02x| \le 1.64$
$-1.64 \le 2.25 - 1.02x \le 1.64$
$-3.89 \le -1.02x \le -0.61$
$3.81 \ge x \ge 0.598$
 to three significant digits
$.598 \le x \le 3.81$

63. $|21.7 - 11.3x| = 15.2$
$21.7 - 11.3x = 15.2$ or $21.7 - 11.3x = -15.2$
$-11.3x = -6.5$ or $-11.3x = -36.9$
$x = 0.575$ or $x = 3.27$
 to three significant digits

65. $0 < |x - 3| < 0.1$
The distance between x and 3 is between 0 and 0.1, that is, less than 0.1 but $x \ne 3$.
$-0.1 < x - 3 < 0.1$ except $x \ne 3$
$2.9 < x < 3.1$ but $x \ne 3$
$2.9 < x < 3$ or $3 < x < 3.1$
$(2.9, 3) \cup (3, 3.1)$

67. $0 < |x - a| < \dfrac{1}{10}$

The distance between x and a is between 0 and $\dfrac{1}{10}$, that is, less than $\dfrac{1}{10}$ but $x \ne a$.

$-\dfrac{1}{10} < x - a < \dfrac{1}{10}$ except $x \ne a$

$a - \dfrac{1}{10} < x < a + \dfrac{1}{10}$ but $x \ne a$

$a - \dfrac{1}{10} < x < a$ or $a < x < a + \dfrac{1}{10}$

$\left(a - \dfrac{1}{10}, a \right) \cup \left(a, a + \dfrac{1}{10} \right)$

69. We consider two cases for $|x - 2| = 2x - 7$.
Case 1: $x - 2 \ge 0$
For this case, the possible values of x are in the set $x \ge 2$.
Then $|x - 2| = x - 2$
We solve $x - 2 = 2x - 7$
$-x = -5$
$x = 5$ A solution, since 5 is among the possible values of x.
Case 2: $x - 2 < 0$
For this case, the possible values of x are in the set $x < 2$.
Then $|x - 2| = 2 - x$
We solve $2 - x = 2x - 7$
$-3x = -9$
$x = 3$ Not a solution, since 3 is not among the possible values of x.
Solution: $x = 5$

71. We consider two cases for $|3x + 5| = 2x + 6$
Case 1: $3x + 5 \ge 0$
For this case, the possible values of x are in the set $x \ge -\dfrac{5}{3}$.
Then $|3x + 5| = 3x + 5$.
We solve $3x + 5 = 2x + 6$
$x = 1$ A solution, since 1 is among the possible values of x.
Case 2: $3x + 5 < 0$
For this case, the possible values of x are in the set $x < -\dfrac{5}{3}$.
Then $|3x + 5| = -(3x + 5)$
We solve $-(3x + 5) = 2x + 6$
$-3x - 5 = 2x + 6$
$-5x = 11$
$x = -2.2$ A solution, since -2.2 is among the possible values of x.
Solution $x = 1, -2.2$

73.   We consider four cases for $|x| + |x + 3| = 3$.

Case 1: $x \geq 0$ and $x + 3 \geq 0$, that is, $x \geq 0$ and $x \geq -3$ (or simply $x \geq 0$)

$|x| = x$ and $|x + 3| = x + 3$

Hence: $x + x + 3 = 3$

$\qquad 2x + 3 = 3$

$\qquad\quad x = 0$ which is a possible value for x in this case.

Case 2: $x < 0$ and $x + 3 \geq 0$, that is, $x < 0$ and $x \geq -3$ (or simply $-3 \leq x < 0$)

$|x| = -x$ and $|x + 3| = x + 3$

Hence: $-x + x + 3 = 3$

$\qquad\quad 3 = 3$ This is satisfied by all x, but the condition $-3 \leq x < 0$ must be imposed.

Case 3: $x \geq 0$ and $x + 3 < 0$, that is, $x \geq 0$ and $x < -3$. These are mutually contradictory, so no solution is possible in this case.

Case 4: $x < 0$ and $x + 3 \leq 0$, that is, $x < 0$ and $x \leq -3$ (or simply $x \leq -3$)

$|x| = -x$ and $|x + 3| = -(x + 3)$

Hence: $-x + [-(x + 3)] = 3$

$\qquad\quad -x - x - 3 = 3$

$\qquad\qquad -2x = 6$

$\qquad\qquad\quad x = -3$ Combining the results of the four cases, $-3 \leq x \leq 0$ is the solution.

75. We consider two cases for $|3 - x| = 2(4 + x)$

Case 1: $3 - x \geq 0$

For this case, the possible values of x are in the set $x \leq 3$.

Then $|3 - x| = 3 - x$.

We solve $3 - x = 2(4 + x)$

$\qquad 3 - x = 8 + 2x$

$\qquad -3x = 5$

$\qquad\quad x = -\dfrac{5}{3}$

A solution, since $-\dfrac{5}{3}$ is among the possible values of x.

Case 2: $3 - x < 0$

For this case, the possible values of x are in the set $x > 3$.

Then $|3 - x| = x - 3$

We solve $x - 3 = 2(4 + x)$

$\qquad x - 3 = 8 + 2x$

$\qquad\quad -x = 11$

$\qquad\quad\ \ x = -11$ Not a solution, since -11 is not among the possible values of x.

Solution $x = -\dfrac{5}{3}$

77. *Case 1:* $x > 0$. Then $|x| = x$. Hence $\dfrac{x}{|x|} = \dfrac{x}{x} = 1$.

Case 2: $x = 0$. Then $|x| = 0$. Hence $\dfrac{x}{|x|}$ is not defined.

Case 3: $x < 0$. Then $|x| = -x$. Hence $\dfrac{x}{|x|} = \dfrac{x}{-x} = -1$.

Thus, the possible values of $\dfrac{x}{|x|}$ are 1 and -1.

79. The absolute value of no number is negative, thus can never be less than -3.

81. There are three possible relations between real numbers a and b; either $a = b$, $a > b$, or $a < b$. We examine each case separately.

Case 1: $a = b$
$|b - a| = |0| = 0$;
$|a - b| = |0| = 0$

Case 2: $a > b$
$|b - a| = -(b - a) = a - b$
$|a - b| = a - b$

Case 3: $b > a$
$|b - a| = b - a$
$|a - b| = -(a - b) = b - a$

Thus in all three cases $|b - a| = |a - b|$.

85. *Case 1. $m > 0$.* Then $|m| = m$; $|-m| = -(-m) = m$.
Hence $|m| = |-m|$

Case 2. $m < 0$. Then $|m| = -m$; $|-m| = -m$.
Hence $|m| = |-m|$

Case 3. $m = 0$. Then $0 = m = -m$,
hence $|m| = |-m| = 0$.

83. If $m < n$, then $m + m < m + n$ (adding m to both sides)
Also, $m + n < n + n$ (adding n to both sides).
Hence,
$$m + m < m + n < n + n$$
$$2m < m + n < 2n$$
$$m < \frac{m + n}{2} < n$$

87. If $n \neq 0$, $n > 0$ or $n < 0$.

Case 1.

$n > 0$. If $m \geq 0$ $|m| = m$, $\dfrac{m}{n} \geq 0$; $\left|\dfrac{m}{n}\right| = \dfrac{m}{n}$; $|n| = n$.

Hence: $\left|\dfrac{m}{n}\right| = \dfrac{m}{n} = \dfrac{|m|}{|n|}$

If $m < 0$ $|m| = -m$, $\dfrac{m}{n} < 0$; $\left|\dfrac{m}{n}\right| = -\dfrac{m}{n}$; $|n| = n$.

Hence: $\left|\dfrac{m}{n}\right| = -\dfrac{m}{n} = \dfrac{-m}{n} = \dfrac{|m|}{|n|}$

Case 2.

$n < 0$. If $m > 0$ $|m| = m$, $\dfrac{m}{n} < 0$; $\left|\dfrac{m}{n}\right| = -\dfrac{m}{n}$; $|n| = -n$

Hence: $\left|\dfrac{m}{n}\right| = -\dfrac{m}{n} = \dfrac{m}{-n} = \dfrac{|m|}{|n|}$

If $m \leq 0$ $|m| = -m$, $\dfrac{m}{n} > 0$; $\left|\dfrac{m}{n}\right| = \dfrac{m}{n}$; $|n| = -n$

Hence: $\left|\dfrac{m}{n}\right| = \dfrac{m}{n} = \dfrac{-m}{-n} = \dfrac{|m|}{|n|}$

89. First note that $a \leq b$ is true if $a < b$ or if $a = b$. Hence $a < b$ implies $a \leq b$. Also $a = b$ implies $a \leq b$. Now consider three cases ($m > 0$, $m = 0$, $m < 0$).

Case 1. $m > 0$. Then $|m| = m$. Also $-|m| < 0$
Hence $-|m| < 0 < m = |m|$
$-|m| < m = |m|$
$-|m| \leq m \leq |m|$

Case 2. $m = 0$. Then $-|m| = m = |m| = 0$.
Hence $-|m| \leq m \leq |m|$

Case 3. $m < 0$. Then $|m| = -m$, hence $-|m| = m$. Also $|m| > 0$.
Hence $-|m| = m < 0 < |m|$
$-|m| = m < |m|$
$-|m| \leq m \leq |m|$

91. $\left|\dfrac{x-45.4}{3.2}\right| < 1$

$-1 < \dfrac{x-45.4}{3.2} < 1$

$-3.2 < x - 45.4 < 3.2$

$42.2 < x < 48.6$

93. The difference between P and 500 has an absolute value of less than 20.

$|P - 500| < 20$

$-20 < P - 500 < 20$

$480 < P < 520$

Production is between 480 and 520 units.

95. The difference between A and 12.436 has an absolute value of less than the error of 0.001.

$|A - 12.436| < 0.001$

$-0.001 < A - 12.436 < 0.001$

$12.435 < A < 12.437$ or, in interval notation,

$(12.435, 12.437)$

97. The difference between N and 2.37 has an absolute value of no more than 0.005.

$|N - 2.37| \le 0.005$.

Section 1-4

1. In the complex number system, every negative real number has an (imaginary) square root.

3. Yes. The square of any pure imaginary number is a negative real number. For example, the square of $3i$ is -9.

5. (A) is true. Every real number a can be written as a complex number $a + 0i$.

(B) is false. For example, i is a complex number that is not a real number.

7. $2 - 9i = 2 + (-9)i$
(A) real part: 2
(B) imaginary part: $-9i$
(C) conjugate: $2 - (-9)i = 2 + 9i$

9. $-\dfrac{3}{2} + \dfrac{5}{6}i$

(A) real part: $-\dfrac{3}{2}$

(B) imaginary part: $\dfrac{5}{6}i$

(C) conjugate: $-\dfrac{3}{2} - \dfrac{5}{6}i$

11. $6.5 + 2.1i$
(A) real part: 6.5
(B) imaginary part: $2.1i$
(C) conjugate: $6.5 - 2.1i$

13. $i\pi = 0 + \pi i$
(A) real part: 0
(B) imaginary part: πi
(C) conjugate: $0 - \pi i = -\pi i$

15. $4\pi = 4\pi + 0i$
(A) real part: 4π
(B) imaginary part: $0i = 0$
(C) conjugate: $4\pi - 0i = 4\pi$

17. $-5 + i\sqrt{2}$
(A) real part: -5
(B) imaginary part: $i\sqrt{2}$
(C) conjugate: $-5 - i\sqrt{2}$

19. $(3 + 5i) + (2 + 4i) = 3 + 5i + 2 + 4i = 5 + 9i$

21. $(8 - 3i) + (-5 + 6i) = 8 - 3i - 5 + 6i = 3 + 3i$

23. $(9 + 5i) - (6 + 2i) = 9 + 5i - 6 - 2i = 3 + 3i$

25. $(3 - 4i) - (-5 + 6i) = 3 - 4i + 5 - 6i = 8 - 10i$

27. $2 + (3i + 5) = 2 + 3i + 5 = 7 + 3i$

29. $(2i)(4i) = 8i^2 = 8(-1) = -8$

31. $-2i(4 - 6i) = -8i + 12i^2 = -8i + 12(-1)$

$\quad\quad = -12 - 8i$

33. $(1 + 2i)(3 - 4i) = 3 - 4i + 6i - 8i^2 = 3 + 2i - 8(-1)$

$\quad\quad = 3 + 2i + 8 = 11 + 2i$

35. $(3 - i)(4 + i) = 12 + 3i - 4i - i^2 = 12 - i - (-1)$

$\quad = 12 - i + 1 = 13 - i$

37. $(2 + 9i)(2 - 9i) = 4 - 81i^2 = 4 + 81 = 85$ or $85 + 0i$

39.
$$\frac{1}{2+4i} = \frac{1}{(2+4i)}\frac{(2-4i)}{(2-4i)}$$

$$= \frac{2-4i}{4-16i^2} = \frac{2-4i}{4+16}$$

$$= \frac{2-4i}{20} = 0.1-0.2i$$

41.
$$\frac{4+3i}{1+2i} = \frac{(4+3i)}{(1+2i)}\frac{(1-2i)}{(1-2i)}$$

$$= \frac{4-5i-6i^2}{1-4i^2} = \frac{4-5i+6}{1+4}$$

$$= \frac{10-5i}{5} = 2-i$$

43.
$$\frac{7+i}{2+i} = \frac{(7+i)}{(2+i)}\frac{(2-i)}{(2-i)} = \frac{14-5i-i^2}{4-i^2}$$

$$= \frac{14-5i+1}{4+1} = \frac{15-5i}{5} = 3-i$$

45. $\sqrt{2}\,\sqrt{8} = \sqrt{16} = 4$

47. $\sqrt{2}\,\sqrt{-8} = \sqrt{2}\,\sqrt{8}\,\sqrt{-1} = \sqrt{2}\,\sqrt{8}\,i$

$$= \sqrt{16}\,i = 4i$$

49. $\sqrt{-2}\,\sqrt{8} = \sqrt{-1}\,\sqrt{2}\,\sqrt{8} = i\sqrt{2}\,\sqrt{8} = i\sqrt{16} = 4i$

51. $\sqrt{-2}\,\sqrt{-8} = \sqrt{-1}\,\sqrt{2}\,\sqrt{-1}\,\sqrt{8} = i\sqrt{2}\,i\sqrt{8}$

$$= i^2\sqrt{16} = -1 \cdot 4 = -4$$

53. $(2-\sqrt{-4})+(5-\sqrt{-9}) = (2-i\sqrt{4})+(5-i\sqrt{9})$

$$= 2-2i+5-3i = 7-5i$$

55. $(9-\sqrt{-9})-(12-\sqrt{-25})$

$$= (9-i\sqrt{9})-(12-i\sqrt{25})$$

$$= (9-3i)-(12-5i)$$

$$= 9-3i-12+5i = -3+2i$$

57. $(3-\sqrt{-4})(-2+\sqrt{-49}) = (3-i\sqrt{4})(-2+i\sqrt{49})$

$$= (3-2i)(-2+7i)$$

$$= -6+25i-14i^2$$

$$= -6+25i+14 = 8+25i$$

59. $\dfrac{5-\sqrt{-4}}{7} = \dfrac{5-i\sqrt{4}}{7} = \dfrac{5-2i}{7} = \dfrac{5}{7}-\dfrac{2}{7}i$

61.
$$\frac{1}{2-\sqrt{-9}} = \frac{1}{2-i\sqrt{9}} = \frac{1}{2-3i} = \frac{1}{(2-3i)}\frac{(2+3i)}{(2+3i)}$$

$$= \frac{2+3i}{4-9i^2} = \frac{2+3i}{4+9} = \frac{2+3i}{13}$$

$$= \frac{2}{13} + \frac{3}{13}i$$

63. $\dfrac{-5}{i} = -\dfrac{5}{i}\cdot\dfrac{i}{i} = \dfrac{-5i}{i^2} = \dfrac{-5i}{-1} = 5i$ or $0+5i$

65. $(2i)^2 - 5(2i) + 6 = 4i^2 - 10i + 6$

$$= -4-10i+6 = 2-10i$$

67. $(5+2i)^2 - 4(5+2i) - 1$

$$= 25+20i+4i^2-20-8i-1$$

$$= 25+20i-4-20-8i-1 = 12i \text{ or } 0+12i$$

69. $x^2 - 2x + 2 = (1-i)^2 - 2(1-i) + 2$

$$= 1-2i+i^2-2+2i+2$$

$$= 1-2i-1-2+2i+2 = 0 \text{ or } 0+0i$$

71. $\sqrt{3-x}$ represents an imaginary number when $3-x$ is negative.

$$3-x < 0$$
$$-x < -3$$
$$x > 3$$

73. $\sqrt{2-3x}$ represents an imaginary number when $2-3x$ is negative.

$$2-3x < 0$$
$$-3x < -2$$
$$x > \frac{2}{3}$$

75. $(2x - 1) + (3y + 2)i = 5 - 4i$
We note: $a + bi = c + di$ if and only if $a = c$ and $b = d$. Thus
$2x - 1 = 5$ and $3y + 2 = -4$
$2x = 6$ $3y = -6$
$x = 3$ $y = -2$

77. $$\frac{(1+x)+(y-2)i}{1+i} = 2 - i$$
$$(1+i)\,\frac{(1+x)+(y-2)i}{1+i} = (2-i)(1+i)$$
$$(1+x)+(y-2)i = 2 - i + 2i - i^2$$
$$(1+x)+(y-2)i = 3 + i$$
We note: $a + bi = c + di$ if and only if $a = c$ and $b = d$. Thus
$1 + x = 3$ and $y - 2 = 1$
$x = 2$ $y = 3$

79. $(10 - 2i)z + (5 + i) = 2i$
$(10 - 2i)z = -5 + i$
$$z = \frac{-5+i}{10-2i}$$
$$z = \frac{-5+i}{10-2i} \cdot \frac{10+2i}{10+2i}$$
$$z = \frac{-50-10i+10i+2i^2}{100-4i^2}$$
$$z = \frac{-50-2}{100+4} = -\frac{1}{2} \text{ or } -\frac{1}{2} + 0i$$

81. $(4 + 2i)z + (7 - 2i) = (4 - i)z + (3 + 5i)$
$3iz + (7 - 2i) = (3 + 5i)$
$3iz = -4 + 7i$
$$z = \frac{-4+7i}{3i}$$
$$z = \frac{-4+7i}{3i} \cdot \frac{i}{i} = \frac{-4i+7i^2}{3i^2}$$
$$z = \frac{-4i-7}{-3} = \frac{7}{3} + \frac{4}{3}i$$

83. x is a square root of y if $x^2 = y$. Thus,

$(2 - i)^2 = 4 - 4i + i^2$ and $(-2 + i)^2 = 4 - 4i + i^2$
$\qquad\qquad = 4 - 4i - 1$ $\qquad\qquad = 4 - 4i - 1$
$\qquad\qquad = 3 - 4i$ $\qquad\qquad = 3 - 4i$

Hence, $2 - i$ and $-2 + i$ are square roots of $3 - 4i$.

85. The error arises when equating $\sqrt{-1}\,\sqrt{-1}$ with $\sqrt{(-1)(-1)}$.
For positive real numbers a and b,
$$\sqrt{-a}\,\sqrt{-b} \neq \sqrt{(-a)(-b)}.$$

87. $i^{4k} = (i^4)^k = (i^2 \cdot i^2)^k = [(-1)(-1)]^k = 1^k = 1$

89. 1. Definition of addition
2. Commutative property for addition of real numbers.
3. Definition of addition (read from right to left).

91. The product of a complex number and its conjugate is a real number.
$z\,\bar{z} = (x + yi)(x - yi)$
$\qquad = x^2 - (yi)^2$
$\qquad = x^2 - y^2i^2$
$\qquad = x^2 + y^2 \text{ or } (x^2 + y^2) + 0i.$
This is a real number.

93. The conjugate of a complex number is equal to the complex number if and only if the number is real. To prove a theorem containing the phrase "if and only if", it is often helpful to prove two parts separately.

Thus: $\overline{z} = z$ if z is real;

$\overline{z} = z$ only if z is real

Hypothesis:	z is real	Hypothesis:	$\overline{z} = z$
Conclusion:	$\overline{z} = z$	Conclusion:	z is real

Proof: Assume z is real, then
$$z = x + 0i = x$$
$$\overline{z} = x - 0i = x$$

Hence $z = \overline{z}$.

Proof: Assume $\overline{z} = z$,
that is, $x - yi = x + yi$

Then by the definition of equality
$$x = x \qquad -y = y$$
$$-2y = 0$$
$$y = 0$$

Hence $z = x + 0i$, that is, z is real.

95. The conjugate of the sum of two complex numbers is equal to the sum of their conjugates.

$$
\begin{aligned}
\overline{z + w} &= \overline{(x + yi) + (u + vi)} \\
&= \overline{x + yi + u + vi} \\
&= \overline{x + u + (y + v)i} \\
&= (x + u) - (y + v)i \\
&= x + u - yi - vi \\
&= (x - yi) + (u - vi) \\
&= \overline{z} + \overline{w}
\end{aligned}
$$

97. The conjugate of the product of two complex numbers is equal to the product of their conjugates.

$$
\begin{aligned}
\overline{zw} &= \overline{(x + yi)(u + vi)} \\
&= \overline{xu + xvi + yui + yvi^2} \\
&= \overline{xu + (xv + yu)i - yv} \\
&= xu - yv - (xv + yu)i \\
&= xu - xvi - yv - yui \\
&= x(u - vi) - yui + yv(-1) \\
&= x(u - vi) - yui + yvi^2 \\
&= x(u - vi) - yi(u - vi) \\
&= (x - yi)(u - vi) \\
&= \overline{z}\ \overline{w}
\end{aligned}
$$

Section 1-5

1. A quadratic equation can be written in the standard form $ax^2 + bx + c = 0$, where $a \neq 0$.

3. The product of two numbers can only be zero if one or both of the numbers is 0.

5. One would have to choose the quadratic formula, because factoring does not always work and completing the square can require somewhat laborious arithmetic.

7.
$$
\begin{aligned}
2x^2 &= 8x \\
2x^2 - 8x &= 0 \\
2x(x - 4) &= 0 \\
2x = 0 \ &\text{or} \ x - 4 = 0 \\
x = 0 \qquad\ &\qquad x = 4
\end{aligned}
$$

9.
$$
\begin{aligned}
-8 &= 22t - 6t^2 \\
6t^2 - 22t - 8 &= 0 \\
2(3t^2 - 11t - 4) &= 0 \\
2(3t + 1)(t - 4) &= 0 \\
3t + 1 = 0 \ &\text{or} \ t - 4 = 0 \\
t = -\frac{1}{3} \qquad\ &\qquad t = 4
\end{aligned}
$$

11.
$$3w^2 + 13w = 10$$
$$3w^2 + 13w - 10 = 0$$
$$(3w - 2)(w + 5) = 0$$
$$3w - 2 = 0 \text{ or } w + 5 = 0$$
$$3w = 2 \qquad w = -5$$
$$w = \frac{2}{3}$$

13.
$$m^2 - 25 = 0$$
$$m^2 = 25$$
$$m = \pm\sqrt{25}$$
$$m = \pm 5$$

15.
$$c^2 + 9 = 0$$
$$c^2 = -9$$
$$c = \pm\sqrt{-9}$$
$$c = \pm 3i$$

17.
$$4y^2 + 9 = 0$$
$$4y^2 = -9$$
$$y^2 = -\frac{9}{4}$$
$$y = \pm\sqrt{-\frac{9}{4}}$$
$$y = \pm\frac{i\sqrt{9}}{\sqrt{4}}$$
$$y = \pm\frac{3i}{2}$$

19.
$$25z^2 - 32 = 0$$
$$25z^2 = 32$$
$$z^2 = \frac{32}{25}$$
$$z = \pm\sqrt{\frac{32}{25}}$$
$$z = \pm\frac{\sqrt{32}}{\sqrt{25}}$$
$$z = \pm\frac{4\sqrt{2}}{5}$$

21.
$$(2k - 5)^2 = 16$$
$$2k - 5 = \pm\sqrt{16}$$
$$2k - 5 = \pm 4$$
$$2k = 5 \pm 4$$
$$k = \frac{5 \pm 4}{2}$$
$$k = \frac{9}{2} \text{ or } k = \frac{1}{2}$$

23.
$$(n - 3)^2 = -4$$
$$n - 3 = \pm\sqrt{-4}$$
$$n - 3 = \pm 2i$$
$$n = 3 \pm 2i$$

25.
$$x^2 - 2x - 1 = 0$$
$$a = 1,\ b = -2,\ c = -1$$
$$b^2 - 4ac = (-2)^2 - 4(1)(-1)$$
$$= 8$$
The discriminant is positive; there are two real roots.
$$x = \frac{-b \pm \sqrt{b^2 - 4ac}}{2a}$$
$$x = \frac{-(-2) \pm \sqrt{8}}{2(1)} = \frac{2 \pm 2\sqrt{2}}{2}$$
$$x = 1 \pm \sqrt{2}$$

Common Errors:
It is incorrect to cancel this way:
$$\frac{2 \pm 2\sqrt{2}}{2} \neq \pm 2\sqrt{2}$$
or this way $\frac{2 \pm 2\sqrt{2}}{2} \neq 1 \pm 2\sqrt{2}$

27.
$$x^2 - 2x + 3 = 0$$
$$a = 1,\ b = -2,\ c = 3$$
$$b^2 - 4ac = (-2)^2 - 4(1)(3) = -8$$
The discriminant is negative; there are no real roots.
$$x = \frac{-b \pm \sqrt{b^2 - 4ac}}{2a}$$
$$x = \frac{-(-2) \pm \sqrt{-8}}{2(1)}$$
$$x = \frac{2 \pm 2i\sqrt{2}}{2} = 1 \pm i\sqrt{2}$$

29.
$$2t^2 + 8 = 6t$$
$$2t^2 - 6t + 8 = 0$$
$$t^2 - 3t + 4 = 0$$
$$a = 1,\ b = -3,\ c = 4$$
$$b^2 - 4ac = (-3)^2 - 4(1)(4) = -7$$
The discriminant is negative; there are no real roots.
$$t = \frac{-b \pm \sqrt{b^2 - 4ac}}{2a}$$
$$t = \frac{-(-3) \pm \sqrt{-7}}{2(1)} = \frac{3 \pm i\sqrt{7}}{2}$$

31.
$$2t^2 + 1 = 6t$$
$$2t^2 - 6t + 1 = 0$$
$$a = 2,\ b = -6,\ c = 1$$
$$b^2 - 4ac = (-6)^2 - 4(2)(1) = 28$$
The discriminant is positive; there are two real roots.
$$t = \frac{-b \pm \sqrt{b^2 - 4ac}}{2a}$$
$$t = \frac{-(-6) \pm \sqrt{28}}{2(2)} = \frac{6 \pm \sqrt{28}}{4}$$
$$t = \frac{6 \pm 2\sqrt{7}}{4} = \frac{3 \pm \sqrt{7}}{2}$$

33. $x^2 - 4x - 1 = 0$
$$x^2 - 4x = 1$$
$$x^2 - 4x + 4 = 5$$
$$(x - 2)^2 = 5$$
$$x - 2 = \pm\sqrt{5}$$
$$x = 2 \pm \sqrt{5}$$

35. $2r^2 + 10r + 11 = 0$
$$r^2 + 5r + \frac{11}{2} = 0$$
$$r^2 + 5r = -\frac{11}{2}$$
$$r^2 + 5r + \frac{25}{4} = -\frac{11}{2} + \frac{25}{4}$$
$$\left(r + \frac{5}{2}\right)^2 = \frac{3}{4}$$
$$r + \frac{5}{2} = \pm\sqrt{\frac{3}{4}}$$
$$r = -\frac{5}{2} \pm \frac{\sqrt{3}}{\sqrt{4}}$$
$$r = -\frac{5}{2} \pm \frac{\sqrt{3}}{2}$$
$$r = \frac{-5 \pm \sqrt{3}}{2}$$

37. $4u^2 + 8u + 15 = 0$
$$u^2 + 2u + \frac{15}{4} = 0$$
$$u^2 + 2u = -\frac{15}{4}$$
$$u^2 + 2u + 1 = -\frac{15}{4} + 1$$
$$(u + 1)^2 = -\frac{11}{4}$$
$$u + 1 = \pm\sqrt{-\frac{11}{4}}$$
$$u = -1 \pm \frac{i\sqrt{11}}{\sqrt{4}}$$
$$u = -\frac{2}{2} \pm \frac{i\sqrt{11}}{2}$$
$$u = \frac{-2 \pm i\sqrt{11}}{2}$$

39. $3w^2 + 4w + 3 = 0$
$$w^2 + \frac{4}{3}w + 1 = 0$$
$$w^2 + \frac{4}{3}w = -1$$
$$w^2 + \frac{4}{3}w + \frac{4}{9} = -1 + \frac{4}{9}$$
$$\left(w + \frac{2}{3}\right)^2 = -\frac{5}{9}$$
$$w + \frac{2}{3} = \pm\sqrt{-\frac{5}{9}}$$
$$w = -\frac{2}{3} \pm \frac{i\sqrt{5}}{\sqrt{9}}$$
$$w = -\frac{2}{3} \pm \frac{i\sqrt{5}}{3}$$
$$w = \frac{-2 \pm i\sqrt{5}}{3}$$

41. $12x^2 + 7x = 10$
$$12x^2 + 7x - 10 = 0$$
$(4x + 5)(3x - 2) = 0$ Polynomial is factorable.

$4x + 5 = 0$ or	$3x - 2 = 0$
$4x = -5$	$3x = 2$
$x = -\dfrac{5}{4}$	$x = \dfrac{2}{3}$

43. $(2y - 3)^2 = 5$ Format for the square root method.
$$2y - 3 = \pm\sqrt{5}$$
$$2y = 3 \pm \sqrt{5}$$
$$y = \frac{3 \pm \sqrt{5}}{2}$$

45.
$$x^2 = 3x + 1$$
$$x^2 - 3x - 1 = 0 \quad \text{Polynomial is not factorable,}$$
$$\text{use quadratic formula.}$$
$$x = \frac{-b \pm \sqrt{b^2 - 4ac}}{2a}$$
$$a = 1, b = -3, c = -1$$
$$x = \frac{-(-3) \pm \sqrt{(-3)^2 - 4(1)(-1)}}{2(1)}$$
$$x = \frac{3 \pm \sqrt{13}}{2}$$

47.
$$7n^2 = -4n$$
$$7n^2 + 4n = 0$$
$$n(7n + 4) = 0 \quad \text{Polynomial is}$$
$$\text{factorable.}$$
$$n = 0 \text{ or } 7n + 4 = 0$$
$$7n = -4$$
$$n = -\frac{4}{7}$$

49.
$$1 + \frac{8}{x^2} = \frac{4}{x}$$
Excluded value: $x \neq 0$
$$x^2 + 8 = 4x$$
$$x^2 - 4x + 8 = 0$$
Polynomial is not factorable,
use quadratic formula, or
complete the square.
$$x^2 - 4x = -8$$
$$x^2 - 4x + 4 = -4$$
$$(x - 2)^2 = -4$$
$$x - 2 = \pm\sqrt{-4}$$
$$x - 2 = \pm i\sqrt{4}$$
$$x - 2 = \pm 2i$$
$$x = 2 \pm 2i$$

51. $\dfrac{24}{10 + m} + 1 = \dfrac{24}{10 - m}$ Excluded value: $m \neq -10, 10$:

LCD is $(10 + m)(10 - m)$

$$(10 + m)(10 - m)\frac{24}{10 + m} + (10 + m)(10 - m) = (10 + m)(10 - m)\frac{24}{10 - m}$$
$$24(10 - m) + 100 - m^2 = 24(10 + m)$$
$$240 - 24m + 100 - m^2 = 240 + 24m$$
$$340 - 24m - m^2 = 240 + 24m$$
$$0 = m^2 + 48m - 100$$
$$m^2 + 48m - 100 = 0 \quad \text{Polynomial is}$$
$$\text{factorable.}$$
$$(m + 50)(m - 2) = 0$$
$$m + 50 = 0 \text{ or } m - 2 = 0$$
$$m = -50 \qquad m = 2$$

53. $\dfrac{2}{x - 2} = \dfrac{4}{x - 3} - \dfrac{1}{x + 1}$ Excluded values: $x \neq 2, 3, -1$

$$(x - 2)(x - 3)(x + 1)\frac{2}{x - 2} = (x - 2)(x - 3)(x + 1)\frac{4}{x - 3} - (x - 2)(x - 3)(x + 1)\frac{1}{x + 1}$$
$$2(x - 3)(x + 1) = 4(x - 2)(x + 1) - (x - 2)(x - 3)$$
$$2(x^2 - 2x - 3) = 4(x^2 - x - 2) - (x^2 - 5x + 6)$$
$$2x^2 - 4x - 6 = 4x^2 - 4x - 8 - x^2 + 5x - 6$$
$$2x^2 - 4x - 6 = 3x^2 + x - 14$$
$$0 = x^2 + 5x - 8$$
$$x^2 + 5x - 8 = 0 \text{ Polynomial is not factorable, use quadratic formula.}$$
$$x = \frac{-b \pm \sqrt{b^2 - 4ac}}{2a} \quad a = 1, b = 5, c = -8$$
$$x = \frac{-5 \pm \sqrt{(5)^2 - 4(1)(-8)}}{2(1)} = \frac{-5 \pm \sqrt{57}}{2}$$

55. $\dfrac{x+2}{x+3} - \dfrac{x^2}{x^2-9} = 1 - \dfrac{x-1}{3-x}$ Excluded values: $x \neq 3, -3$

$$(x-3)(x+3)\dfrac{(x+2)}{x+3} - (x-3)(x+3)\dfrac{x^2}{x^2-9} = (x-3)(x+3) - (x-3)(x+3)\dfrac{x-1}{3-x}$$

$$(x-3)(x+2) - x^2 = x^2 - 9 + (x-1)(x+3)$$
$$x^2 - x - 6 - x^2 = x^2 - 9 + x^2 + 2x - 3$$
$$-x - 6 = 2x^2 + 2x - 12$$
$$0 = 2x^2 + 3x - 6$$
$$2x^2 + 3x - 6 = 0 \qquad \text{Polynomial is not factorable,}$$
$$\text{use quadratic formula.}$$

$$x = \dfrac{-b \pm \sqrt{b^2 - 4ac}}{2a} \quad a = 2, b = 3, c = -6$$

$$x = \dfrac{-3 \pm \sqrt{(3)^2 - 4(2)(-6)}}{2(2)}$$

$$x = \dfrac{-3 \pm \sqrt{57}}{4}$$

57. $s = \dfrac{1}{2}gt^2$

$$\dfrac{1}{2}gt^2 = s$$
$$gt^2 = 2s$$
$$t^2 = \dfrac{2s}{g}$$
$$t = \sqrt{\dfrac{2s}{g}}$$

59.
$$P = EI - RI^2$$
$$RI^2 - EI + P = 0$$

$$I = \dfrac{-b \pm \sqrt{b^2 - 4ac}}{2a} \quad a = R, b = -E, c = P$$

$$I = \dfrac{-(-E) \pm \sqrt{(-E)^2 - 4(R)(P)}}{2(R)}$$

$$I = \dfrac{E + \sqrt{E^2 - 4RP}}{2R} \quad \text{(positive square root)}$$

61. In this problem, $a = 1$, $b = 4$, $c = c$.
Thus, the discriminant
$b^2 - 4ac = (4)^2 - 4(1)(c) = 16 - 4c$.
Hence,
if $16 - 4c > 0$, thus $16 > 4c$ or $c < 4$, there are two distinct real roots.
if $16 - 4c = 0$, thus $c = 4$, there is one real double root,
and if $16 - 4c < 0$, thus $16 < 4c$ or $c > 4$, there are two distinct imaginary roots.

63. $x^2 + 3ix - 2 = 0$

$$x = \dfrac{-b \pm \sqrt{b^2 - 4ac}}{2a} \quad a = 1, b = 3i, c = -2$$

$$x = \dfrac{-3i \pm \sqrt{(3i)^2 - 4(1)(-2)}}{2(1)} = \dfrac{-3i \pm \sqrt{-9+8}}{2}$$

$$x = \dfrac{-3i \pm \sqrt{-1}}{2} = \dfrac{-3i \pm i}{2}$$

$$x = -i, -2i$$

65. $x^2 + 2ix = 3$

$x^2 + 2ix - 3 = 0$

$x = \dfrac{-b \pm \sqrt{b^2 - 4ac}}{2a} \quad a = 1 \ b = 2i \ c = -3$

$x = \dfrac{-2i \pm \sqrt{(2i)^2 - 4(1)(-3)}}{2(1)}$

$x = \dfrac{-2i \pm \sqrt{-4 + 12}}{2}$

$x = \dfrac{-2i \pm \sqrt{8}}{2}$

$x = \dfrac{-2i \pm 2\sqrt{2}}{2}$

$x = \dfrac{2(-i \pm \sqrt{2})}{2}$

$x = -i \pm \sqrt{2}$

$x = \sqrt{2} - i, -\sqrt{2} - i$

67. $x^3 - 1 = 0$

$(x - 1)(x^2 + x + 1) = 0$

$x - 1 = 0 \quad \text{or} \quad x^2 + x + 1 = 0$

$x = 1$

$x = \dfrac{-b \pm \sqrt{b^2 - 4ac}}{2a} \quad a = 1, b = 1, c = 1$

$x = \dfrac{-1 \pm \sqrt{(1)^2 - 4(1)(1)}}{2(1)}$

$x = \dfrac{-1 \pm \sqrt{1 - 4}}{2}$

$x = \dfrac{-1 \pm \sqrt{-3}}{2}$

$x = \dfrac{-1 \pm i\sqrt{3}}{2} \text{ or } -\dfrac{1}{2} \pm \dfrac{1}{2} i\sqrt{3}$

69. The solutions of $ax^2 + bx + c = 0$ are given by $\dfrac{-b \pm \sqrt{b^2 - 4ac}}{2a}$. If $b^2 - 4ac$ is negative, it can be written as $-(4ac - b^2)$, where $4ac - b^2$ is positive. Then

$$\dfrac{-b \pm \sqrt{b^2 - 4ac}}{2a} = \dfrac{-b \pm \sqrt{-(4ac - b^2)}}{2a}$$

$$= \dfrac{-b \pm i\sqrt{4ac - b^2}}{2a}$$

$$= -\dfrac{b}{2a} \pm \dfrac{i\sqrt{4ac - b^2}}{2a}$$

The last expression clearly represents two imaginary numbers, the two imaginary solutions of the equation.

71. If a quadratic equation has two roots, they are $\dfrac{-b + \sqrt{b^2 - 4ac}}{2a}$ and $\dfrac{-b - \sqrt{b^2 - 4ac}}{2a}$. If a, b, c are rational,

then so are $-b, 2a$, and $b^2 - 4ac$. Then, *either* $\sqrt{b^2 - 4ac}$ is rational, hence $\dfrac{-b + \sqrt{b^2 - 4ac}}{2a}$ and

$\dfrac{-b - \sqrt{b^2 - 4ac}}{2a}$ are both rational, *or*, $\sqrt{b^2 - 4ac}$ is irrational, hence $\dfrac{-b + \sqrt{b^2 - 4ac}}{2a}$ and $\dfrac{-b - \sqrt{b^2 - 4ac}}{2a}$

are both irrational, *or*, $\sqrt{b^2 - 4ac}$ is imaginary, hence $\dfrac{-b + \sqrt{b^2 - 4ac}}{2a}$ and $\dfrac{-b + \sqrt{b^2 - 4ac}}{2a}$ are both

imaginary. There is no other possibility; hence, one root cannot be rational while the other is irrational.

73. $r_1 = \dfrac{-b+\sqrt{b^2-4ac}}{2a}$ $r_2 = \dfrac{-b-\sqrt{b^2-4ac}}{2a}$

$r_1 r_2 = \dfrac{(-b+\sqrt{b^2-4ac})}{2a} \dfrac{(-b-\sqrt{b^2-4ac})}{2a}$

$= \dfrac{(-b)^2 - (\sqrt{b^2-4ac})^2}{4a^2} = \dfrac{b^2 - (b^2-4ac)}{4a^2}$

$= \dfrac{b^2 - b^2 + 4ac}{4a^2} = \dfrac{4ac}{4a^2} = \dfrac{c}{a}$

75. The $\pm$ in front still yields the same two numbers even if a is negative.

77. Let x = one number.
Since their sum is 21,
$21 - x$ = other number
Then, since their product is 104,

$$x(21-x) = 104$$
$$21x - x^2 = 104$$
$$0 = x^2 - 21x + 104$$
$$x^2 - 21x + 104 = 0$$
$$(x-13)(x-8) = 0$$
$$x - 13 = 0 \text{ or } x - 8 = 0$$
$$x = 13 \qquad x = 8$$

The numbers are 8 and 13.

79. Let x = first of the two consecutive even integers.

Then $x + 2$ = second of these integers

Since their product is 168,

$$x(x+2) = 168$$
$$x^2 + 2x = 168$$
$$x^2 + 2x - 168 = 0$$
$$(x-12)(x+14) = 0$$
$$x - 12 = 0 \text{ or } \quad x + 14 = 0$$
$$x = 12 \qquad\qquad x = -14$$

If $x = 12$, the two consecutive positive even integers must be 12 and 14. We discard the other solution, since the numbers must be positive.

81. The per person consumption in 1960 is found by setting the number of years after 1960 = x = 0. Then $y = 122$ ounces. To find the year when consumption is again 122, set $y = 122$ and solve.

$$122 = -0.0665x^2 + 3.58x + 122$$
$$-0.0665x^2 + 3.58x = 0$$
$$x(-0.0665x + 3.58) = 0$$
$$x = 0 \quad \text{or} \quad -0.0665x + 3.58 = 0$$

(year 1960) $\qquad x = \dfrac{3.58}{0.0665} \approx 54$

The model predicts consumption at 122 ounces per person in 1960+54 or 2014.

83. From the diagram, the dimension of the planting area are $30 - 2x$ and $20 - 2x$. Then

Area $= 400 = (30 - 2x)(20 - 2x)$

$$400 = 600 - 100x + 4x^2$$
$$0 = 4x^2 - 100x + 200$$
$$x^2 - 25x + 50 = 0$$

$$x = \dfrac{-b \pm \sqrt{b^2 - 4ac}}{2a} \qquad a = 1, b = -25, c = 50$$

$$x = \dfrac{-(-25) \pm \sqrt{(-25)^2 - 4(1)(50)}}{2(1)} \; ; \; x = 2.19 \text{ or } x = 22.81$$

Since x must be less than 20, the second solution is discarded. The walkway should be 2.19 ft wide.

85. From the area formula, Area $= 1,200 = \ell w$. From the perimeter formula, Perimeter $= 150 = 2\ell + 2w$. Solve for w and substitute the result in for w in the first equation.

$$2w = 150 - 2\ell$$

$$w = 75 - \ell$$

Then

$$1,200 = \ell(75 - \ell)$$

$$1,200 = 75\ell - \ell^2$$

$$\ell^2 - 75\ell + 1,200 = 0$$

$$\ell = \frac{-b \pm \sqrt{b^2 - 4ac}}{2a} \quad a = 1, \, b = -75, \, c = 1,200$$

$$\ell = \frac{-(-75) \pm \sqrt{(-75)^2 - 4(1)(1,200)}}{2(1)} \quad \ell = 23.1 \quad \text{or} \quad \ell = 51.9$$

If $\ell = 23.1$, then $w = 75 - 23.1 = 51.9$, so there is actually only one solution, 23.1 feet by 51.9 feet.

89. The revenue equation is $R = qp = (1,600 - 200p)p$.

Solve

(A) $2,800 = (1,600 - 200p)p$
   $200p^2 - 1,600p + 2,800 = 0$
   $p^2 - 8p + 14 = 0$

$$p = \frac{-(-8) \pm \sqrt{(-8)^2 - 4(1)(14)}}{2(1)} = \frac{8 \pm \sqrt{8}}{2}$$

$$p = \$2.59 \text{ or } p = \$5.41$$

87. If $p = 3$, the demand is given by
   $q = 1,600 - 200p = 1,600 - 200(3) = 1,000$
   hamburgers.
   The revenue is given by
   $$R = qp = 1,000 \cdot 3 = \$3,000$$

(B) $3,200 = (1,600 - 200p)p$
   $200p^2 - 1,600p + 3,200 = 0$
   $p^2 - 8p + 16 = 0$
   $(p - 4)^2 = 0$
   $p = \$4$

(C) $3,400 = (1,600 - 200p)p$
   $200p^2 - 1,600p + 3,400 = 0$
   $p^2 - 8p + 17 = 0$
Since the discriminant $b^2 - 4ac = (-8)^2 - 4(1)(17) = -4$ is negative, there is no solution.

91.   Let $r =$ rate of slow plane.
   Then $r + 140 =$ rate of fast plane.

After 1 hour $r(1) = r =$ distance traveled by slow plane.

$(r + 140)(1) = r + 140 =$ distance traveled by fast plane.
Applying the Pythagorean theorem, we have
$$r^2 + (r + 140)^2 = 260^2$$
$$r^2 + r^2 + 280r + 19,600 = 67,600$$
$$2r^2 + 280r - 48,000 = 0$$
$$r^2 + 140r - 24,000 = 0$$
$$(r + 240)(r - 100) = 0$$
$$r + 240 = 0 \text{ or } r - 100 = 0$$
$$r = -240 \qquad r = 100$$

Discarding the negative solution, we have
   $r = 100$ miles per hour $=$ rate of slow plane
$r + 140 = 240$ miles per hour $=$ rate of fast plane

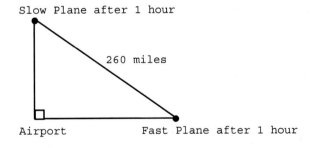

93. Let t = time to travel 500 miles.

Then $200t$ = distance travelled by plane going north

$170t$ = distance travelled by plane going east

Applying the Pythagorean theorem, we have

$$(200t)^2 + (170t)^2 = 500^2$$

$$40,000t^2 + 28,900t^2 = 250,000$$

$$68,900t^2 = 250,000$$

$$t^2 = \frac{250,000}{68,900}$$

$$t = \pm\sqrt{\frac{250,000}{68,900}}$$

$$t = \pm 1.91 \text{ hours}$$

Discarding the negative solution, we have
t = 1.91 hours or 1.91(60) = 114 minutes.
114 minutes after 6:00AM is 7:54AM.

95. Let t = time for smaller pipe to fill tank alone
$t - 5$ = time for larger pipe to fill tank alone
5 = time for both pipes to fill tank together

Then $\dfrac{1}{t}$ = rate for smaller pipe

$\dfrac{1}{t-5}$ = rate for larger pipe

$$\begin{pmatrix} \text{Part of job} \\ \text{completed by} \\ \text{smaller pipe} \end{pmatrix} + \begin{pmatrix} \text{Part of job} \\ \text{completed by} \\ \text{larger pipe} \end{pmatrix} = 1 \text{ whole job}$$

$$\frac{1}{t}(5) + \frac{1}{t-5}(5) = 1$$

$$\frac{5}{t} + \frac{5}{t-5} = 1 \quad \text{Excluded values: } t \neq 0, 5$$

$$t(t-5)\frac{5}{t} + t(t-5)\frac{5}{t-5} = t(t-5)$$

$$5(t-5) + 5t = t(t-5)$$

$$5t - 25 + 5t = t^2 - 5t$$

$$10t - 25 = t^2 - 5t$$

$$0 = t^2 - 15t + 25$$

$$t^2 - 15t + 25 = 0$$

$$t = \frac{-b \pm \sqrt{b^2 - 4ac}}{2a} \quad a = 1, b = -15, c = 25$$

$$t = \frac{-(-15) \pm \sqrt{(-15)^2 - 4(1)(25)}}{2(1)} = \frac{15 \pm \sqrt{125}}{2}$$

$$t = 13.09, 1.91$$

$$t - 5 = 8.09, -3.09$$

Discarding the answer for t which results in a negative answer for $t - 5$, we have 13.09 hours for smaller pipe alone, 8.09 hours for larger pipe alone.

97. Let v = speed of car. Applying the given formula, we have

$$165 = 0.044v^2 + 1.1v$$

$$0 = 0.044v^2 + 1.1v - 165$$

$$0.044v^2 + 1.1v - 165 = 0$$

$$v = \frac{-b \pm \sqrt{b^2 - 4ac}}{2a} \quad a = 0.044, b = 1.1, c = -165$$

$$v = \frac{-1.1 \pm \sqrt{(1.1)^2 - 4(0.044)(-165)}}{2(0.044)} = \frac{-1.1 \pm 5.5}{0.088}$$

$$v = -75 \text{ or } 50$$

Discarding the negative answer, we have v = 50 miles per hour.

99. (A) Let ℓ = length of building
w = width of building.
Then, using the hint, in the similar triangles *ABC* and *AFE*, we have

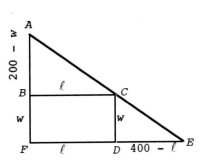

$$\frac{\ell}{200-w} = \frac{400}{200}$$

$$\frac{\ell}{200-w} = 2$$

$$\ell = 2(200 - w)$$

$$\ell = 400 - 2w$$

Since the cross-sectional area of the building is given as 15,000 ft^2, we have

$$\ell w = 15,000$$

Substituting, we get,

$$(400 - 2w)w = 15,000$$

$$400w - 2w^2 = 15,000$$

$$0 = 2w^2 - 400w + 15,000$$

$$0 = w^2 - 200w + 7,500$$

$$0 = (w - 50)(w - 150)$$

$w - 50 = 0$ or	$w - 150 = 0$
$w = 50$	$w = 150$
$\ell = 400 - 2w$	$\ell = 400 - 2w$
$= 400 - 2(50)$	$= 400 - 2(150)$
$= 300$	$= 100$

Thus, there are two solutions: the building is 50 ft wide and 300 ft long or 150 ft wide and 100 ft long.

(B) Preceding as in (A), but with the cross-sectional area given as 25,000 ft^2, we have $\ell w = 25,000$.

$$(400 - 2w)w = 25,000$$

$$400w - 2w^2 = 25,000$$

$$0 = 2w^2 - 400w + 25,000$$

$$0 = w^2 - 200w + 12,500$$

However, since $b^2 - 4ac = (-200)^2 - 4(1)(12,500) = -10,000$ is negative, there are no real solutions; the builder cannot meet this condition.

101. Let x = distance from the warehouse to Factory *A*. Since the distance from the warehouse to Factory *B* via Factory *A* is known (it is the difference in odometer readings: 52937 — 52846) to be 91 miles, then

$91 - x$ = distance from Factory *A* to Factory *B*.

The distance from Factory *B* to the warehouse is known (it is the difference in odometer readings: 53002—52937) to be 65 miles. Applying the Pythagorean theorem, we have

$$x^2 + (91 - x)^2 = 65^2$$
$$x^2 + 8281 - 182x + x^2 = 4225$$
$$2x^2 - 182x + 4056 = 0$$
$$x^2 - 91x + 2028 = 0$$
$$(x - 52)(x - 39) = 0$$
$$x - 52 = 0 \quad \text{or} \quad x - 39 = 0$$
$$x = 52 \text{ mi} \qquad x = 39 \text{ mi}$$

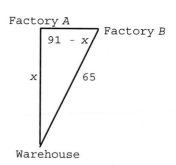

Since we are told that the distance from the warehouse to Factory *A* was greater than the distance from Factory *A* to Factory *B*, we discard the solution $x = 39$, which would lead to $91 - x = 52$ miles, a contradiction. 52 miles.

Section 1-6

1. If an equation is solved by raising both sides to the same power, the resulting equation may have solutions that are not solutions of the original equation; these are called extraneous solutions.

3. Since $|x| = \sqrt{x^2}$, an absolute value equation can be regarded as a radical equation; these can often be solved by squaring both sides.

5. This statement is true, since $\pm\sqrt{5}$ are the only two solutions of $x^2 = 5$. T

7. This statement is false. The left side, $(x + 5)^2$, is not equal to $x^2 + 10x + 25$. This only equals $x^2 + 25$ when $x = 0$. F

9. This statement is false.
    $(\sqrt{x-1} + 1)^2$ is not equal to $x - 1 + 1$ or x, in general.
    In fact
    $(\sqrt{x-1} + 1)^2 = x - 1 + 2\sqrt{x-1} + 1 = x + 2\sqrt{x-1}$.
    This is only equal to x in case $x = 1$.   F

11. This statement is false. If $x^3 = 2$ then $x = \sqrt[3]{2}$ or x is equal to one of two non-real complex numbers whose cube is 2. If $x = 8$, x^3 must equal 512. F

13. $\sqrt{x+2} = 4$
    $x + 2 = 16$
    $x = 14$
    Check:
    $\sqrt{14+2} \overset{?}{=} 4$
    $\sqrt{16} \overset{?}{=} 4$
    $4 \overset{\checkmark}{=} 4$
    Solution: 14

15. $\sqrt{3y-5} + 10 = 0$
    $\sqrt{3y-5} = -10$

    This equation has no solution, since the left side can never be a negative.

17. $\sqrt{3y-2} = y - 2$
    $3y - 2 = y^2 - 4y + 4$
    $0 = y^2 - 7y + 6$
    $y^2 - 7y + 6 = 0$
    $(y - 1)(y - 6) = 0$
    $y = 1, 6$

    Check: 1: $\sqrt{3(1)-2} \overset{?}{=} 1 - 2$
    $\sqrt{1} \overset{?}{=} -1$
    $1 \neq -1$
    Not a solution

    6: $\sqrt{3(6)-2} \overset{?}{=} 6 - 2$
    $\sqrt{16} \overset{?}{=} 4$
    $4 \overset{\checkmark}{=} 4$
    A solution

    Solution: 6

19. $\sqrt{5w+6}\ - w = 2$

$\qquad \sqrt{5w+6}\ = w + 2$

$\qquad 5w + 6\ = w^2 + 4w + 4$

$\qquad 0 = w^2 - w - 2$

$w^2 - w - 2 = 0$

$(w - 2)(w + 1) = 0$

$\qquad w = 2, -1$

$$\boxed{\begin{array}{c} \text{Common Error}: 5w + 6 - w^2 = 4 \\ \text{or} \quad 5w + 6 + w^2 = 4 \\ \text{are not equivalent to the} \\ \text{original equation.} \end{array}}$$

Check:

2:   $\qquad \sqrt{5(2)+6}\ - 2 \overset{?}{=} 2$

$\qquad\qquad\qquad 4 - 2 \overset{\checkmark}{=} 2$

A solution

Solution: 2, −1

−1: $\qquad \sqrt{5(-1)+6}\ -(-1) \overset{?}{=} 2$

$\qquad\qquad\qquad 1 + 1 \overset{\checkmark}{=} 2$

A solution

21. $|2x + 1| = x + 2$

$|2x + 1|^2 = (x + 2)^2$

$\qquad 4x^2 + 4x + 1 = x^2 + 4x + 4$

$\qquad\qquad 3x^2 = 3$

$\qquad\qquad x^2 = 1$

$\qquad\qquad x = 1 \text{ or } x = -1$

Check: $x = 1$

$|2x + 1| = x + 2$

$|2 \cdot 1 + 1| \overset{?}{=} 1 + 2$

$|3| \overset{?}{=} 3$

$3 \overset{\checkmark}{=} 3$

A solution

Solution: 1, −1

$x = -1$

$|2x + 1| = x + 2$

$|2(-1) + 1| \overset{?}{=} (-1) + 2$

$|-1| \overset{?}{=} 1$

$1 \overset{\checkmark}{=} 1$

A solution

23. $|x - 5| = 7 - 2x$

$|x - 5|^2 = (7 - 2x)^2$

$x^2 - 10x + 25 = 49 - 28x + 4x^2$

$\qquad 0 = 3x^2 - 18x + 24$

$3(x - 2)(x - 4) = 0$

$x - 2 = 0 \text{ or } x - 4 = 0$

$\qquad x = 2 \qquad\qquad x = 4$

Check: $x = 2$

$|x - 5| = 7 - 2x$

$|2 - 5| \overset{?}{=} 7 - 2 \cdot 2$

$|-3| \overset{?}{=} 3$

$3 \overset{\checkmark}{=} 3$

A solution

Solution: 2

$x = 4$

$|x - 5| = 7 - 2x$

$|4 - 5| \overset{?}{=} 7 - 2 \cdot 4$

$|-1| \overset{?}{=} -1$

$1 \ne -1$

Not a solution

25. $|3x - 4| \quad = 2x - 5$

$|3x - 4|^2 \quad = (2x - 5)^2$

$9x^2 - 24x + 16 = 4x^2 - 20x + 25$

$5x^2 - 4x - 9 = 0$

$(5x - 9)(x + 1) = 0$

$5x - 9 = 0 \text{ or } x + 1 = 0$

$\qquad x = \dfrac{9}{5} \qquad\qquad x = -1$

Check: $x = \dfrac{9}{5}$

$|3x - 4| = 2x - 5$

$\left|3\left(\dfrac{9}{5}\right) - 4\right| \overset{?}{=} 2\left(\dfrac{9}{5}\right) - 5$

$\left|\dfrac{7}{5}\right| \overset{?}{=} -\dfrac{7}{5}$

$\dfrac{7}{5} \ne -\dfrac{7}{5}$

Not a solution

No solution

$x = -1$

$|3x - 4| = 2x - 5$

$|3(-1) - 4| \overset{?}{=} 2(-1) - 5$

$|-7| \overset{?}{=} -7$

$7 \ne -7$

Not a solution

27.   If we set $u = x^{-3}$ then $u^2 = x^{-6}$ and the equation would become $2u^2 - 4u = 0$; hence, the equation is of quadratic type.

29.   Since $x^3 \ne (x)^2$ this is not an equation of quadratic type.

31. If we set $u = \dfrac{1}{x^2}$ then $u^2 = \dfrac{1}{x^4}$ and the equation would become

$\dfrac{10}{9} + 4u - 7u^2 = 0$; hence, the equation is of quadratic type.

33.
$$\sqrt{3t-2} = 1 - 2\sqrt{t}$$
$$3t - 2 = 1 - 4\sqrt{t} + 4t$$
$$-t - 3 = -4\sqrt{t}$$
$$t^2 + 6t + 9 = 16t$$
$$t^2 - 10t + 9 = 0$$
$$(t - 9)(t - 1) = 0$$
$$t = 9, 1$$

Check: 9: $\quad \sqrt{3 \cdot 9 - 2} \overset{?}{=} 1 - 2\sqrt{9}$

$$\sqrt{25} \overset{\checkmark}{=} 1 - 6$$
$$5 \neq -5$$
Not a solution

1: $\quad \sqrt{3 \cdot 1 - 2} \overset{?}{=} 1 - 2\sqrt{1}$

$$\sqrt{1} \overset{?}{=} 1 - 2$$
$$1 \neq -1$$
Not a solution

No solution

35. $m^4 + 2m^2 - 15 = 0$
Let $u = m^2$, then
$$u^2 + 2u - 15 = 0$$
$$(u + 5)(u - 3) = 0$$
$$u = -5, 3$$
$$m^2 = -5 \qquad m^2 = 3$$
$$m = \pm i\sqrt{5} \qquad m = \pm\sqrt{3}$$

37.
$$3x = \sqrt{x^2 - 2}$$
$$9x^2 = x^2 - 2$$
$$8x^2 = -2$$
$$x^2 = -\dfrac{1}{4}$$
$$x = \pm\sqrt{-\dfrac{1}{4}}$$
$$x = \pm\dfrac{1}{2}i$$

Solution: $\dfrac{1}{2}i$

Check: $\quad \dfrac{1}{2}i: 3\left(\dfrac{1}{2}i\right) \overset{?}{=} \sqrt{\left(\dfrac{1}{2}i\right)^2 - 2}$

$$\dfrac{3}{2}i \overset{?}{=} \sqrt{-\dfrac{1}{4} - 2}$$
$$\dfrac{3}{2}i \overset{?}{=} \sqrt{-\dfrac{9}{4}}$$
$$\dfrac{3}{2}i \overset{\checkmark}{=} \dfrac{3}{2}i$$
A solution

$-\dfrac{1}{2}i: 3\left(-\dfrac{1}{2}i\right) \overset{?}{=} \sqrt{\left(-\dfrac{1}{2}i\right)^2 - 2}$

$$-\dfrac{3}{2}i \overset{?}{=} \sqrt{-\dfrac{1}{4} - 2}$$
$$-\dfrac{3}{2}i \overset{?}{=} \sqrt{-\dfrac{9}{4}}$$
$$-\dfrac{3}{2}i \neq \dfrac{3}{2}i$$
Not a solution

39. $2y^{2/3} + 5y^{1/3} - 12 = 0$
Let $u = y^{1/3}$, then
$$2u^2 + 5u - 12 = 0$$
$$(2u - 3)(u + 4) = 0$$
$$2u - 3 = 0 \qquad u + 4 = 0$$
$$u = \dfrac{3}{2} \qquad u = -4$$
$$y^{1/3} = \dfrac{3}{2} \qquad y^{1/3} = -4$$
$$y = \dfrac{27}{8} \qquad y = -64$$

41. $(m^2 - 2m)^2 + 2(m^2 - 2m) = 15$
Let $u = m^2 - 2m$, then
$$u^2 + 2u = 15$$
$$u^2 + 2u - 15 = 0$$
$$(u + 5)(u - 3) = 0$$
$$u = -5 \qquad\qquad u = 3$$
$$m^2 - 2m = -5 \qquad m^2 - 2m = 3$$
$$m^2 - 2m + 1 = -4 \qquad m^2 - 2m - 3 = 0$$
$$(m - 1)^2 = -4 \qquad (m - 3)(m + 1) = 0$$
$$m - 1 = \pm 2i \quad m - 3 = 0 \quad m + 1 = 0$$
$$m = 1 \pm 2i \quad m = 3 \qquad m = -1$$

43.

$$\sqrt{2t+3} + 2 = \sqrt{t-2}$$

$$\begin{aligned}
2t + 3 + 4\sqrt{2t+3} + 4 &= t - 2 \\
2t + 7 + 4\sqrt{2t+3} &= t - 2 \\
4\sqrt{2t+3} &= -t - 9 \\
16(2t+3) &= t^2 + 18t + 81 \\
32t + 48 &= t^2 + 18t + 81 \\
0 &= t^2 - 14t + 33 \\
0 &= (t - 11)(t - 3) \\
t = 11 \quad t &= 3
\end{aligned}$$

Common Error : $2t + 3 + 4 = t - 2$ is not an equivalent equation to the given equation $(\sqrt{2t+3} + 2)^2 ? \, 2t + 3 + 4$

Check: 11: $\sqrt{2(11)+3} + 2 \overset{?}{=} \sqrt{11-2}$

$$\sqrt{25} + 2 \overset{?}{=} \sqrt{9}$$
$$5 + 2 \neq 3$$

Not a solution

3: $\sqrt{2(3)+3} + 2 \overset{?}{=} \sqrt{3-2}$

$$\sqrt{9} + 2 \overset{?}{=} \sqrt{1}$$
$$3 + 2 \neq 1$$

Not a solution
No solution

45. $\sqrt{w+3} + \sqrt{2-w} = 3$

$$\begin{aligned}
\sqrt{w+3} &= 3 - \sqrt{2-w} \\
w + 3 &= 9 - 6\sqrt{2-w} + 2 - w \\
w + 3 &= 11 - w - 6\sqrt{2-w} \\
2w - 8 &= -6\sqrt{2-w} \\
w - 4 &= -3\sqrt{2-w} \\
w^2 - 8w + 16 &= 9(2-w) \\
w^2 - 8w + 16 &= 18 - 9w \\
w^2 + w - 2 &= 0 \\
(w+2)(w-1) &= 0 \\
w = -2 \qquad w &= 1
\end{aligned}$$

Check: -2: $\sqrt{(-2)+3} + \sqrt{2-(-2)} \overset{?}{=} 3$

$$\sqrt{1} + \sqrt{4} \overset{?}{=} 3$$
$$1 + 2 \overset{\checkmark}{=} 3$$

A solution

1: $\sqrt{1+3} + \sqrt{2-1} \overset{?}{=} 3$

$$\sqrt{4} + \sqrt{1} \overset{\checkmark}{=} 3$$

A solution
Solution: -2, 1

47. $\sqrt{8-z} = 1 + \sqrt{z+5}$

$$\begin{aligned}
8 - z &= 1 + 2\sqrt{z+5} + z + 5 \\
8 - z &= z + 6 + 2\sqrt{z+5} \\
2 - 2z &= 2\sqrt{z+5} \\
1 - z &= \sqrt{z+5} \\
z^2 - 2z + 1 &= z + 5 \\
z^2 - 3z - 4 &= 0 \\
(z-4)(z+1) &= 0 \\
z = 4 \qquad z &= -1
\end{aligned}$$

Check: 4: $\sqrt{8-4} \overset{?}{=} 1 + \sqrt{4+5}$

$$\sqrt{4} \overset{?}{=} 1 + \sqrt{9}$$
$$2 \neq 1 + 3$$

Not a solution

-1: $\sqrt{8-(-1)} \overset{?}{=} 1 + \sqrt{(-1)+5}$

$$\sqrt{9} \overset{?}{=} 1 + \sqrt{4}$$
$$3 \overset{\checkmark}{=} 1 + 2$$

A solution
Solution: -1

49.

$$\sqrt{4x^2 + 12x + 1} - 6x = 9$$

$$\sqrt{4x^2 + 12x + 1} = 6x + 9$$

$$4x^2 + 12x + 1 = 36x^2 + 108x + 81$$

$$0 = 32x^2 + 96x + 80$$

$$0 = 2x^2 + 6x + 5$$

$$x = \frac{-b \pm \sqrt{b^2 - 4ac}}{2a} \quad a = 2 \; b = 6 \; c = 5$$

$$x = \frac{-6 \pm \sqrt{6^2 - 4(2)(5)}}{2(2)}$$

$$x = \frac{-6 \pm \sqrt{36 - 40}}{4}$$

$$x = \frac{-6 \pm \sqrt{-4}}{4}$$

$$x = \frac{-6 \pm 2i}{4}$$

$$x = -\frac{3}{2} \pm \frac{1}{2}i$$

Check: $\quad -\dfrac{3}{2} + \dfrac{1}{2}i$:

$$\sqrt{4\left(-\frac{3}{2} + \frac{1}{2}i\right)^2 + 12\left(-\frac{3}{2} + \frac{1}{2}i\right) + 1} - 6\left(-\frac{3}{2} + \frac{1}{2}i\right) \overset{?}{=} 9$$

$$\sqrt{(-3 + i)^2 - 18 + 6i + 1} + 9 - 3i \overset{?}{=} 9$$

$$\sqrt{9 - 6i + i^2 - 18 + 6i + 1} + 9 - 3i \overset{?}{=} 9$$

$$\sqrt{9 - 6i - 1 - 18 + 6i + 1} + 9 - 3i \overset{?}{=} 9$$

$$\sqrt{-9} + 9 - 3i \overset{?}{=} 9$$

$$3i + 9 - 3i \overset{\checkmark}{=} 9 \quad \text{A solution}$$

$-\dfrac{3}{2} - \dfrac{1}{2}i$:

$$\sqrt{4\left(-\frac{3}{2} - \frac{1}{2}i\right)^2 + 12\left(-\frac{3}{2} - \frac{1}{2}i\right) + 1} - 6\left(-\frac{3}{2} - \frac{1}{2}i\right) \overset{?}{=} 9$$

$$\sqrt{(-3 - i)^2 - 18 - 6i + 1} + 9 + 3i \overset{?}{=} 9$$

$$\sqrt{9 + 6i + i^2 - 18 - 6i + 1} + 9 + 3i \overset{?}{=} 9$$

$$\sqrt{9 + 6i - 1 - 18 - 6i + 1} + 9 + 3i \overset{?}{=} 9$$

$$\sqrt{-9} + 9 + 3i \overset{?}{=} 9$$

$$3i + 9 + 3i \overset{?}{=} 9$$

$$9 + 6i \neq 9 \quad \text{Not a solution}$$

Solution: $-\dfrac{3}{2} + \dfrac{1}{2}i$

51. $y^2 - 2y^{-1} + 3 = 0$
Let $u = y^{-1}$, then
$$u^2 - 2u + 3 = 0$$
$$u^2 - 2u = -3$$
$$u^2 - 2u + 1 = -2$$
$$(u - 1)^2 = -2$$
$$u - 1 = \pm i\sqrt{2}$$
$$u = 1 \pm i\sqrt{2}$$
$$y^{-1} = 1 \pm i\sqrt{2}$$
$$\frac{1}{y} = 1 \pm i\sqrt{2}$$

$$y = \frac{1}{1 \pm i\sqrt{2}} = \frac{1}{(1 \pm i\sqrt{2})}\frac{(1 \mp i\sqrt{2})}{(1 \mp i\sqrt{2})}$$

$$y = \frac{1 \pm i\sqrt{2}}{1 - (-2)} = \frac{1 \pm i\sqrt{2}}{3}$$

53. $2t^4 - 5t^2 + 2 = 0$
Let $u = t^2$, then
$$2u^2 - 5u + 2 = 0$$
$$(2u - 1)(u - 2) = 0$$
$$2u - 1 = 0 \quad \text{or} \quad u - 2 = 0$$
$$u = \frac{1}{2} \qquad\qquad u = 2$$
$$t^2 = \frac{1}{2} \qquad\qquad t^2 = 2$$

$$t^2 = 2 \qquad\qquad t^2 = \frac{1}{2}$$

$$t = \pm\sqrt{2} \qquad\quad t = \pm\sqrt{\frac{1}{2}}$$
$$t = \pm\frac{1}{\sqrt{2}}$$
$$t = \pm\frac{\sqrt{2}}{2}$$

or alternatively, write
$$\frac{1}{y^2} - \frac{2}{y} + 3 = 0 \quad y \neq 0 \;\; LCD = y^2$$
$$1 - 2y + 3y^2 = 0$$
$$3y^2 - 2y + 1 = 0$$
$$y = \frac{-b \pm \sqrt{b^2 - 4ac}}{2a} \quad a = 3, b = -2, c = 1$$
$$y = \frac{-(-2) \pm \sqrt{(-2)^2 - 4(3)(1)}}{2(3)}$$
$$y = \frac{2 \pm \sqrt{-8}}{6}$$
$$y = \frac{2 \pm i2\sqrt{2}}{6} = \frac{1 \pm i\sqrt{2}}{3}$$

55. $3z^{-1} - 3z^{-1/2} + 1 = 0$
Let $u = z^{-1/2}$, then
$$3u^2 - 3u + 1 = 0$$
$$u = \frac{-b \pm \sqrt{b^2 - 4ac}}{2a} \quad a = 3, b = -3, c = 1$$
$$u = \frac{-(-3) \pm \sqrt{(-3)^2 - 4(3)(1)}}{2(3)}$$
$$u = \frac{3 \pm i\sqrt{3}}{6}$$
$$z^{-1/2} = \frac{3 \pm i\sqrt{3}}{6}$$
$$z^{-1} = \left(\frac{3 \pm i\sqrt{3}}{6}\right)^2$$
$$= \frac{9 \pm 2(3)\ i\sqrt{3} + (i\sqrt{3})^2}{36}$$
$$z^{-1} = \frac{9 \pm 6i\sqrt{3} - 3}{36}$$
$$z^{-1} = \frac{6 \pm 6i\sqrt{3}}{36}$$
$$z^{-1} = \frac{1 \pm i\sqrt{3}}{6}$$
$$z = \frac{6}{1 \pm i\sqrt{3}} = \frac{6}{(1 \pm i\sqrt{3})}\frac{(1 \mp i\sqrt{3})}{(1 \mp i\sqrt{3})}$$
$$z = \frac{6(1 \pm i\sqrt{3})}{1 - (-3)} = \frac{6(1 \pm i\sqrt{3})}{4} \text{ or } \frac{3 \pm 3i\sqrt{3}}{2}$$

57. By squaring: $m - 7\sqrt{m} + 12 = 0$

$$m + 12 = 7\sqrt{m}$$
$$m^2 + 24m + 144 = 49m$$
$$m^2 - 25m + 144 = 0$$
$$(m - 9)(m - 16) = 0$$
$$m - 9 = 0 \text{ or } m - 16 = 0$$
$$m = 9, 16$$

By substitution:

$$m - 7\sqrt{m} + 12 = 0$$

Let $u = \sqrt{m}$, then

$$u^2 - 7u + 12 = 0$$
$$(u - 4)(u - 3) = 0$$
$$u - 4 = 0 \text{ or } u - 3 = 0$$
$$u = 3, 4$$
$$\sqrt{m} = 3 \qquad \sqrt{m} = 4$$
$$m = 9 \qquad m = 16$$

These answers have already been checked.

Check: $m = 9$ $m = 16$

$$9 - 7\sqrt{9} + 12 \overset{?}{=} 0 \qquad 16 - 7\sqrt{16} + 12 \overset{?}{=} 0$$
$$0 \overset{\surd}{=} 0 \qquad\qquad\qquad 0 \overset{\surd}{=} 0$$

A solution   A solution

Solution: $m = 9, 16$

59. $t - 11\sqrt{t} + 18 = 0$

By squaring:

$$t - 11\sqrt{t} + 18 = 0$$
$$t + 18 = 11\sqrt{t}$$
$$t^2 + 36w + 324 = 121t$$
$$t^2 - 85w + 324 = 0$$
$$(t - 4)(t - 81) = 0$$
$$t - 4 = 0 \qquad t - 81 = 0$$
$$t = 4, 81$$

Check:

$$4 - 11\sqrt{4} + 18 \overset{?}{=} 0$$
$$0 \overset{\surd}{=} 0$$
$$81 - 11\sqrt{81} + 18 \overset{?}{=} 0$$
$$0 \overset{\surd}{=} 0$$

Solution: $t = 4, 81$

By substitution: $t - 11\sqrt{t} + 18 = 0$

Let $u = \sqrt{t}$, then

$$u^2 - 11u + 18 = 0$$
$$(u - 9)(u - 2) = 0$$
$$u = 2, 9$$
$$u = 2 \qquad u = 9$$
$$\sqrt{t} = 2 \qquad \sqrt{t} = 9$$
$$t = 4 \qquad t = 81$$

These answers have already been checked.

61. $\sqrt{7 - 2x} - \sqrt{x + 2} = \sqrt{x + 5}$

$$7 - 2x - 2\sqrt{7 - 2x}\sqrt{x + 2} + x + 2 = x + 5$$
$$-2\sqrt{7 - 2x}\sqrt{x + 2} - x + 9 = x + 5$$
$$-2\sqrt{7 - 2x}\sqrt{x + 2} = 2x - 4$$
$$-\sqrt{7 - 2x}\sqrt{x + 2} = x - 2$$
$$(7 - 2x)(x + 2) = x^2 - 4x + 4$$
$$7x + 14 - 2x^2 - 4x = x^2 - 4x + 4$$
$$0 = 3x^2 - 7x - 10$$
$$0 = (3x - 10)(x + 1)$$
$$3x - 10 = 0 \qquad x + 1 = 0$$
$$x = \frac{10}{3} \qquad x = -1$$

Check: $x = \dfrac{10}{3}$: $\sqrt{7 - 2\left(\frac{10}{3}\right)} - \sqrt{\frac{10}{3} + 2} \overset{?}{=} \sqrt{\frac{10}{3} + 5}$

$$\sqrt{\frac{21}{3} - \frac{20}{3}} - \sqrt{\frac{10}{3} + \frac{6}{3}} \overset{?}{=} \sqrt{\frac{10}{3} + \frac{15}{3}}$$

$$\sqrt{\frac{1}{3}} - \sqrt{\frac{16}{3}} \overset{?}{=} \sqrt{\frac{25}{3}}$$

$$\frac{1}{\sqrt{3}} - \frac{4}{\sqrt{3}} \neq \frac{5}{\sqrt{3}}$$

Not a solution

$x = -1$: $\sqrt{7 - 2(-1)} - \sqrt{(-1) + 2} \overset{?}{=} \sqrt{(-1) + 5}$

$$\sqrt{9} - \sqrt{1} \overset{?}{=} \sqrt{4}$$

$$3 - 1 \overset{\surd}{=} 2$$

A solution

Solution: -1

63.
$$3 + x^{-4} = 5x^{-2} \quad x \neq 0, \text{LCD} = x^4$$
$$3x^4 + 1 = 5x^2$$
$$3x^4 - 5x^2 + 1 = 0$$

Let $u = x^2$, then
$$3u^2 - 5u + 1 = 0$$
$$u = \frac{-b \pm \sqrt{b^2 - 4ac}}{2a} \quad a = 3, b = -5, c = 1$$
$$u = \frac{-(-5) \pm \sqrt{(-5)^2 - 4(3)(1)}}{2(3)}$$
$$u = \frac{5 \pm \sqrt{13}}{6}$$
$$x^2 = \frac{5 \pm \sqrt{13}}{6}$$
$$x = \pm \sqrt{\frac{5 \pm \sqrt{13}}{6}} \quad \text{(four roots)}$$

65.
$$2\sqrt{x+5} = 0.01x + 2.04$$
$$200\sqrt{x+5} = x + 204$$
$$40{,}000(x + 5) = (x + 204)^2$$
$$40{,}000x + 200{,}000 = x^2 + 408x + 41{,}616$$
$$0 = x^2 - 39{,}592x - 158{,}384$$

Although this is factorable in the integers, one is unlikely to notice this or to detect the factors, so the quadratic formula is used

$$x = \frac{-b \pm \sqrt{b^2 - 4ac}}{2a} \quad a = 1$$
$$b = -39{,}592$$
$$c = -158{,}384$$

$$x = \frac{-(-39{,}592) \pm \sqrt{(-39{,}592)^2 - 4(1)(-158{,}384)}}{2(1)}$$
$$x = \frac{39{,}592 \pm 39{,}600}{2}$$
$$x = -4, x = 39{,}596$$

Check:

$$-4: \quad 2\sqrt{-4+5} \overset{?}{=} 0.01(-4) + 2.04$$
$$2 \overset{\checkmark}{=} 2$$

$$39{,}596: \quad 2\sqrt{39{,}596+5} \overset{?}{=} 0.01(39{,}596) + 2.04$$
$$398 \overset{\checkmark}{=} 398$$

Solution: $-4, 39596$

67. $2x^{-2/5} - 5x^{-1/5} + 1 = 0$

Let $u = x^{-1/5}$, then

$$2u^2 - 5u + 1 = 0$$

$$u = \frac{-b \pm \sqrt{b^2 - 4ac}}{2a} \qquad a = 2, b = -5, c = 1$$

$$u = \frac{-(-5) \pm \sqrt{(-5)^2 - 4(2)(1)}}{2(2)}$$

$$u = \frac{5 \pm \sqrt{17}}{4}$$

$$x^{-1/5} = \frac{5 + \sqrt{17}}{4} \qquad\qquad x^{-1/5} = \frac{5 - \sqrt{17}}{4}$$

$$x^{1/5} = \frac{4}{5 + \sqrt{17}} \qquad\qquad x^{1/5} = \frac{4}{5 - \sqrt{17}}$$

$$x = \left(\frac{4}{5 + \sqrt{17}}\right)^5 \qquad x = \left(\frac{4}{5 - \sqrt{17}}\right)^5$$

$$x \approx 0.016203 \qquad\qquad x \approx 1974.98$$

69. The "solution" is incorrect because an incorrect attempt at squaring both sides was made. The square of $\sqrt{x+3} + 5$ is $x + 3 + 10\sqrt{x+3} + 25$ not $x + 3 + 25$.

71. Substitute $t = 14$ into the given formula and solve.

$$14 = \frac{\sqrt{x}}{4} + \frac{x}{1,100}$$

Let $u = \sqrt{x}$, then

$$14 = \frac{u}{4} + \frac{u^2}{1,100}$$

$$15,400 = 275u + u^2$$

$$0 = u^2 + 275u - 15,400$$

$$u = \frac{-b \pm \sqrt{b^2 - 4ac}}{2a} \quad a = 1, b = 275, c = -15,400$$

$$u = \frac{-275 \pm \sqrt{(275)^2 - 4(1)(-15,400)}}{2(1)}$$

$$u = 47.72 \text{ or } -322.72$$

The negative "solution" for $\sqrt{x}$ is discarded

$$\sqrt{x} = 47.72$$
$$x = (47.72)^2$$
$$x = 2,277 \text{ feet}$$

73. Let $x = $ length and $y = $ width, then $A = xy = 45$. From the Pythagorean theorem, since the diagonal is 10 inches, $x^2 + y^2 = 10^2$. Solve $xy = 45$ for y in terms of x to obtain $y = \dfrac{45}{x}$, then substitute this for y into

$$x^2 + y^2 = 10^2.$$

$$x^2 + \left(\frac{45}{x}\right)^2 = 10^2$$

$$x^2 + \frac{2,025}{x^2} = 100$$

$$x^4 + 2,025 = 100x^2$$

$$x^4 - 100x^2 + 2,025 = 0$$

Let $u = x^2$, then

$$u^2 - 100u + 2,025 = 0$$

$$u = \frac{-b \pm \sqrt{b^2 - 4ac}}{2a} \quad a = 1, b = -100, c = 2,025$$

$$u = \frac{-(-100) \pm \sqrt{(-100)^2 - 4(1)(2,025)}}{2(1)}$$

$u = 71.79$ or $u = -28.21$
$x^2 = 71.79 \qquad x^2 = -28.21$
$x = 8.5$ in $\qquad$ impossible
$y = \dfrac{45}{x} = 5.3$ in $\qquad\qquad$ Dimensions: 5.3 in by 8.5 in

75. Let x = width of cross-section of the beam
      y = depth of cross-section of the beam
From the Pythagorean theorem
      $x^2 + y^2 = 16^2$
Thus, $y = \sqrt{256 - x^2}$

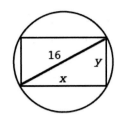

Since the area of the rectangle is given by xy, we have
$$xy = 120$$
$$x\sqrt{256 - x^2} = 120$$
$$x^2(256 - x^2) = 14{,}400$$
$$256x^2 - x^4 = 14{,}400$$
$$-x^4 + 256x^2 - 14{,}400 = 0$$
$$(x^2)^2 - 256x^2 + 14{,}400 = 0$$

$$x^2 = \frac{-b \pm \sqrt{b^2 - 4ac}}{2a} \qquad a = 1,\, b = -256,\, c = 14{,}400$$

$$x^2 = \frac{-(-256) \pm \sqrt{(-256)^2 - 4(1)(14{,}400)}}{2(1)}$$

$$x^2 = \frac{256 \pm \sqrt{65{,}536 - 57{,}600}}{2}$$

$$x^2 = \frac{256 \pm \sqrt{7{,}936}}{2}$$

$$x^2 = 128 \pm \sqrt{1{,}984}$$

$$x = \sqrt{128 \pm \sqrt{1{,}984}}$$

If $x = \sqrt{128 + \sqrt{1{,}984}} \approx 13.1$ then

$$y = \sqrt{256 - x^2} = \sqrt{256 - (128 + \sqrt{1{,}984})} = \sqrt{128 - \sqrt{1{,}984}} \approx 9.1$$

Thus the dimensions of the rectangle are 13.1 inches by 9.1 inches. Notice that if $x = \sqrt{128 - \sqrt{1{,}984}}$, then

$y = \sqrt{128 + \sqrt{1{,}984}}$ and the dimensions are still 13.1 inches by 9.1 inches.

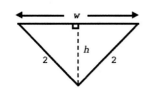

Let w = width of trough
h = altitude of triangular end

77.

Examining the triangular end of the trough sketched above, we see that

$h^2 + \left(\dfrac{1}{2}w\right)^2 = 2^2$. The area of this end, $A = \dfrac{1}{2}wh$. Since the volume of the trough

V is given by $V = A \cdot 6$, we have

$$9 = 6A$$
$$9 = 6\left(\dfrac{1}{2}wh\right)$$
$$9 = 3wh$$
$$3 = wh$$

Since $h^2 = 2^2 - \left(\dfrac{1}{2}w\right)^2$

$$h^2 = 2^2 - \dfrac{1}{4}w^2$$

$$h = \sqrt{4 - \dfrac{1}{4}w^2}$$

Hence we solve

$$3 = w\sqrt{4 - \dfrac{1}{4}w^2}$$

$$9 = w^2\left(4 - \dfrac{1}{4}w^2\right)$$

$$9 = 4w^2 - \dfrac{1}{4}(w^2)^2$$

$$36 = 16w^2 - (w^2)^2$$

$$(w^2)^2 - 16w^2 + 36 = 0$$

$$w^2 = \dfrac{-b \pm \sqrt{b^2 - 4ac}}{2a} \quad a = 1, b = -16, c = 36$$

$$w^2 = \dfrac{-(-16) \pm \sqrt{(-16)^2 - 4(1)(36)}}{2(1)}$$

$$w^2 = \dfrac{16 \pm \sqrt{256 - 144}}{2}$$

$$w^2 = \dfrac{16 \pm \sqrt{112}}{2}$$

$$w^2 = 8 \pm 2\sqrt{7}$$

$$w = \sqrt{8 \pm 2\sqrt{7}}$$

$$w = 1.65 \text{ ft or } 3.65 \text{ ft}$$

CHAPTER 1 REVIEW

1. $8x + 10 = 4x - 30$
$\quad 4x + 10 = -30$
$\quad\quad 4x = -40$
$\quad\quad\; x = -10$
$\quad\quad\quad\quad (1\text{-}1)$

2. $4 - 3(x + 2) = 5x - 7(4 - x)$
$\quad 4 - 3x - 6 = 5x - 28 + 7x$
$\quad\quad -3x - 2 = 12x - 28$
$\quad\quad -15x - 2 = -28$
$\quad\quad\quad -15x = -26$
$\quad\quad\quad\quad\; x = \dfrac{26}{15}$
$\quad\quad\quad\quad\quad\quad (1\text{-}1)$

3. $\dfrac{y+10}{15} - \dfrac{1}{5} = \dfrac{y+1}{6} - \dfrac{1}{10}$ LCD: 30

$30 \cdot \dfrac{(y+10)}{15} - 30 \cdot \dfrac{1}{5} = 30 \cdot \dfrac{(y+1)}{6} - 30 \cdot \dfrac{1}{10}$

$\quad 2(y + 10) - 6 = 5(y + 1) - 3$
$\quad 2y + 20 - 6 = 5y + 5 - 3$
$\quad\quad 2y + 14 = 5y + 2$
$\quad\quad -3y + 14 = 2$
$\quad\quad\quad -3y = -12$
$\quad\quad\quad\; y = 4 \quad\quad (1\text{-}1)$

4. $3(2 - x) - 2 \leq 2x - 1$
$\quad 6 - 3x - 2 \leq 2x - 1$
$\quad\quad -3x + 4 \leq 2x - 1$
$\quad\quad\quad -5x \leq -5$
$\quad\quad\quad\;\; x \geq 1 \quad\quad [1, \infty)$

$\quad\quad\quad\quad\quad\quad (1\text{-}2)$

5. $|y + 9| < 5$
$\quad -5 < y + 9 < 5$
$\quad -14 < y < -4$
$\quad (-14, -4)$

$\quad\quad\quad\quad\quad\quad (1\text{-}3)$

6. $|3 - 2x| \leq 5$
$\quad -5 \leq 3 - 2x \leq 5$
$\quad -8 \leq -2x \leq 2$
$\quad\; 4 \geq x \geq -1$
$\quad -1 \leq x \leq 4$

$[-1, 4]$
$\quad (1\text{-}3)$

7. (A) $9 - 4i = 9 + (-4)i$
Real part: 9
Imaginary part: $-4i$
Conjugate: $9 - (-4)i = 9 + 4i$

(B) $5i = 0 + 5i$
Real part $= 0$
Imaginary part: $5i$
Conjugate: $0 + (-5)i = -5i$

(C) $-10 = -10 + 0i$
Real part: -10
Imaginary part: 0
Conjugate: $-10 - 0i = -10$ $\quad\quad (1\text{-}4)$

8. (A) $(4 + 7i) + (-2 - 3i) = 4 + 7i - 2 - 3i = 2 + 4i$

(B) $(-3 + 5i) - (4 - 8i) = -3 + 5i - 4 + 8i = -7 + 13i$

(C) $(1 - 2i)(3 + 4i) = 3 + 4i - 6i - 8i^2 = 3 - 2i + 8 = 11 - 2i$

(D) $\dfrac{21 + 9i}{5 - 2i} = \dfrac{(21 + 9i)}{(5 - 2i)} \dfrac{(5 + 2i)}{(5 + 2i)}$

$\quad\quad = \dfrac{105 + 42i + 45i + 18i^2}{25 - 4i^2} = \dfrac{105 + 87i - 18}{25 + 4} = \dfrac{87 + 87i}{29} = 3 + 3i \quad\quad (1\text{-}4)$

9. $2x^2 - 7 = 0$

$2x^2 = 7$

$x^2 = \dfrac{7}{2}$

$x = \pm\sqrt{\dfrac{7}{2}} = \pm\dfrac{\sqrt{14}}{2}$

(1-5)

10. $5x^2 + 20 = 0$

$5x^2 = -20$

$x^2 = -4$

$x = \pm\sqrt{-4}$

$x = \pm 2i$ *(1-5)*

11. $2x^2 = 4x$

$2x^2 - 4x = 0$

$2x(x - 2) = 0$

$2x = 0 \quad x - 2 = 0$

$x = 0 \qquad\quad x = 2$

(1-5)

12. $2x^2 = 7x - 3$

$2x^2 - 7x + 3 = 0$

$(2x - 1)(x - 3) = 0$

$2x - 1 = 0 \quad x - 3 = 0$

$x = \dfrac{1}{2} \qquad x = 3$

(1-5)

13. $m^2 + m + 1 = 0$

$m = \dfrac{-b \pm \sqrt{b^2 - 4ac}}{2a} \qquad a = 1 \; b = 1 \; c = 1$

$m = \dfrac{-1 \pm \sqrt{(1)^2 - 4(1)(1)}}{2(1)} = \dfrac{-1 \pm \sqrt{-3}}{2} = \dfrac{-1 \pm i\sqrt{3}}{2} = -\dfrac{1}{2} \pm \dfrac{\sqrt{3}}{2}i$ *(1-5)*

14. $y^2 = \dfrac{3}{2}(y + 1)$

$2y^2 = 3(y + 1)$

$2y^2 = 3y + 3$

$2y^2 - 3y - 3 = 0$

$y = \dfrac{-b \pm \sqrt{b^2 - 4ac}}{2a} \qquad a = 2 \; b = -3 \; c = -3$

$y = \dfrac{-(-3) \pm \sqrt{(-3)^2 - 4(2)(-3)}}{2(2)}$

$y = \dfrac{3 \pm \sqrt{33}}{4}$ *(1-5)*

15. $\sqrt{5x - 6} - x = 0$

$\sqrt{5x - 6} = x$

$5x - 6 = x^2$

$0 = x^2 - 5x + 6$

$x^2 - 5x + 6 = 0$

$(x - 3)(x - 2) = 0$

$x = 2, 3$

Check: $\sqrt{5(2) - 6} - 2 \overset{?}{=} 0$

$0 \overset{\checkmark}{=} 0$

$\sqrt{5(3) - 6} - 3 \overset{?}{=} 0$

$0 \overset{\checkmark}{=} 0$

Solution: 2, 3 *(1-6)*

16. $\sqrt{15 + 6x}$ represents a real number exactly when

$15 + 6x$ is positive or zero.

We can write this as an inequality statement and solve for x.

$15 + 6x \geq 0$

$6x \geq -15$

$x \geq -\dfrac{5}{2}$

(1-2)

17. $\dfrac{7}{2 - x} = \dfrac{10 - 4x}{x^2 + 3x - 10}$

$\dfrac{7}{2 - x} = \dfrac{10 - 4x}{(x - 2)(x + 5)}$ Excluded values: $x \neq 2, -5$

$\overset{-1}{(x - 2)}(x + 5)\dfrac{7}{2 - x} = (x - 2)(x + 5)\dfrac{10 - 4x}{(x - 2)(x + 5)}$

$-7(x + 5) = 10 - 4x$

$-7x - 35 = 10 - 4x$

$-3x = 45$

$x = -15$ *(1-1)*

18.

$$\frac{u-3}{2u-2} = \frac{1}{6} - \frac{1-u}{3u-3}$$

$$\frac{u-3}{2(u-1)} = \frac{1}{6} - \frac{1-u}{3(u-1)} \quad \text{Excluded value: } u \neq 1$$

$$6(u-1)\frac{(u-3)}{2(u-1)} = 6(u-1)\frac{1}{6} - 6(u-1)\frac{(1-u)}{3(u-1)}$$

$$3(u-3) = u-1 - 2(1-u)$$
$$3u-9 = u-1-2+2u$$
$$3u-9 = 3u-3$$
$$-9 = -3$$

No solution $\qquad (1\text{-}1)$

19.

$$\frac{x+3}{8} \leq 5 - \frac{2-x}{3}$$

$$24\frac{(x+3)}{8} \leq 120 - 24\frac{(2-x)}{3}$$

$$3(x+3) \leq 120 - 8(2-x)$$
$$3x+9 \leq 120 - 16 + 8x$$
$$3x+9 \leq 8x + 104$$
$$-5x \leq 95$$
$$x \geq -19$$

$[-19, \infty)$

$\qquad (1\text{-}2)$

20.

$$|3x-8| > 2$$

$$3x-8 < -2 \quad \text{or} \quad 3x-8 > 2$$
$$3x < 6 \qquad\qquad 3x > 10$$

$$x < 2 \quad \text{or} \qquad x > \frac{10}{3}$$

$$\left(-\infty, 2\right) \cup \left(\frac{10}{3}, \infty\right)$$

$\qquad (1\text{-}3)$

21.

$$\sqrt{(1-2m)^2} \leq 3$$
$$|1-2m| \leq 3$$
$$-3 \leq 1-2m \leq 3$$
$$-4 \leq -2m \leq 2$$
$$2 \geq m \geq -1$$
$$-1 \leq m \leq 2$$

$[-1, 2]$

$\qquad (1\text{-}3)$

22. (A) $d(A,B) = |20 - 5| = |15| = 15$
(B) $d(A,C) = |(-8) - 5| = |-13| = 13$
(C) $d(B,C) = |(-8) - 20| = |-28| = 28$ $(1\text{-}3)$

23. (A) $(3+i)^2 - 2(3+i) + 3 = 9 + 6i + i^2 - 6 - 2i + 3$
$$= 9 + 6i - 1 - 6 - 2i + 3$$
$$= 5 + 4i$$

(B) $i^{27} = i^{26}i = (i^2)^{13}i = (-1)^{13}i = (-1)i = -i$ $(1\text{-}4)$

24. (A) $(2 - \sqrt{-4}) - (3 - \sqrt{-9}) = (2 - i\sqrt{4}) - (3 - i\sqrt{9}) = (2 - 2i) - (3 - 3i) = 2 - 2i - 3 + 3i = -1 + i$

(B) $\dfrac{2 - \sqrt{-1}}{3 + \sqrt{-4}} = \dfrac{2 - i\sqrt{1}}{3 + i\sqrt{4}} = \dfrac{2 - i}{3 + 2i} = \dfrac{(2-i)}{(3+2i)}\dfrac{(3-2i)}{(3-2i)} = \dfrac{6 - 7i + 2i^2}{9 - 4i^2} = \dfrac{6 - 7i - 2}{9 + 4} = \dfrac{4 - 7i}{13} = \dfrac{4}{13} - \dfrac{7}{13}i$

(C) $\dfrac{4 + \sqrt{-25}}{\sqrt{-4}} = \dfrac{4 + i\sqrt{25}}{i\sqrt{4}} = \dfrac{4 + 5i}{2i} = \dfrac{4 + 5i}{2i}\dfrac{i}{i} = \dfrac{4i + 5i^2}{2i^2} = \dfrac{4i - 5}{-2} = \dfrac{5}{2} - 2i$ $(1\text{-}4)$

25. $\left(y + \dfrac{11}{3}\right)^2 = 20$

$$y + \frac{11}{3} = \pm\sqrt{20}$$

$$y = -\frac{11}{3} \pm \sqrt{20} = -\frac{11}{3} \pm \frac{3\sqrt{4 \cdot 5}}{3}$$

$$y = \frac{-11 \pm 3 \cdot 2\sqrt{5}}{3} = \frac{-11 \pm 6\sqrt{5}}{3} \quad (1\text{-}5)$$

26. $1 + \dfrac{3}{u^2} = \dfrac{2}{u}$ Excluded value: $u \neq 0$

$$u^2 + 3 = 2u$$
$$u^2 - 2u = -3$$
$$u^2 - 2u + 1 = -2$$
$$(u-1)^2 = -2$$
$$u - 1 = \pm\sqrt{-2}$$
$$u = 1 \pm \sqrt{-2}$$
$$u = 1 \pm i\sqrt{2} \qquad (1\text{-}5)$$

27. $\dfrac{x}{x^2-x-6} - \dfrac{2}{x-3} = 3$

$\dfrac{x}{(x-3)(x+2)} - \dfrac{2}{x-3} = 3$ Excluded values: $x \ne 3, -2$

$(x-3)(x+2)\dfrac{x}{(x-3)(x+2)} - (x-3)(x+2)\dfrac{2}{x-3} = 3(x-3)(x+2)$

$x - 2(x+2) = 3(x-3)(x+2)$

$x - 2x - 4 = 3(x^2 - x - 6)$

$-x - 4 = 3x^2 - 3x - 18$

$0 = 3x^2 - 2x - 14$

$3x^2 - 2x - 14 = 0$

$x = \dfrac{-b \pm \sqrt{b^2 - 4ac}}{2a}$ $a = 3, b = -2, c = -14$

$x = \dfrac{-(-2) \pm \sqrt{(-2)^2 - 4(3)(-14)}}{2(3)}$

$x = \dfrac{2 \pm \sqrt{172}}{6}$

$x = \dfrac{2 \pm 2\sqrt{43}}{6} = \dfrac{1 \pm \sqrt{43}}{3}$ *(1-5)*

28. $2x^{2/3} - 5x^{1/3} - 12 = 0$
Let $u = x^{1/3}$, then
$2u^2 - 5u - 12 = 0$
$(2u + 3)(u - 4) = 0$

$u = -\dfrac{3}{2}, 4$

$x^{1/3} = -\dfrac{3}{2}$ $x^{1/3} = 4$

$x = -\dfrac{27}{8}$ $x = 64$ *(1-6)*

29. $m^4 + 5m^2 - 36 = 0$
Let $u = m^2$, then
$u^2 + 5u - 36 = 0$
$(u + 9)(u - 4) = 0$

$u = -9, 4$

$m^2 = -9$ $m^2 = 4$
$m = \pm 3i$ $m = \pm 2$

30. $\sqrt{y-2} - \sqrt{5y+1} = -3$

$-\sqrt{5y+1} = -3 - \sqrt{y-2}$

$5y + 1 = 9 + 6\sqrt{y-2} + y - 2$

$5y + 1 = y + 7 + 6\sqrt{y-2}$

$4y - 6 = 6\sqrt{y-2}$

$2y - 3 = 3\sqrt{y-2}$

$4y^2 - 12y + 9 = 9(y-2)$

$4y^2 - 12y + 9 = 9y - 18$

$4y^2 - 21y + 27 = 0$

$(4y - 9)(y - 3) = 0$

$y = \tfrac{9}{4}, 3$

> **Common Error:**
> $y - 2 - 5y + 1 = 9$
> is not equivalent to the equation formed by squaring both members of the given equation.

Check: $\sqrt{\tfrac{9}{4}-2} - \sqrt{5\left(\tfrac{9}{4}\right)+1} \overset{?}{=} -3$

$\sqrt{\tfrac{1}{4}} - \sqrt{\tfrac{49}{4}} \overset{?}{=} -3$

$-3 \overset{\checkmark}{=} -3$

$\sqrt{3-2} - \sqrt{5(3)+1} \overset{?}{=} -3$

$-3 \overset{\checkmark}{=} -3$

Solution: $\tfrac{9}{4}, 3$ *(1-6)*

31. $2.15x - 3.73(x - 0.930) = 6.11x$
$2.15x - 3.73x + 3.4689 = 6.11x$
$-1.58x + 3.4689 = 6.11x$
$3.4689 = 7.69x$
$x = 0.451$ *(1-1)*

32. $-1.52 \le 0.770 - 2.04x \le 5.33$
$-2.29 \le -2.04x \le 4.56$
$1.12 \ge x \ge -2.24$
$-2.24 \le x \le 1.12$ or $[-2.24, 1.12]$
   (1-2)

33. $|9.71 - 3.62x| > 5.48$

$9.71 - 3.62x > 5.48$ or $9.71 - 3.62x < -5.48$

$-3.62x > -4.23$ $\qquad\qquad -3.62x < -15.19$

$x < 1.17$ $\qquad\qquad\qquad x > 4.20$

$(1\text{-}3)$

34. $\left|\dfrac{8}{3} - \dfrac{4}{5}t\right| \le \dfrac{1}{2}$

$-\dfrac{1}{2} \le \dfrac{8}{3} - \dfrac{4}{5}t \le \dfrac{1}{2}$

$30\left(-\dfrac{1}{2}\right) \le 30\left(\dfrac{8}{3}\right) - 30\left(\dfrac{4}{5}t\right) \le 30\left(\dfrac{1}{2}\right)$

$-15 \le 80 - 24t \le 15$ $\qquad\qquad (1\text{-}3)$

$-95 \le -24t \le -65$

$\dfrac{95}{24} \ge t \ge \dfrac{65}{24}$

$\dfrac{65}{24} \le t \le \dfrac{95}{24}$

35. $6.09x^2 + 4.57x - 8.86 = 0$

$x = \dfrac{-b \pm \sqrt{b^2 - 4ac}}{2a}$ $a = 6.09,\ b = 4.57,\ c = -8.86$

$x = \dfrac{-4.57 \pm \sqrt{(4.57)^2 - 4(6.09)(-8.86)}}{2(6.09)}$

$x = \dfrac{-4.57 \pm \sqrt{236.7145}}{12.18}$

$x = \dfrac{-4.57 \pm 15.3855}{12.18}$

$x = -1.64,\ 0.888$ $\qquad\qquad (1\text{-}5)$

36. $P = M - Mdt$

$M - Mdt = P$

$M(1 - dt) = P$

$M = \dfrac{P}{1 - dt}$ $\qquad (1\text{-}1)$

37. $P = EI - RI^2$

$RI^2 - EI + P = 0$

$I = \dfrac{-b \pm \sqrt{b^2 - 4ac}}{2a}$ $a = R,\ b = -E,\ c = P$

$I = \dfrac{-(-E) \pm \sqrt{(-E)^2 - 4(R)(P)}}{2(R)}$

$I = \dfrac{E \pm \sqrt{E^2 - 4PR}}{2R}$ $\qquad (1\text{-}5)$

38. $x = \dfrac{4y + 5}{2y + 1}$

$x(2y + 1) = (2y + 1)\dfrac{4y + 5}{2y + 1}$

$2xy + x = 4y + 5$

$2xy + x - 4y = 5$

$2xy - 4y = 5 - x$

$y(2x - 4) = 5 - x$

$y = \dfrac{5 - x}{2x - 4}$ $\qquad (1\text{-}1)$

39. The original equation can be rewritten as
$$\frac{4}{(x-1)(x-3)} = \frac{3}{(x-1)(x-2)}$$
Thus, $x = 1$ cannot be a solution of this equation. This extraneous solution was introduced when both sides were multiplied by $x - 1$ in the second line. $x = 1$ must be discarded and the only correct solution is $x = -1$. *(1-1)*

40. In this problem, $a = 1$, $b = -8$, $c = c$. Thus, the discriminant $b^2 - 4ac = (-8)^2 - 4(1)(c) = 64 - 4c$. Hence,
if $c = -16$, the discriminant is $64 - 4(-16) = 128 > 0$. Therefore there are two real solutions.
if $c = 16$, the disciminant is $64 - 4(16) = 0$. Therefore, there is one real solution.
if $c = 32$, the discriminant is $64 - 4(32) = -128 < 0$. Therefore, there are two imaginary solutions.
In general
if $64 - 4c > 0$, thus $64 > 4c$ or $c < 16$, there are two real solutions.
if $64 - 4c = 0$, thus $c = 16$, there is one real solution.
if $64 - 4c < 0$, thus $64 < 4c$ or $c > 16$, there are imaginary solutions. *(1-5)*

41. The given inequality $a + b < b - a$ is equivalent to, successively,
$a < -a$
$2a < 0$
$a < 0$
Thus its truth is independent of the value of b, and dependent on a being negative. True for all real b and all negative a. *(1-2)*

42. If $a > b$ and b is negative, then $\dfrac{a}{b} < \dfrac{b}{b}$, that is,
$\dfrac{a}{b} < 1$, since dividing both sides by b reverses the
order of the inequality. $\dfrac{a}{b}$ is less than 1. *(1-2)*

43.
$$y = \frac{1}{1 - \frac{1}{1-x}}$$
$$y = \frac{1(1-x)}{(1-x)1 - (1-x)\frac{1}{1-x}}$$
$$y = \frac{1-x}{1-x-1}$$
$$y = \frac{1-x}{-x}$$
$$-xy = 1 - x$$
$$x - xy = 1$$
$$x(1-y) = 1$$
$$x = \frac{1}{1-y}$$ *(1-1)*

44. $0 < |x - 6| < d$ means: the distance between x and 6 is between 0 and d, that is, less than d but $x \neq 6$.
$$-d < x - 6 < d \text{ except } x \neq 6$$
$$6 - d < x < 6 + d \text{ but } x \neq 6$$
$$6 - d < x < 6 \text{ or } 6 < x < 6 + d$$
$$(6 - d, 6) \cup (6, 6 + d)$$
$6 - d \quad 6 \quad 6 - d$ *(1-3)*

45.
$$2x^2 = \sqrt{3}x - \frac{1}{2}$$
$$4x^2 = 2\sqrt{3}x - 1$$
$$4x^2 - 2\sqrt{3}x + 1 = 0$$
$$x = \frac{-b \pm \sqrt{b^2 - 4ac}}{2a} \quad a = 4, b = -2\sqrt{3}, c = 1$$
$$x = \frac{-(-2\sqrt{3}) \pm \sqrt{(-2\sqrt{3})^2 - 4(4)(1)}}{2(4)}$$

46.
$$4 = 8x^{-2} - x^{-4}$$
$$4x^4 = 8x^2 - 1 \quad x \neq 0 \quad LCD = x^4$$
$$4x^4 - 8x^2 + 1 = 0$$
Let $u = x^2$, then
$$4u^2 - 8u + 1 = 0$$
$$u = \frac{-b \pm \sqrt{b^2 - 4ac}}{2a} \quad a = 4, b = -8, c = 1$$
$$u = \frac{-(-8) \pm \sqrt{(-8)^2 - 4(4)(1)}}{2(4)}$$

$$x = \frac{2\sqrt{3} \pm \sqrt{-4}}{8}$$

$$x = \frac{2\sqrt{3} \pm 2i}{8}$$

$$x = \frac{\sqrt{3} \pm i}{4} \text{ or } \frac{\sqrt{3}}{4} \pm \frac{1}{4}i \qquad (1\text{-}5)$$

$$u = \frac{8 \pm \sqrt{48}}{8} = \frac{8 \pm 4\sqrt{3}}{8} \quad \boxed{\begin{array}{l}\text{Common Error: It is incorrect}\\\text{to "cancel" the 8's at this point}\end{array}}$$

$$u = \frac{4(2 \pm \sqrt{3})}{8} = \frac{2 \pm \sqrt{3}}{2}$$

$$x^2 = \frac{2 \pm \sqrt{3}}{2}$$

$$x = \pm\sqrt{\frac{2 \pm \sqrt{3}}{2}} \quad \text{(four real roots)} \quad (1\text{-}6)$$

47. $2ix^2 + 3ix - 5i = 0$

$$i(2x^2 + 3x - 5) = 0$$

$$i(2x + 5)(x - 1) = 0$$

$$2x + 5 = 0 \qquad \text{or} \qquad x - 1 = 0$$

$$2x = -5 \qquad\qquad\qquad x = 1$$

$$x = -\frac{5}{2}$$

$$(1\text{-}5)$$

48. $(a + bi)\left(\dfrac{a}{a^2 + b^2} - \dfrac{b}{a^2 + b^2}i\right)$

$$= \frac{(a + bi)}{1}\left(\frac{a}{a^2 + b^2} - \frac{bi}{a^2 + b^2}\right)$$

$$= \frac{a(a + bi)}{a^2 + b^2} - \frac{bi(a + bi)}{a^2 + b^2}$$

$$= \frac{a^2 + abi - abi - b^2i^2}{a^2 + b^2}$$

$$= \frac{a^2 + b^2}{a^2 + b^2} = 1 \qquad (1\text{-}4)$$

49. Let x = the number

$\dfrac{1}{x}$ = its reciprocal

Then $x - \dfrac{1}{x} = \dfrac{16}{15}$ Excluded value:

$\qquad\qquad\qquad\qquad x \neq 0$

$$15x^2 - 15 = 16x$$

$$15x^2 - 16x - 15 = 0$$

$$(5x + 3)(3x - 5) = 0$$

$$5x + 3 = 0 \text{ or } 3x - 5 = 0$$

$$x = -\frac{3}{5} \qquad x = \frac{5}{3} \qquad (1\text{-}5)$$

50. (A) $H = 0.7(220 - A)$

(B) We are to find H when $A = 20$.

$\qquad H = 0.7(220 - 20)$

$\qquad H = 140$ beats per minute.

(C) We are to find A when

$\qquad H = 126$.

$\qquad 126 = 0.7(220 - A)$

$\qquad 126 = 154 - 0.7A$

$\qquad -28 = -0.7A$

$\qquad A = 40$ years old. $\qquad (1\text{-}1)$

51. Let $\qquad x$ = amount of 80% solution

Then $50 - x$ = amount of 30% solution

since $\quad 50$ = amount of 60% solution

$$\begin{array}{ccc}\text{acid in} & \text{acid in} & \text{acid in} \\ \text{80\% solution} + \text{30\% solution} = \text{60\% solution}\end{array}$$

$$0.8(x) + 0.3(50 - x) = 0.6(50)$$

$$0.8x + 15 - 0.3x = 30$$

$$15 + 0.5x = 30$$

$$0.5x = 15$$

$$x = \frac{15}{0.5}$$

52. Let $\quad x$ = the wind speed

Then $300 + x$ = the speed flying with the wind

$\quad 300 - x$ = the speed flying against the wind

Solving $d = rt$ for t, we have $t = \dfrac{d}{r}$. We use this formula, together with

time down (with the wind) = time back (against the wind) $- \dfrac{3}{2}$

$$\text{time flying down} = \frac{\text{distance flown}}{\text{rate down}} = \frac{1,200}{300 + x}$$

$$\text{time flying back} = \frac{\text{distance back}}{\text{rate back}} = \frac{1,200}{300 - x}$$

$x = 30$ milliliters of 80% solution
$50 - x = 20$ milliliters of 30% solution $(1\text{-}2)$

So, $\dfrac{1,200}{300+x} = \dfrac{1,200}{300-x} - \dfrac{3}{2}$ Excluded values: $x \neq -300, 300$

$2(300-x)(1,200) = 2(300+x)(1,200) - 3(300-x)(300+x)$

$720,000 - 2,400x = 720,000 + 2,400x - 270,000 + 3x^2$

$0 = 3x^2 + 4,800x - 270,000$

$0 = x^2 + 1,600x - 90,000$

$x = \dfrac{-b \pm \sqrt{b^2 - 4ac}}{2a}$ $a = 1, b = 1,600, c = -90,000$

$x = \dfrac{-1,600 \pm \sqrt{(1,600)^2 - 4(1)(-90,000)}}{2(1)}$

$x = -1,654.4$ or $x = 54.4$

Discarding the negative answer, we have
wind speed = 54.4 miles per hour. $(1\text{-}5)$

53. (A) Let $x = $ distance rowed
then $15 - 3 = 12$ km/hr = the rate rowed upstream
$15 + 3 = 18$ km/hr = the rate rowed downstream

Using $t = \dfrac{d}{r}$ as in the previous problem yield

time upstream $= \dfrac{x}{12}$ time downstream $= \dfrac{x}{18}$

So $\dfrac{x}{12} + \dfrac{x}{18} = \dfrac{25}{60}$ LCD = 180

$\dfrac{180}{1} \cdot \dfrac{x}{12} + \dfrac{180}{1} \cdot \dfrac{x}{18} = \dfrac{180}{1} \cdot \dfrac{25}{60}$

$15x + 10x = 75$

$25x = 75$

$x = 3$ km

(B) Now let $x = $ still-water speed
$x - 3 = $ the rate rowed upstream
$x + 3 = $ the rate rowed downstream

time upstream $= \dfrac{3}{x-3}$ time downstream $= \dfrac{3}{x+3}$

So $\dfrac{3}{x-3} + \dfrac{3}{x+3} = \dfrac{23}{60}$ Excluded values: $x = 3, -3$

$60(x+3)3 + 60(x-3)3 = 23(x+3)(x-3)$
$180x + 540 + 180x - 540 = 23x^2 - 207$
$0 = 23x^2 - 360x - 207$

$x = \dfrac{-b \pm \sqrt{b^2 - 4ac}}{2a}$ $a = 23, b = -360, c = -207$

$x = \dfrac{-(-360) \pm \sqrt{(-360)^2 - 4(23)(-207)}}{2(23)}$

$x = 16.2$ or -0.6

Discarding the negative answer, we have $x = 16.2$ km/hr.

(C) Now $18 - 3 = 15$ km/hr = the rate rowed upstream
$18 + 3 = 21$ km/hr = the rate rowed downstream

So $\dfrac{3}{15} + \dfrac{3}{21} = $ round trip time

$= 0.343$ hr

$= 0.343 \times 60$ min

$= 20.6$ min $(1\text{-}1, 1\text{-}5)$

54. (A) Apply the given formula with
$C = 15$.
$$15 = x^2 - 10x + 31$$
$$0 = x^2 - 10x + 16$$
$$x^2 - 10x + 16 = 0$$
$$(x - 8)(x - 2) = 0$$
$$x = 2 \text{ or } 8$$
Thus the output could be either 2,000 or 8,000 units.

(B) Apply the given formula with
$C = 6$.
$$6 = x^2 - 10x + 31$$
$$0 = x^2 - 10x + 25$$
$$x^2 - 10x + 25 = 0$$
$$(x - 5)^2 = 0$$
$$x = 5$$
Thus the output must be 5,000 units. *(1-5)*

55. The break-even points are defined by
$C = R$ (cost = revenue). Applying the formulas
in this problem and the previous one, we have
$$x^2 - 10x + 31 = 3x$$
$$x^2 - 13x + 31 = 0$$
$$x = \frac{-b \pm \sqrt{b^2 - 4ac}}{2a} \quad a = 1, b = -13, c = 31$$
$$x = \frac{-(-13) \pm \sqrt{(-13)^2 - 4(1)(31)}}{2(1)}$$
$$x = \frac{13 \pm \sqrt{45}}{2} \text{ thousand or approximately}$$
$$3,146 \text{ and } 9,854 \text{ units } (1\text{-}5)$$

56. Let P = the percentage required. Then the distance of
P from 54 is less than or equal to 1.2, thus
$$|P - 54| \leq 1.2$$
Solving, we obtain
$$-1.2 \leq P - 54 \leq 1.2$$
$$52.8 \leq P \leq 55.2$$
(1-3)

57. Let x = width of page

y = height of page

Then $xy = 480$, thus $y = \dfrac{480}{x}$.

Since the printed portion is surrounded by margins of 2 cm on each side, we have

$x - 4$ = width of printed portion

$y - 4$ = height of printed portion

Hence

$(x - 4)(y - 4) = 320$, that is

$(x - 4)\left(\dfrac{480}{x} - 4\right) = 320$

Solving this, we obtain:

$x\left(\dfrac{480}{x}\right) - 4x - 4\left(\dfrac{480}{x}\right) + 16 = 320$

$480 - 4x - \dfrac{1{,}920}{x} + 16 = 320$

$-4x - \dfrac{1{,}920}{x} = -176$ LCD: x $x \neq 0$

$-4x^2 - 1{,}920 = -176x$

$0 = 4x^2 - 176x + 1{,}920$

$0 = x^2 - 44x + 480$

$0 = (x - 20)(x - 24)$

$x - 20 = 0$ or $x - 24 = 0$

$x = 20 \qquad\quad x = 24$

$\dfrac{480}{x} = 24 \qquad \dfrac{480}{x} = 20$

Thus, the dimensions of the page are 20 cm by 24 cm.

(1-5)

58.

In the isosceles triangle we note:

$\dfrac{1}{2}Bh = A = 24$

Hence

$h = \dfrac{48}{B}$

Applying the Pythagorean theorem, we have

$$h^2 + \left(\frac{B}{2}\right)^2 = 8^2$$

$$\left(\frac{48}{B}\right)^2 + \left(\frac{B}{2}\right)^2 = 8^2$$

$$\frac{2{,}304}{B^2} + \frac{B^2}{4} = 64$$

$$4B^2\left(\frac{2{,}304}{B^2}\right) + 4B^2\left(\frac{B^2}{4}\right) = 4B^2(64)$$

$$9{,}216 + B^4 = 256B^2$$

$$(B^2)^2 - 256B^2 + 9{,}216 = 0$$

$$B^2 = \frac{-b \pm \sqrt{b^2 - 4ac}}{2a} \quad a = 1, b = -256, c = 9{,}216$$

$$B^2 = \frac{-(-256) \pm \sqrt{(-256)^2 - 4(1)(9{,}216)}}{2(1)}$$

$$B^2 = \frac{256 \pm \sqrt{65{,}536 - 36{,}864}}{2}$$

$$B^2 = \frac{256 \pm \sqrt{28{,}672}}{2}$$

$$B^2 = 128 \pm 32\sqrt{7}$$

$$B = \sqrt{128 \pm 32\sqrt{7}}$$

$$B = 14.58 \text{ ft or } 6.58 \text{ ft} \qquad\qquad \textit{(1-6)}$$

CHAPTER 2

Section 2-1

1. To each point P in the plane there corresponds a single ordered pair of numbers (a, b) called the coordinates of the point. To each ordered pair of numbers (a, b) there corresponds a single point, called the graph of the pair.

3. This can be done by imagining a mirror placed along the y axis; draw a graph so that its reflection in this mirror would be the graph already present; each coordinate given as (a, b) is reflected as $(-a, b)$.

5. The set of all points for which the x coordinate is 0 is the y axis.

7. The set of all points for which the x and y coordinates are negative is quadrant III.

9. The set of all points for which the x coordinate is positive and the y coordinate is negative is quadrant IV.

11. The set of all points for which x is positive, excluding those points for which $y = 0$ (positive x axis), includes quadrants I and IV.

13. The set of all points for which $xy < 0$ includes those points for which the x coordinate is positive and the y coordinate is negative (quadrant IV) and also those points for which the x coordinate is negative and the y coordinate is positive (quadrant II).

15.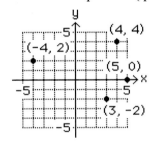

17.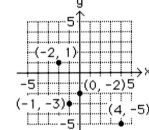

19. Point A has coordinates $(2, 4)$. Its reflection through the y axis is $A'(-2, 4)$.
    Point B has coordinates $(3, -1)$. Its reflection through the y axis is $B'(-3, -1)$.
    Point C has coordinates $(-4, 0)$. Its reflection through the y axis is $C'(4, 0)$.
    Point D has coordinates $(-5, 2)$. Its reflection through the y axis is $D'(5, 2)$.

21. Point A has coordinates $(-3, -3)$. Its reflection through the origin is $A'(3, 3)$.
    Point B has coordinates $(0, 4)$. Its reflection through the origin is $B'(0, -4)$.
    Point C has coordinates $(-3, 2)$. Its reflection through the origin is $C'(3, -2)$.
    Point D has coordinates $(5, -1)$. Its reflection through the origin is $D'(-5, 1)$.

23. $y = 2x - 4$

Test y axis	Test x axis	Test origin
Replace x with $-x$:	Replace y with $-y$:	Replace x with $-x$ and y with $-y$:
$y = 2(-x) - 4$	$-y = 2x - 4$	$-y = 2(-x) - 4$
$y = -2x - 4$	$y = -2x + 4$	$y = 2x + 4$

x	y
0	-4
2	0
4	4

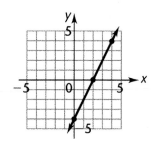

The graph has none of these symmetries.

25. $y = \dfrac{1}{2}x$

Test y axis
Replace x with $-x$:

$y = \dfrac{1}{2}(-x)$

$y = -\dfrac{1}{2}x$

Test x axis
Replace y with $-y$:

$-y = \dfrac{1}{2}x$

$y = -\dfrac{1}{2}x$

Test origin
Replace x with $-x$ and y with $-y$:

$-y = \dfrac{1}{2}(-x)$

$y = \dfrac{1}{2}x$

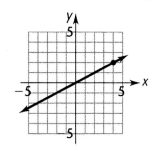

x	y
0	0
4	2

The graph has symmetry with respect to the origin.

We reflect the portion of the graph in quadrant I through the origin, using the origin symmetry.

27. $|y| = x$
Test y axis
Replace x with $-x$:
$|y| = -x$

Test x axis
Replace y with $-y$:
$|-y| = x$
$|y| = x$

Test origin
Replace x with $-x$ and y with $-y$:
$|-y| = -x$
$|y| = -x$

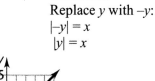

x	y
0	0
4	4

The graph has symmetry with respect to the x axis.

We reflect the portion of the graph where $y \geq 0$ through the x axis, using the x axis symmetry.

29. $|x| = |y|$
Test y axis
Replace x with $-x$:
$|-x| = |y|$
$|x| = |y|$

Test x axis
Replace y with $-y$:
$|x| = |-y|$
$|x| = |y|$

Origin symmetry
follows automatically.

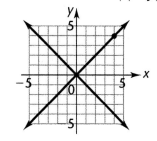

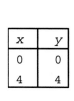

x	y
0	0
4	4

The graph has all three symmetries.

We reflect the portion of the graph in quadrant I through the y axis, and the x axis, and the origin, using all three symmetries.

31. (A) When $x = 8$, the corresponding y value on the graph is 6, to the nearest integer.
    (B) When $x = -5$, the corresponding y value on the graph is -5, to the nearest integer.
    (C) When $x = 0$, the corresponding y value on the graph is -1, to the nearest integer.
    (D) When $y = 6$, the corresponding x value on the graph is 8, to the nearest integer.
    (E) When $y = -5$, the corresponding x value on the graph is -5, to the nearest integer.
    (F) When $y = 0$, the corresponding x value on the graph is 5, to the nearest integer.

33. (A) When $x = 1$, the corresponding y value on the graph is 6, to the nearest integer.
    (B) When $x = -8$, the corresponding y value on the graph is 4, to the nearest integer.
    (C) When $x = 0$, the corresponding y value on the graph is 4, to the nearest integer.
    (D) When $y = -6$, the corresponding x value on the graph is 8, to the nearest integer.
    (E) Three values of x correspond to $y = 4$ on the graph. To the nearest integer they are -8, 0, and 6.
    (F) Three values of x correspond to $y = 0$ on the graph. To the nearest integer they are -7, -2, and 7.

35. (A) Reflect the given graph across the x axis.   (B) Reflect the given graph across the y axis.   (C) Reflect the given graph through the origin.   (D) Reflect the given graph across the y axis, then reflect the resulting curve across the x axis.

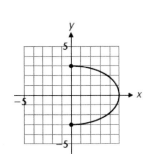 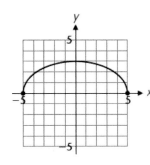 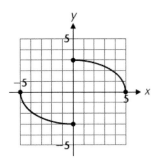 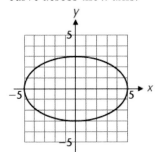

37. $2x + 7y = 0$

Test y axis	Test x axis	Test origin
Replace x with $-x$:	Replace y with $-y$:	Replace x with $-x$ and y with $-y$:
$2(-x) + 7y = 0$	$2x + 7(-y) = 0$	$2(-x) + 7(-y) = 0$
$-2x + 7y = 0$	$2x - 7y = 0$	$-2x - 7y = 0$
		$2x + 7y = 0$

The graph has symmetry with respect to the origin.

39. $x^2 - 4xy^2 = 3$

Test y axis	Test x axis	Test origin
Replace x with $-x$:	Replace y with $-y$:	Replace x with $-x$ and y with $-y$:
$(-x)^2 - 4(-x)y^2 = 3$	$x^2 - 4x(-y)^2 = 3$	$(-x)^2 - 4(-x)(-y)^2 = 3$
$x^2 + 4xy^2 = 3$	$x^2 - 4xy^2 = 3$	$x^2 + 4xy^2 = 3$

The graph has symmetry with respect to the x axis.

41. $x^4 - 5x^2y + y^4 = 1$

Test y axis	Test x axis	Test origin
Replace x with $-x$:	Replace y with $-y$:	Replace x with $-x$ and y with $-y$:
$(-x)^4 - 5(-x)^2y + y^4 = 1$	$x^4 - 5x^2(-y) + (-y)^4 = 1$	$(-x)^4 - 5(-x)^2(-y) + (-y)^4 = 1$
$x^4 - 5x^2y + y^4 = 1$	$x^4 + 5x^2y + y^4 = 1$	$x^4 + 5x^2y + y^4 = 1$

The graph has symmetry with respect to the y axis.

43. $x^3 - y^3 = 8$

Test y axis	Test x axis	Test origin
Replace x with $-x$:	Replace y with $-y$:	Replace x with $-x$ and y with $-y$:
$(-x)^3 - y^3 = 8$	$x^3 - (-y)^3 = 8$	$(-x)^3 - (-y)^3 = 8$
$-x^3 - y^3 = 8$	$x^3 + y^3 = 8$	$-x^3 + y^3 = 8$

The graph has none of these symmetries.

45. $x^4 - 4x^2y^2 + y^4 = 81$

Test y axis	Test x axis	Origin symmetry
Replace x with $-x$:	Replace y with $-y$:	follows automatically
$(-x)^4 - 4(-x)^2y^2 + y^4 = 81$	$x^4 - 4x^2(-y)^2 + (-y)^4 = 81$	
$x^4 - 4x^2y^2 + y^4 = 81$	$x^4 - 4x^2y^2 + y^4 = 81$	

The graph has symmetry with respect to the x axis, the y axis, and the origin.

47. $y^2 = x + 2$

Test y axis	Test x axis	Test origin
Replace x with $-x$:	Replace y with $-y$:	Replace x with $-x$ and y with $-y$:
$y^2 = -x + 2$	$(-y)^2 = x + 2$	$(-y)^2 = (-x) + 2$
	$y^2 = x + 2$	$y^2 = -x + 2$

x	y
-2	0
-1	1
2	2

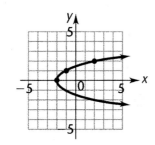

The graph has symmetry with respect to the x axis. To obtain the portion of the graph for $y \geq 0$, we sketch $y = \sqrt{x+2}$, $x \geq -2$. We reflect the portion of the graph for $y \geq 0$ across the x axis, using the x axis symmetry.

49. $y = x^2 + 1$

Test y axis	Test x axis	Test origin
Replace x with $-x$:	Replace y with $-y$:	Replace x with $-x$ and y with $-y$:
$y = (-x)^2 + 1$	$(-y) = x^2 + 1$	$(-y) = (-x)^2 + 1$
$y = x^2 + 1$	$y = -x^2 - 1$	$y = -x^2 - 1$

x	y
0	1
1	2
2	5

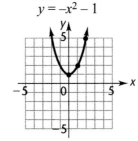

The graph has symmetry with respect to the y axis. We reflect the portion of the graph for $x \geq 0$ across the y axis, using the y axis symmetry.

51. $4y^2 - x^2 = 1$

Test y axis	Test x axis	Origin symmetry
Replace x with $-x$:	Replace y with $-y$:	follows automatically.
$4y^2 - (-x)^2 = 1$	$4(-y)^2 - x^2 = 1$	
$4y^2 - x^2 = 1$	$4y^2 - x^2 = 1$	

The graph has all three symmetries. $y = \pm\dfrac{1}{2}\sqrt{x^2 + 1}$.

x	y
0	$\frac{1}{2}$
2	$\frac{1}{2}\sqrt{5} \approx 1.1$
4	$\frac{1}{2}\sqrt{17} \approx 2.0$

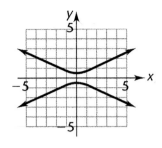

The graph has all three symmetries.
To obtain the quadrant I portion of the graph, we sketch $y = \dfrac{1}{2}\sqrt{x^2 + 1}$, $x \geq 0$. We reflect this graph across the y axis, then reflect everything across the x axis.

53. $y^3 = x$

Test y axis
Replace x with $-x$:
$y^3 = -x$

Test x axis
Replace y with $-y$:
$(-y)^3 = x$
$y^3 = -x$

Test origin
Replace x with $-x$ and y with $-y$:
$(-y)^3 = -x$
$y^3 = x$

x	y
0	0
1	1
8	2

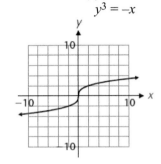

The graph has symmetry with respect to the origin. We reflect the portion of the graph in quadrant I through the origin, using the origin symmetry.

55. $y = 0.6x^2 - 4.5$

Test y axis
Replace x with $-x$:
$y = 0.6(-x)^2 - 4.5$
$y = 0.6x^2 - 4.5$

Test x axis
Replace y with $-y$:
$-y = 0.6x^2 - 4.5$
$y = -0.6x^2 + 4.5$

Test origin
Replace x with $-x$ and y with $-y$:
$-y = 0.6(-x)^2 - 4.5$
$y = -0.6x^2 + 4.5$

x	y
0	-4.5
1	-3.9
2	-2.1
3	0.9
4	5.1

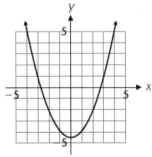

The graph has symmetry with respect to the y axis. We reflect the portion of the graph in quadrant I through the y axis, using the y axis symmetry.

57. $y = x^{2/3}$

Test y axis
Replace x with $-x$:
$y = (-x)^{2/3}$
$y = x^{2/3}$

Test x axis
Replace y with $-y$:
$-y = x^{2/3}$
$y = -x^{2/3}$

Test origin
Replace x with $-x$ and y with $-y$:
$-y = (-x)^{2/3}$
$y = -x^{2/3}$

x	y
0	0
1	1
2	$2^{2/3} \approx 1.6$
3	$3^{2/3} \approx 2.1$

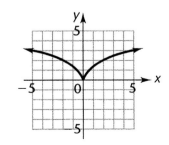

The graph has symmetry with respect to the y axis. We reflect the portion of the graph for $x \geq 0$ across the y axis, using the y axis symmetry.

59. (A) and (B)

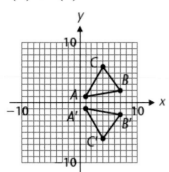

(C) The triangles are mirror images of each other, reflected across the x axis. Changing the sign of the y coordinate reflects the graph across the x axis.

61. (A) and (B)

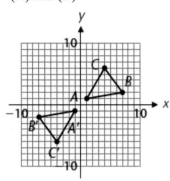

(C) The triangles are mirror images of each other, reflected across the origin. Changing the signs of both coordinates reflects the graph through the origin.

63.
$$2x + y^2 = 3$$
$$y^2 = 3 - 2x$$
$$y = \pm\sqrt{3 - 2x}$$

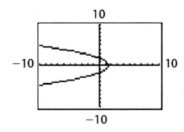

65.
$$x^2 - (y + 1)^2 = 4$$
$$-(y + 1)^2 = 4 - x^2$$
$$(y + 1)^2 = x^2 - 4$$
$$y + 1 = \pm\sqrt{x^2 - 4}$$
$$y = -1 \pm \sqrt{x^2 - 4}$$

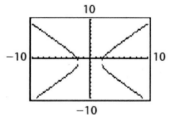

67. $y^3 = |x|$

Test y axis
Replace x with $-x$:
$y^3 = |-x|$
$y^3 = |x|$

Test x axis
Replace y with $-y$:
$(-y)^3 = |x|$
$y^3 = -|x|$

Test origin
Replace x with $-x$ and y with $-y$:
$(-y)^3 = |-x|$
$y^3 = -|x|$

x	y
0	0
1	1
8	2

The graph has symmetry with respect to the y axis. We reflect the portion of the graph for $x \geq 0$ across the y axis using the y axis symmetry.

69. $xy = 1$

Test y axis	Test x axis	Test origin
Replace x with $-x$:	Replace y with $-y$:	Replace x with $-x$ and y with $-y$:
$(-x)y = 1$	$x(-y) = 1$	$(-x)(-y) = 1$
$xy = -1$	$xy = -1$	$xy = 1$

x	y
1	1
2	$\frac{1}{2}$
3	$\frac{1}{3}$
$\frac{1}{2}$	2
$\frac{1}{3}$	3

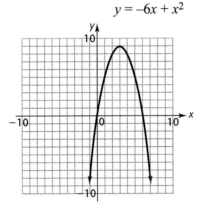

The graph has symmetry with respect to the origin. We reflect the portion of the graph in quadrant I through the origin, using the origin symmetry.

71. $y = 6x - x^2$

Test y axis	Test x axis	Test origin
Replace x with $-x$:	Replace y with $-y$:	Replace x with $-x$ and y with $-y$:
$y = 6(-x) - (-x)^2$	$-y = 6x - x^2$	$-y = 6(-x) - (-x)^2$
$y = -6x - x^2$	$y = -6x + x^2$	$y = 6x + x^2$

x	y
-1	-7
0	0
1	5
2	8
3	9
4	8
5	5
6	0
7	-7

The graph has none of these three symmetries. A larger table of values is needed since we have no symmetry information.

73. $y^2 = |x| + 1$

Test y axis	Test x axis	Origin symmetry
Replace x with $-x$:	Replace y with $-y$:	follows automatically.
$y^2 = |-x| + 1$	$(-y^2) = |x| + 1$	
$y^2 = |x| + 1$	$y^2 = |x| + 1$	

x	y
0	1
1	$\sqrt{2} \approx 1.4$
3	2

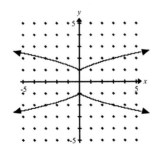

The graph has symmetry with respect to the x axis, the y axis, and the origin. $y = \pm\sqrt{|x| + 1}$ To obtain the quadrant I portion of this graph, we sketch $y = \sqrt{|x| + 1}$ $x \geq 0$. We reflect this graph across the y axis, then reflect everything across the x axis.

75. $|xy| + 2|y| = 6$

Test y axis	Test x axis	Origin symmetry
Replace x with $-x$:	Replace y with $-y$:	follows automatically.
$|(-x)y| + 2|y| = 6$	$|x(-y)| + 2|-y| = 6$	
$|xy| + 2|y| = 6$	$|xy| + 2|y| = 6$	

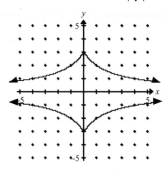

x	y
0	3
1	2
4	1

The graph has symmetry with respect to the x axis, the y axis, and the origin. We reflect the portion of the graph in quadrant I across the y axis, then reflect everything across the x axis.

77. Reflecting a point (x, y) across the x axis yields the point $(x, -y)$. Reflecting this point through the origin yields the point $(-x, y)$. This point is the same point that would result from reflecting the original point across the y axis. Therefore, if the graph is unchanged by reflecting across the x axis and across the origin, it will be unchanged by reflecting across the y axis and will necessarily have symmetry with respect to the y axis.

79. No. For example, the graph of $xy = 1$ is symmetric with respect to the origin, and the equation is unchanged when x is replaced by $-x$ and y is replaced by $-y$ to obtain $(-x)(-y) = 1$ or $xy = 1$. However, it is not symmetric with respect to the x axis, as is seen when only y is replaced by $-y$ to obtain $x(-y)=1$ or $-xy = 1$.

81.

P	$R = (10 - p)p$
5	25
6	24
7	21
8	16
9	9
10	0

83. (A) $6.00 on the price scale corresponds to 3,000 cases on the demand scale.

(B) The demand decreases from 3,000 to 2,600 cases, that is, by 400 cases.

(C) The demand increases from 3,000 to 3,600 cases, that is, by 600 cases.

(D) Demand decreases with increasing price and increases with decreasing price. To increase demand from 2,000 to 4,000 cases, a price decrease from $6.90 to $5.60 is necessary.

85. (A) 9:00 is halfway from 6 AM to noon, and corresponds to a temperature of 53°.

(B) The highest temperature occurs halfway from noon to 6 PM, at 3 PM. This temperature is 68°.

(C) This temperature occurs at 1 AM, 7 AM, and 11 PM.

87. (A) There is no obvious symmetry. A table of values yields the following approximate values:

x	0	0.5	1	1.5	2
v	0.7	0.6	0.5	0.35	0

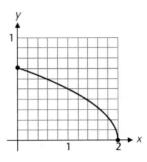

(B) For a displacement of 2 cm, the ball is stationary ($v = 0$). As the vertical displacement approaches 0, the ball gathers speed until $v = 0.5\sqrt{2} \approx 0.7$ m/sec. The velocity carries the ball through the equilibrium position ($x = 0$) to rise again to displacement 2 cm and velocity 0.

Section 2-2

1. In a right triangle, the square of the length of the hypotenuse is equal to the sum of the square of the lengths of the other two sides.

3. The x coordinate of the midpoint is the average (or arithmetic mean) of the x coordinate of the endpoints. The y coordinate of the midpoint is the average of the y coordinates of the endpoints.

5. $d = \sqrt{(4-1)^2 + (4-0)^2} = \sqrt{9+16} = \sqrt{25} = 5$

Midpoint $= \left(\dfrac{1+4}{2}, \dfrac{0+4}{2}\right) = \left(\dfrac{5}{2}, 2\right)$

7. $d = \sqrt{(5-0)^2 + (10-(-2))^2} = \sqrt{5^2 + 12^2} = \sqrt{25+144} = \sqrt{169} = 13$

Midpoint $= \left(\dfrac{0+5}{2}, \dfrac{-2+10}{2}\right) = \left(\dfrac{5}{2}, 4\right)$

9. $d = \sqrt{(3-(-6))^2 + (4-(-4))^2} = \sqrt{9^2 + 8^2} = \sqrt{81+64} = \sqrt{145}$

Midpoint $= \left(\dfrac{-6+3}{2}, \dfrac{-4+4}{2}\right) = \left(\dfrac{-3}{2}, 0\right)$

11. $d = \sqrt{(-6-(-2))^2 + (-3-(-1))^2} = \sqrt{20} = 2\sqrt{5}$

Midpoint $= \left(\dfrac{(-6)+(-2)}{2}, \dfrac{(-3)+(-1)}{2}\right) = (-4, -2)$

13.
$(x-0)^2 + (y-0)^2 = 7^2$
$x^2 + y^2 = 49$

15.
$(x-2)^2 + (y-3)^2 = 6^2$
$(x-2)^2 + (y-3)^2 = 36$

17.
$[x-(-4)]^2 + (y-1)^2 = (\sqrt{7})^2$
$(x+4)^2 + (y-1)^2 = 7$

Common Error: not $(x-4)^2$

19.
$[x-(-3)]^2 + [y-(-4)]^2 = (\sqrt{2})^2$
$(x+3)^2 + (y+4)^2 = 2$

21. This is a circle with center $(0, 0)$ and radius 2.

$$x^2 + y^2 = 4$$

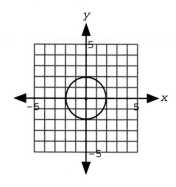

23. This is a circle with center $(1, 0)$ and radius 1.

$$(x - 1)^2 + y^2 = 1$$

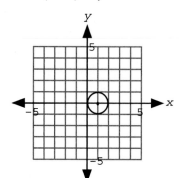

25. This is a circle with center $(-2, 1)$ and radius 3.

$$(x - (-2))^2 + (y - 1)^2 = 9$$
$$\text{or } (x + 2)^2 + (y - 1)^2 = 9$$

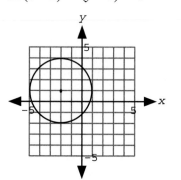

27. (A) $-2 = \dfrac{a_1 + 1}{2}$ (B) $6 = \dfrac{a_2 + 3}{2}$

$\quad -4 = a_1 + 1 \qquad 12 = a_2 + 3$

$\quad -5 = a_1 \qquad\quad\; 9 = a_2$

(C) From parts (A) and (B), $A = (-5, 9)$

$$d(A, M) = \sqrt{(-2 - (-5))^2 + (6 - 9)^2} = \sqrt{3^2 + (-3)^2} = \sqrt{9 + 9} = \sqrt{18}$$

$$d(M, B) = \sqrt{(1 - (-2))^2 + (3 - 6)^2} = \sqrt{3^2 + (-3)^2} = \sqrt{9 + 9} = \sqrt{18}$$

As expected, the distances are the same.

29. The distance formula requires that $\sqrt{[x - (-4)]^2 + (7 - 1)^2} = 10$

Solving, we have
$$\sqrt{(x + 4)^2 + (6)^2} = 10$$
$$(x + 4)^2 + (6)^2 = 10^2$$
$$(x + 4)^2 + 36 = 100$$
$$(x + 4)^2 = 64$$
$$x + 4 = \pm 8$$
$$x = -4 \pm 8$$
$$x = -12, 4$$

31. The distance formula requires that $\sqrt{[2 - (-1)]^2 + (y - 4)^2} = 3$

Solving, we have
$$\sqrt{(3)^2 + (y - 4)^2} = 3$$
$$(3)^2 + (y - 4)^2 = (3)^2$$
$$(y - 4)^2 = 0$$
$$y - 4 = 0$$
$$y = 4$$

33. This is a circle with center $(0, 2)$ and radius 2; that is, the set of all points that are 2 units away from $(0, 2)$.

$$x^2 + (y - 2)^2 = 4$$

35. This is a circle with center $(1, 1)$ and radius 4; that is, the set of all points that are 4 units away from $(1, 1)$.

$$(x - 1)^2 + (y - 1)^2 = 16$$

37. $M = \left(\dfrac{-4.3+9.6}{2}, \dfrac{5.2+(-1.7)}{2} \right) = \left(\dfrac{5.3}{2}, \dfrac{3.5}{2} \right) = (2.65,\ 1.75)$

$d(A,\ M) = \sqrt{(2.65-(-4.3))^2 + (1.75-5.2)^2} = \sqrt{6.95^2 + (-3.45)^2} = \sqrt{48.3025+11.9025}$
$$= \sqrt{60.205} = 7.76$$

$d(M,\ B) = \sqrt{(9.6-2.65)^2 + (-1.7-1.75)^2} = \sqrt{6.95^2 + (-3.45)^2} = \sqrt{48.3025+11.9025}$
$$= \sqrt{60.205} = 7.76$$

$d(A,\ B) = \sqrt{(9.6-(-4.3))^2 + (-1.7-5.2)^2} = \sqrt{13.9^2 + (-6.9)^2} = \sqrt{193.21+47.61}$
$$= \sqrt{240.82} = 15.52$$

$\dfrac{1}{2}\,d(A,\ B) = \dfrac{1}{2}\,(15.52) = 7.76$

39. Write $B = (b_1,\ b_2)$. -5 is the average of 25 and b_1, so $-5 = \dfrac{25+b_1}{2}$

$$-10 = 25 + b_1$$
$$-35 = b_1$$

-2 is the average of 10 and b_2, so $-2 = \dfrac{10+b_2}{2}$

$$-4 = 10 + b_2$$
$$-14 = b_2$$

So $B = (-35,\ -14)$.

$d(A,\ M) = \sqrt{(-5-25)^2 + (-2-10)^2} = \sqrt{(-30)^2 - (12)^2} = \sqrt{900+144} = \sqrt{1{,}044} = 32.3$

$d(M,\ B) = \sqrt{(-35-(-5))^2 + (-14-(-2))^2} = \sqrt{(-30)^2 + (-12)^2} = \sqrt{900+144} = \sqrt{1{,}044} = 32.3$

$d(A,\ B) = \sqrt{(-35-25)^2 + (-14-10)^2} = \sqrt{(-60)^2 + (-24)^2} = \sqrt{3{,}600+576} = \sqrt{4{,}176} = 64.6$

$\dfrac{1}{2}\,d(A,\ B) = \dfrac{1}{2}\,(64.6) = 32.3$

41. Write $A = (a_1,\ a_2)$. -8 is the average of a_1 and 2, so $-8 = \dfrac{a_1+2}{2}$

$$-16 = a_1 + 2$$
$$-18 = a_1$$

-6 is the average of a_2 and 4, so $-6 = \dfrac{a_2+4}{2}$

$$-12 = a_2 + 4$$
$$-16 = a_2$$

So $A = (-18,\ -16)$.

$d(A,\ M) = \sqrt{(-8-(-18))^2 + (-6-(-16))^2} = \sqrt{10^2 + 10^2} = \sqrt{100+100} = \sqrt{200} = 14.14$

$d(M,\ B) = \sqrt{(2-(-8))^2 + (4-(-6))^2} = \sqrt{10^2 + 10^2} = \sqrt{100+100} = \sqrt{200} = 14.14$

$d(A,\ B) = \sqrt{(2-(-18))^2 + (4-(-16))^2} = \sqrt{20^2 + 20^2} = \sqrt{400+400} = \sqrt{800} = 28.28$

$\dfrac{1}{2}\,d(A,\ B) = \dfrac{1}{2}\,(28.28) = 14.14$

43. $x^2 + (y + 2)^2 = 9$
$(x - 0)^2 + (y - (-2))^2 = 3^2$
Center (0, –2); Radius = 3

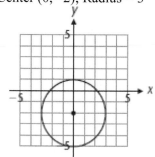

45. $(x + 4)^2 + (y - 2)^2 = 7$
$[x - (-4)]^2 + (y - 2)^2 = (\sqrt{7})^2$
Center (–4, 2); Radius = $\sqrt{7}$

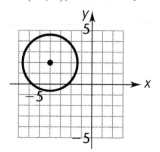

47. $x^2 + 6x + y^2 = 16$
$x^2 + 6x + 9 + y^2 = 16 + 9$
$(x + 3)^2 + y^2 = 25$
Center (–3, 0); Radius = 5

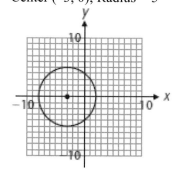

49. $x^2 + y^2 - 6x - 4y = 36$
$x^2 - 6x + y^2 - 4y = 36$
$x^2 - 6x + 9 + y^2 - 4y + 4 = 36 + 9 + 4$
$(x - 3)^2 + (y - 2)^2 = 49$
Center (3, 2); Radius = 7

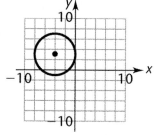

51. $3x^2 + 3y^2 + 24x - 18y + 24 = 0$
$x^2 + y^2 + 8x - 6y + 8 = 0$
$x^2 + 8x + y^2 - 6y = -8$
$x^2 + 8x + 16 + y^2 - 6y + 9 = -8 + 16 + 9$
$(x + 4)^2 + (y - 3)^2 = 17$
Center (–4, 3); Radius = $\sqrt{17}$

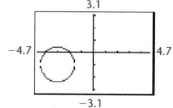

53. $x^2 + y^2 = 3$
$y^2 = 3 - x^2$
$y = \pm\sqrt{3 - x^2}$

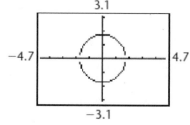

55. $(x + 3)^2 + (y + 1)^2 = 2$
$(y + 1)^2 = 2 - (x + 3)^2$
$y + 1 = \pm\sqrt{2 - (x + 3)^2}$
$y = -1 \pm \sqrt{2 - (x + 3)^2}$

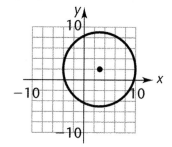

57. Let $A = (-3, 2)$, $B = (1, -2)$, $C = (8, 5)$

$$d(A, B) = \sqrt{(1-(-3))^2 + (-2-2)^2} = \sqrt{4^2 + (-4)^2} = \sqrt{16+16} = \sqrt{32}$$

$$d(B, C) = \sqrt{(8-1)^2 + (5-(-2))^2} = \sqrt{7^2 + 7^2} = \sqrt{49+49} = \sqrt{98}$$

$$d(A, C) = \sqrt{(8-(-3))^2 + (5-2)^2} = \sqrt{11^2 + 3^2} = \sqrt{121+9} = \sqrt{130}$$

Notice that $(d(A, B))^2 + (d(B, C))^2 = 32 + 98 = 130 = (d(A, C))^2$

Since these distances satisfy the Pythagorean Theorem, the three points are vertices of a right triangle. The segment connecting A and C is the hypotenuse (it's the longest side) so we need to find its midpoint.

$$M = \left(\frac{-3+8}{2}, \frac{2+5}{2}\right) = \left(\frac{5}{2}, \frac{7}{2}\right)$$

The vertex opposite the hypotenuse is B

$$d(M, B) = \sqrt{\left(1-\frac{5}{2}\right)^2 + \left(-2-\frac{7}{2}\right)^2} = \sqrt{\left(\frac{-3}{2}\right)^2 + \left(\frac{-11}{2}\right)^2} = \sqrt{\frac{9}{4}+\frac{121}{4}} = \sqrt{\frac{130}{4}} = \sqrt{32.5}$$

59. Perimeter = sum of lengths of all three sides

$$= \sqrt{[1-(-3)]^2 + [(-2)-1]^2} + \sqrt{(4-1)^2 + [3-(-2)]^2} + \sqrt{[4-(-3)]^2 + (3-1)^2}$$

$$= \sqrt{16+9} + \sqrt{9+25} + \sqrt{49+4} = \sqrt{25} + \sqrt{34} + \sqrt{53} = 18.11 \text{ to two decimal places}$$

61.
$$d(P_1, M) = \sqrt{\left(\frac{x_1+x_2}{2} - x_1\right)^2 + \left(\frac{y_1+y_2}{2} - y_1\right)^2}$$

$$= \sqrt{\left(\frac{x_1+x_2-2x_1}{2}\right)^2 + \left(\frac{y_1+y_2-2y_1}{2}\right)^2} = \sqrt{\left(\frac{x_2-x_1}{2}\right)^2 + \left(\frac{y_2-y_1}{2}\right)^2}$$

$$d(M, P_2) = \sqrt{\left(x_2 - \frac{x_1+x_2}{2}\right)^2 + \left(y_2 - \frac{y_1+y_2}{2}\right)^2}$$

$$= \sqrt{\left(\frac{2x_2-x_1-x_2}{2}\right)^2 + \left(\frac{2y_2-y_1-y_2}{2}\right)^2} = \sqrt{\left(\frac{x_2-x_1}{2}\right)^2 + \left(\frac{y_2-y_1}{2}\right)^2}$$

$$\frac{1}{2}d(P_1, P_2) = \frac{1}{2}\sqrt{(x_2-x_1)^2 + (y_2-y_1)^2} = \sqrt{\frac{1}{4}\left[(x_2-x_1)^2 + (y_2-y_1)^2\right]}$$

Note: The $\frac{1}{2}$ becomes $\frac{1}{4}$ when moved inside the radical symbol.

$$= \sqrt{\frac{(x_2-x_1)^2}{4} + \frac{(y_2-y_1)^2}{4}} = \sqrt{\left(\frac{x_2-x_1}{2}\right)^2 + \left(\frac{y_2-y_1}{2}\right)^2}$$

All three of these distances are equal.

63. The center of the circle is at the midpoint of the given diameter. From the midpoint formula, then, the center is at

$$\left(\frac{x_1+x_2}{2},\frac{y_1+y_2}{2}\right)=\left(\frac{-4+6}{2},\frac{3+3}{2}\right)=(1,3)=(h,k)$$

The radius of the circle is the distance from this midpoint to either endpoint. From the distance formula, then, the radius is

$$\sqrt{(x_2-x_1)^2+(y_2-y_1)^2}=\sqrt{(6-1)^2+(3-3)^2}=5=r$$

Substitute into the standard form of the equation of a circle.

$(x-h)^2+(y-k)^2=r^2$

$(x-1)^2+(y-3)^2=5^2$
$(x-1)^2+(y-3)^2=25$

65. The center of the circle is at the midpoint of the given diameter. From the midpoint formula, then, the center is at

$$\left(\frac{x_1+x_2}{2},\frac{y_1+y_2}{2}\right)=\left(\frac{4+0}{2},\frac{0+10}{2}\right)=(2,5)=(h,k)$$

The radius of the circle is the distance from this midpoint to either endpoint. From the distance formula, then, the radius is

$$\sqrt{(x_2-x_1)^2+(y_2-y_1)^2}=\sqrt{(4-2)^2+(0-5)^2}=\sqrt{4+25}=\sqrt{29}=r$$

Substitute into the standard form of the equation of a circle.

$(x-h)^2+(y-k)^2=r^2$

$(x-2)^2+(y-5)^2=(\sqrt{29})^2$
$(x-2)^2+(y-5)^2=29$

67. The center of the circle is at the midpoint of the given diameter. From the midpoint formula, then, the center is at

$$\left(\frac{x_1+x_2}{2},\frac{y_1+y_2}{2}\right)=\left(\frac{11+3}{2},\frac{(-2)+(-4)}{2}\right)=(7,-3)=(h,k)$$

The radius of the circle is the distance from this midpoint to either endpoint. From the distance formula, then, the radius is

$$\sqrt{(x_2-x_1)^2+(y_2-y_1)^2}=\sqrt{(3-7)^2+[(-4)-(-3)]^2}=\sqrt{16+1}=\sqrt{17}=r$$

Substitute into the standard form of the equation of a circle.

$(x-h)^2+(y-k)^2=r^2$

$(x-7)^2+(y-(-3))^2=(\sqrt{17})^2$
$(x-7)^2+(y+3)^2=17$

69. The radius of the circle is the distance from the given center to the given point. From the distance formula, then, the radius is

$$\sqrt{(x_2-x_1)^2+(y_2-y_1)^2}=\sqrt{(2-0)^2+[(-4)-5]^2}=\sqrt{4+81}=\sqrt{85}=r$$

Substitute into the standard form of the equation of a circle.

$(x-h)^2+(y-k)^2=r^2$

$(x-0)^2+(y-5)^2=(\sqrt{85})^2$
$x^2+(y-5)^2=85$

71. The radius of the circle is the distance from the given center to the given point. From the distance formula, then, the radius is

$$\sqrt{(x_2 - x_1)^2 + (y_2 - y_1)^2} = \sqrt{[8-(-2)]^2 + [(-7)-9]^2} = \sqrt{100 + 256} = \sqrt{356} = r$$

Substitute into the standard form of the equation of a circle.

$$(x - h)^2 + (y - k)^2 = r^2$$
$$[x - (-2)]^2 + (y - 9)^2 = (\sqrt{356})^2$$
$$(x + 2)^2 + (y - 9)^2 = 356$$

73.

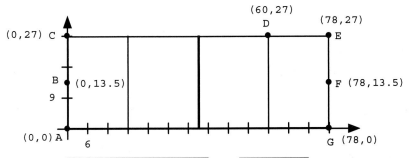

$$d(B, D) = \sqrt{(60-0)^2 + (27-13.5)^2} = \sqrt{60^2 + 13.5^2} = \sqrt{3600 + 182.25} = \sqrt{3,782.25} = 62 \text{ ft.}$$

$$d(F, C) = \sqrt{(78-0)^2 + (13.5-27)^2} = \sqrt{78^2 + (-13.5)^2} = \sqrt{6,084 + 182.25} = \sqrt{6,266.25} = 79 \text{ ft.}$$

75. Using the hint, we note that $(2, r - 1)$ must satisfy $x^2 + y^2 = r^2$, that is

$$2^2 + (r - 1)^2 = r^2$$
$$4 + r^2 - 2r + 1 = r^2$$
$$-2r + 5 = 0$$
$$r = \frac{5}{2} \text{ or 2.5 ft.}$$

77. (A) From the drawing, we can write:

$$\begin{pmatrix} \text{Distance from tower} \\ \text{to town B} \end{pmatrix} = 2 \times \begin{pmatrix} \text{Distance from tower} \\ \text{to town A} \end{pmatrix}$$

$$\begin{pmatrix} \text{Distance from } (x,y) \\ \text{to } (36,15) \end{pmatrix} = 2 \times \begin{pmatrix} \text{Distance from } (x,y) \\ \text{to } (0,0) \end{pmatrix}$$

$$\sqrt{(36-x)^2 + (15-y)^2} = 2\sqrt{(0-x)^2 + (0-y)^2}$$

$$\sqrt{(36-x)^2 + (15-y)^2} = 2\sqrt{x^2 + y^2}$$

$$(36 - x)^2 + (15 - y)^2 = 4(x^2 + y^2)$$

$$1,296 - 72x + x^2 + 225 - 30y + y^2 = 4x^2 + 4y^2$$

$$1,521 = 3x^2 + 3y^2 + 72x + 30y$$

$$507 = x^2 + y^2 + 24x + 10y$$

$$144 + 25 + 507 = x^2 + 24x + 144 + y^2 + 10y + 25$$

$$676 = (x + 12)^2 + (y + 5)^2$$

The circle has center $(-12, -5)$ and radius 26.

(B) All points due east of Town A have y coordinate 0 in this coordinate system. The points on the circle for which $y = 0$ are found by substituting $y = 0$ into the equation of the circle and solving for x.

$$(x + 12)^2 + (y + 5)^2 = 676$$
$$(x + 12)^2 + 25 = 676$$
$$(x + 12)^2 = 651$$
$$x + 12 = \pm\sqrt{651}$$
$$x = -12 \pm \sqrt{651}$$

Choosing the positive square root so that x is greater than -12 (east rather than west) we have
$$x = -12 + \sqrt{651} \approx 13.5 \text{ miles.}$$

Section 2-3

1. Given $Ax + By = C$ as the equation, the x intercept is found by setting $y = 0$ and solving to obtain $x = C/A$. The y intercept is found by setting $x = 0$ and solving to obtain $y = C/B$. If either A or B is 0 there is no corresponding intercept.

3. m is then the slope and b is the y intercept for the line.

5. If the two equations are $A_1x + B_1y = C_1$ and $A_2x + B_2y = C_2$, then the lines will be parallel if $A_2/A_1 = B_2/B_1$ but this ratio is not equal to C_2/C_1. Also note that two distinct vertical lines are parallel and so are two distinct horizontal lines, so if $A_2/A_1 \neq C_2/C_1$ and $B_2 = B_1 = 0$, the lines are parallel; likewise if $B_2/B_1 \neq C_2/C_1$ and $A_2 = A_1 = 0$ the lines are parallel.

7. The vertical segment has length 3 so rise = 3. The horizontal segment has length 5 so run = 5.

   Slope $= \dfrac{\text{rise}}{\text{run}} = \dfrac{3}{5}$. $(2, 2)$ is on the graph.

   Use the point-slope form.

   Common Error: Multiplying both $\dfrac{3}{5}$ and $(x - 2)$ by 5 on the right side.

   $$y - 2 = \frac{3}{5}(x - 2) \quad \text{(Multiply both sides by 5)}$$
   $$5y - 10 = 3(x - 2)$$
   $$5y - 10 = 3x - 6$$
   $$-3x + 5y = +4$$
   $$3x - 5y = -4$$

9. The vertical segment has length 2 so rise = 2. The horizontal segment has length 8 so run = 8.

   Slope $= \dfrac{\text{rise}}{\text{run}} = \dfrac{2}{8} = \dfrac{1}{4}$. $(-4, 1)$ is on the graph.

   Use the point-slope form.

   $$y - 1 = \frac{1}{4}(x - (-4)) \quad \text{(Multiply both sides by 4)}$$
   $$4y - 4 = (x + 4)$$
   $$-x + 4y = 8$$
   $$x - 4y = -8$$

11. The vertical segment has length 3 and goes downward so rise = -3. The horizontal segment has length 5 so run = 5.

    Slope $= \dfrac{\text{rise}}{\text{run}} = \dfrac{-3}{5}$. $(-4, 2)$ is on the graph.

    Use the point-slope form.

    $$y - 2 = \frac{-3}{5}(x - (-4)) \quad \text{(Multiply both sides by 5)}$$
    $$5y - 10 = -3(x + 4)$$
    $$5y - 10 = -3x - 12$$
    $$3x + 5y = -2$$

13. The x intercept is -2. The y intercept is 2. From the point $(-2, 0)$ to the point $(0, 2)$, the value of y increases by 2 units as the value of x increases by 2 units. Thus slope $= \dfrac{\text{rise}}{\text{run}} = \dfrac{2}{2} = 1.$

Equation: $y = mx + b$
$y = 1x + 2$ or $y = x + 2$

15. The x intercept is -2. The y intercept is -4. From the point $(-2, 0)$ to the point $(0, -4)$ the value of y decreases by 4 units as the value of x increases by 2 units. Thus, the slope $= \dfrac{\text{rise}}{\text{run}} = \dfrac{-4}{2} = -2.$

Equation: $y = mx + b$
$y = -2x + (-4)$ or $y = -2x - 4$

17. The x intercept is 3. The y intercept is -1. From the point $(0, -1)$ to the point $(3, 0)$ the value of y increases by 1 unit as the value of x increases by 3 units. Thus, the slope $= \dfrac{\text{rise}}{\text{run}} = \dfrac{1}{3}.$

Equation: $y = mx + b$
$y = \dfrac{1}{3}x + (-1)$ or $y = \dfrac{1}{3}x - 1$

19. $y = -\dfrac{3}{5}x + 4$ slope $-\dfrac{3}{5}$

x	y
0	4
5	1
-5	7

21. $y = -\dfrac{3}{4}x$ slope $-\dfrac{3}{4}$

x	y
0	0
4	-3
-4	3

23. $4x + 2y = 0$
$2y = -4x$

$y = -2x$ slope -2

x	y
0	0
1	-2
2	-4

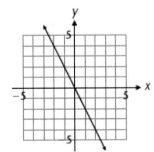

25. $4x - 5y = -24$
$-5y = -4x - 24$

$y = \dfrac{4}{5}x + \dfrac{24}{5}$ slope $= \dfrac{4}{5}$

x	y
-1	4
4	8
9	12

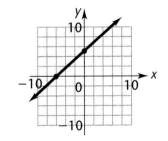

27. $\dfrac{y}{8} - \dfrac{x}{4} = 1$

$\dfrac{y}{8} = \dfrac{x}{4} + 1$

$y = 2x + 8$ slope 2

x	y
0	8
−4	0
−8	−8

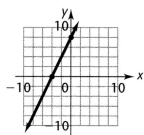

29. $x = -3$
slope not defined
vertical line

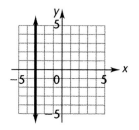

31. $y = 3.5$
slope 0
horizontal line

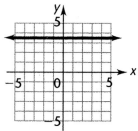

33. Slope and y intercept are given;
We use slope-intercept form.
$y = -3x + 7$
$3x + y = 7$

35. Slope and y intercept are given;
We use slope-intercept form.
$y = \dfrac{7}{2}x - \dfrac{1}{3}$
$6y = 21x - 2$
$-21x + 6y = -2$
$21x - 6y = 2$

37. The equation of this horizontal line
is $y = \dfrac{2}{3}$ or $3y = 2$.

39. A point and the slope are given; we use point-slope form.
$y - 3 = -2(x - 0)$
$y - 3 = -2x$
$\qquad y = -2x + 3$

41. A point and the slope are given; we use point-slope form.
$y - 4 = \dfrac{3}{2}[x - (-5)]$

$y - 4 = \dfrac{3}{2}[x + 5]$

$y - 4 = \dfrac{3}{2}x + \dfrac{15}{2}$

$y = \dfrac{3}{2}x + \dfrac{23}{2}$

43. A point and the slope are given; we use point-slope form.
$y - (-3) = -\dfrac{1}{2}[x - (-2)]$

$y + 3 = -\dfrac{1}{2}[x + 2]$

$y + 3 = -\dfrac{1}{2}x - 1$

$y = -\dfrac{1}{2}x - 4$

45. A point and the slope are given; we use point-slope form:
$y - 4 = -3(x - 0)$
$y - 4 = -3x$
$\qquad y = -3x + 4$

47. A point and the slope are given; we use point-slope form:
$y - 4 = -\dfrac{2}{5}[x - (-5)]$

$y - 4 = -\dfrac{2}{5}[x + 5]$

$y - 4 = -\dfrac{2}{5}x - 2$

$y = -\dfrac{2}{5}x + 2$

49. Two points are given; we first find the slope, then we use point-slope form.
$m = \dfrac{-2-6}{5-1} = \dfrac{-8}{4} = -2$ $y - 6 = (-2)(x - 1)$
$\qquad\qquad\qquad\qquad\qquad y - 6 = -2x + 2$
$\qquad\qquad\qquad\qquad\qquad\quad y = -2x + 8$
or $\qquad\qquad y - (-2) = (-2)(x - 5)$
$\qquad\qquad\qquad\qquad\quad y + 2 = -2x + 10$
$\qquad\qquad\qquad\qquad\qquad\quad y = -2x + 8$

Thus, it does not matter which point is chosen in substituting into the point-slope form; both points must give rise to the same equation.

51. We proceed as in problem 49.

$$m = \frac{8-0}{-4-2} = \frac{8}{-6} = -\frac{4}{3}$$

$$y - 0 = -\frac{4}{3}(x-2)$$

$$y = -\frac{4}{3}x + \frac{8}{3}$$

53. We proceed as in problem 49.

$$m = \frac{4-4}{5-(-3)} = \frac{0}{8} = 0$$

$$y - 4 = 0(x - 5)$$

$$y - 4 = 0$$

$$y = 4$$

55. We proceed as in problem 49.

$$m = \frac{-3-6}{4-4} = \frac{-9}{0}$$

slope is undefined.
A vertical line through (4, 6) has equation $x = 4$.

57. We proceed as in problem 49, using $(-4, 0)$ and $(0, 3)$ as the two given points.

$$m = \frac{3-0}{0-(-4)} = \frac{3}{4}$$

$$y - 0 = \frac{3}{4}[x-(-4)]$$

$$y = \frac{3}{4}x + 3$$

59. A line parallel to $y = 3x - 5$ will have the same slope, namely 3. We now use the point slope form.

$$y - 4 = 3[x - (-3)]$$

$$y - 4 = 3x + 9$$

$$y = 3x + 13$$

$$-3x + y = 13$$

$$3x - y = -13$$

61. A line perpendicular to

$$y = -\frac{1}{3}x \text{ will have slope satisfying}$$

$$-\frac{1}{3}m = -1, \text{ or } m = 3.$$

We use the point-slope form.

$$y - (-3) = 3(x - 2)$$

$$y + 3 = 3x - 6$$

$$9 = 3x - y$$

$$3x - y = 9$$

63. A line parallel to $3x - 2y = 4$ will have the same slope. The slope of $3x - 2y = 4$, or $2y = 3x - 4$, or

$$y = \frac{3}{2}x - 2 \text{ is } \frac{3}{2}. \text{ We use the point-slope form,}$$

$$y - 0 = \frac{3}{2}(x - 5)$$

$$y = \frac{3}{2}x - \frac{15}{2}$$

$$\frac{15}{2} = \frac{3}{2}x - y$$

$$15 = 3x - 2y$$

$$3x - 2y = 15$$

Alternatively, we could notice that a line parallel to $3x - 2y = 4$ will have an equation of the form $3x - 2y = C$.
Since the required line must contain $(5, 0)$, $(5, 0)$ must satisfy its equation. Therefore, $3(5) - 2(0) = C$. Since $15 = C$, the equation desired is $3x - 2y = 15$.

65. A line perpendicular to $x + 3y = 9$, which has slope $-\frac{1}{3}$, will have slope

satisfying $-\frac{1}{3}m = -1$, or $m = 3$.

We use the point-slope form.

$$y - (-4) = 3(x - 0)$$

$$y + 4 = 3x$$

$$4 = 3x - y$$

$$3x - y = 4$$

67. slope of $AB = \frac{-1-2}{4-0} = -\frac{3}{4}$

slope of $DC = \frac{-5-(-2)}{1-(-3)} = -\frac{3}{4}$

Therefore $AB \parallel DC$.

69. slope of $AB = -\frac{3}{4}$

slope of $BC = \frac{-5-(-1)}{1-4} = \frac{4}{3}$

$(\text{slope } AB)(\text{slope } BC) = \left(-\frac{3}{4}\right)\left(\frac{4}{3}\right) = -1$

Therefore $AB \perp BC$.

71. midpoint of $AD = \left(\dfrac{0+(-3)}{2}, \dfrac{2+(-2)}{2}\right) = \left(-\dfrac{3}{2}, 0\right)$

slope of $AD = \dfrac{-2-2}{-3-0} = \dfrac{4}{3}$

We require the equation of a line, through the midpoint of AD, which is perpendicular to AD. Its slope will satisfy $\dfrac{4}{3}m = -1$, or $m = -\dfrac{3}{4}$. We use the point-slope form.

$y - 0 = -\dfrac{3}{4}\left[x - \left(-\dfrac{3}{2}\right)\right]$

$y = -\dfrac{3}{4}\left(x + \dfrac{3}{2}\right)$

$y = -\dfrac{3}{4}x - \dfrac{9}{8}$

$8y = -6x - 9$

$6x + 8y = -9$

73. Two points are given; we first find the slope, then use the point-slope form.

$m = \dfrac{0-b}{a-0} = -\dfrac{b}{a} \quad a \neq 0$

$y - b = -\dfrac{b}{a}(x - 0)$

$y - b = -\dfrac{bx}{a}$

Divide both sides by b, then $(b \neq 0)$

$\dfrac{y-b}{b} = -\dfrac{x}{a}$

$\dfrac{y}{b} - 1 = -\dfrac{x}{a}$

$\dfrac{y}{b} = 1 - \dfrac{x}{a}$

$\dfrac{x}{a} + \dfrac{y}{b} = 1$

75. The circle has center $(0, 0)$. The radius drawn from $(0, 0)$ to the given point $(3, 4)$ has slope given by

$M_R = \dfrac{4-0}{3-0} = \dfrac{4}{3}$.

Therefore, the slope of the tangent line is given by

$\dfrac{4}{3}m = -1 \quad \text{or} \quad m = -\dfrac{3}{4}$

We require the equation of a line through $(3, 4)$ with slope $-\dfrac{3}{4}$. We use the point-slope form.

$y - 4 = -\dfrac{3}{4}(x - 3)$

$y - 4 = -\dfrac{3}{4}x + \dfrac{9}{4}$

$4y - 16 = -3x + 9$

$3x + 4y = 25$

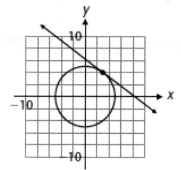

77. The circle has center $(0, 0)$. The radius drawn from $(0, 0)$ to the given point $(5, -5)$ has slope given by

$M_R = \dfrac{-5-0}{5-0} = -1$

Therefore, the slope of the tangent line is given by

$(-1)m = -1 \quad \text{or} \quad m = 1$

We require the equation of a line through $(5, -5)$ with slope 1. We use the point-slope form.

$y - (-5) = 1(x - 5)$

$y + 5 = x - 5$

$x - y = 10$

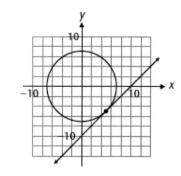

79. The circle has center (3, –4). The radius drawn from (3, –4) to the given point (8, –16) has slope given by

$$M_R = \frac{-16-(-4)}{8-3} = -\frac{12}{5}$$

Therefore, the slope of the tangent line is given by

$$\left(-\frac{12}{5}\right)m = -1 \quad \text{or} \quad m = \frac{5}{12}$$

We require the equation of a line through (8, –16) with slope $\frac{5}{12}$. We use the point-slope form.

$$y-(-16) = \frac{5}{12}(x-8)$$

$$y+16 = \frac{5}{12}x - \frac{40}{12}$$

$$12y+192 = 5x - 40$$

$$232 = 5x - 12y$$

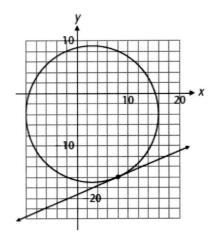

81. (A)

x	0	5,000	10,000	15,000	20,000	25,000	30,000
$212 - 0.0018x = B$	212	203	194	185	176	167	158

(B)   The boiling point drops 9°F for each 5,000 foot increase in altitude.

83.   Total cost = Fixed cost + variable cost. If x = the number of doughnuts produced, variable cost is $0.12x$ ($0.12 per doughnut times the number of doughnuts produced.) If C represents total cost,

$$C = 124 + 0.12x \quad \text{Plug in 250 for } C:$$
$$250 = 124 + 0.12x$$
$$126 = 0.12x$$
$$1,050 = x$$

The shop can produce 1,050 doughnuts for $250.

85. (A) We write $s = mw + b$. If $w = 0$, $s = 0$, hence
$0 = m \cdot 0 + b$, $b = 0$.
If $w = 5$, $s = 2$, hence $2 = m \cdot 5$, $m = 0.4$.
$s = 0.4w$
(B) $s = 0.4(20) = 8$ inches
(C) Solve $3.6 = 0.4w$ to obtain $w = 9$ pounds.

87. (A) We write $F = mC + b$. If $C = 0$, $F = 32$,
hence $32 = m \cdot 0 + b$, $b = 32$.
If $C = 100$, $F = 212$, hence
$212 = m \cdot 100 + 32$,
$100m = 180$, $m = \frac{9}{5}$.

$$F = \frac{9}{5}C + 32$$

(B) If $C = 20$, $F = \frac{9}{5}(20) + 32 = 68°F$

If $F = 86$, solve

$$86 = \frac{9}{5}C + 32$$

$$54 = \frac{9}{5}C$$

$$C = \frac{5}{9}(54) = 30°C$$

89.(A) If h is linearly related to t, then we are looking for an equation whose graph passes through $(t_1, h_1) = (9, 23)$ and $(t_2, h_2) = (24, 40)$. We find the slope, and then we use the point-slope form to find the equation.

$$m = \frac{h_2 - h_1}{t_2 - t_1} = \frac{40-23}{24-9} = \frac{17}{15} \approx 1.13$$

$$h - h_1 = m(t - t_1)$$

$$h - 23 = \frac{17}{15}(t-9)$$

$$h - 23 = \frac{17}{15}t - \frac{51}{5}$$

$$h = \frac{17}{15}t - \frac{51}{5} + 23 = 1.13t + 12.8$$

(B) We are asked for t when $h = 50$.
$$50 = 1.13t + 12.8$$
$$37.2 = 1.13t$$
$$t = 32.9 \text{ hours}$$

91. (A) If L is linearly related to t, then we are looking for an equation whose graph passes through $(t_1, L_1) = (0, 49.2)$ and $(t_2, L_2) = (100, 77.3)$. We find the slope, then we use the point-slope form to find the equation.

$$m = \frac{L_2 - L_1}{t_2 - t_1} = \frac{77.3 - 49.2}{100 - 0} = 0.281$$

$$L - L_1 = m(t - t_1)$$
$$L - 49.2 = 0.281(t - 0)$$
$$L - 49.2 = 0.281t$$
$$L = 0.281t + 49.2$$

(B) We are asked for L when $t = 120$.
$$L = 0.281(120) + 49.2$$
$$L = 82.9 \text{ years}$$

93.

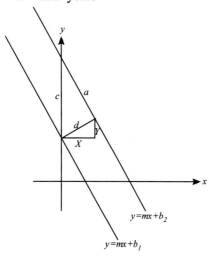

In general, we can show that $d = \dfrac{c}{\sqrt{1 + m^2}}$ as follows:

The Pythagorean Theorem gives: $d^2 + a^2 = c^2$

The two triangles shown are similar, hence corresponding sides are proportional. Thus

$$\frac{a}{d} = \frac{x}{y}$$

The slope of the line segment labeled d is the negative reciprocal of m.

Thus $\dfrac{y}{x} = -\dfrac{1}{m}$

$$\frac{x}{y} = -m$$

It follows that $a = \dfrac{x}{y} d = -md$.

Hence $d^2 + (-md)^2 = c^2$
$$d^2(1 + m^2) = c^2$$
$$d^2 = \frac{c^2}{1 + m^2}$$
$$d = \frac{c}{\sqrt{1 + m^2}}$$

In particular, avenue A is shown to have a rise of -5000 and a run of 4000, hence $m = -\dfrac{5000}{4000} = -1.25$. The equation of avenue A is then (using the slope-intercept form $y = mx + b$) $y = -1.25x + 5000$. Avenue B has the same slope, and y intercept 4000. Substituting in the above formula, with $c = 5000 - 4000 = 1000$, yields

$$d_1 = \frac{1000}{\sqrt{1 + (-1.25)^2}} = 625 \text{ ft.}$$

Section 2-4

1. The process of mathematical modeling consists of three steps.
    Step 1: Construct the mathematical model, a mathematics problem that, when solved, will provide information about the real-world problem.
    Step 2: Solve the mathematical model.
    Step 3: Interpret the solution to the mathematical model in terms of the original real-world problem.

3. Calculate the values y_1 and y_2 associated with x_1 and x_2 respectively,
    Then, average rate of change $= \dfrac{\text{change in } y}{\text{change in } x} = \dfrac{y_2 - y_1}{x_2 - x_1}$.

5. (A) If cost y is linearly related to the number of golf clubs x_1 then we are looking for an equation whose graph passes through $(x_1, y_1) = (80, 8{,}147)$ and $(x_2, y_2) = (100, 9{,}647)$. We find the slope and then use the point-slope form to find the equation.
$$m = \frac{y_2 - y_1}{x_2 - x_1} = \frac{9{,}647 - 8{,}147}{100 - 80} = 75$$
$$y - y_1 = m(x - x_1)$$
$$y - 8{,}147 = 75(x - 80)$$
$$y - 8{,}147 = 75x - 6{,}000$$
$$y = 75x + 2{,}147$$

   (B) The slope of 75 is the rate of change of cost with respect to production, \$75 per golf club.

   (C) Increasing production by 1 unit increases cost by \$75.

7. (A) The rate of change of height with respect to DBH is 4.06 feet per inch.

   (B) Increasing DBH by 1 inch increases height by 4.06 feet.

   (C) Substitute $d = 12$ into $h = 4.06d + 24.1$ to obtain
$$h = 4.06(12) + 24.1$$
$$h = 73 \text{ feet}$$

   (D) Substitute $h = 100$ into $h = 4.06d + 24.1$ and solve.
$$100 = 4.06d + 24.1$$
$$75.9 = 4.06d$$
$$d = 19 \text{ inches}$$

9. (A) Robinson: The rate of change of weight with respect to height is 3.7 pounds per inch.
    Miller: The rate of change of weight with respect to height is 3 pounds per inch.

   (B) 5'6" = 6 inches over 5 feet
    Substitute $h = 6$ into each model.
    Robinson: $w = 108 + 3.7(6) = 130.2$ pounds
    Miller: $w = 117 + 3.0(6) = 135$ pounds

   (C) Substitute $w = 140$ into each model and solve.
    Robinson: $140 = 108 + 3.7h$
$$32 = 3.7h$$
$$h = 9 \text{ inches, predicting 5'9".}$$
    Miller: $140 = 117 + 3.0h$
$$23 = 3.0h$$
$$h = 8 \text{ inches, predicting 5'8".}$$

11. If speed s is linearly related to temperature t, then we are looking for an equation whose graph passes through $(t_1, s_1) = (32, 741)$ and $(t_2, s_2) = (72, 771)$. We find the slope and then use the point-slope form to find the equation.

$$m = \frac{s_2 - s_1}{t_2 - t_1} = \frac{771 - 741}{72 - 32} = 0.75$$
$$s - s_1 = m(t - t_1)$$
$$s - 741 = 0.75(t - 32)$$
$$s - 741 = 0.75t - 24$$
$$s = 0.75t + 717$$

The speed of sound at sea level increases by 0.75 mph for each 1°F change in temperature.

13. If percentage m is linearly related to time t, then we are looking for an equation whose graph passes through $(t_1, m_1) = (0, 25.7)$ and $(t_2, m_2) = (6, 23.9)$. We find the slope and then use the point-slope form to find the equation. M is used for slope to avoid confusion.

$$M = \frac{m_2 - m_1}{t_2 - t_1} = \frac{23.9 - 25.7}{6 - 0} = -0.3$$
$$m - m_1 = M(t - t_1)$$
$$m - 25.7 = -0.3\,(t - 0)$$
$$m = -0.3t + 25.7$$

To find t when $m = 18$, substitute $m = 18$ and solve.
$$18 = -0.3t + 25.7$$
$$-7.7 = -0.3t$$
$$t = 25.67$$

Rounding up to 26, 26 years after 2000 will be 2026.

15. (A) If value V is linearly related to time t, then we are looking for an equation whose graph passes through $(t_1, V_1) = (0, 142{,}000)$ and $(t_2, V_2) = (10, 67{,}000)$. We find the slope and then use the point-slope form to find the equation.

$$m = \frac{V_2 - V_1}{t_2 - t_1} = \frac{67{,}000 - 142{,}000}{10 - 0} = -7{,}500$$
$$V - V_1 = m(t - t_1)$$
$$V - 142{,}000 = -7{,}500(t - 0)$$
$$V = -7{,}500t + 142{,}000$$

(B) The tractor's value decreases at the rate of $7,500 per year.

(C) When $t = 6$, $V = -7{,}500(6) + 142{,}000 = $97,000.

17. (A) If price R is linearly related to cost C, then we are looking for an equation whose graph passes through $(C_1, R_1) = (85, 112)$ and $(C_2, R_2) = (175, 238)$. We find the slope and then use the point-slope form to find the equation.

$$m = \frac{R_2 - R_1}{C_2 - C_1} = \frac{238 - 112}{175 - 85} = 1.4$$
$$R - R_1 = m(C - C_1)$$
$$R - 112 = 1.4(C - 85)$$
$$R - 112 = 1.4C - 119$$
$$R = 1.4C - 7$$

(B) The slope is 1.4. This is the rate of change of retail price with respect to cost.

(C) To find C when $R = 185$, substitute $R = 185$ and solve.
$$185 = 1.4C - 7$$
$$192 = 1.4C$$
$$C = \$137$$

19. (A) If temperature T is linearly related to altitude A, then we are looking for an equation whose graph passes through $(A_1, T_1) = (0, 70)$ and $(A_2, T_2) = (18, -20)$. We find the slope and then use the point-slope form to find the equation.

$$m = \frac{T_2 - T_1}{A_2 - A_1} = \frac{-20 - 70}{18 - 0} = -5$$
$$T - T_1 = m(A - A_1)$$
$$T - 70 = -5(A - 0)$$
$$T = -5A + 70$$

21. (A) If altitude a is linearly related to time t, then we are looking for an equation whose graph passes through $(t_1, a_1) = (0, 2{,}880)$ and $(t_2, a_2) = (120, 0)$. We find the slope and then use the point-slope form to find the equation.

$$m = \frac{a_2 - a_1}{t_2 - t_1} = \frac{0 - 2{,}880}{120 - 0} = -24$$
$$a - a_1 = m(t - t_1)$$
$$a - 2{,}880 = -24(t - 0)$$
$$a = -24t + 2{,}880$$

(B) To find A when $T = 0$, substitute $T = 0$ and solve.

$$0 = -5A + 70$$
$$A = 14, \text{ that is, } 14{,}000 \text{ feet}$$

(B) Since altitude is decreasing at the rate of 24 feet per second, this is the rate of descent.

23. (A)

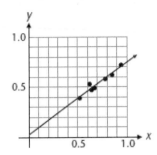

(B) Substitute $x = 1.3$ into $y = 0.72x + 0.03$ to obtain

$$y = 0.72(1.3) + 0.03 \approx 0.97 \text{ million}$$

(C) Substitute $x = 1.8$ into $y = 0.72x + 0.03$ to obtain

$$y = 0.72(1.8) + 0.03 \approx 1.3 \text{ million}$$

25. The entered data is shown here along with the results of the linear regression calculations.

 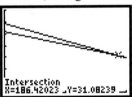

The linear regression model for men's 100-meter freestyle data is seen to be $y = -0.1102x + 51.62$. The linear regression model for women's 100- meter freestyle data is seen to be $y = -0.1469x + 58.47$. A plausible window is shown here, along with the results of the intersection calculation.

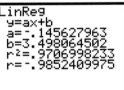

The fact that the lines intersect indicates that, according to this model, the women will eventually catch up with the men.

27.   Entering the data (note: price is entered as y) and applying the linear regression routine yields the following:

 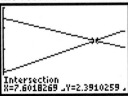

The linear regression model for the price-supply data is seen to be $y = 0.200x + 0.872$. The linear regression model for the price-demand data is seen to be $y = -0.146x + 3.50$. A plausible window is shown here, along with the results of the intersection calculation.

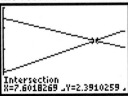

The intersection for $y = 2.39$ implies an equilibrium price of $2.39.

CHAPTER 2 REVIEW

1.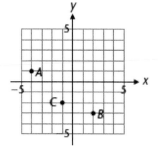

$(2\text{-}1)$

2.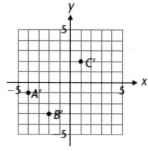

The reflection of A in the x axis is $A'(-4, -1)$.
The reflection of B in the y axis is $B'(-2, -3)$.
The reflection of C in the origin is $C'(1, 2)$. $(2\text{-}1)$

3. (A) $y = 2x$

Test y axis	Test x axis	Test origin
Replace x with $-x$:	Replace y with $-y$:	Replace x with $-x$ and y with $-y$:
$y = 2(-x)$	$-y = 2x$	$-y = 2(-x)$
$y = -2x$	$y = -2x$	$y = 2x$

x	y
0	0
1	2
2	4

The graph has symmetry with respect to the origin. We reflect the portion of the graph in quadrant I through the origin, using the origin symmetry.

(B) $y = 2x - 1$

Test y axis	Test x axis	Test origin
Replace x with $-x$:	Replace y with $-y$:	Replace x with $-x$ and y with $-y$:
$y = 2(-x) - 1$	$-y = 2x - 1$	$-y = 2(-x) - 1$
$y = -2x - 1$	$y = -2x + 1$	$y = 2x + 1$

x	y
0	−1
1	1
−1	−3
2	3
−2	−5

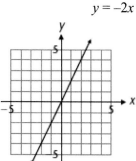

The graph has none of these three symmetries.

(C) $y = 2|x|$

Test y axis	Test x axis	Test origin
Replace x with $-x$:	Replace y with $-y$:	Replace x with $-x$ and y with $-y$:
$y = 2|-x|$	$-y = 2|x|$	$-y = 2|-x|$
$y = 2|x|$	$y = -2|x|$	$y = -2|x|$

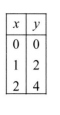

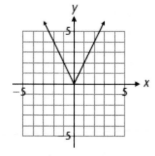

The graph has symmetry with respect to the y axis. We reflect the portion of the graph in quadrant I through the y axis, using the y axis symmetry.

(D) $|y| = 2x$

Test y axis	Test x axis	Test origin
Replace x with $-x$:	Replace y with $-y$:	Replace x with $-x$ and y with $-y$:
$|y| = 2(-x)$	$|-y| = 2x$	$|-y| = 2(-x)$
$|y| = -2x$	$|y| = 2x$	$|y| = -2x$

The graph has symmetry with respect to the x axis. We reflect the portion of the graph in quadrant I through the x axis, using the x axis symmetry.

x	y
0	0
1	2
2	4

(2-1)

4. (A) -2 (B) $-2, 1$ (C) $-3, 2$ *(2-1)*

5. (A) $d(A, B) = \sqrt{[4-(-2)]^2 + (0-3)^2}$
$$= \sqrt{36+9} = \sqrt{45}$$

(B) $m = \dfrac{0-3}{4-(-2)} = \dfrac{-3}{6} = -\dfrac{1}{2}$

(C) The slope m_1 of a line perpendicular to AB must satisfy $m_1\left(-\dfrac{1}{2}\right) = -1.$

Therefore, $m_1 = 2.$ *(2-2, 2-3)*

6. (A) Center at $(0, 0)$ and radius $\sqrt{7}$
$$x^2 + y^2 = r^2$$
$$x^2 + y^2 = (\sqrt{7})^2$$
$$x^2 + y^2 = 7$$

(B) Center at $(3, -2)$ and radius $\sqrt{7}$
$$(h, k) = (3, -2)$$
$$r = \sqrt{7}$$
$$(x - h)^2 + (y - k)^2 = r^2$$
$$(x - 3)^2 + [y - (-2)]^2 = (\sqrt{7})^2$$
$$(x - 3)^2 + (y + 2)^2 = 7 \qquad (2-2)$$

7.
$$(x + 3)^2 + (y - 2)^2 = 5$$
$$[x - (-3)]^2 + (y - 2)^2 = (\sqrt{5})^2$$

Center: $C(h, k) = (-3, 2)$ Radius: $r = \sqrt{5}$ *(2-2)*

8. (A) -4 is the average of a_1 and 2, so $-4 = \dfrac{a_1 + 2}{2}$
$$-8 = a_1 + 2$$
$$-10 = a_1$$

(B) 3 is the average of a_2 and -5, so $3 = \dfrac{a_2 + (-5)}{2}$
$$6 = a_2 - 5$$
$$11 = a_2$$

(C) $A = (-10, 11)$

$$d(A, M) = \sqrt{(-10-(-4))^2 + (11-3)^2} = \sqrt{(-6)^2 + 8^2} = \sqrt{36+64} = \sqrt{100} = 10$$

$$d(M, B) = \sqrt{(-4-2)^2 + (3-(-5)^2} = \sqrt{(-6)^2 + 8^2} = \sqrt{36+64} = \sqrt{100} = 10 \quad (2\text{-}2)$$

9. $A = (-1, -2)$, $B = (4, 3)$, $C = (1, 4)$

(A)

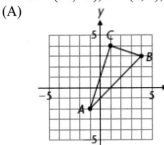

(B) $d(A, B) = \sqrt{(4-(-1))^2 + (3-(-2))^2} = \sqrt{5^2 + 5^2} = \sqrt{25+25} = \sqrt{50}$

$d(B, C) = \sqrt{(1-4)^2 + (4-3)^2} = \sqrt{(-3)^2 + 1^2} = \sqrt{9+1} = \sqrt{10}$

$d(A, C) = \sqrt{(1-(-1))^2 + (4-(-2))^2} = \sqrt{2^2 + 6^2} = \sqrt{4+36} = \sqrt{40} = 2\sqrt{10}$

Perimeter = sum of lengths of all three sides

$= \sqrt{50} + \sqrt{10} + 2\sqrt{10} = 16.56$ to two decimal places

(C) Since $(\sqrt{50})^2 = (\sqrt{10})^2 + (2\sqrt{10})^2$, that is, $50 = 10 + 40$, the triangle is a right triangle.

(D) Midpoint of $AB = \left(\dfrac{-1+4}{2}, \dfrac{-2+3}{2}\right) = (1.5, 0.5)$

Midpoint of $BC = \left(\dfrac{4+1}{2}, \dfrac{3+4}{2}\right) = (2.5, 3.5)$

Midpoint of $AC = \left(\dfrac{-1+1}{2}, \dfrac{-2+4}{2}\right) = (0, 1)$ $\qquad (2\text{-}3)$

10. The points at two of the vertices of the triangle are $(-4, 3)$ and $(1, 1)$. The line moves 2 units down between these points so the rise is -2. The line moves 5 units to the right between these points so the run is 5.

The slope is thus $m = \dfrac{-2}{5}$.

$$y - 1 = \dfrac{-2}{5}(x - 1)$$

$$y - 1 = -\dfrac{2}{5}x + \dfrac{2}{5}$$

$$5y - 5 = -2x + 2$$

$$2x + 5y = 7 \qquad (2\text{-}3)$$

11.
$$3x + 2y = 9$$
$$2y = -3x + 9$$
$$y = -\dfrac{3}{2}x + \dfrac{9}{2}$$

slope: $-\dfrac{3}{2}$

x	y
0	$\dfrac{9}{2}$
3	0
1	3

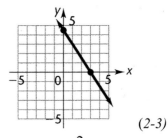

$(2\text{-}3)$

12. The line passes through the two given points, $(6, 0)$ and $(0, 4)$. Thus, its slope is given by

$$m = \dfrac{0-4}{6-0} = \dfrac{-4}{6} = -\dfrac{2}{3}$$

The equation of the line is, therefore, using the point-slope form,

$$y - 0 = -\dfrac{2}{3}(x - 6)$$

or $3y = -2(x - 6)$

or $3y = -2x + 12$.

$$2x + 3y = 12 \qquad (2\text{-}3)$$

13. $y = mx + b$ $\qquad m = -\dfrac{2}{3}$ $\qquad b = 2$

$$y = -\dfrac{2}{3}x + 2 \qquad (2\text{-}3)$$

14. *vertical:* $x = -3$, slope not defined;
horizontal: $y = 4$, slope $= 0$ *(2-3)*

15. $y = x^2 - 2$

Test y axis
Replace x with $-x$:
$y = (-x)^2 - 2$
$y = x^2 - 2$

Test x axis
Replace y with $-y$:
$-y = x^2 - 2$
$y = -x^2 + 2$

Test origin
Replace x with $-x$ and y with $-y$:
$-y = (-x)^2 - 2$
$y = -x^2 + 2$

The graph has symmetry with respect to the y axis.

We reflect the portion of the graph in quadrant I through the y axis, using the y axis symmetry.

x	y
0	-2
1	-1
2	2

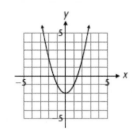

(2-1)

16. $y^2 = x - 2$

Test y axis
Replace x with $-x$:
$y^2 = -x - 2$

Test x axis
Replace y with $-y$:
$(-y)^2 = x - 2$
$y^2 = x - 2$

Test origin
Replace x with $-x$ and y with $-y$:
$(-y)^2 = -x - 2$
$y^2 = -x - 2$

The graph has symmetry with respect to the x axis. We reflect the portion of the graph in quadrant I through the x axis, using the x axis symmetry.

x	y
2	0
3	± 1
6	± 2

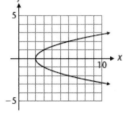

(2-1)

17. $9y^2 + 4x^2 = 36$

Test y axis
Replace x with $-x$:
$9y^2 + 4(-x)^2 = 36$
$9y^2 + 4x^2 = 36$

Test x axis
Replace y with $-y$:
$9(-y)^2 + 4x^2 = 36$
$9y^2 + 4x^2 = 36$

Origin symmetry
follows automatically.

The graph has symmetry with respect to the x axis, the y axis, and the origin. $y = \pm\dfrac{1}{3}\sqrt{36 - 4x^2}$

We reflect the portion of the graph of $y = \dfrac{1}{3}\sqrt{36 - 4x^2}$ in quadrant I through the y axis, then reflect everything through the x axis.

x	y
0	± 2
1	$\pm\frac{1}{3}\sqrt{32} \approx \pm 1.9$
2	$\pm\frac{1}{3}\sqrt{20} \approx \pm 1.5$
3	0

(2-1)

18. $9y^2 - 4x^2 = 36$

Test y axis
Replace x with $-x$:
$9y^2 - 4(-x)^2 = 36$
$9y^2 - 4x^2 = 36$

Test x axis
Replace y with $-y$:
$9(-y)^2 - 4x^2 = 36$
$9y^2 - 4x^2 = 36$

Origin symmetry
follows automatically.

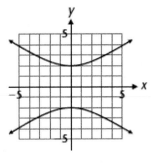

x	y
0	± 2
1	$\pm \frac{1}{3}\sqrt{40} \approx \pm 2.1$
2	$\pm \frac{1}{3}\sqrt{52} \approx \pm 2.4$
3	$\pm \frac{1}{3}\sqrt{72} \approx \pm 2.8$
4	$\pm \frac{10}{3} \approx \pm 3.3$

The graph has symmetry with respect to the

x axis, the y axis, and the origin. $y = \pm \dfrac{1}{3}\sqrt{36 + 4x^2}$

We reflect the portion of the graph of $y = \dfrac{1}{3}\sqrt{36 + 4x^2}$ in

quadrant I through the y axis, then reflect everything through the x axis.

$(2\text{-}1)$

19. The graph is a circle with center (2, 0) and radius 2.
$$(x - h)^2 + (y - k)^2 = r^2$$
$$(x - 2)^2 + (y - 0)^2 = 2^2$$
$$(x - 2)^2 + y^2 = 4$$

$(2\text{-}2)$

20. (A) Since two points are given, we find the slope, then apply the point-slope form.
$$m = \frac{-3 - 3}{0 - (-4)} = \frac{-6}{4} = -\frac{3}{2}$$
$$y - 3 = -\frac{3}{2}\,[x - (-4)]$$
$$2(y - 3) = -3(x + 4)$$
$$2y - 6 = -3x - 12$$
$$3x + 2y = -6$$

(B) $d(P, Q) = \sqrt{(-3 - 3)^2 + [0 - (-4)]^2}$
$$= \sqrt{36 + 16}$$
$$= \sqrt{52}$$
$$= 2\sqrt{13}$$

$(2\text{-}2, 2\text{-}3)$

21. The line $6x + 3y = 5$, or $3y = -6x + 5$, or $y = -2x + \dfrac{5}{3}$,

has slope -2.

(A) We require a line through $(-2, 1)$, with slope -2.

Applying the point-slope form, we have
$$y - 1 = -2[x - (-2)]$$
$$y - 1 = -2x - 4$$
$$y = -2x - 3$$

(B) We require a line with slope m satisfying $-2m = -1$, or

$m = \dfrac{1}{2}$. Again applying the point-slope form, we have

$$y - 1 = \frac{1}{2}\,[x - (-2)]$$
$$y - 1 = \frac{1}{2}x + 1$$
$$y = \frac{1}{2}x + 2 \qquad (2\text{-}3)$$

22. We are given $C(h, k) = (3, 0)$.
To find r we use the distance formula.
$r =$ distance from the center to
$(-1, 4)$
$$= \sqrt{[(-1) - 3]^2 + (4 - 0)^2}$$
$$= \sqrt{16 + 16}$$
$$= \sqrt{32}$$

Then the equation of the circle is
$$(x - h)^2 + (y - k)^2 = r^2$$
$$(x - 3)^2 + (y - 0)^2 = (\sqrt{32})^2$$
$$(x - 3)^2 + y^2 = 32 \qquad (2\text{-}2)$$

23.
$$x^2 + y^2 + 4x - 6y = 3$$
$$(x^2 + 4x + ?) + (y^2 - 6y + ?) = 3$$
$$(x^2 + 4x + 4) + (y^2 - 6y + 9) = 3 + 4 + 9$$
$$(x + 2)^2 + (y - 3)^2 = 16$$
$$[x - (-2)]^2 + (y - 3)^2 = 4^2$$

Center: $C(h, k) = C(-2, 3)$ Radius $r = \sqrt{16} = 4$

$(2\text{-}2)$

24. Let (x, y) be a point equidistant from $(3, 3)$ and $(6, 0)$. Then

$$\sqrt{(x-3)^2+(y-3)^2} = \sqrt{(x-6)^2+(y-0)^2}$$
$$(x-3)^2+(y-3)^2 = (x-6)^2+y^2$$
$$x^2-6x+9+y^2-6y+9 = x^2-12x+36+y^2$$
$$-6x-6y+18 = -12x+36$$
$$6x-6y = 18$$
$$x-y = 3$$

This is the equation of a line. $(2\text{-}2, 2\text{-}3)$

25. If $m = 0$, the equations are reduced to $-y = b$ (a horizontal line) and $x = b$ (a vertical line). In this case, the graphs are perpendicular. Otherwise, $m \neq 0$. Solving for y yields

$$mx - y = b \qquad\qquad x + my = b$$
$$mx = y + b \qquad\qquad my = -x + b$$
$$y = mx - b \qquad\qquad y = -\frac{1}{m}x + \frac{b}{m}$$

The first line has slope m and the second has slope $-\dfrac{1}{m}$.

The graphs are perpendicular in this case also. $(2\text{-}3)$

26.
$$x^2-4x+y^2-2y-3 = 0$$
$$(x^2-4x+?)+(y^2-2y+?) = 3$$
$$(x^2-4x+4)+(y^2-2y+1) = 3+4+1$$
$$(x-2)^2+(y-1)^2 = 8$$
$$(x-2)^2+(y-1)^2 = (\sqrt{8})^2$$

Center: $(2, 1)$; radius: $\sqrt{8} = 2\sqrt{2}$ $(2\text{-}2)$

27. The line tangent to the circle is perpendicular to the radius drawn to the point of tangency. The radius drawn to $(4, 3)$ is a line through $(4, 3)$ and $(2, 1)$ and therefore has slope

$$m_1 = \frac{1-3}{2-4} = 1$$

The tangent line therefore has slope

$$m_2 = -\frac{1}{m_1} = -\frac{1}{1} = -1 \text{ and passes through } (4, 3).$$

Applying the point-slope form yields
$$y-3 = (-1)(x-4)$$
$$y-3 = -x+4$$
$$y = -x+7$$

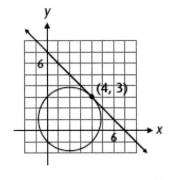

$(2\text{-}2, 2\text{-}3)$

28. The radius of a circle is the distance from the center to any point on the circle. Since the center of this circle is $(4, -3)$ and $(1, 2)$ is a point on the circle, the radius is given by

$$r = \sqrt{(1-4)^2+(2-(-3))^2} = \sqrt{9+25} = \sqrt{34}$$

Hence the equation of the circle is given by

$$(x-4)^2+(y-(-3))^2 = (\sqrt{34})^2$$
$$(x-4)^2+(y+3)^2 = 34$$

$(2\text{-}2)$

29. (A) 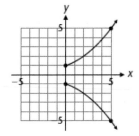   (B)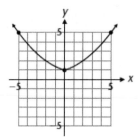

(C) 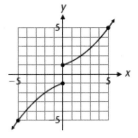   (D)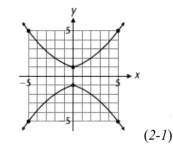

(2-1)

30. $b = 5h$ *(2-3)*   **31.** $h = 0.25b$ *(2-3)*

32. (A) If value V is linearly related to time t, then we are looking for an equation whose graph passes through $(t_1, V_1) = (0, 12{,}000)$ and $(t_2, V_2) = (8, 2{,}000)$. We find the slope, and then we use the point-slope form to find the equation.

$$m = \frac{V_2 - V_1}{t_2 - t_1} = \frac{2{,}000 - 12{,}000}{8 - 0} = -1{,}250$$

$$V - V_1 = m(t - t_1)$$
$$V - 12{,}000 = -1{,}250(t - 0)$$
$$V = -1{,}250t + 12{,}000$$

(B) Substitute $t = 5$ to obtain $V = -1{,}250(5) + 12{,}000 = \$5{,}750$.   *(2-4)*

33. If x is the number of CD's produced, then the variable cost is $5x$. Since the fixed cost is \$24,900, the cost C of producing x CD's is given by $C = 5x + 24{,}900$. To find how many CD's can be produced for \$62,000, substitute $C = 62{,}000$ and solve.

$$62{,}000 = 5x + 24{,}900$$
$$37{,}100 = 5x$$
$$x = 7{,}420 \text{ CD's}$$

(2-4)

34. (A) The rate of change of height with respect to DBH is 2.9.
(B) Increasing DBH by 1 inch increases height by 2.9 feet.
(C) Substitute $d = 3$ into $h = 2.9d + 30.2$ to obtain

$$h = 2.9(3) + 30.2$$
$$h = 38.9$$
$$h = 39 \text{ feet to the nearest foot.}$$

(D) Substitute $h = 45$ into $h = 2.9d + 30.2$ and solve

$$45 = 2.9d + 30.2$$
$$14.8 = 2.9d$$
$$d = 5 \text{ inches}$$

(2-4)

35. (A) The rate of change of body surface area with respect to weight is 0.3433.

   (B) Increasing the weight by 100 grams increases the BSA by 0.3433(100) = 34.33 square centimeters.

   (C) Substitute wt = 15,000 grams into BSA = 1,321 + 0.3433 wt to obtain
BSA = 1,321 + 0.3433(15,000) = 6470.5 cm². *(2-4)*

36. In the sketch, we note that the point (4, r − 2) is on the circle with equation

$x^2 + y^2 = r^2$, hence (4, r − 2) must satisfy this equation.
$$4^2 + (r-2)^2 = r^2$$
$$16 + r^2 - 4r + 4 = r^2$$
$$-4r + 20 = 0$$
$$r = 5 \text{ feet}$$

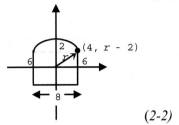

(2-2)

37. (A) $H = 0.7(220 - A)$

   (B) To find H when $A = 20$, substitute $A = 20$ into $H = 0.7(220 - A)$ to
obtain $H = 0.7(220 - 20) = 140$ beats per minute.

   (C) To find A when $H = 126$, substitute $H = 126$ into $H = 0.7(220 - A)$ and solve.
$$126 = 0.7(220 - A)$$
$$180 = 220 - A$$
$$-40 = -A$$
$$A = 40 \text{ years old.}$$ *(2-4)*

38. (A) In this example, the independent variable is years since 1900 so the first list under the STAT EDIT screen comes from the first column of Table 1. (Note that x is years after 1900, so the values we input are 12, 32, 52, 72 and 92. The dependent variable is time, so the second list is 5.41, 4.81, 4.51, 4.00, 3.75.)

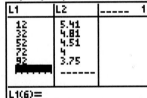  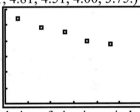

The second screen shows the appropriate plot settings; the third shows a good choice of viewing window; the last is the scatter plot of the data from the table. To compare the algebraic function, we enter y_1 $= -0.021x + 5.57$ in the equation editor, choose the "ask" option for independent variable in the table setup window, then enter x-values 12, 32, 52, 72, and 92.

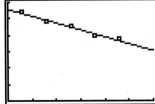 

Comparing the two tables, we see that the corresponding times match very closely. Finally, we look at the graphs of both the function and the scatter plot:

As expected, the graph of the function matches the points from the scatter plot very well.

   (B) The year 2024 corresponds to $x = 124$. Substitute $x = 124$ to obtain $-0.021(124) + 5.57 = 2.966$ minutes
(2-4)

CHAPTER 3

Section 3-1

1. No. A correspondence between two sets is a function only if exactly one element of the second set corresponds to each element of the first set.

3. The domain of a function is the set of all first components in the ordered pairs defining the function; the range is the set of all second components.

5. The symbol $f(x)$ does not denote multiplication of x by f.

7. A function

9. Not a function (two range values correspond to domain values 3 and 5)

11. A function

13. A function; domain = {2, 3, 4, 5}; range = {4, 6, 8, 10}

15. Not a function (two range values correspond to domain values 5 and 10)

17. A function; domain = {Ohio, Alabama, West Virginia, California}; range = {Obama, McCain}

19. A function

21. Not a function (fails vertical line test since the y axis crosses the graph three times.)

23. Not a function (fails vertical line test since the graph itself is vertical)

25. (A) A function.   (B) Not a function, as long as there is more than one student in any Math 125 class.

27. $f(x) = 3x - 5$
    (A) $f(3) = 3(3) - 5 = 4$
    (B) $f(h) = 3h - 5$
    (C) $f(3) + f(h) = 4 + (3h - 5) = 3h - 1$
    (D) $f(3 + h) = 3(3 + h) - 5 = 9 + 3h - 5 = 3h + 4$

    Common Error: $f(3 + h)$ is not the same as $f(3) + h$ or $f(3) + f(h)$.

29. $F(w) = -w^2 + 2w$
    (A) $F(4) = -(4)^2 + 2(4) = -16 + 8 = -8$
    (B) $F(-4) = -(-4)^2 + 2(-4) = -16 - 8 = -24$
    (C) $F(4 + a) = -(4 + a)^2 + 2(4 + a)$
    $$= -(16 + 8a + a^2) + 8 + 2a$$
    $$= -16 - 8a - a^2 + 8 + 2a$$
    $$= -a^2 - 6a - 8$$
    (D) $F(2 - a) = -(2 - a)^2 + 2(2 - a)$
    $$= -(4 - 4a + a^2) + 4 - 2a$$
    $$= -4 + 4a - a^2 + 4 - 2a$$
    $$= -a^2 + 2a$$

31. $f(t) = 2 - 3t^2$
    (A) $f(-2) = 2 - 3(-2)^2 = 2 - 12 = -10$
    (B) $f(-t) = 2 - 3(-t)^2 = 2 - 3t^2$
    (C) $-f(t) = -(2 - 3t^2) = -2 + 3t^2$
    (D) $-f(-t) = -(2 - 3t^2) = -2 + 3t^2$

33. $F(u) = u^2 - u - 1$
    (A) $F(10) = (10)^2 - (10) - 1 = 89$
    (B) $F(u^2) = (u^2)^2 - (u^2) - 1 = u^4 - u^2 - 1$
    (C) $F(5u) = (5u)^2 - (5u) - 1 = 25u^2 - 5u - 1$
    (D) $5F(u) = 5(u^2 - u - 1) = 5u^2 - 5u - 5$

35. (A) When $x = -2$, $y = 6$, so $f(-2) = 6$.
    (B) When $y = -4$, x can equal -6, 2, or 4.

37. Solving for the dependent variable y, we have
    $$y - x^2 = 1$$
    $$y = x^2 + 1$$
    Since $x^2 + 1$ is a real number for each real number x, the equation defines a function with domain all real numbers.

39. Solving for the dependent variable y, we have
$$2x^3 + y^2 = 4$$
$$y^2 = 4 - 2x^3$$
$$y = \pm\sqrt{4 - 2x^3}$$
Since each positive number has two real square roots, the equation does not define a function. For example, when $x = 0$, $y = \pm\sqrt{4 - 2(0)^3} = \pm\sqrt{4} = \pm 2$.

41. Solving for the dependent variable y, we have
$$x^3 - y = 2$$
$$-y = 2 - x^3$$
$$y = x^3 - 2$$
Since $x^3 - 2$ is a real number for each real number x, the equation defines a function with domain all real numbers.

43. If $2x + |y| = 7$, then $|y| = -2x + 7$. This equation does not define a function. For example, if $x = 0$, then $|y| = 7$, so $y = 7$ or $y = -7$.

45. Solving for the dependent variable y, we have
$$3y + 2|x| = 12$$
$$3y = 12 - 2|x|$$
$$y = \frac{12 - 2|x|}{3}$$
Since $\dfrac{12 - 2|x|}{3}$ is a real number for each real number x, the equation defines a function with domain all real numbers.

47. Since $f(x)$ is a polynomial, the domain is the set of all real numbers R, $-\infty < x < \infty$, $(-\infty, \infty)$.

49. Since $3u^2 + 4$ is never negative, $\sqrt{3u^2 + 4}$ represents a real number for all replacements of u by real numbers.
The domain is R, $-\infty < u < \infty$, $(-\infty, \infty)$.

51. If the denominator of the fraction is zero, the function will be undefined, since division by zero is undefined.
For any other values of z, $h(z)$ represents a real number. Solve the equation $4 - z = 0$; $z = 4$. Thus, the domain is all real numbers except 4 or $(-\infty, 4) \cup (4, \infty)$; $z < 4$ or $z > 4$.

53. The square root of a number is defined only if the number is nonnegative.
Thus, $\sqrt{t - 4}$ is defined if $t - 4 \geq 0$ and undefined if $t - 4 < 0$.
Note that $t - 4 \geq 0$ when $t \geq 4$, so the domain is all real numbers greater than or equal to 4 or $[4, \infty)$.

55. The formula $\sqrt{7 + 3w}$ is defined only if $7 + 3w \geq 0$, since the square root is only defined if the number inside is nonnegative.
We solve the inequality:
$$7 + 3w \geq 0$$
$$3w \geq -7$$
$$w \geq -\frac{7}{3}$$
Thus, the domain is all real numbers greater than or equal to $-\dfrac{7}{3}$ or $\left[-\dfrac{7}{3}, \infty\right)$.

57. The fraction $\dfrac{u}{u^2 + 4}$ is defined for any value of u that does <u>not</u> make the denominator zero, so we solve the equation $u^2 + 4 = 0$ to find values that make the function undefined.
$$u^2 + 4 = 0$$
$$u^2 = -4$$
This equation has no solution since the square of a number can't be negative. So there are no values of u that make the fraction undefined and the domain is all real numbers or $(-\infty, \infty)$.

59. There are two issues to consider: we need to make certain that $x + 4 \geq 0$ so that the number inside the square root is nonnegative, and we need to avoid x-values that make the denominator zero.

First, $x + 4 \geq 0$ whenever $x \geq -4$. So x must be greater than or equal to -4 to avoid a negative under the root. Also, $x - 1 = 0$ when $x = 1$, so x cannot be 1. The domain is all real numbers greater than or equal to -4 except 1, or $[-4, 1) \cup (1, \infty)$; $-4 \leq x < 1$ or $x > 1$.

61. There are two issues to consider: the number inside the square root has to be nonnegative, and the denominator of the fraction has to be nonzero. Since we just have t inside the square root, t has to be greater than or equal to zero. Next, we solve $3 - \sqrt{t} = 0$ to find any t-values that make the denominator zero.

$$3 - \sqrt{t} = 0$$
$$3 = \sqrt{t}$$
$$9 = t$$

Thus, t cannot be 9. The domain is all real numbers greater than or equal to zero except 9, or [0, 9) $\cup$ (9, ∞); $0 \le t < 9$ or $t > 9$.

63. $g(x) = 2x^3 - 5$

65. $G(x) = 8\sqrt{x} - 4(x + 2)$

67. Function f multiplies the square of the domain element by 2, then adds 5 to the result.

69. Function Z multiplies the domain element by 4, adds 5 to the result, then divides <u>this</u> result by the square root of the domain element.

71.
$$F(s) = 3s + 15$$
$$F(2 + h) = 3(2 + h) + 15$$
$$F(2) = 3(2) + 15$$

$$\frac{F(2+h) - F(2)}{h} = \frac{[3(2+h)+15] - [3(2)+15]}{h} = \frac{[6+3h+15] - [21]}{h} = \frac{3h + 21 - 21}{h} = \frac{3h}{h} = 3$$

73.
$$g(x) = 2 - x^2$$
$$g(3 + h) = 2 - (3 + h)^2$$
$$g(3) = 2 - (3)^2$$

$$\frac{g(3+h) - g(3)}{h} = \frac{[2-(3+h)]^2 - [2-(3)^2]}{h} = \frac{[2-9-6h-h^2] - [-7]}{h}$$

$$= \frac{-6h - h^2}{h} = \frac{h(-6-h)}{h} = -6 - h$$

75. (A)
$$f(x) = 4x - 7$$
$$f(x + h) = 4(x + h) - 7$$
$$\frac{f(x+h) - f(x)}{h} = \frac{[4(x+h)-7] - [4x-7]}{h}$$
$$= \frac{4x + 4h - 7 - 4x + 7}{h}$$
$$= \frac{4h}{h} = 4$$

(B)
$$f(x) = 4x - 7$$
$$f(a) = 4a - 7$$
$$\frac{f(x) - f(a)}{x - a} = \frac{(4x-7) - (4a-7)}{x - a}$$
$$= \frac{4x - 7 - 4a + 7}{x - a}$$
$$= \frac{4x - 4a}{x - a}$$
$$= \frac{4(x-a)}{x - a} = 4$$

Common Errors: $f(x + h) \ne f(x) + f(h)$
  or $4x - 7 + 4h - 7$
  $f(x + h) \ne f(x) + h$
  or $4x - 7 + h$
Also note: $-f(x) \ne -4x - 7$
Parentheses must be supplied.

77. (A)

$$f(x) = 2x^2 - 4$$
$$f(x+h) = 2(x+h)^2 - 4$$

$$\frac{f(x+h) - f(x)}{h} = \frac{[2(x+h)^2 - 4] - [2x^2 - 4]}{h}$$

$$= \frac{2(x^2 + 2xh + h^2) - 4 - 2x^2 + 4}{h}$$

$$= \frac{2x^2 + 4xh + 2h^2 - 4 - 2x^2 + 4}{h}$$

$$= \frac{4xh + 2h^2}{h}$$

$$= \frac{h(4x + 2h)}{h}$$

$$= 4x + 2h$$

(B)

$$f(x) = 2x^2 - 4$$
$$f(a) = 2a^2 - 4$$

$$\frac{f(x) - f(a)}{x - a} = \frac{(2x^2 - 4) - (2a^2 - 4)}{x - a}$$

$$= \frac{2x^2 - 4 - 2a^2 + 4}{x - a}$$

$$= \frac{2x^2 - 2a^2}{x - a}$$

$$= \frac{2(x - a)(x + a)}{x - a}$$

$$= 2(x + a)$$
$$= 2x + 2a$$

79. (A)

$$f(x) = -4x^2 + 3x - 2$$
$$f(x+h) = -4(x+h)^2 + 3(x+h) - 2$$

$$\frac{f(x+h) - f(x)}{h} = \frac{[-4(x+h)^2 + 3(x+h) - 2] - [-4x^2 + 3x - 2]}{h}$$

$$= \frac{-4(x^2 + 2xh + h^2) + 3(x+h) - 2 + 4x^2 - 3x + 2}{h}$$

$$= \frac{-4x^2 - 8xh - 4h^2 + 3x + 3h - 2 + 4x^2 - 3x + 2}{h}$$

$$= \frac{-8xh - 4h^2 + 3h}{h}$$

$$= \frac{h(-8x - 4h + 3)}{h}$$

$$= -8x - 4h + 3$$

(B)

$$f(x) = -4x^2 + 3x - 2$$
$$f(a) = -4a^2 + 3a - 2$$

$$\frac{f(x) - f(a)}{x - a} = \frac{(-4x^2 + 3x - 2) - (-4a^2 + 3a - 2)}{x - a}$$

$$= \frac{-4x^2 + 3x - 2 + 4a^2 - 3a + 2}{x - a}$$

$$= \frac{-4x^2 + 4a^2 + 3x - 3a}{x - a}$$

$$= \frac{-4(x - a)(x + a) + 3(x - a)}{x - a}$$

$$= \frac{(x - a)[-4(x + a) + 3]}{x - a}$$

$$= -4(x + a) + 3$$
$$= -4x - 4a + 3$$

81. (A) $f(x) = \sqrt{x+2}$

$f(x+h) = \sqrt{x+h+2}$

$\dfrac{f(x+h) - f(x)}{h} = \dfrac{\sqrt{x+h+2} - \sqrt{x+2}}{h}$

$= \dfrac{\sqrt{x+h+2} - \sqrt{x+2}}{h} \cdot \dfrac{\sqrt{x+h+2} + \sqrt{x+2}}{\sqrt{x+h+2} + \sqrt{x+2}}$

$= \dfrac{(\sqrt{x+h+2})^2 - (\sqrt{x+2})^2}{h(\sqrt{x+h+2} + \sqrt{x+2})}$

$= \dfrac{x+h+2 - (x+2)}{h(\sqrt{x+h+2} + \sqrt{x+2})}$

$= \dfrac{h}{h(\sqrt{x+h+2} + \sqrt{x+2})}$

$= \dfrac{1}{\sqrt{x+h+2} + \sqrt{x+2}}$

(B) $f(x) = \sqrt{x+2}$

$f(a) = \sqrt{a+2}$

$\dfrac{f(x) - f(a)}{x-a} = \dfrac{\sqrt{x+2} - \sqrt{a+2}}{x-a}$

$= \dfrac{\sqrt{x+2} - \sqrt{a+2}}{x-a} \cdot \dfrac{\sqrt{x+2} + \sqrt{a+2}}{\sqrt{x+2} + \sqrt{a+2}}$

$= \dfrac{(\sqrt{x+2})^2 - (\sqrt{a+2})^2}{(x-a)(\sqrt{x+2} + \sqrt{a+2})}$

$= \dfrac{x+2 - (a+2)}{(x-a)(\sqrt{x+2} + \sqrt{a+2})} = \dfrac{x-a}{(x-a)(\sqrt{x+2} + \sqrt{a+2})}$

$= \dfrac{1}{\sqrt{x+2} + \sqrt{a+2}}$

83. (A) $f(x) = \dfrac{4}{x}$

$f(x+h) = \dfrac{4}{x+h}$

$\dfrac{f(x+h) - f(x)}{h} = \dfrac{\frac{4}{x+h} - \frac{4}{x}}{h}$

$= \dfrac{4x - 4(x+h)}{hx(x+h)}$

$= \dfrac{-4h}{hx(x+h)}$

$= \dfrac{-4}{x(x+h)}$

(B) $f(x) = \dfrac{4}{x}$

$f(a) = \dfrac{4}{a}$

$\dfrac{f(x) - f(a)}{x-a} = \dfrac{\frac{4}{x} - \frac{4}{a}}{x-a}$

$= \dfrac{4a - 4x}{ax(x-a)}$

$= \dfrac{-4(x-a)}{ax(x-a)}$

$= \dfrac{-4}{ax}$

85. Given w = width and Area = 64, we use $A = \ell w$ to write $\ell = \dfrac{A}{w} = \dfrac{64}{w}$.

Then $P = 2w + 2\ell = 2w + 2\left(\dfrac{64}{w}\right) = 2w + \dfrac{128}{w}$. Since w must be positive, the domain of $P(w)$ is $w > 0$.

87.

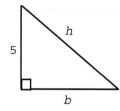

Using the given letters, the Pythagorean theorem gives
$$h^2 = b^2 + 5^2$$
$$h^2 = b^2 + 25$$
$$h = \sqrt{b^2 + 25} \text{ (since } h \text{ is positive)}$$
Since b must be positive, the domain of $h(b)$ is $b > 0$.

89.   Daily cost = fixed cost + variable cost

$C(x) = \$300 + (\$1.75$ per dozen doughnuts) $\times$ (number of dozen doughnuts)

$C(x) = 300 + 1.75x$

91.   The cost is a flat \$17 per month, plus \$2.40 for each hour of airtime.

93.   (A) $S(0) = 16(0)^2 = 0$; $S(1) = 16(1)^2 = 16$; $S(2) = 16(2)^2 = 16(4) = 64$;

$S(3) = 16(3)^2 = 16(9) = 144$ (Note: Remember that the order of operations requires that we apply the exponent first then multiply by 16.)

(B) $\dfrac{S(2+h) - S(2)}{h} = \dfrac{16(2+h)^2 - 16(2)^2}{h} = \dfrac{16(4 + 4h + h^2) - 16(4)}{h}$

$= \dfrac{64 + 64h + 16h^2 - 64}{h} = \dfrac{64h + 16h^2}{h} = \dfrac{h(64 + 16h)}{h} = 64 + 16h$

(Note: Be careful when evaluating $S(2 + h)$! You need to replace the variable t in the function with $(2 + h)$. $S(2 + h)$ is <u>not</u> the same thing as $S(2) + h$!)

(C) $h = 1$: $64 + 16(1) = 80$

$h = -1$: $64 + 16(-1) = 64 - 16 = 48$

$h = 0.1$: $64 + 16(0.1) = 64 + 1.6 = 65.6$;

$h = -0.1$: $64 + 16(-0.1) = 64 - 1.6 = 62.4$

$h = 0.01$: $64 + 16(0.01) = 64 + 0.16 = 64.16$:

$h = -0.01$: $64 + 16(-0.01) = 64 - 0.16 = 63.84$

$h = 0.001$: $64 + 16(0.001) = 64 + 0.016 = 64.016$

$h = -0.001$: $64 + 16(-0.001) = 64 - 0.016 = 63.984$

(D) The smaller h gets the closer the result is to 64. The numerator of the fraction, $S(2 + h) - S(2)$, is the difference between how far an object has fallen after $2 + h$ seconds and how far it's fallen after 2 seconds. This difference is how far the object falls in the small period of time from 2 to $2 + h$ seconds. When you divide that distance by the time (h), you get the average velocity of the object between 2 and $2 + h$ seconds. Part (C) shows that this average velocity approaches 64 feet per second as h gets smaller.

95.

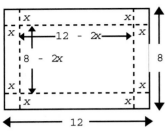 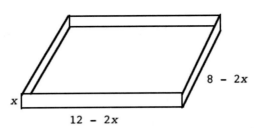

From the above figures it should be clear that
V = length × width × height = $(12 - 2x)(8 - 2x)x$.
Since all distances must be positive, $x > 0$, $8 - 2x > 0$, $12 - 2x > 0$.
Thus, $0 < x$, $4 > x$, $6 > x$, or $0 < x < 4$ (the last condition, $6 > x$, will be automatically satisfied if $x < 4$.)
Domain: $0 < x < 4$.

97. From the text diagram, since each pen must have area 50 square feet, we see

$$\text{Area} = (\text{length})(\text{width}) \text{ or } 50 = (\text{length})x. \text{ Thus, the length of each pen is } \frac{50}{x} \text{ ft.}$$

The total amount of fencing = 4(width) + 5(length) + 4(width – gate width)

$$F(x) = 4x + 5\left(\frac{50}{x}\right) + 4(x - 3)$$

$$F(x) = 4x + \frac{250}{x} + 4x - 12$$

$$F(x) = 8x + \frac{250}{x} - 12$$

Then $F(4) = 8(4) + \dfrac{250}{4} - 12 = 82.5$ $F(5) = 8(5) + \dfrac{250}{5} - 12 = 78$

$F(6) = 8(6) + \dfrac{250}{6} - 12 = 77.7$ $F(7) = 8(7) + \dfrac{250}{7} - 12 = 79.7$

99.

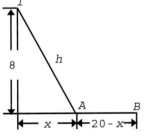

We note that the pipeline consists of the lake section IA, and shore section AB.
The shore section has length $20 - x$.

The lake section has length h, where $h^2 = 8^2 + x^2$, thus $h = \sqrt{64 + x^2}$.

$$\text{The cost of all the pipeline} = \left(\begin{array}{c} cost\ of\ shore \\ section\ per\ mile \end{array}\right)\left(\begin{array}{c} number\ of \\ shore\ miles \end{array}\right) + \left(\begin{array}{c} cost\ of\ lake \\ section\ per\ mile \end{array}\right)\left(\begin{array}{c} number\ of \\ lake\ miles \end{array}\right)$$

$C(x) = 10,000(20 - x) + 15,000\sqrt{64 + x^2}$

From the diagram we see that x must be non-negative, but no more than 20.
Domain: $0 \le x \le 20$

Section 3-2

1.   The graph of a function $f(x)$ is the set of all points whose first coordinate is an element of the domain of f and whose second coordinate is the associated element of the range.

3.   The graph of a function can have one y intercept (when $y = f(0)$) or none (if 0 is not in the domain). The graph can have any number of x intercepts.

5.   A function is increasing on an interval if for any choice x_1, x_2 of x values on that interval, if $x_2 > x_1$, then $f(x_2) > f(x_1)$).

7.   A function is defined piecewise if it is defined by different expressions for different parts of its domain.

9.   (A) $[-4, 4)$ (B) $[-3, 3)$ (C) 0 (D) 0 (E) $[-4, 4)$ (F) None   (G) None   (H) None

11.   (A) $(-\infty, \infty)$ (B) $[-4, \infty)$ (C) $-3, 1$ (D) -3 (E) $[-1, \infty)$ (F) $(-\infty, -1]$ (G) None   (H) None

13.   (A) $(-\infty, 2) \cup (2, \infty)$ (The function is not defined at $x = 2$.)   (B) $(-\infty, -1) \cup [1, \infty)$ (C) None
       (D) 1   (E) None   (F) $(-\infty, -2] \cup (2, \infty)$ (G) $[-2, 2)$ (H) $x = 2$

15. $f(-4) = -3$ since the point $(-4, -3)$ is on the graph; $f(0) = 0$ since the point $(0,0)$ is on the graph; $f(4)$ is undefined since there is no point on the graph at $x = 4$.

17. $h(-3) = 0$ since the point $(-3, 0)$ is on the graph; $h(0) = -3$ since the point $(0, -3)$ is on the graph; $h(2) = 5$ since the point $(2, 5)$ is on the graph.

19. $p(-2) = 1$ since the point $(-2, 1)$ is on the graph; $p(2)$ is undefined since there is no point on the graph at $x = 2$; $p(5) = -4$ since the point $(5, -4)$ is on the graph.

21. One possible answer:

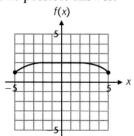

23. One possible answer:

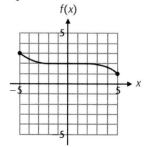

25. One possible answer:

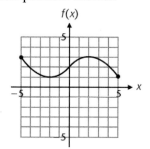

27.

$$f(x) = \underset{\text{slope}}{2}x + 4$$

The y intercept is $f(0) = 4$, and the slope is 2.
To find the x intercept, we solve the equation $f(x) = 0$ for x.
$$f(x) = 0$$
$$2x + 4 = 0$$
$$2x = -4$$
$$x = -2 \qquad \text{The } x \text{ intercept is } -2.$$

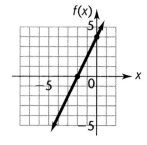

29. $f(x) = -\dfrac{1}{2}x - \dfrac{5}{3}$

The y intercept is $f(0) = -\dfrac{5}{3}$, and the slope is $-\dfrac{1}{2}$. To find the x intercept, we solve the equation $f(x) = 0$ for x.

$$f(x) = 0$$
$$-\frac{1}{2}x - \frac{5}{3} = 0$$
$$-\frac{1}{2}x = \frac{5}{3}$$
$$x = (-2)\frac{5}{3} = \frac{-10}{3} \qquad \text{The } x \text{ intercept is } \frac{-10}{3}.$$

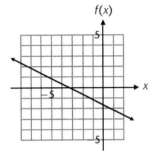

31. $f(x) = -2.3x + 7.1$

The y intercept is $f(0) = 7.1$, and the slope is -2.3. To find the x intercept, we solve the equation $f(x) = 0$ for x.

$$f(x) = 0$$
$$-2.3x + 7.1 = 0$$
$$-2.3x = -7.1$$
$$x = \frac{-7.1}{-2.3}$$
$$x = 3.1 \qquad \text{The } x \text{ intercept is } 3.1.$$

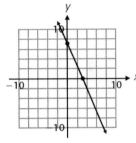

33. A linear function must have the form $f(x) = mx + b$. We are given $f(0) = 10$, hence $10 = f(0) = m(0) + b$.
Thus $b = 10$. Since $f(-2) = 2$, we also have $2 = f(-2) = m(-2) + b = -2m + 10$. Solving for m, we have

$$2 = -2m + 10$$
$$-8 = -2m$$
$$m = 4$$

Hence $f(x) = mx + b$ becomes $f(x) = 4x + 10$.

35. A linear function must have the form $f(x) = mx + b$.
We are given $f(-2) = 7$, hence $7 = f(-2) = m(-2) + b$.
Thus $b = 7 + 2m$. Since $f(4) = -2$, we also have
$-2 = f(4) = 4m + b$. Substituting, we have

$$b = 7 + 2m$$
$$-2 = 4m + b$$
$$-2 = 4m + 7 + 2m$$
$$-2 = 6m + 7$$
$$-9 = 6m$$
$$m = -\frac{3}{2}$$

$$b = 7 + 2m = 7 + 2\left(-\frac{3}{2}\right) = 4$$

Hence $f(x) = mx + b$ becomes $f(x) = -\dfrac{3}{2}x + 4$.

37. The rational expression $\dfrac{3x - 12}{2x + 4}$ is defined

everywhere except at the zero of the denominator:

$$2x + 4 = 0$$
$$2x = -4$$
$$x = -2 \qquad \text{The domain of } f \text{ is } \{x \mid x \neq -2\}.$$

A rational expression is 0 if and only if the numerator is zero:

$$3x - 12 = 0$$
$$3x = 12$$
$$x = 4$$

The x intercept of f is 4.

The y intercept of f is $f(0) = \dfrac{3(0) - 12}{2(0) + 4} = -3.$

39. The rational expression $\dfrac{3x-2}{4x-5}$ is defined
everywhere except at the zero of the denominator:
$$4x - 5 = 0$$
$$4x = 5$$
$$x = \frac{5}{4}$$ The domain of f is $\left\{x \mid x \neq \dfrac{5}{4}\right\}$.
A rational expression is 0 if and only if the
numerator is zero:
$$3x - 2 = 0$$
$$3x = 2$$
$$x = \frac{2}{3}$$
The x intercept of f is $\dfrac{2}{3}$.

The y intercept of f is $f(0) = \dfrac{3(0)-2}{4(0)-5} = \dfrac{2}{5}$.

41. The rational expression $\dfrac{4x}{(x-2)^2}$ is defined
everywhere except at the zero of the denominator:
$$(x - 2)^2 = 0$$
$$x - 2 = 0$$
$$x = 2$$
The domain of f is $\{x \mid x \neq 2\}$.
A rational expression is 0 if and only if the
numerator is zero:
$$4x = 0$$
$$x = 0$$
The x intercept of f is 0.

The y intercept of f is $f(0) = \dfrac{4(0)}{(0-2)^2} = 0$.

43. The rational expression $\dfrac{x^2-16}{x^2-9}$ is defined
everywhere except at the zeros of the denominator:
$$x^2 - 9 = 0$$
$$(x - 3)(x + 3) = 0$$
$$x = 3 \text{ or } -3$$
The domain of f is $\{x \mid x \neq -3, 3\}$.
A rational expression is 0 if and only if the
numerator is zero:
$$x^2 - 16 = 0$$
$$(x - 4)(x + 4) = 0$$
$$x = 4 \text{ or } -4$$
The x intercepts of f are ± 4.

The y intercept of f is $f(0) = \dfrac{0^2-16}{0^2-9} = \dfrac{16}{9}$.

45. The rational expression $\dfrac{x^2+7}{x^2-25}$ is defined
everywhere except at the zeros of the denominator:
$$x^2 - 25 = 0$$
$$(x - 5)(x + 5) = 0$$
$$x = 5 \text{ or } -5$$
The domain of f is $\{x \mid x \neq -5, 5\}$.
A rational expression is 0 if and only if the
numerator is zero.

$x^2 + 7 = 0$ has no real solutions, hence f has no x
intercept.

The y intercept of f is $f(0) = \dfrac{0^2+7}{0^2-25} = -\dfrac{7}{25}$.

47. (A)   For $-1 \leq x < 0$, $f(x) = x + 1$, so $f(-1) = -1 + 1 = 0$.
For $0 \leq x \leq 1$, $f(x) = -x + 1$, so $f(0) = -0 + 1 = 1$ and $f(1) = -1 + 1 = 0$.

(B)

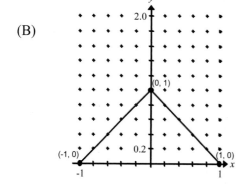

(C) The domain is the union of the intervals used in the
definition of f: $[-1, 1]$.
From the graph, the range is $[0, 1]$.
The function is continuous on its domain.

49. (A) For $-3 \leq x < -1$, $f(x) = -2$, so $f(-3) = -2$.
$f(-1)$ is not defined.
For $-1 < x \leq 2$, $f(x) = 4$, so $f(2) = 4$.

(B)

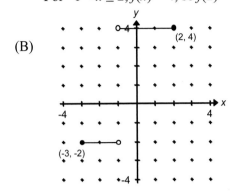

(C) The domain is the union of the intervals used in the definition of f:
$[-3, -1) \cup (-1, 2]$.
From the graph, the range is the set of numbers $\{-2, 4\}$.
The function is discontinuous at $x = -1$.

51. (A) For $x < -1$, $f(x) = x + 2$, so $f(-2) = -2 + 2 = 0$.
$f(-1)$ is not defined.
For $x > -1$, $f(x) = x - 2$, so $f(0) = 0 - 2 = -2$.

(B)

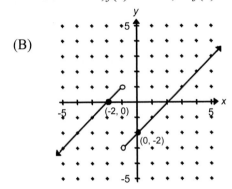

(C) The domain is the union of the intervals used in the definition of f:
$(-\infty, -1) \cup (-1, \infty)$.
From the graph, the range is R.
The function is discontinuous at $x = -1$.

53. (A) For $x < -2$, $f(x) = -2x - 6$, so $f(-3) = -2(-3) - 6 = 0$.
For $-2 \leq x < 3$, $f(x) = -2$, so $f(-2) = f(0) = -2$.
For $x \geq 3$, $f(x) = 6x - 20$, so $f(3) = 6 \cdot 3 - 20 = -2$ and $f(4) = 6 \cdot 4 - 20 = 4$.

(B)

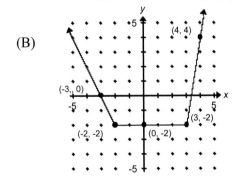

(C) The domain is the union of the intervals used in the definition of f.
The domain is therefore R.
From the graph, the range is $[-2, \infty)$.
The function is continuous on its domain.

55. (A) For $x < -2$, $f(x) = \dfrac{5}{2}x + 6$, so $f(-3) = \dfrac{5}{2}(-3) + 6 = -\dfrac{3}{2}$.

For $-2 \leq x \leq 3$, $f(x) = 1$, so $f(-2) = f(0) = f(3) = 1$.

For $x > 3$, $f(x) = \dfrac{3}{2}x - \dfrac{7}{2}$, so $f(4) = \dfrac{3}{2}(4) - \dfrac{7}{2} = \dfrac{5}{2}$.

(B)

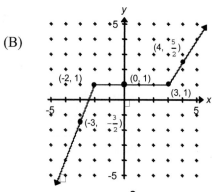

(C) The domain is the union of the intervals used in the definition of f.
The domain is therefore R.
From the graph, the range is R.
The function is continuous on its domain.

57. (A) For $x < 0$, $f(x) = \dfrac{2}{3}x + 4$, so $f(-1) = \dfrac{2}{3}(-1) + 4 = \dfrac{10}{3}$.

$f(0)$ is not defined.

For $0 < x < 2$, $f(x) = -\dfrac{1}{2}x + 3$, so $f(1) = -\dfrac{1}{2}(1) + 3 = \dfrac{5}{2}$.

$f(2)$ is not defined.

For $x > 2$, $f(x) = -\dfrac{1}{2}x$, so $f(3) = -\dfrac{1}{2}(3) = -\dfrac{3}{2}$.

(B)

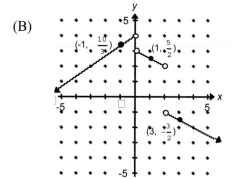

(C) The domain is the union of the intervals used in the definition of f.
$(-\infty, 0) \cup (0, 2) \cup (2, \infty)$.
From the graph, the range is $(-\infty, 4)$.
The function is discontinuous at $x = 0$ and $x = 2$.

59. For $x \le 0$, the graph is a line with slope $\dfrac{1-3}{0-(-2)} = -1$ and y intercept 1, that is, $y = -x + 1$.

For $x > 0$, the graph is a line with slope $\dfrac{(-3)-(-1)}{2-0} = -1$ and y intercept -1, that is, $y = -x - 1$.

Therefore,

$$f(x) = \begin{cases} -x+1 & \text{if} \quad x \le 0 \\ -x-1 & \text{if} \quad x > 0 \end{cases}$$

61. For $x \le -1$, the graph is the horizontal line $y = 3$. For $x > -1$, the graph is a line with slope $\dfrac{-3-3}{1-(-1)} = -3$

passing through $(1, -3)$. The point-slope form yields $y - (-3) = -3(x - 1)$ or $y = -3x$.
Therefore,

$$f(x) = \begin{cases} 3 & \text{if} \quad x \le -1 \\ -3x & \text{if} \quad x > -1 \end{cases}$$

An equally valid solution would be

$$f(x) = \begin{cases} 3 & \text{if} \quad x < -1 \\ -3x & \text{if} \quad x \ge -1 \end{cases}$$

63. For $x < -2$, the graph is the horizontal line $y = 3$. The function is not defined at $x = -2$ or at $x = 1$.

For $-2 < x < 1$, the graph is a line with slope $\dfrac{(-4)-2}{1-(-2)} = -2$ which would, if extended, pass through $(-2, 2)$.

The point-slope form yields $y - 2 = -2[x - (-2)]$, that is, $y = -2x - 2$. For $x > 1$, the graph is the horizontal line $y = -1$.

Therefore,

$$f(x) = \begin{cases} 3 & \text{if} & x < -2 \\ -2x - 2 & \text{if} & -2 < x < 1 \\ -1 & \text{if} & x > 1 \end{cases}$$

65. If $x < 0$, then $|x| = -x$ and $f(x) = 1 + |x| = 1 + (-x) = 1 - x$.
If $x \geq 0$, then $|x| = x$ and $f(x) = 1 + x$.
Therefore,

$$f(x) = \begin{cases} 1 - x & \text{if} & x < 0 \\ 1 + x & \text{if} & x \geq 0 \end{cases}$$

The function is defined for all real numbers; the domain is R. From the graph, the range is $[1, \infty)$. The function is continuous on its domain.

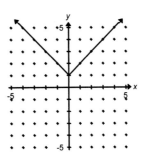

67. If $x - 2 < 0$, that is, $x < 2$, $f(x) = |x - 2| = -(-x - 2) = -x + 2$.
If $x - 2 \geq 0$, that is, $x \geq 2$, $f(x) = |x - 2| = x - 2$.
Therefore,

$$f(x) = \begin{cases} -x + 2 & \text{if} & x < 2 \\ x - 2 & \text{if} & x \geq 2 \end{cases}$$

The function is defined for all real numbers; the domain is R. From the graph, the range is $[0, \infty)$. The function is continuous on its domain.

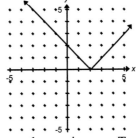

69. (A) One possible answer:

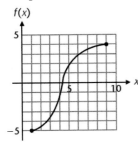

(B) This graph crosses the x axis once. To meet the conditions specified a graph must cross the x axis exactly once. If it crossed more times the function would have to be decreasing somewhere; if it did not cross at all the function would have to be discontinuous somewhere.

71. (A) One possible answer:

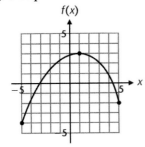

(B) This graph crosses the x axis twice. To meet the conditions specified a graph must cross the x axis at least twice. If it crossed fewer times the function would have to be discontinuous somewhere. However, the graph could cross more times; in fact there is no upper limit on the number of times it can cross the x axis.

73.   Graphs of f and g

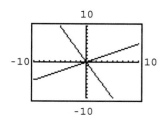

Graph of
$$m(x) = 0.5[-2x + 0.5x + |-2x - 0.5x|]$$
$$= 0.5[-1.5x + |-2.5x|]$$

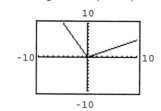

Graph of
$$n(x) = 0.5[-2x + 0.5x - |-2x - 0.5x|]$$
$$= 0.5[-1.5x - |-2.5x|]$$

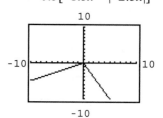

75.   Graphs of f and g

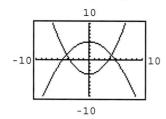

Graph of
$$m(x) = 0.5[5 - 0.2x^2 + 0.3x^2 - 4 + |5 - 0.2x^2 - (0.3x^2 - 4)|]$$
$$= 0.5[1 + 0.1x^2 + |9 - 0.5x^2|]$$

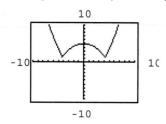

Graph of
$$n(x) = 0.5[5 - 0.2x^2 + 0.3x^2 - 4 - |5 - 0.2x^2 - (0.3x^2 - 4)|]$$
$$= 0.5[1 + 0.1x^2 - |9 - 0.5x^2|]$$

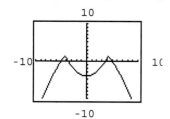

77. Graphs of f and g

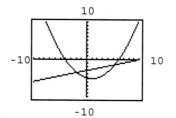

Graph of
$$m(x) = 0.5[0.2x^2 - 0.4x - 5 + 0.3x - 3$$
$$+ |0.2x^2 - 0.4x - 5 - (0.3x - 3)|]$$
$$= 0.5[0.2x^2 - 0.1x - 8 + |0.2x^2 - 0.7x - 2|]$$

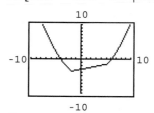

Graph of
$$n(x) = 0.5[0.2x^2 - 0.4x - 5 + 0.3x - 3$$
$$- |0.2x^2 - 0.4x - 5 - (0.3x - 3)|]$$
$$= 0.5[0.2x^2 - 0.1x - 8 - |0.2x^2 - 0.7x - 2|]$$

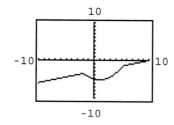

79.   The graphs of $m(x)$ show that the value of $m(x)$ is always the larger of the two values for $f(x)$ and $g(x)$. In other words, $m(x) = \max[f(x), g(x)]$.

81.   Since 100 miles are included, only the daily charge of \$32 applies for mileage between 0 and 100. So if $R(x)$ is the daily cost of rental where x is miles driven, $R(x) = 32$ if $0 \leq x \leq 100$. After 100 miles, the charge is an extra \$0.16 for each mile: the mileage charge will be 0.16 times the number of miles over 100 which is $x - 100$. So the mileage charge is $0.16(x - 100)$ or $0.16x - 16$. The \$32 charge still applies so when $x \geq 100$ the rental charge is $32 + 0.16x - 16$, or $16 + 0.16x$.

$$R(x) = \begin{cases} 32 & 0 \leq x \leq 100 \\ 16 + 0.16x & x > 100 \end{cases}$$

83. If $0 \le x \le 3{,}000$, $E(x) = 200$

	Base Salary	+ Commission on Sales Over \$3,000
If \$3,000 < x < 8,000, E(x)	= 200	+ 0.04(x − 3000)
	= 200	+ 0.04x − 120
	= 80	+ 0.04x

Common Error: Commission is not $0.04x$ (4% of sales) nor is it $0.04x + 200$ (base salary plus 4% of sales).

There is a point of discontinuity at $x = 8{,}000$.

	Salary	+ Bonus
If x ≥ 8,000. E(x) =	80 + 0.04x	+ 100
	= 180	+ 0.04x

Summarizing, $E(x) = \begin{cases} 200 & \text{if} & 0 \le x \le 3{,}000 \\ 80 + 0.04x & \text{if} & 3{,}000 < x < 8{,}000 \\ 180 + 0.04x & \text{if} & 8{,}000 \le x \end{cases}$

$E(5{,}750) = 80 + 0.04(5{,}750) = \$310$
$E(9{,}200) = 180 + 0.04(9{,}200) = \$548$

x	y = 200	x	y = 80 + 0.04x	x	y = 180 + 0.04x
0	200	3,000	200	8,000	500
2,000	200	7,000	360	10,000	580

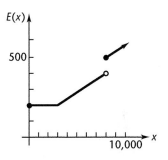

85.

$$
\begin{aligned}
f(4) &= 10[\![0.5+0.4]\!] &= 10(0) &= 0 \\
f(-4) &= 10[\![0.5-0.4]\!] &= 10(0) &= 0 \\
f(6) &= 10[\![0.5+0.6]\!] &= 10(1) &= 10 \\
f(-6) &= 10[\![0.5-0.6]\!] &= 10(-1) &= -10 \\
f(24) &= 10[\![0.5+2.4]\!] &= 10(2) &= 20 \\
f(25) &= 10[\![0.5+2.5]\!] &= 10(3) &= 30 \\
f(247) &= 10[\![0.5+24.7]\!] &= 10(25) &= 250 \\
f(-243) &= 10[\![0.5-24.3]\!] &= 10(-24) &= -240 \\
f(-245) &= 10[\![0.5-24.5]\!] &= 10(-24) &= -240 \\
f(-246) &= 10[\![0.5-24.6]\!] &= 10(-25) &= -250
\end{aligned}
$$

f rounds numbers to the tens place

87. Since $f(x) = [\![10x + 0.5]\!]/10$ rounds numbers to the nearest tenth, (see text example 6) we try
$[\![100x + 0.5]\!]/100 = f(x)$ to round to the nearest hundredth.

$f(3.274) = [\![327.9]\!]/100 = 3.27$
$f(7.846) = [\![785.1]\!]/100 = 7.85$
$f(-2.8783) = [\![-287.33]\!]/100 = -2.88$

A few examples suffice to convince us that this is probably correct.
(A proof would be out of place in this book.)
$f(x) = [\![100x + 0.5]\!]/100$.

89. (A)

$$C(x) = \begin{cases} 15 & 0 < x \le 1 \\ 18 & 1 < x \le 2 \\ 21 & 2 < x \le 3 \\ 24 & 3 < x \le 4 \\ 27 & 4 < x \le 5 \\ 30 & 5 < x \le 6 \end{cases}$$

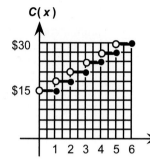

(B) The two functions appear to coincide, for example

$$C(3.5) = 24 \quad f(3.5) = 15 + 3[\![3.5]\!] = 15 + 3 \cdot 3 = 24$$

However,

$$C(1) = 15 \quad f(1) = 15 + 3[\![1]\!] = 15 + 3 \cdot 1 = 18$$

The functions are not the same, therefore. In fact, $f(x) \ne C(x)$ at $x = 1, 2, 3, 4, 5, 6$.

91. On the interval [0, 10,000], the tax is 0.03x. On the interval (10,000, ∞), the tax is 0.03(10,000) + 0.05(x – 10,000) or 300 + 0.05x – 500, that is, 0.05x – 200.

Combining the intervals with the above linear expressions, we have

$$T(x) = \begin{cases} 0.03x & \text{if} \quad 0 \le x \le 10,000 \\ 0.05x - 200 & \text{if} \quad x > 10,000 \end{cases}$$

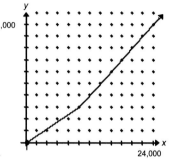

93. A tax of 5.35% on any amount up to $19,890 is calculated by multiplying 0.0535 by the income, which is represented by x. So the tax due, $t(x)$, is 0.0535x if x is between 0 and 19,890. For x-values between 19,890 and 65,330, the percentage is computed only on the portion over 19,890. To find that portion we subtract 19,890 from the income (x – 19,890); then multiply by 0.0705 to get the percentage portion of the tax. The total tax is $1,064 plus the percentage portion, so $t(x) = 1,064 + 0.0705(x – 19,890)$ if x is between 19,890 and 65,330. The tax for incomes over $65,340 is computed in a similar manner: $4,268 plus 7.85% of the portion over 65,330, which is x – 65,330. We get $4,268 + 0.0785(x – 65,330)$ if x is over 65,330. Combined we get

$$t(x) = \begin{cases} 0.0535x & \text{if} \quad 0 \le x \le 19,890 \\ 1,064 + 0.0705(x - 19,890) & \text{if} \quad 19,890 < x \le 65,330 \\ 4,268 + 0.0785(x - 65,330) & \text{if} \quad x > 65,330 \end{cases}$$

or, after simplifying,

$$t(x) = \begin{cases} 0.0535x & \text{if} \quad 0 \le x \le 19,890 \\ 0.0705x - 338.25 & \text{if} \quad 19,890 < x \le 65,330 \\ 0.0785x - 860.41 & \text{if} \quad x > 65,330 \end{cases}$$

$t(10,000) = 0.0535(10,000) = 535$; the tax is $535
$t(30,000) = 0.0705(30,000) - 338.25 = \$1,776.75$
$t(100,000) = 0.0785(100,000) - 860.41 = \$6,989.59$

Section 3-3

1. For each point with coordinates (x, $f(x)$) on the graph of $y = f(x)$ there is a corresponding point with coordinates (x, $f(x) +k$) on the graph of $y = f(x) + k$. Since this point is k units above the first point, each point, and thus the entire graph, has been moved upward k units.

3. For each point with coordinates (x, $f(x)$) on the graph of $y = f(x)$ there is a corresponding point with coordinates (x, $-f(x)$) on the graph of $y = -f(x)$. Since this point is the reflection of the first point with respect to the x axis, the entire graph is a reflection of the graph of $y = f(x)$. Similarly for $y = f(-x)$.

5. Domain: Since $x \geq 0$, the domain is $[0, \infty)$

Range: Since the range of $f(x) = \sqrt{x}$ is $y \geq 0$, for $h(x) = -\sqrt{x}$, $y \leq 0$.
Thus, the range of h is $(-\infty, 0]$.

7. Domain: R

Range: Since the range of $f(x) = x^2$ is $y \geq 0$, for $g(x) = -2x^2$, $y \leq 0$.
Thus, the range of g is $(-\infty, 0]$.

9. Domain: R; Range: R

11. The graph of $y = h(x)$ is the graph of $y = f(x)$ shifted up 2 units.
The domain of h is the domain of f, $[-2, 2]$.
The range of h is the range of f shifted up 2 units, $[0, 4]$.

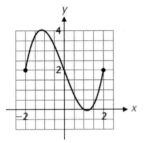

13. The graph of $y = h(x)$ is the graph of $y = g(x)$ shifted up 2 units.
The domain of h is the domain of g, $[-2, 2]$.
The range of h is the range of g shifted up 2 units, $[1, 3]$.

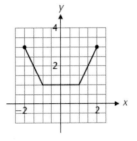

15. The graph of h is the graph of f shifted right 2 units.
The domain of h is the domain of f shifted right 2 units, $[0, 4]$.
The range of h is the range of f, $[-2, 2]$.

Common Error:
$x - 2$ does not indicate shifting left.

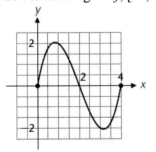

17. The graph of h is the graph of g shifted left 2 units.
The domain of h is the domain of g shifted left 2 units, $[-4, 0]$.
The range of h is the range of g, $[-1, 1]$.

19. The graph of h is the graph of f reflected through the x axis.
The domain of h is the domain of f, $[-2, 2]$.
The range of h is the range of f reflected through the x axis, $[-2, 2]$.

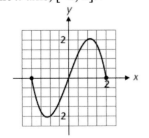

21. The graph of h is the graph of g stretched vertically by a factor of 2.
The domain of h is the domain of g, $[-2, 2]$.
The range of f is the range of g stretched vertically by a factor of 2, $[-2, 2]$.

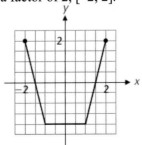

23. The graph of h is the graph of g shrunk horizontally by a factor of $\frac{1}{2}$.

The domain of h is the domain of g shrunk horizontally by a factor of $\frac{1}{2}$, $[-1, 1]$.

The range of h is the range of g, $[-1, 1]$.

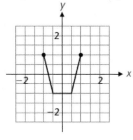

25. The graph of h is the graph of f reflected through the y axis.

The domain of h is the domain of f reflected through the y axis, $[-2, 2]$.

The range of h is the range of f, $[-2, 2]$.

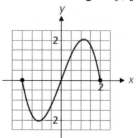

27. $g(-x) = (-x)^3 + (-x) = -x^3 - x = -(x^3 + x) = -g(x)$. Odd

29. $m(-x) = (-x)^4 + 3(-x)^2 = x^4 + 3x^2 = m(x)$. Even

31. $F(-x) = (-x)^5 + 1 = -x^5 + 1$
$-F(x) = -(x^5 + 1) = -x^5 - 1$
Therefore $F(-x) \neq F(x)$. $F(-x) \neq -F(x)$.
$F(x)$ is neither even nor odd.

33. $G(-x) = (-x)^4 + 2 = x^4 + 2 = G(x)$. Even

35. $q(-x) = (-x)^2 + (-x) - 3 = x^2 - x - 3$.
$-q(x) = -(x^2 + x - 3) = -x^2 - x + 3$
Therefore $q(-x) \neq q(x)$. $q(-x) \neq -q(x)$.
$q(x)$ is neither even nor odd.

37. $g(x) = \sqrt[3]{x+4} - 5$.
The graphs of $f(x) = \sqrt[3]{x}$ (thin curve) and $g(x)$ (thick curve) are shown.

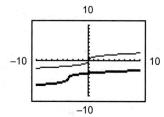

39. $g(x) = -0.5(6 + \sqrt{x})$

The graphs of $f(x) = \sqrt{x}$ (thin curve) and $g(x)$ (thick curve) are shown.

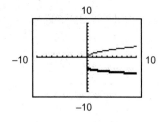

41. $g(x) = -2(x + 4)^2 - 2$
The graphs of $f(x) = x^2$ (thin curve) and $g(x)$ (thick curve) are shown.

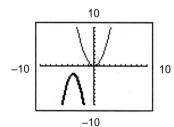

43. $g(x) = \sqrt{-\dfrac{1}{2}(x+2)}$.

The graph of $f(x) = \sqrt{x}$ and $g(x)$ are shown.

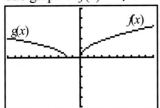

```
WINDOW
 Xmin=-10
 Xmax=10
 Xscl=1
 Ymin=-5
 Ymax=5
 Yscl=1
 Xres=1
```

45. The graph of $y = x^2$ is stretched vertically by a factor of 4 (**or** shrunk horizontally by a factor of 2.)

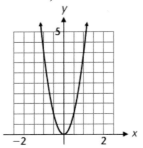

47. The graph of $y = |x|$ is shifted left 2 units.

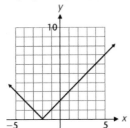

49. $m(x) = -|4x - 8| = -|4(x - 2)|$

The graph of $y = |x|$ is shifted right 2 units, stretched vertically by a factor of 4, and reflected through the x axis.

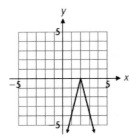

51.   The graph of $y = \sqrt{x}$ is reflected through the x axis and shifted up 3 units.

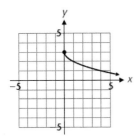

53.   The graph of $y = \sqrt{x}$ is shifted right 1 unit, stretched vertically by a factor of 3, and shifted up 2 units.

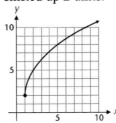

55.   The graph of $y = x^2$ is shifted up 3 units.

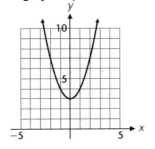

57.   The graph of $y = x^3$ is stretched vertically by a factor of 2 and shifted up 1 unit.

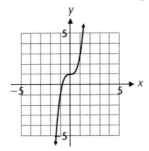

59. The graph of $y = x^2$ is shifted left 2 units.

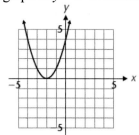

61. The graph of $y = x^2$ is shifted right 2 units, shrunk vertically by a factor of $\frac{1}{2}$, reflected through the x axis, and shifted up 4 units.

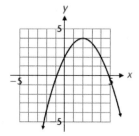

63. The graph of $y = x^2$ has been shifted 2 units right.

$y = (x - 2)^2$

65. The graph of $y = x^3$ has been shifted 2 units down. $y = x^3 - 2$

67. The graph of $y = |x|$ has been shrunk vertically by a factor of $\frac{1}{4}$. $y = \frac{1}{4}|x|$ or $y = 0.25|x|$

69. The graph of $y = x^3$ has been reflected through the y axis, (or the x axis). $y = -x^3$

71. The graph of $y = |x|$ has been shifted left 2 units and up 2 units. $y = |x + 2| + 2$

73. The graph of $y = \sqrt{x}$ has been reflected through the x axis and shifted up 4 units. $y = 4 - \sqrt{x}$

75. The graph of $y = x^2$ has been reflected through the x axis and shifted right 1 unit and up 4 units.
$y = 4 - (x - 1)^2$

77. The graph of $y = x^3$ has been shrunk vertically by a factor of $\frac{1}{2}$ and shifted right 3 units and up 1 unit.

$y = \frac{1}{2}(x - 3)^3 + 1$ or $y = 0.5(x - 3)^3 + 1$

79. (A) The function f is a horizontal shrink of $y = \sqrt[3]{x}$ by a factor of 1/8, while g is a vertical stretch of
$y = \sqrt[3]{x}$ by a factor of 2.

(B) The graphs are shown below in a standard window: they are identical.

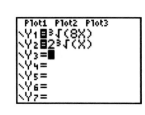
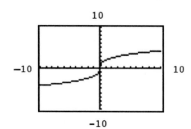

(C) $\sqrt[3]{8x} = \sqrt[3]{8} \cdot \sqrt[3]{x} = 2\sqrt[3]{x}$

81.   (A) The graphs are shown below.

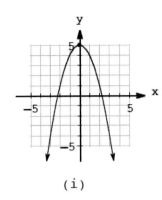

(i)

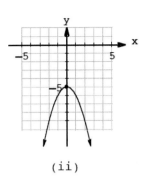

(ii)

The graphs are different, so order is significant when performing multiple transformations.

(B) (i): $y = -\left(x^2 - 5\right)$; (ii): $y = -x^2 - 5$

These functions are different. In the second one, order of operations tells us to first multiply by -1, then subtract 5. In the first, the parentheses indicate that this order should be reversed.

83. $f(x) = x$ is an odd function, since $f(-x) = -x = -f(x)$.
$g(x) = |x|$ is an even function, since $g(-x) = |-x| = |x| = g(x)$.
$h(x) = x^2$ is an even function, since $h(-x) = (-x)^2 = x^2 = h(x)$.
$m(x) = x^3$ is an odd function, since $m(-x) = (-x)^3 = -x^3 = -m(x)$.
$n(x) = \sqrt{x}$ is neither even nor odd. $n(-x) = \sqrt{-x} \neq \sqrt{x}$ and $n(-x) = \sqrt{-x} \neq -\sqrt{x}$.
$p(x) = \sqrt[3]{x}$ is an odd function, since $p(-x) = \sqrt[3]{-x} = -\sqrt[3]{x} = -p(x)$

85.   The graph of $y = f(x - h)$ represents a horizontal shift from the graph of $y = f(x)$. The graph of $y = f(x) + k$ represents a vertical shift from the graph of $y = f(x)$. The graph of $y = f(x - h) + k$ represents both a horizontal and a vertical shift but the order does not matter:
Vertical first then horizontal: $y = f(x) \rightarrow y = f(x) + k \rightarrow y = f(x - h) + k$
Horizontal first then vertical: $y = f(x) \rightarrow y = f(x - h) \rightarrow y = f(x - h) + k$
The same result is achieved; reversing the order does not change the result.

87.   Consider the graph of $y = x^2$.
If a vertical shift is performed the equation becomes $y = x^2 + k$.
If a reflection is now performed the equation becomes $y = -(x^2 + k)$ or $y = -x^2 - k$.
If the reflection is performed first the equation becomes $y = -x^2$.
If the vertical shift is now performed the equation becomes $y = -x^2 + k$.
Since $y = -x^2 - k$ and $y = -x^2 + k$ differ (unless $k = 0$), reversing the order changes the result.

89.   The graph of $y = f(x - h)$ represents a horizontal shift from the graph of $y = f(x)$. The graph of $y = -f(x)$ represents a reflection of the graph of $y = f(x)$ in the x axis. The graph of $y = -f(x - h)$ represents both a horizontal shift and a reflection but the order does not matter:
Shift first then reflection: $y = f(x) \rightarrow y = f(x - h) \rightarrow y = -f(x - h)$
Reflection first then shift: $y = f(x) \rightarrow y = -f(x) \rightarrow y = -f(x - h)$
The same result is achieved; reversing the order does not change the result.

91.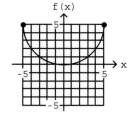

93.

95. (A) $E(x) = \dfrac{1}{2}\,[f(x) + f(-x)]$

$E(-x) = \dfrac{1}{2}\,[f(-x) + f\{-(-x)\}]$

$= \dfrac{1}{2}\,[f(-x) + f(x)]$

$= \dfrac{1}{2}\,[f(x) + f(-x)] = E(x).$

Thus, $E(x)$ is even.

(B) $O(x) = \dfrac{1}{2}\,[f(x) - f(-x)]$

$O(-x) = \dfrac{1}{2}\,[f(-x) - f\{-(-x)\}]$

$= \dfrac{1}{2}\,[f(-x) - f(x)]$

$= -\dfrac{1}{2}\,[f(x) - f(-x)] = -O(x).$

Thus, $O(x)$ is odd.

(C) $E(x) + O(x) = \dfrac{1}{2}\,[f(x) + f(-x)] + \dfrac{1}{2}\,[f(x) - f(-x)]$

$= \dfrac{1}{2}f(x) + \dfrac{1}{2}f(-x) + \dfrac{1}{2}f(x) - \dfrac{1}{2}f(-x) = f(x)$

Conclusion: Any function can be written as the sum of two other functions, one even and the other odd.

97. The graph of the function $C(x) = 30{,}000 + f(x)$ is the same as the given graph of the function $f(x)$ shifted up 30,000 units ($).

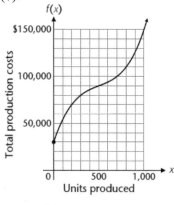

99. $y = 10 + 0.004(x - 10)^3$,
$y = 15 + 0.004(x - 10)^3$,
$y = 20 + 0.004(x - 10)^3$.
Each graph is a vertical shift of the graph of $y = 0.004(x - 10)^3$.

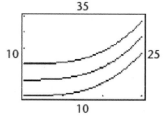

101. $V(t) = \dfrac{64}{C^2}(C - t)^2 \quad 0 \le t \le C$

t	$C = 1$ $V = 64(1 - t)^2$	$C = 2$ $V = 16(2 - t)^2$	$C = 4$ $V = 4(4 - t)^2$	$C = 8$ $V = (8 - t)^2$
0	64	64	64	64
1	0	16	36	49
2	not defined for $t>1$	0	16	36
4		not defined for $t>2$	0	16
8			not defined for $t > 4$	0

Each graph is a portion of the graph of a
horizontal translation followed by a vertical
stretch (except for $C = 8$) of the graph of $y = t^2$.

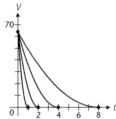

The height of the graph represents the volume of water left in the tank, so we see that for larger values of
C, the water stays in the tank longer. We can conclude that larger values of C correspond to a smaller
opening.

Section 3-4

1. The graph of a quadratic function $f(x) = ax^2 + bx + c$ is a parabola with vertex at $x = -b/2a$, opening upward
if a is positive, and opening downward if a is negative.

3. False. A quadratic function $f(x) = ax^2 + bx + c$ has a maximum if and only if a is negative; if a is positive it
has no maximum.

5. If a is positive the graph opens upward and has a minimum at the vertex; if a is negative the graph opens
downward and has a maximum at the vertex.

7. $f(x) = (x + 3)^2 - 4$
   $= [x - (-3)]^2 - 4$
   Vertex: $(-3, -4)$
   axis: $x = -3$

9. $f(x) = -\left(x - \dfrac{3}{2}\right)^2 - 5$

   Vertex: $\left(\dfrac{3}{2}, -5\right)$

   axis: $x = \dfrac{3}{2}$

11. $f(x) = 2(x + 10)^2 + 20$
   $= 2[x - (-10)]^2 + 20$
   Vertex: $(-10, 20)$
   axis: $x = -10$

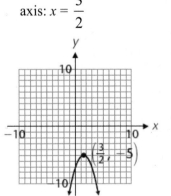

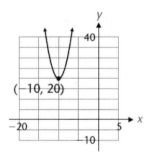

13. The graph of $y = x^2$ is shifted right 2 units and up 1
unit.

15. The graph of $y = x^2$ is shifted left 1 unit and
reflected in the x axis.

17. The graph of $y = x^2$ is shifted right 2 units and down
3 units.

19. The graph of $y = x^2$ has been shifted to the right 2
units. This is the graph of $y = (x - 2)^2$, corresponding to
the function k.

21. The graph of $y = x^2$ has been shifted to the right 2
units and down 3 units. This is the graph of
$y = (x - 2)^2 - 3$, corresponding to the function m.

23. The graph of $y = x^2$ has been reflected in the x axis
and shifted to the left 1 unit, corresponding to the
function h.

25.   Begin by grouping the first two terms with parentheses:

$$f(x) = \left(x^2 - 4x\right) + 5 \qquad \text{Find the number needed to complete the square}$$

$$= \left(x^2 - 4x + ?\right) + 5 \qquad (-4/2)^2 = 4\text{; add and subtract 4}$$

$$= \left(x^2 - 4x + 4\right) + 5 - 4 \qquad \text{Factor parentheses, combine like terms}$$

$$= (x-2)^2 + 1$$

The vertex form is $f(x) = (x-2)^2 + 1$. The vertex is (2, 1) and the axis is $x = 2$.

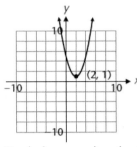

27.   Begin by grouping the first two terms with parentheses, then factoring -1 out of those two terms so that the coefficient of x^2 is 1:

$$h(x) = -1\left(x^2 + 2x\right) - 3 \qquad \text{Find the number needed to complete the square}$$

$$= -1\left(x^2 + 2x + ?\right) - 3 \qquad (2/2)^2 = 1\text{; add 1 inside the parentheses}$$

$$= -1\left(x^2 + 2x + 1\right) - 3 + ? \qquad \text{We actually added } -1(1)\text{, so add 1 as well}$$

$$= -1\left(x^2 + 2x + 1\right) - 3 + 1 \qquad \text{Factor parentheses, combine like terms}$$

$$= -1(x+1)^2 - 2$$

The vertex form is $h(x) = -1(x+1)^2 - 2$. The vertex is (−1, −2) and the axis is $x = -1$.

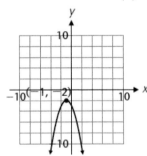

29.   Begin by grouping the first two terms with parentheses, then factoring 2 out of those two terms so that the coefficient of x^2 is 1:

$$m(x) = 2\left(x^2 - 6x\right) + 22 \qquad \text{Find the number needed to complete the square}$$

$$= 2\left(x^2 - 6x + ?\right) + 22 \qquad (-6/2)^2 = 9\text{; add 9 inside the parentheses}$$

$$= 2\left(x^2 - 6x + 9\right) + 22 + ? \qquad \text{We actually added } 2(9)\text{, so subtract 18 as well}$$

$$= 2\left(x^2 - 6x + 9\right) + 22 - 18 \qquad \text{Factor parentheses, combine like terms}$$

$$= 2(x-3)^2 + 4$$

The vertex form is $m(x) = 2(x-3)^2 + 4$. The vertex is (3, 4) and the axis is $x = 3$.

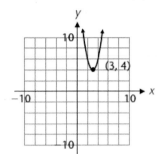

31. Begin by grouping the first two terms with parentheses, then factoring 1/2 out of those two terms so that the coefficient of x^2 is 1:

$$f(x) = \frac{1}{2}(x^2 + 6x) - \frac{7}{2}$$ Find the number needed to complete the square

$$= \frac{1}{2}(x^2 + 6x + ?) - \frac{7}{2}$$ $(6/2)^2 = 9$; add 9 inside the parentheses

$$= \frac{1}{2}(x^2 + 6x + 9) - \frac{7}{2} + ?$$ We actually added $\frac{1}{2}(9)$; subtract $\frac{9}{2}$ as well

$$= \frac{1}{2}(x^2 + 6x + 9) - \frac{7}{2} - \frac{9}{2}$$ Factor the parentheses, combine like terms

$$= \frac{1}{2}(x+3)^2 - 8$$

The vertex form is $f(x) = \frac{1}{2}(x+3)^2 - 8$. The vertex is (–3, –8) and the axis is $x = -3$.

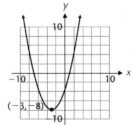

33. Begin by grouping the first two terms with parentheses, then factoring 2 out of those two terms so that the coefficient of x^2 is 1:

$$f(x) = 2(x^2 - 12x) + 90$$ Find the number needed to complete the square

$$= 2(x^2 - 12x + ?) + 90$$ $(-12/2)^2 = 36$; add 36 inside the parentheses

$$= 2(x^2 - 12x + 36) + 90 + ?$$ We actually added 2(36); subtract 72 as well

$$= 2(x^2 - 12x + 36) + 90 - 72$$ Factor the parentheses, combine like terms

$$= 2(x-6)^2 + 18$$

The vertex form is $f(x) = 2(x-6)^2 + 18$. The vertex is (6, 18) and the axis is $x = 6$.

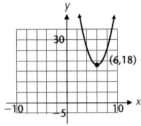

35. $x = -\dfrac{b}{2a} = -\dfrac{8}{2(1)} = -4;\ f(-4) = (-4)^2 + 8(-4) + 8 = 16 - 32 + 8 = -8$

The vertex is (–4,–8). The coefficient of x^2 is positive, so the parabola opens up. The graph is symmetric about its axis, $x = -4$. It decreases until reaching a minimum at (–4, –8), then increases.
The range is [–8, ∞).

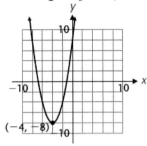

37. $x = -\dfrac{b}{2a} = -\dfrac{-7}{2(-1)} = -\dfrac{7}{2}$

$$f\left(-\frac{7}{2}\right) = -\left(-\frac{7}{2}\right)^2 - 7\left(-\frac{7}{2}\right) + 4 = -\frac{49}{4} + \frac{49}{2} + 4 = -\frac{49}{4} + \frac{98}{4} + \frac{16}{4} = \frac{65}{4}$$

The vertex is $\left(-\dfrac{7}{2}, \dfrac{65}{4}\right)$. The coefficient of x^2 is negative, so the parabola opens down. The graph is

symmetric about its axis, $x = -\dfrac{7}{2}$. It increases until reaching a maximum at $\left(-\dfrac{7}{2}, \dfrac{65}{4}\right)$, then decreases.

The range is $\left(-\infty, \dfrac{65}{4}\right]$.

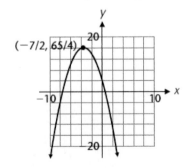

39. $x = -\dfrac{b}{2a} = -\dfrac{-18}{2(4)} = \dfrac{18}{8} = \dfrac{9}{4}$

$$f\left(\dfrac{9}{4}\right) = 4\left(\dfrac{9}{4}\right)^2 - 18\left(\dfrac{9}{4}\right) + 25 = 4\left(\dfrac{81}{16}\right) - \dfrac{162}{4} + 25 = \dfrac{81}{4} - \dfrac{162}{4} + \dfrac{100}{4} = \dfrac{19}{4}$$

The vertex is $\left(\dfrac{9}{4}, \dfrac{19}{4}\right)$. The coefficient of x^2 is positive, so the parabola opens up. The graph is symmetric

about its axis, $x = \dfrac{9}{4}$. It decreases until reaching a minimum at $\left(\dfrac{9}{4}, \dfrac{19}{4}\right)$, then increases.

The range is $\left[\dfrac{19}{4}, \infty\right)$.

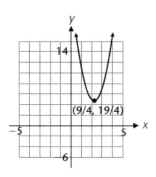

41. $x = -\dfrac{b}{2a} = -\dfrac{50}{2(-10)} = \dfrac{50}{20} = \dfrac{5}{2}$

$$f\left(\dfrac{5}{2}\right) = -10\left(\dfrac{5}{2}\right)^2 + 50\left(\dfrac{5}{2}\right) + 12 = -10\left(\dfrac{25}{4}\right) + 125 + 12 = -\dfrac{125}{2} + \dfrac{250}{2} + \dfrac{24}{2} = \dfrac{149}{2}$$

The vertex is $\left(\dfrac{5}{2}, \dfrac{149}{2}\right)$. The coefficient of x^2 is negative, so the parabola opens down. The graph is

symmetric about its axis, $x = \dfrac{5}{2}$. It increases until reaching a maximum at $\left(\dfrac{5}{2}, \dfrac{149}{2}\right)$, then decreases. The

range is $\left(-\infty, \dfrac{149}{2}\right]$.

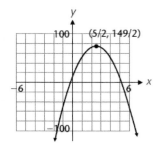

43. $x = -\dfrac{b}{2a} = -\dfrac{3}{2(1)} = \dfrac{-3}{2}$

$f\left(-\dfrac{3}{2}\right) = \left(-\dfrac{3}{2}\right)^2 + 3\left(-\dfrac{3}{2}\right) = \dfrac{9}{4} - \dfrac{9}{2} = \dfrac{9}{4} - \dfrac{18}{4} = -\dfrac{9}{4}$

The vertex is $\left(-\dfrac{3}{2}, -\dfrac{9}{4}\right)$. The coefficient of x^2 is positive, so the parabola opens up. The graph is

symmetric about its axis, $x = -\dfrac{3}{2}$. It decreases until reaching a minimum at $\left(-\dfrac{3}{2}, -\dfrac{9}{4}\right)$, then increases.

The range is $\left[-\dfrac{9}{4}, \infty\right)$.

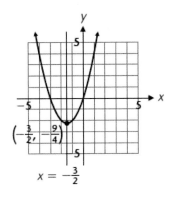

45. $x = -\dfrac{b}{2a} = -\dfrac{-2}{2(0.5)} = 2$

$f(2) = 0.5(2)^2 - 2(2) - 7 = 0.5(4) - 4 - 7 = 2 - 4 - 7 = -9$

The vertex is $(2, -9)$. The coefficient of x^2 is positive, so the parabola opens up. The graph is symmetric

about its axis, $x = 2$. It decreases until reaching a minimum at $(2, -9)$, then increases. The range

is $[-9, \infty)$.

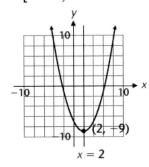

47. $x^2 < 10 - 3x$

$f(x) = x^2 + 3x - 10 < 0$

$f(x) = (x + 5)(x - 2) < 0$

The zeros of f are –5 and 2. Plotting the graph of $f(x)$, we see that $f(x) < 0$ for $-5 < x < 2$, or $(-5, 2)$.

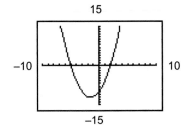

49. $x^2 + 21 > 10x$

$f(x) = x^2 - 10x + 21 > 0$

$f(x) = (x - 3)(x - 7) > 0$

The zeros of f are 3 and 7. Plotting the graph of $f(x)$, we see that $f(x) > 0$ for $x < 3$ and $x > 7$, or $(-\infty, 3) \cup (7, \infty)$.

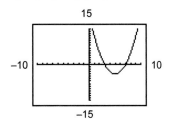

51. $x^2 \leq 8x$

$f(x) = x^2 - 8x \leq 0$

$f(x) = x(x - 8) \leq 0$

The zeros of f are 0 and 8. Plotting the graph of $f(x)$, we see that $f(x) \leq 0$ for $0 \leq x \leq 8$ or $[0, 8]$.

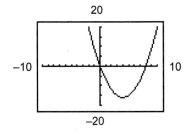

53. $x^2 + 5x \leq 0$

$f(x) = x^2 + 5x \leq 0$

$f(x) = x(x + 5) \leq 0$

The zeros of f are –5 and 0. Plotting the graph of $f(x)$, we see that $f(x) \leq 0$ for $-5 \leq x \leq 0$ or $[-5, 0]$.

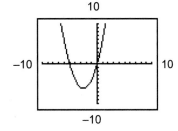

55.

$$x^2 + 1 < 2x$$
$$x^2 - 2x + 1 < 0$$
$$(x - 1)^2 < 0$$

Since the square of no real number is negative, these statements are never true for any real number x.   No solution; $\varnothing$ is the solution set.

57. $x^2 < 3x - 3$

$x^2 - 3x + 3 < 0$

We attempt to find all real zeros of the polynomial.

$$x^2 - 3x + 3 = 0$$

$$x = \frac{-b \pm \sqrt{b^2 - 4ac}}{2a} \quad a = 1, b = -3, c = 3$$

$$x = \frac{-(-3) \pm \sqrt{(-3)^2 - 4(1)(3)}}{2(1)}$$

$$x = \frac{3 \pm \sqrt{-3}}{2}$$

The polynomial has no real zeros. Hence the statement is either true for all real x or for no real x. To determine which, we choose a test number, say 0.

59. $x^2 - 1 \geq 4x$

$f(x) = x^2 - 4x - 1 \geq 0$

Find all real zeros of $f(x)$.

$$x^2 - 4x - 1 = 0$$

$$x = \frac{-b \pm \sqrt{b^2 - 4ac}}{2a} \quad a = 1, b = -4, c = -1$$

$$x = \frac{-(-4) \pm \sqrt{(-4)^2 - 4(1)(-1)}}{2(1)}$$

$$x = \frac{4 \pm \sqrt{16 + 4}}{2} = \frac{4 \pm \sqrt{20}}{2}$$

$$x = 2 \pm \sqrt{5} \approx -0.236, 4.236$$

Common Error:
$x \neq 2 \pm \sqrt{20}$

$x^2 < 3x - 3$

$0^2 \overset{?}{<} 3(0) - 3$

$0 \overset{?}{<} -3$ False.

The statement is never true for any real number x. No solution. $\varnothing$ is the solution set.

Plotting the graph of $f(x)$ we see that $f(x) \geq 0$ for

$x \leq 2 - \sqrt{5}$ and $x \geq 2 + \sqrt{5}$,

or $(-\infty, 2 - \sqrt{5}] \cup [2 + \sqrt{5}, \infty)$.

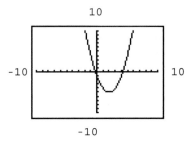

61. The vertex of the parabola is at $(1, -4)$. Therefore the equation must have form
$y = a(x - 1)^2 - 4$
Since the parabola passes through $(3, 4)$, these coordinates must satisfy the equation
$4 = a(3 - 1)^2 - 4$
$8 = 4a$
$a = 2.$
The equation is
$y = 2(x - 1)^2 - 4$
$y = 2(x^2 - 2x + 1) - 4$
$y = 2x^2 - 4x + 2 - 4$
$y = 2x^2 - 4x - 2$

63. The vertex of the parabola is at $(-1, 4)$. Therefore the equation must have form
$y = a(x + 1)^2 + 4$
Since the parabola passes through $(1, 2)$, these coordinates must satisfy the equation.
$2 = a(1 + 1)^2 + 4$
$2 = 4a + 4$
$-2 = 4a$
$a = -0.5$
The equation is
$y = -0.5(x + 1)^2 + 4$
$y = -0.5(x^2 + 2x + 1) + 4$
$y = -0.5x^2 - x - 0.5 + 4$
$y = -0.5x^2 - x + 3.5$

65. Notice that the graph does not provide the exact coordinates of the vertex, so we can't tell for certain what they are. We know that $f(-1)$ and $f(3)$ are both zero, so the axis of symmetry is halfway between $x = -1$ and $x = 3$. In other words, the x-coordinate of the vertex is 1; the equation looks like
$f(x) = a(x - 1)^2 + k.$
Plug in $x = -1$:
$f(-1) = a(-1 - 1)^2 + k = a(-2)^2 + k = 4a + k = 0$ (since $(-1, 0)$ is on the graph)
$4a + k = 0$
$k = -4a$
Substitute $-4a$ in for k: $f(x) = a(x - 1)^2 - 4a$
Plug in $x = 0$:
$f(0) = a(0 - 1)^2 - 4a = a - 4a = -3a = -3$ (since $(0, -3)$ is on the graph)
$-3a = -3$
$a = 1$
$f(x) = (x - 1)^2 - 4$ or $f(x) = x^2 - 2x - 3$

67. Notice that the graph does not provide the exact coordinates of the vertex, so we can't tell for certain what they are. We know that $f(-1)$ and $f(5)$ are equal, so the axis of symmetry is halfway between $x = -1$ and $x = 5$. In other words, the x-coordinate of the vertex is 2; the equation looks like
$f(x) = a(x - 2)^2 + k$
Plug in $x = -1$: $f(-1) = a(-1 - 2)^2 + k = a(-3)^2 + k = 9a + k = 0$ (since $(-1, 0)$ is on the graph)
$9a + k = 0$
$k = -9a$

Substitute $-9a$ in for k: $f(x) = a(x-2)^2 - 9a$

Plug in $x = 0$: $f(0) = a(0-2)^2 - 9a = a(-2)^2 - 9a = 4a - 9a = -5a = 2.5$ (since $(0, 2.5)$ is on the graph)
$$-5a = 2.5$$
$$a = -0.5$$
$f(x) = -0.5(x-2)^2 + 4.5$ or $f(x) = -0.5x^2 + 2x + 2.5$

69.   The vertex of the parabola is at $(4, 8)$.
Therefore the equation must have form
$$y = a(x-4)^2 + 8$$
Since the x intercept is 6, $(6, 0)$ must satisfy the equation
$$0 = a(6-4)^2 + 8$$
$$0 = 4a + 8$$
$$a = -2$$
The equation is
$$y = -2(x-4)^2 + 8$$
$$y = -2(x^2 - 8x + 16) + 8$$
$$y = -2x^2 + 16x - 32 + 8$$
$$y = -2x^2 + 16x - 24$$

71.   The vertex of the parabola is at $(-4, 12)$.
Therefore the equation must have form
$$y = a(x+4)^2 + 12$$
Since the y intercept is 4, $(0, 4)$ must satisfy the equation.
$$4 = a(0+4)^2 + 12$$
$$4 = 16a + 12$$
$$-8 = 16a$$
$$a = -0.5$$
The equation is
$$y = -0.5(x+4)^2 + 12$$
$$y = -0.5(x^2 + 8x + 16) + 12$$
$$y = -0.5x^2 - 4x - 8 + 12 = -0.5x^2 - 4x + 4$$

73.   The vertex of the parabola is at $(-5, -25)$.
Therefore the equation must have form
$$y = a(x+5)^2 - 25$$
Since the parabola passes through $(-2, 20)$, these coordinates must satisfy the equation.
$$20 = a(-2+5)^2 - 25$$
$$20 = 9a - 25$$
$$45 = 9a$$
$$a = 5$$

The equation is $y = 5(x+5)^2 - 25$
$$y = 5(x^2 + 10x + 25) - 25$$
$$y = 5x^2 + 50x + 125 - 25$$
$$y = 5x^2 + 50x + 100$$

75. $a(x-h)^2 + k = a(x^2 - 2xh + h^2) + k$
$$= ax^2 - 2axh + ah^2 + k$$
$$= ax^2 - (2ah)x + (ah^2 + k)$$

77.   The graphs shown are $f(x) = x^2 + 6x + 1$,
$f(x) = x^2 + 1$, and $f(x) = x^2 - 4x + 1$.
These correspond to $f(x) = x^2 + kx + 1$ with $k = 6, 0$, and -4 respectively.

Note that all have the same shape but a different vertex. In fact, all three are translations of the graph $y = x^2$.

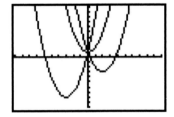

79.   The graphs of $f(x) = (x-1)^2$,
$g(x) = (x-1)^2 + 4$, and
$h(x) = (x-1)^2 - 5$ are shown.

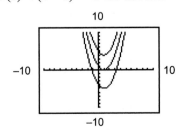

It is clear that $f(x)$ has one x intercept (at $x = 1$), $g(x)$ has no x intercepts and $h(x)$ has two x intercepts.

In general, for $a > 0$, the graph of $f(x) = a(x-h)^2 + k$ can be expected to have no intercepts for $k > 0$, one intercept at $x = h$ for $k = 0$, and two intercepts for $k < 0$.

81. Let one number $= x$. Then the other number is $x - 30$. The product is a function of x given by $f(x) = x(x - 30) = x^2 - 30x$. This is a quadratic function with $a > 0$, therefore it has a minimum value at the vertex of its graph (a parabola). Completing the square yields

$$f(x) = x^2 - 30x \qquad\qquad \frac{1}{2}(-30) = -15; \quad (-15)^2 = 225$$

$$= x^2 - 30x + 225 - 225$$
$$= (x - 15)^2 - 225$$

Thus the minimum product is -225, when $x = 15$ and $x - 30 = -15$. There is no "highest point" on this parabola and no maximum product.

83. Find the vertex, using $a = -1.2$ and $b = 62.5$:

$$x = -\frac{b}{2a} = -\frac{62.5}{2(-1.2)} \approx 26; \quad P(26) = -1.2(26)^2 + 62.5(26) - 491 = 322.8$$

The company should hire 26 employees to make a maximum profit of \$322,800.

85. (A) Find the first coordinate of the vertex, using $a = -0.19$ and $b = 1.2$:

$$x = -\frac{b}{2a} = -\frac{1.2}{2(-0.19)} = 3.2$$

The maximum box office revenue was three years after 2002, which is 2005.

(B) The function specifies yearly totals for revenue, so the domain should be restricted to whole numbers. The exact vertex occurs at $x = 3.2$, so we needed to round down to 3.

87. (A) Since the four sides needing fencing are x, y, $x + 50$, and y, we have $x + y + (x + 50) + y = 250$. (Since both x and $100 - x$ must be nonnegative, the domain of $A(x)$ is $0 \le x \le 100$.)
Solving for y, we get
$y = 100 - x$.
Therefore the area
$A(x) = (x + 50)y = (x + 50)(100 - x) = -x^2 + 50x + 5000$.
(B) This is a quadratic function with $a < 0$, so it has a maximum value at the vertex:

$$x = -\frac{b}{2a} = -\frac{50}{2(-1)} = 25; \quad A(25) = -(25)^2 + 50(25) + 5{,}000 = -625 + 1{,}250 + 5{,}000 = 5{,}625$$

The maximum area is 5,625 square feet when $x = 25$.
(C) When $x = 25$, $y = 100 - 25 = 75$. The dimensions of the corral are then $x + 50$ by y, or 75 ft by 75 ft.

89. According to Example 7, the function describing the height of the sandbag is $h(t) = 10{,}000 - 16t^2$ (since the initial height is 10,000 feet). We want to know when it reaches ground level, so plug in zero for $h(t)$, then solve for t.

$$0 = 10{,}000 - 16t^2$$
$$16t^2 = 10{,}000$$
$$t^2 = 625$$
$$t = 25$$

It hits the ground 25 seconds after it's dropped.

91. According to Example 7, the function describing the height of the diver is $h(t) = h_0 - 16t^2$, where h_0 is the initial height in feet. (This initial height is the height of the cliff.) We know that $h(2.5) = 0$ since it takes 2.5 seconds to reach the water; we plug in 2.5 for t and 0 for $h(t)$, which allows us to solve for h_0.

$$0 = h_0 - 16(2.5)^2$$
$$0 = h_0 - 100$$
$$100 = h_0$$

The cliff is 100 feet high.

93. (A) Since $d(t)$ is a quadratic function with maximum value 484 when $t = 5.5$, an equation for $d(t)$ must be of the form

$$d(t) = a(t - 5.5)^2 + 484$$

Since $d(0) = 0$,

$$0 = d(0) = a(0 - 5.5)^2 + 484$$
$$0 = 30.25a + 484$$
$$a = -16$$

Hence $d(t) = -16(t - 5.5)^2 + 484$
$$= -16(t^2 - 11t + 30.25) + 484$$
$$= -16t^2 + 176t - 484 + 484$$
$$= -16t^2 + 176t$$

Since the graph of d must be symmetric with respect to $t = 5.5$, and $d(0) = 0$, $d(11)$ must also equal 0. The distance above the ground will be nonnegative only for values of t between 0 and 11, hence the domain of the function is $0 \le t \le 11$.

(B) Solve $250 = -16t^2 + 176t$ by graphing Y1 = 250 and Y2 = $-16x^2 + 176x$ and applying a built-in routine.

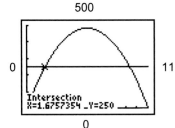 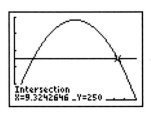

From the graphs $t = 1.68$ sec and $t = 9.32$ sec, to two decimal places.

95. (A) If coordinates are chosen with origin at the center of the base, the parabola is the graph of a quadratic function $h(x)$ with maximum value 14 when $x = 0$. The equation must be of form $h(x) = ax^2 + 14$

Since $h(10) = 0$ (why?)

$$0 = h(10) = a(10)^2 + 14$$
$$0 = 100a + 14$$
$$a = -0.14$$

Hence $h(x) = -0.14x^2 + 14$ $-10 \le x \le 10$

(B) Suppose the truck were to drive so as to maximize its clearance, that is, in the center of the roadway. Then half its width, or 4 ft, would extend to each side. But if $x = 4$, $h(x) = -0.14(4)^2 + 14 = 11.76$ ft. The arch is only 11.76 feet high, but the truck is 12 feet high. The truck cannot pass through the arch.

(C) From part (B), if $x = 4$, $h(x) = 11.76$ ft is the height of the tallest truck.

(D) Find x so that $h(x) = 12$. Solve the equation

$$12 = 0.14x^2 + 14$$

$$-2 = -0.14x^2 \qquad \text{(The negative solution doesn't make sense)}$$

$$x = \sqrt{\frac{2}{0.14}} = 3.78$$

The width of the truck is at most $2x = 2(3.78) = 7.56$ feet

97. (A)   The entered data is shown here along with the results of the quadratic regression calculation.

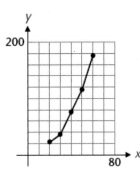

The quadratic model for the skid mark length is $L(x) = 0.061x^2 - 1.2x + 26$

(B)

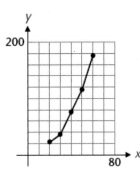

(C)   Solve $150 = 0.06x^2 - 1.2x + 26$

$$0 = 0.06x^2 - 1.2x - 124$$

$$x = \frac{-(-1.2) \pm \sqrt{(-1.2)^2 - 4(0.06)(-124)}}{2(0.06)}$$

$$x = \frac{1.2 \pm 5.59}{0.12}$$

$x = 57$ mph
(the negative answer doesn't make sense)

99. (A) Beer consumption in 1960 is given as 0.99.

Solve $0.99 = -0.0006x^2 + 0.03x + 1$

$$0 = -0.0006x^2 + 0.03x + 0.01$$

$$0 = -6x^2 + 300x + 100 \text{ (for convenience)}$$

$$x = \frac{-300 \pm \sqrt{(300)^2 - 4(-6)(100)}}{2(-6)}$$

$x = 50$ (discarding the negative answer)
This represents the year 2010.

(B) Substitute $x = 45$ to obtain

$$B(45) = -0.0006(45)^2 + 0.03(45) + 1$$
$$= 1.14 \text{ gallons}$$

101. A profit will result if $C(x) < R(x)$.

Solve $245 + 1.6x < 10x - 0.04x^2$

$$0.04x^2 - 8.4x + 245 < 0$$

$$f(x) = 0.04x^2 - 8.4x + 245 < 0$$

Find the zeros of $f(x)$.

$$x = \frac{-(-8.4) \pm \sqrt{(-8.4)^2 - 4(0.04)(245)}}{2(0.04)}$$

$x = 35$ or 175

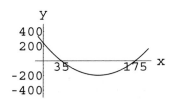

Plotting the graph of $f(x)$ we see that $f(x) < 0$ for $35 < x < 175$. The break-even points are therefore
$(35, R(35)) = (35, 301)$ and $(175, R(175)) = (175, 525)$.

103.   The revenue function is $R(x) = xd(x) = x(9.3 - 0.15x)$ or
$R(x) = -0.15x^2 + 9.3x$.
$R(x)$ has a maximum value at the vertex of this parabola, which is given by

$$x = -\frac{b}{2a} = -\frac{9.3}{2(-0.15)} = 31$$

Then $p = d(31) = 9.3 - 0.15(31) = \$4.65$ is the price which maximizes the revenue.

105.   (A) The revenue function is $R(x) = xd(x) = x(3.5 - 0.00007x)$
$$= 3.5x - 0.00007x^2.$$

The domain is given by $x(3.5 - 0.00007x) \geq 0$ or $0 \leq x \leq 50,000$.
The cost function $C(x)$ is given by
$C(x) = $ Fixed Cost + Variable Cost $= 24,500 + 0.35x$.
  The domain is given by $x \geq 0$ or $[0, \infty)$.
The company will break even when $R(x) = C(x)$.
   Solve

$$3.5x - 0.00007x^2 = 24,5000 + 0.35x$$
$$0 = 0.00007x^2 - 3.15x + 24,500$$
$$x =$$

$$\frac{-(-3.15) \pm \sqrt{(-3.15)^2 - 4(0.00007)(24,500)}}{2(0.00007)}$$

$$x = 10,000 \text{ or } 35,000.$$

The company will break even for sales of 10,000 or 35,000 gallons.

(B)

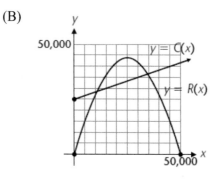

(C)   The company makes a profit for those sales levels for which the graph of the revenue function is above the graph of the cost function, that is, if the sales are between 10,000 and 35,000 gallons. The company suffers a loss for those sales levels for which the graph of the revenue function is below the graph of the cost function, that is, if the sales are between 0 and 10,000 gallons or between 35,000 and 50,000 gallons.

(D)   The profit function is given by $P(x) = R(x) - C(x)$. Thus
$$P(x) = (3.5x - 0.00007x^2) - (24,500 + 0.35x)$$
$$= -0.00007x^2 + 3.15x - 24,500$$
The maximum value of this function occurs at the vertex of its parabola graph. This is given by the formulas (h, k) where

$$h = -\frac{b}{2a} = -\frac{3.15}{2(-0.00007)} = 22,500$$

and

$$k = C - \frac{b^2}{4a} = -24,500 - \frac{3.15^2}{4(-0.00007)} = 10,937.5$$

That is, the maximum profit is $10,937.50 when 22,500 gallons are sold. Substitute $x = 22,500$ to find
$p = d(22,500) = 3.5 - 0.00007(22,500) = \$1.92$ per gallon.

Section 3-5

1.   The sum of two functions is found by adding the expressions for the two functions and finding the intersection of their domains.

3.   Answers will vary.

5. The simplification may obscure values that are not in the domain of one of the functions.

7. Construct a table of values of $f(x)$ and $g(x)$ from the graph, then add to obtain $(f + g)(x)$.

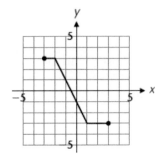

x	–3	–2	–1	0	1	2	3
$f(x)$	1	0	–1	–2	–3	–2	–1
$g(x)$	2	3	2	1	0	–1	–2
$(f + g)(x)$	3	3	1	–1	–3	–3	–3

9. Construct a table of values of $f(x)$ and $g(x)$ from the graph, then multiply to obtain $(fg)(x)$.

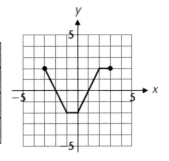

x	–3	–2	–1	0	1	2	3
$f(x)$	1	0	–1	–2	–3	–2	–1
$g(x)$	2	3	2	1	0	–1	–2
$(f g)(x)$	2	0	–2	–2	0	2	2

11. $(f \circ g)(-1) = f[g(-1)]$. From the graph of g, $g(-1) = 2$. From the graph of f, $f[g(-1)] = f(2) = -2$.

13. $(g \circ f)(-2) = g[f(-2)]$. From the graph of f, $f(-2) = 0$. From the graph of g, $g[f(-2)] = g(0) = 1$.

15. From the graph of g, $g(1) = 0$. From the graph of f, $f[g(1)] = f(0) = -2$.

17. From the graph of f, $f(2) = -2$. From the graph of g, $g[f(2)] = g(-2) = 3$.

19. $(f + g)(-3) = f(-3) + g(-3) = [2 - (-3)] + \sqrt{3 - (-3)} = 5 + \sqrt{6}$

21. $(fg)(-1) = f(-1)g(-1)$
$= [2 - (-1)] \sqrt{3 - (-1)}$
$= 3\sqrt{4} = 3 \cdot 2 = 6$

23. $f \circ g(-2) = f(g(-2))$
$= f(\sqrt{3 - (-2)})$
$= f(\sqrt{5}) = 2 - \sqrt{5}$

25. $g \circ f(1) = g(f(1))$
$= g(2 - 1)$
$= g(1)$
$= \sqrt{3 - 1} = \sqrt{2}$

27. Using values from the table, $g(-7) = 4$, so $(f \circ g)(-7) = f(g(-7)) = f(4) = 3$. Similarly,
$(f \circ g)(0) = f(g(0)) = f(-2) = 9$, and $(f \circ g)(4) = f(g(4)) = f(6) = -10$.

29.
$(f + g)(x) = f(x) + g(x) = 4x + x + 1 = 5x + 1$ Domain: $(-\infty, \infty)$
$(f - g)(x) = f(x) - g(x) = 4x - (x + 1) = 3x - 1$ Domain: $(-\infty, \infty)$
$(fg)(x) = f(x)g(x) = 4x(x + 1) = 4x^2 + 4x$ Domain: $(-\infty, \infty)$

$\left(\dfrac{f}{g}\right)(x) = \dfrac{f(x)}{g(x)} = \dfrac{4x}{x + 1}$ Domain: $\{x \mid x \neq -1\}$, or $(-\infty, -1) \cup (-1, \infty)$

> **Common Error:**
> $f(x) - g(x) \neq 4x - x + 1$. The parentheses are necessary.

31. $(f + g)(x) = f(x) + g(x) = 2x^2 + x^2 + 1 = 3x^2 + 1$ Domain: $(-\infty, \infty)$
$(f - g)(x) = f(x) - g(x) = 2x^2 - (x^2 + 1) = x^2 - 1$ Domain: $(-\infty, \infty)$
$(fg)(x) = f(x)g(x) = 2x^2(x^2 + 1) = 2x^4 + 2x^2$ Domain: $(-\infty, \infty)$

$$\left(\frac{f}{g}\right)(x) = \frac{f(x)}{g(x)} = \frac{2x^2}{x^2 + 1}$$ Domain: $(-\infty, \infty)$ (since $g(x)$ is never 0.)

33. $(f + g)(x) = f(x) + g(x) = 3x + 5 + x^2 - 1$
$= x^2 + 3x + 4$ Domain: $(-\infty, \infty)$
$(f - g)(x) = f(x) - g(x) = 3x + 5 - (x^2 - 1)$
$= 3x + 5 - x^2 + 1 = -x^2 + 3x + 6$ Domain: $(-\infty, \infty)$
$(fg)(x) = f(x)g(x) = (3x + 5)(x^2 - 1)$
$= 3x^3 - 3x + 5x^2 - 5 = 3x^3 + 5x^2 - 3x - 5$ Domain: $(-\infty, \infty)$

$$\left(\frac{f}{g}\right)(x) = \frac{f(x)}{g(x)} = \frac{3x + 5}{x^2 - 1}$$ Domain: $\{x \mid x \neq \pm 1\}$, or $(-\infty, -1) \cup (-1, 1) \cup (1, \infty)$

35. $(f + g)(x) = f(x) + g(x) = \sqrt{2 - x} + \sqrt{x + 3}$
$(f - g)(x) = f(x) - g(x) = \sqrt{2 - x} - \sqrt{x + 3}$
$(fg)(x) = f(x)g(x) = \sqrt{2 - x}\,\sqrt{x + 3} = \sqrt{(2 - x)(3 + x)} = \sqrt{6 - x - x^2}$

$$\left(\frac{f}{g}\right)(x) = \frac{f(x)}{g(x)} = \frac{\sqrt{2 - x}}{\sqrt{x + 3}} = \sqrt{\frac{2 - x}{x + 3}}$$

The domains of f and g are:
Domain of $f = \{x \mid 2 - x \geq 0\} = (-\infty, 2]$ Domain of $g = \{x \mid x + 3 \geq 0\} = [-3, \infty)$
The intersection of these domains is $[-3, 2]$. This is the domain of the functions of $f + g, f - g$, and fg.

Since $g(-3) = 0$, $x = -3$ must be excluded from the domain of $\dfrac{f}{g}$, so its domain is $(-3, 2]$.

37. $(f + g)(x) = f(x) + g(x) = \sqrt{x} + 2 + \sqrt{x} - 4 = 2\sqrt{x} - 2$
$(f - g)(x) = f(x) - g(x) = \sqrt{x} + 2 - (\sqrt{x} - 4) = \sqrt{x} + 2 - \sqrt{x} + 4 = 6$
$(fg)(x) = f(x)g(x) = (\sqrt{x} + 2)(\sqrt{x} - 4) = x - 2\sqrt{x} - 8$

$$\left(\frac{f}{g}\right)(x) = \frac{f(x)}{g(x)} = \frac{\sqrt{x} + 2}{\sqrt{x} - 4}$$

The domains of f and g are both $\{x \mid x \geq 0\} = [0, \infty)$ This is the domain of $f + g, f - g$, and fg.

We note that in the domain of $\dfrac{f}{g}$, $g(x) \neq 0$. Thus $\sqrt{x} - 4 \neq 0$. To solve this, we solve

$\sqrt{x} - 4 = 0$
$\sqrt{x} = 4$ $\boxed{\textbf{Common Error: } x \neq \sqrt{4}}$
$x = 16$

Hence, 16 must be excluded from $\{x \mid x \geq 0\}$ to find the domain of $\dfrac{f}{g}$.

Domain of $\dfrac{f}{g} = \{x \mid x \geq 0, x \neq 16\} = [0, 16) \cup (16, \infty)$.

39.
$$(f+g)(x) = f(x) + g(x) = \sqrt{x^2 + x - 6} + \sqrt{7 + 6x - x^2}$$
$$(f-g)(x) = f(x) - g(x) = \sqrt{x^2 + x - 6} - \sqrt{7 + 6x - x^2}$$
$$(fg)(x) = f(x)g(x) = \sqrt{x^2 + x - 6}\ \sqrt{7 + 6x - x^2} = \sqrt{-x^4 + 5x^3 + 19x^2 - 29x - 42}$$
$$\left(\frac{f}{g}\right)(x) = \frac{f(x)}{g(x)} = \frac{\sqrt{x^2 + x - 6}}{\sqrt{7 + 6x - x^2}} = \sqrt{\frac{x^2 + x - 6}{7 + 6x - x^2}}$$

The domains of f and g are:
Domain of $f = \{x \mid x^2 + x - 6 \geq 0\} = \{x \mid (x+3)(x-2) \geq 0\} = (-\infty, -3] \cup [2, \infty)$
Domain of $g = \{x \mid 7 + 6x - x^2 \geq 0\} = \{x \mid (7-x)(1+x) \geq 0\} = [-1, 7]$
The intersection of these domains is $[2, 7]$. This is the domain of the functions $f + g$, $f - g$, and fg.
Since $g(x) = 7 + 6x - x^2 = (7-x)(1+x)$, $g(7) = 0$ and $g(-1) = 0$, hence 7 must be excluded from the domain
of $\dfrac{f}{g}$, so its domain is $[2, 7)$.

41.
$$(f+g)(x) = f(x) + g(x) = x + \frac{1}{x} + x - \frac{1}{x} = 2x$$

$$(f-g)(x) = f(x) - g(x) = x + \frac{1}{x} - \left(x - \frac{1}{x}\right) = \frac{2}{x}$$

$$(fg)(x) = f(x)g(x) = \left(x + \frac{1}{x}\right)\left(x - \frac{1}{x}\right) = x^2 - \frac{1}{x^2}$$

$$\left(\frac{f}{g}\right)(x) = \frac{f(x)}{g(x)} = \frac{x + \frac{1}{x}}{x - \frac{1}{x}} = \frac{x^2 + 1}{x^2 - 1}$$

> **Common Error:**
> Domain is not $(-\infty, \infty)$. See below.

The domains of f and g are both $\{x \mid x \neq 0\} = (-\infty, 0) \cup (0, \infty)$.

This is therefore the domain of $f + g$, $f - g$, and fg. To find the domain of $\dfrac{f}{g}$, we must exclude from this

domain the set of values of x for which $g(x) = 0$.
$$x - \frac{1}{x} = 0$$
$$x^2 - 1 = 0$$
$$x^2 = 1$$
$$x = -1, 1$$

Hence, the domain of $\dfrac{f}{g}$ is $\{x \mid x \neq 0, -1, \text{ or } 1\}$ or $(-\infty, -1) \cup (-1, 0) \cup (0, 1) \cup (1, \infty)$.

43. $(f \circ g)(x) = f[g(x)] = f(x^2 - x + 1) = (x^2 - x + 1)^3$ Domain: $(-\infty, \infty)$
$(g \circ f)(x) = g[f(x)] = g(x^3) = (x^3)^2 - x^3 + 1 = x^6 - x^3 + 1$ Domain: $(-\infty, \infty)$

45. $(f \circ g)(x) = f[g(x)] = f(2x + 3) = |2x + 3 + 1| = |2x + 4|$ Domain: $(-\infty, \infty)$
$(g \circ f)(x) = g[f(x)] = g(|x + 1|) = 2|x + 1| + 3$ Domain: $(-\infty, \infty)$

47. $(f \circ g)(x) = f[g(x)] = f(2x^3 + 4) = (2x^3 + 4)^{1/3}$ Domain: $(-\infty, \infty)$
$(g \circ f)(x) = g[f(x)] = g(x^{1/3}) = 2(x^{1/3})^3 + 4 = 2x + 4$ Domain: $(-\infty, \infty)$

49. $(f \circ g)(x) = f[g(x)] = f(x - 4) = \sqrt{x - 4}$ Domain: $\{x \mid x \geq 4\}$ or $[4, \infty)$
$(g \circ f)(x) = g[f(x)] = g(\sqrt{x}) = \sqrt{x} - 4$ Domain: $\{x \mid x \geq 0\}$ or $[0, \infty)$

51. $(f \circ g)(x) = f[g(x)] = f\left(\dfrac{1}{x}\right) = \dfrac{1}{x} + 2$ Domain: $\{x \mid x \neq 0\}$ or $(-\infty, 0) \cup (0, \infty)$

$(g \circ f)(x) = g[f(x)] = g(x + 2) = \dfrac{1}{x + 2}$ Domain: $\{x \mid x \neq -2\}$ or $(-\infty, -2) \cup (-2, \infty)$

53. $(f \circ g)(x) = f[g(x)] = f(x^2) = \sqrt{4 - x^2}$

The domain of f is $(-\infty, 4]$. The domain of g is all real numbers. Hence the domain of $f \circ g$ is the set of those real numbers x for which $g(x)$ is in $(-\infty, 4]$, that is, for which $x^2 \leq 4$, or $-2 \leq x \leq 2$.
Domain of $f \circ g = \{x \mid -2 \leq x \leq 2\} = [-2, 2]$

$(g \circ f)(x) = g[f(x)] = g(\sqrt{4 - x}) = (\sqrt{4 - x})^2 = 4 - x$

The domain of $g \circ f$ is the set of those numbers x in $(-\infty, 4]$ for which $f(x)$ is in $(-\infty, \infty)$, that is, $(-\infty, 4]$.

55. $(f \circ g)(x) = f[g(x)] = f\left(\dfrac{x}{x - 2}\right) = \dfrac{\frac{x}{x-2} + 5}{\frac{x}{x-2}} = \dfrac{x + 5(x - 2)}{x} = \dfrac{x + 5x - 10}{x} = \dfrac{6x - 10}{x}$

The domain of f is $\{x \mid x \neq 0\}$. The domain of g is $\{x \mid x \neq 2\}$. Hence the domain of $f \circ g$ is the set of those numbers in $\{x \mid x \neq 2\}$ for which $g(x)$ is in $\{x \mid x \neq 0\}$. Thus we must exclude from $\{x \mid x \neq 2\}$ those numbers x for which $\dfrac{x}{x - 2} = 0$, or $x = 0$. Hence the domain of $f \circ g$ is $\{x \mid x \neq 0, x \neq 2\}$, or $(-\infty, 0) \cup (0, 2) \cup (2, \infty)$.

$(g \circ f)(x) = g[f(x)] = g\left(\dfrac{x + 5}{x}\right) = \dfrac{\frac{x+5}{x}}{\frac{x+5}{x} - 2} = \dfrac{x + 5}{x + 5 - 2x} = \dfrac{x + 5}{5 - x}$

The domain of $g \circ f$ is the set of those numbers in $\{x \mid x \neq 0\}$ for which $f(x)$ is in $\{x \mid x \neq 2\}$. Thus we must exclude from $\{x \mid x \neq 0\}$ those numbers x for which $\dfrac{x + 5}{x} = 2$, or $x + 5 = 2x$, or $x = 5$. Hence the domain of $g \circ f$ is $\{x \mid x \neq 0, x \neq 5\}$ or $(-\infty, 0) \cup (0, 5) \cup (5, \infty)$.

57. $(f \circ g)(x) = f[g(x)] = f\left(\dfrac{1}{x - 2}\right) = \dfrac{2\left(\frac{1}{x-2}\right) + 1}{\frac{1}{x-2}} = \dfrac{2 + x - 2}{1} = x$

The domain of f is $\{x \mid x \neq 0\}$. The domain of g is $\{x \mid x \neq 2\}$. Hence the domain of $f \circ g$ is the set of those numbers in $\{x \mid x \neq 2\}$ for which $g(x)$ is in $\{x \mid x \neq 0\}$. Thus we must exclude from $\{x \mid x \neq 2\}$ those numbers x for which $\dfrac{1}{x - 2} = 0$; however, there are none. Hence the domain of $f \circ g$ is $\{x \mid x \neq 2\}$ or $(-\infty, 2) \cup (2, \infty)$.

$(g \circ f)(x) = g[f(x)] = g\left(\dfrac{2x + 1}{x}\right) = \dfrac{1}{\frac{2x+1}{x} - 2} = \dfrac{x}{2x + 1 - 2x} = \dfrac{x}{1} = x$

The domain of $g \circ f$ is the set of those numbers in $\{x \mid x \neq 0\}$ for which $f(x)$ is in $\{x \mid x \neq 2\}$. Thus we must exclude from $\{x \mid x \neq 0\}$ those numbers x for which $\dfrac{2x + 1}{x} = 2$; however, there are none. Hence the domain of $g \circ f$ is $\{x \mid x \neq 0\}$ or $(-\infty, 0) \cup (0, \infty)$.

59. $(f \circ g)(x) = f[g(x)] = f(\sqrt{9 + x^2}) = \sqrt{25 - (\sqrt{9 + x^2})^2} = \sqrt{25 - (9 + x^2)} = \sqrt{16 - x^2}$

The domain of f is $[-5, 5]$. The domain of g is $(-\infty, \infty)$. Hence the domain of $f \circ g$ is the set of those real numbers x for which $g(x)$ is in $[-5, 5]$, that is, $\sqrt{9 + x^2} \le 5$, or $9 + x^2 \le 25$, or $x^2 \le 16$, or $-4 \le x \le 4$. Hence the domain of $f \circ g$ is $\{x \mid -4 \le x \le 4\}$ or $[-4, 4]$.

$(g \circ f)(x) = g[f(x)] = g(\sqrt{25 - x^2}) = \sqrt{9 + (\sqrt{25 - x^2})^2} = \sqrt{9 + 25 - x^2} = \sqrt{34 - x^2}$

The domain of $g \circ f$ is the set of those numbers x in $[-5, 5]$ for which $g(x)$ is real. Since $g(x)$ is real for all x, the domain of $g \circ f$ is $[-5, 5]$.

> **Common Error:** The domain of $g \circ f$ is not evident from the final form $\sqrt{34 - x^2}$. It is not $\left[-\sqrt{34}, \sqrt{34}\right]$

In Problems #61 through 63, f and g are linear functions. f has slope –2 and y intercept 2, so
f(x) = –2x + 2. g has slope 1 and y intercept –2, so g(x) = x – 2.

61. $(f + g)(x) = f(x) + g(x) = (-2x + 2) + (x - 2) = -x.$
The graph of $f + g$ is a straight line with slope -1 passing through the origin. This corresponds to graph (d).

63. $(g - f)(x) = g(x) - f(x) = (x - 2) - (-2x + 2) = x - 2 + 2x - 2 = 3x - 4.$
The graph of $g - f$ is a straight line with slope 3 and y intercept -4. This corresponds to graph (a).

65. $(f \circ g)(x) = f[g(x)] = f(2x - 2) = \dfrac{1}{2}(2x - 2) + 1 = x - 1 + 1 = x$

$(g \circ f)(x) = g[f(x)] = g\left(\dfrac{1}{2}x + 1\right) = 2\left(\dfrac{1}{2}x + 1\right) - 2 = x + 2 - 2 = x$

Graphing $f, g, f \circ g$, and $g \circ f$, we obtain the graph at the right.

The graphs of f and g are reflections of each other in the line $y = x$, which is the graph of $f \circ g$ and $g \circ f$.

67. $(f \circ g)(x) = f[g(x)] = f\left(-\dfrac{3}{2}x - \dfrac{5}{2}\right) = -\dfrac{2}{3}\left(-\dfrac{3}{2}x - \dfrac{5}{2}\right) - \dfrac{5}{3} = x + \dfrac{5}{3} - \dfrac{5}{3} = x$

$(g \circ f)(x) = g[f(x)] = g\left(-\dfrac{2}{3}x - \dfrac{5}{3}\right) = -\dfrac{3}{2}\left(-\dfrac{2}{3}x - \dfrac{5}{3}\right) - \dfrac{5}{2} = x + \dfrac{5}{2} - \dfrac{5}{2} = x$

Graphing $f, g, f \circ g$, and $g \circ f$, we obtain the graph at the right.

The graphs of f and g are reflections of each other in the line $y = x$, which is the graph of $f \circ g$ and $g \circ f$.

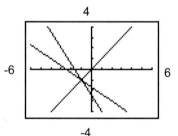

69. $f \circ g(x) = f[g(x)] = f(2\sqrt[3]{x}\,) = \dfrac{\left(2\sqrt[3]{x}\,\right)^3}{8} = \dfrac{8x}{8} = x$

$g \circ f(x) = g[f(x)] = g\left(\dfrac{x^3}{8}\right) = 2\sqrt[3]{\dfrac{x^3}{8}} = 2\left(\dfrac{x}{2}\right) = x$

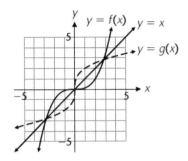

Graphing f, g, $f \circ g$, and $g \circ f$, we obtain the graph at the right.
The graphs of f and g are reflections of each other in the line $y = x$,
which is the graph of $f \circ g$ and $g \circ f$.

71. $f \circ g(x) = f[g(x)] = f(x^3 + 2) = \sqrt[3]{x^3 + 2 - 2} = \sqrt[3]{x^3} = x$

$g \circ f(x) = g[f(x)] = g(\sqrt[3]{x-2}\,) = (\sqrt[3]{x-2}\,)^3 + 2 = x - 2 + 2 = x$

Graphing f, g, $f \circ g$, and $g \circ f$, we obtain the graph at the right.

The graphs of $f \circ g$ and $g \circ f$ are reflections of each other in the line
$y = x$, which is the graph of $f \circ g$ and $g \circ f$.

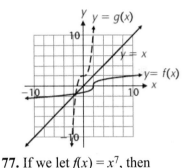

73. If we let $g(x) = 2x - 7$, then

$h(x) = [g(x)]^4$

Now if we let $f(x) = x^4$, we have

$h(x) = [g(x)]^4 = f[g(x)] = (f \circ g)(x)$

75. If we let $g(x) = 4 + 2x$, then

$h(x) = \sqrt{g(x)}$

Now if we let $f(x) = x^{1/2}$, we have

$h(x) = \sqrt{g(x)} = [g(x)]^{1/2}$
$= f[g(x)] = (f \circ g)(x).$

77. If we let $f(x) = x^7$, then
$h(x) = 3f(x) - 5$
Now if we let $g(x) = 3x - 5$, we have
$h(x) = 3f(x) - 5 = g[f(x)] = (g \circ f)(x)$

79. If we let $f(x) = x^{-1/2}$, then

$h(x) = 4f(x) + 3$

Now if we let $g(x) = 4x + 3$, we have

$h(x) = 4f(x) + 3 = g[f(x)] = (g \circ f)(x)$

81. fg and gf are identical, since
$(fg)(x) = f(x)g(x) = g(x)f(x) = (gf)(x)$
by the commutative law for
multiplication of real numbers

83. Yes, the function $g(x) = x$
satisfies these conditions.
$(f \circ g)(x) = f(g(x)) = f(x)$, so $f \circ g = f$
$(g \circ f)(x) = g(f(x)) = f(x)$, so $g \circ f = f$

85.

$(f + g)(x) = f(x) + g(x) = x + \dfrac{1}{x} + x - \dfrac{1}{x} = 2x$

$(f - g)(x) = f(x) - g(x) = x + \dfrac{1}{x} - \left(x - \dfrac{1}{x}\right) = \dfrac{2}{x}$

$(fg)(x) = f(x)g(x) = \left(x + \dfrac{1}{x}\right)\left(x - \dfrac{1}{x}\right) = x^2 - \dfrac{1}{x^2}$

$\left(\dfrac{f}{g}\right)(x) = \dfrac{f(x)}{g(x)} = \dfrac{x + \frac{1}{x}}{x - \frac{1}{x}} = \dfrac{x^2 + 1}{x^2 - 1}$

> **Common Error:**
> Domain is not $(-\infty, \infty)$. See below.

The domains of f and g are both $\{x \mid x \ne 0\} = (-\infty, 0) \cup (0, \infty)$.

This is therefore the domain of $f + g$, $f - g$, and fg. To find the domain of $\dfrac{f}{g}$, we must exclude from this

domain the set of values of x for which $g(x) = 0$.

$$x - \frac{1}{x} = 0$$
$$x^2 - 1 = 0$$
$$x^2 = 1$$
$$x = -1, 1$$

Hence, the domain of $\frac{f}{g}$ is $\{x \mid x \neq 0, -1, \text{ or } 1\}$ or $(-\infty, -1) \cup (-1, 0) \cup (0, 1) \cup (1, \infty)$.

87.
$$(f + g)(x) = f(x) + g(x) = 1 - \frac{x}{|x|} + 1 + \frac{x}{|x|} = 2$$

$$(f - g)(x) = f(x) - g(x) = 1 - \frac{x}{|x|} - \left(1 + \frac{x}{|x|}\right) = 1 - \frac{x}{|x|} - 1 - \frac{x}{|x|} = \frac{-2x}{|x|}$$

$$(fg)(x) = f(x)g(x) = \left(1 - \frac{x}{|x|}\right)\left(1 + \frac{x}{|x|}\right) = (1)^2 - \left(\frac{x}{|x|}\right)^2 = 1 - \frac{x^2}{|x|^2} = 1 - \frac{x^2}{x^2} = 1 - 1 = 0$$

$$\left(\frac{f}{g}\right)(x) = \frac{f(x)}{g(x)} = \frac{1 - \frac{x}{|x|}}{1 + \frac{x}{|x|}} = \frac{|x| - x}{|x| + x}.$$ This can be further simplified

however, when we examine the domain of $\frac{f}{g}$ below.

The domains of f and g are both $\{x \mid x \neq 0\} = (-\infty, 0) \cup (0, \infty)$

This is therefore the domain of $f + g, f - g,$ and fg. To find the domain of $\frac{f}{g}$, we must exclude from this

domain the set of values of x for which $g(x) = 0$.

$$1 + \frac{x}{|x|} = 0$$
$$|x| + x = 0$$
$$|x| = -x$$

This is true when x is negative. The domain of $\frac{f}{g}$ is the positive numbers, $(0, \infty)$.

On this domain, $|x| = x$, so $\left(\frac{f}{g}\right)(x) = \frac{|x| - x}{|x| + x} = \frac{x - x}{x + x} = \frac{0}{2x} = 0$

89. Profit is the difference of the amount of money taken in (Revenue) and the amount of money spent (Cost), so
$$P(x) = R(x) - C(x)$$
$$= \left(20x - \frac{1}{200}x^2\right) - (2x + 8{,}000)$$
$$= 20x - \frac{1}{200}x^2 - 2x - 8{,}000 \text{ (Distribute!)}$$
$$= 18x - \frac{1}{200}x^2 - 8{,}000$$

we have a profit function, but it's a function of the demand (x), not the price (p). We were given $x = 4{,}000 - 200p$, so we can substitute $4{,}000 - 200p$ in for x to get desired function:

$$P(x) = P(4,000 - 200p) = 18(4,000 - 200p) - \frac{1}{200}(4,000 - 200p)^2 - 8,000$$

$$= 72,000 - 3,600p - \frac{1}{200}(16,000,000 - 1,600,000p + 40,000p^2) - 8,000$$

$$= 72,000 - 3,600p - 80,000 + 8,000p - 200p^2 - 8,000$$

$$= -16,000 + 4,400p - 200p^2$$

Now graph the function and use the maximum feature to find the largest profit.

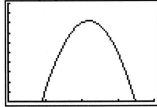

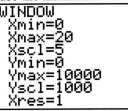
```
WINDOW
 Xmin=0
 Xmax=20
 Xscl=5
 Ymin=0
 Ymax=10000
 Yscl=1000
 Xres=1
```

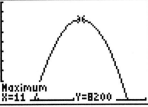
```
Maximum
X=11          Y=8200
```

The maximum is (11, 9,200), so the largest profit occurs when the price is $11.

91. We are given $V(r) = 0.1A(r) = 0.1\pi r^2$ and $r(t) = 0.4t^{1/3}$.

Hence we use composition to express V as a function of the time.

$$(V \circ r)(t) = V[r(t)]$$
$$= 0.1\pi[r(t)]^2$$
$$= 0.1\pi[0.4t^{1/3}]^2$$
$$= 0.1\pi[0.16t^{2/3}]$$
$$= 0.016\pi t^{2/3}$$

We write $V(t) = 0.016\pi t^{2/3}$

93.

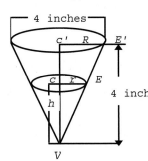

(A) We note: In the figure, triangles VCE and $VC'E'$ are similar. Moreover R = radius of cup = $\frac{1}{2}$ diameter of cup = $\frac{1}{2}(4)$ = 2 inches. Hence $\frac{r}{2} = \frac{h}{4}$ or $r = \frac{1}{2}h$. We write $r(h) = \frac{1}{2}h$.

(B) Since $V = \frac{1}{3}\pi r^2 h$ and $r = \frac{1}{2}h$, $V = \frac{1}{3}\pi\left(\frac{1}{2}h\right)^2 h = \frac{1}{3}\pi\frac{1}{4}h^2 h = \frac{1}{12}\pi h^3$.

We write $V(h) = \frac{1}{12}\pi h^3$.

(C) Since $V(h) = \frac{1}{12}\pi h^3$ and $h(t) = 4 - 0.5\sqrt{t}$, we use composition to express V as a function of t.

$$(V \circ h)(t) = V[h(t)]$$
$$= \frac{1}{12}\pi[h(t)]^3 = \frac{1}{12}\pi(4 - 0.5\sqrt{t})^3$$

Section 3-6

1. The function will be one-to-one if and only if each first component of the ordered pairs corresponds to exactly one second component.

3. If a function is not one-to-one, then at least two input elements correspond to one output element. If the correspondence is reversed, then the result cannot be a function. Example: $\{(1, 3), (2, 3)\}$ when reversed becomes $\{(3, 1), (3, 2)\}$ which is not a function.

5. The result of composing a function with its inverse is the identity function $f(x) = x$. This makes sense because the function and its inverse undo each other's operations.

7. This is a one-to-one function. All of the first coordinates are distinct, and each first coordinate is paired with a different second coordinate. If all of the ordered pairs are reversed, the situation is the same.

9. This is a function but it is not one-to-one. First coordinates 5 and 2 are both paired with 4, and first coordinates 4 and 3 are both paired with 3. If the ordered pairs are reversed, the result is not a function since first coordinates 3 and 4 will each be paired with two different second coordinates.

11. This is not a function: 1 is a first coordinate that is paired with 2 different second coordinates (as is –3). If the ordered pairs are reversed, the result is also not a function since 4 will be a first coordinate paired with 2 different second coordinates (as will 2).

13. One-to-one

15. The range element 7 corresponds to more than one domain element. Not one-to-one.

17. One-to-one

19. Some range elements (0, for example) correspond to more than one domain element. Not one-to-one.

21. One-to-one

23. One-to-one

25. Assume $F(a) = F(b)$
$$\tfrac{1}{2}a + 1 = \tfrac{1}{2}b + 1$$
$$\text{Then } \tfrac{1}{2}a = \tfrac{1}{2}b$$
$$a = b \qquad \text{Therefore } F \text{ is one-to-one.}$$

27. $H(x) = 4x - x^2$
Since $H(1) = 4(1) - 1^2 = 3$ and $H(3) = 4(3) - (3)^2 = 3$, both $(1, 3)$ and $(3, 3)$ belong to H. H is not one-to-one.

29. Assume $M(a) = M(b)$
$$\sqrt{a+1} = \sqrt{b+1}$$
$$\text{Then } a + 1 = b + 1$$
$$a = b \qquad M \text{ is one-to-one.}$$

31. $f(g(x)) = f\left(\dfrac{1}{3}x - \dfrac{5}{3}\right) = 3\left(\dfrac{1}{3}x - \dfrac{5}{3}\right) + 5$
$$= x - 5 + 5 = x$$
$$g(f(x)) = g(3x + 5) = \dfrac{1}{3}(3x + 5) - \dfrac{5}{3} = x + \dfrac{5}{3} - \dfrac{5}{3} = x$$

f and g are inverses

33. $f(g(x)) = f(\sqrt[3]{3-x} - 1) = 2 - ((\sqrt[3]{3-x} - 1) + 1)^3$
$$= 2 - (\sqrt[3]{3-x})^3$$
$$= 2 - (3 - x) = -1 + x$$
f and g are not inverses since $(f \circ g)(x)$ is not x.

35. $f(g(x)) = f\left(\dfrac{3+4x}{2-x}\right) = \dfrac{2\left(\frac{3+4x}{2-x}\right) - 3}{\frac{3+4x}{2-x} + 4} = \dfrac{\frac{6+8x}{2-x} - 3}{\frac{3+4x}{2-x} + 4} = \dfrac{\frac{6+8x}{2-x} - \frac{3(2-x)}{2-x}}{\frac{3+4x}{2-x} + \frac{4(2-x)}{2-x}}$

$$= \dfrac{\frac{6+8x-6+3x}{2-x}}{\frac{3+4x+8-4x}{2-x}} = \dfrac{\frac{11x}{2-x}}{\frac{11}{2-x}} = \dfrac{11x}{2-x} \cdot \dfrac{2-x}{11} = x$$

$$g(f(x)) = g\left(\dfrac{2x-3}{x+4}\right) = \dfrac{3 + 4\left(\frac{2x-3}{x+4}\right)}{2 - \left(\frac{2x-3}{x+4}\right)} = \dfrac{3 + \frac{8x-12}{x+4}}{2 - \frac{2x-3}{x+4}} = \dfrac{\frac{3(x+4)}{x+4} + \frac{8x-12}{x+4}}{\frac{2(x+4)}{x+4} - \frac{2x-3}{x+4}}$$

$$= \dfrac{\frac{3x+12+8x-12}{x+4}}{\frac{2x+8-2x+3}{x+4}} = \dfrac{\frac{11x}{x+4}}{\frac{11}{x+4}} = \dfrac{11x}{x+4} \cdot \dfrac{x+4}{11} = x$$

f and g are inverses.

37. $f(g(x)) = f(\sqrt{x-4}) = 4 + (\sqrt{x-4})^2$
$$= 4 + x - 4 = x$$

$$g(f(x)) = g(4 + x^2) = \sqrt{4 + x^2 - 4}$$

$$= \sqrt{x^2} = x \text{ as long as } x \geq 0.$$
f and g are inverses.

39. $f(g(x)) = f(-\sqrt{1-x}) = 1 - (-\sqrt{1-x})^2 = 1 - (1-x) = x$

$g(f(x)) = g(1-x^2) = -\sqrt{1-(1-x^2)} = -\sqrt{x^2} = -x$ as long as $x \geq 0$.

f and g are not inverses since $g \circ f(x)$ is not x.

41. From the graph:
domain of $f = [-4, 4]$
range of $f = [1, 5]$
Therefore:
domain of $f^{-1} = [1, 5]$
range of $f^{-1} = [-4, 4]$

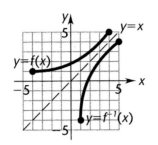

43. From the graph:
domain of $f = [-5, 3]$
range of $f = [-3, 5]$
Therefore:
domain of $f^{-1} = [-3, 5]$
range of $f^{-1} = [-5, 3]$

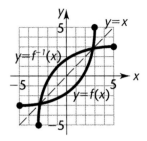

45. The graph of $f(x)$ is a line; f is one-to-one.
The domain of f is therefore $(-\infty, \infty)$ and the range of f is also $(-\infty, \infty)$.

Write $y = f(x)$
$\qquad y = 3x$
Solve $y = 3x$ for x.
$\qquad \dfrac{1}{3}y = x$
Interchange x and y:
$\qquad \dfrac{1}{3}x = y$
$\qquad f^{-1}(x) = \dfrac{1}{3}x$

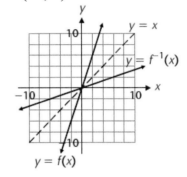

The domain of f^{-1} is $(-\infty, \infty)$ and the range of f^{-1} is $(-\infty, \infty)$.

47. The graph of $f(x)$ is a line; f is one-to-one.
The domain and range of f are therefore $(-\infty, \infty)$.

Write $y = f(x)$
$\qquad y = 4x - 3$
Solve $y = 4x - 3$ for x.
$\qquad y + 3 = 4x$
$\qquad \dfrac{y+3}{4} = x$
Interchange x and y:
$\qquad \dfrac{x+3}{4} = y$
$\qquad f^{-1}(x) = \dfrac{x+3}{4}$

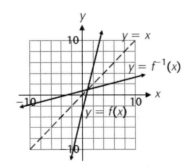

The domain and range of f^{-1} are $(-\infty, \infty)$.

49.   The graph of $f(x)$ is a line; f is one-to-one. The domain and range of f are therefore $(-\infty, \infty)$.

Write $y = f(x)$

$y = 0.2x + 0.4$

Solve for x.

$y - 0.4 = 0.2x$

$5y - 2 = x$

Interchange x and y:

$5x - 2 = y$

$f^{-1}(x) = 5x - 2$

The domain and range of f^{-1} are $(-\infty, \infty)$.

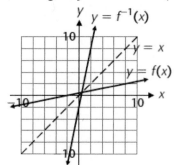

51.   From the graph as shown, f is an increasing function with domain $[0, \infty)$ and range $[3, \infty)$; f is one-to-one.

Write $y = f(x)$

$y = \sqrt{x} + 3$

Solve for x.

$y - 3 = \sqrt{x}$

$(y - 3)^2 = x$

Interchange x and y.

$(x - 3)^2 = y$

$f^{-1}(x) = (x - 3)^2$ domain $[3, \infty)$ range $[0, \infty)$

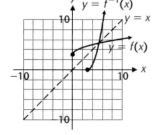

Common error: $f^{-1}(x) \neq (x - 3)^2$ for all x. The graph is only the right-hand half of the parabola.

53.   From the graph as shown, f is a decreasing function with domain $(-\infty, 16]$ and range $[0, \infty)$; f is one-to-one.

Write $y = f(x)$.

$$y = \frac{1}{2}\sqrt{16 - x}$$

Solve for x.

$2y = \sqrt{16 - x}$

$4y^2 = 16 - x$

$x = 16 - 4y^2$

Interchange x and y.

$y = 16 - 4x^2$

$f^{-1}(x) = 16 - 4x^2$ domain $[0, \infty)$ range $(-\infty, 16]$

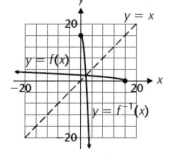

55.   From the graph as shown, f is a decreasing function with domain $[1, \infty)$ and range $(-\infty, 3]$; f is one-to-one.

Write $y = f(x)$.

$y = 3 - \sqrt{x - 1}$

Solve for x.

$y - 3 = -\sqrt{x - 1}$

$(y - 3)^2 = x - 1$

$(y - 3)^2 + 1 = x$

Interchange x and y.

$y = (x - 3)^2 + 1$

$f^{-1}(x) = (x - 3)^2 + 1$ domain $(-\infty, 3]$

range $[1, \infty)$

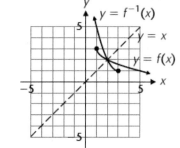

57. The graph of f is the right-hand half of a parabola; f is one-to-one.
The domain of f is $[0, \infty)$ and the range is $[5, \infty)$.

Write $y = f(x)$.

$$y = x^2 + 5 \qquad x \geq 0$$

Solve for x.

$$y - 5 = x^2 \qquad x \geq 0$$

$$\sqrt{y-5} = x \qquad x \geq 0$$

(note: only the positive square root is correct)

Interchange x and y.

$$y = \sqrt{x-5} \qquad y \geq 0$$

$$f^{-1}(x) = \sqrt{x-5} \qquad \text{domain } [5, \infty)$$
$$\text{range } [0, \infty)$$

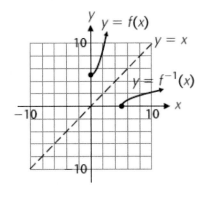

59. The graph of f is the left-hand half of a parabola; f is one-to-one.
The domain of f is $(-\infty, 0]$ and the range is $(-\infty, 4]$.

Write $y = f(x)$.

$$y = 4 - x^2 \qquad x \leq 0$$

Solve for x.

$$y - 4 = -x^2 \qquad x \leq 0$$

$$4 - y = x^2 \qquad x \leq 0$$

$$-\sqrt{4-y} = x \qquad x \leq 0$$

(note: only the negative square root is correct)

Interchange x and y.

$$y = -\sqrt{4-x} \qquad y \leq 0$$

$$f^{-1}(x) = -\sqrt{4-x} \qquad \text{domain } (-\infty, 4]$$
$$\text{range } (-\infty, 0]$$

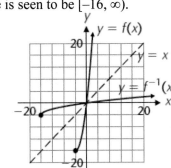

61. The graph of f is the right-hand half of a parabola; f is one-to-one.

Write $x^2 + 8x = (x^2 + 8x + 16) - 16 = (x + 4)^2 - 16$

Then the domain of f is given as $[-4, \infty)$ and the range is seen to be $[-16, \infty)$.

Write $y = f(x)$.

$$y = (x + 4)^2 - 16 \qquad x \geq -4$$

Solve for x.

$$y + 16 = (x + 4)^2 \qquad x \geq -4$$

$$\sqrt{y+16} = x + 4 \qquad x \geq -4$$

$$\sqrt{y+16} - 4 = x \qquad x \geq -4$$

Interchange x and y.

$$y = \sqrt{x+16} - 4 \qquad y \geq -4$$

$$f^{-1}(x) = \sqrt{x+16} - 4 \qquad \text{domain } [-16, \infty)$$
$$\text{range } [-4, \infty)$$

63.   The graph of f is the left-hand half of a parabola; f is one-to-one.
The domain of f is $(-\infty, 2]$ and the range is $[0, \infty)$.
Write $y = f(x)$.

$y = (2 - x)^2$ $x \le 2$

Solve for x.

$\sqrt{y} = 2 - x$ $x \le 2$

$x = 2 - \sqrt{y}$ $x \le 2$

Interchange x and y.

$y = 2 - \sqrt{x}$ $y \le 2$

$f^{-1}(x) = 2 - \sqrt{x}$ domain $[0, \infty)$
                                range $(-\infty, 2]$

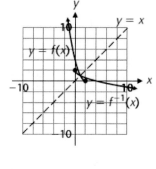

65.   The graph of f is the right-hand half of a parabola; f is one-to-one.
The domain of f is $[1, \infty)$ and the range is $[2, \infty)$.

Write $y = f(x)$.

$y = (x - 1)^2 + 2$ $x \ge 1$

Solve for x.

$y - 2 = (x - 1)^2$ $x \ge 1$

$\sqrt{y - 2} = x - 1$ $x \ge 1$

$1 + \sqrt{y - 2} = x$ $x \ge 1$

Interchange x and y.

$y = 1 + \sqrt{x - 2}$ $y \ge 1$

$f^{-1}(x) = 1 + \sqrt{x - 2}$ domain $[2, \infty)$
                                  range $[1, \infty)$

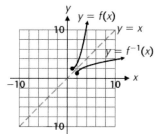

67.   The graph of f is the left-hand half of a parabola; f is one-to-one.
Write $x^2 + 2x - 2 = (x^2 + 2x + 1) - 1 - 2 = (x + 1)^2 - 3$
Then the domain of f is given as $(-\infty, -1]$ and the range is seen to be $[-3, \infty)$.
Write $y = f(x)$.

$y = (x + 1)^2 - 3$ $x \le -1$

Solve for x.

$y + 3 = (x + 1)^2$ $x \le -1$

$-\sqrt{y + 3} = x + 1$ $x \le -1$

$-\sqrt{y + 3} - 1 = x$ $x \le -1$

Interchange x and y.

$y = -\sqrt{x + 3} - 1$ $y \le -1$

$f^{-1}(x) = -\sqrt{x + 3} - 1$ domain $[-3, \infty)$
                                    range $(-\infty, -1]$

69. From the graph as shown, f is an increasing function with domain $[0, 3]$ and range $[-3, 0]$; f is one-to-one. Write $y = f(x)$.

$$y = -\sqrt{9 - x^2} \qquad\qquad 0 \leq x \leq 3$$

Solve for x.

$$y^2 = 9 - x^2 \qquad\qquad 0 \leq x \leq 3$$
$$x^2 = 9 - y^2 \qquad\qquad 0 \leq x \leq 3$$
$$x = \sqrt{9 - y^2} \qquad\qquad 0 \leq x \leq 3$$

Interchange x and y.

$$y = \sqrt{9 - x^2} \qquad\qquad 0 \leq y \leq 3$$
$$f^{-1}(x) = \sqrt{9 - x^2} \qquad\qquad \text{domain } [-3, 0]$$
$$\text{range } [0, 3]$$

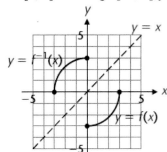

71. From the graph as shown, f is an increasing function with domain $[-3, 0]$ and range $[0, 3]$; f is one-to-one. Write $y = f(x)$.

$$y = \sqrt{9 - x^2} \qquad\qquad -3 \leq x \leq 0$$

Solve for x.

$$y^2 = 9 - x^2 \qquad\qquad -3 \leq x \leq 0$$
$$x^2 = 9 - y^2 \qquad\qquad -3 \leq x \leq 0$$
$$x = -\sqrt{9 - y^2} \qquad\qquad -3 \leq x \leq 0$$

Interchange x and y.

$$y = -\sqrt{9 - x^2} \qquad\qquad -3 \leq y \leq 0$$
$$f^{-1}(x) = -\sqrt{9 - x^2} \quad \text{domain } [0, 3] \quad \text{range } [-3, 0]$$

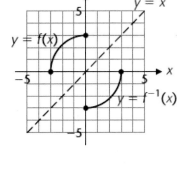

73. From the graph as shown, f is a decreasing function with domain $[-1, 0]$ and range $[0, 1]$; f is one-to-one. Write $y = f(x)$.

$$y = 1 - \sqrt{1 - x^2} \qquad\qquad -1 \leq x \leq 0$$

Solve for x.

$$y - 1 = -\sqrt{1 - x^2} \qquad\qquad -1 \leq x \leq 0$$
$$(y - 1)^2 = 1 - x^2 \qquad\qquad -1 \leq x \leq 0$$
$$y^2 - 2y + 1 = 1 - x^2 \qquad\qquad -1 \leq x \leq 0$$
$$x^2 = 2y - y^2 \qquad\qquad -1 \leq x \leq 0$$
$$x = -\sqrt{2y - y^2} \qquad\qquad -1 \leq x \leq 0$$

Interchange x and y.

$$y = -\sqrt{2x - x^2} \qquad\qquad -1 \leq y \leq 0$$
$$f^{-1}(x) = -\sqrt{2x - x^2} \quad \text{domain } [0, 1] \quad \text{range } [-1, 0]$$

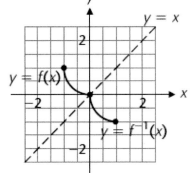

75. Write $y = f(x)$ $\quad y = 3 - \dfrac{2}{x}$

Solve for x.

$$y - 3 = -\dfrac{2}{x}$$
$$x(y - 3) = -2$$
$$x = \dfrac{-2}{y - 3}$$
$$x = \dfrac{2}{3 - y}$$

Interchange x and y.

$$y = \dfrac{2}{3 - x}$$
$$f^1(x) = \dfrac{2}{3 - x}$$

(The student should check that $f \circ f^1(x) = x$ and $f^1 \circ f(x) = x$.)

77. Write $y = f(x)$. $\quad y = \dfrac{2}{x - 1}$

Solve for x.

$$(x - 1)y = 2$$
$$x - 1 = \dfrac{2}{y}$$
$$x = 1 + \dfrac{2}{y}$$
$$x = \dfrac{y}{y} + \dfrac{2}{y}$$
$$x = \dfrac{2 + y}{y}$$

Interchange x and y.

$$y = \dfrac{2 + x}{x}$$
$$f^1(x) = \dfrac{2 + x}{x}$$

79. Write $y = f(x)$. $y = \dfrac{2x}{x + 1}$

Solve for x.

$$y(x + 1) = 2x$$
$$xy + y = 2x$$
$$y = 2x - xy$$
$$y = x(2 - y)$$
$$x = \dfrac{y}{2 - y}$$

Interchange x and y.

$$y = \dfrac{x}{2 - x}$$
$$f^1(x) = \dfrac{x}{2 - x}$$

81. Write $y = f(x)$. $\quad y = \dfrac{2x + 5}{3x - 4}$

Solve for x.

$$y(3x - 4) = 2x + 5$$
$$3xy - 4y = 2x + 5$$
$$3xy - 2x = 4y + 5$$
$$x(3y - 2) = 4y + 5$$
$$x = \dfrac{4y + 5}{3y - 2}$$

Interchange x and y.

$$y = \dfrac{4x + 5}{3x - 2}$$
$$f^1(x) = \dfrac{4x + 5}{3x - 2}$$

83. Write $y = f(x)$. $\quad y = 4 - \sqrt[5]{x + 2}$

Solve for x.

$$y - 4 = -\sqrt[5]{x + 2}$$
$$4 - y = \sqrt[5]{x + 2}$$
$$(4 - y)^5 = x + 2$$
$$x = (4 - y)^5 - 2$$

Interchange x and y.

$$y = (4 - x)^5 - 2$$
$$f^1(x) = (4 - x)^5 - 2$$

85. Since in passing from a function to its inverse, x and y are interchanged, the x intercept of f is the y intercept of f^1 and the y intercept of f is the x intercept of f^1.

87. They are not inverses. The function $f(x) = x^2$ is not one-to-one, so does not have an inverse. If that function is restricted to the domain $[0, \infty)$, then it is one-to-one, and $g(x) = \sqrt{x}$ (which has range $[0, \infty)$) is its inverse.

In problems 89-91, there is more than one possible answer.

89. $f(x) = (2 - x)^2$ One possible answer: domain $x \le 2$

Solve $y = f(x)$ for x:

$$y = (2 - x)^2 \qquad x \le 2$$
$$\sqrt{y} = 2 - x$$

Positive square root
Only since $2 - x \ge 0$

Check:

$$f^{-1}[f(x)] = 2 - \sqrt{(2 - x)^2}$$
$$= 2 - (2 - x) \text{ since } 2 - x \ge 0 \text{ in the domain of } f$$
$$= 2 - 2 + x$$
$$= x$$
$$f[f^{-1}(x)] = [2 - (2 - \sqrt{x})]^2$$

$$\sqrt{y} - 2 = -x$$

$$x = 2 - \sqrt{y} = f^{-1}(y)$$

Interchange x and y:

$$y = f^{-1}(x) = 2 - \sqrt{x} \quad \text{Domain: } x \geq 0$$

$$= [2 - 2 + \sqrt{x}]^2$$
$$= [\sqrt{x}]^2$$
$$= x$$
$$f^{-1}(x) = 2 - \sqrt{x}$$

91. $f(x) = \sqrt{4x - x^2}$

One possible answer: domain $0 \leq x \leq 2$

Solve $y = f(x)$ for x:

$$y = \sqrt{4x - x^2}$$
$$y^2 = 4x - x^2 \qquad y \geq 0$$
$$-y^2 = x^2 - 4x$$
$$4 - y^2 = x^2 - 4x + 4$$
$$4 - y^2 = (x - 2)^2$$
$$\underbrace{-\sqrt{4 - y^2}}_{} = x - 2$$

negative square root only because $x \leq 2$

$$x = 2 - \sqrt{4 - y^2} \quad y \geq 0 \quad f^{-1}(y) = 2 - \sqrt{4 - y^2}$$

Interchange x and y:

$$y = f^{-1}(x) = 2 - \sqrt{4 - x^2} \quad \text{Domain: } 0 \leq x \leq 2$$

Check: $f^{-1}[f(x)] = 2 - \sqrt{4 - (\sqrt{4x - x^2})^2}$

$$= 2 - \sqrt{4 - (4x - x^2)}$$
$$= 2 - \sqrt{4 - 4x + x^2}$$
$$= 2 - \sqrt{(2 - x)^2}$$
$$= 2 - (2 - x) \text{ since } 2 - x \geq 0$$
$$= x$$

$$f[f^{-1}(x)] = \sqrt{4(2 - \sqrt{4 - x^2}) - (2 - \sqrt{4 - x^2})^2}$$

$$= \sqrt{8 - 4\sqrt{4 - x^2} - (4 - 4\sqrt{4 - x^2} + 4 - x^2)}$$
$$= \sqrt{8 - 4\sqrt{4 - x^2} - 4 + 4\sqrt{4 - x^2} - 4 + x^2}$$
$$= \sqrt{x^2}$$
$$= x \text{ since } 0 \leq x$$

$$f^{-1}(x) = 2 - \sqrt{4 - x^2}, \, 0 \leq x \leq 2$$

93. $p = 100 + 5h \quad$ domain $[0, \infty)$ range $[100, \infty)$.

Solve for h

$$p - 100 = 5h$$

$$h = \frac{1}{5}(p - 100) = \frac{1}{5}p - 20 \quad \text{domain } [100, \infty)$$

95. (A) From the graph, d is a decreasing function with domain $[10, 70]$, hence its range is from $d(70) = 200$ to $d(10) = 1{,}000$, $[200, 1000]$

(B) $\quad q = \dfrac{3{,}000}{0.2p + 1}$

Solve for p.

$$q(0.2p + 1) = 3{,}000$$

$$0.2p + 1 = \frac{3{,}000}{q}$$

$$0.2p = \frac{3{,}000}{q} - 1$$

$$p = 5\left(\frac{3{,}000}{q} - 1\right)$$

$$d^{-1}(q) = p = \frac{15{,}000}{q} - 5$$

domain $[200, 1{,}000]$, range $[10, 70]$.

97. (A) If r is linearly related to w, then we are looking for a function whose graph passes through

$(w_1, r_1) = (6, 10.50)$ and $(w_2, r_2) = (10, 15.50)$.

We find the slope, then we use the point-slope form to find the equation.

$$M = \frac{r_2 - r_1}{w_2 - w_1} = \frac{15.50 - 10.50}{10 - 6} = 1.25$$
$$r - r_1 = M(w - w_1)$$
$$r - 10.50 = 1.25(w - 6)$$
$$r - 10.50 = 1.25w - 7.5$$
$$r = m(w) = 1.25w + 3 \quad \text{domain } [0, \infty),$$
$$\text{range } [3, \infty)$$

(B) Solve $r = 1.25w + 3$ for w.
$$r - 3 = 1.25w$$
$$0.8(r - 3) = w$$
$$m^{-1}(r) = w = 0.8r - 2.4 \quad \text{domain } [3, \infty),$$
$$\text{range } [0, \infty)$$

99. $L = 0.06s^2 - 1.2s + 26$ domain $[10, \infty)$
Complete the square to find the range.
$L = 0.06(s^2 - 20s + ?) + 26$
$L = 0.06(s^2 - 20s + 100) - 6 + 26$
$L = 0.06(s - 10)^2 + 20$ therefore, range $[20, \infty)$
Solve for s.

$$L - 20 = 0.06(s - 10)^2$$

$$\frac{50}{3}(L - 20) = (s - 10)^2$$

$$\sqrt{\frac{50}{3}(L - 20)} = s - 10 \quad \text{(positive square root only, since } s \geq 10)$$

$$f^{-1}(L) = s = 10 + \sqrt{\frac{50}{3}(L - 20)} \quad \text{domain } [20, \infty), \text{ range } [10, \infty)$$

CHAPTER 3 REVIEW

1. (A) A function   (B) A function
(C) Not a function; two range elements correspond to the domain element 10.   *(3-1)*

2. (A) All of the first coordinates are distinct, so this is a function with domain {1, 2, 3}. All of the second coordinates are distinct, so the function is one-to-one. The range is {1, 4, 9}. The inverse function is obtained by reversing the order of the ordered pairs: {(1, 1), (4, 2), (9, 3)}. It has domain {1, 4, 9} and range {1, 2, 3}.
(B) This is not a function: both 1 and 2 are first coordinates that get matched with two different second coordinates.
(C) All of the first coordinates are distinct, so this is a function with domain {Albany, Utica, Akron, Dayton}. The range is {New York, Ohio}. It is not one-to-one since two first components are matched with Ohio, for example.
(D) All of the first components are distinct, so this is a function with domain {Albany, Akron, Tucson, Atlanta, Muncie}. The range is {New York, Ohio, Arizona, Georgia, Indiana}. All of the second components are distinct, so the function is one-to-one. The inverse function is {(New York, Albany), (Ohio, Akron), (Arizona, Tucson), (Georgia, Atlanta), (Indiana, Muncie)}. The domain of the inverse function is {New York, Ohio, Arizona, Georgia, Indiana}. The range of the inverse is {Albany, Akron, Tucson, Atlanta, Muncie}.   *(3-1, 3-6)*

3. If there is at least one team that has won more than one Super Bowl, then the correspondence is not a function because one input (team) will correspond with more than one output (year). There are several teams that have won at least two Super Bowls, so this is not a function.   *(3-6)*

4. (A)   Not a function (fails vertical line test)
(B)   A function
(C)   A function
(D)   Not a function (fails vertical line test)   *(3-1)*

5. (A) Function
(B) Not a function—two range elements correspond to some domain elements; for example 2 and –2 correspond to 4.
(C) Function
(D) Not a function—two range elements correspond to some domain elements; for example 2 and –2 correspond to 2.   *(3-1)*

6. $f(2) = 3(2) + 5 = 11$
$g(-2) = 4 - (-2)^2 = 0$
$k(0) = 5$
Therefore
$f(2) + g(-2) + k(0)$
$= 11 + 0 + 5 = 16$ $(3\text{-}1)$

7. $m(-2) = 2|-2| - 1 = 3$
$g(2) = 4 - (2)^2 = 0$
Therefore $\dfrac{m(-2) + 1}{g(2) + 4} = \dfrac{3 + 1}{0 + 4} = 1$ $(3\text{-}1)$

8. $\dfrac{f(2 + h) - f(2)}{h} = \dfrac{[3(2 + h) + 5] - [3(2) + 5]}{h}$
$= \dfrac{6 + 3h + 5 - 11}{h}$
$= \dfrac{3h}{h}$
$= 3$ $(3\text{-}1)$

9. $\dfrac{g(a + h) - g(a)}{h} = \dfrac{[4 - (a + h)^2] - [4 - a^2]}{h}$
$= \dfrac{4 - a^2 - 2ah - h^2 - 4 + a^2}{h}$
$= \dfrac{-2ah - h^2}{h}$
$= \dfrac{h(-2a - h)}{h} = -2a - h$ $(3\text{-}1)$

10. $(f + g)(x) = f(x) + g(x)$
$= 3x + 5 + 4 - x^2 = 9 + 3x - x^2$ $(3\text{-}5)$

11. $(f - g)(x) = f(x) - g(x) = 3x + 5 - (4 - x^2)$
$= 3x + 5 - 4 + x^2 = x^2 + 3x + 1$ $(3\text{-}5)$

12. $(fg)(x) = f(x)g(x) = (3x + 5)(4 - x^2)$
$= 12x - 3x^3 + 20 - 5x^2$
$= 20 + 12x - 5x^2 - 3x^3$ $(3\text{-}5)$

13. $\left(\dfrac{f}{g}\right)(x) = \dfrac{f(x)}{g(x)} = \dfrac{3x + 5}{4 - x^2}$
Domain: $\{x \mid 4 - x^2 \neq 0\}$ or $\{x \mid x \neq \pm 2\}$ $(3\text{-}5)$

14. $(f \circ g)(x) = f[g(x)] = f(4 - x^2) = 3(4 - x^2) + 5$
$= 12 - 3x^2 + 5 = 17 - 3x^2$ $(3\text{-}5)$

15. $(g \circ f)(x) = g[f(x)] = g(3x + 5) = 4 - (3x + 5)^2$
$= 4 - (9x^2 + 30x + 25) = 4 - 9x^2 - 30x - 25$
$= -21 - 30x - 9x^2$ $(3\text{-}5)$

16. (A) $f(1) = (1)^2 - 2(1) = -1$
(B) $f(-4) = (-4)^2 - 2(-4) = 24$
(C) $f(2) \cdot f(-1) = [(2)^2 - 2(2)] \cdot [(-1)^2 - 2(-1)]$
$= 0 \cdot 3 = 0$
(D) $\dfrac{f(0)}{f(3)} = \dfrac{(0)^2 - 2(0)}{(3)^2 - 2(3)} = \dfrac{0}{3} = 0$ $(3\text{-}5)$

17. When $x = -4$, the corresponding value of $f(x)$ on the graph is 4. $f(-4) = 4$.
When $x = 0$, the corresponding value of $f(x)$ on the graph is -4. $f(0) = -4$.
When $x = 3$, the corresponding value of $f(x)$ on the graph is 0. $f(3) = 0$.
When $x = 5$, there is no corresponding value of $f(x)$ on the graph.
$f(5)$ is not defined. $(3\text{-}1, 3\text{-}2)$

18. Two values of x correspond to $f(x) = -2$ on the graph. They are $x = -2$ and $x = 1$. $(3\text{-}1, 3\text{-}2)$

19. Domain: $[-4, 5)$. Range: $[-4, 4]$ $(3\text{-}2)$

20. The graph is increasing on $[0, 5)$ and decreasing on $[-4, 0]$. $(3\text{-}2)$

21. The graph is discontinuous at $x = 0$. $(3\text{-}2)$

22. Construct a table of values of $f(x)$ and $g(x)$ from the graph, then subtract to obtain $(f-g)(x)$.

x	-3	-2	-1	0	1	2	3
$f(x)$	3	2	1	0	1	2	3
$g(x)$	-4	-3	-2	-1	0	1	2
$(f-g)(x)$	7	5	3	1	1	1	1

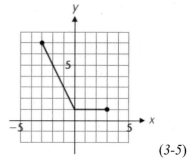

(3-5)

23. Use the top 3 rows of the table in problem 22 and multiply to get a table of values for $(fg)(x)$.

(Note that from the graphs of f and g, we can see that

$$f\left(\frac{1}{2}\right) = \frac{1}{2} \text{ and } g\left(\frac{1}{2}\right) = -\frac{1}{2}, \text{ so } (fg)\left(\frac{1}{2}\right) = -\frac{1}{4}.)$$

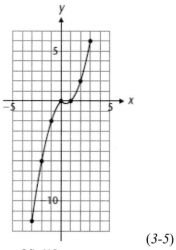

(3-5)

24. $(f \circ g)(-1) = f[g(-1)]$.
From the graph of g, $g(-1) = -2$.
From the graph of f, $f[g(-1)] = f(-2) = 2$. *(3-5)*

25. $g \circ f(-2) = g[f(-2)]$.
From the graph of f, $f(-2) = 2$.
From the graph of g, $g[f(-2)] = g(2) = 1$. *(3-5)*

26. From the graph of g, $g(1) = 0$.
From the graph of f, $f[g(1)] = f(0) = 0$. *(3-5)*

27. From the graph of f, $f(-3) = 3$.
From the graph of g, $g[f(-3)] = g(3) = 2.(3-5)$

28. Some range elements (1 for example) correspond to more than one domain element. Not one-to-one. *(3-6)*

29. Yes, one-to-one. *(3-6)*

30.   (A) $f(-x) = (-x)^5 + 6(-x) = -x^5 - 6x$
$= -(x^5 + 6x) = -f(x)$. Odd
(B) $g(-t) = (-t)^4 + 3(-t)^2 = t^4 + 3t^2 = g(t)$. Even
(C) $h(-z) = (-z)^5 + 4(-z)^2 = -z^5 + 4z^2$
$-h(z) = -(z^5 + 4z^2) = -z^5 - 4z^2$
Therefore, $h(-z) \neq h(z)$; $h(-z) \neq -h(z)$.
h is neither even nor odd.

(3-2)

31. The graph of $f(x)$ is shifted up 1 unit.

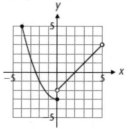

(3-3)

32. The graph of $f(x)$ is shifted left 1 unit

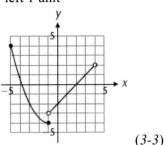

$(3-3)$

33. The graph of $f(x)$ is reflected in the x axis.

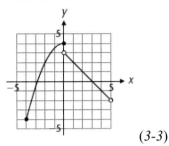

$(3-3)$

34. The graph of $f(x)$ is vertically shrunk by a factor of 0.5.

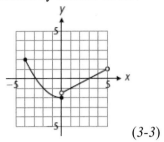

$(3-3)$

35. The graph is horizontally shrunk by a factor of $\dfrac{1}{2}$.

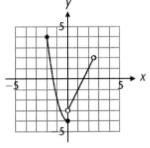

$(3-3)$

36. The graph is reflected about both axes.

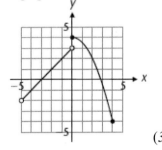

$(3-3)$

37. (A) The graph that is decreasing, then increasing, and has a minimum at $x = 2$ is g.

(B) The graph that is increasing, then decreasing, and has a maximum at $x = -2$ is m.

(C) The graph that is increasing, then decreasing, and has a maximum at $x = 2$ is n.

(D) The graph that is decreasing, then increasing, and has a minimum at $x = -2$ is f. $(3-3)$

38. The equation corresponding to graph f is $y = (x + 2)^2 - 4$.

(A) y intercept: Set $x = 0$, then $y = (0 + 2)^2 - 4 = 0$
  x intercepts: Set $y = 0$, then $0 = (x + 2)^2 - 4$
  $$(x + 2)^2 = 4$$
  $$x + 2 = \pm 2$$
  $$x = 0, -4$$

(B) $(-2, -4)$

(C) The minimum of -4 occurs at the vertex.

(D) Since y is never less than -4, the range is $[-4, \infty)$.

(E) y is increasing on $[-2, \infty)$.

(F) y is decreasing on $(-\infty, -2]$. $(3-4)$

39. (A) $\left(\dfrac{f}{g}\right)(x) = \dfrac{f(x)}{g(x)} = \dfrac{x^2 - 4}{x + 3}$ Domain: $\{x \mid x \neq -3\}$, or $(-\infty, -3) \cup (-3, \infty)$

(B) $\left(\dfrac{g}{f}\right)(x) = \dfrac{g(x)}{f(x)} = \dfrac{x + 3}{x^2 - 4}$ Domain: $\{x \mid x^2 - 4 \neq 0\}$, or $\{x \mid x \neq -2, 2\}$ or $(-\infty, -2) \cup (-2, 2) \cup (2, \infty)$

(C) $(f \circ g)(x) = f[g(x)] = f(x + 3) = (x + 3)^2 - 4 = x^2 + 6x + 5$ Domain: $(-\infty, \infty)$

(D) $(g \circ f)(x) = g[f(x)] = g(x^2 - 4) = x^2 - 4 + 3 = x^2 - 1$ Domain: $(-\infty, \infty)$ $(3-5)$

40. (A) Comparing with the vertex $N f(x) = a(x - h)^2 + k$, we see that since $a = -2$ is negative, the function has a maximum $h = -4$ and $k = -10$ at $x = -4$. The maximum value is $f(-4) = -10$.
The vertex is at $(h, k) = (-4, -10)$.

(B) $f(x) = x^2 - 6x + 11$. Complete the square:
  $f(x) = (x^2 - 6x + 9) - 9 + 11$
  $\qquad = (x - 3)^2 + 2$
Comparing with $f(x) = a(x - h)^2 + k$; $h = 3$ and $k = 2$. Thus, the minimum value is 2 and the vertex is $(3, 2)$. $(3-4)$

41. $q(x) = 2x^2 - 14x + 3$
$\quad = 2(x^2 - 7x) + 3$

$\frac{1}{2}(-7) = -\frac{7}{2}, \quad \left(-\frac{7}{2}\right)^2 = \frac{49}{4}$

$\quad = 2(x^2 - 7x + \frac{49}{4}) - \frac{49}{2} + 3 \quad$ We actually added $2\left(\frac{49}{4}\right)$ so subtract $\frac{49}{2}$

$\quad = 2(x - \frac{7}{2})^2 - \frac{49}{2} + \frac{6}{2}$

$q(x) = 2(x - \frac{7}{2})^2 - \frac{43}{2}$

(3-4)

42.
(A) Reflected across x axis
(B) Shifted down 3 units
(C) Shifted left 3 units

(3-5)

43. (A) When $x = 0$, the corresponding y value on the graph is 0, to the nearest integer.
(B) When $x = 1$, the corresponding y value on the graph is 1, to the nearest integer.
(C) When $x = 2$, the corresponding y value on the graph is 2, to the nearest integer.
(D) When $x = -2$, the corresponding y value on the graph is 0, to the nearest integer. *(3-2)*

44. (A) Two values of x correspond to $y = 0$ on the graph. To the nearest integer, they are -2 and 0.
(B) Two values of x correspond to $y = 1$ on the graph. To the nearest integer, they are -1 and 1.
(C) No value of x corresponds to $y = -3$ on the graph.
(D) To the nearest integer, $x = 3$ corresponds to $y = 3$ on the graph. Also, every value of x such that $x < -2$ corresponds to $y = 3$. *(3-2)*

45. Domain: $(-\infty, \infty)$. Range: $(-3, \infty)$. *(3-2)*

46. Increasing: $[-2, -1]$, $[1, \infty)$. Decreasing: $[-1, 1)$. Constant: $(-\infty, -2)$ *(3-2)*

47. The graph of q is discontinuous at $x = -2$ and $x = 1$. *(3-2)*

48. $f(x) = 4x^3 - \sqrt{x}$ *(3-1)*

49. The function f multiplies the square of the domain element by 3, adds 4 times the domain element, and then subtracts 6. *(3-1)*

50. This equation defines a function. If you solve the equation for y, you get $y = 5 - 0.5x$. This tells us that for any choice of x, we can calculate a unique y that corresponds to it. *(3-1)*

51. This equation does not define a function since most choices of x will result in two corresponding values of y. For example, the pairs $(2, 2)$ and $(2, -2)$ both make the equation a true statement. *(3-1)*

52. Since $m(x)$ is a polynomial, the domain is the set of all real numbers R, $(-\infty, \infty)$.
To find the x intercepts, solve $m(x) = 0$:
$$x^2 - 4x + 5 = 0$$
$$x = \frac{-(-4) \pm \sqrt{(-4)^2 - 4(1)(5)}}{2(1)}$$
$$x = \frac{4 \pm \sqrt{-4}}{2} \quad \text{(no real solutions)}$$
There are no x intercepts. The y intercept is $m(0) = 0^2 - 4(0) + 5 = 5$. *(3-1, 3-2)*

53. The domain is the set of all real numbers for which $\sqrt{x}$ is defined, that is, $[0, \infty)$. Since $2 + 3\sqrt{x}$ is never less than 2, $r(x)$ is never 0 and there are no x intercepts. The y intercept is $r(0) = 2 + 3\sqrt{0} = 2$. *(3-1, 3-2)*

54. The rational expression $\frac{1 - x^2}{x^3}$ is defined everywhere except at zeros of the denominator, $x = 0$. The domain is $(-\infty, 0) \cup (0, \infty)$.
A rational expression is 0 if and only if the numerator is zero:

$$1 - x^2 = 0$$
$$1 = x^2$$
$$x = \pm 1$$

The x intercepts of p are -1, 1. The y intercept is $p(0)$, which is not defined, so there is no y intercept. *(3-1, 3-2)*

55. The fractional expression $\dfrac{x}{\sqrt{3-x}}$ is defined everywhere except at zeros of the denominator, as long as

$\sqrt{3-x}$ is defined, thus
$$3 - x > 0$$
$$x < 3$$

The domain is $(-\infty, 3)$. A fractional expression is 0 if and only if the numerator is 0.

Thus $x = 0$ is the x intercept. The y intercept is $f(0) = \dfrac{0}{\sqrt{3-0}} = 0$.   *(3-1, 3-2)*

56. The rational expression $\dfrac{2x+3}{x^2-4}$ is defined everywhere except at zeros of the denominator.

$$x^2 - 4 = 0$$
$$x^2 = 4$$
$$x = \pm 2$$

The domain is $(-\infty, -2) \cup (-2, 2) \cup (2, \infty)$.
A rational expression is 0 if and only if the numerator is 0.
$$2x + 3 = 0$$
$$x = -\frac{3}{2}$$

The x intercept is $-\dfrac{3}{2}$ or -1.5. The y intercept is $g(0) = \dfrac{2(0)+3}{0^2-4} = -\dfrac{3}{4}$ or -0.75.   *(3-1, 3-2)*

57. The fractional expression $\dfrac{1}{4-\sqrt{x}}$ is defined everywhere except at zeros of the denominator, as long as

$\sqrt{x}$ is defined, thus we must restrict $x \geq 0$ as well as $4 - \sqrt{x}$ to being non-zero.
$$4 - \sqrt{x} = 0$$
$$4 = \sqrt{x}$$
$$16 = x$$

The domain is $[0, 16) \cup (16, \infty)$. Since the numerator is never 0, there are no x intercepts.

The y intercept is $h(0) = \dfrac{1}{4-\sqrt{0}} = \dfrac{1}{4}$ or 0.25.   *(3-1, 3-2)*

58. (A) $f(x) = 0.5x^2 - 4x + 5$
$= 0.5(x^2 - 8x) + 5$
$= 0.5(x^2 - 8x + 16) + 5 - 0.5(16)$
$= 0.5(x - 4)^2 - 3$

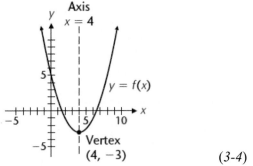

Therefore the line $x = 4$ is the axis of symmetry of the parabola and $(4, -3)$ is its vertex.

(B) The parabola opens upward, since $0.5 = a > 0$. Thus the parabola is decreasing on $(-\infty, 4]$ and increasing on $[4, \infty)$. The range is $[-3, \infty)$.

(3-4)

59. g is a linear function. Its graph passes through $(x_1, y_1) = (-1, 0)$ and $(x_2, y_2) = (1, 4)$. Therefore the slope of the line is

$m = \dfrac{y_2 - y_1}{x_2 - x_1} = \dfrac{4 - 0}{1 - (-1)} = 2$. The equation of the line is obtained from the point-slope form:

$y - y_1 = m(x - x_1)$
$y - 0 = 2[x - (-1)]$
$y = 2x + 2$

The function is given by $g(x) = 2x + 2$.

f is a quadratic function. Its equation must be of the form $f(x) = y = a(x - h)^2 + k$. The vertex of the parabola is at $(1, 2)$. Therefore the equation must have form

$y = a(x - 1)^2 + 2$

Since the parabola passes through $(3, 0)$, these coordinates must satisfy the equation.

$0 = a(3 - 1)^2 + 2$
$0 = 4a + 2$
$-2 = 4a$
$a = -0.5$

The equation is

$y = f(x) = -0.5(x - 1)^2 + 2$
$f(x) = -0.5(x^2 - 2x + 1) + 2$
$f(x) = -0.5x^2 + x - 0.5 + 2$
$f(x) = -0.5x^2 + x + 1.5$

(3-4)

60. (A) For $-4 \le x < 0$, $f(x) = -x - 5$, so $f(-4) = -(-4) - 5 = -1$ and $f(-2) = -(-2) - 5 = -3$

For $0 \le x \le 5$, $f(x) = 0.2x^2$, so $f(0) = 0.2(0)^2 = 0$, $f(2) = 0.2(2)^2 = 0.8$, and $f(5) = 0.2(5)^2 = 5$.

(B)

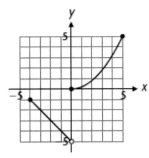

(C) Domain: $[-4, 5]$, range: $(-5, -1] \cup [0, 5]$

(D) The graph is discontinuous at $x = 0$.

(E) Decreasing on $[-4, 0)$, increasing on $[0, 5]$.

(3-2, 3-4)

61. $f(x) = \sqrt{x} - 8 \quad g(x) = |x|$

(A) $(f \circ g)(x) = f[g(x)] = f(|x|) = \sqrt{|x|} - 8$

$(g \circ f)(x) = g[f(x)] = g(\sqrt{x} - 8) = |\sqrt{x} - 8|$

(B) The domain of f is $\{x \mid x \geq 0\}$. The domain of g is all real numbers. Hence the domain of $f \circ g$ is the set of those real numbers x for which $g(x)$ is non-negative, that is, all real numbers. The domain of $(g \circ f)$ is the set of all those non-negative numbers x for which $f(x)$ is real, that is all $\{x \mid x \geq 0\}$ or $[0, \infty)$ *(3-5)*

62. (A) $f(x) = x^3$.

Assume $f(a) = f(b)$
$$a^3 = b^3$$
$$a^3 - b^3 = 0$$
$$(a - b)(a^2 + ab + b^2) = 0$$
The only real solutions of this equation are those for which $a - b = 0$, hence $a = b$. Thus $f(x)$ is one-to-one.

(B) $g(x) = (x - 2)^2$. Since $g(3) = g(1) = 1$, g is not one-to-one.

(C) $h(x) = 2x - 3$

Assume $h(a) = h(b)$
$$2a - 3 = 2b - 3$$
Then $2a = 2b$
$$a = b$$
Thus h is one-to-one.

(D) $F(x) = (x + 3)^2 \quad x \geq -3$

Assume $F(a) = F(b) \quad a \geq -3, \ b \geq -3$
$$(a + 3)^2 = (b + 3)^2$$
$$a^2 + 6a + 9 = b^2 + 6b + 9$$
$$a^2 - b^2 + 6a - 6b = 0$$
$$(a - b)(a + b + 6) = 0$$
Either $a + b + 6 = 0$, that is, $a = b = -3$ (since $a \geq -3, \ b \geq -3$) or $a - b = 0$ that is, $a = b$. In either case, $a = b$.
Thus F is one-to-one.   *(3-6)*

63. Find the composition of the 2 functions in both orders.
$$(u \circ v)(x) = u(v(x)) = u(0.25x + 2)$$
$$= 4(0.25x + 2) - 8 = x + 8 - 8 = x$$
$$(v \circ u)(x) = v(u(x)) = v(4x - 8)$$
$$= 0.25(4x - 8) + 2 = x - 2 + 2 = x$$
The functions are inverses. *(3-6)*

64. (A) The graph of $y = x^2$ is shifted to the right 3 units, then vertically stretched by a factor of 2.

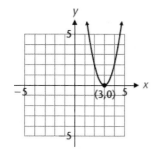

(B) Once choice is $x \leq 3$.
Another choice is $x \geq 3$.

(C) If $x \leq 3$,
Write $y = f(x)$
$$y = 2(x - 3)^2 \quad x \leq 3$$
Solve for x.
$$\frac{y}{2} = (x - 3)^2 \quad x \leq 3$$
$$-\sqrt{\frac{y}{2}} = x - 3 \quad x \leq 3$$
(note: only the negative square root is correct)
$$x = 3 - \sqrt{\frac{y}{2}} \quad y \leq 3$$
Interchange x and y.
$$y = 3 - \sqrt{\frac{x}{2}} \quad x \geq 0$$

If $x \geq 3$,
Write $y = f(x)$
$$y = 2(x - 3)^2 \quad x \geq 3$$
Solve for x.
$$\frac{y}{2} = (x - 3)^2 \quad x \geq 3$$
$$\sqrt{\frac{y}{2}} = x - 3 \quad x \geq 3$$
(note: only the positive square root is correct)
$$x = 3 + \sqrt{\frac{y}{2}} \quad y \geq 3$$
Interchange x and y.
$$y = 3 + \sqrt{\frac{x}{2}} \quad x \geq 0$$

(3-6)

65. (A) The graph of $f(x)$ is a line; f is one-to-one.
Write $y = f(x)$.
$$y = 3x - 7$$
Solve for x.
$$y + 7 = 3x$$
$$\frac{y + 7}{3} = x \quad \text{Interchange } x \text{ and } y:$$
$$y = \frac{x + 7}{3}$$
$$f^{1}(x) = \frac{x + 7}{3}$$

(B) $f^{1}(5) = \dfrac{5 + 7}{3} = 4$

(C) $f^{1}[f(x)] = f^{1}(3x - 7) = \dfrac{3x - 7 + 7}{3} = \dfrac{3x}{3} = x$

(D) Since $a < b$ implies $3a < 3b$, which implies $3a - 7 < 3b - 7$, or $f(a) < f(b)$, f is increasing.

(3-6)

66. The graph of $y = x^2$ is vertically stretched by a factor of 2, reflected through the x axis and shifted to the left 3 units.
Equation: $y = -2(x + 3)^2$.

(3-3)

67. $g(x) = 5 - 3|x - 2|$

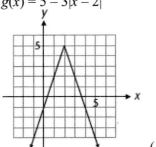

(3-3)

68. The graph of $y = x^2$ has been reflected through the x axis, shifted right 4 units and up 3 units so that the parabola has vertex   (4, 3).
Equation: $y = -(x - 4)^2 + 3$.   *(3-3, 3-4)*

69. The graph of $y = \sqrt[3]{x}$ is vertically stretched by a factor of 2, reflected through the x axis, shifted 1 unit left and 1 unit down.
Equation: $y = -2\sqrt[3]{x + 1} - 1$.   *(3-3)*

70. It is the same as the graph of g shifted to the right 2 units and down 1 unit, then reflected through the x axis.
(3-3)

71. (A) The graph of $y = x^2$ is shifted 2 units to the right, reflected through the x axis, and shifted up 4 units: $y = -(x - 2)^2 + 4$
Check: $y = -(x - 2)^2 + 4$ is graphed on a graphing utility.

(B) The graph of $y = \sqrt{x}$ is reflected through the x axis, stretched by a factor of 4, and shifted up 4 units: $y = 4 - 4\sqrt{x}$
Check: $y = 4 - 4\sqrt{x}$ is graphed on a graphing utility.

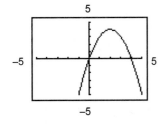

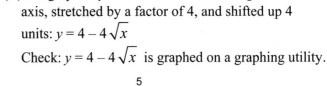

(3-3)

72. $g(x) = 8 - 3|x - 4|$
The -4 shifts 4 units right, the 3 stretches vertically by a factor of 3, and the 8 shifts 8 units up.

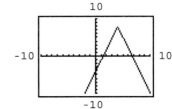

(3-3)

73. The equation is $t(x) = \left(\dfrac{1}{2}(x+2)\right)^2 - 4$. The $\dfrac{1}{2}$ stretches

horizontally by 2, the +2 shifts 2 units left, and the –4 shifts 4 units down. This function can be simplified:

$$\left(\dfrac{1}{2}(x+2)\right)^2 - 4 = \left(\dfrac{1}{2}x+1\right)^2 - 4 = \dfrac{1}{4}x^2 + x + 1 - 4 = \dfrac{1}{4}x^2 + x - 3.$$

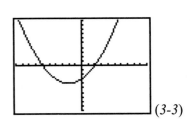

(3-3)

74. The graph of $y = |x|$ is shifted 1 unit left.

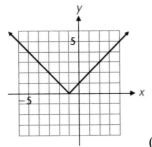

(3-3)

75. The graph of $y = \sqrt[3]{x}$ is shifted 1 unit right, reflected through the x axis, and shifted 1 unit up.

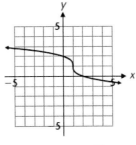

(3-3)

76. The graph of $y = |x|$ is shifted 2 units down.

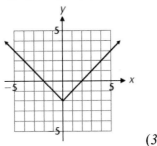

(3-3)

77. The graph of $y = \sqrt{x}$ is reflected through the x axis, stretched vertically by a factor of 3, and shifted up 9 units.

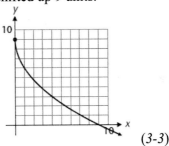

(3-3)

78. The graph of $y = |x|$ is shrunk vertically by a factor of $\dfrac{1}{2}$.

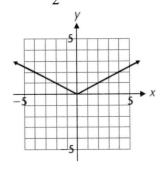

(3-3)

79. $\sqrt[3]{4-0.5x} = \sqrt[3]{0.5(8-x)}$

The graph of $y = \sqrt[3]{x}$ is stretched horizontally by a factor of 2, reflected across the y axis, and shifted 8 units right.

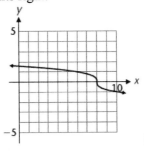

(3-3)

80.   The graph of $y = x^3$ is shifted right 1 unit, stretched vertically by a factor of 3, reflected through the x axis, and shifted up 2 units.

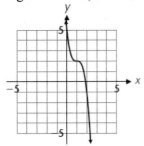

(3-3)

81.   The graph of $y = |x|$ is shifted left 1 unit, reflected through the x axis, and shifted down 1 unit.

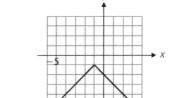

(3-3)

82. $x^2 + x < 20$
$f(x) = x^2 + x - 20 < 0$
$f(x) = (x + 5)(x - 4) < 0$
The zeros of f are -5 and 4. Plotting the graph of $f(x)$, we see that $f(x) < 0$ for $-5 < x < 4$, or $(-5, 4)$.

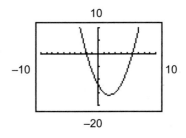

(3-4)

83. $x^2 > 4x + 12$
$f(x) = x^2 - 4x - 12 > 0$
$f(x) = (x + 2)(x - 6) > 0$
The zeros of f are -2 and 6. Plotting the graph of $f(x)$, we see that $f(x) > 0$ for $x < -2$ and $x > 6$ or $(-\infty, -2) \cup (6, \infty)$.

(3-4)

84.   The domain is the set of all real numbers x such that $\sqrt{25 - x^2}$ is a real number, that is, such that $25 - x^2 \geq 0$ or $-5 \leq x \leq 5$, $[-5, 5]$.

(3-1)

85.   (A) $(fg)(x) = f(x)g(x) = x^2\sqrt{1 - x}$
The domain of f is $(-\infty, \infty)$. The domain of g is $(-\infty, 1]$. Hence the domain of fg is the intersection of these sets, that is, $(-\infty, 1]$.

(B) $\left(\dfrac{f}{g}\right)(x) = \dfrac{f(x)}{g(x)} = \dfrac{x^2}{\sqrt{1 - x}}$

To find the domain of $\dfrac{f}{g}$, we exclude from $(-\infty, 1]$ the set of values of x for which $g(x) = 0$

$$\sqrt{1 - x} = 0$$
$$1 - x = 0$$
$$x = 1$$

Thus the domain of $\dfrac{f}{g}$ is $(-\infty, 1)$

(C) $(f \circ g)(x) = f[g(x)] = f(\sqrt{1 - x}) = [\sqrt{1 - x}]^2 = 1 - x$.
The domain of $f \circ g$ is the set of those numbers in $(-\infty, 1]$ for which $g(x)$ is real, that is $(-\infty, 1]$.

(D) $(g \circ f)(x) = g[f(x)] = g(x^2) = \sqrt{1 - x^2}$
The domain of $g \circ f$ is the set of those real numbers for which $f(x)$ is in $(-\infty, 1]$, that is, $x^2 \leq 1$, or $-1 \leq x \leq 1$. $[-1, 1]$.

(3-5)

86. (A) Write $y = f(x)$.

$$y = \frac{x+2}{x-3}$$

Solve for x.

$$y(x-3) = x+2$$
$$xy - 3y = x+2$$
$$xy - x = 3y+2$$
$$x(y-1) = 3y+2$$
$$x = \frac{3y+2}{y-1}$$

Interchange x and y:

$$f^1(x) = y = \frac{3x+2}{x-1}$$

(B) $f^1(3) = \dfrac{3(3)+2}{3-1} = \dfrac{11}{2}$

(C) $f^1[f(x)] = f^1\left(\dfrac{x+2}{x-3}\right)$

$$= \frac{3\left(\frac{x+2}{x-3}\right)+2}{\frac{x+2}{x-3}-1}$$

$$= \frac{3(x+2)+2(x-3)}{x+2-(x-3)}$$

$$= \frac{3x+6+2x-6}{x+2-x+3}$$

$$= \frac{5x}{5} = x \qquad\qquad (3\text{-}6)$$

87. (A) Write $y = f(x)$.

$$y = \sqrt{x-1}$$

Domain of f: $[1, \infty)$, Range: $[0, \infty)$.

Solve for x.

$$y^2 = x-1$$
$$y^2 + 1 = x$$

Interchange x and y.

$$x^2 + 1 = y$$
$$f^1(x) = x^2 + 1 \quad \text{Domain of } f^1: [0, \infty),$$
$$\text{Range: } [1, \infty)$$

(B) See part (A)

(C)

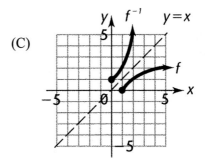

$(3\text{-}6)$

88. (A) Domain of $f = [0, \infty) = $ Range of f^1

Since $x^2 \geq 0$, $x^2 - 1 \geq -1$, so

Range of $f = [-1, \infty) = $ Domain of f^1

(B) $f(x) = x^2 - 1$ $x \geq 0$

f is one-to-one on its domain (steps omitted)

Solve $y = f(x)$ for x:

$$y = x^2 - 1 \quad x \geq 0$$
$$x^2 = y+1 \quad x \geq 0$$
$$x = \underbrace{\sqrt{y+1}}_{} = f^1(y)$$

positive square root since $x \geq 0$

Interchange x and y:

$$y = f^1(x) = \sqrt{x+1} \quad \text{Domain: } [-1, \infty)$$

Check:

$$f^1[f(x)] = \sqrt{x^2-1+1} \quad x \geq 0$$
$$= \sqrt{x^2} \quad x \geq 0$$
$$= x \text{ since } x \geq 0$$
$$f[f^1(x)] = (\sqrt{x+1})^2 - 1$$
$$= x+1-1$$
$$= x$$

(C) $f^1(3) = \sqrt{3+1} = 2$

(D) $f^1[f(4)] = 4$

(E) $f^1[f(x)] = x$

$(3\text{-}6)$

89. (A) Reflect the given graph across the *y* axis: (B) Reflect the given graph across the origin:

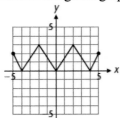

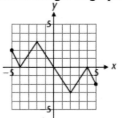

(3-3)

90. (A) The graph must cross the *x* axis exactly once. Some possible graphs are shown:

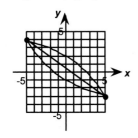

(B) The graph may cross the *x* axis once, but it may fail to cross the *x* axis at all. A possible graph of the latter type is shown:

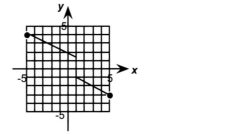

(3-2)

91.   (A) If $0 \le x \le 2{,}000$, $E(x) = 6 \cdot 20 = 120$

If $2{,}000 < x \le 5{,}000$,

	$E(x)$	= Base salary	+ Commission on sales over $2,000
		= 120	+ 0.1(x − 2,000)
		= 120	+ 0.1x − 200
		= 0.1x	− 80

If $x > 5{,}000$, $E(x)$ = Salary + Bonus
= $(0.1x - 80) + 250$
= $0.1x + 170$

Summarizing,

$$E(x) = \begin{cases} 120 & \text{if} \quad 0 \le x \le 2{,}000 \\ 0.1x - 80 & \text{if} \quad 2{,}000 < x \le 5{,}000 \\ 0.1x + 170 & \text{if} \quad x > 5{,}000 \end{cases}$$

(B)   If $0 \le x \le 2{,}000$, $E(x) = 120$, so $E(2{,}000) = \$120$.
If $2{,}000 < x \le 5{,}000$, $E(x) = 0.1x - 80$, so $E(4{,}000) = 0.1(4{,}000) - 80 = \$320$.
If $x > 5{,}000$, $E(x) = 0.1x + 170$, so $E(6{,}000) = 0.1(6{,}000) + 170 = \$770$.

(C)   In order to average more than $400 a week, she must sell more than $2,000. Can she earn $400 a week if she sells between $2,000 and $5,000?
Solve
$$0.1x - 80 = 400$$
$$0.1x = 480$$
$$x = \$4{,}800$$
This is between $2,000 and $5,000, so, yes, she can average $400 a week if she can sell $4,800 on average each week. (3-2)

92. The function describing the height of the stuntman is $h(t) = 120 - 16t^2$, since the initial height is 120 feet. Substitute 0 for $h(t)$ and solve.
$$0 = 120 - 16t^2$$
$$16t^2 = 120$$
$$t^2 = 7.5$$
$$t = 2.7 \text{ seconds after jumping}$$

(3-4)

93. (A) If r is linearly related to c, then we are looking for a function whose graph passes through $(c_1, r_1) = (30, 48)$ and $(c_2, r_2) = (20, 32)$. We find the slope, then we use the point-slope form to find the equation.

$$m = \frac{r_2 - r_1}{c_2 - c_1} = \frac{32 - 48}{20 - 30} = 1.6$$

$$r - r_1 = m(c - c_1)$$
$$r - 48 = 1.6(c - 30)$$
$$r - 48 = 1.6c - 48$$
$$f(c) = r = 1.6c \quad \text{domain: } [10, \infty) \text{ range: } [16, \infty)$$

(B) $f(105) = 1.6(105) = \$168$

(C) Solve $r = 1.6c$ for c.
$$0.625r = c = f^{-1}(r)$$
Domain: $[16, \infty)$, range: $[10, \infty)$

(D) $f^{-1}(39.99) = 0.625(39.99) = \$24.99$

(3-6)

94. (A)

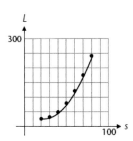

(C)

Substitute $L = 200$ into $f^{-1}(L)$ to obtain

$$S = 20 + \sqrt{\frac{50}{3}(200 - 26)} = 74 \text{ mph}$$

(B) $L = 0.06s^2 - 2.4s + 50$ domain $[20, \infty)$
Complete the square to find the range.
$$L = 0.06(s^2 - 40s + \,?) + 50$$
$$L = 0.06(s^2 - 40s + 400) - 0.06(400) + 50$$
$$L = 0.06(s - 20)^2 + 26 \quad \text{therefore, range } [26, \infty)$$
Solve for s.
$$L - 26 = 0.06(s - 20)^2$$
$$\frac{50}{3}(L - 26) = (s - 20)^2$$
$$\sqrt{\frac{50}{3}(L - 26)} = s - 20 \quad \begin{array}{l}\text{(positive square root} \\ \text{only, since } s \geq 20)\end{array}$$
$$f^{-1}(L) = s = 20 + \sqrt{\frac{50}{3}(L - 26)} \quad \begin{array}{l}\text{domain } [26, \infty), \\ \text{range } [20, \infty).\end{array}$$

(3-6)

95. (A)   Examining the graph of p, we obtain

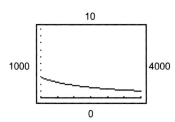

Clearly, d is a decreasing function, passing the horizontal line test, so d is one-to-one.

When $q = 1000$, $p = d(1000) = \dfrac{9}{1 + 0.002(1000)} = 3$

When $q = 4000$, $p = d(4000) = \dfrac{9}{1 + 0.002(4000)} = 1$

Thus the range of d is $1 \leq p \leq 3$ or $[1, 3]$.

(B) Solve $p = d(q)$ for q.

$$p = \frac{9}{1 + 0.002q}$$
$$p(1 + 0.002q) = 9$$
$$1 + 0.002q = \frac{9}{p}$$
$$0.002q = \frac{9}{p} - 1$$
$$q = \frac{4,500}{p} - 500 = d^{-1}(p)$$

Domain d^{-1} = range d = $[1, 3]$
Range d^{-1} = domain d = $[1000, 4000]$.

C) Revenue is price times number sold, so we need to multiply the variable p (price) by the function q (number sold) that we obtained in part B:

$$p \cdot q = p \cdot \left(\frac{4,500}{p} - 500 \right) = 4,500 - 500p$$

(D) Revenue is price times number sold, so we need to multiply the function p (price) times the variable q (numbers sold):

$$p \cdot q = \frac{9}{1+0.002q} \cdot q = \frac{9q}{1+0.002q} \qquad (3\text{-}6)$$

96. Profit is revenue minus cost so we start by subtracting the revenue and cost functions:

$$\begin{aligned} P(x) &= R(x) - C(x) = (50x - 0.1x^2) - (10x + 1,500) \\ &= 50x - 0.1x^2 - 10x - 1,500 = -0.1x^2 + 40x - 1,500 \end{aligned}$$

The variable is x but we're asked to find profit in terms of price (p) so we need to substitute $500 - 10p$ in for x.

$$\begin{aligned} p(500 - 10p) &= -0.1(500 - 10p)^2 + 40(500 - 10p) - 1,500 \\ &= -0.1(250,000 - 10,000p + 100p^2) + 20,000 - 400p - 1,500 \\ &= -25,000 + 1,000p - 10p^2 + 20,000 - 400p - 1,500 \\ &= -10p^2 + 600p - 6,500 \end{aligned}$$

so $P(p) = -10p^2 + 600p - 6,500$

This is a quadratic function, so its maximum occurs at the vertex of its parabola graph which is found at

$$p = -\frac{b}{2a} = -\frac{600}{2(-10)} = 30$$

Then $f(p) = f\left(-\frac{b}{2a} \right) = f(30) = -10(30)^2 + 600(30) - 6,500 = 2,500$

Thus the price that produces the largest profit is \$30 and this profit is \$2,500. $\qquad (3\text{-}4)$

97. (A) From the figure, we see that $A = x(y + y) = 2xy$. Since the fence consists of four pieces of length y and three pieces of length x, we have $3x + 4y = 120$. Hence $4y = 120 - 3x$

$$y = 30 - \frac{3}{4}x$$

$$A = 2x\left(30 - \frac{3}{4}x \right)$$

$$A(x) = 60x - \frac{3}{2}x^2$$

(B) Since both x and y must be positive, we have $x > 0$

$$30 - \frac{3}{4}x > 0 \text{ or } -\frac{3}{4}x > -30 \text{ or } x < 40$$

Hence $0 < x < 40$ is the domain of A.

(C) The function A is a quadratic function. Completing the square yields:

$$\begin{aligned} A(x) &= -\frac{3}{2}x^2 + 60x \\ &= -\frac{3}{2}(x^2 - 40x) \\ &= -\frac{3}{2}(x^2 - 40x + 400) + \frac{3}{2} \cdot 400 \\ &= -\frac{3}{2}(x - 20)^2 + 600 \end{aligned}$$

Comparing with $f(x) = a(x - h)^2 + k$, the total area will be maximum when $x = 20$.

Then $y = 30 - \frac{3}{4}x = 30 - \frac{3}{4}(20) = 15 \qquad (3\text{-}4)$

98. (A) $f(1) = 1 - (\llbracket\sqrt{1}\rrbracket)^2 = 1 - 1 = 0$

$f(2) = 2 - (\llbracket\sqrt{2}\rrbracket)^2 = 2 - 1 = 1$

$f(3) = 3 - (\llbracket\sqrt{3}\rrbracket)^2 = 3 - 1 = 2$

$f(4) = 4 - (\llbracket\sqrt{4}\rrbracket)^2 = 4 - 4 = 0$

$f(5) = 5 - (\llbracket\sqrt{5}\rrbracket)^2 = 5 - 4 = 1$

$f(6) = 6 - (\llbracket\sqrt{6}\rrbracket)^2 = 6 - 4 = 2$

$f(7) = 7 - (\llbracket 7\rrbracket)^2 = 7 - 4 = 3$

$f(8) = 8 - (\llbracket 8\rrbracket)^2 = 8 - 4 = 4$

$f(9) = 9 - (\llbracket 9\rrbracket)^2 = 9 - 9 = 0$

$f(10) = 10 - (\llbracket 10\rrbracket)^2 = 10 - 9 = 1$

$f(11) = 11 - (\llbracket 11\rrbracket)^2 = 11 - 9 = 2$

$f(12) = 12 - (\llbracket 12\rrbracket)^2 = 12 - 9 = 3$

$f(13) = 13 - (\llbracket 13\rrbracket)^2 = 13 - 9 = 4$

$f(14) = 14 - (\llbracket 14\rrbracket)^2 = 14 - 9 = 5$

$f(15) = 15 - (\llbracket 15\rrbracket)^2 = 15 - 9 = 6$

$f(16) = 16 - (\llbracket 16\rrbracket)^2 = 16 - 16 = 0$

(B) $f(n^2) = n^2 - (\llbracket\sqrt{n^2}\rrbracket)^2$

$= n^2 - (\llbracket n\rrbracket)^2$ since $\sqrt{n^2} = n$ if n is positive

$= n^2 - (n)^2$ since $\llbracket n\rrbracket = n$ if n is a (positive) integer.

$= 0$

(C) It determines if an integer is a perfect square integer. If $f(x) = 0$, then x is a perfect square and if $f(x) \neq 0$, x is not a perfect square integer.

(3-2)

99. Amounts less than $3,000: Tax is 2% of income $(x) = 0.02x$

Amounts between $3,000 and $5,000: Tax is $60 + 3% of income over 3,000 $(x - 3,000)$ so tax $= 60 + 0.03(x - 3,000) = 0.03x - 30$

Amounts between $5,000 and $17,000: Tax is $120 + 5% of income over 5,000 $(x - 5,000)$ so tax $= 120 + 0.05(x - 5,000) = 0.05x - 130$

Amounts over $17,000: Tax is $720 + 5.75% of income over 17,000 $(x - 17,000)$ so tax $= 720 + 0.0575(x - 17,000) = 0.0575x - 257.5$

Combined, we get $t(x) = \begin{cases} 0.02x & 0 \leq x \leq 3,000 \\ 0.03x - 30 & 3,000 < x \leq 5,000 \\ 0.05x - 130 & 5,000 < x \leq 17,000 \\ 0.0575x - 257.5 & x > 17,000 \end{cases}$

$t(2,000) = 0.02(2,000) = 40$. The tax on $2,000 is $40.

$t(4,000) = 0.03(4,000) - 30 = 120 - 30 = 90$. The tax on $4,000 is $90.

$t(10,000) = 0.05(10,000) - 130 = 500 - 130 = 370$. The tax on $10,000 is $130.

$t(30,000) = 0.0575(30,000) - 257.5 = 1,725 - 257.5 = 1,467.5$. The tax on $30,000 is $1,467.50.

CHAPTER 4

Section 4-1

1. A function that can be written in the form $P(x) = a_nx^n + a_{n-1}x^{n-1} + \ldots + a_1x + a_0$, $a_n \neq 0$, n a nonnegative integer, is a polynomial function.

3. 0 must be inserted as the coefficient of the missing term of degree 3.

5. True. A quadratic function can be written as $P(x) = a_2x^2 + a_1x + a_0$, $a_2 \neq 0$. (See problem 1).

7. False. If a polynomial of degree greater than 0, for example $f(x) = x^2 + 1$, has no x intercepts, it has imaginary zeros (in this case $\pm i$).

9. The degree is odd and the coefficient is positive, so $f(x)$ increases without bound as $x \to \infty$ and decreases without bound as $x \to -\infty$. This matches graph c.

11. The degree is even and the coefficient is positive, so $h(x)$ increases without bound both as $x \to \infty$ and $x \to -\infty$. This matches graph d.

13. The real zeros are the x intercepts: -1 and 3. The turning point is $(1, 4)$. $P(x) \to -\infty$ as $x \to \infty$ and $P(x) \to -\infty$ as $x \to -\infty$.

15. The real zeros are the x intercepts: -2 and 1. The turning points are $(-1, 4)$ and $(1, 0)$. $P(x) \to -\infty$ as $x \to -\infty$ and $P(x) \to \infty$ as $x \to \infty$.

17. The graph of a polynomial always increases or decreases without bound as $x \to \infty$ and $x \to -\infty$. This graph does not.

19. The graph of a polynomial always has a finite number of turning points--at most one less than the degree. This graph has infinitely many turning points.

21. Set each factor equal to zero:

$$x = 0 \quad x^2 - 9 = 0 \quad x^2 + 4 = 0$$
$$x^2 = 9 \quad x^2 = -4$$
$$x = 3, -3 \quad x = 2i, -2i$$

The zeros are 0, 3, -3, $2i$, and $-2i$; of these 0, 3, and -3 are x-intercepts.

23. Set each factor equal to zero:

$$x + 5 = 0 \quad x^2 + 9 = 0 \quad x^2 + 16 = 0$$
$$x = -5 \quad x^2 = -9 \quad x^2 = -16$$
$$x = 3i, -3i \quad x = 4i, -4i$$

The zeros are -5, $3i$, $-3i$, $4i$, and $-4i$. Only -5 is an x intercept.

25.
$$
\begin{array}{r}
3x + 2 \\
x+1\overline{\smash{\big)}\,3x^2 + 5x + 6} \\
\underline{3x^2 + 3x} \\
2x + 6 \\
\underline{2x + 2} \\
4
\end{array}
$$
$3x + 2$, $R = 4$

27.
$$
\begin{array}{r}
4m + 4 \\
m-1\overline{\smash{\big)}\,4m^2 + 0m - 1} \\
\underline{4m^2 - 4m} \\
4m - 1 \\
\underline{4m - 4} \\
3
\end{array}
$$
$4m + 4$, $R = 3$

29.
$$
\begin{array}{r}
8x - 14 \\
x+1\overline{\smash{\big)}\,8x^2 - 6x + 6} \\
\underline{8x^2 + 8x} \\
-14x + 6 \\
\underline{-14x - 14} \\
20
\end{array}
$$
$8x - 14$, $R = 20$

31.
$$
\begin{array}{r}
x^2 + x\ \ + 1 \\
x-1\overline{\smash{\big)}\,x^3 - 0x^2 + 0x - 1} \\
\underline{x^3 - x^2} \\
x^2 + 0x \\
\underline{x^2 - x} \\
x - 1 \\
\underline{x - 1} \\
0
\end{array}
$$
$x^2 + x + 1$, $R = 0$

33.
$$\begin{array}{r} 2y^2 - 5y + 13 \\ y+2\overline{\smash{\big)}\,2y^3 - y^2 + 3y - 1} \\ \underline{2y^3 + 4y^2} \\ -5y^2 + 3y \\ \underline{-5y^2 - 10y} \\ 13y - 1 \\ \underline{13y + 26} \\ -27 \end{array}$$
$2y^2 - 5y + 13, \; R = -27$

35.
$$\begin{array}{r} 1 \;\; 3 \; -7 \\ 2 \;\; 10 \\ 2\overline{\smash{\big)}\,1 \;\; 5 \;\; 3} \end{array}$$
$$\frac{x^2 + 3x - 7}{x - 2} = x + 5 + \frac{3}{x - 2}$$

37.
$$\begin{array}{r} 4 \;\; 10 \; -9 \\ -12 \;\; 6 \\ -3\overline{\smash{\big)}\,4 - 2 - 3} \end{array}$$
$$\frac{4x^2 + 10x - 9}{x + 3} = 4x - 2 - \frac{3}{x + 3}$$

39.
$$\begin{array}{r} 2 \;\; 0 \; -3 \;\; 1 \\ 4 \;\; 8 \;\; 10 \\ 2\overline{\smash{\big)}\,2 \;\; 4 \;\; 5 \;\; 11} \end{array}$$
$$\frac{2x^3 - 3x + 1}{x - 2} = 2x^2 + 4x + 5 + \frac{11}{x - 2}$$

Common Error:
The first row is not
$2 - 31$
The 0 must be inserted for the missing power.

41.
$$\begin{array}{r} 1 \quad\;\; 4 \; -221 \\ -17 \quad 221 \\ -17\overline{\smash{\big)}\,1 \; -13 \quad 0} \end{array}$$
The remainder is 0, hence -17 is a zero.

43.
$$\begin{array}{r} 2 \quad 38 \quad -1 \quad 19 \\ -38 \quad 0 \quad 19 \\ -19\overline{\smash{\big)}\,2 \quad 0 \quad -1 \quad 38} \end{array}$$
The remainder is non-zero, hence -19 is not a zero.

45. $x - 1$ will be a factor of $P(x)$ if $P(1) = 0$. Since $P(x) = x^{18} - 1$, $P(1) = 1^{18} - 1 = 0$. Therefore $x - 1$ is a factor of $x^{18} - 1$.

47. $x + 1$ will be a factor of $P(x)$ if $P(-1) = 0$. Since $P(x) = 3x^3 - 7x^2 - 8x + 2$, $P(-1) = 3(-1)^3 - 7(-1)^2 - 8(-1) + 2 = -3 - 7 + 8 + 2 = 0$. Therefore $x + 1$ is a factor of $3x^3 - 7x^2 - 8x + 2$.

49.
$$\begin{array}{r} 3 \; -1 \; -10 \\ -6 \;\; 14 \\ -2\overline{\smash{\big)}\,3 - 7 \;\; 4} \end{array} \quad P(-2) = 4$$

51.
$$\begin{array}{r} 2 \; -5 \;\; 7 \; -7 \\ 4 \; -2 \;\; 10 \\ 2\overline{\smash{\big)}\,2 \; -1 \;\; 5 \;\; 3} \end{array} \quad P(2) = 3$$

53.
$$\begin{array}{r} 1 \;\; 0 \; -10 \;\; 25 \; -2 \\ -4 \;\; 16 \; -24 \; -4 \\ -4\overline{\smash{\big)}\,1 - 4 \;\; 6 \;\; 1 \; -6} \end{array} \quad P(-4) = -6$$

55.
$$\begin{array}{r} 3 \;\; 0 \;\; 0 \; -1 \; -4 \\ -3 \;\; 3 \; -3 \;\; 4 \\ -1\overline{\smash{\big)}\,3 \; -3 \;\; 3 \; -4 \;\; 0} \end{array}$$
$3x^3 - 3x^2 + 3x - 4, \quad R = 0$

57.
$$\begin{array}{r} 1 \;\; 0 \; 0 \;\; 0 \; 0 \;\; 1 \\ -1 \; 1 \; -1 \; 1 \; -1 \\ -1\overline{\smash{\big)}\,1 \; -1 \; 1 \; -1 \; 1 \; 0} \end{array}$$
$x^4 - x^3 + x^2 - x + 1, \, R = 0$

59.
$$\begin{array}{r} 3 \;\; 2 \;\; 0 \; -4 \; -1 \\ -9 \;\; 21 \; -63 \;\; 201 \\ -3\overline{\smash{\big)}\,3 \; -7 \;\; 21 \; -67 \;\; 200} \end{array}$$
$3x^3 - 7x^2 + 21x - 67, R = 200$

61.
$$\begin{array}{r} 2 \; -13 \quad 0 \;\; 75 \; 2 \;\; 0 \; -50 \\ 10 \; -15 \; -75 \; 0 \; 10 \;\; 50 \\ 5\overline{\smash{\big)}\,2 \; -3 \; -15 \;\; 0 \; 2 \; 10 \;\; 0} \end{array}$$
$2x^5 - 3x^4 - 15x^3 + 2x + 10, R = 0$

63. $P(x) = x^3 - 5x^2 + 2x + 6 \quad n = 3 \quad a_n = 1$
Since $a_n > 0$ and n is odd $P(x) \to \infty$ as $x \to \infty$ and $P(x) \to -\infty$ as $x \to -\infty$. Since the degree of $P(x)$ is 3, $P(x)$ can have a maximum of three x intercepts and two local extrema.

65. $P(x) = -x^3 + 4x^2 + x + 5 \quad n = 3 \quad a_n = -1$
Since $a_n < 0$ and n is odd $P(x) \to -\infty$ as $x \to \infty$ and $P(x) \to \infty$ as $x \to -\infty$. Since the degree of $P(x)$ is 3, $P(x)$ can have a maximum of three x intercepts and two local extrema.

67. $P(x) = x^4 + x^3 - 5x^2 - 3x + 12 \quad n = 4 \quad a_n = 1$
Since $a_n > 0$ and n is even $P(x) \to \infty$ as $x \to \infty$ and $P(x) \to \infty$ as $x \to -\infty$. Since the degree of $P(x)$ is 4, $P(x)$ can have a maximum of four x intercepts and three local extrema.

69. $P(x) = x^3$ is an example of a third-degree polynomial with one x intercept $(x = 0)$.

71. No such polynomial exists; the graph of a third-degree polynomial must cross the x axis at least once.

73.

$$\begin{array}{r|rrrr} & 1 & -3 & 1 & -3 \\ & & i & -3i-1 & 3 \\ \hline i & 1 & -3+i & -3i & 0 \end{array}$$

$x^2 + (-3 + i)x - 3i, R = 0$

75. We apply the remainder theorem to evaluate using synthetic division.

(A)
$$\begin{array}{r|rrr} & 1 & 2i & -10 \\ & & 2-i & 5 \\ \hline 2-i & 1 & 2+i & -5 \end{array}$$
$P(2 - i) = -5$

(B)
$$\begin{array}{r|rrr} & 1 & 2i & -10 \\ & & 5-5i & 10-40i \\ \hline 5-5i & 1 & 5-3i & -40i \end{array}$$
$P(5 - 5i) = -40i$

(C)
$$\begin{array}{r|rrr} & 1 & 2i & -10 \\ & & 3-i & 10 \\ \hline 3-i & 1 & 3+i & 0 \end{array}$$
$P(3 - i) = 0$

(D)
$$\begin{array}{r|rrr} & 1 & 2i & -10 \\ & & -3-i & 10 \\ \hline -3-i & 1 & -3+i & 0 \end{array}$$
$P(-3 - i) = 0$

77. Graphing and applying built-in routines yields:

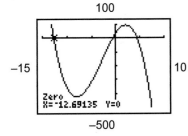
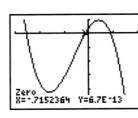
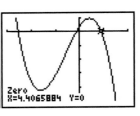

x intercepts at $x = -12.69, -0.72, 4.41$

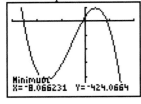

Local minimum at $P(-8.07) \approx -424.07$

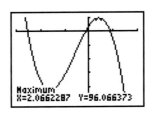

Local maximum at $P(2.07) \approx 96.07$

79. Graphing and applying built-in routines yields:

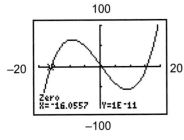
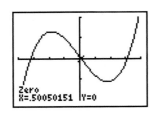
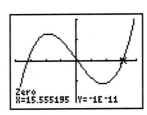

x intercepts at $-16.06, 0.50, 15.56$

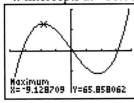

Local maximum at $P(-9.13) \approx 65.86$

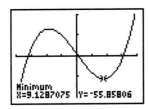

Local minimum at $P(9.13) \approx -55.86$

81.   Graphing and applying built-in routines yields:

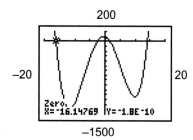
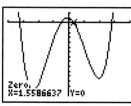
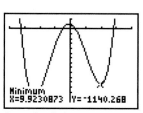
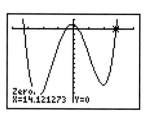

x intercepts at −16.15, −2.53, 1.56, 14.12.

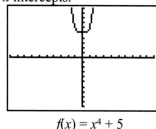
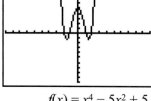

Local minimum at
$P(-11.68) \approx -1{,}395.99$

Local maximum at
$P(-0.50) \approx 95.72$

Local minimum at
$P(9.92) \approx -1{,}140.27$

83.   (A) If the degree is even the graph has to approach +∞ both to the right and left, so there has to be at least one turning point. $f(x) = x^4$, graphed below, has only 1 turning point. A degree 4 polynomial can't have any more than 3 turning points. $f(x) = x^4 - 5x^2$, graphed below, has 3 turning points.

$f(x) = x^4$ $f(x) = x^4 - 5x^2$

(B) An even degree polynomial can have no *x* intercepts as illustrated by $f(x) = x^4 + 5$ (graphed below). A polynomial of degree 4 can have at most 4 *x* intercepts. For example, $f(x) = x^4 - 5x^2 + 5$, graphed below, has 4 *x* intercepts.

$f(x) = x^4 + 5$ $f(x) = x^4 - 5x^2 + 5$

85.   No. If $f(x)$ is an even function, then $f(x) = f(-x)$ for any *x*. But $f(x) = x^2 + x$ is an even degree polynomial and $f(1) = 2$ while $f(-1) = 0$.

87.   (A) From the division algorithm, when $P(x)$ is divided by $x - r$,
$$P(x) = (x - r)Q(x) + R$$
(B) If $x = r$, then
$$P(r) = (r - r)Q(r) + R$$
$$P(r) = 0{\cdot}Q(r) + R$$
$$P(r) = R$$
When a polynomial $P(x)$ is divided by $x - r$, the remainder is equal to $P(r)$.

89. (A) The revenue $R(x)$ is given by revenue = (number sold)(price per object)

$$R(x) = xp(x)$$
$$= x(0.0004x^2 - x + 569)$$
$$= 0.0004x^3 - x^2 + 569x$$

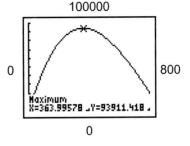

(B) Graphing and applying a built-in routine yields the graph at the right. The number of air conditioners that maximizes the revenue = 364. The maximum revenue = \$93,911.

The price $p(x) = \dfrac{R(x)}{x} = \dfrac{93,911}{364} = \$258$

91.

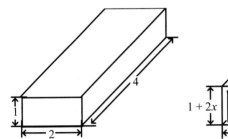 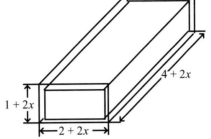

(A) The volume of the shielding is equal to the volume of the shielded box (right hand picture) minus the volume of the unshielded box (left hand picture). Thus, we have

$$\begin{pmatrix} \text{Volume of} \\ \text{shielding} \end{pmatrix} = \begin{pmatrix} \text{Volume of} \\ \text{shielded box} \end{pmatrix} - \begin{pmatrix} \text{Volume of} \\ \text{unshielded box} \end{pmatrix}$$

$$\begin{aligned} V &= (1 + 2x)(2 + 2x)(4 + 2x) - 1 \cdot 2 \cdot 4 \\ &= (2 + 6x + 4x^2)(4 + 2x) - 8 \\ &= 8 + 24x + 16x^2 + 4x + 12x^2 + 8x^3 - 8 \\ &= 28x + 28x^2 + 8x^3 \end{aligned}$$

(B) Substitute $x = 0.05$ to find
$$V = 28(0.05) + 28(0.05)^2 + 8(0.05)^3 = 1.471 \text{ cubic feet}$$

93. (A) The independent variable is years since 1960, so enter 0, 10, 20, 30, 40, 47 as L_1. The dependent variable is total expenditures, so enter the total expenditures column as L_2. Then choose the cubic regression from the STAT CALC menu.

L1	L2	L3 3	EDIT **CALC** TESTS	CubicReg L₁,L₂	CubicReg
0	28		1:1-Var Stats		y=ax³+bx²+cx+d
10	75		2:2-Var Stats		a=.0210939441
20	253		3:Med-Med		b=-.1287915774
30	714		4:LinReg(ax+b)		c=6.192857497
40	1353		5:QuadReg		d=20.84904986
47	2241		**6**CubicReg		
L3(1)=			7↓QuartReg		

The cubic regression polynomial is
$$y = 0.021094x^3 - 0.12879x^2 + 6.19286x + 20.84905$$

(B) 2018 is 58 years after 1960, so substitute 58 into the regression model.
$$y = 0.021094(58)^3 - 0.12879(58)^2 + 6.19286(58) + 20.84905 = \$4,062 \text{ billion}.$$

95. (A) The independent variable is years since 1950, so enter 0, 10, 20, 30, 40, 50 as L_1. The dependent variable is marriage rate, so enter the marriage column as L_2. Then choose the cubic regression from the STAT CALC menu.

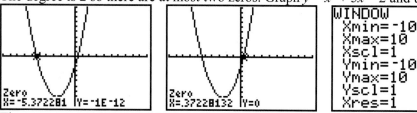

$$y = -0.0002185x^3 + 0.01521x^2 - 0.27073x + 10.81984$$

(B) 2016 is 66 years after 1950, so substitute 66 into the regression model.

$$y = -0.0002185(66)^3 + 0.01521(66)^2 - 0.27073(66) + 10.81984 = -3.6 \text{ (an utterly implausible estimate)}$$

Section 4-2

1. A polynomial of degree $n > 0$ can have at most n zeros. Any set of real numbers, with n members or fewer, will have a largest and a smallest element, so it will have an upper and a lower bound.

3. Yes. 5 is an upper bound and so is any number larger than 5.

5. Answers will vary.

7. The degree is 2 so there are at most two zeros. Graph $y = x^2 + 5x - 2$ and use the zero command.

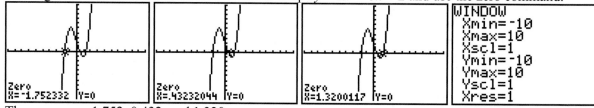

The zeros are -5.372 and 0.372.

9. The degree is 3 so there are at most three zeros. Graph $y = 2x^3 - 5x + 2$ and use the zero command.

The zeros are -1.752, 0.432, and 1.320.

11. This inequality is true wherever the graph of $P(x)$ is above the x axis or intersects the x-axis. This is $[-2, -1] \cup \{1\} \cup [3, \infty)$.

13. This inequality is true only when $P(x)$ is above the x axis but not where it intersects the x-axis. This is $(-2, -1) \cup (3, \infty)$.

15. See the graph of $P(x) = x^2 + 5x - 2$ in Problem 7. It is positive (above the x axis) on $(-\infty, -5.372) \cup (0.372, \infty)$.

17. See the graph of $P(x) = 2x^3 - 5x + 2$ in Problem 9. It is negative (below the x axis) or zero (on the x axis) on $(-\infty, -1.752] \cup [0.432, 1.320]$.

19. We form a synthetic division table.

	1	0	–3	1	
0	1	0	–3	1	
1	1	1	–2	–1	
2	1	2	1	3	an upper bound
–1	1	–1	–2	3	
–2	1	–2	1	–1	a lower bound

2 is an upper bound; –2 is a lower bound.

21. We form a synthetic division table.

	1	–3	4	2	–9	
0	1	–3	4	2	–9	
1	1	–2	2	4	–5	
2	1	–1	2	6	3	
3	1	0	4	14	33	an upper bound
–1	1	–4	8	–6	–3	
–2	1	–5	14	–26	43	a lower bound

3 is an upper bound; –2 is a lower bound.

23. We form a synthetic division table.

	1	0	–3	3	2	–2	
0	1	0	–3	3	2	–2	
1	1	1	–2	1	3	1	
2	1	2	1	5	12	22	an upper bound
–1	1	–1	–2	5	–3	1	
–2	1	–2	1	1	0	–2	
–3	1	–3	6	–15	47	–143	a lower bound

2 is an upper bound; –3 is a lower bound.

25. (A) $P(3) = 3^3 - 2(3)^2 - 5(3) + 4 = -2$ Different signs, so there is a zero between 3 and 4.
  $P(4) = 4^3 - 2(4)^2 - 5(4) + 4 = 16$

  (B) Midpoint of [3, 4]: 3.5; $P(3.5) = 4.875$; New interval: [3, 3.5]
  Midpoint of [3, 3.5]: 3.25; $P(3.25) = 0.953$; New interval: [3, 3.25]
  Midpoint of [3, 3.25]: 3.125; $P(3.125) = -0.639$; New interval: [3.125, 3.25]
  Midpoint of [3.125, 3.25]: 3.1875; $P(3.1875) = 0.128$; New interval: [3.125, 3.1875]
  Midpoint of [3.125, 3.1875]: 3.15625; $P(3.15625) = -0.263$

The sign is different for $P(3.15625)$ and $P(3.1875)$; both of these x-values round to 3.2, so 3.2 is the zero to
one decimal place accuracy. It took 5 intervals.

Calculator Note: Here's a convenient way to repeatedly plug different numbers into the same
function as we did in Problem 25. Enter the function as y_1 in the equation editor and use the
"value" command from the calculate menu. All you have to do is key in the x-value you want to
plug in.

27. (A) $P(-2) = -9$ Different signs, so there's a zero between –2 and –1.
  $P(-1) = 3$

  (B) Midpoint of [–2, –1] = –1.5; $P(-1.5) = -1.375$; New interval: [–1.5, –1]
  Midpoint of [–1.5, –1] = –1.25; $P(-1.25) = 1.17$; New interval: [–1.5, –1.25]
  Midpoint of [–1.5, –1.25] = –1.375; $P(-1.375) = -0.006$; New interval: [–1.375, –1.25]
  Midpoint of [–1.375, –1.25] = –1.3125; $P(-1.3125) = 0.606$; New interval: [–1.375, –1.3125]
  Midpoint of [–1.375, –1.3125] = –1.34375; $P(-1.34375) = 0.306$; New interval: [–1.375, –1.34375]
  Midpoint of [–1.375, –1.34375] = –1.359375; $P(-1.359375) = 0.15$
  $P(-1.375)$ and $P(-1.359375)$ have opposite signs and both x-values round to –1.4, so –1.4 is the zero to
  one decimal place accuracy. It took 6 intervals.

29. (A) $P(3) = -2$
   $P(4) = 59$ Different signs, so there's a zero between 3 and 4.

(B) Midpoint of [3, 4] = 3.5; $P(3.5) = 17.1$; New interval: [3, 3.5]
   Midpoint of [3, 3.5] = 3.25; $P(3.25) = 5.2$; New interval: [3, 3.25]
   Midpoint of [3, 3.25] = 3.125; $P(3.125) = 1.1$; New interval: [3, 3.125]
   Midpoint of [3, 3.125] = 3.0625; $P(3.0625) = -0.6$

$P(3.0625)$ and $P(3.125)$ have opposite signs and both x-values round to 3.1,
so 3.1 is the zero to one decimal place accuracy. It took 4 intervals.

31. (A) We form a synthetic division table.

	1	-2	3	-8
0	1	-2	3	-8
1	1	-1	2	-6
2	1	0	3	-2
3	1	1	6	10
-1	1	-3	6	-14

From the table, 3 is an upper bound and –1 is a lower bound.

(B) The only interval in which a real zero is indicated is (2, 3). We search for this real zero. We organize our calculations in a table.

Sign Change Interval (a, b)	Midpoint m	Sign of P		
		$P(a)$	$P(m)$	$P(b)$
(2, 3)	2.5	–	+	+
(2, 2.5)	2.25	–	+	+
(2, 2.25)	2.125	–	–	+
(2.125, 2.25)	2.1875	–	–	+
(2.1875, 2.25)	We stop here	–	+	

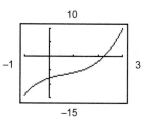

Since each endpoint rounds to 2.2 (using scientific rounding), a real zero lies on this last interval and is given by 2.2 to one decimal place accuracy. A glance at the graph of $P(x)$ on [–1, 3] confirms that this is the only real zero.

33. (A) We form a synthetic division table.

	2	1	2	1
0	2	1	2	1
1	2	3	5	6
-1	2	-1	3	-2

From the table, 1 is an upper bound and –1 is a lower bound.

(B) The only interval in which a real zero is indicated is (–1, 0). Bisection immediately yields –0.5 as a zero.

35. (A) We form a synthetic division table.

	1	0	1	0	-6
0	1	0	1	0	-6
1	1	1	2	2	-4
2	1	2	5	10	14
-1	1	-1	2	-2	-4
-2	1	-2	5	-10	14

From the table, 2 is an upper bound and –2 is a lower bound.

(B) Real zeros are indicated in the intervals (–2, –1) and (1, 2). Since $P(x)$ is an even function, we need only to search in one of these intervals; if a is a real zero, then $-a$ is also a real zero. We organize our calculations in a table.

Sign Change Interval (a, b)	Midpoint m	Sign of P P(a)	P(m)	P(b)
(1, 2)	1.5	−	+	+
(1, 1.5)	1.25	−	−	+
(1.25, 1.5)	1.375	−	−	+
(1.375, 1.5)	1.4375	−	+	+
(1.375, 1.4375)	We stop here	−		+

Since each endpoint rounds to 1.4, a real zero lies on this last interval and is given by 1.4 to one decimal place accuracy. As noted, −1.4 is also a zero.

Algebraically, since $x^4 + x^2 - 6 = (x^2 + 3)(x^2 - 2) = (x^2 + 3)(x - \sqrt{2})(x + \sqrt{2})$, $\sqrt{2} \approx 1.4$ and $-\sqrt{2} \approx -1.4$ are zeros. Thus the approximate answers are confirmed.

37. Since 1 is a zero of multiplicity 2, $P(x)$ does not change sign at $x = 1$. The bisection method fails. (The TI-83, using a more complicated routine, can find the zero.)

39. Since 3 is a zero of multiplicity 4, $P(x)$ does not change sign at $x = 3$. The bisection method fails. (The TI-83 cannot find this zero.)

41. The graph in a standard window shows two zeros that are turning points. The degree is 4 so there could be more zeros. We'll make a synthetic division table to see if $x = \pm 10$ are bounds for the real zeros.

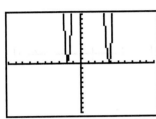

$$
\begin{array}{r|rrrrr}
 & 1 & -4 & -10 & 28 & 49 \\
\hline
-10 & 1 & -14 & 130 & -1272 & 12769 \\
10 & 1 & 6 & 50 & 528 & 5329 \\
\end{array}
$$

The signs alternate for −10 so it's a lower bound for the real zeros, and all signs are positive for 10 so it's an upper bound. In other words, the only real zeros are the two we see on the standard screen.

43. The graph in a standard window shows three zeros two of which are turning points. The degree is 5 so there could be more zeros. We'll make a synthetic division table to see if $x = \pm 10$ are bounds for the real zeros.

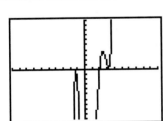

$$
\begin{array}{r|rrrrrr}
 & 1 & -6 & 4 & 24 & -16 & -32 \\
\hline
-10 & 1 & -16 & 164 & -1616 & 16144 & -161472 \\
10 & 1 & 4 & 44 & 464 & 4624 & 46208 \\
\end{array}
$$

The signs alternate for −10 so it's a lower bound for the real zeros, and all signs are positive for 10 so it's an upper bound. In other words, the only real zeros are the two we see on the standard screen.

To find the zero that's not a turning point, we use the zero command; and to find the two that are, we use the maximum and minimum commands:

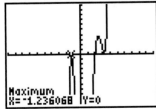
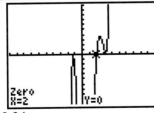
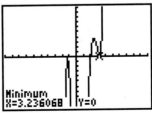

The zeros are −1.24, 2, and 3.24.

45. On a standard viewing window it's difficult to see what's happening close to $x = 2$, so we examine that area closer.

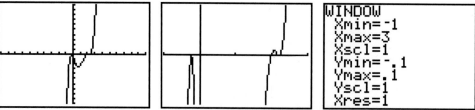

Now we can see that there are three zeros, two of which are turning points. The degree is five so there could be other zeros. A synthetic division table will help us check.

$$\begin{array}{r|rrrrrr} & 1 & -6 & 11 & -4 & -3.75 & -0.5 \\ \hline -2 & 1 & -8 & 27 & -58 & 112.25 & -225 \\ 10 & 1 & 4 & 51 & 506 & 5056.25 & 50562 \end{array}$$

The signs alternate for -2 so it's a lower bound for the zeros. The signs are all positive for 10 so it's an upper bound for the zeros and we know that we have seen all of them. To find the zero that's not a turning point we use the zero command; and to find the two that are, we use the maximum and minimum commands.

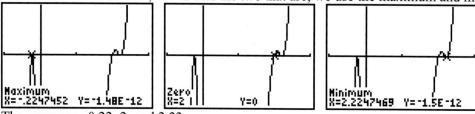

The zeros are -0.22, 2, and 2.22.

47. $x^2 > 9$

$x^2 - 9 > 0$

Let $P(x) = x^2 - 9$, then $P(x) = (x + 3)(x - 3)$. The zeros of P are -3 and 3. They partition the x axis into the three intervals shown in the table. Choose a test number in each interval to determine the sign of P in that interval.

Interval	$(-\infty, -3)$	$(-3, 3)$	$(3, \infty)$
Test number x	-4	0	4
$P(x)$	7	-9	7
Sign of P	$+$	$-$	$+$

We conclude that the solution set of the inequality is $(-\infty, -3) \cup (3, \infty)$.

49. $x^3 \leq 16x$

$x^3 - 16x \leq 0$

Let $P(x) = x^3 - 16x$, then $P(x) = x(x^2 - 16) = x(x - 4)(x + 4)$. The zeros of P are -4, 0, and 4. They partition the x axis into the four intervals shown in the table. Choose a test number in each interval to determine the sign of P in that interval. The equality holds at the zeros.

Interval	$(-\infty, -4)$	$(-4, 0)$	$(0, 4)$	$(4, \infty)$
Test number x	-5	-2	2	5
$P(x)$	-45	24	-24	45
Sign of P	$-$	$+$	$-$	$+$

We conclude that the solution set of the inequality is $(-\infty, -4] \cup [0, 4]$.

51. $x^4 + 4 \geq 5x^2$

$x^4 - 5x^2 + 4 \geq 0$

Let $P(x) = x^4 - 5x^2 + 4$, then $P(x) = (x^2 - 4)(x^2 - 1) = (x + 2)(x - 2)(x + 1)(x - 1)$. The zeros of P are $-2, -1,$ $1, 2$. They partition the x axis into the five intervals shown in the table. Choose a test number in each interval to determine the sign of P in that interval. The equality holds at the zeros.

Interval	$(-\infty, -2)$	$(-2, -1)$	$(-1, 1)$	$(1, 2)$	$(2, \infty)$
Test number x	-3	-1.5	0	1.5	3
$P(x)$	40	-2.1875	4	-2.1875	40
Sign of P	$+$	$-$	$+$	$-$	$+$

We conclude that the solution set of the inequality is $(-\infty, -2] \cup [-1, 1] \cup [2, \infty)$.

53.
$$x^2 + 7x - 3 \leq x^3 + x + 4$$
$$-x^3 + x^2 + 6x - 7 \leq 0$$

Find the zeros of $P(x) = -x^3 + x^2 + 6x - 7$ graphically:

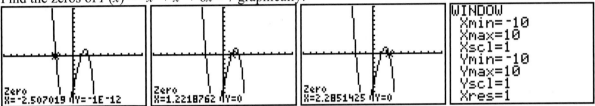

The zeros are $-2.507, 1.222,$ and 2.285. $P(x)$ is negative or zero (below, or on, the x axis) on $[-2.507, 1.222] \cup [2.285, \infty)$.

55. $x^4 < 8x^3 - 17x^2 + 9x - 2$

$x^4 - 8x^3 + 17x^2 - 9x + 2 < 0$

Find the zeros of $P(x) = x^4 - 8x^3 + 17x^2 - 9x + 2$ graphically:

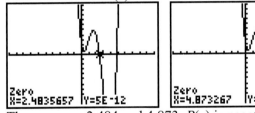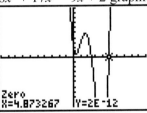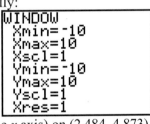

The zeros are 2.484 and 4.873. $P(x)$ is negative (below the x axis) on $(2.484, 4.873)$.

57.
$$(x^2 + 2x - 2)^2 \geq 2$$
$$(x^2 + 2x - 2)^2 - 2 \geq 0$$

Find the zeros of $P(x) = (x^2 + 2x - 2)^2 - 2$ graphically:

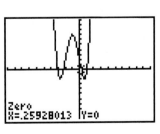

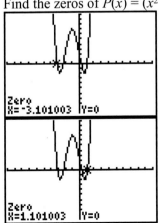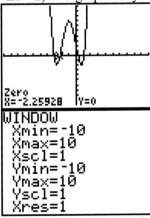

The zeros are $-3.101, -2.259, 0.259,$ and 1.101. $P(x)$ is positive or zero (above, or on, the x axis) on $(-\infty, -3.101] \cup [-2.259, 0.259] \cup [1.101, \infty)$.

59. (A) We form a synthetic division table.

	1	−24	−25	10
0	1	−24	−25	10
10	1	−14	−165	−1640
20	1	−4	−105	−2090
30	1	6	155	4660
−10	1	−34	315	−3140

From the table, 30 is an upper bound and −10 is a lower bound.

(B) Graphing $P(x)$ using the window suggested by part (A), we obtain

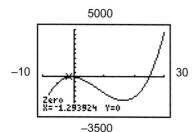
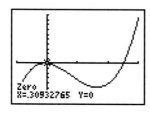
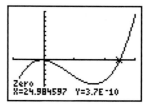

The zeros are −1.29, 0.31, and 24.98.

61. (A) We form a synthetic division table.

	1	12	−900	0	5,000
0	1	12	−900	0	5,000
10	1	22	−680	−680	−63,000
20	1	32	−260	−5200	−99,000
30	1	42	360	10,800	329,000
−10	1	2	−920	9,200	−87,000
−20	1	−8	−740	14,800	−291,000
−30	1	−18	−360	10,800	−319,000
−40	1	−28	220	−8,800	357,000

From the table, 30 is an upper bound and −40 is a lower bound.

(B) Graphing $P(x)$ using the window suggested in part (A), we obtain

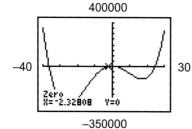
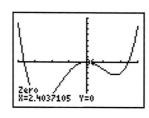
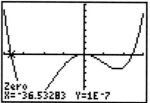
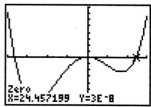

The zeros are −36.53, −2.33, 2.40, and 24.46.

63. (A) We form a synthetic division table.

	1	0	−100	−1,000	−5,000
0	1	0	−100	−1,000	−5,000
10	1	10	0	−1,000	−15,000
20	1	20	300	5,000	95,000
−10	1	−10	0	−1,000	5,000

From the table, 20 is an upper bound and −10 is a lower bound.

(B) Graphing $P(x)$ using the window suggested in part (A), we obtain

100000

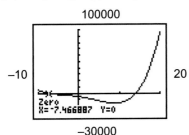

−10

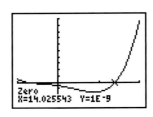

20

−30000

The real zeros are −7.47 and 14.03.

65. Yes. According to the Remainder Theorem, if the remainder is 10 when $P(x)$ is divided by $x + 4$, then $P(-4) = 10$. Similarly, if the remainder is −8 when dividing by $x + 5$, then $P(-5) = -8$. Since $P(-5)$ and $P(-4)$ have opposite signs, there must be a zero between −5 and −4.

67. Step 1: $P(x)$ can be written in the form

$P(x) = (x - r)Q(x) + R$ where the coefficients of $Q(x)$ and R are positive. This is the assumption, stated in terms of the division algorithm.

Step 2: Suppose $s > r > 0$. Then $P(s) > 0$. $s - r > 0$, $Q(r) > 0$, $R > 0$, so $P(s)$ must be > 0.

Step 3: r is an upper bound for the real zeros of $P(x)$. $P(x)$ cannot be 0 for any $s > r$, so r is an upper bound.

69. If all coefficients of $P(x)$ are nonnegative, then no positive replacement of x could possibly make $P(x) = 0$; hence, there are no positive zeros of $P(x)$. All zeros must therefore be less than or equal to 0, and 0 is an upper bound for the zeros.

71. Let (x, x^2) be a point on the graph of $y = x^2$. Then the distance from $(1, 2)$ to (x, x^2) must equal 1 unit. Applying the distance formula, we have,

$$\sqrt{(x-1)^2 + (x^2 - 2)^2} = 1$$
$$(x - 1)^2 + (x^2 - 2)^2 = 1$$
$$x^2 - 2x + 1 + x^4 - 4x^2 + 4 = 1$$
$$x^4 - 3x^2 - 2x + 4 = 0$$

Let $P(x) = x^4 - 3x^2 - 2x + 4$
The only rational zero is 1.

```
    1  0  −3  −2   4
       1   1  −2  −4
  1 | 1  1  −2  −4   0      P(x) = (x − 1)(x³ + x² − 2x − 4)
```

We examine $Q(x) = x^3 + x^2 - 2x - 4$. Graphing $y = Q(x)$ we obtain the graph shown at the right. $Q(x)$ (and $P(x)$) has a second zero at $x = 1.7$. Therefore, the two real zeros of $P(x)$ are 1 and 1.7. Hence the two required points are $(1, 1)$ and $(1.7, 1.7^2) = (1.7, 2.9)$.

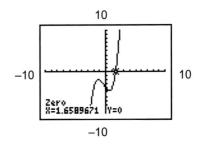

10

−10

10

−10

73.

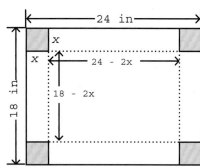
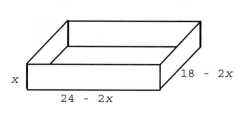

From the above figures it should be clear that

$V = \text{length} \times \text{width} \times \text{height} = (24 - 2x)(18 - 2x)x \quad 0 < x < 9 \quad \text{(why?)}$

We solve $(24 - 2x)(18 - 2x)x = 600$

$$432x - 84x^2 + 4x^3 = 600$$
$$4x^3 - 84x^2 + 432x - 600 = 0$$
$$x^3 - 21x^2 + 108x - 150 = 0$$

Let $P(x) = x^3 - 21x^2 + 108x - 150$. Graphing $y = P(x)$ on the interval $0 < x < 9$, we obtain

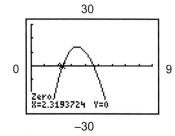
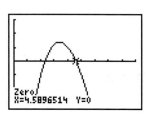

The zeros of $P(x)$ are 2.3 and 4.6, $0 < x < 9$. $x = 2.3$ inches or 4.6 inches.

75.   We note:

$$\begin{pmatrix} \text{Volume} \\ \text{of} \\ \text{tank} \end{pmatrix} = \begin{pmatrix} \text{Volume of} \\ \text{two hemispheres} \\ \text{of radius } x \end{pmatrix} + \begin{pmatrix} \text{Volume of cylinder} \\ \text{with radius } x, \\ \text{height } 10 - 2x \end{pmatrix}$$

$$20\pi = \frac{4}{3}\pi x^3 + \pi x^2(10 - 2x)$$

$$20 = \frac{4}{3}x^3 + 10x^2 - 2x^3$$

$$60 = 4x^3 + 30x^2 - 6x^3$$

$$2x^3 - 30x^2 + 60 = 0$$

$$x^3 - 15x^2 + 30 = 0 \quad \text{From physical considerations, } x > 0 \text{ and } 10 - 2x > 0,$$
$$\text{hence we are interested only in solutions in } (0, 5).$$

Let $P(x) = x^3 - 15x^2 + 30$

Graphing $y = P(x)$ on the interval $0 < x < 5$, we obtain

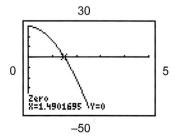

The only zero of $P(x)$, $0 < x < 5$, is 1.5. $x = 1.5$ feet.

Section 4-3

1. Every polynomial of degree $n > 0$ with complex coefficients has a complex zero.

3. The multiplicity of a zero c is the number of times $x - c$ appears in the factorization of the polynomial into linear factors.

5. | Zero | Multiplicity |
   |------|--------------|
   | –8 | 3 |
   | 6 | $\underline{2}$ |
   | | 5 = degree of $P(x)$ |

7. | Zero | Multiplicity |
   |------|--------------|
   | –4 | 3 |
   | 3 | 2 |
   | –1 | $\underline{1}$ |
   | | 6 = degree of $P(x)$ |

9. $x^3(2x + 1)^2 = (x - 0)^3\, 2^2\left(x + \dfrac{1}{2}\right)^2$

Zero	Multiplicity
0	3
–1/2	$\underline{2}$
	5 = degree of $P(x)$

11. $(x^2 + 4)^3(x^2 - 4)^5(x + 2i)$
    $= [(x + 2i)(x - 2i)]^3[(x - 2)(x + 2)]^5(x + 2i)$
    $= (x + 2i)^4(x - 2i)^3(x - 2)^5(x + 2)^5$

Zero	Multiplicity
–2i	4
2i	3
2	5
–2	$\underline{5}$
	17 = degree of $P(x)$

13. $P(x) = (x - 3)^2(x + 4)$; degree 3

15. $P(x) = (x + 7)^3[x - (-3 + \sqrt{2}\,)][x - (-3 - \sqrt{2}\,)]$; degree 5

17. $P(x) = [x - (2 - 3i)][x - (2 + 3i)](x + 4)^2$; degree 4

19. Since –2, 1, and 3 are zeros, $P(x) = (x + 2)(x - 1)(x - 3)$ is the lowest degree polynomial that has this graph. The degree of $P(x)$ is 3.

21. Since –2 and 1 are zeros, each with multiplicity 2, $P(x) = (x + 2)^2(x - 1)^2$ is the lowest degree polynomial that has this graph. The degree of $P(x)$ is 4.

23. –3, –2, and 2 are zeros, each with multiplicity 1. 0 is a zero with multiplicity 2.
    $P(x) = x^2(x + 3)(x + 2)(x - 2)$ is the lowest degree polynomial that has this graph. The degree of $P(x)$ is 5.

25. (A) Let $u = x^2$; then $x^4 + 5x^2 + 4 = u^2 + 5u + 4 = (u + 4)(u + 1)$. Thus $P(x) = (x^2 + 4)(x^2 + 1)$
    (B) The zeros of $x^2 + 4$ are $2i$ and $-2i$, so it factors as $(x - 2i)(x + 2i)$.
    The zeros of $x^2 + 1$ are i and $-i$, so it factors as $(x - i)(x + i)$. Thus $P(x) = (x - 2i)(x + 2i)(x - i)(x + i)$

27. (A) Factor by grouping:
    $P(x) = (x^3 - x^2) + (25x - 25) = x^2(x - 1) + 25(x - 1) = (x^2 + 25)(x - 1)$
    (B) The zeros of $x^2 + 25$ are $5i$ and $-5i$ so it factors as $(x - 5i)(x + 5i)$. Thus $P(x) = (x - 5i)(x + 5i)(x - 1)$

29. $a_n = 1$, $a_0 = -4$. Possible factors of –4 are ±1, ±2, ±4. Possible factors of 1 are ±1. Therefore the possible rational zeros are ±1, ±2, ±4.

31. $a_n = 10$, $a_0 = 1$. Possible factors of 1 are ±1. Possible factors of 10 are ±1, ±2, ±5, ±10. Therefore the possible rational zeros are $\pm 1, \pm\dfrac{1}{2}, \pm\dfrac{1}{5}, \pm\dfrac{1}{10}$

33. $a_n = 7$, $a_0 = -2$. Possible factors of -2 are ± 1, ± 2. Possible factors of 7 are ± 1, ± 7. Therefore the possible rational zeros are ± 1, ± 2, $\pm\dfrac{1}{7}$, $\pm\dfrac{2}{7}$.

35. $P(x) = x^3 + 9x^2 + 24x + 16$. Since -1 is a zero of $P(x)$, we can write

$$
\begin{array}{r|rrrr}
 & 1 & 9 & 24 & 16 \\
 & & -1 & -8 & -16 \\
\hline
-1 & 1 & 8 & 16 & 0
\end{array}
$$

$P(x) = (x + 1)(x^2 + 8x + 16) = (x + 1)Q(x)$
Since $Q(x)$ is a quadratic with obvious factors we can write $P(x) = (x + 1)(x + 4)(x + 4)$.

37. $P(x) = x^4 + 2x^2 + 1$; Since i is a double zero, we can write

$$
\begin{array}{r|rrrrr}
 & 1 & 0 & 2 & 0 & 1 \\
 & & i & -1 & i & -1 \\
\hline
i & 1 & i & 1 & i & 0 \\
 & & i & -2 & -i & \\
\hline
i & 1 & 2i & -1 & 0 &
\end{array}
\quad \Rightarrow x^2 + 2ix - 1
$$

$x = \dfrac{-2i \pm \sqrt{4i^2 - 4(-1)}}{2} = \dfrac{-2i \pm \sqrt{0}}{2} = -i$ (double zero) $P(x) = (x - i)(x - i)(x + i)(x + i)$

39. $P(x) = 2x^3 - 17x^2 + 90x - 41$. Since $\dfrac{1}{2}$ is a zero of $P(x)$, we can write

$$
\begin{array}{r|rrrr}
 & 2 & -17 & 90 & -41 \\
 & & 1 & -8 & 41 \\
\hline
\frac{1}{2} & 2 & -16 & 82 & 0
\end{array}
$$

$P(x) = \left(x - \dfrac{1}{2}\right)(2x^2 - 16x + 82) = \left(x - \dfrac{1}{2}\right)2(x^2 - 8x + 41) = (2x - 1)(x^2 - 8x + 41) = (2x - 1)\ Q(x)$

Since $Q(x)$ is a quadratic, we can find its zeros by the quadratic formula
$x^2 - 8x + 41 = 0$ $a = 1$ $b = -8$ $c = 41$

$x = \dfrac{-b \pm \sqrt{b^2 - 4ac}}{2a} = \dfrac{-(-8) \pm \sqrt{(-8)^2 - 4(1)(41)}}{2(1)} = \dfrac{8 \pm \sqrt{-100}}{2} = \dfrac{8 \pm 10i}{2} = 4 \pm 5i$

Since the zeros of $Q(x)$ are $4 + 5i$ and $4 - 5i$, by the factor theorem
$Q(x) = [x - (4 + 5i)][x - (4 - 5i)]$ and $P(x) = (2x - 1)[x - (4 + 5i)][x - (4 - 5i)]$

41.   Let $P(x) = 2x^3 - 5x^2 + 1$. Possible rational zeros: ± 1, $\pm\dfrac{1}{2}$.

Examining the graph of $y = P(x)$, we see that there is a zero between -1 and 0, between 0 and 1, and between 2 and 3.

We test the likely candidates, $\dfrac{1}{2}$ and $-\dfrac{1}{2}$, and find

$$
\begin{array}{r|rrrr}
 & 2 & -5 & 0 & 1 \\
 & & 1 & -2 & -1 \\
\hline
\frac{1}{2} & 2 & -4 & -2 & 0
\end{array}
$$

$\dfrac{1}{2}$ is a zero.

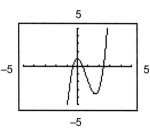

So $P(x) = \left(x - \dfrac{1}{2}\right)(2x^2 - 4x - 2)$
$= (2x - 1)(x^2 - 2x - 1)$

To find the remaining zeros, we solve
$x^2 - 2x - 1 = 0$, by completing the square:
$$x^2 - 2x = 1$$
$$x^2 - 2x + 1 = 2$$
$$(x - 1)^2 = 2$$
$$x - 1 = \pm\sqrt{2}$$
$$x = 1 \pm \sqrt{2}$$

Hence the zeros are $\dfrac{1}{2}$, $1 \pm \sqrt{2}$. These are the roots of the equation.

43. Let $P(x) = x^4 + 4x^3 - x^2 - 20x - 20$. Possible rational zeros: $\pm 1, \pm 2,$
$\pm 4, \pm 5, \pm 10, \pm 20$.
Examining the graph of $y = P(x)$, we see that there is a zero between
2 and 3, and possibly a double zero near –2. We test –2.

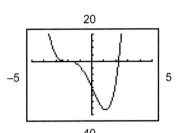

$$\begin{array}{r} 1 \quad 4 \quad -1 \quad -20 \quad -20 \\ -2 \quad -4 \quad 10 \quad 20 \\ \hline -2\,\overline{\smash{)}\,1 \quad 2 \quad -5 \quad -10 \quad\ 0} \end{array} \quad \text{–2 is a zero.}$$

Testing whether it is a double zero, we examine the reduced polynomial $x^3 + 2x^2 - 5x - 10$.

$$\begin{array}{r} 1 \quad 2 \quad -5 \quad -10 \\ -2 \quad\ 0 \quad 10 \\ \hline -2\,\overline{\smash{)}\,1 \quad 0 \quad -5 \quad\ 0} \end{array} \qquad \text{–2 is a double zero.}$$

So $P(x) = (x + 2)^2(x^2 - 5) = (x + 2)^2(x - \sqrt{5})(x + \sqrt{5})$. So the zeros of the polynomial are –2 (double), $\pm\sqrt{5}$.
These are the roots of the equation.

45. Let $P(x) = x^4 - 2x^3 - 5x^2 + 8x + 4$. Possible rational zeros: $\pm 1, \pm 2, \pm 4$.
Examining the graph of $y = P(x)$ we see that there is a zero between –
1 and 0 and between 2 and 3. The possible integer zeros are –2 and 2,
which we test.

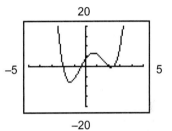

$$\begin{array}{r} 1 \ -2 \quad -5 \quad\ 8 \quad\ 4 \\ 2 \quad\ 0 \quad -10 \quad -4 \\ \hline 2\,\overline{\smash{)}\,1 \quad 0 \quad -5 \quad -2 \quad\ 0} \end{array} \qquad \text{2 is a zero.}$$

We examine the reduced polynomial $x^3 - 5x - 2$.

$$\begin{array}{r} 1 \quad\ 0 \quad -5 \quad -2 \\ -2 \quad\ 4 \quad\ 2 \\ \hline -2\,\overline{\smash{)}\,1 \quad -2 \quad -1 \quad\ 0} \end{array} \qquad \text{–2 is a zero.}$$

So $P(x) = (x - 2)(x + 2)(x^2 - 2x - 1)$. The zeros of $x^2 - 2x - 1$ are $1 \pm \sqrt{2}$. Hence the zeros of the polynomial are $\pm 2, 1 \pm \sqrt{2}$. These are the roots of the equation.

47. Factoring is the simplest method of solving. Let $u = x^2$.
$$\begin{aligned} x^4 + 10x^2 + 9 &= 0 \\ u^2 + 10u + 9 &= 0 \\ (u + 9)(u + 1) &= 0 \end{aligned}$$
$$\begin{array}{ll} u = -9, & u = -1 \\ x^2 = -9, & x^2 = -1 \\ x = 3i, -3i, & i, -i \end{array}$$

49. The possible rational zeros are $\pm 1, \pm 2, \pm 3, \pm 5, \pm 6, \pm 10, \pm 15, \pm 30$.
Examining a portion of the graph of $y = P(x)$ we see that there are
possible integer zeros at 2, 3, and –5. We test the likely candidates
and find

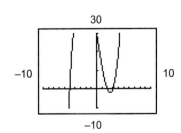

$$\begin{array}{r} 1 \ 0 \ -19 \quad 30 \\ 2 \quad 4 \quad -30 \\ \hline 2\,\overline{\smash{)}\,1 \ 2 \ -15 \quad 0} \end{array} \qquad \text{2 is a zero.}$$

So $P(x) = (x - 2)(x^2 + 2x - 15) = (x - 2)(x - 3)(x + 5)$
So the zeros of $P(x)$ are 2, 3, –5.

51. $P(x) = x^4 - \dfrac{21}{10}x^3 + \dfrac{2}{5}x = \dfrac{1}{10}(10x^4 - 21x^3 + 4x) = \dfrac{1}{10}x(10x^3 - 21x^2 + 4).$

Clearly, 0 is a zero.

We examine $Q(x) = 10x^3 - 21x^2 + 4$. Possible factors of 4 are $\pm 1, \pm 2,$ ± 4. Possible factors of 10 are $\pm 1, \pm 2, \pm 5, \pm 10$.

Hence the possible rational zeros of

$Q(x)$ are $\pm 1, \pm 2, \pm 4, \pm \dfrac{1}{2}, \pm \dfrac{1}{5}, \pm \dfrac{2}{5}, \pm \dfrac{4}{5}, \pm \dfrac{1}{10}.$

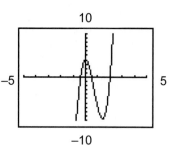

10

−5   5

−10

Examining the graph of $y = Q(x)$ we see that there are zeros between −1 and 0, and between 0 and 1, and a possible integer zero at 2.

Testing 2, we obtain

$$\begin{array}{r|rrrr} & 10 & -21 & 0 & 4 \\ & & 20 & -2 & -4 \\ \hline 2 & 10 & -1 & -2 & 0 \end{array}$$ 2 is a zero.

So $P(x) = \dfrac{1}{10}x(x-2)(10x^2 - x - 2)$

$\qquad\qquad = \dfrac{1}{10}x(x-2)(5x+2)(2x-1)$

So the zeros of $P(x)$ are $0, 2, -\dfrac{2}{5}, \dfrac{1}{2}.$

53. $P(x) = x^4 - 5x^3 + \dfrac{15}{2}x^2 - 2x - 2 = \dfrac{1}{2}(2x^4 - 10x^3 + 15x^2 - 4x - 4).$

Possible factors of −4 are $\pm 1, \pm 2, \pm 4$. Possible factors of 2 are $\pm 1,$ ± 2. Hence the possible rational zeros are $\pm 1, \pm 2, \pm 4, \pm \dfrac{1}{2}.$

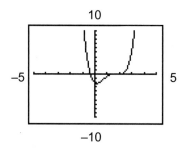

10

−5   5

−10

Examining the graph of $y = P(x)$ we see that there are zeros between −1 and 0, and between 1 and 2, and a possible double zero at 2. Testing 2, we obtain

$$\begin{array}{r|rrrrr} & 2 & -10 & 15 & -4 & -4 \\ & & 4 & -12 & 6 & 4 \\ \hline 2 & 2 & -6 & 3 & 2 & 0 \end{array}$$ 2 is a zero.

Testing whether it is a double zero, we examine the reduced polynomial $2x^3 - 6x^2 + 3x + 2$.

$$\begin{array}{r|rrrr} & 2 & -6 & 3 & 2 \\ & & 4 & -4 & -2 \\ \hline 2 & 2 & -2 & -1 & 0 \end{array}$$ Thus 2 is a double zero of $P(x)$.

$P(x) = \dfrac{1}{2}(x-2)^2(2x^2 - 2x - 1)$

To find the remaining zeros, we solve $2x^2 - 2x - 1 = 0$.

Applying the quadratic formula with $a = 2, b = -2, c = -1$, we obtain

$$x = \dfrac{-(-2)\pm\sqrt{(-2)^2 - 4(2)(-1)}}{2(2)} = \dfrac{2\pm\sqrt{12}}{4} = \dfrac{1\pm\sqrt{3}}{2} \text{ or } \dfrac{1}{2}\pm\dfrac{1}{2}\sqrt{3}.$$

So the zeros of $P(x)$ are 2 (double), $\dfrac{1}{2}\pm\dfrac{1}{2}\sqrt{3}.$

55. The possible rational zeros are $\pm 1, \pm 2, \pm 4, \pm \dfrac{1}{2}, \pm \dfrac{1}{3}, \pm \dfrac{2}{3}, \pm \dfrac{4}{3}, \pm \dfrac{1}{6}.$

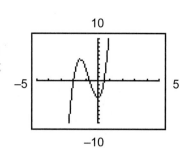

10

−5   5

−10

Examining the graph of $y = P(x)$, we see that there is a zero between −1 and 0, between 0 and 1, and a possible integer zero at −2. Testing −2, we obtain

$$\begin{array}{r|rrrr} & 6 & 13 & 0 & -4 \\ & & -12 & -2 & 4 \\ \hline -2 & 6 & 1 & -2 & 0 \end{array}$$ −2 is a zero.

$P(x) = (x+2)(6x^2 + x - 2) = (x+2)(3x+2)(2x-1)$

57. The possible rational zeros are ±1, ±2, ±4.
Examining the graph of $y = P(x)$, we see that there is a zero between
−1 and 0, between 2 and 3, and a possible integer zero at −4. Testing
−4, we obtain

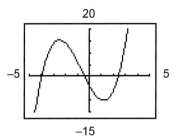

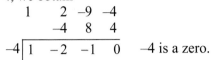

$$\begin{array}{r} 1 \quad\; 2 \; -9 \; -4 \\ -4 \quad 8 \quad 4 \\ \hline -4\,|\,1 \; -2 \; -1 \quad 0 \end{array}$$ −4 is a zero.

So $P(x) = (x + 4)(x^2 - 2x - 1)$. The zeros of $x^2 - 2x - 1$ are $1 \pm \sqrt{2}$.
Hence $P(x) = (x + 4)[x - (1 + \sqrt{2})][x - (1 - \sqrt{2})]$

59. The possible rational zeros are $\pm 1, \pm 2, \pm\frac{1}{2}, \pm\frac{1}{4}$.

Examining the graph of $y = P(x)$, we see that there is a zero between
−1 and 0, between 0 and 1, and possible integer zeros at −1 and 2.
Testing 2, we obtain

$$\begin{array}{r} 4 \; -4 \; -9 \quad 1 \quad 2 \\ 8 \quad 8 \; -2 \; -2 \\ \hline 2\,|\,4 \quad 4 \; -1 \; -1 \quad 0 \end{array}$$ 2 is a zero.

Testing −1, we examine the reduced polynomial $4x^3 + 4x^2 - x - 1$.

$$\begin{array}{r} 4 \quad 4 \; -1 \; -1 \\ -4 \quad 0 \quad 1 \\ \hline -1\,|\,4 \quad 0 \; -1 \quad 0 \end{array}$$ −1 is a zero.

So $P(x) = (x - 2)(x + 1)(4x^2 - 1) = (x - 2)(x + 1)(2x - 1)(2x + 1)$.

61. If $2 - 5i$ is a zero, $2 + 5i$ is a zero.
$$\begin{aligned} P(x) &= [x - (2 - 5i)][x - (2 + 5i)] \\ &= [x - 2 + 5i][x - 2 - 5i] \\ &= [(x - 2) + 5i][(x - 2) - 5i] \\ &= (x - 2)^2 - (5i)^2 \\ &= x^2 - 4x + 4 + 25 \\ &= x^2 - 4x + 29 \end{aligned}$$

63. If $6 + i$ is a zero, $6 - i$ is a zero.
$$\begin{aligned} P(x) &= a[x - (6 + i)][x - (6 - i)] \\ &= a[x - 6 - i][x - 6 + i] \\ &= a[(x - 6) - i][(x - 6) + i] \\ &= a[(x - 6)^2 - i^2] \\ &= a(x^2 - 12x + 36 + 1) \\ P(x) &= a(x^2 - 12x + 37) \\ P(x) &= ax^2 - 12ax + 37a. \end{aligned}$$
Since $P(0) = 74 = 37a$, $a = 2$. Hence $P(x) = 2x^2 - 24x + 74$

65. If $8i$ is a zero, $-8i$ is a zero.
$$\begin{aligned} P(x) &= (x + 5)(x - 8i)(x + 8i) \\ &= (x + 5)(x^2 + 64) \\ &= x^3 + 64x + 5x^2 + 320 \\ P(x) &= x^3 + 5x^2 + 64x + 320 \end{aligned}$$

67. If i is a zero, $-i$ is a zero. If $1 - i$ is a zero, $1 + i$ is a zero.
$$\begin{aligned} P(x) &= a(x - i)(x + i)[x - (1 - i)][x - (1 + i)] \\ &= a(x^2 - i^2)\,[x - 1 + i][x - 1 - i] \\ &= a(x^2 + 1)[(x - 1)^2 - i^2] \\ &= a(x^2 + 1)[x^2 - 2x + 1 + 1] \\ &= a(x^2 + 1)(x^2 - 2x + 2) \\ &= a(x^4 - 2x^3 + 2x^2 + x^2 - 2x + 2) \\ &= a(x^4 - 2x^3 + 3x^2 - 2x + 2) \end{aligned}$$
Since $P(1) = 10 = a(1^4 - 2\cdot 1^3 + 3\cdot 1^2 - 2\cdot 1 + 2)$, $10 = 2a$, $5 = a$.
Hence $P(x) = 5(x^4 - 2x^3 + 3x^2 - 2x + 2) = 5x^4 - 10x^3 + 15x^2 - 10x + 10$

69. $\begin{aligned}[t] [x - (4 - 5i)][x - (4 + 5i)] &= [x - 4 + 5i][x - 4 - 5i] \\ &= [(x - 4) + 5i][(x - 4) - 5i] \\ &= (x - 4)^2 - 25i^2 \\ &= x^2 - 8x + 16 + 25 \\ &= x^2 - 8x + 41 \end{aligned}$

71. $\begin{aligned}[t] [x - (3 + 4i)][x - (3 - 4i)] &= [x - 3 - 4i][x - 3 + 4i] \\ &= [(x - 3) - 4i][(x - 3) + 4i] \\ &= (x - 3)^2 - 16i^2 \\ &= x^2 - 6x + 9 + 16 \\ &= x^2 - 6x + 25 \end{aligned}$

73. $[x - (a + bi)][x - (a - bi)] = [x - a - bi][x - a + bi]$
$$= [(x - a) - bi][(x - a) + bi]$$
$$= (x - a)^2 - b^2 i^2$$
$$= (x - a)^2 + b^2$$
$$= x^2 - 2ax + a^2 + b^2$$

75. If $3 - i$ is a zero, then $3 + i$ is a zero.
So $Q(x) = [x - (3 - i)][x - (3 + i)]$ divides $P(x)$ evenly.
Applying problem 73,
$Q(x) = x^2 - 6x + 9 + 1 = x^2 - 6x + 10$.
Dividing, we see

$$
\begin{array}{r}
x + 1 \\
x^2 - 6x + 10 \overline{\smash{\big)}\ x^3 - 5x^2 + 4x + 10} \\
\underline{x^3 - 6x^2 + 10x} \\
x^2 - 6x + 10 \\
\underline{x^2 - 6x + 10} \\
0
\end{array}
$$

So $P(x) = (x + 1)Q(x)$ and the two other zeros are -1 and $3 + i$.

77. If $-5i$ is a zero, then so is $5i$.
So $Q(x) = (x - 5i)(x + 5i)$ divides $P(x)$ evenly.
$Q(x) = x^2 - 25i^2 = x^2 + 25$. Dividing, we see

$$
\begin{array}{r}
x - 3 \\
x^2 + 25 \overline{\smash{\big)}\ x^3 - 3x^2 + 25x - 75} \\
\underline{x^3 \qquad\ + 25x} \\
-3x^2 \qquad -75 \\
\underline{-3x^2 \qquad -75} \\
0
\end{array}
$$

So $P(x) = (x - 3)Q(x)$ and the two other zeros are $5i$ and 3.

79. If $2 + i$ is a zero, then $2 - i$ is a zero.
So $Q(x) = [x - (2 + i)][x - (2 - i)]$ divides $P(x)$ evenly.
Applying problem 73,
$Q(x) = x^2 - 4x + 4 + 1 = x^2 - 4x + 5$. Dividing, we see

$$
\begin{array}{r}
x^2 - 2 \\
x^2 - 4x + 5 \overline{\smash{\big)}\ x^4 - 4x^3 + 3x^2 + 8x - 10} \\
\underline{x^4 - 4x^3 + 5x^2} \\
-2x^2 + 8x - 10 \\
\underline{-2x^2 + 8x - 10} \\
0
\end{array}
$$

So $P(x) = Q(x)(x^2 - 2)$. $x^2 - 2$ has two zeros: $\sqrt{2}$ and $-\sqrt{2}$.
Summarizing, $P(x)$ has 4 zeros: $2 + i, 2 - i, \sqrt{2}, -\sqrt{2}$.

81.   Here is a graph of
$P(x) = 3x^3 - 37x^2 + 84x - 24$.

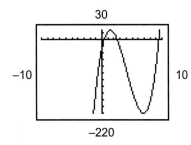

The rational zero theorem gives $\pm 1, \pm 2, \pm 3, \pm 4, \pm 6, \pm 8, \pm 12, \pm 24,$
$\pm \frac{1}{3}, \pm \frac{2}{3}, \pm \frac{4}{3}, \pm \frac{8}{3}$ as possible rational zeros. However, the graph
suggests that $P(x)$ has no integer zeros; there are no negative zeros, and the positive zeros would
appear to lie between 0 and 1, 2 and 3, and 9 and 10. This suggests that we consider only the possible zeros
$\frac{1}{3}, \frac{2}{3}$, and $\frac{8}{3}$.

Testing $\frac{1}{3}$, we obtain

$$
\begin{array}{r}
\phantom{\tfrac{1}{3}|}\ \ 3 \quad -37 \quad\ 84 \ -24 \\
\phantom{\tfrac{1}{3}|\ \ 3} 1 \ -12 \quad 24 \\
\hline
\tfrac{1}{3}\big|\ \ 3 \quad -36 \quad 72 \quad\ \ 0
\end{array}
\qquad \frac{1}{3} \text{ is a zero.}
$$

So $P(x) = \left(x - \dfrac{1}{3}\right)(3x^2 - 36x + 72) = \left(x - \dfrac{1}{3}\right)3(x^2 - 12x + 24)$

To find the remaining zeros, we solve $x^2 - 12x + 24 = 0$ by completing the square: $x^2 - 12x = -24$

$$x^2 - 12x + 36 = 12$$
$$(x - 6)^2 = 12$$
$$x - 6 = \pm\sqrt{12}$$
$$x = 6 \pm \sqrt{12} \text{ or } 6 \pm 2\sqrt{3} \qquad \text{So the zeros of } P(x) \text{ are } \frac{1}{3}, 6 \pm 2\sqrt{3}.$$

83. Here is a graph of
$P(x) = 4x^4 + 4x^3 + 49x^2 + 64x - 240.$

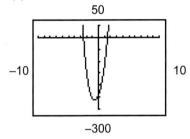

The rational zero theorem gives $\pm1, \pm2, \pm3, \pm4, \pm5, \pm6, \pm8, \pm10,$ $\pm12, \pm15, \pm16, \pm20, \pm24, \pm30, \pm40, \pm48, \pm60, \pm80, \pm120, \pm240,$ $\pm\frac{1}{2}, \pm\frac{3}{2}, \pm\frac{5}{2}, \pm\frac{15}{2}, \pm\frac{1}{4}, \pm\frac{3}{4}, \pm\frac{5}{4}, \pm\frac{15}{4}$ as possible rational zeros.

However, the graph suggests that $P(x)$ has no integer zeros, and the zeros appear to lie between -3 and -2, and 1 and 2.

This suggests that we consider only the possible zeros $\frac{3}{2}$, $\frac{5}{4}$, and $-\frac{5}{2}$. Testing $\frac{3}{2}$, we obtain

$$
\begin{array}{r}
\phantom{\frac{3}{2}}\ \ 4 \quad\ \ 4 \quad\ 49 \quad\ \ 64 \quad -240 \\
\phantom{\frac{3}{2}}\ \ \ \quad\ \ 6 \quad\ 15 \quad\ \ 96 \quad\ \ 240 \\
\hline
\frac{3}{2}\ \vert\ 4 \quad 10 \quad 64 \quad 160 \quad\ \ \ 0
\end{array}
\qquad \frac{3}{2} \text{ is a zero.}
$$

So $P(x) = \left(x - \frac{3}{2}\right)(4x^3 + 10x^2 + 64x + 160)$

$$= \left(x - \frac{3}{2}\right)2(2x^3 + 5x^2 + 32x + 80)$$

We consider the reduced polynomial $Q(x) = 2x^3 + 5x^2 + 32x + 80$. The graph suggests that the other real zero is negative, so we try $-\frac{5}{2}$ next.

$$
\begin{array}{r}
\phantom{-\frac{5}{2}}\ \ 2 \quad\ \ 5 \quad\ 32 \quad\ \ 80 \\
\phantom{-\frac{5}{2}}\ -5 \quad\ \ 0 \quad -80 \\
\hline
-\frac{5}{2}\ \vert\ 2 \quad\ 0 \quad 32 \quad\ \ \ 0
\end{array}
\qquad -\frac{5}{2} \text{ is a zero.}
$$

So $P(x) = \left(x - \frac{3}{2}\right)2\left(x + \frac{5}{2}\right)(2x^2 + 32) = 4\left(x - \frac{3}{2}\right)\left(x + \frac{5}{2}\right)(x^2 + 16).$

The remaining zeros of $P(x)$ are the zeros of $x^2 + 16$, that is, $\pm 4i$. So the zeros of $P(x)$ are $\frac{3}{2}, -\frac{5}{2}, \pm 4i$.

85. Here is a graph of $P(x) = 4x^4 - 44x^3 + 145x^2 - 192x + 90$.
The rational zero theorem gives $\pm1, \pm2, \pm3, \pm5, \pm6, \pm9, \pm10, \pm15,$ $\pm18, \pm30, \pm45, \pm90, \pm\frac{1}{2}, \pm\frac{3}{2}, \pm\frac{5}{2}, \pm\frac{9}{2}, \pm\frac{15}{2}, \pm\frac{45}{2}, \pm\frac{1}{4}, \pm\frac{3}{4}, \pm\frac{5}{4},$ $\pm\frac{9}{4}, \pm\frac{15}{4}, \pm\frac{45}{4}$ as possible rational zeros. However, the graph

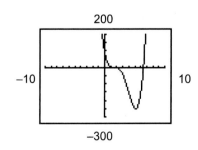

suggests that the only possible integer zeros are 1 and 2; there are no negative zeros, and the zeros appear to lie between 0 and 3, and between 6 and 7. This suggests that we consider only the possible zeros $1, 2, \frac{1}{2}, \frac{3}{2}, \frac{5}{2}, \frac{1}{4}, \frac{3}{4}, \frac{5}{4}, \frac{9}{4}.$

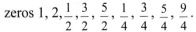

Testing the possible candidates, we obtain $P(1) = 3$, $P(2) = -2$, and

$$
\begin{array}{r}
\phantom{\frac{3}{2}}\;\; 4 \quad -44 \quad 145 \quad -192 \quad 90 \\
6 \quad -57 \quad 132 \quad -90 \\
\hline
\tfrac{3}{2}\; \big|\;\; 4 \quad -38 \quad\;\; 88 \quad\;\; -60 \quad\;\; 0
\end{array}
\qquad \tfrac{3}{2} \text{ is a zero.}
$$

So $P(x) = \left(x - \dfrac{3}{2}\right)(4x^3 - 38x^2 + 88x - 60) = \left(x - \dfrac{3}{2}\right)2(2x^3 - 19x^2 + 44x - 30)$

We consider the reduced polynomial $Q(x) = 2x^3 - 19x^2 + 44x - 30$. The remaining possibilities from the reduced list are $\dfrac{1}{2}, \dfrac{3}{2}, \dfrac{5}{2}$. Testing for a possible double zero at $\dfrac{3}{2}$, we obtain

$$
\begin{array}{r}
\phantom{\tfrac{3}{2}}\;\; 2 \quad -19 \quad\;\; 44 \quad -30 \\
3 \quad -24 \quad\;\; 30 \\
\hline
\tfrac{3}{2}\; \big|\;\; 2 \quad -16 \quad\;\; 20 \quad\;\; 0
\end{array}
\qquad \tfrac{3}{2} \text{ is a double zero.}
$$

So $P(x) = \left(x - \dfrac{3}{2}\right)^2 2(2x^2 - 16x + 20) = \left(x - \dfrac{3}{2}\right)^2 4(x^2 - 8x + 10)$

To find the remaining zeros, we solve $x^2 - 8x + 10 = 0$, by completing the square.

$$
\begin{aligned}
x^2 - 8x &= -10 \\
x^2 - 8x + 16 &= 6 \\
(x - 4)^2 &= 6 \\
x - 4 &= \pm\sqrt{6} \\
x &= 4 \pm \sqrt{6} \qquad \text{So the zeros of } P(x) \text{ are } \tfrac{3}{2} \text{ (double)}, 4 \pm \sqrt{6}.
\end{aligned}
$$

87.   (A) Since 1 is a root, let $P(x) = x^3 - 1$ and write

$$
\begin{array}{r}
\;\; 1 \quad 0 \quad 0 \quad -1 \\
1 \quad 1 \quad\;\; 1 \\
\hline
1\; \big|\;\; 1 \quad 1 \quad 1 \quad\;\; 0
\end{array}
$$

$P(x) = (x - 1)(x^2 + x + 1)$

The other cube roots of 1 will be solutions to $x^2 + x + 1 = 0$.

Applying the quadratic formula with $a = b = c = 1$, we have

$x = \dfrac{-1 \pm \sqrt{(1)^2 - 4(1)(1)}}{2(1)} = \dfrac{-1 \pm \sqrt{-3}}{2} = \dfrac{-1 \pm i\sqrt{3}}{2}$. Thus, $-\dfrac{1}{2} + \dfrac{\sqrt{3}}{2}i$ and $-\dfrac{1}{2} - \dfrac{\sqrt{3}}{2}i$ are the other cube roots of 1.

(B) Thus, there are 3 distinct cube roots of 1.

89.   Step 1: $a_2\left(\dfrac{b}{c}\right)^2 + a_1\left(\dfrac{b}{c}\right) + a_0 = 0$ Substitute $\dfrac{b}{c}$ into $a_2 x^2 + a_1 x + a_0 = 0$

Step 2: $a_2 b^2 + a_1 bc + a_0 c^2 = 0$ Multiply both sides by c^2.

Step 3: $a_2 b^2 + a_1 bc = -a_0 c^2$ Subtract $a_0 c^2$ from both sides.

Step 4: b is a factor of $-a_0 c^2$, so b is a factor of a_0 b and c have no factors in common.

Step 5: Modify steps 3 and 4 to conclude   Write $a_2 b^2 = -a_1 bc + a_0 c^2$.

     that c is a factor of a_2.   Then c is a factor of $a_2 b^2$, so c is a factor of a_2.

91. $P(2 + i) = (2 + i)^2 + 2i(2 + i) - 5$

     $= 4 + 4i + i^2 + 4i + 2i^2 - 5$

     $= 4 + 4i - 1 + 4i - 2 - 5$

     $= -4 + 8i$

So $P(2 + i) \neq 0$ and $2 + i$ is not a zero of $P(x)$. This does not contradict the theorem, since $P(x)$ is not a polynomial with real coefficients (the coefficient of x is the imaginary number $2i$).

93. Let x = the amount of increase.

Then old volume = $1 \times 2 \times 3 = 6$

new volume = $(x + 1)(x + 2)(x + 3) = x^3 + 6x^2 + 11x + 6$

Since (new volume) = 10 (old volume), we must solve

$$x^3 + 6x^2 + 11x + 6 = 10(6)$$
$$x^3 + 6x^2 + 11x + 6 = 60$$
$$P(x) = x^3 + 6x^2 + 11x - 54 = 0$$

The possible rational zeros are ±1, ±2, ±3, ±6, ±9, ±18, ±27, ±54.

Testing in order, we obtain $P(1) = -36$ $P(2) = 0$

$$
\begin{array}{r|rrrr}
 & 1 & 6 & 11 & -54 \\
 &   & 2 & 16 & 54 \\
\hline
2 & 1 & 8 & 27 & 0 \\
\end{array}
$$

Thus, $x^3 + 6x^2 + 11x - 54 = (x - 2)(x^2 + 8x + 27)$. Since $x^2 + 8x + 27 = 0$ has no positive zeros, 2 is the only positive solution of the equation. The increase must equal 2 feet.

95.

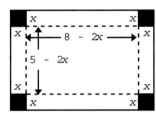 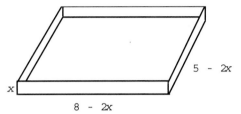

From the figure, it should be clear that Volume = $x(5 - 2x)(8 - 2x) = 14$

Since x, $5 - 2x$, and $8 - 2x$ must all be positive, the domain of x is $0 < x < \dfrac{5}{2}$ or $(0, 2.5)$.

We solve $x(5 - 2x)(8 - 2x) = 14$, or $4x^3 - 26x^2 + 40x = 14$, for x in this domain.

$$4x^3 - 26x^2 + 40x = 14$$
$$4x^3 - 26x^2 + 40x - 14 = 0$$
$$P(x) = 2x^3 - 13x^2 + 20x - 7 = 0$$

Possible rational zeros: ±1, ±7, $\pm\dfrac{1}{2}$, $\pm\dfrac{7}{2}$. Testing the possibilities, we obtain

$P(1) = 2$ $P(7) = 182$ $P\left(\dfrac{1}{2}\right) = 0$

$$
\begin{array}{r|rrrr}
 & 2 & -13 & 20 & -7 \\
 &   & 1 & -6 & 7 \\
\hline
\frac{1}{2} & 2 & -12 & 14 & 0 \\
\end{array}
$$
   $\dfrac{1}{2}$ is a zero.

So $2x^3 - 13x^2 + 20x - 7 = \left(x - \dfrac{1}{2}\right)(2x^2 - 12x + 14) = (2x - 1)(x^2 - 6x + 7)$

To find the remaining zeros, we solve $x^2 - 6x + 7 = 0$, by completing the square:

$$x^2 - 6x = -7$$
$$x^2 - 6x + 9 = 2$$
$$(x - 3)^2 = 2$$
$$x - 3 = \pm\sqrt{2}$$
$$x = 3 \pm \sqrt{2}$$

Hence the zeros are $\dfrac{1}{2}$, $3 - \sqrt{2}$, $3 + \sqrt{2}$, or 0.5, 1.6, 4.4 to two significant digits. We discard $3 + \sqrt{2}$ or 4.4, since it is not in the interval $(0, 2.5)$. The square should be 0.5×0.5 inches or 1.6×1.6 inches.

Section 4-4

1.   Yes. Since 1 is a polynomial (of degree 0), $P(x) = \dfrac{P(x)}{1}$ is a rational function if $P(x)$ is a polynomial.

3.   A vertical asymptote is a vertical line $x = a$ that the graph of a function approaches ever more closely, but does not cross, as x approaches a from left and/or right, while function values increase or decrease without bound.

5.   An oblique asymptote is a line of non-zero slope that the graph of a function approaches ever more closely as x increases and/or decreases without bound.

7.   This graph has a vertical asymptote $x = 2$, and a horizontal asymptote $y = -2$. This corresponds to $g(x)$.

9.   This graph has a vertical asymptote $x = 2$, and a horizontal asymptote $y = 2$. This corresponds to $h(x)$.

11.   (A) ∞ (B) $-\infty$ (C) 2 (D) 2   13. (A) $-\infty$ (B) ∞ (C) 2 (D) 2

15. $f(x) = \dfrac{3x - 9}{x} = \dfrac{n(x)}{d(x)}$ *Domain:* $d(x) = x$

zero: $x = 0$

domain: all real numbers except 0, $(-\infty, 0) \cup (0, \infty)$
x intercepts: $n(x) = 3x - 9$ zero: $x = 3$ *x intercept:* 3

17. $h(x) = \dfrac{x + 6}{x^2 - 4} = \dfrac{n(x)}{d(x)}$ *Domain:* $d(x) = x^2 - 4$

zeros: $x^2 - 4 = 0$
$x^2 = 4$
$x = \pm 2$

domain: all real numbers except ± 2
$(-\infty, -2) \cup (-2, 2) \cup (2, \infty)$
x intercepts: $n(x) = x + 6$ zero: $x = -6$ *x intercept:* -6

19. $r(x) = \dfrac{x^2 + 3x - 4}{x^2 + 12} = \dfrac{n(x)}{d(x)}$ *Domain:* $d(x) = x^2 + 1$

zeros: $x^2 + 1 = 0$
$x^2 = -1$
$x = \pm i$ No real zeros
domain: all real numbers
x intercepts: $n(x) = x^2 + 3x - 4$
zeros: $x^2 + 3x - 4 = 0$
$(x + 4)(x - 1) = 0$
$x = -4, 1$
x intercepts: $-4, 1$

21. $F(x) = \dfrac{x^4 + 16}{x^2 - 36} = \dfrac{n(x)}{d(x)}$ *Domain:* $d(x) = x^2 - 36$

zeros: $x^2 - 36 = 0$
$x^2 = 36$
$x = \pm 6$

domain: all real numbers except ± 6
$(-\infty, -6) \cup (-6, 6) \cup (6, \infty)$
x intercepts: $n(x) = x^4 + 16$ No real zeros
no *x* intercepts

23. $f(x) = \dfrac{5x + 1}{x + 2} = \dfrac{n(x)}{d(x)}$

vertical asymptotes: $d(x) = x + 2$
zero: $x = -2$
vertical asymptote $x = -2$

horizontal asymptotes: Since $n(x)$ and $d(x)$ have the same degree, the line $y = 5$ is a horizontal asymptote.

25. $s(x) = \dfrac{2x - 3}{x^2 - 16} = \dfrac{n(x)}{d(x)}$

vertical asymptotes: $d(x) = x^2 - 16$
zeros: $x^2 - 16 = 0$
$x^2 = 16$
$x = \pm 4$
vertical asymptotes: $x = 4$, $x = -4$
horizontal asymptote: Since the degree of $n(x)$ is less than the degree of $d(x)$, the x axis is a horizontal asymptote.   horizontal asymptote: $y = 0$

27. $p(x) = \dfrac{x^2 + 2x + 1}{x} = \dfrac{n(x)}{d(x)}$

vertical asymptotes: $d(x) = x$ zero: $x = 0$
vertical asymptote: $x = 0$
horizontal asymptote: Since the degree of $n(x)$ is
greater than the degree of $d(x)$, there are no
horizontal asymptotes.

29. $h(x) = \dfrac{3x^2 + 8}{2x^2 + 6x} = \dfrac{n(x)}{d(x)}$

vertical asymptotes: $d(x) = 2x^2 + 6x$
zeros: $2x^2 + 6x = 0$
$2x(x + 3) = 0$
$x = 0, -3$
vertical asymptotes: $x = -3, x = 0$
horizontal asymptote: Since $n(x)$ and $d(x)$ have
the same degree, the line $y = \dfrac{3}{2}$ is a horizontal
asymptote.

31. The graph has more than one horizontal asymptote.

33. The graph has a sharp corner at $(0, 0)$.

35. $\dfrac{x^2 + 2x}{x} = \dfrac{x(x + 2)}{x} = x + 2$ if $x \neq 0$. The graph of
f is the same as the graph of g except that f has a
hole at $(0, 2)$.

37. $\dfrac{x + 2}{x^2 + 10x + 16} = \dfrac{x + 2}{(x + 2)(x + 8)} = \dfrac{1}{x + 8}$
if $x \neq -2$. The graph of f is the same as the graph of
g except that f has a hole at $\left(-2, \dfrac{1}{6}\right)$.

Complete the sketch. Plot a few points.

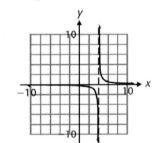

x	$f(x)$
4.5	2
5	1
6	0.5
3.5	-2
3	-1
2	-0.5

39. $f(x) = \dfrac{1}{x - 4} = \dfrac{n(x)}{d(x)}$

Intercepts.
There are no real zeros of $n(x) = 1$. No x intercept
$f(0) = -\dfrac{1}{4}$ $y = -\dfrac{1}{4}$ y intercept
Vertical asymptotes. $d(x) = x - 4$ zeros: 4 $x = 4$
Horizontal asymptotes. Since the degree of $n(x)$ is
less that the degree of $d(x)$, the x axis is a
horizontal asymptote.

Common Error: Entering $1/x - 4$ in the calculator.
Parentheses are needed: $1/(x - 4)$.

Complete the sketch. Plot a few additional points.

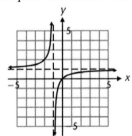

41. $f(x) = \dfrac{x}{x + 1} = \dfrac{n(x)}{d(x)}$

Intercepts. Real zeros of $n(x) = x$ $x = 0$ x intercept
$f(0) = 0$ $y = 0$ y intercept
The graph crosses the coordinate axes only at the origin.
Vertical asymptotes. $d(x) = x + 1$ zeros: -1 $x = -1$
Horizontal asymptotes. Since $n(x)$ and $d(x)$ have the same
degree, the line $y = 1$ is a horizontal asymptote.

43. $g(x) = \dfrac{1-x^2}{x^2} = \dfrac{n(x)}{d(x)}$

Intercepts. Real zeros of $n(x) = 1 - x^2$
$$1 - x^2 = 0$$
$$x^2 = 1$$
$$x = \pm 1 \quad x \text{ intercepts}$$
$g(0)$ is not defined   no y intercepts
Vertical asymptotes. $d(x) = x^2$ zeros: 0 $x = 0$
Horizontal asymptotes. Since $n(x)$ and $d(x)$ have the same degree, the line $y = -1$ is a horizontal asymptote.

Complete the sketch. Plot a few additional points

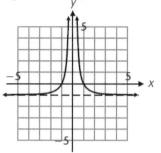

45. $f(x) = \dfrac{9}{x^2 - 9} = \dfrac{n(x)}{d(x)}$

Intercepts. There are no real zeros of $n(x) = 9$. No x intercept $f(0) = -1$ y intercept
Vertical asymptotes. $d(x) = x^2 - 9$ zeros: $x^2 - 9 = 0$
$$x^2 = 9$$
$$x = \pm 3$$
Horizontal asymptotes. Since the degree of $n(x)$ is less than the degree of $d(x)$, the x axis is a horizontal asymptote.

Complete the sketch. Plot a few additional points.

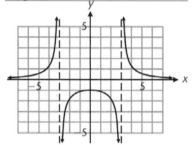

47. $f(x) = \dfrac{x}{x^2 - 1} = \dfrac{n(x)}{d(x)}$

Intercepts. Real zeros of $n(x) = x$ $x = 0$ x intercept
$$f(0) = 0 \quad y = 0 \quad y \text{ intercept}$$
The graph crosses the coordinate axes only at the origin.
Vertical asymptotes. $d(x) = x^2 - 1$ zeros: $x^2 - 1 = 0$
$$x^2 = 1$$
$$x = \pm 1$$
Horizontal asymptotes. Since the degree of $n(x)$ is less than the degree of $d(x)$, the x axis is a horizontal asymptote.

Complete the sketch. Plot a few additional points.

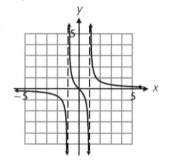

49. $g(x) = \dfrac{2}{x^2 + 1} = \dfrac{n(x)}{d(x)}$

Intercepts. There are no real zeros of $n(x) = 2$. No x intercept $g(0) = 2$ y intercept
Vertical asymptotes. There are no real zeros of $d(x) = x^2 + 1$ No vertical asymptotes
Horizontal asymptotes. Since the degree of $n(x)$ is less than the degree of $d(x)$, the x axis is a horizontal asymptote.

Complete the sketch. Plot a few additional points.

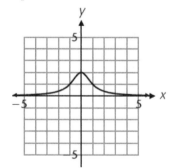

51. $f(x) = \dfrac{12x^2}{(3x+5)^2} = \dfrac{n(x)}{d(x)}$

Intercepts. Real zeros of $n(x) = 12x^2$ $x = 0$ x intercept
$\qquad\qquad\quad f(0) = 0$ $y = 0$ y intercept
The graph crosses the coordinate axes only at the origin.
Vertical asymptotes. $d(x) = (3x + 5)^2$ zeros: $(3x + 5)^2 = 0$
$\qquad\qquad\qquad\qquad\qquad\qquad\qquad 3x + 5 = 0$
$\qquad\qquad\qquad\qquad\qquad\qquad\qquad\quad x = -\dfrac{5}{3}$

Horizontal asymptotes. Since $n(x)$ and $d(x)$ have the same

degree, the line $y = \dfrac{12}{3^2} = \dfrac{4}{3}$ is a horizontal asymptote.

Complete the sketch. Plot a few additional points.

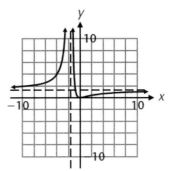

53. To have zeros $-2, -1, 1,$ and 2, the numerator must have factors $(x + 2), (x + 1), (x - 1),$ and $(x - 2)$. To have a horizontal asymptote at $y = 3$, the degree of the denominator should be the same as the numerator, and the leading coefficient of the numerator should be 3 times as large. To have no vertical asymptote, the denominator should have no real zeros.

$f(x) = \dfrac{3(x+2)(x-2)(x+1)(x-1)}{x^4 + 1}$ or $f(x) = \dfrac{3(x^2-4)(x^2-1)}{x^4+1}$ will work.

55. To get $y = 2x + 5$ as an oblique asymptote, our function should look like $f(x) = 2x + 5 + \dfrac{r(x)}{q(x)}$ where the

degree of $q(x)$ is greater than the degree of $r(x)$. If $q(x) = x - 10$, we'll have $x = 10$ as vertical asymptote. In that case $r(x)$ will have to be constant so that its power is less than $q(x)$; $r(x) = 100$ will do.

$f(x) = 2x + 5 + \dfrac{100}{x-10} = \dfrac{(2x+5)(x-10)}{x-10} + \dfrac{100}{x-10} = \dfrac{(2x+5)(x-10)+100}{x-10}$

57. $\dfrac{x}{x-2} \le 0$ Let $f(x) = \dfrac{p(x)}{q(x)} = \dfrac{x}{x-2}$

> **Common Error:**
> It is not correct to "multiply both sides" by $x - 2$.

The zero of $p(x) = x$ is 0. The zero of $q(x) = x - 2$ is 2. These two zeros partition the x axis into the three intervals shown in the table. A test number is chosen from each interval to determine the sign of $f(x)$.

Interval	Test number x	$f(x)$	Sign of f
$(-\infty, 0)$	-1	$\dfrac{1}{3}$	$+$
$(0, 2)$	1	-1	$-$
$(2, \infty)$	3	3	$+$

The equality is satisfied at $x = 0$, but not at $x = 2$. We conclude that the solution set is $[0, 2)$.

59. $\dfrac{x^2 - 16}{5x - 2} > 0$ Let $f(x) = \dfrac{p(x)}{q(x)} = \dfrac{x^2 - 16}{5x - 2}$

The zeros of $p(x) = x^2 - 16 = (x + 4)(x - 4)$ are -4 and 4. The zero of $q(x) = 5x - 2$ is $\dfrac{2}{5}$.

These three zeros partition the x axis into the four intervals shown in the table. A test number is chosen from each interval to determine the sign of $f(x)$.

Interval	Test number x	$f(x)$	Sign of f
$(-\infty, -4)$	-5	$-\dfrac{1}{3}$	$-$
$\left(-4, \dfrac{2}{5}\right)$	0	8	$+$
$\left(\dfrac{2}{5}, 4\right)$	1	-5	$-$
$(4, \infty)$	5	$\dfrac{9}{23}$	$+$

We conclude that the solution set is $\left(-4, \dfrac{2}{5}\right) \cup (4, \infty)$.

61. $\dfrac{x^2 + 4x - 20}{3x} \geq 4$

$\dfrac{x^2 + 4x - 20}{3x} - 4 \geq 0$

$\dfrac{x^2 + 4x - 20}{3x} - \dfrac{12x}{3x} \geq 0$

$\dfrac{x^2 - 8x - 20}{3x} \geq 0$

Let $f(x) = \dfrac{p(x)}{q(x)} = \dfrac{x^2 - 8x - 20}{3x}$.

The zeros of $p(x) = x^2 - 8x - 20 = (x + 2)(x - 10)$ are -2 and 10. The zero of $q(x)$ is 0.

These three zeros partition the x axis into the four intervals shown in the table. A test number is chosen from each interval to determine the sign of $f(x)$.

Interval	Test number x	$f(x)$	Sign of f
$(-\infty, -2)$	-3	$-\dfrac{13}{9}$	$-$
$(-2, 0)$	-1	$\dfrac{11}{3}$	$+$
$(0, 10)$	1	-9	$-$
$(10, \infty)$	11	$\dfrac{13}{33}$	$+$

The equality holds at -2 and 10, but not at 0. We conclude that the solution set is $[-2, 0) \cup [10, \infty)$

63. $\dfrac{5x}{x^2 - 1} < \dfrac{9}{x}$

$\dfrac{5x}{x^2 - 1} - \dfrac{9}{x} < 0$

$\dfrac{5x^2 - 9(x^2 - 1)}{x(x^2 - 1)} < 0$

$\dfrac{-4x^2 + 9}{x(x^2 - 1)}$

Let $f(x) = \dfrac{p(x)}{q(x)} = \dfrac{-4x^2 + 9}{x(x^2 - 1)}$.

The zeros of $p(x) = -4x^2 + 9 = 9 - 4x^2 = (3 + 2x)(3 - 2x)$ are $-\dfrac{3}{2}$ and $\dfrac{3}{2}$.

The zeros of $q(x) = x(x^2 - 1) = x(x + 1)(x - 1)$ are 0, 1, and -1. These five zeros partition the x axis into the six intervals shown in the table. A test number is chosen from each interval to determine the sign of $f(x)$.

Interval	Test number x	$f(x)$	Sign of f
$\left(-\infty,-\dfrac{3}{2}\right)$	-2	$\dfrac{7}{6}$	$+$
$\left(-\dfrac{3}{2},-1\right)$	$-\dfrac{5}{4}$	$-\dfrac{176}{45}$	$-$
$(-1, 0)$	$-\dfrac{1}{2}$	$\dfrac{64}{3}$	$+$
$(0, 1)$	$\dfrac{1}{2}$	$-\dfrac{64}{3}$	$-$
$\left(1,\dfrac{3}{2}\right)$	$\dfrac{5}{4}$	$\dfrac{176}{45}$	$+$
$\left(\dfrac{3}{2},\infty\right)$	2	$-\dfrac{7}{6}$	$-$

We conclude that the solution set is $\left(-\dfrac{3}{2},-1\right)\cup(0,1)\cup\left(\dfrac{3}{2},\infty\right)$.

65. $\dfrac{x^2+7x+3}{x+2}>0$

zeros of the numerator $x^2+7x+3=0$ $a=1, b=7, c=3$

$$x=\frac{-7\pm\sqrt{7^2-4(1)(3)}}{2(1)}=\frac{-7\pm\sqrt{37}}{2}=\frac{-7\pm6.083}{2}=-6.541, -0.459$$

zeros of the denominator: $x=-2$

The three zeros partition the x axis into the four intervals shown in the table below. A test number is chosen from each interval to determine the sign of the rational expression.

Interval	$(-\infty,-6.541)$	$(-6.541,-2)$	$(-2,-0.459)$	$(-0.459,\infty)$
Test number x	-10	-5	-1	0
$f(x)$	$-\dfrac{33}{8}$	$\dfrac{7}{3}$	-3	$\dfrac{3}{2}$
Sign of f	$-$	$+$	$-$	$+$

The expressions is positive on $(-6.541, -2)\cup(-0.459,\infty)$. We need to exclude all endpoints, so this is the solution.

Graphical check:

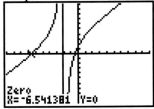 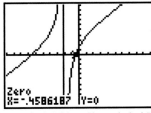

```
WINDOW
 Xmin=-10
 Xmax=10
 Xscl=1
 Ymin=-10
 Ymax=10
 Yscl=1
 Xres=1
```

The graph is above the x axis on $(-6.541, -2)\cup(-0.459,\infty)$.

67. $\dfrac{9}{x} - \dfrac{5}{x^2} \le 1$ (Simplify)

$\dfrac{9}{x} - \dfrac{5}{x^2} - 1 \le 0$

$\dfrac{9x}{x^2} - \dfrac{5}{x^2} - \dfrac{x^2}{x^2} \le 0$

$\dfrac{-x^2 + 9x - 5}{x^2} \le 0$

zeros of the numerator: $-x^2 + 9x - 5 = 0$ $a = -1, b = 9, c = -5$

$x = \dfrac{-9 \pm \sqrt{9^2 - 4(-1)(-5)}}{2(-1)} = \dfrac{-9 \pm \sqrt{61}}{-2} = \dfrac{-9 \pm 7.810}{-2} = 0.595, 8.405$

zeros of the denominator: $x = 0$

These three zeros partition the x axis into the four intervals shown in the table below. A test number is chosen from each interval to determine the sign of the rational expression.

Interval	$(-\infty, 0)$	$(0, 0.595)$	$(0.595, 8.405)$	$(8.405, \infty)$
Test number x	-1	0.5	1	10
$f(x)$	-15	-3	3	$-\dfrac{3}{20}$
Sign of f	$-$	$-$	$+$	$-$

The expression is negative on $(-\infty, 0)$, $(0, 0.595)$, and $(8.405, \infty)$. It's equal to zero when $x = 0.595$ and 8.405, so we include those endpoints, but we exclude $x = 0$ since the expression is undefined there. The solution is $(-\infty, 0) \cup (0, 0.595] \cup [8.405, \infty)$.

Graphical check:

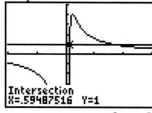 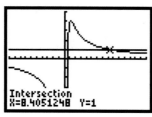 

The graph of $y_1 = \dfrac{9}{x} - \dfrac{5}{x^2}$ is below the graph of $y_2 = 1$ on $(-\infty, 0)$, $(0, 0.595)$ and $(8.405, \infty)$ and they intersect at $x = 0.595$ and $x = 8.405$.

69. $\dfrac{3x + 2}{x - 5} > 10$ (Simplify)

$\dfrac{3x + 2}{x - 5} - 10 > 0$

$\dfrac{3x + 2}{x - 5} - \dfrac{10(x - 5)}{x - 5} > 0$

$\dfrac{3x + 2 - 10x + 50}{x - 5} > 0$

$\dfrac{-7x + 52}{x - 5} > 0$

zeros of the numerator: $-7x + 52 = 0$

$-7x = -52$

$x = 7.429$

zeros of the denominator: $x = 5$

These two zeros partition the x axis into the 3 intervals shown in the table below. A test number is chosen from each interval to determine the sign of the rational expression.

Interval	$(-\infty, 5)$	$(5, 7.429)$	$(7.429, \infty)$
Test number x	0	6	8
$f(x)$	$-\dfrac{52}{5}$	10	$-\dfrac{4}{3}$
Sign of f	$-$	$+$	$-$

The expression is positive on $(5, 7.429)$. We need to exclude the endpoints, so this is the solution.

Graphical check:

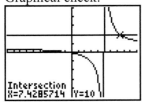

The graph of $y_1 = \dfrac{3x+2}{x-5}$ is above the graph of $y_2 = 10$ on $(5, 7.429)$.

71. $\dfrac{4}{x+1} \geq \dfrac{7}{x}$ (Simplify)

$\dfrac{4}{x+1} - \dfrac{7}{x} \geq 0$

$\dfrac{4x}{x(x+1)} - \dfrac{7(x+1)}{x(x+1)} \geq 0$

$\dfrac{4x - 7x - 7}{x(x+1)} \geq 0$

$\dfrac{-3x - 7}{x(x+1)} \geq 0$

zeros of the numerator: $-3x - 7 = 0$

$-3x = 7$

$x = -2.333$

zeros of the denominator: $x(x + 1) = 0$

$x = 0, -1$

These three zeros partition the x axis into the four intervals shown in the table below. A test number is chosen from each interval to determine the sign of the rational expression.

Interval	$(-\infty, -2.333)$	$(-2.333, -1)$	$(-1, 0)$	$(0, \infty)$
Test number x	-3	-2	-0.5	1
$f(x)$	$\dfrac{1}{3}$	$-\dfrac{1}{2}$	22	-5
Sign of f	$+$	$-$	$+$	$-$

The expression is positive on $(-\infty, -2.333) \cup (-1, 0)$. We include $x = -2.333$ because it makes the expression zero, but exclude 0 and -1 as they make the expression undefined.

The solution is $(-\infty, -2.333] \cup (-1, 0)$.

Graphical check:

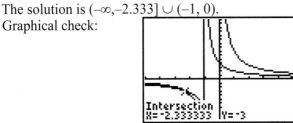

The graph of $y_1 = \dfrac{4}{x+1}$ is above the graph of $y_2 = \dfrac{7}{x}$ on $(-\infty, -2.333] \cup (-1, 0)$.

73. $f(x) = \dfrac{2x^2}{x-1} = \dfrac{n(x)}{d(x)}$

Vertical asymptotes. Real zeroes of $d(x) = x - 1$ $x = 1$

Horizontal asymptote. Since the degree of $n(x)$ is greater than the degree of $d(x)$, there is no horizontal asymptote.

75. $p(x) = \dfrac{x^3}{x^2 + 1} = \dfrac{n(x)}{d(x)}$

Vertical asymptotes. There are no real zeros of $d(x) = x^2 + 1$. No vertical asymptotes.

Horizontal asymptotes. Since the degree of $n(x)$ is greater than the degree of $d(x)$, there is no horizontal asymptote.

Oblique asymptote.

$$\begin{array}{r} 2x+2 \\ x-1\overline{\smash{\big)}2x^2} \\ \underline{2x^2-2x} \\ 2x \\ \underline{2x-2} \\ 2 \end{array}$$

Thus, $f(x) = 2x + 2 + \dfrac{2}{x-1}$.

Hence, the line $y = 2x + 2$ is an oblique asymptote.

Oblique asymptote:

$$\begin{array}{r} x \\ x^2+1\overline{\smash{\big)}x^3} \\ \underline{x^3+x} \\ -x \end{array}$$

Thus, $p(x) = x + \dfrac{-x}{x^2+1}$.

Hence, the line $y = x$ is an oblique asymptote.

77. $r(x) = \dfrac{2x^2-3x+5}{x} = \dfrac{n(x)}{d(x)}$

Vertical asymptotes. Real zeros of $d(x) = x$ $x = 0$

Horizontal asymptote. Since the degree of $n(x)$ is greater than the degree of $d(x)$, there is no horizontal asymptote.

Oblique asymptote. $\dfrac{2x^2-3x+5}{x} = \dfrac{2x^2}{x} - \dfrac{3x}{x} + \dfrac{5}{x} = 2x - 3 + \dfrac{5}{x}$

Thus $r(x) = 2x - 3 + \dfrac{5}{x}$. Hence the line $y = 2x - 3$ is an oblique asymptote.

79. $f(x) = \dfrac{x^2+1}{x} = \dfrac{n(x)}{d(x)}$

Intercepts. There are no real zeros of $n(x) = x^2 + 1$.
No x intercept. $f(0)$ is not defined. No y intercept.
Vertical asymptotes. Real zeros of $d(x) = x$. $x = 0$
Horizontal asymptote. Since the degree of $n(x)$ is greater than the degree of $d(x)$, there is no horizontal asymptote.

Oblique asymptote. $f(x) = \dfrac{x^2+1}{x} = \dfrac{x^2}{x} + \dfrac{1}{x} = x + \dfrac{1}{x}$

Hence, the line $y = x$ is an oblique asymptote.
Complete the sketch. Plot a few points.

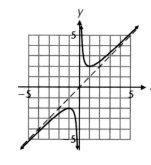

x	$f(x)$
$\frac{1}{2}$	$\frac{5}{2}$
1	2
2	$\frac{5}{2}$
$-\frac{1}{2}$	$-\frac{5}{2}$
-1	-2
-2	$-\frac{5}{2}$

81. $k(x) = \dfrac{x^2-4x+3}{2x-4} = \dfrac{n(x)}{d(x)}$

Intercepts. Real zeros of $n(x) = x^2 - 4x + 3$ $x^2 - 4x + 3 = 0$
$(x-1)(x-3) = 0$
$x = 1, 3$ x intercepts
$k(0) = -\dfrac{3}{4}$ y intercept

Vertical asymptotes. Real zeros of $d(x) = 2x - 4$ $2x - 4 = 0$
$2x = 4$
$x = 2$

Horizontal asymptote. Since the degree of $n(x)$ is greater than the degree of $d(x)$, there is no horizontal asymptote.

Oblique asymptote:

$$\begin{array}{r} \frac{1}{2}x-1 \\ 2x-4\overline{\smash{\big)}x^2-4x+3} \\ \underline{x^2-2x} \\ -2x+3 \\ \underline{-2x+4} \\ -1 \end{array}$$

Thus, $k(x) = \dfrac{1}{2}x - 1 + \dfrac{-1}{2x-4}$.

Hence, the line $y = \frac{1}{2}x - 1$ is an oblique asymptote.

Complete the sketch. Plot a few additional points.

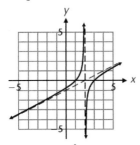

83. $F(x) = \dfrac{8 - x^3}{4x^2} = \dfrac{n(x)}{d(x)}$

Intercepts. Real zeros of $n(x) = 8 - x^3$ $8 - x^3 = 0$

$$(2 - x)(4 + 2x + x^2) = 0$$

$$2 - x = 0 \quad 4 + 2x + x^2 = 0$$

$$x = 2 \quad \text{No real zeros}$$

$$x = 2 \quad x \text{ intercept}$$

$F(0)$ is not defined. No y intercept.

Vertical asymptotes. Real zeros of $d(x) = 4x^2$. $x = 0$

Horizontal asymptote. Since the degree of $n(x)$ is greater than the degree of $d(x)$, there is no horizontal asymptote.

Oblique asymptote. $F(x) = \dfrac{8 - x^3}{4x^2} = \dfrac{8}{4x^2} - \dfrac{x^3}{4x^2}$

$$= -\frac{1}{4}x + \frac{2}{x^2}.$$

85. $f(x) = \dfrac{x^2 - 4}{x - 2}$. $f(x)$ is not defined if $x - 2 = 0$, that is, $x = 2$

$$\text{Domain: } (-\infty, 2) \cup (2, \infty)$$

$$f(x) = \dfrac{(x - 2)(x + 2)}{(x - 2)}$$

$$f(x) = x + 2$$

The graph is a straight line with slope 1 and y intercept 2, except that the point $(2, 4)$ is not on the graph. There are no asymptotes.

87. $r(x) = \dfrac{x + 2}{x^2 - 4}$. $f(x)$ is not defined if $x^2 - 4 = 0$, that is,

$$x^2 = 4$$

$$x = \pm 2$$

$$\text{Domain: } (-\infty, -2) \cup (-2, 2) \cup (2, \infty)$$

$$r(x) = \dfrac{x + 2}{(x + 2)(x - 2)}$$

$$r(x) = \dfrac{1}{x - 2}$$

The graph is the same as the graph of the function $\dfrac{1}{x - 2}$,

except that the point $\left(-2, -\dfrac{1}{4}\right)$ is not on the graph.

Hence, the line $y = -\dfrac{1}{4}x$ is an oblique asymptote.

Complete the sketch. Plot a few additional points.

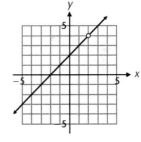

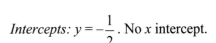

Intercepts: $y = -\dfrac{1}{2}$. No x intercept.

Vertical asymptote: $x = 2$

Horizontal asymptote: $y = 0$

Complete the sketch. Plot a few additional points

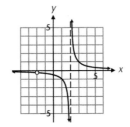

89. $N(t) = \dfrac{50t}{t+4}$ $t \geq 0$

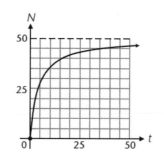

Intercepts: Real zeros of $50t$: $t = 0$ $N(0) = 0$
Vertical asymptotes: None, since -4, the only zero of $t + 4$, is not in the domain of N.
Horizontal asymptote: $N = 50$. As $t \to \infty$, $N \to 50$
Complete the sketch. Plot a few additional points.

91. $N(t) = \dfrac{5t+30}{t}$ $t \geq 1$

Intercepts: Real zeros of $5t + 30$, $t \geq 1$. None, since -6, the only zero of $5t + 30$, is not in the domain of N.
Vertical asymptotes: None, since 0, the only zero of t, is not in the domain of N.
Horizontal asymptote: $N = 5$. As $t \to \infty$, $N \to 5$
Complete the sketch. Plot a few points.

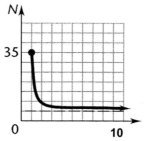

t	$N(t)$
1	35
3	15
5	11
10	8

93.   (A) $\overline{C}(n) = \dfrac{C(n)}{n} = \dfrac{2{,}500 + 175n + 25n^2}{n} = 25n + 175 + \dfrac{2{,}500}{n}$

(B) The minimum value of the function $\overline{C}(n)$ is $\overline{C}\left(\sqrt{\dfrac{c}{a}}\right)$, where $a = 25$ and $c = 2{,}500$

$\quad$ min $\overline{C}(n) = \overline{C}\left(\sqrt{\dfrac{2{,}500}{25}}\right) = \overline{C}\left(\sqrt{100}\right) = \overline{C}(10)$ This minimum occurs when $n = 10$, after 10 years.

(C) *Intercepts:* Real zeros of $2{,}500 + 175n + 25n^2$. None. No n intercepts.

$\quad$ 0 is not in the domain of n, so there are no $\overline{C}$ intercepts.
Vertical asymptotes: Real zeros of n. The line $n = 0$ is a vertical asymptote.

Sign behavior: $\overline{C}$ is always positive since $n \geq 0$.
Horizontal asymptote: None, since the degree of $C(n)$ is greater than the degree of n.

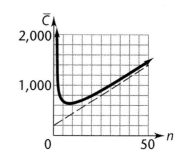

Oblique asymptote: The line $\overline{C} = 25n + 175$ is an oblique asymptote.

95.   (A) Since Area = length × width, length = $\dfrac{\text{Area}}{\text{width}} = \dfrac{225}{x}$.

$\quad$ Then total length of fence = 2 × width + 2 × length

$\quad L(x) = 2x + \dfrac{450}{x} = \dfrac{2x^2 + 450}{x}$

(B) x can be any positive number, thus, domain = $(0, \infty)$

(C) The minimum value of the function $L(x)$ is $L\left(\sqrt{\dfrac{c}{a}}\right)$ where $a = 2$ and $c = 450$.

$$\min L(x) = L\left(\sqrt{\dfrac{450}{2}}\right) = L(\sqrt{225}) = L(15) \qquad \text{This minimum occurs when } x = 15.$$

Width = 15 feet. Length = $\dfrac{225}{15}$ = 15 feet.

(D) *Intercepts:* Real zeros of $2x^2 + 450$. None, hence, no x intercepts. 0 is not in the domain of L, so there are no L intercepts.
Vertical asymptotes: Real zeros of x. The line $x = 0$ is a vertical asymptote.
Sign behavior: $L(x)$ is always positive since $x > 0$.
Horizontal asymptote: None, since the degree of $2x^2 + 450$ is greater than the degree of x.
Oblique asymptote: The line $L = 2x$ is an oblique asymptote.

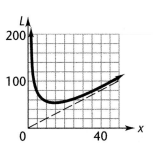

Section 4-5

1. y increases, for if $x_2 > x_1$, $kx_2 > kx_1$ so $y_2 > y_1$.

3. y decreases, for if $x_2 > x_1$, $\dfrac{1}{x_1} > \dfrac{1}{x_2}$, $\dfrac{k}{x_1} > \dfrac{k}{x_2}$, so $y_2 < y_1$.

5. If y varies directly with x, then $y = kx$. If $x = 0$, $y = k \cdot 0 = 0$.

7. $F = \dfrac{k}{x}$

9. $R = kST$

11. $L = km^3$

13. $A = kc^2d$

15. $P = kx$

17. $h = \dfrac{k}{\sqrt{s}}$

19. $R = k\dfrac{m}{d^2}$

21. $D = k\dfrac{xy^2}{z}$

23. Write $u = k\sqrt{v}$. Substitute $u = 3$ and $v = 4$ and solve for k.

$$3 = k\sqrt{4}$$
$$3 = 2k$$
$$k = \dfrac{3}{2}$$

The equation of variation is $u = \dfrac{3}{2}\sqrt{v}$.

When $v = 10$, $u = \dfrac{3}{2}\sqrt{10}$.

25. Write $L = \dfrac{k}{M^2}$. Substitute $L = 9$ and $M = 9$ and solve for k.

$$9 = \dfrac{k}{9^2}$$
$$k = 9^3 = 729$$

The equation of variation is $L = \dfrac{729}{M^2}$.

When $M = 6$, $L = \dfrac{729}{6^2} = \dfrac{81}{4}$.

27. Write $Q = k\dfrac{mn^2}{P}$. Substitute $Q = 2$, $m = 3$, $n = 6$, and $P = 12$ and solve for k.

$$2 = k\dfrac{3(6)^2}{12}$$
$$2 = 9k$$
$$k = \dfrac{2}{9}$$

The equation of variation is $Q = \dfrac{2}{9}\dfrac{mn^2}{P}$.

When $m = 4$, $n = 18$, and $P = 2$, $Q = \dfrac{2}{9}\dfrac{4(18)^2}{2} = 144$.

29. $t = \dfrac{k}{T}$

31. $L = k\dfrac{wh^2}{x}$

33. $N = \dfrac{F}{d}$

35. Write $f = kx$. Then $f_1 = kx_1$ and $f_2 = kx_2$.

Therefore
$$\frac{kx_1}{kx_2} = \frac{f_1}{f_2}$$
$$\frac{x_1}{x_2} = \frac{f_1}{f_2}$$

37. Write $w = \dfrac{k}{d^2}$. Substitute $w = 100$ and $d = 4{,}000$ and solve for k.
$$100 = \frac{k}{(4{,}000)^2}$$
$$k = 100(4{,}000)^2 = 1.6 \times 10^9$$

The equation of variation is $w = \dfrac{1.6 \times 10^9}{d^2}$.

When she is 400 miles above the earth's surface, $d = 4{,}000 + 400 = 4{,}400$.
Substitute to find
$$w = \frac{1.6 \times 10^9}{(4{,}400)^2} = 83 \text{ lbs to the nearest pound}$$

39. Write $I = k\dfrac{E}{R}$. Substitute $I = 22$, $E = 110$, and $R = 5$ and solve for k.
$$22 = k\frac{110}{5}$$
$$k = 1$$

The equation of variation is $I = \dfrac{E}{R}$.

When $E = 220$ and $R = 11$, $I = \dfrac{220}{11} = 20$ amperes

41. Write $P = kv^3$. Let $P_1 = kv_1^3$ and $v_2 = 2v_1$, then $P_2 = kv_2^3 = k(2v_1)^3 = 8kv_1^3 = 8P_1$. Hence P must be multiplied by 8 to double the speed of the boat.

43. Write $f = k\dfrac{\sqrt{T}}{L}$. Let $f_1 = k\dfrac{\sqrt{T_1}}{L_1}$, $T_2 = 4T_1$, and $L_2 = 2L_1$, then $f_2 = k\dfrac{\sqrt{T_2}}{L_2} = k\dfrac{\sqrt{4T_1}}{2L_1} = k\dfrac{\sqrt{T_1}}{L_1} = f_1$.

There would be no net effect.

45. Write $t = k\dfrac{r}{v}$. Substitute $t = 1.42$, $r = 4{,}050$, and $v = 18{,}000$ and solve for k.
$$1.42 = k\frac{4{,}050}{18{,}000}$$
$$k = 1.42\frac{18{,}000}{4{,}050}$$
$$k = 6.311$$

The equation of variation is $t = 6.311\dfrac{r}{v}$.

When $r = 4{,}300$ and $v = 18{,}500$,
$$t = 6.311\frac{4{,}300}{18{,}500} = 1.47 \text{ hours}$$

47. Write $d = kh$. Substitute $d = 4$ and $h = 500$ and solve for k.
$$4 = k(500)$$
$$k = \frac{1}{125}$$

The equation of variation is $d = \dfrac{1}{125}h$.

When $h = 2{,}500$, $d = \dfrac{1}{125}(2{,}500) = 20$ days.

49. Write $L = kv^2$. Let $L_1 = kv_1^2$ and $v_2 = 2v_1$.
Then
$$L_2 = kv_2^2 = k(2v_1)^2 = 4kv_1^2 = 4L_1.$$
The length would be quadrupled.

51. Write $P = kAv^2$. Substitute $P = 120$, $A = 100$, and $v = 20$ and solve for k.
$$120 = k(100)20^2$$
$$120 = 40{,}000k$$
$$k = \frac{3}{1000}$$

The equation of variation is $P = \dfrac{3}{1000}Av^2$.

When $A = 200$ and $v = 30$,
$$P = \frac{3}{1000}(200)(30)^2 = 540 \text{ lb}$$

53. (A) $\Delta S = kS$
(B) Substitute $\Delta S = 1$ and $S = 50$ and solve for k.
$$1 = k(50)$$
$$k = \frac{1}{50}$$
The equation of variation is $\Delta S = \frac{1}{50}S$.

When $S = 500$, $\Delta S = \frac{1}{50}(500) = 10$ oz.

(C) Substitute $\Delta S = 1$ and $S = 60$ and solve for k.
$$1 = k(60)$$
$$k = \frac{1}{60}$$
The equation of variation is $\Delta S = \frac{1}{60}S$.

When $S = 480$, $\Delta S = \frac{1}{60}(480) = 8$ candlepower.

55. Write $V = kr^3$. Let $V_1 = kr_1^3$ and $r_2 = 2r_1$, then
$$V_2 = kr_2^3 = k(2r_1)^3 = 8kr_1^3 = 8V_1$$
The volume would be 8 times the original.

57. Write frequency $= f$, length $= x$, $f = \frac{k}{x}$. Substitute $f = 16$ and $x = 32$ and solve for k.
$$16 = \frac{k}{32}$$
$$k = 512$$
The equation of variation is $f = \frac{512}{x}$.

When $x = 16$, $f = \frac{512}{16} = 32$ times per second.

CHAPTER 4 REVIEW

1. The zeros are -1 and 3; the turning points are $(-1, 0)$, $(1, 2)$, and $(3, 0)$; $P(x) \to \infty$ as $x \to -\infty$ and $P(x) \to \infty$ as $x \to \infty$.   (*4-1*)

2.
$$\begin{array}{r} 2 \quad 3 \quad 0 \quad -1 \\ -4 \quad 2 \quad -4 \\ \hline -2 \,\lvert\, 2 \quad -1 \quad 2 \quad -5 \end{array}$$
$$2x^3 + 3x^2 - 1 = (x + 2)(2x^2 - x + 2) - 5 \quad (\textit{4-1})$$

3.
$$\begin{array}{r} 1 \quad -4 \quad 0 \quad 9 \quad 0 \quad -8 \\ 3 \quad -3 \quad -9 \quad 0 \quad 0 \\ \hline 3 \,\lvert\, 1 \quad -1 \quad -3 \quad 0 \quad 0 \quad -8 \end{array}$$
$P(3) = -8$ (*4-1*)

4. $2, -4, -1$ (*4-1*)

5. Since complex zeros come in conjugate pairs, $1 - i$ is a zero.   (*4-3*)

6. (A) Since the graph has x intercepts -2, 0, and 2, these are zeros of $P(x)$.
Therefore, $P(x) = (x + 2)x(x - 2) = x^3 - 4x$.
(B) $P(x) \to \infty$ as $x \to \infty$ and $P(x) \to -\infty$ as $x \to -\infty$.   (*4-1*)

7. We form a synthetic division table:

	1	-4	0	2	
-2	1	-6	12	-22	both are lower bounds, since
-1	1	-5	5	-3	both rows alternate in sign
3	1	-1	-3	-7	
4	1	0	0	2	upper bound

(*4-2*)

8. We investigate $P(1)$ and $P(2)$ by forming a synthetic division table.

	2	-3	1	-5
1	2	-1	0	-5
2	2	1	3	1

Since $P(1)$ and $P(2)$ have opposite signs, there is at least one real zero between 1 and 2.   (*4-2*)

9. Possible factors of -15 are $\pm1, \pm3, \pm5, \pm15$. Possible factors of 5 are $\pm1, \pm5$. Therefore the possible rational zeros are $\pm1, \pm3, \pm5, \pm15, \pm\dfrac{1}{5}, \pm\dfrac{3}{5}$.   *(4-3)*

10. $P(x) = 5x^2 + 74x - 15 = (5x - 1)(x + 15) = 0$ if $5x - 1 = 0$, $x = \dfrac{1}{5}$ or $x + 15 = 0$, $x = -15$.

zeros: $\dfrac{1}{5}, -15$ (compare with Problem 9)   *(4-3)*

11. (A) $f(x) = \dfrac{6x}{x - 5} = \dfrac{n(x)}{d(x)}$

Domain: $d(x) = x - 5$ zero: $x = 5$ domain: all real numbers except 5, $(-\infty, 5) \cup (5, \infty)$.
x intercepts: $n(x) = 6x$ zero: $x = 0$ x intercept $= 0$

(B) $g(x) = \dfrac{7x + 3}{x^2 + 2x - 8} = \dfrac{n(x)}{d(x)}$

Domain: $d(x) = x^2 + 2x - 8$ zero: $x^2 + 2x - 8 = 0$
$$(x - 2)(x + 4) = 0$$
$$x = 2 \text{ or } x = -4$$
domain: all real numbers except $2, -4$, $(-\infty, -4) \cup (-4, 2) \cup (2, \infty)$

x intercepts: $n(x) = 7x + 3$ zero: $x = -\dfrac{3}{7}$ x intercept: $-\dfrac{3}{7}$ *(4-4)*

12. (A) $f(x) = \dfrac{6x}{x - 5} = \dfrac{n(x)}{d(x)}$

vertical asymptotes: zero of $d(x) = 5$ (from problem 11A) vertical asymptote: $x = 5$
horizontal asymptote: Since $n(x)$ and $d(x)$ have the same degree, the line $y = 6$ is a horizontal asymptote.

(B) $g(x) = \dfrac{7x + 3}{x^2 + 2x - 8} = \dfrac{n(x)}{d(x)}$

vertical asymptotes: zeros of $d(x) = 2, -4$ (from problem 11B) vertical asymptotes: $x = 2$, $x = -4$
horizontal asymptote: Since the degree of $n(x)$ is less than the degree of $d(x)$, the x axis is a horizontal asymptote. horizontal asymptote: $y = 0$ *(4-4)*

13. The graph of a polynomial has to approach ∞ or $-\infty$ as $x \to \infty$ and $x \to -\infty$. This graph approaches zero.   *(4-1)*

14. $F = k\sqrt{x}$ *(4-5)* **15.** $G = kxy^2$ *(4-5)*

16. $H = \dfrac{k}{z^3}$ *(4-5)*   **17.** $R = kx^2y^2$ *(4-5)*   **18.** $S = \dfrac{k}{u^2}$ *(4-5)*   **19.** $T = k\dfrac{v}{w}$ *(4-5)*

20. $P(x) = x^3 - 3x^2 - 3x + 4$

(A)

10

−10   10

−10

(B) Applying a built-in routine yields:

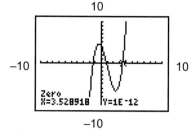

10

−10   10

−10

The graph of $P(x)$ has three x intercepts and two turning points. $P(x) \to \infty$ as $x \to \infty$ and $P(x) \to -\infty$ as $x \to -\infty$.

The largest x intercept is 3.53.   *(4-1)*

21. We use synthetic division:

$$\begin{array}{r|rrrrr} & 8 & -14 & -13 & -4 & 7 \\ & & 2 & -3 & -4 & -2 \\ \hline \frac{1}{4} & 8 & -12 & -16 & -8 & 5 \end{array}$$

Thus, $P(x) = \left(x - \dfrac{1}{4}\right)(8x^3 - 12x^2 - 16x - 8) + 5$

$$P\left(\frac{1}{4}\right) = 5 \hspace{3cm} (4\text{-}1)$$

22.

$$\begin{array}{r|rrrr} & 4 & -8 & -3 & -3 \\ & & -2 & 5 & -1 \\ \hline -\frac{1}{2} & 4 & -10 & 2 & -4 \end{array}$$

$$P\left(-\frac{1}{2}\right) = -4 \hspace{1.5cm} (4\text{-}1)$$

23. The quadratic formula tells us that $x^2 - 2x - 1 = 0$ if

$$x = \frac{-b \pm \sqrt{b^2 - 4ac}}{2a} \quad a = 1, b = -2, c = -1$$

$$x = \frac{-(-2) \pm \sqrt{(-2)^2 - 4(1)(-1)}}{2(1)} = \frac{2 \pm \sqrt{8}}{2} = 1 \pm \sqrt{2}$$

Since $1 \pm \sqrt{2}$ are zeros of $x^2 - 2x - 1$, its factors are $x - (1 + \sqrt{2})$ and $x - (1 - \sqrt{2})$, that is,

$x^2 - 2x - 1 = [x - (1 + \sqrt{2})][x - (1 - \sqrt{2})]$ *(4-1)*

24. $x + 1$ will be a factor of $P(x)$ if $P(-1) = 0$.

$P(-1) = 9(-1)^{26} - 11(-1)^{17} + 8(-1)^{11} - 5(-1)^4 - 7 = 9 + 11 - 8 - 5 - 7 = 0$, so the answer is yes, $x + 1$ is a factor.

$\hspace{12cm} (4\text{-}1)$

25. The possible rational zeros are $\pm 1, \pm 2, \pm 4, \pm 8, \pm \dfrac{1}{2}$. We form a synthetic division table:

$$\begin{array}{r|rrrr} & 2 & -3 & -18 & -8 \\ \hline 1 & 2 & -1 & -19 & -27 \\ 2 & 2 & 1 & -16 & -40 \\ 4 & 2 & 5 & 2 & 0 \end{array}$$

So $2x^3 - 3x^2 - 18x - 8 = (x - 4)(2x^2 + 5x + 2) = (x - 4)(2x + 1)(x + 2)$

Zeros: $4, -\dfrac{1}{2}, -2$ $\hspace{6cm} (4\text{-}3)$

26. $(x - 4)(2x + 1)(x + 2)$ $\hspace{5cm} (4\text{-}3)$

27. The possible rational zeros are $\pm 1, \pm 5$. We form a synthetic division table:

$$\begin{array}{r|rrrr} & 1 & -3 & 0 & 5 \\ \hline 1 & 1 & -2 & -2 & 3 \\ 5 & 1 & 2 & 10 & 55 \\ -1 & 1 & -4 & 4 & 1 \\ -5 & 1 & -8 & 40 & -195 \end{array}$$

There are no rational zeros, since all possibilities fail. $\hspace{2cm} (4\text{-}3)$

28. $P(x) = 2x^4 - x^3 + 2x - 1$.

Possible rational zeros: $\pm 1, \pm \dfrac{1}{2}$

Examining the graph of $y = P(x)$, we see that there is a zero between 0 and 1, and possibly a zero at -1. We test the likely candidates, and find

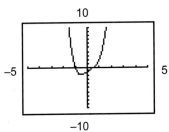

$$\begin{array}{r|rrrrr} & 2 & -1 & 0 & 2 & -1 \\ & & -2 & 3 & -3 & 1 \\ \hline -1 & 2 & -3 & 3 & -1 & 0 \end{array}$$

-1 is a zero. So $P(x) = (x + 1)(2x^3 - 3x^2 + 3x - 1) = (x + 1)Q(x)$

Testing $\dfrac{1}{2}$ in the reduced polynomial $Q(x)$, we obtain

$$
\begin{array}{r}
2 \quad -3 \quad\;\; 3 \quad -1 \\
1 \quad -1 \quad\;\; 1 \\
\hline
\tfrac{1}{2}\big|\; 2 \quad -2 \quad\;\; 2 \quad\;\; 0
\end{array}
$$

$\dfrac{1}{2}$ is a zero. So $P(x) = (x + 1)\left(x - \dfrac{1}{2}\right)(2x^2 - 2x + 2) = (x + 1)(2x - 1)(x^2 - x + 1)$

To find the remaining zeros, we solve $x^2 - x + 1 = 0$, by the quadratic formula.

$x^2 - x + 1 = 0$

$$x = \frac{-b \pm \sqrt{b^2 - 4ac}}{2a} \qquad a = 1, b = -1, c = 1$$

$$x = \frac{-(-1) \pm \sqrt{(-1)^2 - 4(1)(1)}}{2(1)} = \frac{1 \pm \sqrt{-3}}{2} = \frac{1 \pm i\sqrt{3}}{2}$$

The four zeros are -1, $\dfrac{1}{2}$, and $\dfrac{1 \pm i\sqrt{3}}{2}$ (4-3)

29. $(x + 1)\left(x - \dfrac{1}{2}\right)2\left(x - \dfrac{1 + i\sqrt{3}}{2}\right)\left(x - \dfrac{1 - i\sqrt{3}}{2}\right) = (x + 1)(2x - 1)\left(x - \dfrac{1 + i\sqrt{3}}{2}\right)\left(x - \dfrac{1 - i\sqrt{3}}{2}\right)$ (4-3)

30. The degree is 9. The zeros are 1 (multiplicity 3), -1 (multiplicity 4), i and $-i$.   (4-3)

31. (A) Let $u = x^2$.

Then $P(x) = x^4 + 5x^2 - 36$
$= u^2 + 5u - 36 = (u + 9)(u - 4)$
$= (x^2 + 9)(x^2 - 4) = (x^2 + 9)(x + 2)(x - 2)$

(B) $x^2 + 9$ has zeros $-3i$ and $3i$, so it factors as
$(x + 3i)(x - 3i)$.
Thus $P(x) = (x + 3i)(x - 3i)(x + 2)(x - 2)$ (4-3)

32. (A) Examining the graph of $P(x)$, we see that there may be zeros of even multiplicity between -1 and 0, and between 4 and 5, and a possible integer zero at 2. Testing 2, we obtain

$$
\begin{array}{r}
1 \quad -10 \quad\;\; 30 \quad -20 \quad -15 \quad -2 \\
2 \quad -16 \quad\;\; 28 \quad\;\; 16 \quad\;\; 2 \\
\hline
2\big|\; 1 \quad\; -8 \quad\;\; 14 \quad\;\;\; 8 \quad\;\;\; 1 \quad\;\; 0
\end{array}
$$

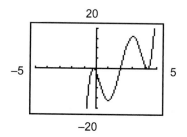

2 is a zero. Applying built-in routines, we obtain

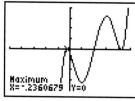 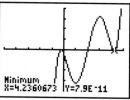

There are zeros of even multiplicity at -0.24 and 4.24. Since $P(x)$ is a fifth-degree polynomial, they must be double zeros and 2 must be a simple zero.

(B) -0.24 can be approximated with a maximum routine; 2 can be approximated by the bisection method; 4.24 can be approximated with a minimum routine.   (4-2)

33. (A) We form a synthetic division table.

	1	−2	−30	0	−25	
0	1	−2	−30	0	−25	
1	1	−1	−31	−31	−56	
2	1	0	−30	−60	−145	
3	1	1	−27	−81	−268	
4	1	2	−22	−88	−377	
5	1	3	−15	−75	−400	
6	1	4	−6	−36	−241	
7	1	5	5	35	220	7 is an upper bound
−1	1	−3	−27	27	−52	
−2	1	−4	−22	44	−113	
−3	1	−5	−15	45	−160	
−4	1	−6	−6	24	−121	
−5	1	−7	5	−25	100	−5 is a lower bound

(B) We search for the real zero in (6, 7) indicated in the table. We organize our calculations in a table.

Sign Change Interval (a, b)	Midpoint m	Sign of P		
		$P(a)$	$P(m)$	$P(b)$
(6, 7)	6.5	−	−	+
(6.5, 7)	6.75	−	+	+
(6.5, 6.75)	6.625	−	+	+
(6.5, 6.625)	6.5625	−	−	+
(6.5625, 6.625)	We stop here	−		+

Since each endpoint rounds to 6.6, a real zero lies on this interval and is given by 6.6 to one decimal place accuracy. 4 intervals were required.

(C) Graphing and applying a built-in routine, we obtain:

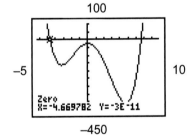
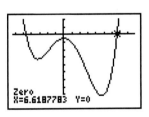

The zeros are −4.67 and 6.62.

(4-2)

34. $f(x) = \dfrac{x-1}{2x+2} = \dfrac{n(x)}{d(x)}$

(A) The domain of f is the set of all real numbers x such that $d(x) = 2x + 2 \neq 0$, that is $(-\infty, -1) \cup (-1, \infty)$.

f has an x intercept where $n(x) = x - 1 = 0$, that is, $x = 1$. $f(0) = -\dfrac{1}{2}$, hence f has a y intercept at $y = -\dfrac{1}{2}$

(B) Vertical asymptote: $x = -1$. Horizontal asymptote: since $n(x)$ and $d(x)$ have the same degree, the line $y = \dfrac{1}{2}$ is a horizontal asymptote.

(C) Complete the sketch. Plot a few additional points.

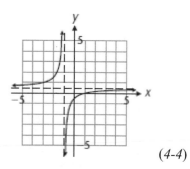

(4-4)

35.   (A) Find the zeros of $P(x) = x^3 - 5x + 4$ graphically:

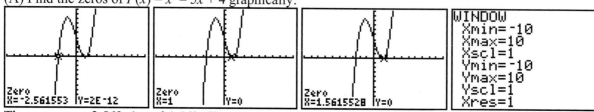

The zeros are –2.562, 1, and 1.562. (Two are very close together, so you may need to look closely at that portion of the graph to see that there are two.) $P(x)$ is negative (below the x axis) on $(-\infty, -2.562) \cup (1, 1.562)$.

(B) Keeping $y_1 = x^3 - 5x + 4$, graph $y_2 = 2$.

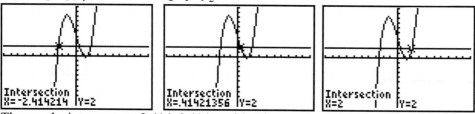

The graphs intersect at –2.414, 0.414, and 2. The graph of $x^3 - 5x + 4$ is below the graph of 2 on $(-\infty, -2.414) \cup (0.414, 2)$.

(4-2)

36.   The graph is discontinuous at $x = 0$, but $x = 0$ is not a vertical asymptote.

(4-4)

37. Write $B = \dfrac{k}{\sqrt{c}}$. Substitute $B = 5$ and $c = 4$ and solve for k.

$$5 = \frac{k}{\sqrt{4}}$$

$$k = 10$$

The equation of variation is $B = \dfrac{10}{\sqrt{c}}$.

When $c = 25$, $B = \dfrac{10}{\sqrt{25}} = \dfrac{10}{5} = 2$

(4-5)

38.   Write $D = kxy$. Substitute $D = 10$, $x = 3$, and $y = 2$ and solve for k.

$$10 = k(3)(2)$$

$$k = \frac{5}{3}$$

The equation of variation is $D = \dfrac{5}{3}xy$.

When $x = 9$ and $y = 8$, $D = \dfrac{5}{3}(9)(8) = 120$

(4-5)

39.

$$\begin{array}{ccccc} & 1 & 0 & 3 & 2 \\ & & 1+i & 2i & 1+5i \end{array}$$

$$1+i \overline{\smash{\big)}\ 1 \quad 1+i \quad 3+2i \quad 3+5i}$$

$(1 + i)^2 = (1 + i)(1 + i) = 1 + 2i + i^2 = 1 + 2i - 1 = 2i$

$(1 + i)(3 + 2i) = 3 + 5i + 2i^2 = 3 + 5i - 2 = 1 + 5i$

$\quad P(x) = [x^2 + (1 + i)x + (3 + 2i)][x - (1 + i)] + 3 + 5i$ *(4-1)*

40. $P(x) = \left(x + \dfrac{1}{2}\right)^2 (x + 3)(x - 1)^3.$

The degree is 6.   *(4-3)*

41. $P(x) = (x + 5)[x - (2 - 3i)][x - (2 + 3i)].$
The degree is 3.   *(4-3)*

42. The possible rational zeros are $\pm 1, \pm 2, \pm 4, \pm \dfrac{1}{2}$.

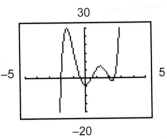

Examining the graph of $y = P(x)$, we see that there are zeros between
-1 and 0, between 0 and 1, between 2 and 3, and possible integer
zeros at -2 and 2. Testing 2, we obtain

$$\begin{array}{r|rrrrrr} & 2 & -5 & -8 & 21 & 0 & -4 \\ & & 4 & -2 & -20 & 2 & 4 \\ \hline 2 & 2 & -1 & -10 & 1 & 2 & 0 \end{array} \quad \text{2 is a zero.}$$

So $P(x) = (x - 2)(2x^4 - x^3 - 10x^2 + x + 2)$. Testing -2 in the reduced polynomial, we obtain

$$\begin{array}{r|rrrrr} & 2 & -1 & -10 & 1 & 2 \\ & & -4 & 10 & 0 & -2 \\ \hline -2 & 2 & -5 & 0 & 1 & 0 \end{array} \quad \text{-2 is a zero.}$$

Hence $P(x) = (x - 2)(x + 2)(2x^3 - 5x^2 + 1)$. $2x^3 - 5x^2 + 1$ has been shown (see Section 4-3, problem 41 for
details) to have zeros $\dfrac{1}{2}$, $1 \pm \sqrt{2}$. Hence $P(x)$ has zeros $\dfrac{1}{2}, \pm 2, 1 \pm \sqrt{2}$.   *(4-3)*

43. $(x - 2)(x + 2)\left(x - \dfrac{1}{2}\right)2[x - (1 - \sqrt{2})][x - (1 + \sqrt{2})] = (x - 2)(x + 2)(2x - 1)[x - (1 - \sqrt{2})][x - (1 + \sqrt{2})]$ *(4-3)*

44. Graphing $y = P(x)$, we obtain:

Clearly there is a local maximum near -4. Applying a built-in
routine, we obtain

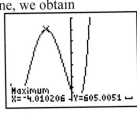

To find the other required points, we need different windows. Redrawing and applying built-in routines, we
obtain

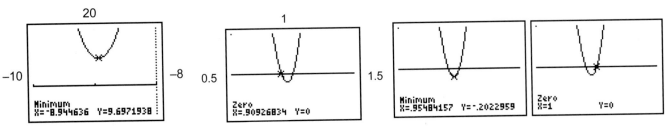

Summarizing, $P(x)$ has zeros at 0.91 and 1. It has a local minimum $P(-8.94) \approx 9.7$. It has a local maximum
$P(-4.01) \approx 605.01$. It has a local minimum $P(0.95) \approx -0.20$.   *(4-2)*

45. $P(x)$ changes sign three times. Therefore, it has three zeros and its minimal degree is 3.   *(4-1)*

46. Since $1 + 2i$ is a zero, $1 - 2i$ is also a zero.

Hence $[x - (1 - 2i)][x - (1 + 2i)] = [(x - 1) + 2i][(x - 1) - 2i] = (x - 1)^2 - 4i^2 = x^2 - 2x + 5$ is a factor.

Since $P(x)$ is a cubic polynomial, it must be of the form $a(x - r)(x^2 - 2x + 5)$. Since the constant term of this polynomial, $-5ar$, must be an integer, r must be a rational number. Thus there can be no irrational zeros. *(4-3)*

47. (A) Since $x^3 - 27$ is a cubic polynomial, it has 3 zeros and there are 3 cube roots of 27.

(B) $x^3 - 27 = (x - 3)(x^2 + 3x + 3^2) = (x - 3)(x^2 + 3x + 9)$. We solve $x^2 + 3x + 9 = 0$ by applying the quadratic formula with $a = 1$, $b = 3$, $c = 9$,

to obtain $x = \dfrac{-3 \pm \sqrt{3^2 - 4(1)(9)}}{2(1)} = \dfrac{-3 \pm \sqrt{-27}}{2} = \dfrac{-3 \pm 3i\sqrt{3}}{2}$ or $-\dfrac{3}{2} \pm \dfrac{3i}{2}\sqrt{3}$ *(4-3)*

48. (A) We form a synthetic division table.

	1	2	−500	0	−4,000
0	1	2	−500	0	−4,000
10	1	12	−380	−3,800	−42,000
20	1	22	−60	−1,200	−28,000
30	1	32	460	13,800	410,000
−10	1	−8	−420	4,200	−46,000
−20	1	−18	−140	2,800	−60,000
−30	1	−28	340	−10,200	302,000

From the table, 30 is an upper bound and −30 is a lower bound.

(B) Graphing $P(x)$ in the window suggested by part (A), we obtain

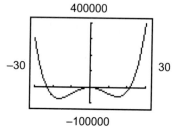 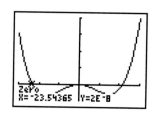 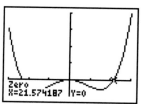

The zeros are −23.54 and 21.57. Examining the graph more closely near $x = 0$, we obtain

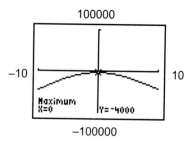

There is no other real zero.   *(4-2)*

49. $f(x) = \dfrac{x^2 + 2x + 3}{x+1} = \dfrac{n(x)}{d(x)}$

Intercepts. There are no real zeros of $n(x) = x^2 + 2x + 3$.
   No x intercept $f(0) = 3$ y intercept
Vertical asymptotes. Real zeros of $d(x) = x + 1$ $x = -1$
Horizontal asymptotes. Since the degree of $n(x)$ is
   greater than the degree of $d(x)$, there is no horizontal
   asymptote.
Oblique asymptote:

$$\begin{array}{r} x + 1 \\ x+1\overline{)\,x^2 + 2x + 3} \\ \underline{x^2 + x} \\ x + 3 \\ \underline{x + 1} \\ 2 \end{array}$$

Thus, $f(x) = x + 1 + \dfrac{2}{x+1}$.

Hence, the line $y = x + 1$ is an oblique asymptote.
Complete the sketch. Plot a few additional points.

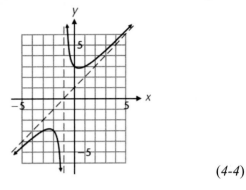

(4-4)

50. Graphing $y = f(x)$, we obtain the graph at the right.
From the graph, we can see that $f(x) \to 2$ as $x \to \infty$ and
$f(x) \to -2$ as $x \to -\infty$; the lines $y = 2$ and $y = -2$ are
horizontal asymptotes.

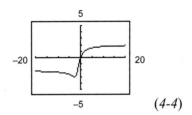

(4-4)

51. (A) $\dfrac{x-2}{5-x} \le 0$

> **Common Error:**
> It is not correct to "multiply both sides" by $5 - x$.

Let $f(x) = \dfrac{p(x)}{q(x)} = \dfrac{x-2}{5-x}$

The zero of $p(x) = x - 2$ is 2. The zero of $q(x) = 5 - x$ is 5. These two zeros partition the x axis into the three
intervals shown in the table. A test number is chosen from each interval to determine the sign of f.

Interval	Test number x	$f(x)$	Sign of f
$(-\infty, 2)$	1	$-\dfrac{1}{4}$	$-$
$(2, 5)$	4	2	$+$
$(5, \infty)$	6	-4	$-$

The equality is satisfied at $x = 2$, but not at $x = 5$. We conclude that the solution set is $(-\infty, 2] \cup (5\ \infty)$.

(B) $\dfrac{17}{x+3} > \dfrac{5}{x}$

$\dfrac{17}{x+3} - \dfrac{5}{x} > 0$

$\dfrac{17x - 5(x+3)}{x(x+3)} > 0$

$\dfrac{12x - 15}{x(x+3)} > 0$

Let $f(x) = \dfrac{p(x)}{q(x)} = \dfrac{12x-15}{x(x+3)}$ The zero of $p(x) = 12x - 15$ is $\dfrac{15}{12}$ or $\dfrac{5}{4}$. The zeros of $q(x) = x(x + 3)$ are 0
and -3.

These three zeros partition the x axis into the four intervals shown in the table. A test number is chosen from each interval to determine the sign of $f(x)$.

Interval	Test number x	$f(x)$	Sign of f
$(-\infty, -3)$	-4	$-\dfrac{63}{4}$	$-$
$(-3, 0)$	-1	$\dfrac{27}{2}$	$+$
$\left(0, \dfrac{5}{4}\right)$	1	$-\dfrac{3}{4}$	$-$
$\left(\dfrac{5}{4}, \infty\right)$	2	$\dfrac{9}{10}$	$+$

We conclude that the solution set is $(-3, 0) \cup \left(\dfrac{5}{4}, \infty\right)$.   (4-4)

52. (A) $\dfrac{x^2 - 3}{x^3 - 3x + 1} \le 0$

zeros of the numerator: $x^2 - 3 = 0$
$$x^2 = 3$$
$$x = \sqrt{3}, -\sqrt{3} \text{ or } 1.732, -1.732$$

zeros of the denominator: Find graphically:

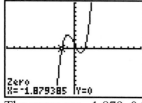 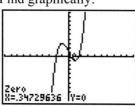 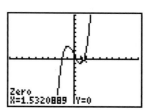

The zeros are $-1.879, 0.347, 1.532$.

Interval	$(-\infty, -1.879)$	$(-1.879, -1.732)$	$(-1.732, 0.347)$	$(0.347, 1.532)$	$(1.532, 1.732)$	$(1.732, \infty)$
Test number x	-2	-1.8	0	1	1.6	2
$f(x)$	-1	0.423	-3	2	-1.49	$\frac{1}{3}$
Sign of f	$-$	$+$	$-$	$+$	$-$	$+$

The expression is negative on $(-\infty, -1.879)$, $(-1.732, 0.347)$, and $(1.532, 1.732)$. We should include -1.732 and 1.732 (since the expression is zero there) and exclude $-1.879, 0.347$, and 1.532 (since the expression is undefined there.) The solution is $(-\infty, -1.879) \cup [-1.732, 0.347) \cup (1.532, 1.732]$.

Graphical check:

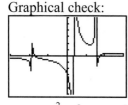

The graph is below the x axis on $(-\infty, -1.879) \cup (-1.732, 0.347) \cup (1.532, 1.732)$, and intersects the x axis at -1.732 and 1.732.

(B) $\dfrac{x^2 - 3}{x^3 - 3x + 1} > \dfrac{5}{x^2}$

$$\dfrac{x^2 - 3}{x^3 - 3x + 1} - \dfrac{5}{x^2} > 0$$

$$\frac{x^2(x^2-3)}{x^2(x^3-3x+1)} - \frac{5(x^3-3x+1)}{x^2(x^3-3x+1)} > 0$$

$$\frac{x^4-3x^2-5x^3+15x-5}{x^2(x^3-3x+1)} > 0$$

zeros of the numerator: Find graphically:

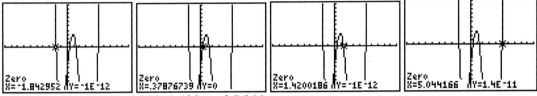

The zeros are -1.843, 0.379, 1.420, and 5.044.

zeros of the denominator:

$x^2(x^3-3x+1)=0$

$x^2=0 \qquad\qquad x^3-3x+1=0$

$x=0 \qquad\qquad\quad x=-1.879, 0.347, 1.532$ (From part A)

Interval	$(-\infty,-1.879)$	$(-1.879,-1.843)$	$(-1.843,0)$	$(0,0.347)$	$(0.347,0.379)$
Test number x	-2	-1.85	-1	0.1	0.35
$f(x)$	-2.25	0.47	-5.7	-504.3	363
Sign of f	$-$	$+$	$-$	$-$	$+$

Interval	$(0.379,1.420)$	$(1.420,1.532)$	$(1.532,5.044)$	$(5.044,\infty)$
Test number x	1	1.5	2	6
$f(x)$	-3	3.8	-0.92	0.03
Sign of f	$-$	$+$	$-$	$+$

The expression is positive on $(-1.879, -1.843) \cup (0.347, 0.379) \cup (1.420, 1.532) \cup (5.044, \infty)$ (4-4)

53. The potential rational zeros are ± 1, ± 2, and ± 4. A look at the graph shows 3 zeros, none of which occur at integer values, so none of the candidates for rational zeros are actually zeros.

(4-3)

54. To have real zeros -3, 0, and 2, we should have factors $(x+3)$, x, and $(x-2)$ in the numerator. To have vertical asymptotes $x=-1$ and $x=4$, we should have factors $(x+1)$ and $(x-4)$ in the denominator. At the moment, our function is

$$f(x) = \frac{x(x+3)(x-2)}{(x+1)(x-4)}$$

But the degree of the numerator is greater than the degree of the denominator, so there will be no horizontal asymptote. We can fix that by squaring one of the factors in the denominator. Multiplying the numerator by 5 will then make $y=5$ a horizontal asymptote.

$$f(x) = \frac{5x(x+3)(x-2)}{(x+1)^2(x-4)}$$

(There are other answers.)

(4-4)

55. In the given figure, let y = height of door

$2x$ = width of door

Then Area of door = $48 = 2xy$

Since (x, y) is a point on the parabola $y = 16 - x^2$, its coordinates satisfy the equation of the parabola.

Hence $\qquad 48 = 2x(16 - x^2)$

$\qquad\qquad 48 = 32x - 2x^3$

$\quad 2x^3 - 32x + 48 = 0$

$\qquad x^3 - 16x + 24 = 0$

The possible rational solutions of this equation are $\pm 1, \pm 2, \pm 3, \pm 4, \pm 6, \pm 8, \pm 12, \pm 24$. Testing the likely candidates, we obtain

$$
\begin{array}{r}
1 \quad 0 \quad -16 \quad 24 \\
2 \quad 4 \quad -24 \\
\hline
2\overline{\smash{\big)}\ 1 \quad 2 \quad -12 \quad 0}
\end{array}
$$

2 is a solution. Thus the equation can be factored $(x - 2)(x^2 + 2x - 12) = 0$.
To find the remaining zeros, we solve $x^2 + 2x - 12 = 0$, by completing the square.

$$
\begin{aligned}
x^2 + 2x &= 12 \\
x^2 + 2x + 1 &= 13 \\
(x + 1)^2 &= 13 \\
x + 1 &= \pm\sqrt{13} \\
x &= -1 + \sqrt{13} \text{ (discarding the negative solution)} \approx 2.61
\end{aligned}
$$

Thus the positive zeros are $x = 2, 2.61$. Thus the dimensions of the door are either $2x = 4$ feet by $16 - x^2 = 12$ feet, or $2x = 5.2$ feet by $16 - x^2 = 9.2$ feet. *(4-2)*

56. We note:

$$
\left(\begin{array}{c} \text{Volume} \\ \text{of} \\ \text{silo} \end{array}\right) = \left(\begin{array}{c} \text{Volume of} \\ \text{hemisphere} \\ \text{of radius } x \end{array}\right) + \left(\begin{array}{c} \text{Volume of} \\ \text{cylinder with} \\ \text{radius } x, \text{ height } 18 \end{array}\right)
$$

$$
\begin{aligned}
486\pi &= \frac{2}{3}\pi x^3 + \pi x^2 \cdot 18 \\
486 &= \frac{2}{3}x^3 + 18x^2 \\
0 &= x^3 + 27x^2 - 729
\end{aligned}
$$

There are no rational zeros of $P(x) = x^3 + 27x^2 - 729$ (details omitted). Examining the graph of $y = P(x)$, we obtain, for positive x: The radius is 4.8 feet.

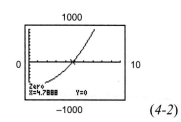

(4-2)

57.

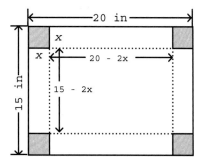

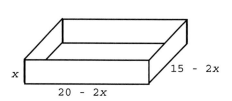

From the above figures it should be clear that

$$
V = \text{length} \times \text{width} \times \text{height} = (20 - 2x)(15 - 2x)x \quad 0 < x < 7.5
$$

$$
\begin{aligned}
\text{We solve } (20 - 2x)(15 - 2x)x &= 300 \\
300x - 70x^2 + 4x^3 &= 300 \\
4x^3 - 70x^2 + 300x - 300 &= 0
\end{aligned}
$$

There are no rational zeros of $P(x) = 4x^3 - 70x^2 + 300x - 300$ (details omitted).
Examining the graph of $y = P(x)$
for $0 < x < 7.5$, we obtain

$x = 1.4$ inches or $x = 4.5$ inches.

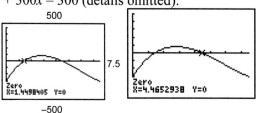

(4-2)

58. Write $F = \dfrac{k}{r}$. Let $F_1 = \dfrac{k}{r_1}$ and $r_2 = 2r_1$. Then $F_2 = \dfrac{k}{r_2} = \dfrac{k}{2r_1} = \dfrac{1}{2}\,\dfrac{k}{r_1} = \dfrac{1}{2}F_1$.   **59.** $v = k\dfrac{\sqrt{T}}{\sqrt{w}}$ *(4-5)*

The force would be $\dfrac{1}{2}$ the original.   *(4-5)*

60. Write $A = kWt$. Substitute $A = A_0$, $W = 10$ and $t = 8$ and solve for k.

$$A_0 = k(10)(8)$$

$$k = \frac{A_0}{80}$$

The equation of variation for this job is $A = \frac{A_0}{80} Wt$.

Substitute $A = A_0$ (again) and $W = 4$ and solve for t.

$$A_0 = \frac{A_0}{80}(4)t$$

$$A_0 = \frac{A_0}{20}t$$

$$t = 20 \text{ days}$$

(4-5)

61. Write $I = kpr$. Substitute $I = 8$, $p = 100$, and $r = 0.04$ and solve for k.

$$8 = k(100)(0.04)$$

$$k = 2$$

The equation of variation is $I = 2pr$. When $p = 150$ and $r = 0.03$,

$$I = 2(150)(0.03)$$

$$I = \$9.00$$

(4-5)

62. (A)

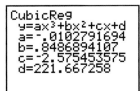

Enter the data.

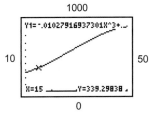

Compute the regression equation.

(B)

Transfer the regression equation to the equation editor.

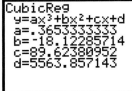

Graph the regression equation and determine the value of y corresponding to $x = 15$.

The model predicts that 339 refrigerators would be sold if 15 ads were placed. *(4-1)*

63. (A)

Enter the data.   Compute the regression equation.

The cubic regression model is $y = 0.36533x^3 - 18.1229x^2 + 89.6238x + 5563.857$.

(B) Substitute x = 2020 – 1987 = 33 into the model equation to obtain y = 1,915.

(C) No. Extrapolations are seldom reliable in any situation; this model has a positive coefficient for the x^3, predicting that the crime index will eventually be infinite; finally, crime statistics are affected by far too many sociological factors to be predicted by any simple model. *(4-1)*

CHAPTER 5

Section 5-1

1. An exponential function is a function where the variable appears in an exponent.
3. If $b > 1$, the function is an increasing function. If $0 < b < 1$, the function is a decreasing function.
5. A positive number raised to any real power will give a positive result.
7. (A) The graph of $y = (0.2)^x$ is decreasing and passes through the point $(-1, 0.2^{-1}) = (-1, 5)$.
    This corresponds to graph g.
    (B) The graph of $y = 2^x$ is increasing and passes through the point $(1, 2)$. This corresponds to graph n.
    (C) The graph of $y = \left(\frac{1}{3}\right)^x$ is decreasing and passes through the point $(-1, 3)$. This corresponds to graph f.
    (D) The graph of $y = 4^x$ is increasing and passes through the point $(1, 4)$. This corresponds to graph m.

9. 16.24   11. 7.524   13. 1.649   15. 4.469   17. $10^{3x-1}10^{4-x} = 10^{3x-1+4-x} = 10^{2x+3}$

19. $\dfrac{3x}{3^{1-x}} = 3^{x-(1-x)} = 3^{x-1+x} = 3^{2x-1}$ 21. $\left(\dfrac{4^x}{5^y}\right)^{3z} = \dfrac{4^{3xz}}{5^{3yz}}$ 23. $\dfrac{e^{5x}}{e^{2x+1}} = e^{5x-(2x+1)} = e^{5x-2x-1} = e^{3x-1}$

25. The graph of g is the same as the graph of f stretched vertically by a factor of 3. Therefore g is increasing and the graph has horizontal asymptote $y = 0$.

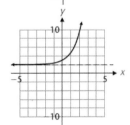

27. The graph of g is the same as the graph of f reflected through the y axis and shrunk vertically by a factor of $\frac{1}{3}$. Therefore g is decreasing and the graph has horizontal asymptote $y = 0$.

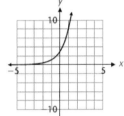

29. The graph of g is the same as the graph of f shifted upward 2 units. Therefore g is increasing and the graph has horizontal asymptote $y = 2$.

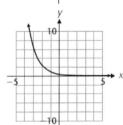

31. The graph of g is the same as the graph of f shifted 2 units to the left. Therefore g is increasing and the graph has horizontal asymptote $y = 0$.

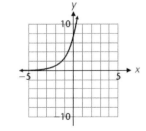

33. $5^{3x} = 5^{4x-2}$ if and only if
$$3x = 4x - 2$$
$$-x = -2$$
$$x = 2$$

35. $7^{x^2} = 7^{2x+3}$ if and only if
$$x^2 = 2x + 3$$
$$x^2 - 2x - 3 = 0$$
$$(x - 3)(x + 1) = 0$$
$$x = -1, 3$$

37. $\left(\dfrac{4}{5}\right)^{6x+1} = \dfrac{5}{4}$

$\left(\dfrac{4}{5}\right)^{6x+1} = \left(\dfrac{4}{5}\right)^{-1}$ if and only if
$$6x + 1 = -1$$
$$6x = -2$$
$$x = -\dfrac{1}{3}$$

39. $(1 - x)^5 = (2x - 1)^5$ if and only if
$$1 - x = 2x - 1$$
$$-3x = -2$$
$$x = \dfrac{2}{3}$$

41. $2xe^{-x} = 0$ if $2x = 0$ or $e^{-x} = 0$. Since e^{-x} is never 0, the only solution is $x = 0$.

43. $x^2e^x - 5xe^x = 0$
$$xe^x(x - 5) = 0$$
$$x = 0 \text{ or } e^x = 0 \text{ or } x - 5 = 0$$
$$\phantom{x = 0 \text{ or }} \text{never} \phantom{\text{ or }} x = 5$$
$$x = 0, 5$$

45. $9^{x^2} = 3^{3x-1}$
$$(3^2)^{x^2} = 3^{3x-1}$$
$$3^{2x^2} = 3^{3x-1} \text{ if and only if}$$
$$2x^2 = 3x - 1$$
$$2x^2 - 3x + 1 = 0$$
$$(2x - 1)(x - 1) = 0$$
$$x = \dfrac{1}{2}, 1$$

47. $25^{x+3} = 125^x$
$$(5^2)^{x+3} = (5^3)^x$$
$$5^{2x+6} = 5^{3x} \text{ if and only if}$$
$$2x + 6 = 3x$$
$$x = 6$$

49. $4^{2x+7} = 8^{x+2}$
$$(2^2)^{2x+7} = (2^3)^{x+2}$$
$$2^{4x+14} = 2^{3x+6} \text{ if and only if}$$
$$4x + 14 = 3x + 6$$
$$x = -8$$

51.
$$a^2 = a^{-2}$$
$$a^2 = \dfrac{1}{a^2}$$
$$a^4 = 1 \quad (a \neq 0)$$
$$a^4 - 1 = 0$$
$$(a - 1)(a + 1)(a^2 + 1) = 0$$
$$a = 1 \text{ or } a = -1$$
This does not violate the exponential property mentioned because $a = 1$ and a negative are excluded from consideration in the statement of the property.

53. $1^{-3} = \dfrac{1}{1^3} = 1, 1^{-2} = \dfrac{1}{1^2} = 1, 1^{-1} = \dfrac{1}{1^1} = 1,$
$1^0 = 1, 1^2 = 1, 1^3 = 1.$

$1^x = 1$ for all real x; the function $f(x) = 1^x$ is neither increasing nor decreasing and is equal to $f(x) = 1$, thus the variable is effectively not in the exponent at all.

55. The graph of g is the same as the graph of f reflected through the x axis; g is increasing; horizontal asymptote: $y = 0$.

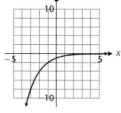

57. The graph of g is the same as the graph of f stretched horizontally by a factor of 2 and shifted upward 3 units; g is decreasing; horizontal asymptote: $y = 3$.

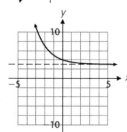

59. The graph of g is the same as the graph of f stretched vertically by a factor of 500; g is increasing; horizontal asymptote: $y = 0$.

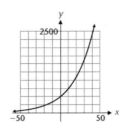

61. The graph of g is the same as the graph of f shifted 3 units to the right, stretched vertically by a factor of 2, and shifted upward 1 unit; g is increasing; horizontal asymptote: $y = 1$.

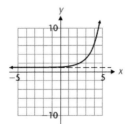

63. The graph of g is the same as the graph of f shifted 2 units to the right, reflected in the origin, stretched vertically by a factor of 4, and shifted upward 3 units; g is increasing; horizontal asymptote: $y = 3$.

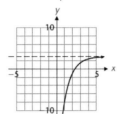

65. $\dfrac{-2x^3 e^{-2x} - 3x^2 e^{-2x}}{x^6} = \dfrac{x^2 e^{-2x}(-2x-3)}{x^6} = \dfrac{e^{-2x}(-2x-3)}{x^4}$

67. $(e^x + e^{-x})^2 + (e^x - e^{-x})^2 = (e^x)^2 + 2(e^x)(e^{-x}) + (e^{-x})^2 + (e^x)^2 - 2(e^x)(e^{-x}) + (e^{-x})^2$

Common Errors:	$= e^{2x} + 2 + e^{-2x} + e^{2x} - 2 + e^{-2x}$
$\left(e^x\right)^2 \neq e^{x^2}$	$= 2e^{2x} + 2e^{-2x}$
$e^{2x} + e^{2x} \neq e^{4x}$	

69. Examining the graph of $y = f(x)$, we obtain

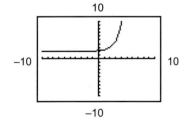

There are no local extrema and no x intercepts. The y intercept is 2.14. As $x \to -\infty$, $y \to 2$, so the line $y = 2$ is a horizontal asymptote.

71. Examining the graph of $y = s(x)$, we obtain

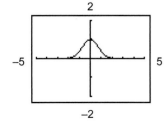

There is a local maximum at $s(0) = 1$, and 1 is the y intercept. There is no x intercept. As $x \to \infty$ or $x \to -\infty$, $y \to 0$, so the line $y = 0$ (the x axis) is a horizontal asymptote

73. Examining the graph of $y = F(x)$, we obtain

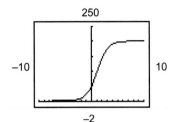

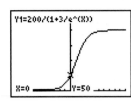

There are no local extrema and no x intercepts.

When $x = 0$, $F(0) = \dfrac{200}{1+3e^{-0}} = 50$ is the y intercept.

As $x \to -\infty$, $y \to 0$, so the line $y = 0$ (the x axis) is a horizontal asymptote. As $x \to \infty$, $y \to 200$, so the line $y = 200$ is also a horizontal asymptote.

75.

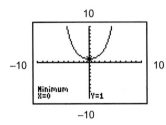

The local minimum is $f(0) = 1$, so zero is the y intercept. There are no x intercepts or horizontal asymptotes; $f(x) \to \infty$ as $x \to \infty$ and $x \to -\infty$.

77. Examining the graph of $y = f(x)$, we obtain

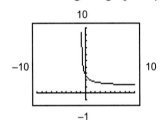

As $x \to 0$, $f(x) = (1 + x)^{1/x}$ seems to approach a value near 3. A table of values near $x = 0$ yields

Although $f(0)$ is not defined, as $x \to 0$, $f(x)$ seems to approach a number near 2.718. In fact, it approaches

e, since as $x \to 0$, $u = \dfrac{1}{x} \to \infty$, and $f(x) = \left(1 + \dfrac{1}{u}\right)^{u}$ must approach e as $u \to \infty$.

79. Make a table of values, substituting in each requested x value:

x	1.4	1.41	1.414	1.4142	1.41421	1.414214
2^x	2.639016	2.657372	2.664750	2.665119	2.665138	2.665145

The approximate value of $2^{\sqrt{2}}$ is 2.665145 to six decimal places. Using a calculator to compute directly, we get 2.665144.

81.

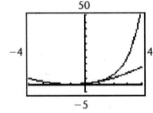

83.

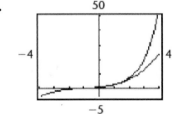

85. Here are graphs of $f_1(x) = \dfrac{x}{e^x}$, $f_2(x) = \dfrac{x^2}{e^x}$, and $f_3(x) = \dfrac{x^3}{e^x}$. In each case as $x \to \infty$, $f_n(x) \to 0$. The line $y = 0$ is a horizontal asymptote. As $x \to -\infty$, $f_1(x) \to -\infty$ and $f_3(x) \to -\infty$, while $f_2(x) \to \infty$. It appears that as $x \to -\infty$, $f_n(x) \to \infty$ if n is even and $f_n(x) \to -\infty$ if n is odd.

f_1:

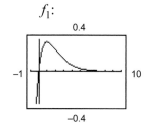

f_2:

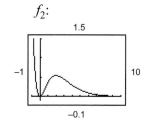

f_3:

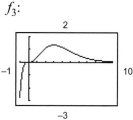

As confirmation of these observations, we show the graph of $f_4 = \dfrac{x^4}{e^x}$

(not required).

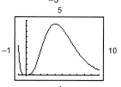

87. We use the compound interest formula

$A = P\left(1 + \dfrac{r}{m}\right)^n$ to find P: $P = \dfrac{A}{\left(1 + \frac{r}{m}\right)^n}$

$m = 365$ $r = 0.0625$ $A = 100{,}000$ $n = 365 \cdot 17$

$P = \dfrac{100{,}000}{\left(1 + \frac{0.0625}{365}\right)^{365 \cdot 17}} = \$34{,}562.00$ to the nearest dollar

89. We use the Continuous Compound Interest Formula

$A = Pe^{rt}$

$P = 5{,}250$ $r = 0.0638$

(A) $t = 6.25$ $A = 5{,}250e^{(0.0638)(6.25)} = \$7822.30$

(B) $t = 17$ $A = 5{,}250e^{(0.0638)(17)} = \$15{,}530.85$

91. We use the compound interest formula $A = P\left(1 + \dfrac{r}{m}\right)^n$

For the first account, $P = 3000$, $r = 0.08$, $m = 365$. Let $y_1 = A$, then $y_1 = 3000(1 + 0.08/365)^x$ where x is the number of compounding periods (days). For the second account, $P = 5000$, $r = 0.05$, $m = 365$. Let $y_2 = A$, then $y_2 = 5000(1 + 0.05/365)^x$

Examining the graphs of y_1 and y_2, we obtain the graphs at the right. The graphs intersect at $x = 6216.15$ days. Comparing the amounts in the accounts, we see that the first account is worth more than the second for $x \geq 6217$ days.

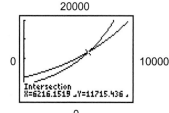

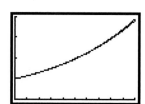

93. We use the compound interest formula $A = P\left(1 + \dfrac{r}{m}\right)^n$

For the first account, $P = 10{,}000$, $r = 0.049$, $m = 365$. Let $y_1 = A$, then $y_1 = 10000(1 + 0.049/365)^x$ where x is the number of compounding periods (days). For the second account, $P = 10{,}000$, $r = 0.05$, $m = 4$. Let $y_2 = A$, then $y_2 = 10000(1 + 0.05/4)^{4x/365}$ where x is the number of days. Examining the graphs of y_1 and y_2, we obtain the graph at the right. The two graphs are just about indistinguishable from one another. Examining a table of values, we obtain:

X	Y1	Y2
0	10000	10000
91.25	10123	10125
182.5	10248	10252
273.75	10374	10380
365	10502	10509
456.25	10632	10641
547.5	10763	10774

X=0

X	Y1	Y2
638.75	10895	10909
730	11030	11045
821.25	11165	11183
912.5	11303	11323
1003.8	11442	11464
1095	11583	11608
1186.25	11726	11753

X=1186.25

The two accounts are extremely close in value, but the second account is always larger than the first. The first will never be larger than the second.

95. We use the Continuous Compound Interest Formula

$$A = Pe^{rt}$$

$$P = \frac{A}{e^{rt}} \text{ or } P = Ae^{-rt}$$

$$A = 30{,}000 \quad r = 0.06 \quad t = 10$$

$$P = 30{,}000e^{(-0.06)(10)}$$

$$P = \$16{,}464.35$$

97. We use the compound interest formula $A = P\left(1+\dfrac{r}{m}\right)^n$

Flagstar Bank: $P = 5{,}000 \quad r = 0.0312 \quad m = 4 \quad n = (4)(3)$

$$A = 5{,}000\left(1+\frac{0.0312}{4}\right)^{(4)(3)} = \$5{,}488.61$$

UmbrellaBank.com: $P = 5{,}000 \quad r = 0.03 \quad m = 365 \quad n = (365)(3)$

$$A = 5{,}000\left(1+\frac{0.03}{365}\right)^{(365)(3)} = \$5{,}470.85$$

Allied First Bank: $P = 5{,}000 \quad r = 0.0296 \quad m = 12 \quad n = (12)(3)$

$$A = 5{,}000\left(1+\frac{0.0296}{12}\right)^{(12)(3)} = \$5{,}463.71$$

99. We use the compound interest formula

$$A = P\left(1+\frac{r}{m}\right)^n \quad m = 52 \qquad \text{[Note: If } m = 365/7 \text{ is used the answers will differ very slightly.]}$$

$$P = 4{,}000 \quad r = 0.06$$

$$A = 4{,}000\left(1+\frac{0.06}{52}\right)^n$$

(A) $n = (52)(0.5)$, hence

$$A = 4{,}000\left(1+\frac{0.06}{52}\right)^{(52)(0.5)}$$

$$= \$4{,}121.75$$

(B) $n = (52)(10) = 520$, hence

$$A = 4{,}000\left(1+\frac{0.06}{52}\right)^{520}$$

$$= \$7{,}285.95$$

Section 5-2

1. Doubling time is the time it takes a population to double. Half-life is the time it takes for half of an initial quantity of a radioactive substance to decay.

3. Exponential growth is the simple model $A = A_0 e^{kt}$, i.e. unlimited growth. Limited growth models more realistically incorporate the fact that there is a reasonable maximum value for A.

5. Use the doubling time model $A = A_0(2)^{t/d}$ with $A_0 = 200, d = 5$. $A = 200(2)^{t/5}$

7. Use the continuous growth model $A = A_0 e^{rt}$ with $A_0 = 2{,}000, r = 0.02$. $A = 2{,}000e^{0.02t}$

9. Use the half-life model $A = A_0\left(\dfrac{1}{2}\right)^{t/h}$ with $A_0 = 100, h = 6$. $A = 100\left(\dfrac{1}{2}\right)^{t/6}$

11. Use the exponential decay model $A = A_0 e^{-kt}$ with $A_0 = 4, k = 0.124$. $A = 4e^{-0.124t}$

13.

n	L
1	2
2	4
3	8
4	16
5	32
6	64
7	128
8	256
9	512
10	1,024

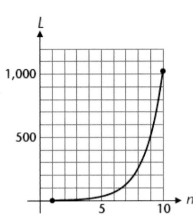

15. Use the doubling time model: $P = P_0 2^{t/d}$

Substituting $P_0 = 10$ and $d = 2.4$, we have
$P = 10(2^{t/2.4})$

(A) $t = 7$, hence $P = 10(2^{7/2.4})$
$\qquad\qquad = 75.5 \qquad\qquad$ 76 flies

(B) $t = 14$, hence $P = 10(2^{14/2.4})$
$\qquad\qquad\qquad = 570.2 \qquad\qquad$ 570 flies

17. Use the doubling time model $A = A_0 \left(\dfrac{1}{2}\right)^{t/h}$

with $A_0 = 2,200, d = 2$. $A = 2,200(2)^{t/2}$ where t is years after 1970.

(A) For $t = 20$: $A = 2,200(2)^{20/2} = 2,252,800$

(B) For $t = 35$: $A = 2,200(2)^{35/2} = 407,800,360$

19. Use the half-life model $A = A_0 \left(\dfrac{1}{2}\right)^{t/h} = A_0 2^{-t/h}$

Substituting $A_0 = 25$ and $h = 12$, we have
$A = 25(2^{-t/12})$

(A) $t = 5$, hence $A = 25(2^{-5/12}) = 19$ pounds

(B) $t = 20$, hence $A = 25(2^{-20/12}) = 7.9$ pounds

21. Use the continuous growth model $A = A_0 e^{rt}$ with $A_0 = 6.8$, $r = 0.01188$, $t = 2020 - 2008 = 12$
$A = 6.8 e^{0.01188(12)} = 7.8$ billion

23. Use the continuous growth model $A = A_0 e^{rt}$.   Below is a graph of A_1 and A_2.

Let A_1 = the population of Russia and
$\qquad A_2$ = the population of Nigeria.

For Russia, $A_0 = 1.43 \times 10^8$, $r = -0.0037$
$\qquad\qquad A_1 = 1.43 \times 10^8 e^{-0.0037t}$

For Nigeria, $A_0 = 1.29 \times 10^8$, $r = 0.0256$
$\qquad\qquad A_2 = 1.29 \times 10^8 e^{0.0256t}$

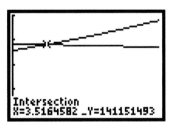

From the graph, assuming $t = 0$ in 2005, it appears that the two populations became equal when t was approximately 3.5, in 2008. After that the population of Nigeria will be greater than that of Russia.

25. A table of values can be generated by a graphing calculator and yields

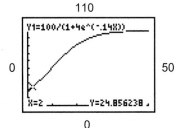

t	P
0	75
10	72
20	70
30	68
40	65
50	63
60	61
70	59
80	57
90	55
100	53

27. $I = I_0 e^{-0.00942d}$

(A) $d = 50$ $I = I_0 e^{-0.00942(50)} = 0.62 I_0$ 62%

(B) $d = 100$ $I = I_0 e^{-0.00942(100)} = 0.39 I_0$ 39%

29. Use the continuous growth model $A = A_0 e^{rt}$ with

$A_0 = 33.2$ million, $r = 0.0237$

(A) In 2014, assuming $t = 0$ in 2007, substitute $t = 7$.
$A = 33.2 e^{0.0237(7)} = 39.2$ million

(B) In 2020, substitute $t = 13$.
$A = 33.2 e^{0.0237(13)} = 45.2$ million

31. $T = T_m + (T_0 - T_m)e^{-kt}$
$T_m = 40°$ $T_0 = 72°$ $k = 0.4$ $t = 3$
$T = 40 + (72 - 40)e^{-0.4(3)}$
$T = 50°$

33. As t increases without bound, $e^{-0.2t}$ approaches 0, hence $q = 0.0009(1 - e^{-0.2t})$ approaches 0.0009. Hence 0.0009 coulomb is the maximum charge on the capacitor.

35. (A) Examining the graph of $N(t)$, we obtain the graphs below.

110

```
Y1=100/(1+4e^(-.14X))
X=2        Y=24.856238
```

0

```
Y1=100/(1+4e^(-.14X))
X=6        Y=36.672457
```

50

0

After 2 years, 25 deer will be present. After 6 years, 37 deer will be present.

(B) Applying a built-in routine, we obtain the graph at the right. It will take 10 years for the herd to grow to 50 deer.

(C) As t increases without bound, $e^{-0.14t}$ approaches 0, hence $N = \dfrac{100}{1 + 4e^{-0.14t}}$

approaches 100. Hence 100 is the number of deer the island can support.

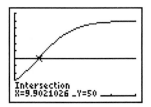

```
Intersection
X=9.9021026  Y=50
```

37.

```
L1    L2     L3    2
1     12575  ------
2     9455
3     8115
4     6845
5     5225
6     4485
------
L2(7) =
```

Enter the data.

```
ExpReg
y=a*b^x
a=14910.20311
b=.8162940177
```

Compute the regression equation.

The model gives $y = 14910.20311(0.8162940177)^x$.
Clearly, when $x = 0$, $y = \$14,910$ is the estimated purchase price.
Applying a built-in routine, we obtain the graph at the right.
When $x = 10$, the estimated value of the van is $\$1,959$.

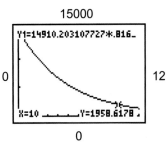

39. (A) The independent variable is years since 1980, so enter 0, 5, 10, 15, 20, and 25 as L_1. The dependent variable is power generation in North America, so enter the North America column as L_2. Then use the logistic regression command from the STAT CALC menu.

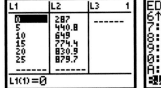  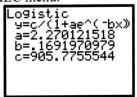

The model is

$$y = \frac{906}{1 + 2.27e^{-0.169x}}$$

(B) Since $x = 0$ corresponds to 1980, use $x = 30$ to predict power generation in 2010.

$$y = \frac{906}{1 + 2.27e^{-0.169(30)}} = 893.3 \text{ billion kilowatt hours}$$

Use $x = 40$ to predict power generation in 2020.

$$y = \frac{906}{1 + 2.27e^{-0.169(40)}} = 903.6 \text{ billion kilowatt hours}$$

Section 5-3

1. The exponential function $f(x) = b^x$ for $b > 0$, $b \ne 1$ and the logarithmic function $g(x) = \log_b x$ are inverse functions for each other.

3. The range of the exponential function is the positive real numbers, hence the domain of the logarithmic function must also be the positive real numbers.

5. $\log_5 3 = \log_e 3 / \log_e 5$ or $\log_{10} 3 / \log_{10} 5$.

7. $81 = 3^4$ **9.** $0.001 = 10^{-3}$ **11.** $\dfrac{1}{36} = 6^{-2}$ **13.** $\log_4 8 = \dfrac{3}{2}$ **15.** $\log_{32} \dfrac{1}{2} = -\dfrac{1}{5}$ **17.** $\log_{2/3} \dfrac{8}{27} = 3$

19. Make a table of values for each function:

x	$f(x) = 3^x$	x	$f^{-1}(x) = \log_3 x$
-3	$1/27$	$1/27$	-3
-2	$1/9$	$1/9$	-2
-1	$1/3$	$1/3$	-1
0	1	1	0
1	3	3	1
2	9	9	2
3	27	27	3

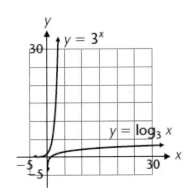

21. Make a table of values for each function:

x	$f(x)=(2/3)^x$	x	$f^{-1}(x)=\log_{2/3}x$
-3	$27/8$	$27/8$	-3
-2	$9/4$	$9/4$	-2
-1	$3/2$	$3/2$	-1
0	1	1	0
1	$2/3$	$2/3$	1
2	$4/9$	$4/9$	2
3	$8/27$	$8/27$	3

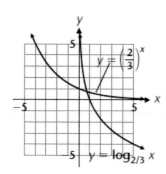

23. 0   **25.** 1   **27.** 4   **29.** $\log_{10}0.01=\log_{10}10^{-2}=-2$ **31.** $\log_3 27=\log_3 3^3=3$

33. $\log_{1/2}2=\log_{1/2}\left(\dfrac{1}{2}\right)^{-1}=-1$ **35.** 5   **37.** $\log_5\sqrt[3]{5}=\log_5 5^{1/3}=\dfrac{1}{3}$ **39.** 4.6923   **41.** 3.9905

43. $\log_7 13=\dfrac{\ln 13}{\ln 7}=1.3181$
  using the change of base formula

45. $\log_5 120.24=\dfrac{\ln 120.24}{\ln 5}=2.9759$
  using the change of base formula

47. $x=10^{5.3027}=200{,}800$

49. $x=10^{-3.1773}=6.648\times 10^{-4}=0.0006648$

51. $x=e^{3.8655}=47.73$

53. $x=e^{-0.3916}=0.6760$

55. Write $\log_2 x=2$ in equivalent exponential form.
  $$x=2^2=4$$

57. $\log_4 16=\log_4 4^2=2$
  $$y=2$$

59. Write $\log_b 16=2$ in equivalent exponential form.
  $$16=b^2$$
  $$b^2=16$$
  $$b=4$$
  since bases are required to be positive

61. Write $\log_b 1=0$ in equivalent exponential form.
  $$1=b^0$$
  This statement is true if b is any real number except 0. However, bases are required to be positive and 1 is not allowed, so the original statement is true if b is any positive real number except 1.

63. Write $\log_4 x=\dfrac{1}{2}$ in equivalent exponential form.
  $$x=4^{1/2}=2$$

65. $\log_{1/3}9=\log_{1/3}3^2=\log_{1/3}\dfrac{1}{\left(\frac{1}{3}\right)^2}=\log_{1/3}\left(\dfrac{1}{3}\right)^{-2}=-2$

67. Write $\log_b 1000=\dfrac{3}{2}$ in equivalent exponential
  form
  $$1000=b^{3/2}$$
  $$10^3=b^{3/2}$$
  $$(10^3)^{2/3}=(b^{3/2})^{2/3}$$
  (If two numbers are equal the results are equal if they are raised to the same exponent.)
  $$10^{3(2/3)}=b^{3/2(2/3)}$$
  $$10^2=b$$
  $$b=100$$

69. Write $\log_8 x=-\dfrac{4}{3}$ in equivalent exponential form.
  $$8^{-4/3}=x$$
  $$x=(8^{1/3})^{-4}=2^{-4}=\dfrac{1}{16}$$

71. Write $\log_{16}8=y$ in equivalent exponential form.
  $$16^y=8$$
  $$(2^4)^y=2^3$$
  $$2^{4y}=2^3 \text{ if and only if}$$
  $$4y=3$$
  $$y=\dfrac{3}{4}$$

73. 4.959   **75.** 7.861   **77.** 2.280   **79.** $\log x-\log y$

81. $\log(x^4y^3) = \log x^4 + \log y^3 = 4\log x + 3\log y$

83. $\ln\left(\dfrac{x}{y}\right)$

85. $2\ln x + 5\ln y - \ln z = \ln x^2 + \ln y^5 - \ln z = \ln(x^2y^5) - \ln z$

$$= \ln\left(\dfrac{x^2y^5}{z}\right)$$

87. $\log(xy) = \log x + \log y = -2 + 3 = 1$

89. $\log\left(\dfrac{\sqrt{x}}{y^3}\right) = \log\sqrt{x} - \log y^3 = \dfrac{1}{2}\log x - 3\log y = \dfrac{1}{2}(-2) - 3\cdot 3 = -10$

91. The graph of g is the same as the graph of f shifted upward 3 units; g is increasing. Domain: $(0, \infty)$ Vertical asymptote: $x = 0$

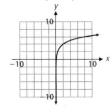

93. The graph of g is the same as the graph of f shifted 2 units to the right; g is decreasing. Domain: $(2, \infty)$ Vertical asymptote: $x = 2$

95. The graph of g is the same as the graph of f reflected through the x axis and shifted downward 1 unit; g is decreasing. Domain: $(0, \infty)$ Vertical asymptote: $x = 0$

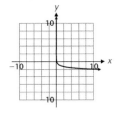

97. The graph of g is the same as the graph of f reflected through the x axis, stretched vertically by a factor of 3, and shifted upward 5 units. g is decreasing. Domain: $(0, \infty)$ Vertical asymptote: $x = 0$

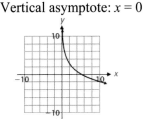

99.   Write $y = \log_5 x$
In exponential form:
$5^y = x$
Interchange x and y:
$5^x = y$
Therefore $f^1(x) = 5^x$.

101.   Write $y = 4\log_3(x + 3)$
$\dfrac{y}{4} = \log_3(x + 3)$
In exponential form:
$3^{y/4} = x + 3$
$x = 3^{y/4} - 3$
Interchange x and y:
$y = 3^{x/4} - 3$
Therefore $f^1(x) = 3^{x/4} - 3$

103.   (A) Write $y = \log_3(2 - x)$
In exponential form:
$3^y = 2 - x$
$x = 2 - 3^y$
Interchange x and y:
$y = 2 - 3^x$
Therefore, $f^1(x) = 2 - 3^x$

(B)   The graph is the same as the graph of $y = 3^x$ reflected through the x axis and shifted 2 units upward.

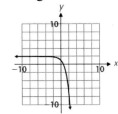

(C)

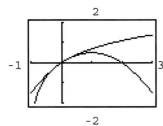

105. The inequality sign in the last step reverses because $\log \frac{1}{3}$ is negative.

107.

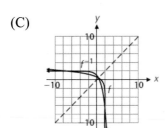

109.

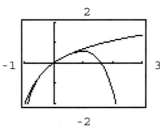

111. Let $u = \log_b M$ and $v = \log_b N$. Changing each equation to exponential form, $b^u = M$ and $b^v = N$.

Then we can write M/N as $\dfrac{M}{N} = \dfrac{b^u}{b^v} = b^{u-v}$ using a familiar property of exponents. Now change this

equation to logarithmic form: $\log_b \left(\dfrac{M}{N} \right) = u - v$

Finally, recall the way we defined u and v in the first line of our proof: $\log_b \left(\dfrac{M}{N} \right) = \log_b M - \log_b N$

Section 5-4

1. Answers will vary.
3. The intensity of a sound and the energy released by an earthquake can vary from extremely small to extremely large. A logarithmic scale can condense this variation into a range that can be easily comprehended.

5. We use the decibel formula $D = 10 \log \dfrac{I}{I_0}$

(A) $I = I_0$

$D = 10 \log \dfrac{I_0}{I_0}$

$D = 10 \log 1$

$D = 0$ decibels

(B) $I_0 = 1.0 \times 10^{-12}$ $I = 1.0$

$D = 10 \log \dfrac{1.0}{1.0 \times 10^{-12}}$

$D = 120$ decibels

7. We use the decibel formula

$D = 10 \log \dfrac{I}{I_0}$

$I_2 = 1000 I_1$

$D_1 = 10 \log \dfrac{I_1}{I_0}$ $D_2 = 10 \log \dfrac{I_2}{I_0}$

$D_2 - D_1 = 10 \log \dfrac{I_2}{I_0} - 10 \log \dfrac{I_1}{I_0}$

$= 10 \log \left(\dfrac{I_2}{I_0} \div \dfrac{I_1}{I_0} \right) = 10 \log \dfrac{I_2}{I_1}$

$= 10 \log \dfrac{1000 I_1}{I_1} = 10 \log 1000 = 30$ decibels

9. We use the magnitude formula

$M = \dfrac{2}{3} \log \dfrac{E}{E_0}$ with $E = 1.99 \times 10^{-17}$, $E_0 = 10\,4.40$

$M = \dfrac{2}{3} \log \dfrac{1.99 \times 10^{-17}}{10^{4.40}} = 8.6$

11. We use the magnitude formula $M = \dfrac{2}{3} \log \dfrac{E}{E_0}$

For the Long Beach earthquake,

$6.3 = \dfrac{2}{3} \log \dfrac{E_1}{E_0}$

$9.45 = \log \dfrac{E_1}{E_0}$

(Change to exponential form)

$\dfrac{E_1}{E_0} = 10^{9.45}$

$E_1 = E_0 \cdot 10^{9.45}$

For the Anchorage earthquake,

$8.3 = \dfrac{2}{3} \log \dfrac{E_2}{E_0}$

$12.45 = \log \dfrac{E_2}{E_0}$

(Change to exponential form)

$\dfrac{E_2}{E_0} = 10^{12.45}$

$E_2 = E_0 \cdot 10^{12.45}$

Now we can compare the energy levels by dividing the more powerful (Anchorage) by the less (Long Beach):

$\dfrac{E_2}{E_1} = \dfrac{E_0 \cdot 10^{12.45}}{E_0 \cdot 10^{9.45}} = 10^3$

$E_2 = 10^3 E_1$, or 1000 times as powerful

13. Use the magnitude formula $M = \dfrac{2}{3}\log\dfrac{E}{E_0}$ with $E = 1.34 \times 10^{14}, E_0 = 10^{4.40}$: $M = \dfrac{2}{3}\log\dfrac{1.34 \times 10^{14}}{10^{4.40}} = 6.5$

15. Use the magnitude formula $M = \dfrac{2}{3}\log\dfrac{E}{E_0}$ with $E = 2.38 \times 10^{21}, E_0 = 10^{4.40}$: $M = \dfrac{2}{3}\log\dfrac{2.38 \times 10^{21}}{10^{4.40}} = 11.3$

17. We use the rocket equation.

$v = c \ln \dfrac{W_t}{W_b}$

$v = 2.57 \ln (19.8)$

$v = 7.67$ km/s

19. (A) $pH = -\log[H^+] = -\log(4.63 \times 10^{-9}) = 8.3$.
Since this is greater than 7, the substance is basic.

(B) $pH = -\log[H^+] = -\log(9.32 \times 10^{-4}) = 3.0$
Since this is less than 7, the substance is acidic.

21. Since $pH = -\log[H^+]$, we have

$5.2 = -\log[H^+]$, or

$[H^+] = 10^{-5.2} = 6.3 \times 10^{-6}$ moles per liter

23. $m = 6 - 2.5 \log \dfrac{L}{L_0}$

(A) We find m when $L = L_0$

$m = 6 - 2.5 \log \dfrac{L_0}{L_0}$

$m = 6 - 2.5 \log 1$

$m = 6$

(B) We compare L_1 for $m = 1$ with L_2 for $m = 6$

$1 = 6 - 2.5 \log \dfrac{L_1}{L_0}$

$-5 = -2.5 \log \dfrac{L_1}{L_0}$

$2 = \log \dfrac{L_1}{L_0}$

$\dfrac{L_1}{L_0} = 10^2$

$L_1 = 100 L_0$

$6 = 6 - 2.5 \log \dfrac{L_2}{L_0}$

$0 = -2.5 \log \dfrac{L_2}{L_0}$

$0 = \log \dfrac{L_2}{L_0}$

$\dfrac{L_2}{L_0} = 1$

$L_2 = L_0$

Hence $\dfrac{L_1}{L_2} = \dfrac{100 L_0}{L_0} = 100$. The star of magnitude 1 is 100 times brighter.

25. (A) Enter the years since 1995 as L_1. Enter the values shown in the column headed "% with home access" as L_2. Use the logarithmic regression model from the STAT CALC menu.

The model is $y = 11.9 + 24.1 \ln x$. Evaluating this for $x = 13$ (year 2008) yields 73.7%. Evaluating for $x = 20$ (year 2015) yields 84.1%.

(B) No; the predicted percentage goes over 100 sometime around 2034.

Section 5-5

1. The logarithm function is the inverse of the exponential function, moreover, $\log_b M^p = p\log_b M$. This property of logarithms can often be used to get a variable out of an exponent in solving an equation.

3. If $\log_b u = \log_b v$, then $u = v$ because the logarithm is a one-to-one function.

5. $\left(\ln x\right)^2$ means to take the logarithm of x, then square the result.

   $\ln x^2$ means to square x, then take the logarithm of the result.

7. $10^{-x} = 0.0347$
   $-x = \log_{10} 0.0347$
   $x = -\log_{10} 0.0347$
   $x = 1.46$

9. $10^{3x+1} = 92$
   $3x + 1 = \log_{10} 92$
   $3x = \log_{10} 92 - 1$
   $x = \dfrac{\log_{10} 92 - 1}{3}$
   $x = 0.321$

11. $e^x = 3.65$
    $x = \ln 3.65$
    $x = 1.29$

13. $e^{2x-1} + 68 = 207$
    $e^{2x-1} = 139$
    $2x - 1 = \ln 139$
    $x = \dfrac{1 + \ln 139}{2}$
    $x = 2.97$

15. $2^3 2^{-x} = 0.426$
    $2^{-x} = \dfrac{0.426}{2^3}$
    $\ln 2^{-x} = \ln \dfrac{0.426}{8}$
    $-x \ln 2 = \ln \dfrac{0.426}{8}$
    $x = \dfrac{\ln \frac{0.426}{8}}{-\ln 2}$
    $x = 4.23$

17. $\log_5 x = 2$
    $5^2 = x$
    $x = 25$

19. $\log(t - 4) = -1$
    $10^{-1} = t - 4$
    $t = 4 + 10^{-1}$
    $t = 4 + \dfrac{1}{10}$
    $t = \dfrac{41}{10}$

21. $\log 5 + \log x = 2$
    $\log(5x) = 2$
    $5x = 10^2$
    $5x = 100$
    $x = 20$

23. $\log x + \log(x - 3) = 1$
    $\log[x(x - 3)] = 1$
    $x(x - 3) = 10^1$
    $x^2 - 3x = 10$
    $x^2 - 3x - 10 = 0$
    $(x - 5)(x + 2) = 0$
    $x = 5$ or -2

    Common Error:
    $\log(x - 3) \ne \log x - \log 3$

    Check:
    $\log 5 + \log(5 - 3) \overset{\checkmark}{=} 1$
    $\log(-2) + \log(-2 - 3)$ is not defined.
    $x = 5$

25. $\log(x + 1) - \log(x - 1) = 1$
    $\log \dfrac{x+1}{x-1} = 1$
    $\dfrac{x+1}{x-1} = 10^1$
    $\dfrac{x+1}{x-1} = 10$
    $x + 1 = 10(x - 1)$
    $x + 1 = 10x - 10$
    $11 = 9x$
    $x = \dfrac{11}{9}$

    Common Error:
    $\dfrac{x+1}{x-1} \ne \log 1$

    Check:
    $\log\left(\dfrac{11}{9} + 1\right) - \log\left(\dfrac{11}{9} - 1\right) \overset{?}{=} 1$
    $\log \dfrac{20}{9} - \log \dfrac{2}{9} \overset{?}{=} 1$
    $\log 10 \overset{\checkmark}{=} 1$

27.
$$2 = 1.05^x$$
$$\ln 2 = x \ln 1.05$$
$$\frac{\ln 2}{\ln 1.05} = x$$
$$x = 14.2$$

29. $e^{-1.4x} + 5 = 0$
No solution. Both terms on the left side are always positive, so they can never add to 0.

31.
$$123 = 500e^{-0.12x}$$
$$\frac{123}{500} = e^{-0.12x}$$
$$\ln\left(\frac{123}{500}\right) = -0.12x$$
$$\frac{\ln\left(\frac{123}{500}\right)}{-0.12} = x$$
$$x = 11.7$$

33.
$$e^{-x^2} = 0.23$$
$$-x^2 = \ln 0.23$$
$$x^2 = -\ln 0.23$$
$$x = \pm\sqrt{-\ln 0.23}$$
$$x = \pm 1.21$$

35.
$$\log(5 - 2x) = \log(3x + 1)$$
$$5 - 2x = 3x + 1$$
$$4 = 5x$$
$$x = \frac{4}{5}$$

37.
$$\log x - \log 5 = \log 2 - \log(x - 3)$$
$$\log \frac{x}{5} = \log \frac{2}{x-3}$$
$$\frac{x}{5} = \frac{2}{x-3}$$
Excluded value: $x \neq 3$
$$5(x - 3)\frac{x}{5} = 5(x - 3)\frac{2}{x-3}$$
$$(x - 3)x = 10$$
$$x^2 - 3x = 10$$
$$x^2 - 3x - 10 = 0$$
$$(x - 5)(x + 2) = 0$$
$$x = 5, -2$$
Solution: 5

Check:
$$\log 5 - \log 5 \overset{\sqrt{}}{=} \log 2 - \log 2$$
$\log(-2)$ is not defined

39.
$$\ln x = \ln(2x - 1) - \ln(x - 2)$$
$$\ln x = \ln \frac{2x-1}{x-2}$$
$$x = \frac{2x-1}{x-2}$$
Excluded value: $x \neq 2$
$$x(x - 2) = (x - 2)\frac{2x-1}{x-2}$$
$$x(x - 2) = 2x - 1$$
$$x^2 - 2x = 2x - 1$$
$$x^2 - 4x + 1 = 0$$
$$x = \frac{-b \pm \sqrt{b^2 - 4ac}}{2a}$$
$$a = 1, b = -4, c = 1$$
$$x = \frac{-(-4) \pm \sqrt{(-4)^2 - 4(1)(1)}}{2(1)}$$
$$x = \frac{4 \pm \sqrt{12}}{2} = 2 \pm \sqrt{3}$$

Check:
$$\ln(2 + \sqrt{3}) \overset{?}{=} \ln[2(2 + \sqrt{3}) - 1]$$
$$- \ln[(2 + \sqrt{3}) - 2]$$
$$\ln(2 + \sqrt{3}) \overset{?}{=} \ln(3 + 2\sqrt{3}) - \ln\sqrt{3}$$
$$\ln(2 + \sqrt{3}) \overset{?}{=} \ln\left(\frac{3 + 2\sqrt{3}}{\sqrt{3}}\right)$$
$$\ln(2 + \sqrt{3}) \overset{\sqrt{}}{=} \ln(\sqrt{3} + 2)$$
$\ln(x - 2)$ is not defined if $x = 2 - \sqrt{3}$
Solution: $2 + \sqrt{3}$

41.

$$\log(2x + 1) = 1 - \log(x - 1)$$
$$\log(2x + 1) + \log(x - 1) = 1$$
$$\log[(2x + 1)(x - 1)] = 1$$
$$(2x + 1)(x - 1) = 10$$
$$2x^2 - x - 1 = 10$$
$$2x^2 - x - 11 = 0$$

$$x = \frac{-b \pm \sqrt{b^2 - 4ac}}{2a}$$

$$a = 2, \, b = -1, \, c = -11$$

$$x = \frac{-(-1) \pm \sqrt{(-1)^2 - 4(2)(-11)}}{2(2)}$$

$$x = \frac{1 \pm \sqrt{89}}{4}$$

Check: $\log\left(2\dfrac{1+\sqrt{89}}{4} + 1\right) \overset{?}{=} 1 - \log\left(\dfrac{1+\sqrt{89}}{4} - 1\right)$

$$\log\left(\frac{1+\sqrt{89}+2}{2}\right) \overset{?}{=} 1 - \log\left(\frac{1+\sqrt{89}-4}{4}\right)$$

$$\log\left(\frac{3+\sqrt{89}}{2}\right) \overset{?}{=} 1 - \log\left(\frac{\sqrt{89}-3}{4}\right)$$

$$\log\left(\frac{3+\sqrt{89}}{2}\right) \overset{?}{=} \log 10 - \log\left(\frac{\sqrt{89}-3}{4}\right)$$

$$\overset{?}{=} \log\left(\frac{40}{\sqrt{89}-3}\right)$$

$$\overset{?}{=} \log\left[\frac{40\left(\sqrt{89}+3\right)}{89-9}\right]$$

$$\overset{\surd}{=} \log\left(\frac{\sqrt{89}+3}{2}\right)$$

$\log(x - 1)$ is not defined if $x = \dfrac{1-\sqrt{89}}{4}$. Solution: $x = \dfrac{1+\sqrt{89}}{4}$

43.

$$\ln(x + 1) = \ln(3x + 3)$$
$$x + 1 = 3x + 3$$
$$-2x = 2$$
$$x = -1$$

Check: $\ln(-1 + 1)$ is not defined

No solution.

45.

$$(\ln x)^3 = \ln x^4$$
$$(\ln x)^3 = 4 \ln x$$
$$(\ln x)^3 - 4 \ln x = 0$$
$$\ln x[(\ln x)^2 - 4] = 0$$
$$\ln x(\ln x - 2)(\ln x + 2) = 0$$

$\ln x = 0$	$\ln x - 2 = 0$	$\ln x + 2 = 0$
$x = 1$	$\ln x = 2$	$\ln x = -2$
	$x = e^2$	$x = e^{-2}$

Check:

$(\ln 1)^3 \overset{?}{=} \ln 1^4$ $(\ln e^2)^3 \overset{?}{=} \ln(e^2)^4$ $(\ln e^{-2})^3 \overset{?}{=} \ln(e^{-2})^4$

$\quad 0 \overset{\surd}{=} 0$ $\quad 8 \overset{\surd}{=} 8$ $\quad -8 \overset{\surd}{=} -8$

Solution: $1, e^2, e^{-2}$

47.

$$\ln(\ln x) = 1$$
$$\ln x = e^1$$
$$\ln x = e$$
$$x = e^e$$

49.

$$A = Pe^{rt}$$
$$\frac{A}{P} = e^{rt}$$
$$\ln \frac{A}{P} = rt$$
$$\frac{1}{t} \ln \frac{A}{P} = r$$
$$r = \frac{1}{t} \ln \frac{A}{P}$$

51.

$$D = 10 \log \frac{I}{I_0}$$
$$\frac{D}{10} = \log \frac{I}{I_0}$$
$$\frac{I}{I_0} = 10^{D/10}$$
$$I = I_0(10^{D/10})$$

53.

$$M = 6 - 2.5 \log \frac{I}{I_0}$$
$$6 - M = 2.5 \log \frac{I}{I_0}$$
$$\frac{6-M}{2.5} = \log \frac{I}{I_0}$$
$$\frac{I}{I_0} = 10^{(6-M)/2.5}$$
$$I = I_0[10^{(6-M)/2.5}]$$

55.

$$I = \frac{E}{R}(1 - e^{-Rt/L})$$

$$RI = E(1 - e^{-Rt/L})$$

$$\frac{RI}{E} = 1 - e^{-Rt/L}$$

$$\frac{RI}{E} - 1 = -e^{-Rt/L}$$

$$-\left(\frac{RI}{E} - 1\right) = e^{-Rt/L}$$

$$-\frac{RI}{E} + 1 = e^{-Rt/L}$$

$$1 - \frac{RI}{E} = e^{-Rt/L}$$

$$\ln\left(1 - \frac{RI}{E}\right) = -\frac{Rt}{L}$$

$$-\frac{L}{R}\ln\left(1 - \frac{RI}{E}\right) = t$$

$$t = -\frac{L}{R}\ln\left(1 - \frac{RI}{E}\right)$$

57.

$$y = \frac{e^x + e^{-x}}{2}$$

$$2y = e^x + e^{-x}$$

$$2y = e^x + \frac{1}{e^x}$$

$$2ye^x = (e^x)^2 + 1$$

$$0 = (e^x)^2 - 2ye^x + 1$$

This equation is quadratic in e^x

$$e^x = \frac{-b \pm \sqrt{b^2 - 4ac}}{2a} \qquad \begin{array}{l} a = 1, \\ b = -2y, \\ c = 1 \end{array}$$

$$e^x = \frac{-(-2y) \pm \sqrt{(-2y)^2 - 4(1)(1)}}{2(1)}$$

$$e^x = \frac{2y \pm \sqrt{4y^2 - 4}}{2}$$

$$e^x = \frac{2(y \pm \sqrt{y^2 - 1})}{2}$$

$$e^x = y \pm \sqrt{y^2 - 1}$$

$$x = \ln(y \pm \sqrt{y^2 - 1})$$

59.

$$y = \frac{e^x - e^{-x}}{e^x + e^{-x}}$$

$$y = \frac{e^x - \frac{1}{e^x}}{e^x + \frac{1}{e^x}}$$

$$y = \frac{e^x e^x - \frac{1}{e^x}e^x}{e^x e^x + \frac{1}{e^x}e^x}$$

$$y = \frac{e^{2x} - 1}{e^{2x} + 1}$$

$$y(e^{2x} + 1) = e^{2x} - 1$$

$$ye^{2x} + y = e^{2x} - 1$$

$$1 + y = e^{2x} - ye^{2x}$$

$$1 + y = (1 - y)e^{2x}$$

$$e^{2x} = \frac{1 + y}{1 - y}$$

$$2x = \ln\frac{1 + y}{1 - y}$$

$$x = \frac{1}{2}\ln\frac{1 + y}{1 - y}$$

61. Graphing $y = 2^{-x} - 2x$ and applying a built-in routine, we obtain

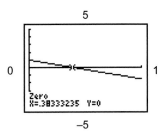

The required solution of $2^{-x} - 2x = 0$, $0 \le x \le 1$, is 0.38.

63. Graphing $y = e^{-x} - x$ and applying a built-in routine, we obtain

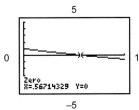

The required solution of $e^{-x} - x = 0$, $0 \le x \le 1$, is 0.57.

65. Graphing $y = \ln x + 2x$ and applying a built-in routine, we obtain

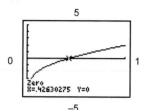

The required solution of $\ln x + 2x = 0$, $0 \le x \le 1$, is 0.43.

67. Graphing $y = \ln x + e^x$ and applying a built-in routine, we obtain

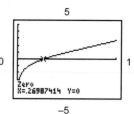

The required solution of $\ln x + e^x = 0$, $0 \le x \le 1$, is 0.27.

69. To find the doubling time we replace A in $A = P(1 + 0.07)^n$ with $2P$ and solve for n.
$$2P = P(1.07)^n$$
$$2 = (1.07)^n$$
$$\ln 2 = n \ln 1.07$$
$$n = \frac{\ln 2}{\ln 1.07}$$
$$n = 10 \text{ years to the nearest year}$$

71. We solve $A = Pe^{rt}$ for r, with $A = 2,500$, $P = 1,000$, $t = 10$
$$2,500 = 1,000 e^{r(10)}$$
$$2.5 = e^{10r}$$
$$10r = \ln(2.5)$$
$$r = \frac{1}{10} \ln 2.5 = 0.0916 \text{ or } 9.16\%$$

73. (A) We're given $P_0 = 10.5$ (we could use 10.5 million, but if you look carefully at the calculations below, you'll see that the millions will cancel out anyhow), 11.3 for P, and 2 for t (since May 2007 is two years after May 2005).
$$11.3 = 10.5 e^{r \cdot 2}$$
$$\frac{11.3}{10.5} = e^{2r}$$
$$\ln\left(\frac{11.3}{10.5}\right) = 2r$$
$$r = \frac{\ln\left(\frac{11.3}{10.5}\right)}{2} \approx 0.0367 \quad \text{The annual growth rate is } 3.67\%.$$

(B) $P = 10.5 e^{0.0367t}$; plug in 20 for P and solve for t.
$$20 = 10.5 e^{0.0367t}$$
$$\frac{20}{10.5} = e^{0.0367t}$$
$$\ln\left(\frac{20}{10.5}\right) = 0.0367t$$
$$t = \frac{\ln\left(\frac{20}{10.5}\right)}{0.0367} \approx 17.6$$

The illegal immigrant population is predicted to reach 20 million near the end of 2022, which is 17.6 years after May 2005.

75. We solve $P = P_0 e^{rt}$ for t with $P = 2P_0$, $r = 0.0114$.
$$2P_0 = P_0 e^{0.0114t}$$
$$2 = e^{0.0114t}$$
$$\ln 2 = 0.0114t$$
$$t = \frac{\ln 2}{0.0114}$$
$$t = 61 \text{ years to the nearest year}$$

77. We're given $A_0 = 5$, $A = 1$, $t = 6$:
$$A = A_0 \left(\frac{1}{2}\right)^{t/h}$$
$$1 = 5\left(\frac{1}{2}\right)^{6/h}$$
$$\frac{1}{5} = \left(\frac{1}{2}\right)^{6/h}$$
$$\ln\frac{1}{5} = \ln\left(\frac{1}{2}\right)^{6/h}$$
$$\ln\frac{1}{5} = \frac{6}{h}\ln\left(\frac{1}{2}\right)$$
$$h \cdot \ln\frac{1}{5} = 6\ln\left(\frac{1}{2}\right)$$
$$h = \frac{6\ln(1/2)}{\ln(1/5)} \approx 2.58$$
The half-life is about 2.58 hours.

79. Let A_0 represent the amount of Carbon-14 originally present. Then the amount left in 2003 was $0.289A_0$. Plug this in for A, and solve for t:

$$0.289A_0 = A_0 e^{-0.000124t}$$
$$0.289 = e^{-0.000124t}$$
$$\ln 0.289 = \ln e^{-0.000124t}$$
$$\ln 0.289 = -0.000124t$$
$$t = \frac{\ln 0.289}{-0.000124} \approx 10{,}010$$

The sample was about 10,010 years old.

83. We solve $q = 0.0009(1 - e^{-0.2t})$ for t with $q = 0.0007$

$$0.0007 = 0.0009(1 - e^{-0.2t})$$
$$\frac{0.0007}{0.0009} = 1 - e^{-0.2t}$$
$$\frac{7}{9} = 1 - e^{-0.2t}$$
$$-\frac{2}{9} = -e^{-0.2t}$$
$$\frac{2}{9} = e^{-0.2t}$$
$$\ln \frac{2}{9} = -0.2t$$
$$t = \frac{\ln \frac{2}{9}}{-0.2}$$
$$t = 7.52 \text{ seconds}$$

87. (A) Plug in $M = 7.0$ and solve for E:

$$7 = \frac{2}{3} \log \frac{E}{10^{4.40}}$$
$$\frac{21}{2} = \log \frac{E}{10^{4.4}}$$
$$10^{21/2} = \frac{E}{10^{4.4}}$$
$$E = 10^{21/2} \cdot 10^{4.4} \approx 7.94 \times 10^{14} \text{ joules}$$

89. First, find the energy released by one magnitude 7.5 earthquake:

$$7.5 = \frac{2}{3} \log \frac{E}{10^{4.40}}$$
$$11.25 = \log \frac{E}{10^{4.4}}$$

81. Let A_0 represent the amount of Carbon-14 originally present. Then the amount left in 2004 was $0.883A_0$. Plug this in for A, and solve for t:

$$0.883A_0 = A_0 e^{-0.000124t}$$
$$0.883 = e^{-0.000124t}$$
$$\ln 0.883 = \ln e^{-0.000124t}$$
$$\ln 0.883 = -0.000124t$$
$$t = \frac{\ln 0.883}{-0.000124} \approx 1{,}003$$

It was 1,003 years old in 2004, so it was made in 1001.

85. First, we solve $T = T_m + (T_0 - T_m)e^{-kt}$ for k, with $T = 61.5°$, $T_m = 40°$, $T_0 = 72°$, $t = 1$

$$61.5 = 40 + (72 - 40)e^{-k(1)}$$
$$21.5 = 32e^{-k}$$
$$\frac{21.5}{32} = e^{-k}$$
$$\ln \frac{21.5}{32} = -k$$
$$k = -\ln \frac{21.5}{32}$$
$$k = 0.40$$

Now we solve $T = T_m + (T_0 - T_m)e^{-0.40t}$ for t, with $T = 50°$, $T_m = 40°$, $T_0 = 72°$

$$50 = 40 + (72 - 40)e^{-0.40t}$$
$$10 = 32e^{-0.40t}$$
$$\frac{10}{32} = e^{-0.40t}$$
$$\ln \frac{10}{32} = -0.40t$$
$$t = \frac{\ln 10/32}{-0.40}$$
$$t = 2.9 \text{ hours}$$

(B) $\dfrac{7.94 \times 10^{14} \text{ joules}}{2.88 \times 10^{14} \text{ joules/day}} = 2.76 \text{ days}$

Finally, divide by the energy consumption per year:

$$\frac{5.364 \times 10^{16} \text{ joules}}{1.05 \times 10^{17} \text{ joules/year}} = 0.510$$

So this energy could power the U.S. for 0.510 years, or about 186 days.

$$10^{11.25} = \frac{E}{10^{4.4}}$$

$$E = 10^{11.25} \cdot 10^{4.4} \approx 4.47 \times 10^{15} \text{ joules}$$

Now multiply by twelve to get the energy released by twelve such earthquakes:

$$12 \cdot 4.47 \times 10^{15} = 5.364 \times 10^{16}$$

CHAPTER 5 REVIEW

1. (A) The graph of $y = \log_2 x$ passes through $(1, 0)$ and $(2, 1)$. This corresponds to graph m.

(B) The graph of $y = 0.5^x$ passes through $(0, 1)$ and $(1, 0.5)$. This corresponds to graph f.

(C) The graph of $y = \log_{0.5} x$ passes through $(1, 0)$ and $(0.5, 1)$. This corresponds to graph n.

(D) The graph of $y = 2^x$ passes through $(0, 1)$ and $(1, 2)$. This corresponds to graph g.   *(5-1, 5-3)*

2. $\log m = n$ *(5-3)*   **3.** $\ln x = y$ *(5-3)*   **4.** $x = 10^y$ *(5-3)*   **5.** $y = e^x$ *(5-3)*

6. (A) Make a table of values:

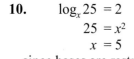

x	-2	-1	0	1	2	3
$\left(\frac{4}{3}\right)^x$	$\frac{9}{16}$	$\frac{3}{4}$	1	$\frac{4}{3}$	$\frac{16}{9}$	$\frac{64}{27}$

(5-1)

(B) The function in part (B) is the inverse of the one graphed in part (A), so its graph is a reflection about the line $y = x$ of the graph to the left. To plot points, just switch the x and y coordinates of the points from the table in part (A).

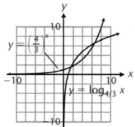

(5-3)

7.
$$\frac{7^{x+2}}{7^{2-x}} = 7^{(x+2)-(2-x)}$$
$$= 7^{x+2-2+x}$$
$$= 7^{2x} \qquad (5\text{-}1)$$

8.
$$\left(\frac{e^x}{e^{-x}}\right)^x = \left[e^{x-(-x)}\right]^x$$
$$= (e^{2x})^x = e^{2x \cdot x}$$
$$= e^{2x^2} \qquad (5\text{-}1)$$

9.
$$\log_2 x = 3$$
$$x = 2^3$$
$$x = 8 \qquad (5\text{-}3)$$

10.
$$\log_x 25 = 2$$
$$25 = x^2$$
$$x = 5$$
since bases are restricted positive
(5-3)

11.
$$\log_3 27 = x$$
$$\log_3 3^3 = x$$
$$x = 3 \qquad (5\text{-}3)$$

12.
$$10^x = 17.5$$
$$x = \log_{10} 17.5$$
$$x = 1.24 \qquad (5\text{-}5)$$

13.
$$e^x = 143{,}000$$
$$x = \ln 143{,}000$$
$$x = 11.9 \qquad (5\text{-}5)$$

14.
$$\ln x = -0.01573$$
$$x = e^{-0.01573}$$
$$x = 0.984 \qquad (5\text{-}3)$$

15.
$$\log x = 2.013$$
$$x = 10^{2.013}$$
$$x = 103 \qquad (5\text{-}3)$$

16. 1.145 *(5-3)*   **17.** Not defined. ($-e$ is not in the domain of the logarithm function.) *(5-3)*   **18.** 2.211 *(5-3)*   **19.** 11.59 *(5-1)*

20. $2\log a - \frac{1}{3}\log b + \log c = \log a^2 + \log c - \log b^{\frac{1}{3}}$
$$= \log\left(a^2 c\right) - \log b^{\frac{1}{3}}$$
$$= \log\left(\frac{a^2 c}{\sqrt[3]{b}}\right) \qquad (5\text{-}3)$$

21. $\ln\frac{a^5}{\sqrt{b}} = \ln a^5 - \ln\sqrt{b}$
$$= 5\ln a - \ln b^{\frac{1}{2}}$$
$$= 5\ln a - \frac{1}{2}\ln b$$
$$(5\text{-}3)$$

22.
$$3^x = 120$$
$$\log_3 3^x = \log_3 120$$
$$x = \log_3 120$$

23.
$$10^{2x} = 500$$
$$\log 10^{2x} = \log 500$$
$$2x = \log 500$$

24. $\log_2(4x - 5) = 5$
$$2^5 = 4x - 5$$
$$32 = 4x - 5$$

or, using the change-of-base
formula $\dfrac{\ln 120}{\ln 3}$ *(5-5)*

$x = \dfrac{\log 500}{2}$

(5-5)

$37 = 4x$

$x = \dfrac{37}{4}$ *(5-5)*

25. $\ln(x - 5) = 0$

$x - 5 = e^0$

$x - 5 = 1$

$x = 6$

(5-5)

26. $\ln(2x - 1) = \ln(x + 3)$

$2x - 1 = x + 3$

$x = 4$

Check:

$\ln(2 \cdot 4 - 1) \overset{?}{=} \ln(4 + 3)$

$\ln 7 \overset{\surd}{=} \ln 7$

(5-5)

27. $\log(x^2 - 3) = 2 \log(x - 1)$

$\log(x^2 - 3) = \log(x - 1)^2$

$x^2 - 3 = (x - 1)^2$

$x^2 - 3 = x^2 - 2x + 1$

$-3 = -2x + 1$

$-4 = -2x$

$x = 2$

Check:

$\log(2^2 - 3) \overset{?}{=} 2 \log(2 - 1)$ $\log 1 \overset{?}{=} 2$

$\log 1$

$0 \overset{\surd}{=} 0$

(5-5)

28. $e^{x^2 - 3} = e^{2x}$

$x^2 - 3 = 2x$

$x^2 - 2x - 3 = 0$

$(x - 3)(x + 1) = 0$

$x = 3, -1$

(5-5)

29. $4^{x-1} = 2^{1-x}$

$(2^2)^{x-1} = 2^{1-x}$

$2^{2(x-1)} = 2^{1-x}$

$2(x - 1) = 1 - x$

$2x - 2 = 1 - x$

$3x = 3$

$x = 1$ *(5-5)*

30. $2x^2 e^{-x} = 18 e^{-x}$

$2x^2 e^{-x} - 18 e^{-x} = 0$

$2e^{-x}(x^2 - 9) = 0$

$2e^{-x}(x - 3)(x + 3) = 0$

$2e^{-x} = 0 \quad x - 3 = 0 \quad x + 3 = 0$

never $\qquad x = 3 \qquad x = -3$

Solution: 3, -3 *(5-5)*

31. $\log_{1/4} 16 = x$

$\log_{1/4} 4^2 = x$

$\log_{1/4}\left(\dfrac{1}{4}\right)^{-2} = x$

$x = -2$

(5-5)

32. $\log_x 9 = -2$

$x^{-2} = 9$

$\dfrac{1}{x^2} = 9$

$1 = 9x^2$

$\dfrac{1}{9} = x^2$

$x = \pm\sqrt{\dfrac{1}{9}}$

$x = \dfrac{1}{3}$ since bases are restricted positive

(5-5)

33. $\log_{16} x = \dfrac{3}{2}$

$16^{3/2} = x$

$64 = x$

$x = 64$

(5-5)

34. $\log_x e^5 = 5$

$e^5 = x^5$

$x = e$ *(5-5)*

35. $10^{\log_{10} x} = 33$

$\log_{10} x = \log_{10} 33$

$x = 33$ *(5-5)*

36. $x = 2(10^{1.32})$

$x = 41.8$ *(5-1)*

37. $x = \log_5 23$

$x = \dfrac{\log 23}{\log 5}$ or $\dfrac{\ln 23}{\ln 5}$

$x = 1.95$ *(5-3)*

38. $\ln x = -3.218$

$x = e^{-3.218}$

$x = 0.0400$ *(5-3)*

39. $x = \log(2.156 \times 10^{-7})$

$x = -6.67$

(5-3)

40. $x = \dfrac{\ln 4}{\ln 2.31}$

$x = 1.66$ *(5-3)*

41. $25 = 5(2)^x$

$\dfrac{25}{5} = 2^x$

$5 = 2^x$

$\ln 5 = x \ln 2$

$\dfrac{\ln 5}{\ln 2} = x$

$x = 2.32$

(5-5)

42. $4{,}000 = 2{,}500 e^{0.12x}$

$\dfrac{4{,}000}{2{,}500} = e^{0.12x}$

$0.12x = \ln \dfrac{4{,}000}{2{,}500}$

$x = \dfrac{1}{0.12} \ln \dfrac{4{,}000}{2{,}500}$

$x = 3.92$ *(5-5)*

43. $0.01 = e^{-0.05x}$

$-0.05x = \ln 0.01$

$x = \dfrac{\ln 0.01}{-0.05}$

$x = 92.1$ *(5-5)*

44. $5^{2x-3} = 7.08$

$(2x - 3)\log 5 = \log 7.08$

$2x - 3 = \dfrac{\log 7.08}{\log 5}$

$x = \dfrac{1}{2}\left[3 + \dfrac{\log 7.08}{\log 5}\right] = 2.11$ *(5-5)*

45.

$$\frac{e^x - e^{-x}}{2} = 1$$

$$e^x - e^{-x} = 2$$

$$e^x - \frac{1}{e^x} = 2$$

$$e^x e^x - e^x\left(\frac{1}{e^x}\right) = 2e^x$$

$$(e^x)^2 - 1 = 2e^x$$

$$(e^x)^2 - 2e^x - 1 = 0$$

This equation is quadratic in e^x: $e^x = \dfrac{-b \pm \sqrt{b^2 - 4ac}}{2a}$ $a = 1,$
$b = -2,$
$c = -1$

$$e^x = \frac{-(-2) \pm \sqrt{(-2)^2 - 4(1)(-1)}}{2}$$

$$e^x = \frac{2 \pm \sqrt{8}}{2} = 1 \pm \sqrt{2}$$

$x = \ln(1 \pm \sqrt{2})$ $1 - \sqrt{2}$ is negative, hence not in the domain of the logarithm function. $x = \ln(1 + \sqrt{2})$
$$x = 0.881 \qquad\qquad (5\text{-}5)$$

46.

$$\log 3x^2 - \log 9x = 2$$

$$\log \frac{3x^2}{9x} = 2$$

$$\frac{3x^2}{9x} = 10^2$$

$$\frac{x}{3} = 100$$

$$x = 300$$

Check:

$$\log(3 \cdot 300^2) - \log(9 \cdot 300) \overset{?}{=} 2$$

$$\log(270{,}000) - \log(2{,}700) \overset{?}{=} 2$$

$$\log \frac{270{,}000}{2{,}700} \overset{?}{=} 2$$

$$\log 100 \overset{\surd}{=} 2 \qquad\qquad (5\text{-}5)$$

47.

$$\log x - \log 3 = \log 4 - \log(x + 4)$$

$$\log \frac{x}{3} = \log \frac{4}{x+4}$$

$$\frac{x}{3} = \frac{4}{x+4} \qquad \begin{array}{l}\text{excluded value:}\\ x \neq -4\end{array}$$

$$3(x + 4)\frac{x}{3} = 3(x + 4)\frac{4}{x+4}$$

$$(x + 4)x = 12$$

$$x^2 + 4x = 12$$

$$x^2 + 4x - 12 = 0$$

$$(x + 6)(x - 2) = 0$$

$$x = -6 \quad x = 2$$

Check: $\log(-6)$ is not defined

$$\log 2 - \log 3 \overset{?}{=} \log 4 - \log(2 + 4)$$

$$\log \frac{2}{3} \overset{?}{=} \log \frac{4}{6}$$

$$\log \frac{2}{3} \overset{\surd}{=} \log \frac{2}{3}$$

Solution: 2 \qquad\qquad (5\text{-}5)

48.

$$\ln(x + 3) - \ln x = 2 \ln 2$$

$$\ln \frac{x+3}{x} = \ln 2^2$$

$$\frac{x+3}{x} = 2^2$$

$$\frac{x+3}{x} = 4$$

$$x + 3 = 4x$$

$$3 = 3x$$

$$x = 1$$

Check:

$$\ln(1 + 3) - \ln 1 \overset{?}{=} 2 \ln 2$$

$$\ln 4 - 0 \overset{?}{=} 2 \ln 2$$

$$\ln 4 \overset{\surd}{=} \ln 4 \qquad\qquad (5\text{-}5)$$

49. $\ln(2x + 1) - \ln(x - 1) = \ln x$

$$\ln \frac{2x+1}{x-1} = \ln x$$

$$\frac{2x+1}{x-1} = x \quad \text{Excluded value: } x \neq 1$$

$$(x - 1)\frac{2x+1}{x-1} = x(x - 1)$$

$$2x + 1 = x^2 - x$$

$$0 = x^2 - 3x - 1$$

Check: $\ln\left(\dfrac{3 - \sqrt{13}}{2}\right)$ is not defined

$$\ln\left(2 \cdot \frac{3 + \sqrt{13}}{2} + 1\right) - \ln\left(\frac{3 + \sqrt{13}}{2} - 1\right) \overset{?}{=} \ln\left(\frac{3 + \sqrt{13}}{2}\right)$$

$$\ln(3 + \sqrt{13} + 1) - \ln\left(\frac{3 + \sqrt{13} - 2}{2}\right) \overset{?}{=} \ln\left(\frac{3 + \sqrt{13}}{2}\right)$$

$$x = \frac{-b \pm \sqrt{b^2 - 4ac}}{2a} \quad a = 1, b = -3, c = -1$$

$$x = \frac{-(-3) \pm \sqrt{(-3)^2 - 4(1)(-1)}}{2(1)} = \frac{3 \pm \sqrt{13}}{2}$$

$$\ln(4 + \sqrt{13}) - \ln\left(\frac{1 + \sqrt{13}}{2}\right) \overset{?}{=} \ln\left(\frac{3 + \sqrt{13}}{2}\right)$$

$$\ln\left(\frac{4 + \sqrt{13}}{1} \cdot \frac{2}{1 + \sqrt{13}}\right) \overset{?}{=} \ln\left(\frac{3 + \sqrt{13}}{2}\right)$$

$$\ln\left(\frac{(4 + \sqrt{13})2}{1 + \sqrt{13}}\right) \overset{?}{=} \ln\left(\frac{3 + \sqrt{13}}{2}\right)$$

$$\ln\left(\frac{(4 + \sqrt{13})2(1 - \sqrt{13})}{(1 + \sqrt{13})(1 - \sqrt{13})}\right) \overset{?}{=} \ln\left(\frac{3 + \sqrt{13}}{2}\right)$$

$$\ln\left(\frac{2(4 - 3\sqrt{13} - 13)}{1 - 13}\right) \overset{?}{=} \ln\left(\frac{3 + \sqrt{13}}{2}\right)$$

$$\ln\left(\frac{-18 - 6\sqrt{13}}{-12}\right) \overset{?}{=} \ln\left(\frac{3 + \sqrt{13}}{2}\right)$$

$$\ln\left(\frac{3 + \sqrt{13}}{2}\right) \overset{\checkmark}{=} \ln\left(\frac{3 + \sqrt{13}}{2}\right)$$

Solution: $\dfrac{3 + \sqrt{13}}{2}$ (5-5)

50.
$$(\log x)^3 = \log x^9$$
$$(\log x)^3 = 9 \log x$$
$$(\log x)^3 - 9 \log x = 0$$
$$\log x[(\log x)^2 - 9] = 0$$
$$\log x(\log x - 3)(\log x + 3) = 0$$
$$\log x = 0 \quad \log x - 3 = 0 \quad \log x + 3 = 0$$
$$x = 1 \qquad \log x = 3 \qquad \log x = -3$$
$$x = 10^3 \qquad x = 10^{-3}$$

Check: $(\log 1)^3 \overset{?}{=} \log 1^9$

$$0 \overset{\checkmark}{=} 0$$

$(\log 10^3)^3 \overset{?}{=} \log(10^3)^9$

$$27 \overset{\checkmark}{=} 27$$

$(\log 10^{-3})^3 \overset{?}{=} \log(10^{-3})^9$

$$-27 \overset{\checkmark}{=} -27$$

Solution: $1, 10^3, 10^{-3}$ (5-5)

51. $\ln(\log x) = 1$
$$\log x = e$$
$$x = 10^e$$
                    (5-5)

52. $(e^x + 1)(e^{-x} - 1) - e^x(e^{-x} - 1) = e^x e^{-x} - e^x + e^{-x} - 1 - e^x e^{-x} + e^x = 1 - e^x + e^{-x} - 1 - 1 + e^x = e^{-x} - 1$ (5-1)

53. $(e^x + e^{-x})(e^x - e^{-x}) - (e^x - e^{-x})^2 = (e^x)^2 - (e^{-x})^2 - [(e^x)^2 - 2e^x e^{-x} + (e^{-x})^2] = e^{2x} - e^{-2x} - [e^{2x} - 2 + e^{-2x}]$
$$= e^{2x} - e^{-2x} - e^{2x} + 2 - e^{-2x} = 2 - 2e^{-2x} \quad (5-1)$$

54. The graph of g is the same as the graph of f reflected through the x axis, shrunk vertically by a factor of $\frac{1}{3}$, and shifted upward 3 units; g is decreasing. Domain: all real numbers
Horizontal asymptote: $y = 3$

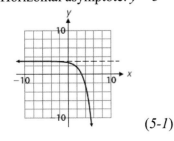

(5-1)

55. The graph of g is the same as the graph of f stretched vertically by a factor of 2 and shifted downward 4 units; g is increasing.
Domain: all real numbers
Horizontal asymptote: $y = -4$

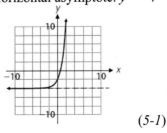

(5-1)

56. The graph of g is the same as the graph of f shifted downward 2 units; g is increasing. Domain: $(0, \infty)$ Vertical asymptote: $x = 0$

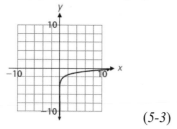

(5-3)

57. The graph of g is the same as the graph of f stretched vertically by a factor of 2 and shifted upward 1 unit; g is decreasing. Domain: $(0, \infty)$ Vertical asymptote: $x = 0$

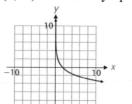

(5-3)

58. If the graph of $y = e^x$ is reflected in the x axis, y is replaced by $-y$ and the graph becomes the graph of $-y = e^x$ or $y = -e^x$.

If the graph of $y = e^x$ is reflected in the y axis, x is replaced by $-x$ and the graph becomes the graph of

$$y = e^{-x} \text{ or } y = \frac{1}{e^x} \text{ or } y = \left(\frac{1}{e}\right)^x.$$

(5-1)

59. (A) For $x > -1$, $y = e^{-x/3}$ decreases from $e^{1/3}$ to 0 while $\ln(x + 1)$ increases from $-\infty$ to ∞. Consequently, the graphs can intersect at exactly one point.

(B) Graphing $y_1 = e^{-x/3}$ and $y_2 = 4\ln(x + 1)$ we obtain

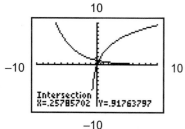

The solution of $e^{-x/3} = 4\ln(x + 1)$ is $x = 0.258$.

(5-5)

60. Examining the graph of $f(x) = 4 - x^2 + \ln x$, we obtain

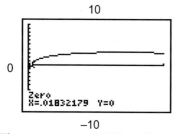

The zeros are at 0.018 and 2.187.

(5-5)

61. Graphing $y_1 = 10^{x-3}$ and $y_2 = 8\log x$, we obtain

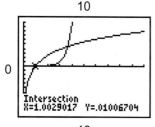

The graphs intersect at (1.003, 0.010) and (3.653, 4.502).

(5-5)

62.
$$D = 10 \log \frac{I}{I_0}$$
$$\frac{D}{10} = \log \frac{I}{I_0}$$
$$10^{D/10} = \frac{I}{I_0}$$
$$I_0 10^{D/10} = I$$
$$I = I_0(10^{D/10})$$
$$(5\text{-}5)$$

63.
$$y = \frac{1}{\sqrt{2\pi}} e^{-x^2/2}$$
$$\sqrt{2\pi}\, y = e^{-x^2/2}$$
$$-\frac{x^2}{2} = \ln(\sqrt{2\pi}\, y)$$
$$x^2 = -2\ln(\sqrt{2\pi}\, y)$$
$$x = \pm\sqrt{-2\ln(\sqrt{2\pi}y)}$$
$$(5\text{-}5)$$

64.
$$x = -\frac{1}{k} \ln \frac{I}{I_0}$$
$$-kx = \ln \frac{I}{I_0}$$
$$\frac{I}{I_0} = e^{-kx}$$
$$I = I_0(e^{-kx}) \ (5\text{-}5)$$

65.
$$r = P\frac{i}{1-(1+i)^{-n}}$$
$$\frac{r}{P} = \frac{i}{1-(1+i)^{-n}}$$
$$\frac{P}{r} = \frac{1-(1+i)^{-n}}{i}$$
$$\frac{Pi}{r} = 1-(1+i)^{-n}$$
$$\frac{Pi}{r} - 1 = -(1+i)^{-n}$$
$$1 - \frac{Pi}{r} = (1+i)^{-n}$$
$$\ln\left(1-\frac{Pi}{r}\right) = -n\ln(1+i)$$
$$\frac{\ln\left(1-\frac{Pi}{r}\right)}{-\ln(1+i)} = n$$
$$n = -\frac{\ln\left(1-\frac{Pi}{r}\right)}{\ln(1+i)} \qquad (5\text{-}5)$$

66.
$$\ln y = -5t + \ln c$$
$$\ln y - \ln c = -5t$$
$$\ln\left(\frac{y}{c}\right) = -5t$$
$$\frac{y}{c} = e^{-5t}$$
$$y = ce^{-5t} \qquad (5\text{-}5)$$

67.

x	$y = \log_2 x$	$x = \log_2 y$	y
1	0	0	1
2	1	1	2
4	2	2	4
8	3	3	8

Domain $f = (0, \infty) = $ Range f^{-1}
Range $f = (-\infty, \infty) = $ Domain f^{-1}

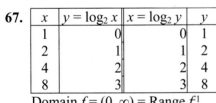

$(5\text{-}3)$

68. If $\log_1 x = y$, then we would have to have $1^y = x$; that is, $1 = x$ for arbitrary positive x,
which is impossible. $(5\text{-}3)$

69. Let $u = \log_b M$ and $v = \log_b N$; then $M = b^u$ and $N = b^v$.
Thus, $\log(MN) = \log_b(b^u b^v) = \log_b b^{u+v} = u + v = \log_b M + \log_b N.$ $(5\text{-}3)$

70. We solve $P = P_0(1.03)^t$ for t, using $P = 2P_0$.
$$2P_0 = P_0(1.03)^t$$
$$2 = (1.03)^t$$
$$\ln 2 = t \ln 1.03$$
$$\frac{\ln 2}{\ln 1.03} = t$$
$$t = 23.4 \text{ years} \qquad (5\text{-}2)$$

71. We solve $P = P_0 e^{0.03t}$ for t using $P = 2P_0$.
$$2P_0 = P_0 e^{0.03t}$$
$$2 = e^{0.03t}$$
$$\ln 2 = 0.03t$$
$$\frac{\ln 2}{0.03} = t$$
$$t = 23.1 \text{ years} \qquad (5\text{-}2)$$

72.
$$A_0 = \text{original amount}$$
$$0.01 A_0 = 1 \text{ percent of original amount}$$
We solve $A = A_0 e^{-0.000124t}$ for t,
using $A = 0.01 A_0$.
$$0.01 A_0 = A_0 e^{-0.000124t}$$
$$0.01 = e^{-0.000124t}$$
$$\ln 0.01 = -0.000124t$$
$$\frac{\ln 0.01}{-0.000124} = t$$
$$t = 37{,}100 \text{ years} \qquad (5\text{-}2)$$

73. (A) When $t = 0$, $N = 1$. As t increases by 1/2, N
doubles. Hence $N = 1 \cdot (2)^{t \div 1/2}$
$$N = 2^{2t} (\text{or } N = 4^t)$$

(B) We solve $N = 4^t$ for t, using
$$N = 10^9$$
$$10^9 = 4^t$$
$$9 = t \log 4$$
$$t = \frac{9}{\log 4}$$
$$t = 15 \text{ days} \qquad (5\text{-}2)$$

74. We use $A = Pe^{rt}$ with $P = 1$, $r = 0.03$, and
$t = 2011 - 1 = 2010$.
$$A = 1 e^{0.03(2010)}$$
$$A = 1.5 \times 10^{26} \text{ dollars } (5\text{-}1)$$

75.(A)

t	p
0	1,000
5	670
10	449
15	301
20	202
25	135
30	91

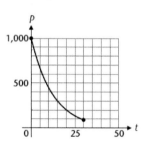

(B) As t tends to infinity, P appears to tend to 0.   (5-1)

76. $M = \dfrac{2}{3} \log \dfrac{E}{E_0}$ $E_0 = 10^{4.40}$

We use $E = 1.99 \times 10^{14}$
$$M = \frac{2}{3} \log \frac{1.99 \times 10^{14}}{10^{4.40}}$$
$$M = \frac{2}{3} \log(1.99 \times 10^{9.6})$$
$$M = \frac{2}{3} (\log 1.99 + 9.6)$$
$$M = \frac{2}{3} (0.299 + 9.6)$$
$$M = 6.6 \qquad (5\text{-}4)$$

77. We solve $M = \dfrac{2}{3} \log \dfrac{E}{E_0}$ for E, using
$$E_0 = 10^{4.40}, M = 8.3$$
$$8.3 = \frac{2}{3} \log \frac{E}{10^{4.40}}$$
$$\frac{3}{2}(8.3) = \log \frac{E}{10^{4.40}}$$
$$12.45 = \log \frac{E}{10^{4.40}}$$
$$\frac{E}{10^{4.40}} = 10^{12.45}$$
$$E = 10^{4.40} \cdot 10^{12.45}$$
$$E = 10^{16.85} \text{ or } 7.08 \times 10^{16} \text{ joules} \qquad (5\text{-}4)$$

78. We use the given formula twice, with
$$I_2 = 100{,}000 I_1$$
$$D_1 = 10 \log \frac{I_1}{I_0} \qquad D_2 = 10 \log \frac{I_2}{I_0}$$
$$D_2 - D_1 = 10 \log \frac{I_2}{I_0} - 10 \log \frac{I_1}{I_0} = 10 \log \left(\frac{I_2}{I_0} \div \frac{I_1}{I_0} \right) = 10 \log \frac{I_2}{I_1}$$
$$= 10 \log \frac{100{,}000 I_1}{I_1} = 10 \log 100{,}000 = 50 \text{ decibels}$$
The level of the louder sound is 50 decibels more.   (5-2)

79. $I = I_0 e^{-kd}$

To find k, we solve for k using $I = \frac{1}{2} I_0$ and $d = 73.6$

$$\frac{1}{2} I_0 = I_0 e^{-k(73.6)}$$

$$\frac{1}{2} = e^{-73.6k}$$

$$-73.6k = \ln \frac{1}{2}$$

$$k = \frac{\ln \frac{1}{2}}{-73.6}$$

$$k = 0.00942$$

We now find the depth at which 1% of the surface light remains. We solve $I = I_0 e^{-0.00942d}$ for d with $I = 0.01 I_0$

$$0.01 I_0 = I_0 e^{-0.00942d}$$

$$0.01 = e^{-0.00942d}$$

$$-0.00942d = \ln 0.01$$

$$d = \frac{\ln 0.01}{-0.00942}$$

$$d = 489 \text{ feet} \qquad (5\text{-}2)$$

80. We solve $N = \dfrac{30}{1 + 29 e^{-1.35t}}$ for t with $N = 20$.

$$20 = \frac{30}{1 + 29 e^{-1.35t}}$$

$$\frac{1}{20} = \frac{1 + 29 e^{-1.35t}}{30}$$

$$1.5 = 1 + 29 e^{-1.35t}$$

$$0.5 = 29 e^{-1.35t}$$

$$\frac{0.5}{29} = e^{-1.35t}$$

$$-1.35t = \ln \frac{0.5}{29}$$

$$t = \frac{\ln \frac{0.5}{29}}{-1.35}$$

$$t = 3 \text{ years} \qquad (5\text{-}2)$$

81. (A) The independent variable is years since 1980, so enter 0, 5, 10, 15, 20, and 25 as L_1. The dependent variable is Medicare expenditures, so enter that column as L_2. Then use the exponential regression command on the STAT CALC menu.

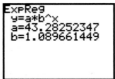

The exponential model is $y = 43.3(1.09)^x$.

To find total expenditures in 2010 and 2020, we plug in 30 and 40 for x:

$$y(30) = 43.3(1.09)^{30} = 574; \quad y(40) = 43.3(1.09)^{40} = 1{,}360$$

Expenditures are predicted to be \$574 billion in 2010 and \$1,360 billion in 2020.

(B) Graph $y_1 = 43.3(1.09)^x$ and $y_2 = 900$ and use the INTERSECT command:

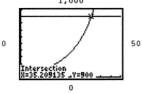

Expenditures are predicted to reach \$900 billion in 2015.   (5-2)

82. (A) The independent variable is years since 1990, so enter 4, 7, 10, 13, 16 as L_1. The dependent variable is the number of subscribers, so enter the subscribers' column as L_2. Then use the logarithmic regression command from the STAT CALC menu.

The model is $y = -199.1 + 143.7 \ln x$. Evaluating this at $x = 25$ (year 2015) gives 263.5 million subscribers.

(B) With the same data as in part (A), use the logistic regression command from the STAT CALC menu.

 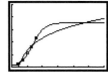

The model is $y = \dfrac{354.9}{1 + 31.94 e^{-0.2556x}}$. Evaluating this at $x = 25$ (year 2015) gives 336.8 million subscribers.

(C) Plot both models, together with the given data points, on the same screen.

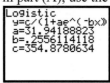

Clearly, the logistic model fits the data better. Moreover, the logarithmic model predicts that the number of subscribers becomes infinite, eventually, which is absurd. The logistic model predicts eventual   leveling off near 354.9 million, which still seems high compared with the US population, but is more reasonable. The logistic model wins on both criteria specified in the problem.

(5-2, 5-4)

CHAPTER 6

SECTION 6-1

1. Circle, ellipse, parabola, hyperbola – plus the degenerate conic sections: point, line, pair of lines.

3. A plane passing through the vertex of a cone produces a degenerate conic, as listed in problem 1 above.

5. The light rays are reflected to converge at a point, called the focus.

7. From the standard equations of a parabola with vertex at $(0, 0)$, if the directrix is $x = 8$, then $8 = -a$, $a = -8$, hence the focus is $(-8, 0)$.

9. From the standard equations of a parabola with vertex at $(0, 0)$, if the directrix is $y = -10$, then $-10 = -a$, $a = 10$, hence the focus is $(0, 10)$.

11. From the standard equations of a parabola with vertex at $(0, 0)$, if the focus is at $(0, -15)$, then $-15 = a$, hence the directrix is $y = 15$.

13. From the standard equations of a parabola with vertex at $(0, 0)$, if the focus is at $(25, 0)$, then $25 = a$, hence the directrix is $x = -25$.

15. To graph $y^2 = 4x$, assign x values that make the right side a perfect square (x must be non-negative for y to be real) and solve for y. Since the coefficient of x is positive, a must be positive, and the parabola opens right.

x	0	1	4
y	0	±2	±4

To find the focus and directrix, solve
$4a = 4$
$a = 1$
Focus: $(1, 0)$ Directrix: $x = -1$

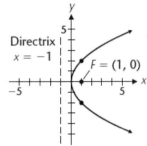

17. To graph $x^2 = 8y$, assign y values that make the right side a perfect square (y must be non-negative for x to be real) and solve for x. Since the coefficient of y is positive, a must be positive, and the parabola opens up.

x	0	±4	±2
y	0	2	½

To find the focus and directrix, solve
$4a = 8$
$a = 2$
Focus: $(0, 2)$ Directrix: $y = -2$

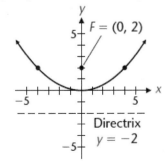

19. To graph $y^2 = -12x$, assign x values that make the right side a perfect square (x must be zero or negative for y to be real) and solve for y. Since the coefficient of x is negative, a must be negative, and the parabola opens left.

x	0	−3	$-\dfrac{1}{3}$
y	0	±6	±2

To find the focus and directrix, solve
$4a = -12$
$a = -3$
Focus: $(-3, 0)$ Directrix: $x = -(-3) = 3$

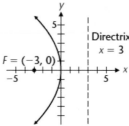

21. To graph $x^2 = -4y$, assign y values that make the right side a perfect square (y must be zero or negative for x to be real) and solve for x. Since the coefficient of y is negative, a must be negative, and the parabola opens down.

x	0	±2	±4
y	0	−1	−4

To find the focus and directrix, solve
$4a = -4$
$a = -1$
Focus: $(0, -1)$ Directrix: $y = -(-1) = 1$

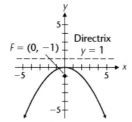

23. To graph $y^2 = -20x$, we may proceed as in problem 19. Alternatively, after noting that x must be zero or negative for y to be real, we may pick convenient values for x and solve for y using a calculator. Since the coefficient of x is negative, a must be negative, and the parabola opens left.

x	0	−1	−2
y	0	$\pm\sqrt{20} \approx \pm4.5$	$\pm\sqrt{40} \approx \pm6.3$

To find the focus and directrix, solve
$4a = -20$
$a = -5$
Focus: $(-5, 0)$ Directrix: $x = -(-5) = 5$

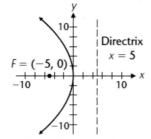

25. Comparing $y^2 = 39x$ with $y^2 = 4ax$, the standard equation of a parabola symmetric with respect to the x axis, we have
$4a = 39$ Focus on x axis
$a = 9.75$
Focus: $(9.75, 0)$

27. Comparing $x^2 = -105y$ with $x^2 = 4ay$, the standard equation of a parabola symmetric with respect to the y axis, we have
$4a = -105$ Focus on y axis
$a = -26.25$
Focus: $(0, -26.25)$

29. Comparing $y^2 = -77x$ with $y^2 = 4ax$, the standard equation of a parabola symmetric with respect to the x axis, we have
$4a = -77$ Focus on x axis
$a = -19.25$
Focus: $(-19.25, 0)$

31. Comparing directrix $y = -3$ with the information in the chart of standard equations for a parabola, we see:
$a = 3$. Axis: the y axis. Equation: $x^2 = 4ay$.
Thus the equation of the parabola must be $x^2 = 4 \cdot 3y$, or $x^2 = 12y$.

33. Comparing focus $(0, -7)$ with the information in the chart of standard equations for a parabola, we see:
$a = -7$ Axis: the y axis. Equation: $x^2 = 4ay$.
Thus the equation of the parabola must be $x^2 = 4(-7)y$, or $x^2 = -28y$.

35. Comparing directrix $x = 6$ with the information in the chart of standard equations for a parabola, we see:
$6 = -a$. $a = -6$. Axis: the x axis. Equation: $y^2 = 4ax$.
Thus the equation of the parabola must be $y^2 = 4(-6)x$, or $y^2 = -24x$.

37. Comparing focus $(2, 0)$ with the information in the chart of standard equations for a parabola, we see:
$a = 2$ Axis: the x axis. Equation: $y^2 = 4ax$.
Thus the equation of the parabola must be $y^2 = 4(2)x$, or $y^2 = 8x$.

39. The parabola is opening up and has an equation of the form $x^2 = 4ay$. Since $(4, 2)$ is on the graph, we have:
$$x^2 = 4ay$$
$$(4)^2 = 4a(2)$$
$$16 = 8a$$
$$2 = a$$
Thus, the equation of the parabola is
$$x^2 = 4(2)y$$
$$x^2 = 8y$$

41. The parabola is opening left and has an equation of the form $y^2 = 4ax$. Since $(-3, 6)$ is on the graph, we have:
$$y^2 = 4ax$$
$$(6)^2 = 4a(-3)$$
$$-3 = a$$
Thus, the equation of the parabola is
$$y^2 = 4(-3)x$$
$$y^2 = -12x$$

43. The parabola is opening down and has an equation of the form $x^2 = 4ay$. Since $(-6, -9)$ is on the graph, we have:
$$x^2 = 4ay$$
$$(-6)^2 = 4a(-9)$$
$$36 = -36a$$
$$-1 = a$$
Thus, the equation of the parabola is $x^2 = 4(-1)y$
$$x^2 = -4y$$

45. $x^2 = 4y$
$y^2 = 4x$
Solve for y in the first equation, then substitute into the second equation.

$$y = \frac{x^2}{4}$$

$$\left(\frac{x^2}{4}\right)^2 = 4x$$

$$\frac{x^4}{16} = 4x$$

$$x^4 = 64x$$
$$x^4 - 64x = 0$$

(4, 4)

(0, 0)

These exact solutions yield more than 3-digit accuracy.

$$x^2 + 4x + 16 = 0$$

$$x(x^3 - 64) = 0 \qquad\qquad \text{No real solutions}$$
$$x(x - 4)(x^2 + 4x + 16) = 0$$
$$x = 0 \qquad\qquad x - 4 = 0$$
$$x = 4$$
$$\text{For } x = 0 \qquad \text{For } x = 4$$
$$y = 0$$
$$y = \frac{4^2}{4}$$
$$y = 4$$

Solutions: $(0, 0)$, $(4, 4)$

47. $y^2 = 6x$
$x^2 = 5y$

Solve for x in the first equation, then substitute into the second equation.

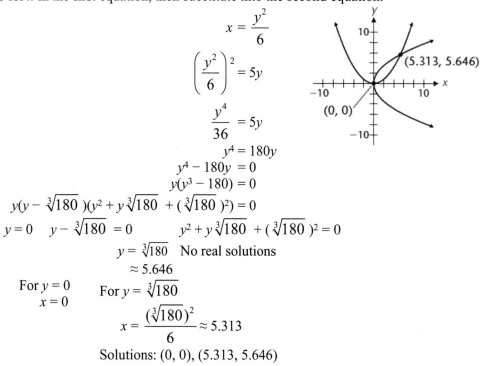

$$x = \frac{y^2}{6}$$
$$\left(\frac{y^2}{6}\right)^2 = 5y$$
$$\frac{y^4}{36} = 5y$$
$$y^4 = 180y$$
$$y^4 - 180y = 0$$
$$y(y^3 - 180) = 0$$
$$y(y - \sqrt[3]{180})(y^2 + y\sqrt[3]{180} + (\sqrt[3]{180})^2) = 0$$
$$y = 0 \quad y - \sqrt[3]{180} = 0 \qquad y^2 + y\sqrt[3]{180} + (\sqrt[3]{180})^2 = 0$$
$$y = \sqrt[3]{180} \quad \text{No real solutions}$$
$$\approx 5.646$$

For $y = 0$ For $y = \sqrt[3]{180}$
$x = 0$

$$x = \frac{(\sqrt[3]{180})^2}{6} \approx 5.313$$

Solutions: $(0, 0)$, $(5.313, 5.646)$

49. **(A)** The line $x = 0$ intersects the parabola $x^2 = 4ay$ only at $(0, 0)$.
The line $y = 0$ intersects the parabola $x^2 = 4ay$ only at $(0, 0)$.
Only these 2 lines intersect the parabola at exactly one point (see part (B)).

(B) A line through $(0, 0)$ with slope $m \neq 0$ has equation $y = mx$.
Solve the system:
$$y = mx$$
$$x^2 = 4ay$$
by substituting y from the first equation into the second equation.
$$x^2 = 4amx$$
$$x^2 - 4amx = 0$$
$$x(x - 4am) = 0$$
$$x = 0 \qquad x = 4am$$
For $x = 0$ For $x = 4am$
$$y = 0 \qquad y = m(4am)$$
$$= 4am^2$$

Solutions: $(0, 0)$, $(4am, 4am^2)$ are the required coordinates.

51. Since A and B lie on the curve $x^2 = 4ay$, their coordinates must satisfy the equation of the curve. Clearly, the y coordinate of A, F, and B is a. Substituting a for y, we have

$$x^2 = 4aa$$
$$x^2 = 4a^2$$
$$x = \pm 2a$$

Therefore, A has coordinates $(-2a, a)$ and B has coordinates $(2a, a)$.

53. Let $P = (x, y)$ be a point on the parabola. Then, by the definition of the parabola, the distance from $P = (x, y)$ to the focus $F = (2, 2)$ must equal the perpendicular distance from P to the directrix at $D = (x, -4)$. Applying the distance formula, we have

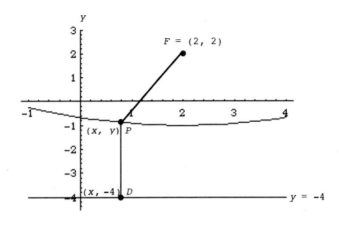

$$d(P, F) = d(P, D)$$
$$\sqrt{(x-2)^2 + (y-2)^2} = \sqrt{(x-x)^2 + [y-(-4)]^2}$$
$$(x-2)^2 + (y-2)^2 = (x-x)^2 + (y+4)^2$$
$$x^2 - 4x + 4 + y^2 - 4y + 4 = 0 + y^2 + 8y + 16$$
$$x^2 - 4x - 12y - 8 = 0$$

55. Let $P = (x, y)$ be a point on the parabola.

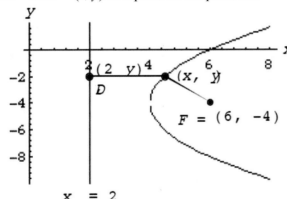

Then, by the definition of the parabola, the distance from $P = (x, y)$ to the focus $F = (6, -4)$ must equal the perpendicular distance from P to the directrix at $D = (2, y)$. Applying the distance formula, we have

$$d(P, F) = d(P, D)$$
$$\sqrt{(x-6)^2 + [y-(-4)]^2} = \sqrt{(x-2)^2 + (y-y)^2}$$
$$(x-6)^2 + (y+4)^2 = (x-2)^2 + (y-y)^2$$
$$x^2 - 12x + 36 + y^2 + 8y + 16 = x^2 - 4x + 4 + 0$$
$$y^2 + 8y - 8x + 48 = 0$$

57. Using Figure 9-5, we note: The point $P = (x, y)$ is a point on the parabola if and only if

$$d_1 = d_2$$
$$d(P, N) = d(P, F)$$
$$\sqrt{(x-x)^2 + (y+a)^2} = \sqrt{(x-0)^2 + (y-a)^2}$$
$$(y+a)^2 = x^2 + (y-a)^2$$
$$y^2 + 2ay + a^2 = x^2 + y^2 - 2ay + a^2$$
$$x^2 = 4ay$$

59. From the figure, we see that the coordinates of P must be $(-100, -50)$.

The parabola is opening down with axis the y axis, hence it has an equation of the form $x^2 = 4ay$. Since $(-100, -50)$ is on the graph, we have

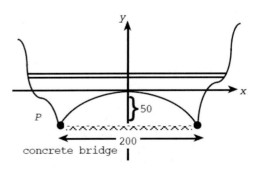

$$(-100)^2 = 4a(-50)$$
$$10{,}000 = -200a$$
$$a = -50$$

Thus, the equation of the parabola is

$$x^2 = 4(-50)y$$
$$x^2 = -200y$$

61. (A) From the figure, we see that the parabola is opening up with axis the y axis, hence it has an equation of the form $x^2 = 4ay$. Since the focus is at $(0, a) = (0, 100)$, $a = 100$ and the equation of the parabola is $x^2 = 400y$ or $y = 0.0025x^2$

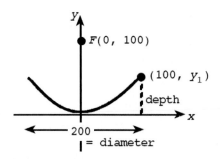

(B) Since the depth represents the y coordinate y_1 of a point on the parabola with $x = 100$, we have
$$y_1 = 0.0025(100)^2$$
$$\text{depth} = 25 \text{ feet}$$

SECTION 6-2

1. An ellipse is the set of all points P in a plane such that the sum of the distances from P to two fixed points in the plane is a constant.

3. Answers will vary.

5. A circle is not an ellipse, however, it can be considered the limiting case of an ellipse as the two fixed points converge to one (this would then be the center of the limiting case circle).

7. Given major axis length $2a = 10$ and minor axis length $2b = 8$, then $a = 5$, $b = 4$, and $c^2 = a^2 - b^2$. Therefore $c^2 = 5^2 - 4^2$, $c^2 = 9$, $c = 3$. The distance between the foci is then $2c$, or 6.

9. Given major axis length $2a = 2$ and minor axis length $2b = 1$, then $a = 1$, $b = \dfrac{1}{2}$, and $c^2 = a^2 - b^2$.

Therefore $c^2 = 1^2 - \left(\dfrac{1}{2}\right)^2$, $c^2 = \dfrac{3}{4}$, $c = \dfrac{\sqrt{3}}{2}$. The distance between the foci is then $2c$, or $\sqrt{3}$.

11. Given distance between foci $2c = 14$ and minor axis length $2b = 48$, then $c = 7$, $b = 24$, and $c^2 = a^2 - b^2$.
Then
$$7^2 = a^2 - 24^2$$
$$49 = a^2 - 576$$
$$625 = a^2$$
$$25 = a$$
The major axis length is then $2a$, or 50.

13. Given distance between foci $2c = 5$ and minor axis length $2b = 5$, then $c = \dfrac{5}{2}$, $b = \dfrac{5}{2}$, and $c^2 = a^2 - b^2$.

Then
$$\left(\frac{5}{2}\right)^2 = a^2 - \left(\frac{5}{2}\right)^2$$
$$\frac{25}{4} = a^2 - \frac{25}{4}$$
$$\frac{50}{4} = a^2$$
$$a = \frac{5\sqrt{2}}{2}$$
The major axis length is then $2a$, or $5\sqrt{2}$.

15. When $y = 0$, $\dfrac{x^2}{25} = 1$. x intercepts: ± 5

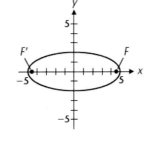

When $x = 0$, $\dfrac{y^2}{4} = 1$. y intercepts: ± 2

Thus, $a = 5$, $b = 2$, and the major axis is on the x axis.

Foci: $c^2 = a^2 - b^2$
$c^2 = 25 - 4$
$c^2 = 21$
$c = \sqrt{21}$

Foci: $F' = (-\sqrt{21}, 0)$, $F = (\sqrt{21}, 0)$

Major axis length $= 2(5) = 10$; Minor axis length $= 2(2) = 4$

17. When $y = 0$, $\dfrac{x^2}{4} = 1$. x intercepts: ± 2

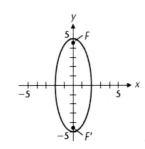

When $x = 0$, $\dfrac{y^2}{25} = 1$. y intercepts: ± 5

Thus, $a = 5$, $b = 2$, and the major axis is on the y axis.

Foci: $c^2 = a^2 - b^2$
$c^2 = 25 - 4$
$c^2 = 21$
$c = \sqrt{21}$

Foci: $F' = (0, -\sqrt{21})$, $F = (0, \sqrt{21})$

Major axis length $= 2(5) = 10$ Minor axis length $= 2(2) = 4$

19. First, write the equation in standard form by dividing both sides by 9.

$x^2 + 9y^2 = 9$

$\dfrac{x^2}{9} + \dfrac{y^2}{1} = 1$

Locate the intercepts.

When $y = 0$, $\dfrac{x^2}{9} = 1$. x intercepts: ± 3

When $x = 0$, $\dfrac{y^2}{1} = 1$. y intercepts: ± 1

Thus $a = 3$, $b = 1$, and the major axis is on the x axis.

Foci: $c^2 = a^2 - b^2$
$c^2 = 9 - 1$
$c^2 = 8$
$c = \sqrt{8}$

Foci: $F' = (-\sqrt{8}, 0)$, $F = (\sqrt{8}, 0)$

Major axis length $= 2(3) = 6$ Minor axis length $= 2(1) = 2$

21. When $y = 0$, $9x^2 = 144$. x intercepts: ± 4
When $x = 0$, $16y^2 = 144$. y intercepts: ± 3
This corresponds to graph (b).

23. When $y = 0$, $4x^2 = 16$. x intercepts: ± 2
When $x = 0$, $y^2 = 16$. y intercepts: ± 4
This corresponds to graph (a).

25. First, write the equation in standard form by dividing both sides by 225.

$$25x^2 + 9y^2 = 225$$

$$\frac{x^2}{9} + \frac{y^2}{25} = 1$$

Locate the intercepts.

When $y = 0$, $\dfrac{x^2}{9} = 1$. x intercepts: ± 3

When $x = 0$, $\dfrac{y^2}{25} = 1$. y intercepts: ± 5

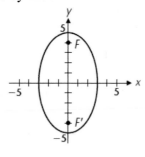

Thus $a = 5$, $b = 3$, and the major axis is on the y axis.

Foci: $c^2 = a^2 - b^2$

$\qquad\quad c^2 = 25 - 9$

$\qquad\quad c^2 = 16$

$\qquad\quad\ c = 4$

Foci: $F' = (0, -4)$, $F = (0, 4)$

Major axis length $= 2(5) = 10$ Minor axis length $= 2(3) = 6$

27. First, write the equation in standard form by dividing both sides by 12.

$$2x^2 + y^2 = 12$$

$$\frac{x^2}{6} + \frac{y^2}{12} = 1$$

Locate the intercepts.

When $y = 0$, $\dfrac{x^2}{6} = 1$. x intercepts: $\pm\sqrt{6}$

When $x = 0$, $\dfrac{y^2}{12} = 1$. y intercepts: $\pm\sqrt{12}$

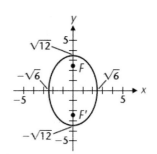

Thus $a = \sqrt{12}$, $b = \sqrt{6}$, and the major axis is on the y axis.

Foci: $c^2 = a^2 - b^2$

$\qquad\quad c^2 = 12 - 6$

$\qquad\quad c^2 = 6$

$\qquad\quad\ c = \sqrt{6}$

Foci: $F' = (0, -\sqrt{6})$, $F = (0, \sqrt{6})$

Major axis length $= 2\sqrt{12} \approx 6.93$ Minor axis length $= 2\sqrt{6} \approx 4.90$

29. First, write the equation in standard form by dividing both sides by 28.

$$4x^2 + 7y^2 = 28$$

$$\frac{x^2}{7} + \frac{y^2}{4} = 1$$

Locate the intercepts.

When $y = 0$, $\dfrac{x^2}{7} = 1$. x intercepts: $\pm\sqrt{7}$

When $x = 0$, $\dfrac{y^2}{4} = 1$. y intercepts: ± 2

Thus $a = \sqrt{7}$, $b = 2$, and the major axis is on the x axis.

Foci: $c^2 = a^2 - b^2$
$c^2 = 7 - 4$
$c^2 = 3$
$c = \sqrt{3}$

Foci: $F' = (-\sqrt{3}, 0), F = (\sqrt{3}, 0)$

Major axis length $= 2\sqrt{7} \approx 5.29$ Minor axis length $= 2(2) = 4$

31. The x intercepts are ± 5. Thus, if $y = 0$, $\dfrac{(\pm 5)^2}{M} = 1$, so $M = 25$.

The y intercepts are ± 4. Thus, if $x = 0$, $\dfrac{(\pm 4)^2}{N} = 1$, so $N = 16$.

Equation: $\dfrac{x^2}{25} + \dfrac{y^2}{16} = 1$

33. The x intercepts are ± 3. Thus, if $y = 0$, $\dfrac{(\pm 3)^2}{M} = 1$, so $M = 9$.

The y intercepts are ± 6. Thus, if $x = 0$, $\dfrac{(\pm 6)^2}{N} = 1$, so $N = 36$.

Equation: $\dfrac{x^2}{9} + \dfrac{y^2}{36} = 1$

35. Make a rough sketch of the ellipse and compute x and y intercepts.

$\dfrac{x^2}{a^2} + \dfrac{y^2}{b^2} = 1 \quad a = \dfrac{10}{2} = 5, b = \dfrac{6}{2} = 3$

$\dfrac{x^2}{25} + \dfrac{y^2}{9} = 1$

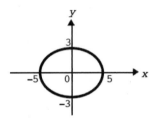

37. Make a rough sketch of the ellipse and compute x and y intercepts.

$\dfrac{x^2}{b^2} + \dfrac{y^2}{a^2} = 1 \quad a = \dfrac{22}{2} = 11, b = \dfrac{16}{2} = 8$

$\dfrac{x^2}{64} + \dfrac{y^2}{121} = 1$

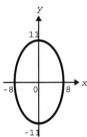

39. Make a rough sketch of the ellipse, locate focus and x intercepts, then determine y intercepts using the special triangle relationship.

$\dfrac{x^2}{a^2} + \dfrac{y^2}{b^2} = 1 \quad a = \dfrac{16}{2} = 8$

$b^2 = 8^2 - 6^2 = 64 - 36 = 28$

$b = \sqrt{28}$

$\dfrac{x^2}{64} + \dfrac{y^2}{28} = 1$

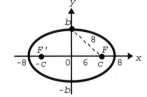

41. Make a rough sketch of the ellipse, locate focus and x intercepts, then determine y intercepts using the special triangle relationship.

$$\frac{x^2}{b^2} + \frac{y^2}{a^2} = 1 \quad b = \frac{20}{2} = 10$$

$$a^2 = 10^2 + (\sqrt{70})^2 = 100 + 70 = 170$$

$$a = \sqrt{170}$$

$$\frac{x^2}{100} + \frac{y^2}{170} = 1$$

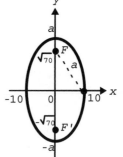

43. The graph does not pass the vertical line test; most vertical lines that intersect an ellipse do so in two places; hence, the equation does not define a function.

45. From the figure, we see that the point $P = (x, y)$ is a point on the curve if and only if

$$d_1 = \frac{1}{2}d_2$$

$$d(P, F) = \frac{1}{2}d(P, M)$$

$$\sqrt{(x-2)^2 + (y-0)^2} = \frac{1}{2}\sqrt{(x-8)^2 + (y-y)^2}$$

$$(x-2)^2 + y^2 = \frac{1}{4}(x-8)^2$$

$$x^2 - 4x + 4 + y^2 = \frac{1}{4}(x^2 - 16x + 64)$$

$$4x^2 - 16x + 16 + 4y^2 = x^2 - 16x + 64$$

$$3x^2 + 4y^2 = 48$$

$$\frac{x^2}{16} + \frac{y^2}{12} = 1$$

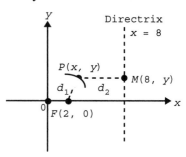

The curve must be an ellipse since its equation can be written in standard form for an ellipse.

47. The only points that could satisfy this condition are those on the line segment $F'F$, and all of those would qualify.

49.

$$d_1 + d_2 = 2a \quad \text{Use the distance formula:}$$

$$\sqrt{(x+c)^2 + y^2} = 2a - \sqrt{(x-c)^2 + y^2} \quad \text{Square both sides:}$$

$$(x+c)^2 + y^2 = 4a^2 - 4a\sqrt{(x-c)^2 + y^2} + (x-c)^2 + y^2 \quad \text{Isolate the square root:}$$

$$\sqrt{(x-c)^2 + y^2} = a - \frac{cx}{a} \quad \text{Square both sides:}$$

$$(x-c)^2 + y^2 = a^2 - 2cx + \frac{c^2 x^2}{a^2} \quad \text{Simplify and collect terms:}$$

$$\left(1 - \frac{c^2}{a^2}\right)x^2 + y^2 = a^2 - c^2 \quad \text{Use } a^2 - c^2 = b^2, \ 1 - \frac{c^2}{a^2} = \frac{b^2}{a^2}, \text{ and divide both sides by } b^2: \ \frac{x^2}{a^2} + \frac{y^2}{b^2} = 1$$

51. From the figure we see that the x and y intercepts of the ellipse must be 20 and 12 respectively. Hence the equation of the ellipse must be

$$\frac{x^2}{(20)^2} + \frac{y^2}{(12)^2} = 1 \quad \text{or} \quad \frac{x^2}{400} + \frac{y^2}{144} = 1$$

To find the clearance above the water 5 feet from the bank, we need the y coordinate y_1 of the point P whose x coordinate is $a - 5 = 15$. Since P is on the ellipse, we have

$$\frac{15^2}{400} + \frac{y_1^2}{144} = 1$$

$$\frac{225}{400} + \frac{y_1^2}{144} = 1$$

$$0.5625 + \frac{y_1^2}{144} = 1$$

$$\frac{y_1^2}{144} = 0.4375$$

$$y_1^2 = 144(0.4375) = 63$$

$$y_1 \approx \pm 7.94$$

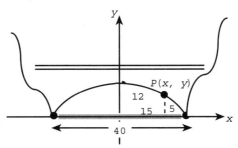

Therefore, the clearance is 7.94 feet, approximately.

53. (A) From the figure we see that the x intercept of the ellipse must be 24.0. Hence the equation of the ellipse must have the form

$$\frac{x^2}{(24.0)^2} + \frac{y^2}{b^2} = 1$$

Since the point (23.0, 1.14) is on the ellipse, its coordinates must satisfy the equation of the ellipse. Hence

$$\frac{(23.0)^2}{(24.0)^2} + \frac{(1.14)^2}{b^2} = 1$$

$$\frac{(1.14)^2}{b^2} = 1 - \frac{(23.0)^2}{(24.0)^2}$$

$$\frac{(1.14)^2}{b^2} = \frac{47}{576}$$

$$b^2 = \frac{576(1.14)^2}{47}$$

$$b^2 = 15.9$$

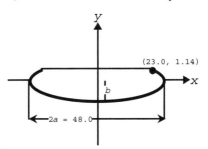

Thus, the equation of the ellipse must be $\dfrac{x^2}{576} + \dfrac{y^2}{15.9} = 1$.

(B) From the figure, we can see that the width of the wing must equal $1.14 + b = 1.14 + \sqrt{15.9} = 5.13$ feet.

SECTION 6-3

1. A hyperbola is the set of all points P in a plane such that the absolute value of the difference of the distances from P to two fixed points in the plane is a positive constant.

3. Answers will vary.

5. No. The axes can be varied independently to achieve various hyperbolic shapes.

7. Given transverse axis length $2a = 24$ and conjugate axis length $2b = 18$, then $a = 12$, $b = 9$, and $c^2 = a^2 + b^2$. Therefore $c^2 = 12^2 + 9^2$, $c^2 = 225$, and $c = 15$. The distance between the foci is then $2c$, or 30.

9. Given transverse axis length $2a = 1$ and conjugate axis length $2b = 3$, then $a = \dfrac{1}{2}$, $b = \dfrac{3}{2}$, and $c^2 = a^2 + b^2$.

   Therefore $c^2 = \left(\dfrac{1}{2}\right)^2 + \left(\dfrac{3}{2}\right)^2$, $c^2 = \dfrac{10}{4}$, and $c = \dfrac{\sqrt{10}}{2}$. The distance between the foci is then $2c$, or $\sqrt{10}$.

11. When $y = 0$, $x^2 = 1$ x intercepts: ± 1
When $x = 0$, $-y^2 = 1$. There are no y intercepts.
This corresponds to graph (d).

13. When $y = 0$, $-x^2 = 4$. There are no x intercepts.
When $x = 0$, $y^2 = 4$. y intercepts: ± 2
This corresponds to graph (c).

15. When $y = 0$, $\dfrac{x^2}{9} = 1$. x intercepts: ± 3 $a = 3$

When $x = 0$, $-\dfrac{y^2}{4} = 1$. There are no y intercepts, but $b = 2$.

Sketch the asymptotes using the asymptote
rectangle, then sketch in the hyperbola.
Foci: $c^2 = 3^2 + 2^2$
$\qquad c^2 = 13$
$\qquad c = \sqrt{13}$
$F' = (-\sqrt{13}, 0)$, $F = (\sqrt{13}, 0)$
Transverse axis length $= 2(3) = 6$
Conjugate axis length $= 2(2) = 4$

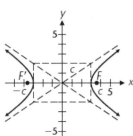

17. When $y = 0$, $-\dfrac{x^2}{9} = 1$. There are no x intercepts, but $b = 3$.

When $x = 0$, $\dfrac{y^2}{4} = 1$. y intercepts: ± 2, $a = 2$

Sketch the asymptotes using the asymptote
rectangle, then sketch in the hyperbola.
Foci: $c^2 = 2^2 + 3^2$
$\qquad c^2 = 13$
$\qquad c = \sqrt{13}$
$F' = (0, -\sqrt{13})$, $F = (0, \sqrt{13})$
Transverse axis length $= 2(2) = 4$
Conjugate axis length $= 2(3) = 6$

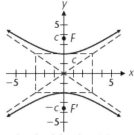

19. First, write the equation in standard form by dividing both sides by 16.
$\qquad 4x^2 - y^2 = 16$

$$\frac{x^2}{4} - \frac{y^2}{16} = 1$$

Locate intercepts: When $y = 0$, $x = \pm 2$. x intercepts: ± 2 $a = 2$

When $x = 0$, $-\dfrac{y^2}{16} = 1$. There are no y intercepts, but $b = 4$.

Sketch the asymptotes using the asymptote rectangle, then sketch
in the hyperbola.
Foci: $c^2 = 2^2 + 4^2$
$\qquad c^2 = 20$
$\qquad c = \sqrt{20}$
$F' = (-\sqrt{20}, 0)$, $F = (\sqrt{20}, 0)$
Transverse axis length $= 2(2) = 4$
Conjugate axis length $= 2(4) = 8$

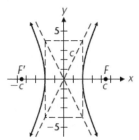

21. First, write the equation in standard form by dividing both sides by 144.
$\qquad 9y^2 - 16x^2 = 144$

$$\frac{y^2}{16} - \frac{x^2}{9} = 1$$

Locate intercepts: When $y = 0$, $-\dfrac{x^2}{9} = 1$. There are no x intercepts, but $b = 3$.

When $x = 0$, $\dfrac{y^2}{16} = 1$, $y = \pm4$. y intercepts: ±4 $a = 4$

Sketch the asymptotes using the asymptote rectangle, then sketch in the hyperbola.

Foci: $c^2 = 4^2 + 3^2$
$\quad\quad c^2 = 25$
$\quad\quad\quad c = 5$

$F' = (0, -5)$, $F = (0, 5)$

Transverse axis length = $2(4) = 8$.

Conjugate axis length = $2(3) = 6$.

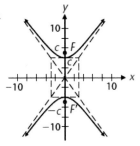

23. First, write the equation in standard form by dividing both sides by 12.

$3x^2 - 2y^2 = 12$

$$\dfrac{x^2}{4} - \dfrac{y^2}{6} = 1$$

Locate intercepts: When $y = 0$, $\dfrac{x^2}{4} = 1$. $x = \pm2$. x intercepts: ±2 $a = 2$

When $x = 0$, $-\dfrac{y^2}{6} = 1$. There are no y intercepts, but $b = \sqrt{6}$.

Sketch the asymptotes using the asymptote rectangle, then sketch in the hyperbola.

Foci: $c^2 = 2^2 + (\sqrt{6})^2$

$\quad c^2 = 10$

$\quad\quad c = \sqrt{10}$

$F' = (-\sqrt{10}, 0)$, $F = (\sqrt{10}, 0)$

Transverse axis length = $2(2) = 4$

Conjugate axis length = $2\sqrt{6} \approx 4.90$

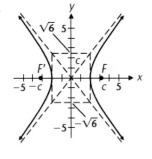

25. First, write the equation in standard form by dividing both sides by 28.

$7y^2 - 4x^2 = 28$

$$\dfrac{y^2}{4} - \dfrac{x^2}{7} = 1$$

Locate intercepts: When $y = 0$, $-\dfrac{x^2}{7} = 1$. There are no x intercepts, but $b = \sqrt{7}$.

When $x = 0$, $\dfrac{y^2}{4} = 1$, $y = \pm2$. y intercepts: ±2 $a = 2$

Sketch the asymptotes using the asymptote rectangle, then sketch in the hyperbola.

Foci: $c^2 = 2^2 + (\sqrt{7})^2$

$\quad c^2 = 11$

$\quad\quad c = \sqrt{11}$

$F' = (0, -\sqrt{11})$, $F = (0, \sqrt{11})$

Transverse axis length = $2(2) = 4$

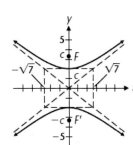

Conjugate axis length $= 2\sqrt{7} \approx 5.29$

27. Since the graph has x intercepts ($x = \pm 3$) but no y intercepts, the equation must be in the form
$$\frac{x^2}{M} - \frac{y^2}{N} = 1$$
and, when $y = 0$, $x = \pm 3$, hence
$$\frac{9}{M} - \frac{0}{N} = 1$$
$$M = 9$$
Since the point $(5, 4)$ is on the graph, its coordinates must satisfy the equation, which is known to be of form

29. Since the graph has y intercepts ($y = \pm 4$) but no x intercepts, the equation must be in the form
$$\frac{y^2}{N} - \frac{x^2}{M} = 1$$
and, when $x = 0$, $y = \pm 4$, hence
$$\frac{16}{N} - \frac{0}{M} = 1$$
$$N = 16$$
Since the point $(3, 5)$ is on the graph, its coordinates must satisfy the equation, which is known to be of form

$$\frac{x^2}{9} - \frac{y^2}{N} = 1$$
Hence $\dfrac{5^2}{9} - \dfrac{4^2}{N} = 1$
$$\frac{25}{9} - \frac{16}{N} = 1$$
$$-\frac{16}{N} = -\frac{16}{9}$$
$$N = 9$$
The equation is therefore $\dfrac{x^2}{9} - \dfrac{y^2}{9} = 1$

$$\frac{y^2}{16} - \frac{x^2}{M} = 1$$
Hence $\dfrac{5^2}{16} - \dfrac{3^2}{M} = 1$
$$\frac{25}{16} - \frac{9}{M} = 1$$
$$-\frac{9}{M} = -\frac{9}{16}$$
$$M = 16$$
The equation is therefore $\dfrac{y^2}{16} - \dfrac{x^2}{16} = 1$

31. Since the transverse axis is on the x axis, start with $\dfrac{x^2}{a^2} - \dfrac{y^2}{b^2} = 1$ and find a and b
$$a = \frac{14}{2} = 7 \text{ and } b = \frac{10}{2} = 5$$
Thus, the equation is $\dfrac{x^2}{49} - \dfrac{y^2}{25} = 1$

33. Since the transverse axis is on the y axis, start with $\dfrac{y^2}{a^2} - \dfrac{x^2}{b^2} = 1$ and find a and b
$$a = \frac{24}{2} = 12 \text{ and } b = \frac{18}{2} = 9$$
Thus, the equation is $\dfrac{y^2}{144} - \dfrac{x^2}{81} = 1$

35. Since the transverse axis is on the x axis, start with
$$\frac{x^2}{a^2} - \frac{y^2}{b^2} = 1 \text{ and find } a \text{ and } b$$
$$a = \frac{18}{2} = 9$$

To find b, sketch the asymptote rectangle, label known parts, and use the Pythagorean Theorem.
$b^2 = 11^2 - 9^2$
$b^2 = 40$
$b = \sqrt{40}$
Thus, the equation is
$$\frac{x^2}{81} - \frac{y^2}{40} = 1$$

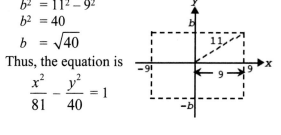

36. Since the conjugate axis is on the x axis, start with
$$\frac{y^2}{a^2} - \frac{x^2}{b^2} = 1 \text{ and find } a \text{ and } b$$
$$b = \frac{14}{2} = 7$$

To find a, sketch the asymptote rectangle, label known parts, and use the Pythagorean Theorem.
$a^2 = (\sqrt{200})^2 - 7^2$
$a^2 = 151$
$a = \sqrt{151}$
Thus, the equation is
$$\frac{y^2}{151} - \frac{x^2}{49} = 1$$

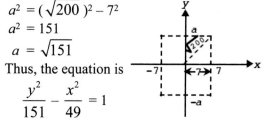

39. The equation $\dfrac{x^2}{25} - \dfrac{y^2}{4} = 1$ is in standard form with $a^2 = 25$, $b^2 = 4$. Since the intercepts are on the x axis, the asymptotes have equations $y = \pm\dfrac{b}{a}x = \pm\dfrac{2}{5}x$.

41. The equation $\dfrac{y^2}{4} - \dfrac{x^2}{16} = 1$ is in standard form with $a^2 = 4$, $b^2 = 16$. Since the intercepts are on the y axis, the asymptotes have equations $y = \pm\dfrac{a}{b}x = \pm\dfrac{2}{4}x$ or $y = \pm\dfrac{1}{2}x$.

43. $9x^2 - y^2 = 9$. In standard form, this becomes $\dfrac{x^2}{1} - \dfrac{y^2}{9} = 1$

Then $a^2 = 1$, $b^2 = 9$. Since the intercepts are on the x axis, the asymptotes have equations $y = \pm\dfrac{b}{a}x = \pm\dfrac{3}{1}x$ or $y = \pm 3x$.

45. $2y^2 - 3x^2 = 1$. In standard form, this becomes $\dfrac{y^2}{1/2} - \dfrac{x^2}{1/3} = 1$

Then $a^2 = \dfrac{1}{2}$, $b^2 = \dfrac{1}{3}$. Since the intercepts are on the y axis, the asymptotes have equations $y = \pm\dfrac{a}{b}x$. Write a
$= \sqrt{\dfrac{1}{2}}$, $b = \sqrt{\dfrac{1}{3}}$, $\dfrac{a}{b} = \sqrt{\dfrac{1}{2}} \div \sqrt{\dfrac{1}{3}} = \sqrt{\dfrac{3}{2}}$ or $\dfrac{\sqrt{3}}{\sqrt{2}}$. Asymptotes: $y = \pm\dfrac{\sqrt{3}}{\sqrt{2}}x$.

47. (A) If a hyperbola has center at $(0, 0)$ and a focus at $(1, 0)$, its equation must be of form $\dfrac{x^2}{a^2} - \dfrac{y^2}{b^2} = 1$
with $c = 1$, thus $a^2 + b^2 = 1$ or $b^2 = 1 - a^2$
Therefore there are an infinite number of such hyperbolas.

Each has an equation of form $\dfrac{x^2}{a^2} - \dfrac{y^2}{1-a^2} = 1$ Note that since $0 < a < c$, we require $0 < a < 1$.

(B) If an ellipse has center at $(0, 0)$ and a focus at $(1, 0)$, its equation must be of form $\dfrac{x^2}{a^2} + \dfrac{y^2}{b^2} = 1$
with $c = 1$, thus $a^2 - 1 = b^2$
Therefore there are an infinite number of such ellipses.

Each has an equation of form $\dfrac{x^2}{a^2} + \dfrac{y^2}{a^2-1} = 1$ Note that since $a > c > 0$, we require $a > 1$.

(C) If a parabola has vertex at $(0, 0)$ and focus at $(1, 0)$, its equation must be of form $y^2 = 4ax$
with $a = 1$. Therefore there is one such parabola; its equation is $y^2 = 4x$.

49. (A) The points of intersection are the solutions of the system
$$x^2 - y^2 = 1$$
$$y = 0.5x = \tfrac{1}{2}x$$
We solve using substitution:
$$x^2 - \left(\tfrac{1}{2}x\right)^2 = 1$$
$$x^2 - \tfrac{1}{4}x^2 = 1$$
$$\tfrac{3}{4}x^2 = 1$$
$$x^2 = \tfrac{4}{3}$$
$$x = \pm\dfrac{2}{\sqrt{3}}$$

(B)
$$x^2 - y^2 = 1$$
$$y = 2x$$
$$x^2 - (2x)^2 = 1$$
$$x^2 - 4x^2 = 1$$
$$-3x^2 = 1$$
$$x^2 = -\tfrac{1}{3} \text{ No solution.}$$

The graphs do not intersect. Repeat the above calculations using $y = mx$ instead of $y = 2x$.
$$x^2 - y^2 = 1$$
$$y = mx$$
$$x^2 - (mx)^2 = 1$$
$$x^2 - m^2x^2 = 1$$
$$x^2(1 - m^2) = 1$$
$$x^2 = \dfrac{1}{1-m^2}$$

If the right side is negative the equation will have no

$y = \frac{1}{2}x$, so when $x = \frac{2}{\sqrt{3}}$, $y = \frac{1}{2} \cdot \frac{2}{\sqrt{3}} = \frac{1}{\sqrt{3}}$

when $x = \frac{-2}{\sqrt{3}}$, $y = \frac{1}{2} \cdot \frac{-2}{\sqrt{3}} = \frac{-1}{\sqrt{3}}$

The points of intersection are

$\left(\frac{2}{\sqrt{3}}, \frac{1}{\sqrt{3}}\right)$ and $\left(\frac{-2}{\sqrt{3}}, \frac{-1}{\sqrt{3}}\right)$.

solution, so the graphs intersect only if $1 - m^2 > 0$. This occurs only if m^2 is between zero and 1; that is,   for $-1 < m < 1$.

In this case, $x = \pm\dfrac{1}{\sqrt{1-m^2}}$; $y = mx = \pm\dfrac{m}{\sqrt{1-m^2}}$.

So if $-1 < m < 1$, the graphs intersect at

$\left(\dfrac{1}{\sqrt{1-m^2}}, \dfrac{m}{\sqrt{1-m^2}}\right)$ and $\left(\dfrac{-1}{\sqrt{1-m^2}}, \dfrac{-m}{\sqrt{1-m^2}}\right)$.

51. (A) The points of intersection are the solutions of the system

$$y^2 - 4x^2 = 1$$
$$y = x$$
$$x^2 - 4x^2 = 1$$
$$-3x^2 = 1$$
$$x^2 = -\frac{1}{3}$$

No solution. The graphs do not intersect.

(B)
$$y^2 - 4x^2 = 1$$
$$y = 3x$$
$$(3x)^2 - 4x^2 = 1$$
$$9x^2 - 4x^2 = 1$$
$$5x^2 = 1$$
$$x^2 = \frac{1}{5}$$
$$x = \pm\frac{1}{\sqrt{5}}$$

$y = 3x$, so when $x = \frac{1}{\sqrt{5}}$, $y = \frac{3}{\sqrt{5}}$ and when

$x = \frac{-1}{\sqrt{5}}$, $y = \frac{-3}{\sqrt{5}}$. The points of intersection

are $\left(\frac{1}{\sqrt{5}}, \frac{3}{\sqrt{5}}\right)$ and $\left(\frac{-1}{\sqrt{5}}, \frac{-3}{\sqrt{5}}\right)$.

Repeat the above calculations with $y = mx$ in place of $y = 3x$.

$$y^2 - 4x^2 = 1$$
$$y = mx$$
$$(mx)^2 - 4x^2 = 1$$
$$m^2x^2 - 4x^2 = 1$$
$$x^2(m^2 - 4) = 1$$
$$x^2 = \frac{1}{m^2 - 4}$$

This equation will have solutions only if $m^2 - 4$ is positive; this occurs when $m > 2$ or $m < -2$. In this case, $x = \pm\dfrac{1}{\sqrt{m^2-4}}$; $y = mx = \pm\dfrac{m}{\sqrt{m^2-4}}$.

So if $m > 2$ or $m < -2$ the points of intersection are

$\left(\dfrac{1}{\sqrt{m^2-4}}, \dfrac{m}{\sqrt{m^2-4}}\right)$ and $\left(\dfrac{-1}{\sqrt{m^2-4}}, \dfrac{-m}{\sqrt{m^2-4}}\right)$.

53. (A) $\dfrac{x^2}{a^2} - \dfrac{y^2}{b^2} = 1$ Solve for y.

$$-\frac{y^2}{b^2} = 1 - \frac{x^2}{a^2}$$
$$\frac{y^2}{b^2} = \frac{x^2}{a^2} - 1$$
$$y^2 = \frac{b^2 x^2}{a^2} - b^2$$

$$y^2 = \frac{b^2}{a^2}x^2\left(1 - \frac{a^2}{x^2}\right)$$

$$y = \pm\frac{b}{a}x\sqrt{1 - \frac{a^2}{x^2}}$$

(B) As $|x| \to \infty$, $\dfrac{a}{|x|} \to 0$, $\dfrac{a^2}{x^2} \to 0$, $1 - \dfrac{a^2}{x^2} \to 1$, and $\sqrt{1 - \dfrac{a^2}{x^2}} \to 1$.

Hence as $|x| \to \infty$, $y \to \pm\dfrac{b}{a}x$. Therefore these lines form asymptotes for the hyperbola.

(C) Since $\sqrt{1 - \dfrac{a^2}{x^2}} < 1$ for $|x| > a$, $\dfrac{b}{a}x\sqrt{1 - \dfrac{a^2}{x^2}} < \dfrac{b}{a}x$, for $x > 0$. Thus in quadrant I, the hyperbola is below

its asymptote $y = \dfrac{b}{a}x$. However, $-\dfrac{b}{a}x < -\dfrac{b}{a}x\sqrt{1 - \dfrac{a^2}{x^2}}$, for $x > 0$, hence, in quadrant IV, the hyperbola is

above its asymptote, $y = -\dfrac{b}{a}x$. Similar arguments applied for $x < 0$ show that in quadrant II the

hyperbola is below its asymptote $y = -\dfrac{b}{a}x$, and in quadrant III, it is above its asymptote $y = \dfrac{b}{a}x$.

55.   By the triangle inequality, no points can satisfy this condition. The set is empty.

57.

$$|d_1 - d_2| = 2a$$
$$d_1 - d_2 = \pm 2a$$
$$d_1 = \pm 2a + d_2 \qquad \text{Use the distance formula}$$
$$\sqrt{(x+c)^2 + y^2} = \pm 2a + \sqrt{(x-c)^2 + y^2} \qquad \text{Square both sides}$$
$$(x+c)^2 + y^2 = 4a^2 \pm 4a\sqrt{(x-c)^2 + y^2} + (x-c)^2 + y^2 \qquad \text{Isolate the square root.}$$
$$\pm\sqrt{(x-c)^2 + y^2} = a - \frac{cx}{a} \qquad \text{Square both sides}$$
$$(x-c)^2 + y^2 = a^2 - 2cx + \frac{c^2x^2}{a^2} \qquad \text{Simplify and collect terms}$$
$$\left(1 - \frac{c^2}{a^2}\right)x^2 + y^2 = a^2 - c^2 \quad \text{Use } a^2 - c^2 = -b^2, \ 1 - \frac{c^2}{a^2} = -\frac{b^2}{a^2} \quad \text{and divide both sides by } -b^2.$$
$$\frac{x^2}{a^2} - \frac{y^2}{b^2} = 1$$

59. From the figure, we see that the point $P(x, y)$ is a point on the curve if and only if $d_1 = \frac{3}{2}d_2$

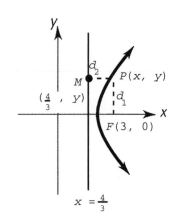

$$d(P, F) = \frac{3}{2}d(P, M)$$

$$\sqrt{(x-3)^2 + (y-0)^2} = \frac{3}{2}\sqrt{\left(x - \frac{4}{3}\right)^2 + (y - y)^2}$$

$$(x-3)^2 + y^2 = \frac{9}{4}\left(x - \frac{4}{3}\right)^2$$

$$x^2 - 6x + 9 + y^2 = \frac{9}{4}\left(x^2 - \frac{8}{3}x + \frac{16}{9}\right)$$

$$4x^2 - 24x + 36 + 4y^2 = 9x^2 - 24x + 16$$

$$-5x^2 + 4y^2 = -20$$

$$\frac{x^2}{4} - \frac{y^2}{5} = 1$$

The curve must be a hyperbola since its equation can be written in standard form for a hyperbola.

61. From the figure, we see that the transverse axis of the hyperbola must be on the y axis and $a = 4$. Hence, the equation of the hyperbola must have the form $\dfrac{y^2}{4^2} - \dfrac{x^2}{b^2} = 1$

To find b, we note that the point $(8, 12)$ is on the hyperbola, hence its coordinates satisfy the equation. Substituting, we have

$$\frac{12^2}{4^2} - \frac{8^2}{b^2} = 1$$

$$9 - \frac{64}{b^2} = 1$$

$$-\frac{64}{b^2} = -8$$

$$-64 = -8b^2$$

$$b^2 = 8$$

The equation required is $\dfrac{y^2}{16} - \dfrac{x^2}{8} = 1$

Using this equation, we can compute y when $x = 6$ to answer the question asked (see figure).

$$\frac{y^2}{16} - \frac{6^2}{8} = 1$$

$$\frac{y^2}{16} - \frac{36}{8} = 1$$

$$y^2 - 72 = 16$$

$$y^2 = 88$$

$$y = 9.38 \text{ to two decimal places}$$

The height above the vertex

$$= y - \text{height of vertex} = 9.38 - 4 = 5.38 \text{ feet}$$

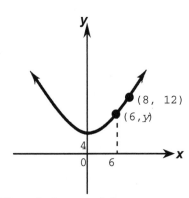

Hyperbola part of dome

63.   From the figure below, we can see:

$FF' = 2c = 120 - 20 = 100$

Thus $c = 50$

$FV = c - a = 120 - 110 = 10$

Thus $a = c - 10 = 50 - 10 = 40$

Since $c^2 = a^2 + b^2$

$50^2 = 40^2 + b^2$

$b = 30$

Thus the equation of the hyperbola, in standard form, is

$$\frac{y^2}{40^2} - \frac{x^2}{30^2} = 1$$

Expressing y in terms of x, we have

$$\frac{y^2}{40^2} = 1 + \frac{x^2}{30^2}$$

$$\frac{y^2}{40^2} = \frac{1}{30^2}(30^2 + x^2)$$

$$y^2 = \frac{40^2}{30^2}(30^2 + x^2)$$

$$y = \frac{4}{3}\sqrt{x^2 + 30^2}$$

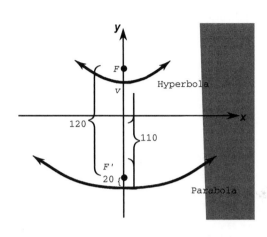

discarding the negative solution, since the reflecting hyperbola is above the x axis.

CHAPTER 6 REVIEW

1.   First write the equation in standard form by dividing both sides by 225.

$9x^2 + 25y^2 = 225$

$$\frac{x^2}{25} + \frac{y^2}{9} = 1$$

In this form the equation is identifiable as that of an ellipse. Locate the intercepts.

When $y = 0$, $\dfrac{x^2}{25} = 1$. x intercepts: ± 5

When $x = 0$, $\dfrac{y^2}{9} = 1$. y intercepts: ± 3

> **Common Error:**
> The relationship $c^2 = a^2 + b^2$ applies to a, b, c as defined for hyperbolas but not for ellipses.

Thus, $a = 5$, $b = 3$, and the major axis is on the x axis.

Foci: $c^2 = a^2 - b^2$

$c^2 = 25 - 9$

$c^2 = 16$

$c = 4$

Foci: $F'(-4, 0)$, $F(4, 0)$

Major axis length $= 2(5) = 10$

Minor axis length $= 2(3) = 6$

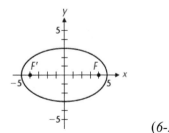

(6-2)

2. $x^2 = -12y$ is the equation of a parabola. To graph, assign y values that make the right side a perfect square (y must be zero or negative for x to be real) and solve for x. Since the coefficient of y is negative, a must be negative, and the parabola opens down.

x	0	± 6	± 2
y	0	-3	$-\frac{1}{3}$

To find the focus and directrix, solve
$$4a = -12$$
$$a = -3$$
Focus: $(0, -3)$ Directrix: $y = -(-3) = 3$

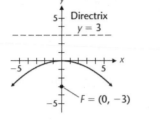

                                                        (6-1)

3. First, write the equation in standard form by dividing both sides by 225.
$$25y^2 - 9x^2 = 225$$
$$\frac{y^2}{9} - \frac{x^2}{25} = 1$$

In this form the equation is identifiable as that of a hyperbola.

When $y = 0$, $-\dfrac{x^2}{25} = 1$. There are no x intercepts, but $b = 5$.

When $x = 0$, $\dfrac{y^2}{9} = 1$. y intercepts: ± 3

Sketch the asymptotes using the asymptote rectangle, then sketch in the hyperbola.
Foci: $c^2 = 3^2 + 5^2$
$$c^2 = 34$$
$$c = \sqrt{34}$$
Foci: $F'(0, -\sqrt{34}\,)$, $F(0, \sqrt{34}\,)$
Transverse axis length = $2(3) = 6$
Conjugate axis length = $2(5) = 10$

                                                        (6-3)

4. First, write the equation in standard form by dividing both sides by 16.
$$x^2 - y^2 = 16$$
$$\frac{x^2}{16} - \frac{y^2}{16} = 1$$

In this form the equation is identifiable as a hyperbola.

When $x = 0$, $-\dfrac{y^2}{16} = 1$. There are no y intercepts, but $b = 4$. When $y = 0$, $\dfrac{x^2}{16} = 1$. x intercepts: ± 4.

Sketch the asymptotes using the asymptote rectangle, then sketch in the hyperbola.
Foci: $c^2 = 4^2 + 4^2$
$$c^2 = 32$$
$$c = 4\sqrt{2}$$
Foci: $F' = (-4\sqrt{2}, 0)$, $F = (4\sqrt{2}, 0)$
Transverse axis length = $2(4) = 8$
Conjugate axis length = $2(4) = 8$

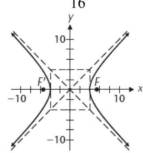

                                                        (6-3)

5. $y^2 = 8x$ is the equation of a parabola. To graph, assign x values that make the right side a perfect square (x must be zero or positive for y to be real) and solve for y. Since the coefficient of x is positive, a must be positive, and the parabola opens right.

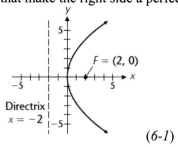

x	0	2	8
y	0	± 4	± 8

To find the focus and directrix, solve $4a = 8$

$$a = 2.$$

Focus: $(2, 0)$ Directrix: $x = -2$ *(6-1)*

6. First, write the equation in standard form by dividing both sides by 8.

$$2x^2 + y^2 = 8$$

$$\frac{x^2}{4} + \frac{y^2}{8} = 1$$

In this form the equation is identifiable as that of an ellipse. Locate the intercepts.

When $y = 0$, $\dfrac{x^2}{4} = 1$ x intercepts: ± 2 When $x = 0$, $\dfrac{y^2}{8} = 1$ y intercepts: $\pm 2\sqrt{2}$

Thus, $a = 2\sqrt{2}$, $b = 2$, and the major axis is on the y axis.

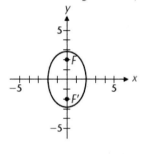

Foci: $c^2 = a^2 - b^2$
$$c^2 = 8 - 4$$
$$c^2 = 4$$
$$c = 2$$

Foci: $F' = (0, -2)$, $F = (0, 2)$
Major axis length $= 2(2\sqrt{2}) = 4\sqrt{2}$
Minor axis length $= 2(2) = 4$ *(6-2)*

7. The parabola is opening either left or right and has an equation of the form $y^2 = 4ax$. Since $(-4, -2)$ is on the graph, we have:

$$(-2)^2 = 4a(-4)$$
$$4 = -16a$$
$$-\frac{1}{4} = a$$

Thus, the equation of the parabola is

$$y^2 = 4\left(-\frac{1}{4}\right)x$$

$$y^2 = -x$$ *(6-1)*

8. Make a rough sketch of the ellipse and compute x and y intercepts:

$$\frac{x^2}{a^2} + \frac{y^2}{b^2} = 1 \qquad a = \frac{12}{2} = 6 \quad b = \frac{10}{2} = 5$$

$$\frac{x^2}{36} + \frac{y^2}{25} = 1$$

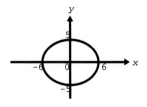

(6-2)

9. Make a rough sketch of the ellipse, locate focus and x intercepts, then determine y intercepts using the special triangle relationship.

$$\frac{x^2}{b^2} + \frac{y^2}{a^2} = 1 \quad b = \frac{12}{2} = 6 \quad a^2 = 6^2 + 8^2 = 100$$

$$a = 10$$

$$\frac{x^2}{36} + \frac{y^2}{100} = 1$$

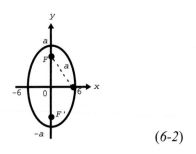

(6-2)

10. Since the transverse axis is on the y axis, start with

$$\frac{y^2}{a^2} - \frac{x^2}{b^2} = 1 \text{ and find } a \text{ and } b. \quad b = \frac{6}{2} = 3, c = \frac{8}{2} = 4$$

To find a, sketch the asymptote rectangle, label known parts, and use the Pythagorean Theorem.

$$a^2 = c^2 - b^2$$
$$a^2 = 4^2 - 3^2$$
$$a^2 = 7$$
$$a = \sqrt{7}$$

Thus, the equation is $\dfrac{y^2}{7} - \dfrac{x^2}{9} = 1$

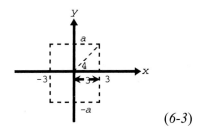

(6-3)

11. Since the transverse axis is on the x axis, start with

$$\frac{x^2}{a^2} - \frac{y^2}{b^2} = 1 \text{ and find } a \text{ and } b. \quad a = \frac{14}{2} = 7 \quad b = \frac{16}{2} = 8$$

Thus, the equation is $\dfrac{x^2}{49} - \dfrac{y^2}{64} = 1$

(6-3)

12. Comparing focus $(0, -5)$ with the information in the chart of standard equations for a parabola, we see: $a = -5$ Axis of symmetry: the y axis. Equation: $x^2 = 4ay$. Thus the equation of the parabola must be $x^2 = 4(-5)y$ or $x^2 = -20y$.

(6-1)

13. Since the major axis is on the x axis, the foci must be at $(\pm c, 0)$ and the equation of the ellipse is of form

$$\frac{x^2}{a^2} + \frac{y^2}{b^2} = 1$$

Since the major axis has twice the length of the minor axis, $a = 2b$. The equation then becomes

$$\frac{x^2}{4b^2} + \frac{y^2}{b^2} = 1$$

Since $(-6, 0)$ is on the graph, its coordinates satisfy the equation, hence

$$\frac{(-6)^2}{4b^2} + \frac{0^2}{b^2} = 1$$

$$\frac{36}{4b^2} = 1$$

$$b^2 = 9$$

Then $a^2 = 4b^2 = 36$ and $c^2 = a^2 - b^2 = 36 - 9 = 27$; $c = \sqrt{27}$. The foci are at $(\pm\sqrt{27}, 0)$, that is, $(-3\sqrt{3}, 0)$ and $(3\sqrt{3}, 0)$.

(6-2)

14. Since the conjugate axis has length 4, $2b = 4$, hence $b = 2$. Since $(0, -3)$ is a focus, $c = 3$.
Hence $a^2 = c^2 - b^2 = 9 - 4 = 5$ and $a = \sqrt{5}$. The y intercepts are $(0, \pm a)$, that is $(0, \sqrt{5})$ and $(0, -\sqrt{5})$. *(6-3)*

15. Since the focus is at $(-4, 0)$, the axis of symmetry is the x axis, the parabola opens left, and the directrix
has equation $x = -(-4)$ or $x = 4$. *(6-1)*

16. $x^2 = 8y \qquad y^2 = -x$
Solve for y in the first equation, then substitute into the second equation

$$y = \frac{x^2}{8}$$

$$\left(\frac{x^2}{8}\right)^2 = -x$$

$$\frac{x^4}{64} = -x$$

$$x^4 = -64x$$
$$x^4 + 64x = 0$$
$$x(x^3 + 64) = 0$$
$$x(x + 4)(x^2 - 4x + 16) = 0$$
$$x = 0 \quad x + 4 = 0 \qquad x^2 - 4x + 16 = 0$$
$$x = -4 \qquad \text{No real solutions.}$$

For $x = 0$ For $x = -4$

$$y = 0 \qquad y = \frac{(-4)^2}{8}$$

$$y = 2 \quad \text{Solutions: } (0, 0), (-4, 2)$$ *(6-1)*

17. Since the major axis has length 14, $2a = 14$, hence $a = 7$. Since $(0, -1)$ is a focus, $c = 1$.
Hence $b^2 = a^2 - c^2 = 49 - 1 = 48$; $b = \sqrt{48}$.
The x intercepts are at $(\pm\sqrt{48}, 0)$, that is $(4\sqrt{3}, 0)$ and $(-4\sqrt{3}, 0)$. *(6-2)*

18. Since the transverse axis is on the y axis, the foci must be at $(0, \pm c)$ and the equation of the hyperbola is of
the form

$$\frac{y^2}{a^2} - \frac{x^2}{b^2} = 1$$

Since the conjugate axis has twice the length of the transverse axis, $b = 2a$. The equation then becomes

$$\frac{y^2}{a^2} - \frac{x^2}{4a^2} = 1$$

Since $(0, -4)$ is on the graph,, its coordinates satisfy the equation, hence

$$\frac{(-4)^2}{a^2} - \frac{0^2}{4a^2} = 1$$

$$\frac{16}{a^2} = 1$$

$$a^2 = 16$$

Then $b^2 = 4a^2 = 64$ and $c^2 = a^2 + b^2 = 16 + 64 = 80$; $c = \sqrt{80}$.
The foci are at $(0, \pm\sqrt{80})$, that is $(0, 4\sqrt{5})$ and $(0, -4\sqrt{5})$. *(6-3)*

19.   From the figure, we see that the point $P(x, y)$ is a point on the curve if and only if

$$d_1 = d_2$$
$$d(F, P) = d(M, P)$$
$$\sqrt{(x-2)^2 + (y-4)^2} = \sqrt{(x-6)^2 + (y-y)^2}$$
$$(x-2)^2 + (y-4)^2 = (x-6)^2$$
$$x^2 - 4x + 4 + (y-4)^2 = x^2 - 12x + 36$$
$$(y-4)^2 = -8x + 32$$
$$(y-4)^2 = -8(x-4) \text{ or}$$
$$y^2 - 8y + 16 = -8x + 32$$
$$y^2 - 8y + 8x - 16 = 0$$

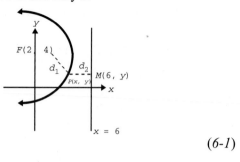

(6-1)

20.   From the figure, we see that the point $P(x, y)$ is a point on the curve if and only if

$$d_1 = 2d_2$$
$$d(F, P) = 2d(N, P)$$
$$\sqrt{(x-4)^2 + (y-0)^2} = 2\sqrt{(x-1)^2 + (y-y)^2}$$
$$(x-4)^2 + y^2 = 4(x-1)^2$$
$$x^2 - 8x + 16 + y^2 = 4(x^2 - 2x + 1)$$
$$x^2 - 8x + 16 + y^2 = 4x^2 - 8x + 4$$
$$-3x^2 + y^2 = -12$$
$$\frac{x^2}{4} - \frac{y^2}{12} = 1$$

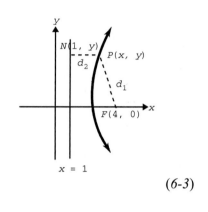

(6-3)

This is the equation of a hyperbola.

21.   From the figure, we see that the point $P(x, y)$ is a point on the curve if and only if

$$d_1 = \frac{2}{3}d_2$$
$$d(F, P) = \frac{2}{3}d(M, P)$$
$$\sqrt{(x-4)^2 + (y-0)^2} = \frac{2}{3}\sqrt{(x-9)^2 + (y-y)^2}$$
$$(x-4)^2 + y^2 = \frac{4}{9}(x-9)^2$$
$$9[(x-4)^2 + y^2] = 4(x-9)^2$$
$$9(x^2 - 8x + 16 + y^2) = 4(x^2 - 18x + 81)$$
$$9x^2 - 72x + 144 + 9y^2 = 4x^2 - 72x + 324$$
$$5x^2 + 9y^2 = 180$$
$$\frac{x^2}{36} + \frac{y^2}{20} = 1$$

(6-2)

This is the equation of an ellipse.

22.   The equation $\dfrac{x^2}{49} - \dfrac{y^2}{25} = 1$ is in standard form with $a^2 = 49$, $b^2 = 25$. Since the intercepts are on the x axis,

the asymptotes have equations $y = \pm\dfrac{b}{a}x = \pm\dfrac{5}{7}x$.

(6-3)

23. The equation $\dfrac{y^2}{64} - \dfrac{x^2}{4} = 1$ is in standard form with $a^2 = 64$, $b^2 = 4$. Since the intercepts are on the y axis,

the asymptotes have equations $y = \pm\dfrac{a}{b}x = \pm\dfrac{8}{2}x$ or $y = \pm 4x$.   (6-3)

24. $4x^2 - y^2 = 1$. In standard form, this becomes $\dfrac{x^2}{1/4} - \dfrac{y^2}{1} = 1$

Then $a^2 = \dfrac{1}{4}$, $b^2 = 1$. Since the intercepts are on the x axis, the asymptotes have equations $\quad y = \pm\dfrac{b}{a}x =$

$\pm\dfrac{1}{1/2}x$ or $y = \pm 2x$.   (6-3)

25. From the figure, we see that the parabola opens up, hence its equation must be of the form $x^2 = 4ay$. Since
(4, 1) is on the graph we have
$\quad 4^2 = 4a\cdot 1$
$\quad 16 = 4a$
$\quad\ \ a = 4$

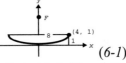

Thus a, the distance of the focus from the vertex, is 4 feet.   (6-1)

26. From the figure, we see that the x intercepts must be at $(-5, 0)$ and $(5, 0)$, the foci at $(-4, 0)$ and $(4, 0)$.
Hence $a = 5$ and $c = 4$. We can determine the y intercepts using the special triangle relationship
$\quad 5^2\ = 4^2 + b^2$
$\quad 25 = 16 + b^2$
$\quad\ \ b\ = 3$

Hence, the equation of the ellipse is $\dfrac{x^2}{5^2} + \dfrac{y^2}{3^2} = 1$

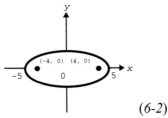

(6-2)

27. From the figure, we can see: $d + a = y_1 =$ the y coordinate of the point on the hyperbola with x coordinate

15. From the equation of the hyperbola $\dfrac{y^2}{40^2} - \dfrac{x^2}{30^2} = 1$, we have $a = 40$, hence $d + 40 = y_1$, or $d = y_1 - 40$.

Since the point $(15, y_1)$ is on the hyperbola, its coordinates must satisfy the equation of the hyperbola.

Thus, $\dfrac{y_1^2}{40^2} - \dfrac{15^2}{30^2} = 1$

$\qquad\qquad \dfrac{y_1^2}{40^2} = 1 + \dfrac{15^2}{30^2}$

$\qquad\qquad \dfrac{y_1^2}{40^2} = \dfrac{5}{4}$

$\qquad\qquad\ \ y_1^2 = 2000$

$\qquad\qquad\ \ \ y_1 = 44.72$

$\qquad \text{depth} = y_1 - 40 = 4.72 \text{ feet.}$

(6-3)

CHAPTER 7

SECTION 7–1

1. Graph the two equations in the same coordinate system. Determine the point of intersection (if shown) by inspection. Check by substitution in both equations.

3. By multiplying both sides of the equations by non–zero constants as required, match coefficients of one variable so that they are equal in absolute value and opposite in sign. Add to eliminate one variable, solve the resulting equation for the other, and substitute into the original equations to find the other variable, and check.

5. No. A system of linear equations can have no solution, one solution, or infinitely many solutions.

7. Both lines in the given system are different, but they have the same slope $\left(\dfrac{1}{2}\right)$ and are therefore parallel.

    This system corresponds to (b) and has no solution.

9. In slope–intercept form, these equations are $y = 2x - 5$ and $y = -\dfrac{3}{2}x - \dfrac{3}{2}$. Thus, one has slope 2 and y

    intercept -5; the other has slope $-\dfrac{3}{2}$ and y intercept $-\dfrac{3}{2}$. This system corresponds to (d) and its solution can

    be read from the graph as $(1, -3)$. Checking, we see that $\quad 2x - y = 2\cdot 1 - (-3) = 5$
    $$3x + 2y = 3\cdot 1 + 2(-3) = -3$$

Note: Checking steps are not shown, but should be performed by the student.

11. $x + y = 7$
     $x - y = 3$
     If we add, we can eliminate y.
     $\begin{aligned} x + y &= 7 \\ \underline{x - y} &= \underline{3} \\ 2x &= 10 \\ x &= 5 \end{aligned}$
     Now substitute $x = 5$ back into the top equation and solve for y.
     $5 + y = 7$
     $\quad y = 2$
     $(5, 2)$

13. $3x - 2y = 12$
     $7x + 2y = 8$
     If we add, we can eliminate y.
     $\begin{aligned} 3x - 2y &= 12 \\ \underline{7x + 2y} &= \underline{8} \\ 10x &= 20 \\ x &= 2 \end{aligned}$
     Now substitute $x = 2$ back into the bottom equation and solve for y.
     $7(2) + 2y = 8$
     $\quad 2y = -6$
     $\quad y = -3$
     $(2, -3)$

15. $3u + 5v = 15$
     $6u + 10v = -30$
     If we multiply the top equation by -2 and add, we eliminate both u and v.
     $\begin{aligned} -6u - 10v &= -30 \\ \underline{6u + 10v} &= \underline{-30} \\ 0 &= -60 \end{aligned}$
     No solution. The equations represent parallel lines.

17. $3x - y = -2$
     $-9x + 3y = 6$
     If we multiply the top equation by 3 and add, we eliminate both x and y.
     $\begin{aligned} 9x - 3y &= -6 \\ \underline{-9x + 3y} &= \underline{6} \\ 0 &= 0 \end{aligned}$
     The system is dependent and has infinite solutions. Solving the first equation for y in terms of x, we obtain $y = 3x + 2$. Thus if we let $x = s$, $y = 3s + 2$, we can express the solution set as
     $\{(s, 3s + 2) \mid s \text{ any real number}\}$

19. $x - y = 4$
$x + 3y = 12$
Solve the first equation for x in terms of y.
$x = 4 + y$
Substitute into the second equation to eliminate x.
$(4 + y) + 3y = 12$
$4y = 8$
$y = 2$
Now replace y with 2 in the first equation to find x.
$x - 2 = 4$
$x = 6$
Solution: $x = 6$, $y = 2$

21. $4x + 3y = 26$
$3x - 11y = -7$
Solve the second equation for x in terms of y.
$3x = 11y - 7$
$x = \dfrac{11y - 7}{3}$
Substitute into the first equation to eliminate x.
$4\left(\dfrac{11y - 7}{3}\right) + 3y = 26$
$\dfrac{44y - 28}{3} + 3y = 26$
$44y - 28 + 9y = 78$
$53y = 106$
$y = 2$
$x = \dfrac{11 \cdot 2 - 7}{3}$
$x = 5$
Solution: $x = 5$, $y = 2$

23. $7m + 12n = -1$
$5m - 3n = 7$
Solve the first equation for n in terms of m.
$12n = -1 - 7m$
$n = \dfrac{-1 - 7m}{12}$
Substitute into the second equation to eliminate n.
$5m - 3\left(\dfrac{-1 - 7m}{12}\right) = 7$
$5m - \dfrac{-1 - 7m}{4} = 7$
$20m + 1 + 7m = 28$
$27m = 27$
$m = 1$
$n = \dfrac{-1 - 7(1)}{12}$
$n = -\dfrac{2}{3}$
Solution: $m = 1$, $n = -\dfrac{2}{3}$

25. $y = 0.08x$
$y = 100 + 0.04x$
Substitute y from the first equation into the second equation to eliminate y.
$0.08x = 100 + 0.04x$
$0.04x = 100$
$x = 2{,}500$
$y = 0.08(2{,}500)$
$y = 200$
Solution: $x = 2{,}500$, $y = 200$

27. $\dfrac{2}{5}x + \dfrac{3}{2}y = 2$

$\dfrac{7}{3}x - \dfrac{5}{4}y = -5$

Eliminate fractions by multiplying both sides of the first equation by 10 and both sides of the second equation by 12.

$$10\left(\dfrac{2}{5}x + \dfrac{3}{2}y\right) = 20$$

$$4x + 15y = 20$$

$$12\left(\dfrac{7}{3}x - \dfrac{5}{4}y\right) = -60$$

$$28x - 15y = -60$$

Solve the first equation for y in terms of x and substitute into the second equation to eliminate y.

$$15y = 20 - 4x$$

$$y = \dfrac{20 - 4x}{15}$$

$$28x - 15\left(\dfrac{20 - 4x}{15}\right) = -60$$

$$28x - (20 - 4x) = -60$$

$$28x - 20 + 4x = -60$$

$$32x = -40$$

$$x = -\dfrac{5}{4}$$

$$y = \dfrac{20 - 4\left(-\frac{5}{4}\right)}{15} = \dfrac{20 + 5}{15} = \dfrac{5}{3}$$ Solution: $x = -\dfrac{5}{4},\ y = \dfrac{5}{3}$

29. $-2.3y + 4.1z = -14.21$

$10.1y - 2.9z = 26.15$

If we multiply the top equation by 2.9 and the bottom equation by 4.1, and add, we can eliminate z.

$$-6.67y + 11.89z = -41.209$$

$$\underline{41.41y - 11.89z = 107.215}$$

$$34.74y \qquad\quad = 66.006$$

$$y = 1.9$$

Now substitute $y = 1.9$ back into the first equation and solve for z.

$$-2.3(1.9) + 4.1z = -14.21$$

$$-4.37 + 4.1z = -14.21$$

$$4.1z = -9.84$$

$$z = -2.4$$

31. $-2x = 2 \qquad E_1$

$x - 3y = 2 \qquad E_2$

$-x + 2y + 3z = -7 \qquad E_3$

Solve E_1 for x.

$$-2x = 2 \qquad E_1$$

$$x = -1$$

Substitute $x = -1$ in E_2 and solve for y.

$$x - 3y = 2 \qquad E_2$$

$$-1 - 3y = 2$$

$$y = -1$$

Substitute $x = -1$ and $y = -1$ in E_3 and solve for z.

$$-x + 2y + 3z = -7 \qquad E_3$$

$$-(-1) + 2(-1) + 3z = -7$$

$$z = -2 \qquad\qquad (-1, -1, -2)$$

33. $2y - z = 2 \qquad E_1$

$-4y + 2z = 1 \qquad E_2$

$x - 2y + 3z = 0 \qquad E_3$

Multiply E_1 by 2 and add to E_2

$$4y - 2z = 4 \qquad 2E_1$$

$$\underline{-4y + 2z = 1} \qquad E_2$$

$$0 = 5 \qquad E_4$$

A contradiction. No solution.

35. $x - 3y = 2 \qquad E_1$

$2y + z = -1 \qquad E_2$

$x - y + z = 1 \qquad E_3$

Multiply E_1 by -1 and add to E_3 to eliminate x.

$$-x + 3y = -2 \qquad (-1)E_1$$

$$\underline{x - y + z = 1} \qquad E_3$$

$$2y + z = -1 \qquad E_4$$

Equivalent system:

$$x - 3y = 2 \qquad E_1$$

$$2y + z = -1 \qquad E_2$$

$$2y + z = -1 \qquad E_4$$

If E_2 is multiplied by -1 and added to E_4, $0 = 0$ results. The system is dependent and equivalent to

$$x - 3y = 2$$

$$2y + z = -1$$

Let $y = s$. Then

$$2s + z = -1$$

$$z = -2s - 1$$

$$x - 3s = 2$$

$$x = 3s + 2$$

Solutions: $\{(3s + 2,\ s,\ -2s - 1)\mid s$ is any real number$\}$

37.

$$2x \quad + z = -5 \qquad E_1$$
$$x \quad - 3z = -6 \qquad E_2$$
$$4x + 2y - z = -9 \qquad E_3$$

Multiply E_1 by 3 and add to E_2 to eliminate z.

$$6x \quad + 3z = -15 \qquad 3E_1$$
$$x \quad - 3z = -6 \qquad E_2$$
$$7x \qquad = -21 \qquad E_4$$
$$x = -3$$

Substitute $x = -3$ into E_1 and solve for z.

$$2x \quad + z = -5 \qquad E_1$$
$$2(-3) \quad + z = -5$$
$$z = 1$$

Substitute $x = -3$ and $z = 1$ into E_3 and solve for y.

$$4(-3) + 2y - 1 = -9$$
$$y = 2$$
$$(-3, 2, 1)$$

41.

$$2a + 4b + 3c = -6 \qquad E_1$$
$$a - 3b + 2c = -15 \qquad E_2$$
$$-a + 2b - c = 9 \qquad E_3$$

Add E_2 to E_3 to eliminate a. Also multiply E_2 by -2 and add to E_1 to eliminate a.

$$a - 3b + 2c = -15 \qquad E_2$$
$$\underline{-a + 2b - c = 9} \qquad E_3$$
$$-b + c = -6 \qquad E_4$$

$$-2a + 6b - 4c = 30 \qquad (-2)E_2$$
$$\underline{2a + 4b + 3c = -6} \qquad E_1$$
$$10b - c = 24 \qquad E_5$$

Equivalent system:

$$a - 3b + 2c = -15 \qquad E_2$$
$$-b + c = -6 \qquad E_4$$
$$10b - c = 24 \qquad E_5$$

39.

$$x - y + z = 1 \qquad E_1$$
$$2x + y + z = 6 \qquad E_2$$
$$7x - y + 5z = 15 \qquad E_3$$

Multiply E_1 by -2 and add to E_2 to eliminate x.
Also multiply E_1 by -7 and add to E_3 to eliminate x.

$$-2x + 2y - 2z = -2 \qquad (-2)E_1$$
$$\underline{2x + y + z = 6} \qquad E_2$$
$$3y - z = 4 \qquad E_4$$

$$-7x + 7y - 7z = -7 \qquad (-7)E_1$$
$$\underline{7x - y + 5z = 15} \qquad E_3$$
$$6y - 2z = 8 \qquad E_5$$

Equivalent system:

$$x - y + z = 1 \qquad E_1$$
$$3y - z = 4 \qquad E_4$$
$$6y - 2z = 8 \qquad E_5$$

If E_4 is multiplied by -2 and added to E_5, $0 = 0$
results. The system is dependent and equivalent to

$$x - y + z = 1$$
$$3y - z = 4$$

Let $y = s$. Then $3s - z = 4$
$$z = 3s - 4$$
$$x - s + (3s - 4) = 1$$
$$x = -2s + 5$$

Solutions: $\{(-2s + 5, s, 3s - 4) \mid s \text{ is any real number}\}$

Add E_4 to E_5 to eliminate c

$$-b + c = -6 \qquad E_4$$
$$\underline{10b - c = 24} \qquad E_5$$
$$9b = 18$$
$$b = 2$$

Substitute $b = 2$ into E_4 and solve for c.

$$-b + c = -6 \qquad E_4$$
$$-2 + c = -6$$
$$c = -4$$

Substitute $b = 2$ and $c = -4$ into E_2 and solve for a.

$$a - 3b + 2c = -15 \qquad E_2$$
$$a - 3(2) + 2(-4) = -15$$
$$a = -1$$
$$(-1, 2, -4)$$

43.
$$2x - 3y + 3z = -5 \qquad E_1$$
$$3x + 2y - 5z = 34 \qquad E_2$$
$$5x - 4y - 2z = 23 \qquad E_3$$

Multiply E_1 by $-\dfrac{3}{2}$ and add to E_2 to eliminate x.

Also multiply E_1 by $-\dfrac{5}{2}$ and add to E_3 to eliminate x.

$$-3x + \frac{9}{2}y - \frac{9}{2}z = \frac{15}{2} \qquad \left(-\frac{3}{2}\right)E_1$$
$$\underline{3x + 2y - 5z = 34 \qquad E_2}$$
$$\frac{13}{2}y - \frac{19}{2}z = \frac{83}{2} \qquad E_4$$

$$-5x + \frac{15}{2}y - \frac{15}{2}z = \frac{25}{2} \qquad \left(-\frac{5}{2}\right)E_1$$
$$\underline{5x - 4y - 2z = 23 \qquad E_3}$$
$$\frac{7}{2}y - \frac{19}{2}z = \frac{71}{2} \qquad E_5$$

Equivalent system:
$$2x - 3y + 3z = -5 \qquad E_1$$
$$\frac{13}{2}y - \frac{19}{2}z = \frac{83}{2} \qquad E_4$$
$$\frac{7}{2}y - \frac{19}{2}z = \frac{71}{2} \qquad E_5$$

45.
$$-x + 2y - z = -4 \qquad E_1$$
$$2x + 5y - 4z = -16 \qquad E_2$$
$$x + y - z = -4 \qquad E_3$$

Multiply E_1 by 2 and add to E_2 to eliminate x. Also add E_1 to E_3 to eliminate x.

$$-2x + 4y - 2z = -8 \qquad 2E_1$$
$$\underline{2x + 5y - 4z = -16 \qquad E_2}$$
$$9y - 6z = -24 \qquad E_4$$
$$-x + 2y - z = -4 \qquad E_1$$
$$\underline{x + y - z = -4 \qquad E_3}$$
$$3y - 2z = -8 \qquad E_5$$

Equivalent system:
$$-x + 2y - z = -4 \quad E_1$$
$$9y - 6z = -24 \quad E_4$$
$$3y - 2z = -8 \quad E_5$$

47.
$$x = 2 + p - 2q$$
$$y = 3 - p + 3q$$
Solve the first equation for p in terms of q, x, and y and substitute into the second equation to eliminate p, then solve for q in terms of x and y.
$$p = x - 2 + 2q$$
$$y = 3 - (x - 2 + 2q) + 3q$$
$$y = 3 - x + 2 - 2q + 3q$$

Multiply E_4 by -1 and add to E_5 to eliminate z.

$$-\frac{13}{2}y + \frac{19}{2}z = -\frac{83}{2} \qquad (-1)E_4$$
$$\underline{\frac{7}{2}y - \frac{19}{2}z = \frac{71}{2} \qquad E_5}$$
$$-3y = -6 \qquad E_6$$

Solve E_6 for y to obtain $y = 2$. Substitute $y = 2$ into E_4 and solve for z.

$$\frac{13}{2}y - \frac{19}{2}z = \frac{83}{2} \quad E_4$$
$$\frac{13}{2}(2) - \frac{19}{2}z = \frac{83}{2}$$
$$-\frac{19}{2}z = \frac{57}{2}$$
$$z = -3$$

Substitute $y = 2$ and $z = -3$ into E_1 and solve for x.
$$2x - 3y + 3z = -5 \quad E_1$$
$$2x - 3(2) + 3(-3) = -5$$
$$x = 5$$

$(5, 2, -3)$

If E_5 is multiplied by -3 and added to E_4, $0 = 0$ results. The system is dependent and equivalent to
$$-x + 2y - z = -4$$
$$3y - 2z = -8$$
Let $z = s$. Then
$$3y - 2s = -8$$
$$y = \frac{2s - 8}{3} \text{ or } \frac{2}{3}s - \frac{8}{3}$$
$$-x + 2\left(\frac{2}{3}s - \frac{8}{3}\right) - s = -4$$
$$-x = -\frac{4}{3}s + \frac{16}{3} + s - 4$$
$$x = \frac{1}{3}s - \frac{4}{3}$$

Solutions: $\left\{\left(\dfrac{1}{3}s - \dfrac{4}{3}, \dfrac{2}{3}s - \dfrac{8}{3}, s\right) \middle| s \text{ is any real number}\right\}$

$$y = 5 - x + q$$
$$q = x + y - 5$$

Now substitute this expression for q into $p = x - 2 + 2q$ to find p in terms of x and y.

$$p = x - 2 + 2(x + y - 5)$$
$$p = x - 2 + 2x + 2y - 10$$
$$p = 3x + 2y - 12 \qquad \text{Solution: } p = 3x + 2y - 12, \, q = x + y - 5$$

To check this solution substitute into the original equations to see if true statements result:

$$x = 2 + p - 2q$$

$$x \overset{?}{=} 2 + (3x + 2y - 12) - 2(x + y - 5)$$

$$x \overset{?}{=} 2 + 3x + 2y - 12 - 2x - 2y + 10$$

$$x \overset{\surd}{=} x$$

$$y = 3 - p + 3q$$

$$y \overset{?}{=} 3 - (3x + 2y - 12) + 3(x + y - 5)$$

$$y \overset{?}{=} 3 - 3x - 2y + 12 + 3x + 3y - 15$$

$$y \overset{\surd}{=} y$$

49. $\quad ax + by = h$
$\qquad cx + dy = k$

Solve the first equation for x in terms of y and the constants.

$$ax = h - by$$

$$x = \frac{h - by}{a} \quad (a \neq 0)$$

Substitute this expression into the second equation to eliminate x.

$$c\left(\frac{h - by}{a}\right) + dy = k$$

$$ac\left(\frac{h - by}{a}\right) + ady = ak$$

$$c(h - by) + ady = ak$$

$$ch - bcy + ady = ak$$

$$(ad - bc)y = ak - ch$$

$$y = \frac{ak - ch}{ad - bc}$$

$$ad - bc \neq 0$$

Similarly, solve the first equation for y in terms of x and the constants.

$$by = h - ax$$

$$y = \frac{h - ax}{b} \quad (b \neq 0)$$

Substitute this expression into the second equation to eliminate y.

$$cx + d\left(\frac{h - ax}{b}\right) = k$$

$$bcx + bd\left(\frac{h - ax}{b}\right) = bk$$

$$bcx + d(h - ax) = bk$$

$$bcx + dh - adx = bk$$

$$(bc - ad)x = bk - dh$$

$$x = \frac{bk - dh}{bc - ad} \quad bc - ad \neq 0$$

or, for consistency with the expression for y, $x = \dfrac{dh - bk}{ad - bc}$

Solution: $x = \dfrac{dh - bk}{ad - bc}, y = \dfrac{ak - ch}{ad - bc} \quad ad - bc \neq 0$

51. Let x = airspeed of the plane
$\qquad y$ = rate at which wind is blowing

Then $x - y$ = ground speed flying from Atlanta to Los Angeles (head wind)

$\qquad x + y$ = ground speed flying from Los Angeles to Atlanta (tail wind)

Then, applying Distance = Rate × Time, we have

$$2,100 = 8.75(x - y)$$
$$2,100 = 5(x + y)$$

After simplification, we have

$$x - y = 240$$
$$x + y = 420$$

Solve the first equation for x in terms of y and substitute into the second equation. $\quad x = 240 + y$

$$240 + y + y = 420$$
$$2y = 180$$
$$y = 90 \text{ mph} = \text{wind rate}$$
$$x = 240 + y$$
$$x = 240 + 90$$
$$x = 330 \text{ mph} = \text{airspeed}$$

53. Let x = time rowed upstream
y = time rowed downstream
Then $x + y = \dfrac{1}{4}$ (15 min $= \dfrac{1}{4}$ hr.)
Since   rate upstream = 20 – 2 = 18 mph and
rate downstream = 20 + 2 = 22 mph,
applying Distance = Rate × Time to the equal
distances upstream and downstream, we have
$18x = 22y$
Solve the first equation for y in terms of x and
substitute into the second equation.
$$y = \dfrac{1}{4} - x$$
$$18x = 22\left(\dfrac{1}{4} - x\right)$$
$$18x = 5.5 - 22x$$
$$40x = 5.5$$
$$x = 0.1375 \text{ hr.}$$
Then the distance rowed upstream
$$= 18x = 18(0.1375) = 2.475 \text{ km.}$$

55.   Let x = amount of first batch
y = amount of second batch
Then the amount of dark chocolate in any mix of these will
be $0.5x + 0.8y$, hence in 100 pounds of a 68% dark
chocolate mix
$0.5x + 0.8y = 0.68(100)$
Also, the amount of milk chocolate in any mix of these will
be $0.5x + 0.2y$, hence since 100 – 68 = 32 percent
$0.5x + 0.2y = 0.32(100)$
For convenience, eliminate decimals by multiplying both
sides of both equations by 10.
$5x + 8y = 680$
$5x + 2y = 320$
If we multiply the second equation by –1 and add, we can
eliminate x.
$$\begin{array}{r} 5x + 8y = 680 \\ \underline{-5x - 2y = -320} \\ 6y = 360 \\ y = 60 \end{array}$$
Since there are 100 pounds in the mix, clearly $x = 40$.
$x = 40$ lbs. of 50–50 mix, $y = 60$ lbs. of 80–20 mix.

57. "Break even" means Cost = Revenue.
Let y = Cost = Revenue.
Let x = number of CDs sold
y = Revenue = number of CDs sold × price per CD
$y = x(8.00)$
y = Cost = Fixed Cost + Variable Cost = 17,680 + number of CDs × cost per CD
$y = 17,680 + x(4.60)$
Substitute y from the first equation into the second equation to eliminate y.
$8.00x = 17,680 + 4.60x$
$3.40x = 17,680$
$$x = \dfrac{17,680}{3.40}$$
$x = 5,200$ CDs

59.   Let x = number of hours Mexico plant is operated
y = number of hours Taiwan plant is operated
Then (Production at Mexico plant)   + (Production at Taiwan plant)   = (Total Production)
$40x$ + $20y$ = 4000 (keyboards)
$32x$ + $32y$ = 4000 (screens)
Solve the first equation for y in terms of x and substitute into the second equation.
$$20y = 4,000 - 40x$$
$$y = 200 - 2x$$
$$32x + 32(200 - 2x) = 4,000$$
$$32x + 6,400 - 64x = 4,000$$
$$-32x = -2,400$$
$$x = 75 \text{ hours Mexico plant}$$
$$y = 200 - 2x = 200 - 2(75) = 50 \text{ hours Taiwan plant}$$

61. (A) If $p = 4$, then $4 = 0.007q + 3$, $q = \dfrac{1}{0.007} = 143$ T–shirts is the number that suppliers are willing to

supply at this price.

$4 = -0.018q + 15$, $q = \dfrac{11}{0.018} = 611$ T–shirts is the number that consumers will purchase.

Demand exceeds supply and the price will rise.

(B) If $p = 8$, then $8 = 0.007q + 3$, $q = \dfrac{5}{0.007} = 714$ T–shirts is the number that suppliers are willing to

supply.

$8 = -0.018q + 15$, $q = \dfrac{7}{0.018} = 389$ T–shirts is the number that consumers will purchase at this price.

Supply exceeds demand and the price will fall.

(C) Solve $p = 0.007q + 3$

$\qquad p = -0.018q + 15$

Substitute the expression for p in terms of q from the first
equation into the second equation.

$\quad 0.007q + 3 = -0.018q + 15$

$\quad 0.025q + 3 = 15$

$\qquad\quad 0.025q = 12$

$\qquad\qquad q = 480$ T–shirts is the equilibrium quantity.

$\qquad\qquad p = 0.007(480) + 3 = \$6.36$ is the equilibrium price.

(D)

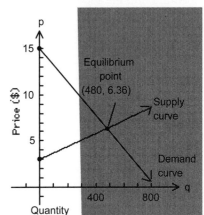

63. (A) Write $p = aq + b$.

Since $p = 0.60$ corresponds to supply $q = 450$, $0.60 = 450a + b$

Since $p = 0.90$ corresponds to supply $q = 750$, $0.90 = 750a + b$

Solve the first equation for b in terms of a and substitute into the second equation.

$\qquad b = 0.60 - 450a$

$\quad 0.90 = 750a + 0.60 - 450a$

$\quad 0.30 = 300a$

$\qquad a = 0.001$

$\qquad b = 0.60 - 450a = 0.60 - 450(0.001) = 0.15$

Thus, the supply equation is $p = 0.001q + 0.15$.

(B) Write $p = cq + d$.

Since $p = 0.60$ corresponds to demand $q = 645$, $0.60 = 645c + d$

Since $p = 0.90$ corresponds to demand $q = 495$, $0.90 = 495c + d$

Solve the first equation for d in terms of c and substitute into the second equation.

$\qquad d = 0.60 - 645c$

$\quad 0.90 = 495c + 0.60 - 645c$

$\quad 0.30 = -150c$

$\qquad c = -0.002$

$\qquad d = 0.60 - 645c = 0.60 - 645(-0.002) = 1.89$

Thus, the demand equation is $p = -0.002q + 1.89$.

(C) Solve the system of equations

$\qquad p = 0.001q + 0.15$

$\qquad p = -0.002q + 1.89$

Substitute p from the first equation into the second equation to eliminate p.

$\quad 0.001q + 0.15 = -0.002q + 1.89$

$\qquad\qquad 0.003q = 1.74$

$\qquad\qquad\quad q = 580$ bushels = equilibrium quantity

$\qquad\qquad\quad p = 0.001q + 0.15 = 0.001(580) + 0.15 = \$0.73$ equilibrium price

65. Let p = time of primary wave
  s = time for secondary wave
We know $s - p = 16$ (time difference)
To find a second equation, we have to use Distance = Rate $\times$ Time
  $5p$ = distance for primary wave
  $3s$ = distance for secondary wave
These distances are equal, hence $5p = 3s$
Solve the first equation for s in terms of p and substitute into the second equation to eliminate s.
  $s = p + 16$
  $5p = 3(p + 16)$
  $5p = 3p + 48$
  $2p = 48$
  $p = 24$ seconds
  $s = 24 + 16$
  $s = 40$ seconds
The distance traveled = $5p = 3s = 120$ miles

67. Let x = number of lawn mowers manufactured each week
  y = number of snowblowers manufactured each week
  z = number of chain saws manufactured each week
Then
$E_1 \quad 20x + 30y + 45z = 35,000$ Labor
$E_2 \quad 35x + 50y + 40z = 50,000$ Materials
$E_3 \quad 15x + 25y + 10z = 20,000$ Shipping
Multiply E_3 by -4.5 and add to E_1 to eliminate z. Also multiply E_3 by -4 and add to E_2 to eliminate z.

$$
\begin{array}{ll}
20x + 30y + 45z = 35,000 & E_1 \\
\underline{-67.5x - 112.5y - 45z = -90,000} & (-4.5)E_3 \\
-47.5x - 82.5y \qquad\;\; = -55,000 & E_4 \\
35x + 50y + 40z = 50,000 & E_2 \\
\underline{-60x - 100y - 40z = -80,000} & (-4)E_3 \\
-25x - 50y \qquad\;\;\;\; = -30,000 & E_5
\end{array}
$$

Equivalent system:
$$
\begin{array}{ll}
15x + 25y + 10z = 20,000 & E_3 \\
-47.5x - 82.5y \qquad = -55,000 & E_4 \\
-25x - 50y \qquad\;\; = -30,000 & E_5
\end{array}
$$
Multiply E_5 by -1.9 and add to E_4 to eliminate x.
$$
\begin{array}{ll}
47.5x + 95y \;\; = 57,000 & (-1.9)E_5 \\
\underline{-47.5x - 82.5y = -55,000} & E_4 \\
12.5y = 2,000 & \\
y = 160 &
\end{array}
$$
Substitute $y = 160$ into E_5 and solve for x.
$$
\begin{array}{ll}
-25x - 50y \qquad = -30,000 & E_5 \\
-25x - 50(160) = -30,000 & \\
x = 880 &
\end{array}
$$
Substitute $x = 880$ and $y = 160$ into E_3 and solve for z.
$$
\begin{array}{ll}
15x + 25y + 10z = 20,000 & E_3 \\
15(880) + 25(160) + 10z = 20,000 & \\
z = 280 &
\end{array}
$$
880 lawn mowers, 160 snow blowers, 280 chain saws.

69. Let x = number of days operating the Michigan plant

y = number of days operating the New York plant

z = number of days operating the Ohio plant

Then

E_1	$10x + 70y + 60z = 2{,}150$	Notebooks
E_2	$20x + 50y + 80z = 2{,}300$	Desktops
E_3	$40x + 30y + 90z = 2{,}500$	Servers

Multiply E_1 by -2 and add to E_2 to eliminate x. Also multiply E_1 by -4 and add to E_3 to eliminate x.

$$-20x - 140y - 120z = -4{,}300 \qquad (-2)E_1$$
$$\underline{20x + 50y + 80z = 2{,}300} \qquad E_2$$
$$-90y - 40z = -2{,}000 \qquad E_4$$

$$-40x - 280y - 240z = -8{,}600 \qquad (-4)E_1$$
$$\underline{40x + 30y + 90z = 2{,}500} \qquad E_3$$
$$-250y - 150z = -6{,}100 \qquad E_5$$

Equivalent system:

$$10x + 70y + 60z = 2{,}150 \qquad E_1$$
$$-90y - 40z = -2{,}000 \qquad E_4$$
$$-250y - 150z = -6{,}100 \qquad E_5$$

Multiply E_5 by -0.36 and add to E_4 to eliminate y.

$$-90y - 40z = -2{,}000 \qquad E_4$$
$$\underline{90y + 54z = 2{,}196} \qquad (0.36)E_5$$
$$14z = 196$$
$$z = 14$$

Substitute $z = 14$ into E_4 and solve for y.

$$-90y - 40z = -2{,}000 \qquad E_4$$
$$-90y - 40(14) = -2{,}000$$
$$y = 16$$

Substitute $y = 16$ and $z = 14$ into E_1 and solve for x.

$$10x + 70y + 60z = 2{,}150 \qquad E_1$$
$$10x + 70(16) + 60(14) = 2{,}150$$
$$x = 19$$

19 days Michigan plant, 16 days New York plant, 14 days Ohio plant

71. Let

 x = amount invested in treasury bonds at 4%
 y = amount invested in municipal bonds at 3.5%
 z = amount invested in corporate bonds at 4.5%

Then

E_1	$x + y + z = 70,000$	total investment
E_2	$0.04x + 0.035y + 0.045z = 2,900$	interest income
E_3	$x = y + z$	tax considerations

Multiply E_2 by 1,000 and rewrite E_3 to obtain:

$$\begin{aligned} x + y + z &= 70,000 \qquad\qquad E_1\\ 40x + 35y + 45z &= 2,900,000 \qquad E_4\\ x - y - z &= 0 \qquad\qquad\quad E_5 \end{aligned}$$

Add E_1 and E_5 to eliminate y and z.

$$\begin{aligned} x + y + z &= 70,000 \qquad E_1\\ \underline{x - y - z = 0} &\qquad\qquad\quad E_5\\ 2x &= 70,000\\ x &= 35,000 \end{aligned}$$

Substitute $x = 35,000$ into E_1 and E_4

$$\begin{aligned} 35,000 + y + z &= 70,000\\ 40(35,000) + 35y + 45z &= 2,900,000 \end{aligned}$$

Simplify to obtain

$$\begin{aligned} y + z &= 35,000 \qquad\qquad E_6\\ 35y + 45z &= 1,500,000 \qquad E_7 \end{aligned}$$

Multiply E_6 by -35 and add to E_7 to eliminate y.

$$\begin{aligned} -35y - 35z &= -1,225,000 \qquad (-35)E_6\\ \underline{35y + 45z = 1,500,000} &\qquad\qquad\quad E_7\\ 10z &= 275,000\\ z &= 27,500 \end{aligned}$$

Substitute $z = 27,500$ into E_6 and solve for y.

$$\begin{aligned} y + 27,500 &= 35,000\\ y &= 7,500 \end{aligned}$$

$35,000 treasury bonds, $7,500 municipal bonds, $27,500 corporate bonds.

SECTION 7–2

1. The size of a matrix is given by $m \times n$, where m is the number of rows and n is the number of columns.

3. A column matrix is a matrix with only one column. Its size is given by $m \times 1$, where m is the number of rows.

5. a_{ij} is the element in row i, column j of a matrix.

7. The augmented coefficient matrix of a system of equations is the coefficient matrix with one added column, the column of constants.

9. The reduced matrix of a system is a matrix row–equivalent to the augmented coefficient matrix, from which the solutions of the system can be directly read off.

11. No. Condition 2 is violated.   **13.** Yes   **15.** No. Condition 4 is violated.   **17.** Yes

19. $\begin{aligned} x_1 &= -2\\ x_2 &= 3\\ x_3 &= 0 \quad \text{The system is already solved.} \end{aligned}$

21.
$$x_1 \quad - 2x_3 = 3$$
$$x_2 + x_3 = -5$$

Solution:
$x_3 = t$
$x_2 = -5 - x_3 = -5 - t$
$x_1 = 3 + 2x_3 = 3 + 2t$
Thus $x_1 = 2t + 3$, $x_2 = -t - 5$, $x_3 = t$ is the solution for t any real number.

23.
$$x_1 \qquad = 0$$
$$x_2 \qquad = 0$$
$$0 \qquad = 1$$
The system has no solution.

25.
$$x_1 - 2x_2 \quad - 3x_4 = -5$$
$$x_3 + 3x_4 = 2$$
Solution:
$x_4 = t$
$x_3 = 2 - 3x_4 = 2 - 3t$
$x_2 = s$
$x_1 = -5 + 2x_2 + 3x_4 = -5 + 2s + 3t$
Thus $x_1 = 2s + 3t - 5$, $x_2 = s$, $x_3 = -3t + 2$, $x_4 = t$
is the solution, for s and t any real numbers.

27. $R_1 \leftrightarrow R_2$ means interchange Rows 1 and 2.
$$\begin{bmatrix} 4 & -6 & | & -8 \\ 1 & -3 & | & 2 \end{bmatrix}$$

29. $-4R_1 \rightarrow R_1$ means multiply Row 1 by -4.
$$\begin{bmatrix} -4 & 12 & | & -8 \\ 4 & -6 & | & -8 \end{bmatrix}$$

31. $2R_2 \rightarrow R_2$ means multiply Row 2 by 2.
$$\begin{bmatrix} 1 & -3 & | & 2 \\ 8 & -12 & | & -16 \end{bmatrix}$$

33. $(-4)R_1 + R_2 \rightarrow R_2$ means replace Row 2 by itself plus -4 times Row 1.
$$\begin{bmatrix} 1 & -3 & | & 2 \\ 4 & -6 & | & -8 \end{bmatrix} \rightarrow \begin{bmatrix} 1 & -3 & | & 2 \\ 0 & 6 & | & -16 \end{bmatrix}$$
$$-4 \quad 12 \quad -8$$

35. $(-2)R_1 + R_2 \rightarrow R_2$ means replace Row 2 by itself plus -2 times Row 1.
$$\begin{bmatrix} 1 & -3 & | & 2 \\ 4 & -6 & | & -8 \end{bmatrix} \rightarrow \begin{bmatrix} 1 & -3 & | & 2 \\ 2 & 0 & | & -12 \end{bmatrix}$$
$$-2 \quad 6 \quad -4$$

37. $(-1)R_1 + R_2 \rightarrow R_2$ means replace Row 2 by itself plus -1 times Row 1.
$$\begin{bmatrix} 1 & -3 & | & 2 \\ 4 & -6 & | & -8 \end{bmatrix} \rightarrow \begin{bmatrix} 1 & -3 & | & 2 \\ 3 & -3 & | & -10 \end{bmatrix}$$
$$-1 \quad 3 \quad -2$$

39. $\begin{bmatrix} 1 & 2 & | & -1 \\ 0 & 1 & | & 3 \end{bmatrix}$ $(-2)R_2 + R_1 \rightarrow R_1$

Need a 0 here
$$\sim \begin{bmatrix} 1 & 0 & | & -7 \\ 0 & 1 & | & 3 \end{bmatrix}$$

41.
$$\begin{bmatrix} 1 & 0 & -3 & | & 1 \\ 0 & 1 & 2 & | & 0 \\ 0 & 0 & 3 & | & -6 \end{bmatrix} \tfrac{1}{3}R_3 \rightarrow R_3$$
↑
Need a 1 here
Need 0's here
↓
$$\sim \begin{bmatrix} 1 & 0 & -3 & | & 1 \\ 0 & 1 & 2 & | & 0 \\ 0 & 0 & 1 & | & -2 \end{bmatrix} \begin{array}{l} 3R_3 + R_1 \rightarrow R_1 \\ (-2)R_3 + R_2 \rightarrow R_2 \end{array}$$
$$\sim \begin{bmatrix} 1 & 0 & 0 & | & -5 \\ 0 & 1 & 0 & | & 4 \\ 0 & 0 & 1 & | & -2 \end{bmatrix}$$

43.
$$\begin{bmatrix} 1 & 2 & -2 & | & -1 \\ 0 & 3 & -6 & | & 1 \\ 0 & -1 & 2 & | & -\frac{1}{3} \end{bmatrix} \frac{1}{3}R_2 \rightarrow R_2$$

Need a 1 here

$$\sim \begin{bmatrix} 1 & 2 & -2 & | & -1 \\ 0 & 1 & -2 & | & \frac{1}{3} \\ 0 & -1 & 2 & | & -\frac{1}{3} \end{bmatrix} \begin{matrix} (-2)R_2 + R_1 \rightarrow R_1 \\ \\ R_3 + R_2 \rightarrow R_3 \end{matrix}$$

Need 0's here

$$\sim \begin{bmatrix} 1 & 0 & 2 & | & -\frac{5}{3} \\ 0 & 1 & -2 & | & \frac{1}{3} \\ 0 & 0 & 0 & | & 0 \end{bmatrix}$$

45.
$$\begin{bmatrix} 1 & -4 & | & -2 \\ -2 & 1 & | & -3 \end{bmatrix} \; 2R_1 + R_2 \rightarrow R_2$$

Need a 0 here
2 -8 -4

$$\sim \begin{bmatrix} 1 & -4 & | & -2 \\ 0 & -7 & | & -7 \end{bmatrix} \; -\frac{1}{7}R_2 \rightarrow R_2$$

Need a 1 here
Need a 0 here
$\downarrow$

$$\sim \begin{bmatrix} 1 & -4 & | & -2 \\ 0 & 1 & | & 1 \end{bmatrix} \; 4R_2 + R_1 \rightarrow R_1$$

0 4 4

$$\sim \begin{bmatrix} 1 & 0 & | & 2 \\ 0 & 1 & | & 1 \end{bmatrix} \qquad \text{Therefore } x_1 = 2 \text{ and } x_2 = 1$$

47.
$$\begin{bmatrix} 1 & 2 & | & 4 \\ 2 & 4 & | & -8 \end{bmatrix} \; (-2)R_1 + R_2 \rightarrow R_2$$

$\uparrow$
Need a 0 here
-2 -4 -8

$$\sim \begin{bmatrix} 1 & 2 & | & 4 \\ 0 & 0 & | & -16 \end{bmatrix}$$

This matrix corresponds to the system
$x_1 + 2x_2 = 4$
$0x_1 + 0x_2 = -16$
This system has no solution.

49.
$$\begin{bmatrix} 3 & -6 & | & -9 \\ -2 & 4 & | & 6 \end{bmatrix} \; \frac{1}{3}R_1 \rightarrow R_1$$

Need a 1 here

$$\sim \begin{bmatrix} 1 & -2 & | & -3 \\ -2 & 4 & | & 6 \end{bmatrix} \; -2R_1 + R_2 \rightarrow R_2$$

Need a 0 here
2 -4 -6

$$\sim \begin{bmatrix} 1 & -2 & | & -3 \\ 0 & 0 & | & 0 \end{bmatrix}$$

This matrix corresponds to the system
$x_1 - 2x_2 = -3$
$0x_1 + 0x_2 = 0$
Thus $x_1 = 2x_2 - 3$.
Hence there are infinitely many solutions: for any real number s, $x_2 = s$, $x_1 = 2s - 3$ is a solution.

51.
$$\begin{bmatrix} 2 & 4 & -10 & | & -2 \\ 3 & 9 & -21 & | & 0 \\ 1 & 5 & -12 & | & 1 \end{bmatrix} R_1 \leftrightarrow R_3$$

Need a 1 here

$$\sim \begin{bmatrix} 1 & 5 & -12 & | & 1 \\ 3 & 9 & -21 & | & 0 \\ 2 & 4 & -10 & | & -2 \end{bmatrix} \begin{matrix} (-3)R_1 + R_2 \to R_2 \\ (-2)R_1 + R_3 \to R_3 \end{matrix}$$

Need 0's here

$$\sim \begin{bmatrix} 1 & 5 & -12 & | & 1 \\ 0 & -6 & 15 & | & -3 \\ 0 & -6 & 14 & | & -4 \end{bmatrix} -\tfrac{1}{6}R_2 \to R_2$$

Need a 1 here

$$\sim \begin{bmatrix} 1 & 5 & -12 & | & 1 \\ 0 & 1 & -\tfrac{5}{2} & | & \tfrac{1}{2} \\ 0 & -6 & 14 & | & -4 \end{bmatrix} \begin{matrix} (-5)R_2 + R_1 \to R_1 \\ \\ 6R_2 + R_3 \to R_3 \end{matrix}$$

Need 0's here

$$\sim \begin{bmatrix} 1 & 0 & \tfrac{1}{2} & | & -\tfrac{3}{2} \\ 0 & 1 & -\tfrac{5}{2} & | & \tfrac{1}{2} \\ 0 & 0 & -1 & | & -1 \end{bmatrix} -R_3 \to R_3$$

Need a 1 here

$$\sim \begin{bmatrix} 1 & 0 & \tfrac{1}{2} & | & -\tfrac{3}{2} \\ 0 & 1 & -\tfrac{5}{2} & | & \tfrac{1}{2} \\ 0 & 0 & 1 & | & 1 \end{bmatrix} \begin{matrix} (-\tfrac{1}{2})R_3 + R_1 \to R_1 \\ \tfrac{5}{2}R_3 + R_2 \to R_2 \end{matrix}$$

Need 0's here

$$\sim \begin{bmatrix} 1 & 0 & 0 & | & -2 \\ 0 & 1 & 0 & | & 3 \\ 0 & 0 & 1 & | & 1 \end{bmatrix}$$

Therefore $x_1 = -2$, $x_2 = 3$, and $x_3 = 1$.

53.
$$\begin{bmatrix} 3 & 8 & -1 & | & -18 \\ 2 & 1 & 5 & | & 8 \\ 2 & 4 & 2 & | & -4 \end{bmatrix} \begin{matrix} \tfrac{1}{2}R_3 \to R_3 \\ \\ R_3 \leftrightarrow R_1 \end{matrix}$$

Need a 1 here

$$\sim \begin{bmatrix} 1 & 2 & 1 & | & -2 \\ 2 & 1 & 5 & | & 8 \\ 3 & 8 & -1 & | & -18 \end{bmatrix} \begin{matrix} (-2)R_1 + R_2 \to R_2 \\ (-3)R_1 + R_3 \to R_3 \end{matrix}$$

Need 0's here

$$\sim \begin{bmatrix} 1 & 2 & 1 & | & -2 \\ 0 & -3 & 3 & | & 12 \\ 0 & 2 & -4 & | & -12 \end{bmatrix} -\tfrac{1}{3}R_2 \to R_2$$

Need a 1 here

$$\sim \begin{bmatrix} 1 & 2 & 1 & | & -2 \\ 0 & 1 & -1 & | & -4 \\ 0 & 2 & -4 & | & -12 \end{bmatrix} \begin{matrix} (-2)R_2 + R_1 \to R_1 \\ \\ (-2)R_2 + R_3 \to R_3 \end{matrix}$$

Need 0's here

$$\sim \begin{bmatrix} 1 & 0 & 3 & | & 6 \\ 0 & 1 & -1 & | & -4 \\ 0 & 0 & -2 & | & -4 \end{bmatrix} -\tfrac{1}{2}R_3 \to R_3$$

Need a 1 here

$$\sim \begin{bmatrix} 1 & 0 & 3 & | & 6 \\ 0 & 1 & -1 & | & -4 \\ 0 & 0 & 1 & | & 2 \end{bmatrix} \begin{matrix} (-3)R_3 + R_1 \to R_1 \\ R_3 + R_2 \to R_2 \end{matrix}$$

Need 0's here

$$\begin{bmatrix} 1 & 0 & 0 & | & 0 \\ 0 & 1 & 0 & | & -2 \\ 0 & 0 & 1 & | & 2 \end{bmatrix}$$ Therefore $x_1 = 0$, $x_2 = -2$, and $x_3 = 2$.

55. $\begin{bmatrix} 2 & -1 & -3 & | & 8 \\ 1 & -2 & 0 & | & 7 \end{bmatrix} R_1 \leftrightarrow R_2$

$\sim \begin{bmatrix} 1 & -2 & 0 & | & 7 \\ 2 & -1 & -3 & | & 8 \end{bmatrix} (-2)R_1 + R_2 \to R_2$

$\sim \begin{bmatrix} 1 & -2 & 0 & | & 7 \\ 0 & 3 & -3 & | & -6 \end{bmatrix} \frac{1}{3}R_2 \to R_2$

$\sim \begin{bmatrix} 1 & -2 & 0 & | & 7 \\ 0 & 1 & -1 & | & -2 \end{bmatrix} 2R_2 + R_1 \to R_1 \sim \begin{bmatrix} 1 & 0 & -2 & | & 3 \\ 0 & 1 & -1 & | & -2 \end{bmatrix}$

Let $x_3 = t$. Then

$x_2 - x_3 = -2$

$\quad x_2 = x_3 - 2 = t - 2$

$x_1 - 2x_3 = 3$

$\quad x_1 = 2x_3 + 3 = 2t + 3$

Solution: $x_1 = 2t + 3$, $x_2 = t - 2$, $x_3 = t$, t any real number.

59. $\begin{bmatrix} 3 & -4 & -1 & | & 1 \\ 2 & -3 & 1 & | & 1 \\ 1 & -2 & 3 & | & 2 \end{bmatrix} R_1 \leftrightarrow R_3$

$\sim \begin{bmatrix} 1 & -2 & 3 & | & 2 \\ 2 & -3 & 1 & | & 1 \\ 3 & -4 & -1 & | & 1 \end{bmatrix} \begin{matrix} (-2)R_1 + R_2 \to R_2 \\ (-3)R_1 + R_3 \to R_3 \end{matrix}$

$\sim \begin{bmatrix} 1 & -2 & 3 & | & 2 \\ 0 & 1 & -5 & | & -3 \\ 0 & 2 & -10 & | & -5 \end{bmatrix} (-2)R_2 + R_3 \to R_3$

$\sim \begin{bmatrix} 1 & -2 & 3 & | & 2 \\ 0 & 1 & -5 & | & -3 \\ 0 & 0 & 0 & | & 1 \end{bmatrix}$

Since the last row corresponds to the equation $0x_1 + 0x_2 + 0x_3 = 1$, there is no solution.

63. $\begin{bmatrix} 2 & -5 & -3 & | & 7 \\ -4 & 10 & 2 & | & 6 \\ 6 & -15 & -1 & | & -19 \end{bmatrix} \begin{matrix} 2R_1 + R_2 \to R_2 \\ (-3)R_1 + R_3 \to R_3 \end{matrix}$

$\sim \begin{bmatrix} 2 & -5 & -3 & | & 7 \\ 0 & 0 & -4 & | & 20 \\ 0 & 0 & 8 & | & -40 \end{bmatrix} \begin{matrix} \frac{1}{2}R_1 \to R_1 \\ -\frac{1}{4}R_2 \to R_2 \end{matrix}$

$\sim \begin{bmatrix} 1 & -2.5 & -1.5 & | & 3.5 \\ 0 & 0 & 1 & | & -5 \\ 0 & 0 & 8 & | & -40 \end{bmatrix} \begin{matrix} 1.5R_2 + R_1 \to R_1 \\ (-8)R_2 + R_3 \to R_3 \end{matrix}$

$\sim \begin{bmatrix} 1 & -2.5 & 0 & | & -4 \\ 0 & 0 & 1 & | & -5 \\ 0 & 0 & 0 & | & 0 \end{bmatrix}$

57. $\begin{bmatrix} 2 & -1 & | & 0 \\ 3 & 2 & | & 7 \\ 1 & -1 & | & -1 \end{bmatrix} R_1 \leftrightarrow R_3$

$\sim \begin{bmatrix} 1 & -1 & | & -1 \\ 3 & 2 & | & 7 \\ 2 & -1 & | & 0 \end{bmatrix} \begin{matrix} (-3)R_1 + R_2 \to R_2 \\ (-2)R_1 + R_3 \to R_3 \end{matrix}$

$\sim \begin{bmatrix} 1 & -1 & | & -1 \\ 0 & 5 & | & 10 \\ 0 & 1 & | & 2 \end{bmatrix} R_2 \leftrightarrow R_3$

$\sim \begin{bmatrix} 1 & -1 & | & -1 \\ 0 & 1 & | & 2 \\ 0 & 5 & | & 10 \end{bmatrix} \begin{matrix} R_2 + R_1 \to R_1 \\ (-5)R_2 + R_3 \to R_3 \end{matrix} \sim \begin{bmatrix} 1 & 0 & | & 1 \\ 0 & 1 & | & 2 \\ 0 & 0 & | & 0 \end{bmatrix}$

Therefore $x_1 = 1$ and $x_2 = 2$.

61. $\begin{bmatrix} 2 & -2 & -4 & | & -2 \\ -3 & 3 & 6 & | & 3 \end{bmatrix} \begin{matrix} \frac{1}{2}R_1 \to R_1 \\ \frac{1}{3}R_2 \to R_2 \end{matrix}$

$\sim \begin{bmatrix} 1 & -1 & -2 & | & -1 \\ -1 & 1 & 2 & | & 1 \end{bmatrix} R_1 + R_2 \to R_2$

$\sim \begin{bmatrix} 1 & -1 & -2 & | & -1 \\ 0 & 0 & 0 & | & 0 \end{bmatrix}$

Let $x_3 = t$, $x_2 = s$. Then

$x_1 - x_2 - 2x_3 = -1$

$\quad x_1 = x_2 + 2x_3 - 1$

$\quad\quad = s + 2t - 1$

Solution: $x_1 = s + 2t - 1$, $x_2 = s$, $x_3 = t$, s and t any real numbers.

Let $x_2 = t$. Then $x_3 = -5$ and

$x_1 - 2.5x_2 = -4$

$\quad x_1 = 2.5x_2 - 4$

$\quad x_1 = 2.5t - 4$

Solution: $x_1 = 2.5t - 4$, $x_2 = t$, $x_3 = -5$, t any real number.

65.

$$\begin{bmatrix} 1 & 2 & -4 & -1 & | & 7 \\ 2 & 5 & -9 & -4 & | & 16 \\ 1 & 5 & -7 & -7 & | & 13 \end{bmatrix} \begin{matrix} \\ (-2)R_1 + R_2 \to R_2 \\ (-1)R_1 + R_3 \to R_3 \end{matrix}$$

$$\sim \begin{bmatrix} 1 & 2 & -4 & -1 & | & 7 \\ 0 & 1 & -1 & -2 & | & 2 \\ 0 & 3 & -3 & -6 & | & 6 \end{bmatrix} \begin{matrix} (-2)R_2 + R_1 \to R_1 \\ \\ (-3)R_2 + R_3 \to R_3 \end{matrix}$$

$$\sim \begin{bmatrix} 1 & 0 & -2 & 3 & | & 3 \\ 0 & 1 & -1 & -2 & | & 2 \\ 0 & 0 & 0 & 0 & | & 0 \end{bmatrix}$$

Let $x_4 = t$, $x_3 = s$. Then

$$x_2 - x_3 - 2x_4 = 2$$
$$x_2 = s + 2t + 2$$
$$x_1 - 2x_3 + 3x_4 = 3$$
$$x_1 = 2s - 3t + 3$$

Solution: $x_1 = 2s - 3t + 3$, $x_2 = s + 2t + 2$, $x_3 = s$, $x_4 = t$, s and t any real numbers.

67.

$$\begin{bmatrix} 1 & -1 & 3 & -2 & | & 1 \\ -2 & 4 & -3 & 1 & | & 0.5 \\ 3 & -1 & 10 & -4 & | & 2.9 \\ 4 & -3 & 8 & -2 & | & 0.6 \end{bmatrix} \begin{matrix} \\ 2R_1 + R_2 \to R_2 \\ (-3)R_1 + R_3 \to R_3 \\ (-4)R_1 + R_4 \to R_4 \end{matrix} \sim \begin{bmatrix} 1 & -1 & 3 & -2 & | & 1 \\ 0 & 2 & 3 & -3 & | & 2.5 \\ 0 & 2 & 1 & 2 & | & -0.1 \\ 0 & 1 & -4 & 6 & | & -3.4 \end{bmatrix} R_4 \leftrightarrow R_2$$

$$\sim \begin{bmatrix} 1 & -1 & 3 & -2 & | & 1 \\ 0 & 1 & -4 & 6 & | & -3.4 \\ 0 & 2 & 1 & 2 & | & -0.1 \\ 0 & 2 & 3 & -3 & | & 2.5 \end{bmatrix} \begin{matrix} R_2 + R_1 \to R_1 \\ \\ (-2)R_2 + R_3 \to R_3 \\ (-2)R_2 + R_4 \to R_4 \end{matrix} \sim \begin{bmatrix} 1 & 0 & -1 & 4 & | & -2.4 \\ 0 & 1 & -4 & 6 & | & -3.4 \\ 0 & 0 & 9 & -10 & | & 6.7 \\ 0 & 0 & 11 & -15 & | & 9.3 \end{bmatrix} (-1)R_4 + R_3 \to R_3$$

$$\sim \begin{bmatrix} 1 & 0 & -1 & 4 & | & -2.4 \\ 0 & 1 & -4 & 6 & | & -3.4 \\ 0 & 0 & -2 & 5 & | & -2.6 \\ 0 & 0 & 11 & -15 & | & 9.3 \end{bmatrix} -\tfrac{1}{2}R_3 \leftrightarrow R_3 \sim \begin{bmatrix} 1 & 0 & -1 & 4 & | & -2.4 \\ 0 & 1 & -4 & 6 & | & -3.4 \\ 0 & 0 & 1 & -2.5 & | & 1.3 \\ 0 & 0 & 11 & -15 & | & 9.3 \end{bmatrix} \begin{matrix} R_3 + R_1 \to R_1 \\ 4R_3 + R_2 \to R_2 \\ \\ (-11)R_3 + R_4 \to R_4 \end{matrix}$$

$$\sim \begin{bmatrix} 1 & 0 & 0 & 1.5 & | & -1.1 \\ 0 & 1 & 0 & -4 & | & 1.8 \\ 0 & 0 & 1 & -2.5 & | & 1.3 \\ 0 & 0 & 0 & 12.5 & | & -5 \end{bmatrix} \tfrac{1}{12.5}R_4 \to R_4 \sim \begin{bmatrix} 1 & 0 & 0 & 1.5 & | & -1.1 \\ 0 & 1 & 0 & -4 & | & 1.8 \\ 0 & 0 & 1 & -2.5 & | & 1.3 \\ 0 & 0 & 0 & 1 & | & -0.4 \end{bmatrix} \begin{matrix} (-1.5)R_4 + R_1 \to R_1 \\ 4R_4 + R_2 \to R_2 \\ 2.5R_4 + R_3 \to R_3 \end{matrix}$$

$$\sim \begin{bmatrix} 1 & 0 & 0 & 0 & | & -0.5 \\ 0 & 1 & 0 & 0 & | & 0.2 \\ 0 & 0 & 1 & 0 & | & 0.3 \\ 0 & 0 & 0 & 1 & | & -0.4 \end{bmatrix}$$

Solution: $x_1 = -0.5$, $x_2 = 0.2$, $x_3 = 0.3$, $x_4 = -0.4$

69.

$$\begin{bmatrix} 1 & -2 & 1 & 1 & 2 & | & 2 \\ -2 & 4 & 2 & 2 & -2 & | & 0 \\ 3 & -6 & 1 & 1 & 5 & | & 4 \\ -1 & 2 & 3 & 1 & 1 & | & 3 \end{bmatrix} \begin{matrix} \\ 2R_1 + R_2 \to R_2 \\ (-3)R_1 + R_3 \to R_3 \\ R_1 + R_4 \to R_4 \end{matrix} \sim \begin{bmatrix} 1 & -2 & 1 & 1 & 2 & | & 2 \\ 0 & 0 & 4 & 4 & 2 & | & 4 \\ 0 & 0 & -2 & -2 & -1 & | & -2 \\ 0 & 0 & 4 & 2 & 3 & | & 5 \end{bmatrix} \begin{matrix} \\ \tfrac{1}{4}R_2 \to R_2 \end{matrix}$$

$$\sim \begin{bmatrix} 1 & -2 & 1 & 1 & 2 & | & 2 \\ 0 & 0 & 1 & 1 & 0.5 & | & 1 \\ 0 & 0 & -2 & -2 & -1 & | & -2 \\ 0 & 0 & 4 & 2 & 3 & | & 5 \end{bmatrix} \begin{matrix} (-1)R_2 + R_1 \to R_1 \\ \\ 2R_2 + R_3 \to R_3 \\ (-4)R_2 + R_4 \to R_4 \end{matrix} \sim \begin{bmatrix} 1 & -2 & 0 & 0 & 1.5 & | & 1 \\ 0 & 0 & 1 & 1 & 0.5 & | & 1 \\ 0 & 0 & 0 & 0 & 0 & | & 0 \\ 0 & 0 & 0 & -2 & 1 & | & 1 \end{bmatrix} \begin{matrix} \\ R_3 \leftrightarrow R_4 \end{matrix}$$

$$\sim \begin{bmatrix} 1 & -2 & 0 & 0 & 1.5 & | & 1 \\ 0 & 0 & 1 & 1 & 0.5 & | & 1 \\ 0 & 0 & 0 & -2 & 1 & | & 1 \\ 0 & 0 & 0 & 0 & 0 & | & 0 \end{bmatrix} \begin{matrix} \\ (-\tfrac{1}{2})R_3 \to R_3 \end{matrix} \sim \begin{bmatrix} 1 & -2 & 0 & 0 & 1.5 & | & 1 \\ 0 & 0 & 1 & 1 & 0.5 & | & 1 \\ 0 & 0 & 0 & 1 & -0.5 & | & -0.5 \\ 0 & 0 & 0 & 0 & 0 & | & 0 \end{bmatrix} \begin{matrix} \\ (-1)R_3 + R_2 \to R_2 \end{matrix}$$

$$\sim \begin{bmatrix} 1 & -2 & 0 & 0 & 1.5 & | & 1 \\ 0 & 0 & 1 & 0 & 1 & | & 1.5 \\ 0 & 0 & 0 & 1 & -0.5 & | & -0.5 \\ 0 & 0 & 0 & 0 & 0 & | & 0 \end{bmatrix}$$

Let $x_5 = t$. Then

$$x_4 - 0.5x_5 = -0.5$$
$$x_4 = 0.5x_5 - 0.5 = 0.5t - 0.5$$
$$x_3 + x_5 = 1.5$$
$$x_3 = -x_5 + 1.5 = -t + 1.5$$

Let $x_2 = s$. Then

$$x_1 - 2x_2 + 1.5x_5 = 1$$
$$x_1 = 2x_2 - 1.5x_5 + 1 = 2s - 1.5t + 1$$

Solution: $x_1 = 2s - 1.5t + 1$, $x_2 = s$, $x_3 = -t + 1.5$, $x_4 = 0.5t - 0.5$, $x_5 = t$, s and t any real numbers.

71. (A) The reduced form matrix will have the form $\begin{bmatrix} 1 & a & b & | & c \\ 0 & 0 & 0 & | & 0 \\ 0 & 0 & 0 & | & 0 \end{bmatrix}$

Thus, the system has been shown equivalent to

$$x_1 + ax_2 + bx_3 = c$$
$$0 = 0$$
$$0 = 0$$

The system is dependent, and x_2 and x_3 may assume any real values. Thus, there are two parameters in the solution.

(B) The reduced form matrix will have the form $\begin{bmatrix} 1 & 0 & a & | & b \\ 0 & 1 & c & | & d \\ 0 & 0 & 0 & | & 0 \end{bmatrix}$

Thus, the system has been shown equivalent to

$$x_1 + ax_3 = b$$
$$x_2 + cx_3 = d$$
$$0 = 0$$

The system is dependent, with a solution for any real value of x_3.

Thus, there is one parameter in the solution.

(C)   The reduced form matrix will have the form $\begin{bmatrix} 1 & 0 & 0 & | & a \\ 0 & 1 & 0 & | & b \\ 0 & 0 & 1 & | & c \end{bmatrix}$

Thus, there is only one solution, $x_1 = a$, $x_2 = b$, $x_3 = c$, and the system is independent.

(D)   This is impossible; there are only 3 equations.

73.   Let
x = the number of CD's
y = the number of DVD's
z = the number of books
Then

$$x + y + z = 13 \qquad \text{total items}$$
$$10x + 12y + 7z = 129 \qquad \text{total amount spent}$$

If we multiply the first equation by –10 and add, we can eliminate x.

$$\begin{aligned} -10x - 10y - 10z &= -130 \\ \underline{10x + 12y + 7z} &= \underline{129} \\ 2y - 3z &= -1 \\ 2y &= 3z - 1 \\ y &= \frac{3z-1}{2} \end{aligned}$$

Since x, y, and z must be positive integers, a solution is achieved, but only for certain values of z.

If $z = 1$, $y = \dfrac{3 \cdot 1 - 1}{2} = 1$, $x + y + z = 13$, hence $x + 1 + 1 = 13$, $x = 11$

11 CD's, 1 DVD, and 1 book

If $z = 3$, $y = \dfrac{3 \cdot 3 - 1}{2} = 4$, $x + y + z = 13$, hence $x + 4 + 3 = 13$, $x = 6$

6 CD's, 4 DVDs, and 3 books

If $z = 5$, $y = \dfrac{3 \cdot 5 - 1}{2} = 7$, $x + y + z = 13$, hence $x + 7 + 5 = 13$, $x = 1$

1 CD, 7 DVDs, and 5 books
No other solutions are possible.

75.   Let x = amount of 20% solution
y = amount of 80% solution
Summarize the given information in a table:

	20% solution	80% solution	62% solution
amount of solution	x	y	100
amount of acid	$0.2x$	$0.8y$	$0.62(100) = 62$

Form equations from the information:

$$\left(\begin{array}{c} \text{Amount of} \\ \text{20\% solution} \end{array} \right) + \left(\begin{array}{c} \text{Amount of} \\ \text{80\% solution} \end{array} \right) = \left(\begin{array}{c} \text{Amount of} \\ \text{62\% solution} \end{array} \right)$$
$$x \qquad + \qquad y \qquad = \qquad 100$$

$$\left(\begin{array}{c} \text{Amount of acid} \\ \text{in 20\% solution} \end{array} \right) + \left(\begin{array}{c} \text{Amount of acid} \\ \text{in 80\% solution} \end{array} \right) = \left(\begin{array}{c} \text{Amount of acid} \\ \text{in 62\% solution} \end{array} \right)$$
$$0.2x \qquad + \qquad 0.8y \qquad = \qquad 62$$

Solve this system using elimination by addition.

$$\begin{aligned} -0.2x - 0.2y &= -20 \\ \underline{0.2x + 0.8y} &= \underline{62} \\ 0.6y &= 42 \\ y &= 70 \\ x + 70 &= 100 \\ x &= 30 \end{aligned}$$

30 liters of 20% solution and 70 liters of 80% solution.

77. If the curve passes through a point, the coordinates of the point satisfy the equation of the curve. Hence,

$3 = a + b(-2) + c(-2)^2$

$2 = a + b(-1) + c(-1)^2$

$6 = a + b(1) + c(1)^2$

After simplification, we have

$a - 2b + 4c = 3$

$a - b + c = 2$

$a + b + c = 6$

We write the augmented matrix and solve by Gauss–Jordan elimination.

$$\begin{bmatrix} 1 & -2 & 4 & | & 3 \\ 1 & -1 & 1 & | & 2 \\ 1 & 1 & 1 & | & 6 \end{bmatrix} \begin{matrix} \\ (-1)R_1 + R_2 \to R_2 \\ (-1)R_1 + R_3 \to R_3 \end{matrix} \sim \begin{bmatrix} 1 & -2 & 4 & | & 3 \\ 0 & 1 & -3 & | & -1 \\ 0 & 3 & -3 & | & 3 \end{bmatrix} \begin{matrix} 2R_2 + R_1 \to R_1 \\ \\ (-3)R_2 + R_3 \to R_3 \end{matrix} \sim \begin{bmatrix} 1 & 0 & -2 & | & 1 \\ 0 & 1 & -3 & | & -1 \\ 0 & 0 & 6 & | & 6 \end{bmatrix} \tfrac{1}{6}R_3 \to R_3$$

$$\sim \begin{bmatrix} 1 & 0 & -2 & | & 1 \\ 0 & 1 & -3 & | & -1 \\ 0 & 0 & 1 & | & 1 \end{bmatrix} \begin{matrix} 2R_3 + R_1 \to R_1 \\ 3R_3 + R_2 \to R_2 \\ \\ \end{matrix} \sim \begin{bmatrix} 1 & 0 & 0 & | & 3 \\ 0 & 1 & 0 & | & 2 \\ 0 & 0 & 1 & | & 1 \end{bmatrix} \quad \text{Thus } a = 3, b = 2, c = 1.$$

79. Let x_1 = number of one–person boats

x_2 = number of two–person boats

x_3 = number of four–person boats

We have

$0.5x_1 + 1.0x_2 + 1.5x_3 = 380$ cutting department

$0.6x_1 + 0.9x_2 + 1.2x_3 = 330$ assembly department

$0.2x_1 + 0.3x_2 + 0.5x_3 = 120$ packing department

> **Common Error:**
> The facts in this problem do not justify the equation
> $0.5x_1 + 0.6x_2 + 0.2x_3 = 380$

Clearing of decimals for convenience:

$x_1 + 2x_2 + 3x_3 = 760$

$6x_1 + 9x_2 + 12x_3 = 3300$

$2x_1 + 3x_2 + 5x_3 = 1200$

We write the augmented matrix and solve by Gauss–Jordan elimination:

$$\begin{bmatrix} 1 & 2 & 3 & | & 760 \\ 6 & 9 & 12 & | & 3300 \\ 2 & 3 & 5 & | & 1200 \end{bmatrix} \begin{matrix} \\ (-6)R_1 + R_2 \to R_2 \\ (-2)R_1 + R_3 \to R_3 \end{matrix} \sim \begin{bmatrix} 1 & 2 & 3 & | & 760 \\ 0 & -3 & -6 & | & -1260 \\ 0 & -1 & -1 & | & -320 \end{bmatrix} -\tfrac{1}{3}R_2 \to R_2$$

$$\sim \begin{bmatrix} 1 & 2 & 3 & | & 760 \\ 0 & 1 & 2 & | & 420 \\ 0 & -1 & -1 & | & -320 \end{bmatrix} \begin{matrix} (-2)R_2 + R_1 \to R_1 \\ \\ R_2 + R_3 \to R_3 \end{matrix} \sim \begin{bmatrix} 1 & 0 & -1 & | & -80 \\ 0 & 1 & 2 & | & 420 \\ 0 & 0 & 1 & | & 100 \end{bmatrix} \begin{matrix} R_3 + R_1 \to R_1 \\ (-2)R_3 + R_2 \to R_2 \\ \\ \end{matrix}$$

$$\begin{bmatrix} 1 & 0 & 0 & | & 20 \\ 0 & 1 & 0 & | & 220 \\ 0 & 0 & 1 & | & 100 \end{bmatrix}$$

Therefore

$x_1 = 20$ one–person boats

$x_2 = 220$ two–person boats

$x_3 = 100$ four–person boats

81. This assumption discards the third equation. The system, cleared of decimals, reads

$$x_1 + 2x_2 + 3x_3 = 760$$
$$6x_1 + 9x_2 + 12x_3 = 3300$$

The augmented matrix becomes $\begin{bmatrix} 1 & 2 & 3 & | & 760 \\ 6 & 9 & 12 & | & 3300 \end{bmatrix}$

We solve by Gauss–Jordan elimination. We start by introducing a 0 into the lower left corner using $(-6)R_1 + R_2$ as in the previous problem:

$$\sim \begin{bmatrix} 1 & 2 & 3 & | & 760 \\ 0 & -3 & -6 & | & -1260 \end{bmatrix} -\tfrac{1}{3}R_2 \to R_2 \sim \begin{bmatrix} 1 & 2 & 3 & | & 760 \\ 0 & 1 & 2 & | & 420 \end{bmatrix} (-2)R_2 + R_1 \to R_1 \sim \begin{bmatrix} 1 & 0 & -1 & | & -80 \\ 0 & 1 & 2 & | & 420 \end{bmatrix}$$

This augmented matrix is in reduced form. It corresponds to the system:

$$x_1 - x_3 = -80$$
$$x_2 + 2x_3 = 420$$

Let $x_3 = t$. Then

$$x_2 = -2x_3 + 420$$
$$= -2t + 420$$
$$x_1 = x_3 - 80$$
$$= t - 80$$

A solution is achieved, not for every real value of t, but for integer values of t that give rise to non–negative x_1, x_2, x_3.

$x_1 \geq 0$ means $t - 80 \geq 0$ or $t \geq 80$

$x_2 \geq 0$ means $-2t + 420 \geq 0$ or $210 \geq t$

Thus we have the solution

$x_1 = (t - 80)$ one–person boats

$x_2 = (-2t + 420)$ two–person boats

$x_3 = t$ four–person boats

$80 \leq t \leq 210$, t an integer

83. In this case we have $x_3 = 0$ from the beginning. The three equations of problem 79, cleared of decimals, read:

$$x_1 + 2x_2 = 760$$
$$6x_1 + 9x_2 = 3300$$
$$2x_1 + 3x_2 = 1200$$

The augmented matrix becomes: $\begin{bmatrix} 1 & 2 & | & 760 \\ 6 & 9 & | & 3300 \\ 2 & 3 & | & 1200 \end{bmatrix}$

Notice that the row operation $(-3)R_3 + R_2 \to R_2$

transforms this into the equivalent augmented matrix: $\begin{bmatrix} 1 & 2 & | & 760 \\ 0 & 0 & | & -300 \\ 2 & 3 & | & 1200 \end{bmatrix}$

Therefore, since the second row corresponds to the equation $0x_1 + 0x_2 = -300$ there is no solution. No production schedule will use all the work–hours in all departments.

85. Let x_1 = number of ounces of food A.

x_2 = number of ounces of food B.

x_3 = number of ounces of food C.

> **Common Error:**
> The facts in this problem do not justify the equation
> $30x_1 + 10x_2 + 10x_3 = 340$

Then

$30x_1 + 10x_2 + 20x_3 = 340$ (calcium)

$10x_1 + 10x_2 + 20x_3 = 180$ (iron)

$10x_1 + 30x_2 + 20x_3 = 220$ (vitamin A)

or

$3x_1 + x_2 + 2x_3 = 34$

$x_1 + x_2 + 2x_3 = 18$

$x_1 + 3x_2 + 2x_3 = 22$

is the system to be solved. We form the augmented matrix and solve by Gauss–Jordan elimination.

$$\begin{bmatrix} 3 & 1 & 2 & | & 34 \\ 1 & 1 & 2 & | & 18 \\ 1 & 3 & 2 & | & 22 \end{bmatrix} R_1 \leftrightarrow R_2 \sim \begin{bmatrix} 1 & 1 & 2 & | & 18 \\ 3 & 1 & 2 & | & 34 \\ 1 & 3 & 2 & | & 22 \end{bmatrix} \begin{array}{l} (-3)R_1 + R_2 \to R_2 \\ \\ (-1)R_1 + R_3 \to R_3 \end{array} \sim \begin{bmatrix} 1 & 1 & 2 & | & 18 \\ 0 & -2 & -4 & | & -20 \\ 0 & 2 & 0 & | & 4 \end{bmatrix} -\tfrac{1}{2} R_2 \to R_2$$

$$\sim \begin{bmatrix} 1 & 1 & 2 & | & 18 \\ 0 & 1 & 2 & | & 10 \\ 0 & 2 & 0 & | & 4 \end{bmatrix} \begin{array}{l} (-1)R_2 + R_1 \to R_1 \\ \\ (-2)R_2 + R_3 \to R_3 \end{array} \sim \begin{bmatrix} 1 & 0 & 0 & | & 8 \\ 0 & 1 & 2 & | & 10 \\ 0 & 0 & -4 & | & -16 \end{bmatrix} -\tfrac{1}{4} R_3 \to R_3 \sim \begin{bmatrix} 1 & 0 & 0 & | & 8 \\ 0 & 1 & 2 & | & 10 \\ 0 & 0 & 1 & | & 4 \end{bmatrix} (-2)R_3 + R_2 \to R_2$$

$$\sim \begin{bmatrix} 1 & 0 & 0 & | & 8 \\ 0 & 1 & 0 & | & 2 \\ 0 & 0 & 1 & | & 4 \end{bmatrix}$$

Thus

$x_1 = 8$ ounces food A

$x_2 = 2$ ounces food B

$x_3 = 4$ ounces food C

87. In this case we have $x_3 = 0$ from the beginning. The three equations of problem 85 become

$30x_1 + 10x_2 = 340$

$10x_1 + 10x_2 = 180$

$10x_1 + 30x_2 = 220$

or

$3x_1 + x_2 = 34$

$x_1 + x_2 = 18$

$x_1 + 3x_2 = 22$

The augmented matrix becomes $\begin{bmatrix} 3 & 1 & | & 34 \\ 1 & 1 & | & 18 \\ 1 & 3 & | & 22 \end{bmatrix}$

We solve by Gauss–Jordan elimination, starting by the row operation

$R_1 \leftrightarrow R_2$

$$\begin{bmatrix} 1 & 1 & | & 18 \\ 3 & 1 & | & 34 \\ 1 & 3 & | & 22 \end{bmatrix} \begin{array}{l} (-3)R_1 + R_2 \to R_2 \\ \\ (-1)R_1 + R_3 \to R_3 \end{array} \sim \begin{bmatrix} 1 & 1 & | & 18 \\ 0 & -2 & | & -20 \\ 0 & 2 & | & 4 \end{bmatrix} R_2 + R_3 \to R_3 \sim \begin{bmatrix} 1 & 1 & | & 18 \\ 0 & -2 & | & -20 \\ 0 & 0 & | & -16 \end{bmatrix}$$

Since the third row corresponds to the equation

$0x_1 + 0x_2 = -16$

there is no solution.

89. In this case we discard the third equation. The system becomes

$$30x_1 + 10x_2 + 20x_3 = 340$$
$$10x_1 + 10x_2 + 20x_3 = 180$$

or

$$3x_1 + x_2 + 2x_3 = 34$$
$$x_1 + x_2 + 2x_3 = 18$$

The augmented matrix becomes $\begin{bmatrix} 3 & 1 & 2 & | & 34 \\ 1 & 1 & 2 & | & 18 \end{bmatrix}$

We solve by Gauss–Jordan elimination, starting by the row operation $R_1 \leftrightarrow R_2$.

$$\begin{bmatrix} 1 & 1 & 2 & | & 18 \\ 3 & 1 & 2 & | & 34 \end{bmatrix} (-3)R_1 + R_2 \to R_2 \sim \begin{bmatrix} 1 & 1 & 2 & | & 18 \\ 0 & -2 & -4 & | & -20 \end{bmatrix} -\tfrac{1}{2}R_2 \to R_2 \sim \begin{bmatrix} 1 & 1 & 2 & | & 18 \\ 0 & 1 & 2 & | & 10 \end{bmatrix} (-1)R_2 + R_1 \to R_1$$

$$\sim \begin{bmatrix} 1 & 0 & 0 & | & 8 \\ 0 & 1 & 2 & | & 10 \end{bmatrix}$$

This augmented matrix is in reduced form. It corresponds to the system

$$x_1 = 8$$
$$x_2 + 2x_3 = 10$$

$$\text{Let } x_3 = t$$
$$\text{Then } x_2 = -2x_3 + 10$$
$$= -2t + 10$$

A solution is achieved, not for every real value t, but for values of t that give rise to non–negative x_2, x_3.

$x_3 \geq 0$ means $t \geq 0$

$x_2 \geq 0$ means $-2t + 10 \geq 0$, $5 \geq t$

Thus we have the solution

$x_1 = 8$ ounces food A

$x_2 = -2t + 10$ ounces food B

$x_3 = t$ ounces food C

$0 \leq t \leq 5$

91. Let x_1 = number of hours company A is to be scheduled

$\quad\quad x_2$ = number of hours company B is to be scheduled

In x_1 hours, company A can handle $30x_1$ telephone and $10x_1$ house contacts.

In x_2 hours, company B can handle $20x_2$ telephone and $20x_2$ house contacts.

We therefore have:

$\quad 30x_1 + 20x_2 = 600$ telephone contacts

$\quad 10x_1 + 20x_2 = 400$ house contacts

We form the augmented matrix and solve by Gauss–Jordan elimination.

$$\begin{bmatrix} 30 & 20 & | & 600 \\ 10 & 20 & | & 400 \end{bmatrix} \begin{matrix} \tfrac{1}{10}R_1 \to R_1 \\ \tfrac{1}{10}R_2 \to R_2 \end{matrix} \sim \begin{bmatrix} 3 & 2 & | & 60 \\ 1 & 2 & | & 40 \end{bmatrix} R_1 \leftrightarrow R_2 \sim \begin{bmatrix} 1 & 2 & | & 40 \\ 3 & 2 & | & 60 \end{bmatrix} (-3)R_1 + R_2 \to R_2$$

$$\sim \begin{bmatrix} 1 & 2 & | & 40 \\ 0 & -4 & | & -60 \end{bmatrix} -\tfrac{1}{4}R_3 \to R_3 \sim \begin{bmatrix} 1 & 2 & | & 40 \\ 0 & 1 & | & 15 \end{bmatrix} (-2)R_2 + R_1 \to R_1$$

$$\sim \begin{bmatrix} 1 & 0 & | & 10 \\ 0 & 1 & | & 15 \end{bmatrix}$$

Therefore

$x_1 = 10$ hours company A

$x_2 = 15$ hours company B

93. Let x = base price
  y = surcharge for each additional pound.
  Since a 5–pound package costs the base price plus 4 surcharges, $x + 4y = 27.75$
  Since a 20–pound package costs the base price plus 19 surcharges, $x + 19y = 64.50$
  Solve using elimination by addition.

$$-x - 4y = -27.75$$
$$\underline{x + 19y = 64.50}$$
$$15y = 36.75$$
$$y = 2.45$$
$$x + 4(2.45) = 27.75$$
$$x = 17.95$$

The base price is \$17.95 and the surcharge per pound is \$2.45.

95. Let x = number of pounds of robust blend
  y = number of pounds of mild blend
  Summarize the given information in a table:

	Robust blend	Mild blend
ozs. of Columbian beans	12	6
ozs. of Brazilian beans	4	10

Form equations from the information:

$$\left(\begin{array}{c}\text{pounds of Columbian} \\ \text{beans needed for} \\ \text{robust blend}\end{array}\right) + \left(\begin{array}{c}\text{pounds of Columbian} \\ \text{beans needed for} \\ \text{mild blend}\end{array}\right) = \left(\begin{array}{c}\text{Total} \\ \text{Columbian beans} \\ \text{available}\end{array}\right)$$

$$\frac{12}{16}x \qquad + \qquad \frac{6}{16}y \qquad = \qquad 50(132)$$

$$\left(\begin{array}{c}\text{pounds of Brazilian} \\ \text{beans needed for} \\ \text{robust blend}\end{array}\right) + \left(\begin{array}{c}\text{pounds of Brazilian} \\ \text{beans needed for} \\ \text{mild blend}\end{array}\right) = \left(\begin{array}{c}\text{Total} \\ \text{Brazilian beans} \\ \text{available}\end{array}\right)$$

$$\frac{4}{16}x \qquad + \qquad \frac{10}{16}y \qquad = \qquad 40(132)$$

Solve using elimination by addition:

$$\frac{12}{16}x + \frac{6}{16}y = 6{,}600$$
$$-\frac{12}{16}x - \frac{30}{16}y = -15{,}840$$
$$-\frac{24}{16}y = -9{,}240$$
$$y = 6{,}160$$
$$\frac{4}{16}x + \frac{10}{16}(6{,}160) = 40(132)$$
$$\frac{1}{4}x + 3{,}850 = 5{,}280$$
$$\frac{1}{4}x = 1{,}430$$
$$x = 5{,}720$$

5,720 pounds of the robust blend and 6,160 pounds of the mild blend.

SECTION 7–3

1. A and B must be the same size.
3. The number of columns of B must equal the number of rows of A, that is, if B is an $m \times n$ matrix, A must be a $n \times p$ matrix.
5. The negative of an $m \times n$ matrix A is an $m \times n$ matrix $-A$ in which each element is -1 times the corresponding element of A.
7. Multiply each element of the matrix by the number.
9. BA is an $n \times n$ matrix is which the element in row i, column j is the product of the element in row i of B times the element in column j of A.

11. $\begin{bmatrix} 5 & -2 \\ 3 & 0 \end{bmatrix} + \begin{bmatrix} -3 & 7 \\ 1 & -6 \end{bmatrix} = \begin{bmatrix} 5+(-3) & (-2)+7 \\ 3+1 & 0+(-6) \end{bmatrix} = \begin{bmatrix} 2 & 5 \\ 4 & -6 \end{bmatrix}$

13. $\begin{bmatrix} 4 & 0 \\ -2 & 3 \\ 8 & 1 \end{bmatrix} + \begin{bmatrix} -1 & 2 \\ 0 & 5 \\ 4 & -6 \end{bmatrix} = \begin{bmatrix} 4+(-1) & 0+2 \\ (-2)+0 & 3+5 \\ 8+4 & 1+(-6) \end{bmatrix} = \begin{bmatrix} 3 & 2 \\ -2 & 8 \\ 12 & -5 \end{bmatrix}$

15. These matrices have different sizes, hence the sum is not defined.

17. $\begin{bmatrix} 5 & -1 & 0 \\ 4 & 6 & 3 \end{bmatrix} - \begin{bmatrix} 2 & 4 & -6 \\ 3 & 5 & -5 \end{bmatrix} = \begin{bmatrix} 5-2 & (-1)-4 & 0-(-6) \\ 4-3 & 6-5 & 3-(-5) \end{bmatrix} = \begin{bmatrix} 3 & -5 & 6 \\ 1 & 1 & 8 \end{bmatrix}$

19. These matrices have different sizes, hence the difference is not defined.

21. $\begin{bmatrix} 2.4 & -2.8 & 3.9 \\ -1.6 & 0 & 4.2 \end{bmatrix} - \begin{bmatrix} 7 & -2.2 & -2.2 \\ -3.2 & -3.2 & 1 \end{bmatrix} = \begin{bmatrix} 2.4-7 & (-2.8)-(-2.2) & (3.9)-(-2.2) \\ (-1.6)-(-3.2) & 0-(-3.2) & 4.2-1 \end{bmatrix} = \begin{bmatrix} -4.6 & -0.6 & 6.1 \\ 1.6 & 3.2 & 3.2 \end{bmatrix}$

23. $\begin{bmatrix} 12 & -16 & 28 \\ -8 & 36 & 20 \end{bmatrix}$ 25. $\begin{bmatrix} 5 & 3 \end{bmatrix} \begin{bmatrix} 4 \\ 7 \end{bmatrix} = [5 \cdot 4 + 3 \cdot 7] = [41]$

27. $\begin{bmatrix} -5 \\ -3 \end{bmatrix} \begin{bmatrix} 4 & -2 \end{bmatrix} = \begin{bmatrix} (-5)4 & (-5)(-2) \\ (-3)4 & (-3)(-2) \end{bmatrix} = \begin{bmatrix} -20 & 10 \\ -12 & 6 \end{bmatrix}$ 29. $\begin{bmatrix} 3 & -2 & -4 \end{bmatrix} \begin{bmatrix} 1 \\ 2 \\ -3 \end{bmatrix} = [3 \cdot 1 + (-2)2 + (-4)(-3)] = [11]$

31. $\begin{bmatrix} 1 \\ 2 \\ -3 \end{bmatrix} \begin{bmatrix} 3 & -2 & -4 \end{bmatrix} = \begin{bmatrix} 1 \cdot 3 & 1(-2) & 1(-4) \\ 2 \cdot 3 & 2(-2) & 2(-4) \\ (-3)3 & (-3)(-2) & (-3)(-4) \end{bmatrix} = \begin{bmatrix} 3 & -2 & -4 \\ 6 & -4 & -8 \\ -9 & 6 & 12 \end{bmatrix}$ 33. $\begin{bmatrix} -6 & 3 \\ 2 & -5 \end{bmatrix} \begin{bmatrix} 1 \\ 3 \end{bmatrix} = \begin{bmatrix} (-6)1+3 \cdot 3 \\ 2 \cdot 1+(-5)3 \end{bmatrix} = \begin{bmatrix} 3 \\ -13 \end{bmatrix}$

35. $\begin{bmatrix} 5 & 1 \\ 4 & 6 \end{bmatrix} \begin{bmatrix} 2 & 0 \\ 3 & 8 \end{bmatrix} = \begin{bmatrix} 5 \cdot 2+1 \cdot 3 & 5 \cdot 0+1 \cdot 8 \\ 4 \cdot 2+6 \cdot 3 & 4 \cdot 0+6 \cdot 8 \end{bmatrix} = \begin{bmatrix} 13 & 8 \\ 26 & 48 \end{bmatrix}$

37. $\begin{bmatrix} 8 & -3 \\ -5 & 3 \end{bmatrix} \begin{bmatrix} 2 & 0 \\ 0 & 6 \end{bmatrix} = \begin{bmatrix} 8 \cdot 2+(-3)0 & 8 \cdot 0+(-3)6 \\ (-5)2+3 \cdot 0 & (-5)0+3 \cdot 6 \end{bmatrix} = \begin{bmatrix} 16 & -18 \\ -10 & 18 \end{bmatrix}$

39. C has 3 columns. A has 2 rows. Therefore, CA is not defined.

41. $BA = \begin{bmatrix} -3 & 1 \\ 2 & 5 \end{bmatrix} \begin{bmatrix} 2 & -1 & 3 \\ 0 & 4 & -2 \end{bmatrix} = \begin{bmatrix} (-3)2+1 \cdot 0 & (-3)(-1)+1 \cdot 4 & (-3)3+1(-2) \\ 2 \cdot 2+5 \cdot 0 & 2(-1)+5 \cdot 4 & 2 \cdot 3+5(-2) \end{bmatrix} = \begin{bmatrix} -6 & 7 & -11 \\ 4 & 18 & -4 \end{bmatrix}$

43. $C^2 = \begin{bmatrix} -1 & 0 & 2 \\ 4 & -3 & 1 \\ -2 & 3 & 5 \end{bmatrix} \begin{bmatrix} -1 & 0 & 2 \\ 4 & -3 & 1 \\ -2 & 3 & 5 \end{bmatrix} = \begin{bmatrix} (-1)(-1)+0 \cdot 4+2(-2) & (-1)0+0(-3)+2 \cdot 3 & (-1)2+0 \cdot 1+2 \cdot 5 \\ 4(-1)+(-3)4+1(-2) & 4 \cdot 0+(-3)(-3)+1 \cdot 3 & 4 \cdot 2+(-3)1+1 \cdot 5 \\ (-2)(-1)+3 \cdot 4+5(-2) & (-2)0+3(-3)+5 \cdot 3 & (-2)2+3 \cdot 1+5 \cdot 5 \end{bmatrix}$

$= \begin{bmatrix} -3 & 6 & 8 \\ -18 & 12 & 10 \\ 4 & 6 & 24 \end{bmatrix}$

45. $DA = \begin{bmatrix} 3 & -2 \\ 0 & -1 \\ 1 & 2 \end{bmatrix} \begin{bmatrix} 2 & -1 & 3 \\ 0 & 4 & -2 \end{bmatrix} = \begin{bmatrix} 3\cdot2+(-2)0 & 3(-1)+(-2)4 & 3\cdot3+(-2)(-2) \\ 0\cdot2+(-1)0 & 0(-1)+(-1)4 & 0\cdot3+(-1)(-2) \\ 1\cdot2+2\cdot0 & 1(-1)+2\cdot4 & 1\cdot3+2(-2) \end{bmatrix} = \begin{bmatrix} 6 & -11 & 13 \\ 0 & -4 & 2 \\ 2 & 7 & -1 \end{bmatrix}$

$C+DA = \begin{bmatrix} -1 & 0 & 2 \\ 4 & -3 & 1 \\ -2 & 3 & 5 \end{bmatrix} + \begin{bmatrix} 6 & -11 & 13 \\ 0 & -4 & 2 \\ 2 & 7 & -1 \end{bmatrix} = \begin{bmatrix} 5 & -11 & 15 \\ 4 & -7 & 3 \\ 0 & 10 & 4 \end{bmatrix}$

47. $0.2CD = 0.2 \begin{bmatrix} -1 & 0 & 2 \\ 4 & -3 & 1 \\ -2 & 3 & 5 \end{bmatrix} \begin{bmatrix} 3 & -2 \\ 0 & -1 \\ 1 & 2 \end{bmatrix} = 0.2 \begin{bmatrix} (-1)3+0\cdot0+2\cdot1 & (-1)(-2)+0(-1)+2\cdot2 \\ 4\cdot3+(-3)0+1\cdot1 & 4(-2)+(-3)(-1)+1\cdot2 \\ (-2)3+3\cdot0+5\cdot1 & (-2)(-2)+3(-1)+5\cdot2 \end{bmatrix}$

$= 0.2 \begin{bmatrix} -1 & 6 \\ 13 & -3 \\ -1 & 11 \end{bmatrix} = \begin{bmatrix} -0.2 & 1.2 \\ 2.6 & -0.6 \\ -0.2 & 2.2 \end{bmatrix}$

49. $DB = \begin{bmatrix} 3 & -2 \\ 0 & -1 \\ 1 & 2 \end{bmatrix} \begin{bmatrix} -3 & 1 \\ 2 & 5 \end{bmatrix} = \begin{bmatrix} 3(-3)+(-2)2 & 3\cdot1+(-2)5 \\ 0(-3)+(-1)2 & 0\cdot1+(-1)5 \\ 1(-3)+2\cdot2 & 1\cdot1+2\cdot5 \end{bmatrix} = \begin{bmatrix} -13 & -7 \\ -2 & -5 \\ 1 & 11 \end{bmatrix}$

$CD = \begin{bmatrix} -1 & 6 \\ 13 & -3 \\ -1 & 11 \end{bmatrix}$ (see problem 47)

Thus, $2DB + 5CD = 2\begin{bmatrix} -13 & -7 \\ -2 & -5 \\ 1 & 11 \end{bmatrix} + 5\begin{bmatrix} -1 & 6 \\ 13 & -3 \\ -1 & 11 \end{bmatrix} = \begin{bmatrix} -26 & -14 \\ -4 & -10 \\ 2 & 22 \end{bmatrix} + \begin{bmatrix} -5 & 30 \\ 65 & -15 \\ -5 & 55 \end{bmatrix} = \begin{bmatrix} -31 & 16 \\ 61 & -25 \\ -3 & 77 \end{bmatrix}$

51. $(-1)AC$ is a matrix of size 2×3. $3DB$ is a matrix of size 3×2. Hence, $(-1)AC + 3DB$ is not defined.

53. $CD = \begin{bmatrix} -1 & 6 \\ 13 & -3 \\ -1 & 11 \end{bmatrix}$ (see problem 47)

Hence $CDA = \begin{bmatrix} -1 & 6 \\ 13 & -3 \\ -1 & 11 \end{bmatrix} \begin{bmatrix} 2 & -1 & 3 \\ 0 & 4 & -2 \end{bmatrix}$

$= \begin{bmatrix} (-1)2+6\cdot0 & (-1)(-1)+6\cdot4 & (-1)3+6(-2) \\ 13\cdot2+(-3)0 & 13(-1)+(-3)4 & 13\cdot3+(-3)(-2) \\ (-1)2+11\cdot0 & (-1)(-1)+11\cdot4 & (-1)3+11(-2) \end{bmatrix} = \begin{bmatrix} -2 & 25 & -15 \\ 26 & -25 & 45 \\ -2 & 45 & -25 \end{bmatrix}$

55. $DB = \begin{bmatrix} -13 & -7 \\ -2 & -5 \\ 1 & 11 \end{bmatrix}$ (see problem 49)

Hence

$DBA = \begin{bmatrix} -13 & -7 \\ -2 & -5 \\ 1 & 11 \end{bmatrix} \begin{bmatrix} 2 & -1 & 3 \\ 0 & 4 & -2 \end{bmatrix} = \begin{bmatrix} (-13)2+(-7)0 & (-13)(-1)+(-7)4 & (-13)3+(-7)(-2) \\ (-2)2+(-5)0 & (-2)(-1)+(-5)4 & (-2)3+(-5)(-2) \\ 1\cdot2+11\cdot0 & 1(-1)+11\cdot4 & 1\cdot3+11(-2) \end{bmatrix} = \begin{bmatrix} -26 & -15 & -25 \\ -4 & -18 & 4 \\ 2 & 43 & -19 \end{bmatrix}$

57. Entering matrix B in a graphing calculator, we obtain the results

```
[B]²                 [B]^4                 [B]^6
    [[.28 .72]          [[.2512 .7488]        [[.250048 .7499…
     [.24 .76]]          [.2496 .7504]]        [.249984 .7500…
[B]³                 [B]^5                 [B]^7
    [[.256 .744]        [[.25024 .74976…      [[.2500096 .749…
     [.248 .752]]        [.24992 .75008…       [.2499968 .750…
```

It appears that $B^n \rightarrow \begin{bmatrix} 0.25 & 0.75 \\ 0.25 & 0.75 \end{bmatrix}$

We calculate $AB, AB^2, AB^3, \ldots$ and obtain the results

```
[A]*[B]               [A]*[B]^4
      [[.26 .74]]         [[.25008 .74992…
[A]*[B]²              [A]*[B]^5
      [[.252 .748]]        [[.250016 .7499…
[A]*[B]³              [A]*[B]^6
   [[.2504 .7496]]         [[.2500032 .749…
```

It appears that $AB^n \rightarrow [0.25 \quad 0.75]$.

59. $\begin{bmatrix} a & b \\ c & d \end{bmatrix} + \begin{bmatrix} 2 & -3 \\ 0 & 1 \end{bmatrix} = \begin{bmatrix} a+2 & b-3 \\ c & d+1 \end{bmatrix} = \begin{bmatrix} 1 & -2 \\ 3 & -4 \end{bmatrix}$

if and only if corresponding elements are equal.

$a+2=1 \quad b-3=-2 \quad c=3 \quad d+1=-4$

$\quad a=-1 \quad\quad b=1 \quad\quad c=3 \quad\quad d=-5$

61. $\begin{bmatrix} 3 & 0 \\ -7 & -11 \end{bmatrix} - \begin{bmatrix} w & x \\ y & z \end{bmatrix} = \begin{bmatrix} 3-w & -x \\ -7-y & -11-z \end{bmatrix} = \begin{bmatrix} 9 & 1 \\ 4 & 6 \end{bmatrix}$

if and only if corresponding elements are equal.

$3-w=9 \quad -x=1 \quad -7-y=4 \quad -11-z=6$

$\quad w=-6 \quad\quad x=-1 \quad\quad y=-11 \quad\quad z=-17$

63. Compute the square matrix A:

$$A^2 = \begin{bmatrix} a & b \\ c & -a \end{bmatrix}\begin{bmatrix} a & b \\ c & -a \end{bmatrix} = \begin{bmatrix} a^2+bc & ab+(-ab) \\ ac+(-ac) & cb+a^2 \end{bmatrix} = \begin{bmatrix} a^2+bc & 0 \\ 0 & a^2+bc \end{bmatrix}$$

Two of the entries are already zero and the other two are both $a^2 + bc$. So if $a^2 + bc = 0$, then $A^2 = 0$.

If $a = 1$, $b = 1$, $c = -1$, then $a^2 + bc = 0$, so the matrix $A = \begin{bmatrix} 1 & 1 \\ -1 & -1 \end{bmatrix}$ will have $A^2 = 0$. If $a = 2$, $b = 4$,

$c = -1$, then $a^2 + bc = 0$, so the matrix $A = \begin{bmatrix} 2 & 4 \\ -1 & -2 \end{bmatrix}$ will have $A^2 = 0$.

65. Compute the product AB:

$$AB = \begin{bmatrix} a & b \\ c & d \end{bmatrix}\begin{bmatrix} 1 & 1 \\ 1 & -1 \end{bmatrix} = \begin{bmatrix} a+b & a+b \\ c+d & c+d \end{bmatrix}$$

Two of the entries are $a + b$ and the other two are $c + d$, so if $a = -b$ and $c = -d$, then $AB = 0$.
The following are a couple of examples of matrices A that will satisfy $AB = 0$:

$$\begin{bmatrix} 2 & -2 \\ 4 & -4 \end{bmatrix} \quad \begin{bmatrix} -5 & 5 \\ 1 & -1 \end{bmatrix}$$

67. $\begin{bmatrix} 1 & 3 \\ -2 & -2 \end{bmatrix}\begin{bmatrix} x & 1 \\ 3 & 2 \end{bmatrix} = \begin{bmatrix} x+9 & 7 \\ -2x-6 & -6 \end{bmatrix} = \begin{bmatrix} y & 7 \\ y & -6 \end{bmatrix}$

if and only if corresponding elements are equal.

$x + 9 = y \quad 7 \overset{\checkmark}{=} 7$　　Two conditions are already met.

$-2x - 6 = y \quad -6 \overset{\checkmark}{=} -6$

To find x and y, we solve the system:

$x + 9 = y$

$-2x - 6 = y$ to obtain $x = -5, y = 4$. (Solution left to the student.)

69.　$\begin{bmatrix} 1 & 3 \\ 1 & 4 \end{bmatrix} \begin{bmatrix} a & b \\ c & d \end{bmatrix} = \begin{bmatrix} a + 3c & b + 3d \\ a + 4c & b + 4d \end{bmatrix} = \begin{bmatrix} 6 & -5 \\ 7 & -7 \end{bmatrix}$

if and only if corresponding elements are equal.

$a + 3c = 6 \quad b + 3d = -5$

$a + 4c = 7 \quad b + 4d = -7$

Solving these systems we obtain $a = 3, b = 1, c = 1, d = -2$. (Solution left to the student.)

71.　(A)　Since $\begin{bmatrix} a_1 & 0 \\ 0 & d_1 \end{bmatrix} + \begin{bmatrix} a_2 & 0 \\ 0 & d_2 \end{bmatrix} = \begin{bmatrix} a_1 + a_2 & 0 \\ 0 & d_1 + d_2 \end{bmatrix}$, the statement is true.

　　(B)　$A + B = B + A$ is true for any matrices for which $A + B$ is defined, as it is in this case.

　　(C)　Since $\begin{bmatrix} a_1 & 0 \\ 0 & d_1 \end{bmatrix} \begin{bmatrix} a_2 & 0 \\ 0 & d_2 \end{bmatrix} = \begin{bmatrix} a_1 a_2 & 0 \\ 0 & d_1 d_2 \end{bmatrix}$, the statement is true.

　　(D)　Since $\begin{bmatrix} a_1 & 0 \\ 0 & d_1 \end{bmatrix} \begin{bmatrix} a_2 & 0 \\ 0 & d_2 \end{bmatrix} = \begin{bmatrix} a_1 a_2 & 0 \\ 0 & d_1 d_2 \end{bmatrix} = \begin{bmatrix} a_2 a_1 & 0 \\ 0 & d_2 d_1 \end{bmatrix} = \begin{bmatrix} a_2 & 0 \\ 0 & d_2 \end{bmatrix} \begin{bmatrix} a_1 & 0 \\ 0 & d_1 \end{bmatrix}$,

　　　　the statement is true.

73.　$\dfrac{1}{2}(A + B) = \dfrac{1}{2}\left(\begin{bmatrix} 30 & 25 \\ 60 & 80 \end{bmatrix} + \begin{bmatrix} 36 & 27 \\ 54 & 74 \end{bmatrix} \right) = \dfrac{1}{2}\begin{bmatrix} 66 & 52 \\ 114 & 154 \end{bmatrix} = \begin{bmatrix} 33 & 26 \\ 57 & 77 \end{bmatrix}$

This result provides the average cost of production for the two plants.

75.　If a quantity is increased by 15%, the result is a multiplication by 1.15.

If a quantity is increased by 10%, the result is a multiplication by 1.1.

Thus we must calculate $1.1N - 1.15M$. The mark–up matrix is:

$1.1N - 1.15M = 1.1\begin{bmatrix} 13{,}900 & 783 & 263 & 215 \\ 15{,}000 & 838 & 395 & 236 \\ 18{,}300 & 967 & 573 & 248 \end{bmatrix} - 1.15\begin{bmatrix} 10{,}400 & 682 & 215 & 182 \\ 12{,}500 & 721 & 295 & 182 \\ 16{,}400 & 827 & 443 & 192 \end{bmatrix}$

$= \begin{bmatrix} 15{,}290 & 861.3 & 289.3 & 236.5 \\ 16{,}500 & 921.8 & 434.5 & 259.6 \\ 20{,}130 & 1{,}063.7 & 630.3 & 272.8 \end{bmatrix} - \begin{bmatrix} 11{,}960 & 784.3 & 247.25 & 209.3 \\ 14{,}375 & 829.15 & 339.25 & 209.3 \\ 18{,}860 & 951.05 & 509.45 & 220.8 \end{bmatrix}$

	Basic Car	Air	CD changer	Cruise Control
Model A	$3,330	$77	$42	$27
Model B	$2,125	$93	$95	$50
Model C	$1,270	$113	$121	$52

$=$ 〔Model A / Model B / Model C table above〕 $=$ Mark up

77.　(A)　$\begin{bmatrix} 0.6 & 0.6 & 0.2 \end{bmatrix} \begin{bmatrix} 8 \\ 10 \\ 5 \end{bmatrix} = (0.6)8 + (0.6)10 + (0.2)5 = 11.80$ dollars per boat

(B) $[1.5 \quad 1.2 \quad 0.4]\begin{bmatrix} 9 \\ 12 \\ 6 \end{bmatrix} = (1.5)9 + (1.2)12 + (0.4)6 = 30.30$ dollars per boat

(C) The matrix NM has no obvious meaning, but the matrix MN gives the labor costs per boat at each plant.

(D) $MN = \begin{bmatrix} 0.6 & 0.6 & 0.2 \\ 1.0 & 0.9 & 0.3 \\ 1.5 & 1.2 & 0.4 \end{bmatrix}\begin{bmatrix} 8 & 9 \\ 10 & 12 \\ 5 & 6 \end{bmatrix} = \begin{bmatrix} (0.6)8+(0.6)10+(0.2)5 & (0.6)9+(0.6)12+(0.2)6 \\ (1.0)8+(0.9)10+(0.3)5 & (1.0)9+(0.9)12+(0.3)6 \\ (1.5)8+(1.2)10+(0.4)5 & (1.5)9+(1.2)12+(0.4)6 \end{bmatrix}$

$$= \begin{bmatrix} \$11.80 & \$13.80 \\ \$18.50 & \$21.60 \\ \$26.00 & \$30.30 \end{bmatrix} \begin{matrix} \text{One-person boat} \\ \text{Two-person boat} \\ \text{Four-person boat} \end{matrix}$$

with column headers Plant I, Plant II.

This matrix gives the labor costs for each type of boat at each plant.

79. (A) $A^2 = AA = \begin{bmatrix} 0 & 1 & 0 & 1 & 0 \\ 0 & 0 & 1 & 0 & 0 \\ 1 & 0 & 0 & 0 & 1 \\ 0 & 0 & 1 & 0 & 0 \\ 0 & 0 & 0 & 1 & 0 \end{bmatrix}\begin{bmatrix} 0 & 1 & 0 & 1 & 0 \\ 0 & 0 & 1 & 0 & 0 \\ 1 & 0 & 0 & 0 & 1 \\ 0 & 0 & 1 & 0 & 0 \\ 0 & 0 & 0 & 1 & 0 \end{bmatrix} = \begin{bmatrix} 0 & 0 & 2 & 0 & 0 \\ 1 & 0 & 0 & 0 & 1 \\ 0 & 1 & 0 & 2 & 0 \\ 1 & 0 & 0 & 0 & 1 \\ 0 & 0 & 1 & 0 & 0 \end{bmatrix}$

The 1 in row 2 and column 1 of A^2 indicates that there is one way to travel from Baltimore to Atlanta with one intermediate connection. The 2 in row 1 and column 3 indicates that there are two ways to travel from Atlanta to Chicago with one intermediate connection. In general, the elements in A^2 indicate the number of different ways to travel from the ith city to the jth city with one intermediate connection.

(B) $A^3 = A^2A = \begin{bmatrix} 0 & 0 & 2 & 0 & 0 \\ 1 & 0 & 0 & 0 & 1 \\ 0 & 1 & 0 & 2 & 0 \\ 1 & 0 & 0 & 0 & 1 \\ 0 & 0 & 1 & 0 & 0 \end{bmatrix}\begin{bmatrix} 0 & 1 & 0 & 1 & 0 \\ 0 & 0 & 1 & 0 & 0 \\ 1 & 0 & 0 & 0 & 1 \\ 0 & 0 & 1 & 0 & 0 \\ 0 & 0 & 0 & 1 & 0 \end{bmatrix} = \begin{bmatrix} 2 & 0 & 0 & 0 & 2 \\ 0 & 1 & 0 & 2 & 0 \\ 0 & 0 & 3 & 0 & 0 \\ 0 & 1 & 0 & 2 & 0 \\ 1 & 0 & 0 & 0 & 1 \end{bmatrix}$

The 1 in row 4 and column 2 of A^3 indicates that there is one way to travel from Denver to Baltimore with two intermediate connections. The 2 in row 1 and column 5 indicates that there are two ways to travel from Atlanta to El Paso with two intermediate connections. In general, the elements in A^3 indicate the number of different ways to travel from the ith city to the the jth city with two intermediate connections.

(C) A is given above.

$A + A^2 = \begin{bmatrix} 0 & 1 & 0 & 1 & 0 \\ 0 & 0 & 1 & 0 & 0 \\ 1 & 0 & 0 & 0 & 1 \\ 0 & 0 & 1 & 0 & 0 \\ 0 & 0 & 0 & 1 & 0 \end{bmatrix} + \begin{bmatrix} 0 & 0 & 2 & 0 & 0 \\ 1 & 0 & 0 & 0 & 1 \\ 0 & 1 & 0 & 2 & 0 \\ 1 & 0 & 0 & 0 & 1 \\ 0 & 0 & 1 & 0 & 0 \end{bmatrix} = \begin{bmatrix} 0 & 1 & 2 & 1 & 0 \\ 1 & 0 & 1 & 0 & 1 \\ 1 & 1 & 0 & 2 & 1 \\ 1 & 0 & 1 & 0 & 1 \\ 0 & 0 & 1 & 1 & 0 \end{bmatrix}$

$A + A^2 + A^3 = \begin{bmatrix} 0 & 1 & 2 & 1 & 0 \\ 1 & 0 & 1 & 0 & 1 \\ 1 & 1 & 0 & 2 & 1 \\ 1 & 0 & 1 & 0 & 1 \\ 0 & 0 & 1 & 1 & 0 \end{bmatrix} + \begin{bmatrix} 2 & 0 & 0 & 0 & 2 \\ 0 & 1 & 0 & 2 & 0 \\ 0 & 0 & 3 & 0 & 0 \\ 0 & 1 & 0 & 2 & 0 \\ 1 & 0 & 0 & 0 & 1 \end{bmatrix} = \begin{bmatrix} 2 & 1 & 2 & 1 & 2 \\ 1 & 1 & 1 & 2 & 1 \\ 1 & 1 & 3 & 2 & 1 \\ 1 & 1 & 1 & 2 & 1 \\ 1 & 0 & 1 & 1 & 1 \end{bmatrix}$

A zero element remains, so we must compute A^4.

$$A^4 = A^3 A = \begin{bmatrix} 2 & 0 & 0 & 0 & 2 \\ 0 & 1 & 0 & 2 & 0 \\ 0 & 0 & 3 & 0 & 0 \\ 0 & 1 & 0 & 2 & 0 \\ 1 & 0 & 0 & 0 & 1 \end{bmatrix} \begin{bmatrix} 0 & 1 & 0 & 1 & 0 \\ 0 & 0 & 1 & 0 & 0 \\ 1 & 0 & 0 & 0 & 1 \\ 0 & 0 & 1 & 0 & 0 \\ 0 & 0 & 0 & 1 & 0 \end{bmatrix} = \begin{bmatrix} 0 & 2 & 0 & 4 & 0 \\ 0 & 0 & 3 & 0 & 0 \\ 3 & 0 & 0 & 0 & 3 \\ 0 & 0 & 3 & 0 & 0 \\ 0 & 1 & 0 & 2 & 0 \end{bmatrix}$$

Then $A + A^2 + A^3 + A^4 = \begin{bmatrix} 2 & 1 & 2 & 1 & 2 \\ 1 & 1 & 1 & 2 & 1 \\ 1 & 1 & 3 & 2 & 1 \\ 1 & 1 & 1 & 2 & 1 \\ 1 & 0 & 1 & 1 & 1 \end{bmatrix} + \begin{bmatrix} 0 & 2 & 0 & 4 & 0 \\ 0 & 0 & 3 & 0 & 0 \\ 3 & 0 & 0 & 0 & 3 \\ 0 & 0 & 3 & 0 & 0 \\ 0 & 1 & 0 & 2 & 0 \end{bmatrix} = \begin{bmatrix} 2 & 3 & 2 & 5 & 2 \\ 1 & 1 & 4 & 2 & 1 \\ 4 & 1 & 3 & 2 & 4 \\ 1 & 1 & 4 & 2 & 1 \\ 1 & 1 & 1 & 3 & 1 \end{bmatrix}$

This matrix indicates that it is possible to travel from any origin to any destination with at most 3 intermediate connections.

81. (A) $[1{,}000 \quad 500 \quad 5{,}000] \begin{bmatrix} \$0.80 \\ \$1.50 \\ \$0.40 \end{bmatrix} = 1{,}000(\$0.80) + 500(\$1.50) + 5{,}000(\$0.40) = \$3{,}550$

(B) $[2{,}000 \quad 800 \quad 8{,}000] \begin{bmatrix} \$0.80 \\ \$1.50 \\ \$0.40 \end{bmatrix} = 2{,}000(\$0.80) + 800(\$1.50) + 8{,}000(\$0.40) = \$6{,}000$

(C) The matrix MN has no obvious interpretations, but the matrix NM represents the total cost of all contacts in each town.

(D) $NM = \begin{bmatrix} 1{,}000 & 500 & 5{,}000 \\ 2{,}000 & 800 & 8{,}000 \end{bmatrix} \begin{bmatrix} \$0.80 \\ \$1.50 \\ \$0.40 \end{bmatrix} = \begin{bmatrix} 1{,}000(0.80) + 500(1.50) + 5{,}000(0.40) \\ 2{,}000(0.80) + 800(1.50) + 8{,}000(0.40) \end{bmatrix}$

$= \begin{bmatrix} \$3{,}550 \\ \$6{,}000 \end{bmatrix} \begin{matrix} \text{Berkeley} \\ \text{Oakland} \end{matrix} = $ cost of all contacts in each town.

(E) The matrix $[1 \quad 1]N$ can be used to find the total number of each of the three types of contact:

$$[1 \quad 1] \begin{bmatrix} 1{,}000 & 500 & 5{,}000 \\ 2{,}000 & 800 & 8{,}000 \end{bmatrix} = [1{,}000 + 2{,}000 \quad 500 + 800 \quad 5{,}000 + 8{,}000]$$

$\text{[Telephone House Letter]} = [3{,}000 \quad 1{,}300 \quad 13{,}000]$

(F) The matrix $N \begin{bmatrix} 1 \\ 1 \\ 1 \end{bmatrix}$ can be used to find the total number of contacts in each town:

$$\begin{bmatrix} 1{,}000 & 500 & 5{,}000 \\ 2{,}000 & 800 & 8{,}000 \end{bmatrix} \begin{bmatrix} 1 \\ 1 \\ 1 \end{bmatrix} = \begin{bmatrix} 1{,}000 + 500 + 5{,}000 \\ 2{,}000 + 800 + 8{,}000 \end{bmatrix} = \begin{bmatrix} 6{,}500 \\ 10{,}800 \end{bmatrix} = \begin{bmatrix} \text{Berkeley contacts} \\ \text{Oakland contacts} \end{bmatrix}$$

83. (A) Since player 1 did not defeat player 1, a 0 is placed in row 1, column 1.
Since player 1 did not defeat player 2, a 0 is placed in row 1, column 2.
Since player 1 defeated player 3, a 1 is placed in row 1, column 3.
Since player 1 defeated player 4, a 1 is placed in row 1, column 4.
Since player 1 defeated player 5, a 1 is placed in row 1, column 5.
Since player 1 did not defeat player 6, a 0 is placed in row 1, column 6.

Proceeding in this manner, we obtain

$$A = \begin{bmatrix} 0 & 0 & 1 & 1 & 1 & 0 \\ 1 & 0 & 0 & 1 & 1 & 0 \\ 0 & 1 & 0 & 1 & 0 & 0 \\ 0 & 0 & 0 & 0 & 0 & 1 \\ 0 & 0 & 1 & 1 & 0 & 1 \\ 1 & 1 & 1 & 0 & 0 & 0 \end{bmatrix}$$

(B) $A^2 = \begin{bmatrix} 0 & 0 & 1 & 1 & 1 & 0 \\ 1 & 0 & 0 & 1 & 1 & 0 \\ 0 & 1 & 0 & 1 & 0 & 0 \\ 0 & 0 & 0 & 0 & 0 & 1 \\ 0 & 0 & 1 & 1 & 0 & 1 \\ 1 & 1 & 1 & 0 & 0 & 0 \end{bmatrix} \begin{bmatrix} 0 & 0 & 1 & 1 & 1 & 0 \\ 1 & 0 & 0 & 1 & 1 & 0 \\ 0 & 1 & 0 & 1 & 0 & 0 \\ 0 & 0 & 0 & 0 & 0 & 1 \\ 0 & 0 & 1 & 1 & 0 & 1 \\ 1 & 1 & 1 & 0 & 0 & 0 \end{bmatrix} = \begin{bmatrix} 0 & 1 & 1 & 2 & 0 & 2 \\ 0 & 0 & 2 & 2 & 1 & 2 \\ 1 & 0 & 0 & 1 & 1 & 1 \\ 1 & 1 & 1 & 0 & 0 & 0 \\ 1 & 2 & 1 & 1 & 0 & 1 \\ 1 & 1 & 1 & 3 & 2 & 0 \end{bmatrix}$

$$A + A^2 = \begin{bmatrix} 0 & 1 & 2 & 3 & 1 & 2 \\ 1 & 0 & 2 & 3 & 2 & 2 \\ 1 & 1 & 0 & 2 & 1 & 1 \\ 1 & 1 & 1 & 0 & 0 & 1 \\ 1 & 2 & 2 & 2 & 0 & 2 \\ 2 & 2 & 2 & 3 & 2 & 0 \end{bmatrix} = B$$

Check (using graphing calculator):

Finally $B^{-1}A^{-1}$ is calculated as $C = \begin{bmatrix} 1 \\ 1 \\ 1 \\ 1 \\ 1 \\ 1 \end{bmatrix}$ Then $BC = \begin{bmatrix} 0 & 1 & 2 & 3 & 1 & 2 \\ 1 & 0 & 2 & 3 & 2 & 2 \\ 1 & 1 & 0 & 2 & 1 & 1 \\ 1 & 1 & 1 & 0 & 0 & 1 \\ 1 & 2 & 2 & 2 & 0 & 2 \\ 2 & 2 & 2 & 3 & 2 & 0 \end{bmatrix} \begin{bmatrix} 1 \\ 1 \\ 1 \\ 1 \\ 1 \\ 1 \end{bmatrix} = \begin{bmatrix} 9 \\ 10 \\ 6 \\ 4 \\ 9 \\ 11 \end{bmatrix}$

(D) BC measures the relative strength of the players, with the larger numbers representing greater strength. Thus, player 6 is the strongest and player 4 the weakest; ranking:
    Frank, Bart, Aaron & Elvis (tie), Charles, Dan.

SECTION 7–4

1. An identity matrix is a square matrix I whose product with any matrix A, if defined, is A.

3. The inverse matrix A^{-1} of a matrix A is a matrix such that $AA^{-1} = A^{-1}A = I$. Not every matrix has an inverse.

5. Answers will vary.   **7.** Answers will vary.   **9.** Gauss–Jordan elimination is the best approach.

11. $\begin{bmatrix} 2 & -3 \\ 4 & 5 \end{bmatrix}$ **13.** $\begin{bmatrix} -2 & 1 & 3 \\ 2 & 4 & -2 \\ 5 & 1 & 0 \end{bmatrix}$ **15.** $\begin{bmatrix} 3 & -4 \\ -2 & 3 \end{bmatrix}\begin{bmatrix} 3 & 4 \\ 2 & 3 \end{bmatrix} = \begin{bmatrix} 3\cdot3+(-4)2 & 3\cdot4+(-4)3 \\ (-2)3+3\cdot2 & (-2)4+3\cdot3 \end{bmatrix} = \begin{bmatrix} 1 & 0 \\ 0 & 1 \end{bmatrix}$

Thus, these two matrices are inverses of each other.

17. $\begin{bmatrix} 2 & 2 \\ -1 & -1 \end{bmatrix}\begin{bmatrix} 1 & 1 \\ -1 & -1 \end{bmatrix} = \begin{bmatrix} 2\cdot1+2(-1) & 2\cdot1+2(-1) \\ (-1)1+(-1)(-1) & (-1)1+(-1)(-1) \end{bmatrix} = \begin{bmatrix} 0 & 0 \\ 0 & 0 \end{bmatrix}$

Thus, these two matrices are not inverses of each other.

19. $\begin{bmatrix} -5 & 2 \\ -8 & 3 \end{bmatrix}\begin{bmatrix} 3 & -2 \\ 8 & -5 \end{bmatrix} = \begin{bmatrix} (-5)3+2\cdot 8 & (-5)(-2)+2(-5) \\ (-8)3+3\cdot 8 & (-8)(-2)+3(-5) \end{bmatrix} = \begin{bmatrix} 1 & 0 \\ 0 & 1 \end{bmatrix}$

Thus, these two matrices are inverses of each other.

21. $\begin{bmatrix} 1 & 2 & 0 \\ 0 & 1 & 0 \\ -1 & -1 & 1 \end{bmatrix}\begin{bmatrix} 1 & -2 & 0 \\ 0 & 1 & 0 \\ 1 & -1 & 0 \end{bmatrix} = \begin{bmatrix} 1\cdot 1+2\cdot 0+0\cdot 1 & 1(-2)+2\cdot 1+0(-1) & 1\cdot 0+2\cdot 0+0\cdot 0 \\ 0\cdot 1+1\cdot 0+0\cdot 1 & 0(-2)+1\cdot 1+0(-1) & 0\cdot 0+1\cdot 0+0\cdot 0 \\ (-1)1+(-1)0+1\cdot 1 & (-1)(-2)+(-1)1+1(-1) & (-1)0+(-1)0+1\cdot 0 \end{bmatrix} = \begin{bmatrix} 1 & 0 & 0 \\ 0 & 1 & 0 \\ 0 & 0 & 0 \end{bmatrix}$

Thus, these two matrices are not inverses of each other.

23. $\begin{bmatrix} 1 & -1 & 1 \\ 0 & 2 & -1 \\ 2 & 3 & 0 \end{bmatrix}\begin{bmatrix} 3 & 3 & -1 \\ -2 & -2 & 1 \\ -4 & -5 & 2 \end{bmatrix} = \begin{bmatrix} 1\cdot 3+(-1)(-2)+1(-4) & 1\cdot 3+(-1)(-2)+1(-5) & 1(-1)+(-1)1+1\cdot 2 \\ 0\cdot 3+2(-2)+(-1)(-4) & 0\cdot 3+2(-2)+(-1)(-5) & 0(-1)+2\cdot 1+(-1)2 \\ 2\cdot 3+3(-2)+0(-4) & 2\cdot 3+3(-2)+0(-5) & 2(-1)+3\cdot 1+0\cdot 2 \end{bmatrix} = \begin{bmatrix} 1 & 0 & 0 \\ 0 & 1 & 0 \\ 0 & 0 & 1 \end{bmatrix}$

Thus, these two matrices are inverses of each other.

25. $\begin{aligned} 2x_1 - x_2 &= 3 \\ x_1 + 3x_2 &= -2 \end{aligned}$

27. $\begin{aligned} -2x_1 \quad\quad + x_3 &= 3 \\ x_1 + 2x_2 + x_3 &= -4 \\ x_2 - x_3 &= 2 \end{aligned}$

29. $\begin{bmatrix} 4 & -3 \\ 1 & 2 \end{bmatrix}\begin{bmatrix} x_1 \\ x_2 \end{bmatrix} = \begin{bmatrix} 2 \\ 1 \end{bmatrix}$

31. $\begin{bmatrix} 1 & -2 & 1 \\ -1 & 1 & 0 \\ 2 & 3 & 1 \end{bmatrix}\begin{bmatrix} x_1 \\ x_2 \\ x_3 \end{bmatrix} = \begin{bmatrix} -1 \\ 2 \\ -3 \end{bmatrix}$

33. Since $\begin{bmatrix} 3 & -2 \\ 1 & 4 \end{bmatrix}\begin{bmatrix} -2 \\ 1 \end{bmatrix} = \begin{bmatrix} 3(-2) & (-2)1 \\ 1(-2) & 4\cdot 1 \end{bmatrix} = \begin{bmatrix} -8 \\ 2 \end{bmatrix}$, $\begin{bmatrix} x_1 \\ x_2 \end{bmatrix} = \begin{bmatrix} -8 \\ 2 \end{bmatrix}$ if and only if $x_1 = -8$ and $x_2 = 2$.

35. Since $\begin{bmatrix} -2 & 3 \\ 2 & -1 \end{bmatrix}\begin{bmatrix} 3 \\ 2 \end{bmatrix} = \begin{bmatrix} (-2)3 & 3\cdot 2 \\ 2\cdot 3 & (-1)2 \end{bmatrix} = \begin{bmatrix} 0 \\ 4 \end{bmatrix}$, $\begin{bmatrix} x_1 \\ x_2 \end{bmatrix} = \begin{bmatrix} 0 \\ 4 \end{bmatrix}$ if and only if $x_1 = 0$ and $x_2 = 4$.

37. $\begin{bmatrix} 1 & -1 \\ 1 & -2 \end{bmatrix}\begin{bmatrix} x_1 \\ x_2 \end{bmatrix} = \begin{bmatrix} 5 \\ 7 \end{bmatrix}$

$\quad\quad A \quad\quad X \quad = B$

$AX = B$ has solution $X = A^{-1}B$.

To find A^{-1}, we perform row operations on

$\begin{bmatrix} 1 & -1 & | & 1 & 0 \\ 1 & -2 & | & 0 & 1 \end{bmatrix}(-1)R_1 + R_2 \to R_2$

$\sim \begin{bmatrix} 1 & -1 & | & 1 & 0 \\ 0 & -1 & | & -1 & 1 \end{bmatrix}(-1)R_2 + R_1 \to R_1$

$\sim \begin{bmatrix} 1 & 0 & | & 2 & -1 \\ 0 & -1 & | & -1 & 1 \end{bmatrix}(-1)R_2 \to R_2$

$\sim \begin{bmatrix} 1 & 0 & | & 2 & -1 \\ 0 & 1 & | & 1 & -1 \end{bmatrix}$

Hence $A^{-1} = \begin{bmatrix} 2 & -1 \\ 1 & -1 \end{bmatrix}$

Check: $A^{-1}A = \begin{bmatrix} 2 & -1 \\ 1 & -1 \end{bmatrix}\begin{bmatrix} 1 & -1 \\ 1 & -2 \end{bmatrix} = \begin{bmatrix} 1 & 0 \\ 0 & 1 \end{bmatrix}$

Then

$\quad X \quad\quad A^{-1} \quad B$

$\begin{bmatrix} x_1 \\ x_2 \end{bmatrix} = \begin{bmatrix} 2 & -1 \\ 1 & -1 \end{bmatrix}\begin{bmatrix} 5 \\ 7 \end{bmatrix} = \begin{bmatrix} 3 \\ -2 \end{bmatrix}$ $\quad x_1 = 3, x_2 = -2.$

39. $\begin{bmatrix} 1 & 1 \\ 2 & -3 \end{bmatrix}\begin{bmatrix} x_1 \\ x_2 \end{bmatrix} = \begin{bmatrix} 15 \\ 10 \end{bmatrix}$

$\quad\quad A \quad\quad X \quad = B$

$AX = B$ has solution $X = A^{-1}B$.

To find A^{-1}, we perform row operations on

$\begin{bmatrix} 1 & 1 & | & 1 & 0 \\ 2 & -3 & | & 0 & 1 \end{bmatrix}(-2)R_1 + R_2 \to R_2$

$\sim \begin{bmatrix} 1 & 1 & | & 1 & 0 \\ 0 & -5 & | & -2 & 1 \end{bmatrix}\left(-\frac{1}{5}\right)R_2 \to R_2$

$\sim \begin{bmatrix} 1 & 1 & | & 1 & 0 \\ 0 & 1 & | & \frac{2}{5} & -\frac{1}{5} \end{bmatrix}(-1)R_2 + R_1 \to R_1$

$\sim \begin{bmatrix} 1 & 0 & | & \frac{3}{5} & \frac{1}{5} \\ 0 & 1 & | & \frac{2}{5} & -\frac{1}{5} \end{bmatrix}$

Hence $A^{-1} = \begin{bmatrix} \frac{3}{5} & \frac{1}{5} \\ \frac{2}{5} & -\frac{1}{5} \end{bmatrix}$

Check: $A^{-1}A = \begin{bmatrix} \frac{3}{5} & \frac{1}{5} \\ \frac{2}{5} & -\frac{1}{5} \end{bmatrix}\begin{bmatrix} 1 & 1 \\ 2 & -3 \end{bmatrix} = \begin{bmatrix} 1 & 0 \\ 0 & 1 \end{bmatrix}$

Then

$\quad X \quad\quad A^{-1} \quad B$

$\begin{bmatrix} x_1 \\ x_2 \end{bmatrix} = \begin{bmatrix} \frac{3}{5} & \frac{1}{5} \\ \frac{2}{5} & -\frac{1}{5} \end{bmatrix}\begin{bmatrix} 15 \\ 10 \end{bmatrix} = \begin{bmatrix} 11 \\ 4 \end{bmatrix}$ $\quad x_1 = 11, x_2 = 4$

41. $\begin{bmatrix} 1 & 9 & | & 1 & 0 \\ 0 & 1 & | & 0 & 1 \end{bmatrix} (-9)R_2 + R_1 \rightarrow R_1 \sim \begin{bmatrix} 1 & 0 & | & 1 & -9 \\ 0 & 1 & | & 0 & 1 \end{bmatrix}$ Hence, $M^{-1} = \begin{bmatrix} 1 & -9 \\ 0 & 1 \end{bmatrix}$

Check: $M^{-1}M = \begin{bmatrix} 1 & -9 \\ 0 & 1 \end{bmatrix}\begin{bmatrix} 1 & 9 \\ 0 & 1 \end{bmatrix} = \begin{bmatrix} 1 \cdot 1 + (-9)0 & 1 \cdot 9 + (-9)1 \\ 0 \cdot 1 + 1 \cdot 0 & 0 \cdot 9 + 1 \cdot 1 \end{bmatrix} = \begin{bmatrix} 1 & 0 \\ 0 & 1 \end{bmatrix}$

43. $\begin{bmatrix} -1 & -2 & | & 1 & 0 \\ 2 & 5 & | & 0 & 1 \end{bmatrix} 2R_1 + R_2 \rightarrow R_2 \sim \begin{bmatrix} -1 & -2 & | & 1 & 0 \\ 0 & 1 & | & 2 & 1 \end{bmatrix} 2R_2 + R_1 \rightarrow R_1 \sim \begin{bmatrix} -1 & 0 & | & 5 & 2 \\ 0 & 1 & | & 2 & 1 \end{bmatrix} (-1)R_1 \rightarrow R_1$

$\sim \begin{bmatrix} 1 & 0 & | & -5 & -2 \\ 0 & 1 & | & 2 & 1 \end{bmatrix}$ Hence, $M^{-1} = \begin{bmatrix} -5 & -2 \\ 2 & 1 \end{bmatrix}$

Check: $M^{-1}M = \begin{bmatrix} -5 & -2 \\ 2 & 1 \end{bmatrix}\begin{bmatrix} -1 & -2 \\ 2 & 5 \end{bmatrix} = \begin{bmatrix} (-5)(-1)+(-2)2 & (-5)(-2)+(-2)5 \\ 2(-1)+1 \cdot 2 & 2(-2)+1 \cdot 5 \end{bmatrix} = \begin{bmatrix} 1 & 0 \\ 0 & 1 \end{bmatrix}$

45. $\begin{bmatrix} -5 & 7 & | & 1 & 0 \\ 2 & -3 & | & 0 & 1 \end{bmatrix} 3R_2 + R_1 \rightarrow R_1 \sim \begin{bmatrix} 1 & -2 & | & 1 & 3 \\ 2 & -3 & | & 0 & 1 \end{bmatrix} (-2)R_1 + R_2 \rightarrow R_2 \sim \begin{bmatrix} 1 & -2 & | & 1 & 3 \\ 0 & 1 & | & -2 & -5 \end{bmatrix} 2R_2 + R_1 \rightarrow R_1$

$\sim \begin{bmatrix} 1 & 0 & | & -3 & -7 \\ 0 & 1 & | & -2 & -5 \end{bmatrix}$ Hence, $M^{-1} = \begin{bmatrix} -3 & -7 \\ -2 & -5 \end{bmatrix}$

Check: $M^{-1}M = \begin{bmatrix} -3 & -7 \\ -2 & -5 \end{bmatrix}\begin{bmatrix} -5 & 7 \\ 2 & -3 \end{bmatrix} = \begin{bmatrix} (-3)(-5)+(-7)2 & (-3)7+(-7)(-3) \\ (-2)(-5)+(-5)2 & (-2)7+(-5)(-3) \end{bmatrix} = \begin{bmatrix} 1 & 0 \\ 0 & 1 \end{bmatrix}$

47. If the inverse existed we would find it by row operations on the following matrix: $= \begin{bmatrix} 3 & 9 & | & 1 & 0 \\ 2 & 6 & | & 0 & 1 \end{bmatrix}$

But consider what happens if we perform $(-\frac{2}{3})R_1 + R_2 \rightarrow R_2 = \begin{bmatrix} 3 & 9 & | & 1 & 0 \\ 0 & 0 & | & -\frac{2}{3} & 1 \end{bmatrix}$

Since a row of zeros results to the left of the vertical line, no inverse exists.

49. $\begin{bmatrix} 2 & 3 & | & 1 & 0 \\ 3 & 5 & | & 0 & 1 \end{bmatrix} \frac{1}{2}R_1 \rightarrow R_1 \sim \begin{bmatrix} 1 & 1.5 & | & 0.5 & 0 \\ 3 & 5 & | & 0 & 1 \end{bmatrix} (-3)R_1 + R_2 \rightarrow R_2 \sim \begin{bmatrix} 1 & 1.5 & | & 0.5 & 0 \\ 0 & 0.5 & | & -1.5 & 1 \end{bmatrix} 2R_2 \rightarrow R_2$

$\sim \begin{bmatrix} 1 & 1.5 & | & 0.5 & 0 \\ 0 & 1 & | & -3 & 2 \end{bmatrix} (-1.5)R_2 + R_1 \rightarrow R_1 \sim \begin{bmatrix} 1 & 0 & | & 5 & -3 \\ 0 & 1 & | & -3 & 2 \end{bmatrix}$ The inverse is $\begin{bmatrix} 5 & -3 \\ -3 & 2 \end{bmatrix}$

The checking steps are omitted for lack of space in this and some subsequent problems.

51. $\begin{bmatrix} 1 & -1 & 0 & | & 1 & 0 & 0 \\ -1 & 1 & -1 & | & 0 & 1 & 0 \\ 0 & -1 & 1 & | & 0 & 0 & 1 \end{bmatrix} R_1 + R_2 \rightarrow R_2 \sim \begin{bmatrix} 1 & -1 & 0 & | & 1 & 0 & 0 \\ 0 & 0 & -1 & | & 1 & 1 & 0 \\ 0 & -1 & 1 & | & 0 & 0 & 1 \end{bmatrix} R_2 \leftrightarrow R_3$

$\sim \begin{bmatrix} 1 & -1 & 0 & | & 1 & 0 & 0 \\ 0 & -1 & 1 & | & 0 & 0 & 1 \\ 0 & 0 & -1 & | & 1 & 1 & 0 \end{bmatrix} (-1)R_2 + R_1 \rightarrow R_1 \sim \begin{bmatrix} 1 & 0 & -1 & | & 1 & 0 & -1 \\ 0 & -1 & 1 & | & 0 & 0 & 1 \\ 0 & 0 & -1 & | & 1 & 1 & 0 \end{bmatrix} \begin{matrix} (-1)R_3 + R_1 \rightarrow R_1 \\ R_3 + R_2 \rightarrow R_2 \end{matrix}$

$\sim \begin{bmatrix} 1 & 0 & 0 & | & 0 & -1 & -1 \\ 0 & -1 & 0 & | & 1 & 1 & 1 \\ 0 & 0 & -1 & | & 1 & 1 & 0 \end{bmatrix} \begin{matrix} (-1)R_2 \rightarrow R_2 \\ (-1)R_3 \rightarrow R_3 \end{matrix} \sim \begin{bmatrix} 1 & 0 & 0 & | & 0 & -1 & -1 \\ 0 & 1 & 0 & | & -1 & -1 & -1 \\ 0 & 0 & 1 & | & -1 & -1 & 0 \end{bmatrix}$ Hence, $M^{-1} = \begin{bmatrix} 0 & -1 & -1 \\ -1 & -1 & -1 \\ -1 & -1 & 0 \end{bmatrix}$

Check: $M^{-1}M = \begin{bmatrix} 0 & -1 & -1 \\ -1 & -1 & -1 \\ -1 & -1 & 0 \end{bmatrix}\begin{bmatrix} 1 & -1 & 0 \\ -1 & 1 & -1 \\ 0 & -1 & 1 \end{bmatrix}$

$= \begin{bmatrix} 0 \cdot 1 + (-1)(-1)+(-1)0 & 0(-1)+(-1)1+(-1)(-1) & 0 \cdot 0+(-1)(-1)+(-1)1 \\ (-1)1+(-1)(-1)+(-1)0 & (-1)(-1)+(-1)1+(-1)(-1) & (-1)0+(-1)(-1)+(-1)1 \\ (-1)1+(-1)(-1)+0 \cdot 0 & (-1)(-1)+(-1)1+0(-1) & (-1)0+(-1)(-1)+0 \cdot 1 \end{bmatrix} = \begin{bmatrix} 1 & 0 & 0 \\ 0 & 1 & 0 \\ 0 & 0 & 1 \end{bmatrix}$

53.
$$\begin{bmatrix} 1 & 2 & 5 & | & 1 & 0 & 0 \\ 3 & 5 & 9 & | & 0 & 1 & 0 \\ 1 & 1 & -2 & | & 0 & 0 & 1 \end{bmatrix} \begin{matrix} \\ (-3)R_1 + R_2 \to R_2 \\ (-1)R_1 + R_3 \to R_3 \end{matrix} \sim \begin{bmatrix} 1 & 2 & 5 & | & 1 & 0 & 0 \\ 0 & -1 & -6 & | & -3 & 1 & 0 \\ 0 & -1 & -7 & | & -1 & 0 & 1 \end{bmatrix} \begin{matrix} 2R_2 + R_1 \to R_1 \\ \\ (-1)R_2 + R_3 \to R_3 \end{matrix}$$

$$\sim \begin{bmatrix} 1 & 0 & -7 & | & -5 & 2 & 0 \\ 0 & -1 & -6 & | & -3 & 1 & 0 \\ 0 & 0 & -1 & | & 2 & -1 & 1 \end{bmatrix} \begin{matrix} (-7)R_3 + R_1 \to R_1 \\ (-6)R_3 + R_2 \to R_2 \\ \end{matrix} \sim \begin{bmatrix} 1 & 0 & 0 & | & -19 & 9 & -7 \\ 0 & -1 & 0 & | & -15 & 7 & -6 \\ 0 & 0 & -1 & | & 2 & -1 & 1 \end{bmatrix} \begin{matrix} \\ (-1)R_2 \to R_2 \\ (-1)R_3 \to R_3 \end{matrix}$$

$$\sim \begin{bmatrix} 1 & 0 & 0 & | & -19 & 9 & -7 \\ 0 & 1 & 0 & | & 15 & -7 & 6 \\ 0 & 0 & 1 & | & -2 & 1 & -1 \end{bmatrix} \quad \text{Hence, } M^{-1} = \begin{bmatrix} -19 & 9 & -7 \\ 15 & -7 & 6 \\ -2 & 1 & -1 \end{bmatrix}$$

Check: $M^{-1}M = \begin{bmatrix} -19 & 9 & -7 \\ 15 & -7 & 6 \\ -2 & 1 & -1 \end{bmatrix} \begin{bmatrix} 1 & 2 & 5 \\ 3 & 5 & 9 \\ 1 & 1 & -2 \end{bmatrix}$

$$= \begin{bmatrix} (-19)1 + 9 \cdot 3 + (-7)1 & (-19)2 + 9 \cdot 5 + (-7)1 & (-19)5 + 9 \cdot 9 + (-7)(-2) \\ 15 \cdot 1 + (-7)3 + 6 \cdot 1 & 15 \cdot 2 + (-7)5 + 6 \cdot 1 & 15 \cdot 5 + (-7)9 + 6(-2) \\ (-2)1 + 1 \cdot 3 + (-1)1 & (-2)2 + 1 \cdot 5 + (-1)1 & (-2)5 + 1 \cdot 9 + (-1)(-2) \end{bmatrix} = \begin{bmatrix} 1 & 0 & 0 \\ 0 & 1 & 0 \\ 0 & 0 & 1 \end{bmatrix}$$

55.
$$\begin{bmatrix} 2 & 2 & -1 & | & 1 & 0 & 0 \\ 0 & 4 & -1 & | & 0 & 1 & 0 \\ -1 & -2 & 1 & | & 0 & 0 & 1 \end{bmatrix} R_1 \leftrightarrow R_3 \sim \begin{bmatrix} -1 & -2 & 1 & | & 0 & 0 & 1 \\ 0 & 4 & -1 & | & 0 & 1 & 0 \\ 2 & 2 & -1 & | & 1 & 0 & 0 \end{bmatrix} 2R_1 + R_3 \to R_3$$

$$\sim \begin{bmatrix} -1 & -2 & 1 & | & 0 & 0 & 1 \\ 0 & 4 & -1 & | & 0 & 1 & 0 \\ 0 & -2 & 1 & | & 1 & 0 & 2 \end{bmatrix} \begin{matrix} (-1)R_3 + R_1 \to R_1 \\ 2R_3 + R_2 \to R_2 \\ \end{matrix} \sim \begin{bmatrix} -1 & 0 & 0 & | & -1 & 0 & -1 \\ 0 & 0 & 1 & | & 2 & 1 & 4 \\ 0 & -2 & 1 & | & 1 & 0 & 2 \end{bmatrix} (-1)R_2 + R_3 \to R_3$$

$$\sim \begin{bmatrix} -1 & 0 & 0 & | & -1 & 0 & -1 \\ 0 & 0 & 1 & | & 2 & 1 & 4 \\ 0 & -2 & 0 & | & -1 & -1 & -2 \end{bmatrix} R_2 \leftrightarrow R_3 \sim \begin{bmatrix} -1 & 0 & 0 & | & -1 & 0 & -1 \\ 0 & -2 & 0 & | & -1 & -1 & -2 \\ 0 & 0 & 1 & | & 2 & 1 & 4 \end{bmatrix} \begin{matrix} (-1)R_1 \to R_1 \\ (-\frac{1}{2})R_2 \to R_2 \\ \end{matrix}$$

$$\sim \begin{bmatrix} 1 & 0 & 0 & | & 1 & 0 & 1 \\ 0 & 1 & 0 & | & \frac{1}{2} & \frac{1}{2} & 1 \\ 0 & 0 & 1 & | & 2 & 1 & 4 \end{bmatrix} \quad \text{The inverse is } \begin{bmatrix} 1 & 0 & 1 \\ \frac{1}{2} & \frac{1}{2} & 1 \\ 2 & 1 & 4 \end{bmatrix}$$

57. If the inverse existed we would find it by row operations on the following matrix: $\begin{bmatrix} 2 & 1 & 1 & | & 1 & 0 & 0 \\ 1 & 1 & 0 & | & 0 & 1 & 0 \\ -1 & -1 & 0 & | & 0 & 0 & 1 \end{bmatrix}$

But consider what happens if we perform $R_2 + R_3 \to R_2$ $\begin{bmatrix} 2 & 1 & 1 & | & 1 & 0 & 0 \\ 0 & 0 & 0 & | & 0 & 1 & 1 \\ -1 & -1 & 0 & | & 0 & 0 & 1 \end{bmatrix}$

Since a row of zeros results to the left of the vertical line, no inverse exists.

59.
$$\begin{bmatrix} 1 & 5 & 10 & | & 1 & 0 & 0 \\ 0 & 1 & 4 & | & 0 & 1 & 0 \\ 1 & 6 & 15 & | & 0 & 0 & 1 \end{bmatrix} \begin{matrix} \\ \\ (-1)R_1 + R_3 \to R_3 \end{matrix} \sim \begin{bmatrix} 1 & 5 & 10 & | & 1 & 0 & 0 \\ 0 & 1 & 4 & | & 0 & 1 & 0 \\ 0 & 1 & 5 & | & -1 & 0 & 1 \end{bmatrix} \begin{matrix} (-5)R_2 + R_1 \to R_1 \\ \\ (-1)R_2 + R_3 \to R_3 \end{matrix}$$

$$\sim \begin{bmatrix} 1 & 0 & -10 & | & 1 & -5 & 0 \\ 0 & 1 & 4 & | & 0 & 1 & 0 \\ 0 & 0 & 1 & | & -1 & -1 & 1 \end{bmatrix} \begin{matrix} 10R_3 + R_1 \to R_1 \\ (-4)R_3 + R_2 \to R_2 \\ \end{matrix} \sim \begin{bmatrix} 1 & 0 & 0 & | & -9 & -15 & 10 \\ 0 & 1 & 0 & | & 4 & 5 & -4 \\ 0 & 0 & 1 & | & -1 & -1 & 1 \end{bmatrix} \quad \text{The inverse is } \begin{bmatrix} -9 & -15 & 10 \\ 4 & 5 & -4 \\ -1 & -1 & 1 \end{bmatrix}$$

61. $\begin{bmatrix} -1 & -2 \\ 2 & 5 \end{bmatrix}\begin{bmatrix} x_1 \\ x_2 \end{bmatrix} = \begin{bmatrix} k_1 \\ k_2 \end{bmatrix}$

$AX = K$ has solution $X = A^{-1}K$.

We find $A^{-1}K$ for each given K. From problem 43, $A^{-1} = \begin{bmatrix} -5 & -2 \\ 2 & 1 \end{bmatrix}$

(A) $K = \begin{bmatrix} 2 \\ 5 \end{bmatrix}$ $A^{-1}K = \begin{bmatrix} -5 & -2 \\ 2 & 1 \end{bmatrix}\begin{bmatrix} 2 \\ 5 \end{bmatrix} = \begin{bmatrix} -20 \\ 9 \end{bmatrix}$ $x_1 = -20, x_2 = 9$

(B) $K = \begin{bmatrix} -4 \\ 1 \end{bmatrix}$ $A^{-1}K = \begin{bmatrix} -5 & -2 \\ 2 & 1 \end{bmatrix}\begin{bmatrix} -4 \\ 1 \end{bmatrix} = \begin{bmatrix} 18 \\ -7 \end{bmatrix}$ $x_1 = 18, x_2 = -7$

(C) $K = \begin{bmatrix} -3 \\ -2 \end{bmatrix}$ $A^{-1}K = \begin{bmatrix} -5 & -2 \\ 2 & 1 \end{bmatrix}\begin{bmatrix} -3 \\ -2 \end{bmatrix} = \begin{bmatrix} 19 \\ -8 \end{bmatrix}$ $x_1 = 19, x_2 = -8$

63. $\begin{bmatrix} -5 & 7 \\ 2 & -3 \end{bmatrix}\begin{bmatrix} x_1 \\ x_2 \end{bmatrix} = \begin{bmatrix} k_1 \\ k_2 \end{bmatrix}$

$AX = K$ has solution $X = A^{-1}K$.

We find $A^{-1}K$ for each given K. From problem 45, $A^{-1} = \begin{bmatrix} -3 & -7 \\ -2 & -5 \end{bmatrix}$

(A) $K = \begin{bmatrix} -5 \\ 1 \end{bmatrix}$ $A^{-1}K = \begin{bmatrix} -3 & -7 \\ -2 & -5 \end{bmatrix}\begin{bmatrix} -5 \\ 1 \end{bmatrix} = \begin{bmatrix} 8 \\ 5 \end{bmatrix}$ $x_1 = 8, x_2 = 5$

(B) $K = \begin{bmatrix} 8 \\ -4 \end{bmatrix}$ $A^{-1}K = \begin{bmatrix} -3 & -7 \\ -2 & -5 \end{bmatrix}\begin{bmatrix} 8 \\ -4 \end{bmatrix} = \begin{bmatrix} 4 \\ 4 \end{bmatrix}$ $x_1 = 4, x_2 = 4$

(C) $K = \begin{bmatrix} 6 \\ 0 \end{bmatrix}$ $A^{-1}K = \begin{bmatrix} -3 & -7 \\ -2 & -5 \end{bmatrix}\begin{bmatrix} 6 \\ 0 \end{bmatrix} = \begin{bmatrix} -18 \\ -12 \end{bmatrix}$ $x_1 = -18, x_2 = -12$

65. $\begin{bmatrix} 1 & -1 & 0 \\ -1 & 1 & -1 \\ 0 & -1 & 1 \end{bmatrix}\begin{bmatrix} x_1 \\ x_2 \\ x_3 \end{bmatrix} = \begin{bmatrix} k_1 \\ k_2 \\ k_3 \end{bmatrix}$

$AX = K$ has solution $X = A^{-1}K$.

We find $A^{-1}K$ for each given K. From problem 51, $A^{-1} = \begin{bmatrix} 0 & -1 & -1 \\ -1 & -1 & -1 \\ -1 & -1 & 0 \end{bmatrix}$

(A) $K = \begin{bmatrix} 1 \\ 1 \\ 2 \end{bmatrix}$ $A^{-1}K = \begin{bmatrix} 0 & -1 & -1 \\ -1 & -1 & -1 \\ -1 & -1 & 0 \end{bmatrix}\begin{bmatrix} 1 \\ 1 \\ 2 \end{bmatrix} = \begin{bmatrix} -3 \\ -4 \\ -2 \end{bmatrix}$ $x_1 = -3, x_2 = -4, x_3 = -2$

(B) $K = \begin{bmatrix} -1 \\ 0 \\ -4 \end{bmatrix}$ $A^{-1}K = \begin{bmatrix} 0 & -1 & -1 \\ -1 & -1 & -1 \\ -1 & -1 & 0 \end{bmatrix}\begin{bmatrix} -1 \\ 0 \\ -4 \end{bmatrix} = \begin{bmatrix} 4 \\ 5 \\ 1 \end{bmatrix}$ $x_1 = 4, x_2 = 5, x_3 = 1$

(C) $K = \begin{bmatrix} 3 \\ -2 \\ 0 \end{bmatrix}$ $A^{-1}K = \begin{bmatrix} 0 & -1 & -1 \\ -1 & -1 & -1 \\ -1 & -1 & 0 \end{bmatrix}\begin{bmatrix} 3 \\ -2 \\ 0 \end{bmatrix} = \begin{bmatrix} 2 \\ -1 \\ -1 \end{bmatrix}$ $x_1 = 2, x_2 = -1, x_3 = -1$

67. $\begin{bmatrix} 1 & 2 & 5 \\ 3 & 5 & 9 \\ 1 & 1 & -2 \end{bmatrix} \begin{bmatrix} x_1 \\ x_2 \\ x_3 \end{bmatrix} = \begin{bmatrix} k_1 \\ k_2 \\ k_3 \end{bmatrix}$

$AX = K$ has solution $X = A^{-1}K$.

We find $A^{-1}K$ for each given K. From problem 53, $A^{-1} = \begin{bmatrix} -19 & 9 & -7 \\ 15 & -7 & 6 \\ -2 & 1 & -1 \end{bmatrix}$

(A) $K = \begin{bmatrix} 0 \\ 1 \\ 4 \end{bmatrix}$ $A^{-1}K = \begin{bmatrix} -19 & 9 & -7 \\ 15 & -7 & 6 \\ -2 & 1 & -1 \end{bmatrix} \begin{bmatrix} 0 \\ 1 \\ 4 \end{bmatrix} = \begin{bmatrix} -19 \\ 17 \\ -3 \end{bmatrix}$ $x_1 = -19, x_2 = 17, x_3 = -3$

(B) $K = \begin{bmatrix} 5 \\ -1 \\ 0 \end{bmatrix}$ $A^{-1}K = \begin{bmatrix} -19 & 9 & -7 \\ 15 & -7 & 6 \\ -2 & 1 & -1 \end{bmatrix} \begin{bmatrix} 5 \\ -1 \\ 0 \end{bmatrix} = \begin{bmatrix} -104 \\ 82 \\ -11 \end{bmatrix}$ $x_1 = -104, x_2 = 82, x_3 = -11$

(C) $K = \begin{bmatrix} -6 \\ 0 \\ 2 \end{bmatrix}$ $A^{-1}K = \begin{bmatrix} -19 & 9 & -7 \\ 15 & -7 & 6 \\ -2 & 1 & -1 \end{bmatrix} \begin{bmatrix} -6 \\ 0 \\ 2 \end{bmatrix} = \begin{bmatrix} 100 \\ -78 \\ 10 \end{bmatrix}$ $x_1 = 100, x_2 = -78, x_3 = 10$

69.

$AX = BX + C$	
$AX + (-BX) = (-BX) + BX + C$	Addition property of equality
$AX - BX = 0 + C$	Additive inverse property; definition of subtraction
$AX - BX = C$	
$(A - B)X = C$	Right distributive property

[To be more careful, we should write
$AX - BX = AX + -BX$ by the definition of subtraction
$= [A + (-B)]X$ by the right distributive property
$= (A - B)X$ by the definition of subtraction
but the distributive properties are
generally understood as applying to subtraction also.]

$(A - B)^{-1}[(A - B)X] = (A - B)^{-1}C$	Left multiplication property of equality
$[(A - B)^{-1}(A - B)]X = (A - B)^{-1}C$	Associative property
$IX = (A - B)^{-1}C$	Multiplicative inverse property
$X = (A - B)^{-1}C$	Multiplicative identity property

71.

$X = AX + C$	
$X + (-AX) = (-AX) + AX + C$	Addition property of equality
$X - AX = 0 + C$	Additive inverse property; definition of subtraction
$X - AX = C$	Additive identity property
$IX - AX = C$	Multiplicative identity property
$(I - A)X = C$	Right distributive property
$(I - A)^{-1}[(I - A)X] = (I - A)^{-1}C$	Left multiplication property of equality
$[(I - A)^{-1}(I - A)]X = (I - A)^{-1}C$	Associative property
$IX = (I - A)^{-1}C$	Multiplicative inverse property
$X = (I - A)^{-1}C$	Multiplicative identity property

73.

$$AX + C = 3X$$
$$AX + (-AX) + C = 3X + (-AX)$$ Addition property of equality
$$0 + C = 3X - AX$$ Additive inverse property; definition of subtraction
$$C = 3X - AX$$ Additive identity property
$$C = 3IX - AX$$ Multiplicative identity property
$$C = (3I - A)X$$ Right distributive property
$$(3I - A)^{-1} C = (3I - A)^{-1} [(3I - A)X]$$ Left multiplication property of equality
$$(3I - A)^{-1} C = [(3I - A)^{-1} (3I - A)]X$$ Associative property
$$(3I - A)^{-1} C = IX$$ Multiplicative inverse property
$$(3I - A)^{-1} C = X$$ Multiplicative inverse property

75. Try to find A^{-1}:

$$\begin{bmatrix} a & 0 & | & 1 & 0 \\ 0 & d & | & 0 & 1 \end{bmatrix} \frac{1}{a}R_1 \to R_1 \sim \begin{bmatrix} 1 & 0 & | & \frac{1}{a} & 0 \\ 0 & d & | & 0 & 1 \end{bmatrix} \frac{1}{d}R_2 \to R_2 \sim \begin{bmatrix} 1 & 0 & | & \frac{1}{a} & 0 \\ 0 & 1 & | & 0 & \frac{1}{d} \end{bmatrix}$$ The inverse is $A^{-1} = \begin{bmatrix} \frac{1}{a} & 0 \\ 0 & \frac{1}{d} \end{bmatrix}$

This will exist unless either a or d is zero, which would make $\frac{1}{a}$ or $\frac{1}{d}$ undefined. So A^{-1} exists exactly when both a and d are non–zero.

77. (A) A^{-1}: $\begin{bmatrix} 3 & 2 & | & 1 & 0 \\ -4 & -3 & | & 0 & 1 \end{bmatrix} R_2 + R_1 \to R_1$

$\sim \begin{bmatrix} -1 & -1 & | & 1 & 1 \\ -4 & -3 & | & 0 & 1 \end{bmatrix} (-1)R_1 \to R_1$

$\sim \begin{bmatrix} 1 & 1 & | & -1 & -1 \\ -4 & -3 & | & 0 & 1 \end{bmatrix} 4R_1 + R_2 \to R_2$

$\sim \begin{bmatrix} 1 & 1 & | & -1 & -1 \\ 0 & 1 & | & -4 & -3 \end{bmatrix} (-1)R_2 + R_1 \to R_1$

$\sim \begin{bmatrix} 1 & 0 & | & 3 & 2 \\ 0 & 1 & | & -4 & -3 \end{bmatrix}$ $A^{-1} = \begin{bmatrix} 3 & 2 \\ -4 & -3 \end{bmatrix}$

A^2: $\begin{bmatrix} 3 & 2 \\ -4 & -3 \end{bmatrix} \begin{bmatrix} 3 & 2 \\ -4 & -3 \end{bmatrix}$

$= \begin{bmatrix} 3 \cdot 3 + 2(-4) & 3 \cdot 2 + 2(-3) \\ (-4)3 + (-3)(-4) & (-4)2 + (-3)(-3) \end{bmatrix}$

$= \begin{bmatrix} 1 & 0 \\ 0 & 1 \end{bmatrix}$

(B) A^{-1}: $\begin{bmatrix} -2 & -1 & | & 1 & 0 \\ 3 & 2 & | & 0 & 1 \end{bmatrix} R_2 + R_1 \to R_1$

$\sim \begin{bmatrix} 1 & 1 & | & 1 & 1 \\ 3 & 2 & | & 0 & 1 \end{bmatrix} (-3)R_1 + R_2 \to R_2$

$\sim \begin{bmatrix} 1 & 1 & | & 1 & 1 \\ 0 & -1 & | & -3 & -2 \end{bmatrix} R_2 + R_1 \to R_1$

$\sim \begin{bmatrix} 1 & 0 & | & -2 & -1 \\ 0 & -1 & | & -3 & -2 \end{bmatrix} (-1)R_2 \to R_2$

$\sim \begin{bmatrix} 1 & 0 & | & -2 & -1 \\ 0 & 1 & | & 3 & 2 \end{bmatrix}$ $A^{-1} = \begin{bmatrix} -2 & -1 \\ 3 & 2 \end{bmatrix}$

A^2: $\begin{bmatrix} -2 & -1 \\ 3 & 2 \end{bmatrix} \begin{bmatrix} -2 & -1 \\ 3 & 2 \end{bmatrix}$

$= \begin{bmatrix} (-2)(-2) + (-1)3 & (-2)(-1) + (-1)2 \\ 3(-2) + 2 \cdot 3 & 3(-1) + 2 \cdot 2 \end{bmatrix}$

$= \begin{bmatrix} 1 & 0 \\ 0 & 1 \end{bmatrix}$

Note that in both cases $A^{-1} = A$ and $A^2 = I$.

79. (A) We calculate A^{-1} by row operations on

$$\begin{bmatrix} 4 & 2 & | & 1 & 0 \\ 1 & 3 & | & 0 & 1 \end{bmatrix} R_1 \leftrightarrow R_2$$

$$\sim \begin{bmatrix} 1 & 3 & | & 0 & 1 \\ 4 & 2 & | & 1 & 0 \end{bmatrix} (-4)R_1 + R_2 \to R_2$$

$$\sim \begin{bmatrix} 1 & 3 & | & 0 & 1 \\ 0 & -10 & | & 1 & -4 \end{bmatrix} \left(-\frac{1}{10}\right)R_2 \to R_2$$

$$\sim \begin{bmatrix} 1 & 3 & | & 0 & 1 \\ 0 & 1 & | & -\frac{1}{10} & \frac{2}{5} \end{bmatrix} (-3)R_2 + R_1 \to R_1$$

$$\sim \begin{bmatrix} 1 & 0 & | & \frac{3}{10} & -\frac{1}{5} \\ 0 & 1 & | & -\frac{1}{10} & \frac{2}{5} \end{bmatrix}$$

Hence $A^{-1} = \begin{bmatrix} \frac{3}{10} & -\frac{1}{5} \\ -\frac{1}{10} & \frac{2}{5} \end{bmatrix}$

(B) We calculate A^{-1} by row operations on

$$\begin{bmatrix} 5 & 5 & | & 1 & 0 \\ -1 & 3 & | & 0 & 1 \end{bmatrix} R_1 \leftrightarrow R_2$$

$$\sim \begin{bmatrix} -1 & 3 & | & 0 & 1 \\ 5 & 5 & | & 1 & 0 \end{bmatrix} 5R_1 + R_2 \to R_2$$

$$\sim \begin{bmatrix} -1 & 3 & | & 0 & 1 \\ 0 & 20 & | & 1 & 5 \end{bmatrix} \frac{1}{20}R_2 \to R_2$$

$$\sim \begin{bmatrix} -1 & 3 & | & 0 & 1 \\ 0 & 1 & | & \frac{1}{20} & \frac{1}{4} \end{bmatrix} (-3)R_2 + R_1 \to R_1$$

$$\sim \begin{bmatrix} -1 & 0 & | & -\frac{3}{20} & \frac{1}{4} \\ 0 & 1 & | & \frac{1}{20} & \frac{1}{4} \end{bmatrix} (-1)R_1 \to R_1$$

$$\sim \begin{bmatrix} 1 & 0 & | & \frac{3}{20} & -\frac{1}{4} \\ 0 & 1 & | & \frac{1}{20} & \frac{1}{4} \end{bmatrix}$$

Hence $A^{-1} = \begin{bmatrix} \frac{3}{20} & -\frac{1}{4} \\ \frac{1}{20} & \frac{1}{4} \end{bmatrix}$

We calculate $(A^{-1})^{-1}$ by row operations on

$$\begin{bmatrix} \frac{3}{10} & -\frac{1}{5} & | & 1 & 0 \\ -\frac{1}{10} & \frac{2}{5} & | & 0 & 1 \end{bmatrix} \frac{10}{3}R_1 \to R_1$$

$$\sim \begin{bmatrix} 1 & -\frac{2}{3} & | & \frac{10}{3} & 0 \\ -\frac{1}{10} & \frac{2}{5} & | & 0 & 1 \end{bmatrix} \frac{1}{10}R_1 + R_2 \to R_2$$

$$\sim \begin{bmatrix} 1 & -\frac{2}{3} & | & \frac{10}{3} & 0 \\ 0 & \frac{1}{3} & | & \frac{1}{3} & 1 \end{bmatrix} 2R_2 + R_1 \to R_1$$

$$\sim \begin{bmatrix} 1 & 0 & | & 4 & 2 \\ 0 & \frac{1}{3} & | & \frac{1}{3} & 1 \end{bmatrix} 3R_2 \to R_2$$

$$\sim \begin{bmatrix} 1 & 0 & | & 4 & 2 \\ 0 & 1 & | & 1 & 3 \end{bmatrix}$$

Hence $(A^{-1})^{-1} = \begin{bmatrix} 4 & 2 \\ 1 & 3 \end{bmatrix}$

We calculate A^{-1} by row operations on

$$\begin{bmatrix} \frac{3}{20} & -\frac{1}{4} & | & 1 & 0 \\ \frac{1}{20} & \frac{1}{4} & | & 0 & 1 \end{bmatrix} \frac{20}{3}R_1 \to R_1$$

$$\sim \begin{bmatrix} 1 & -\frac{5}{3} & | & \frac{20}{3} & 0 \\ \frac{1}{20} & \frac{1}{4} & | & 0 & 1 \end{bmatrix} -\frac{1}{20}R_1 + R_2 \to R_2$$

$$\sim \begin{bmatrix} 1 & -\frac{5}{3} & | & \frac{20}{3} & 0 \\ 0 & \frac{1}{3} & | & -\frac{1}{3} & 1 \end{bmatrix} 5R_2 + R_1 \to R_1$$

$$\sim \begin{bmatrix} 1 & 0 & | & 5 & 5 \\ 0 & \frac{1}{3} & | & -\frac{1}{3} & 1 \end{bmatrix} 3R_2 \to R_2$$

$$\sim \begin{bmatrix} 1 & 0 & | & 5 & 5 \\ 0 & 1 & | & -1 & 3 \end{bmatrix}$$

Hence $(A^{-1})^{-1} = \begin{bmatrix} 5 & 5 \\ -1 & 3 \end{bmatrix}$

Note that in both cases the inverse of the inverse works out to be the original matrix.

81. (A) Using a graphing calculator, we enter A and B and calculate A^{-1} and B^{-1}

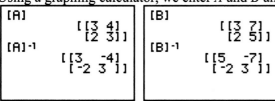

Then $(AB)^{-1}$ and $A^{-1}B^{-1}$ are calculated as

Finally $B^{-1}A^{-1}$ is calculated as

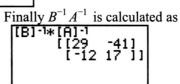

(B) Using a graphing calculator, we enter A and B and calculate A^{-1} and B^{-1}

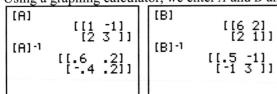

Then $(AB)^{-1}$ and $A^{-1}B^{-1}$ are calculated as   Finally $B^{-1}A^{-1}$ is calculated as

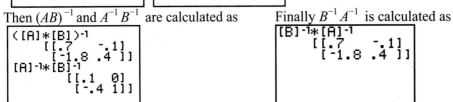

Notice that in each case $(AB)^{-1} = B^{-1}A^{-1}$ but $(AB)^{-1} \neq A^{-1}B^{-1}$.

83. Using the assignation numbers 1 to 27 with the letters of the alphabet and a blank as in the text, write

L E B R O N   J A M E S

12 5 2   18 15 14 27 10 1   13 5 19

and calculate

$$\begin{bmatrix} 3 & 5 \\ 1 & 2 \end{bmatrix}\begin{bmatrix} 12 & 2 & 15 & 27 & 1 & 5 \\ 5 & 18 & 14 & 10 & 13 & 19 \end{bmatrix} = \begin{bmatrix} 61 & 96 & 115 & 131 & 68 & 110 \\ 22 & 38 & 43 & 47 & 27 & 43 \end{bmatrix}$$

The encoded message is thus

61 22 96 38 115 43 131 47 68 27 110 43

85. The inverse of matrix A is easily calculated to be $A^{-1} = \begin{bmatrix} 2 & -5 \\ -1 & 3 \end{bmatrix}$

Putting the coded message into matrix form and multiplying by A^{-1} yields:

$$\begin{bmatrix} 2 & -5 \\ -1 & 3 \end{bmatrix}\begin{bmatrix} 31 & 150 & 57 & 150 & 103 & 160 & 61 & 192 \\ 12 & 55 & 20 & 59 & 39 & 61 & 22 & 73 \end{bmatrix} = \begin{bmatrix} 2 & 25 & 14 & 5 & 11 & 15 & 12 & 19 \\ 5 & 15 & 3 & 27 & 14 & 23 & 5 & 27 \end{bmatrix}$$

This decodes to 2 5 25 15 14 3 5 27 11 14 15 23 12 5 19 27

B E Y O N C E   K N O W L E S

87. Using the assignation of numbers 1 to 27 with the letters of the alphabet and a blank as in the text, write

N E W   E N G L A N D   P A T R I O T S

14 5 23 27 5 14 7 12 1 14 4 27 16 1 20 18 9 15 20 19

and calculate

$$\begin{bmatrix} 1 & 0 & 1 & 0 & 1 \\ 0 & 1 & 1 & 0 & 3 \\ 2 & 1 & 1 & 1 & 1 \\ 0 & 0 & 1 & 0 & 2 \\ 1 & 1 & 1 & 2 & 1 \end{bmatrix}\begin{bmatrix} 14 & 14 & 4 & 18 \\ 5 & 7 & 27 & 9 \\ 23 & 12 & 16 & 15 \\ 27 & 1 & 1 & 20 \\ 5 & 14 & 20 & 19 \end{bmatrix} = \begin{bmatrix} 42 & 40 & 40 & 52 \\ 43 & 61 & 103 & 81 \\ 88 & 62 & 72 & 99 \\ 33 & 40 & 56 & 53 \\ 101 & 49 & 69 & 101 \end{bmatrix}$$

The coded message is thus

42 40 40 52 43 61 103 81 88 62 72 99 33 40 56 53 101 49 69 101.

89. The inverse of B is calculated to be

$$B^{-1} = \begin{bmatrix} -2 & -1 & 2 & 2 & -1 \\ 3 & 2 & -2 & -4 & 1 \\ 6 & 2 & -4 & -5 & 2 \\ -2 & -1 & 1 & 2 & 0 \\ -3 & -1 & 2 & 3 & -1 \end{bmatrix}$$

Putting the coded message into matrix form and multiplying by B^{-1} yields

$$\begin{bmatrix} -2 & -1 & 2 & 2 & -1 \\ 3 & 2 & -2 & -4 & 1 \\ 6 & 2 & -4 & -5 & 2 \\ -2 & -1 & 1 & 2 & 0 \\ -3 & -1 & 2 & 3 & -1 \end{bmatrix} \begin{bmatrix} 32 & 51 & 62 & 58 & 39 \\ 25 & 64 & 109 & 115 & 110 \\ 55 & 103 & 114 & 105 & 85 \\ 19 & 39 & 62 & 73 & 65 \\ 41 & 100 & 92 & 113 & 111 \end{bmatrix} = \begin{bmatrix} 18 & 18 & 27 & 12 & 1 \\ 1 & 19 & 20 & 15 & 18 \\ 9 & 27 & 8 & 19 & 11 \\ 4 & 15 & 5 & 20 & 27 \\ 5 & 6 & 27 & 27 & 27 \end{bmatrix}$$

This decodes to

18 1 9 4 5   18 19 27   15 6 27   20 8 5 27   12 15 19 20 27   1 18 11 27 27
R A I D E R S   O F   T H E   L O S T   A R K

91. The system to be solved, for an arbitrary return, is derived as follows:

Let x_1 = number of \$20 tickets sold

$\qquad x_2$ = number of \$30 tickets sold

Then $x_1 + x_2 = 10{,}000$ number of seats

$\qquad 20x_1 + 30x_2 = k_2$ return required

We solve the system by writing it as a matrix equation.

$$\begin{matrix} A & X & B \end{matrix}$$

$$\begin{bmatrix} 1 & 1 \\ 20 & 30 \end{bmatrix} \begin{bmatrix} x_1 \\ x_2 \end{bmatrix} = \begin{bmatrix} 10{,}000 \\ k_2 \end{bmatrix}$$

If A^{-1} exists, then $X = A^{-1}B$. To find A^{-1}, we perform row operations on

$$\begin{bmatrix} 1 & 1 & | & 1 & 0 \\ 20 & 30 & | & 0 & 1 \end{bmatrix} \begin{matrix} (-20)R_1 + R_2 \to R_2 \end{matrix} \sim \begin{bmatrix} 1 & 1 & | & 1 & 0 \\ 0 & 10 & | & -20 & 1 \end{bmatrix} 0.1R_2 \to R_2 \sim \begin{bmatrix} 1 & 1 & | & 1 & 0 \\ 0 & 1 & | & -2 & 0.1 \end{bmatrix} (-1)R_2 + R_1 \to R_1$$

$$\sim \begin{bmatrix} 1 & 0 & | & 3 & -0.1 \\ 0 & 1 & | & -2 & 0.1 \end{bmatrix}$$

Hence $A^{-1} = \begin{bmatrix} 3 & -0.1 \\ -2 & 0.1 \end{bmatrix}$

Check: $A^{-1}A = \begin{bmatrix} 3 & -0.1 \\ -2 & 0.1 \end{bmatrix} \begin{bmatrix} 1 & 1 \\ 20 & 30 \end{bmatrix} = \begin{bmatrix} 1 & 0 \\ 0 & 1 \end{bmatrix}$

We can now solve the system as

$$\begin{matrix} X & A^{-1} & B \end{matrix}$$

$$\begin{bmatrix} x_1 \\ x_2 \end{bmatrix} = \begin{bmatrix} 3 & -0.1 \\ -2 & 0.1 \end{bmatrix} \begin{bmatrix} 10{,}000 \\ k_2 \end{bmatrix}$$

If $k_2 = 240{,}000$ (Concert 1),

$$\begin{bmatrix} x_1 \\ x_2 \end{bmatrix} = \begin{bmatrix} 3 & -0.1 \\ -2 & 0.1 \end{bmatrix} \begin{bmatrix} 10{,}000 \\ 240{,}000 \end{bmatrix} = \begin{bmatrix} 6{,}000 \\ 4{,}000 \end{bmatrix}$$

Concert 1: 6,000 \$20 tickets and 4,000 \$30 tickets

If $k_2 = 250{,}000$ (Concert 2),

$$\begin{bmatrix} x_1 \\ x_2 \end{bmatrix} = \begin{bmatrix} 3 & -0.1 \\ -2 & 0.1 \end{bmatrix} \begin{bmatrix} 10{,}000 \\ 250{,}000 \end{bmatrix} = \begin{bmatrix} 5{,}000 \\ 5{,}000 \end{bmatrix}$$

Concert 2: 5,000 \$20 tickets and 5,000 \$30 tickets

If $k_2 = 270{,}000$ (Concert 3),

$$\begin{bmatrix} x_1 \\ x_2 \end{bmatrix} = \begin{bmatrix} 3 & -0.1 \\ -2 & 0.1 \end{bmatrix} \begin{bmatrix} 10{,}000 \\ 270{,}000 \end{bmatrix} = \begin{bmatrix} 3{,}000 \\ 7{,}000 \end{bmatrix}$$

Concert 3: 3,000 \$20 tickets and 7,000 \$30 tickets

93. We solve the system, for arbitrary V_1 and V_2, by writing it as a matrix equation.

$$\overset{A}{\begin{bmatrix} 1 & -1 & 1 \\ 1 & 1 & 0 \\ 0 & 1 & 2 \end{bmatrix}} \overset{J}{\begin{bmatrix} I_1 \\ I_2 \\ I_3 \end{bmatrix}} = \overset{B}{\begin{bmatrix} 0 \\ V_1 \\ V_2 \end{bmatrix}}$$

If A^{-1} exists, then $J = A^{-1}B$. To find A^{-1}, we perform row operations on

$$\begin{bmatrix} 1 & -1 & 1 & | & 1 & 0 & 0 \\ 1 & 1 & 0 & | & 0 & 1 & 0 \\ 0 & 1 & 2 & | & 0 & 0 & 1 \end{bmatrix} \begin{matrix} \\ \\ (-1)R_1 + R_2 \to R_2 \end{matrix} \sim \begin{bmatrix} 1 & -1 & 1 & | & 1 & 0 & 0 \\ 0 & 2 & -1 & | & -1 & 1 & 0 \\ 0 & 1 & 2 & | & 0 & 0 & 1 \end{bmatrix} R_2 \leftrightarrow R_3$$

$$\sim \begin{bmatrix} 1 & -1 & 1 & | & 1 & 0 & 0 \\ 0 & 1 & 2 & | & 0 & 0 & 1 \\ 0 & 2 & -1 & | & -1 & 1 & 0 \end{bmatrix} \begin{matrix} R_2 + R_1 \to R_1 \\ \\ (-2)R_2 + R_3 \to R_3 \end{matrix} \sim \begin{bmatrix} 1 & 0 & 3 & | & 1 & 0 & 1 \\ 0 & 1 & 2 & | & 0 & 0 & 1 \\ 0 & 0 & -5 & | & -1 & 1 & -2 \end{bmatrix} -\tfrac{1}{5}R_3 \to R_3$$

$$\sim \begin{bmatrix} 1 & 0 & 3 & | & 1 & 0 & 1 \\ 0 & 1 & 2 & | & 0 & 0 & 1 \\ 0 & 0 & 1 & | & \tfrac{1}{5} & -\tfrac{1}{5} & \tfrac{2}{5} \end{bmatrix} \begin{matrix} (-3)R_3 + R_1 \to R_1 \\ (-2)R_3 + R_2 \to R_2 \end{matrix} \sim \begin{bmatrix} 1 & 0 & 0 & | & \tfrac{2}{5} & \tfrac{3}{5} & -\tfrac{1}{5} \\ 0 & 1 & 0 & | & -\tfrac{2}{5} & \tfrac{2}{5} & \tfrac{1}{5} \\ 0 & 0 & 1 & | & \tfrac{1}{5} & -\tfrac{1}{5} & \tfrac{2}{5} \end{bmatrix}$$

Hence $A^{-1} = \dfrac{1}{5}\begin{bmatrix} 2 & 3 & -1 \\ -2 & 2 & 1 \\ 1 & -1 & 2 \end{bmatrix}$ Check: $A^{-1}A = \dfrac{1}{5}\begin{bmatrix} 2 & 3 & -1 \\ -2 & 2 & 1 \\ 1 & -1 & 2 \end{bmatrix}\begin{bmatrix} 1 & -1 & 1 \\ 1 & 1 & 0 \\ 0 & 1 & 2 \end{bmatrix} = \begin{bmatrix} 1 & 0 & 0 \\ 0 & 1 & 0 \\ 0 & 0 & 1 \end{bmatrix}$

We can now solve the system as

$$\overset{J}{\begin{bmatrix} I_1 \\ I_2 \\ I_3 \end{bmatrix}} = \dfrac{1}{5}\overset{A^{-1}}{\begin{bmatrix} 2 & 3 & -1 \\ -2 & 2 & 1 \\ 1 & -1 & 2 \end{bmatrix}}\overset{B}{\begin{bmatrix} 0 \\ V_1 \\ V_2 \end{bmatrix}}$$

(A) $V_1 = 10$ $V_2 = 10$

$$\begin{bmatrix} I_1 \\ I_2 \\ I_3 \end{bmatrix} = \dfrac{1}{5}\begin{bmatrix} 2 & 3 & -1 \\ -2 & 2 & 1 \\ 1 & -1 & 2 \end{bmatrix}\begin{bmatrix} 0 \\ 10 \\ 10 \end{bmatrix} = \begin{bmatrix} 4 \\ 6 \\ 2 \end{bmatrix}$$

$I_1 = 4, I_2 = 6, I_3 = 2$ (amperes)

(B) $V_1 = 10$ $V_2 = 15$

$$\begin{bmatrix} I_1 \\ I_2 \\ I_3 \end{bmatrix} = \dfrac{1}{5}\begin{bmatrix} 2 & 3 & -1 \\ -2 & 2 & 1 \\ 1 & -1 & 2 \end{bmatrix}\begin{bmatrix} 0 \\ 10 \\ 15 \end{bmatrix} = \begin{bmatrix} 3 \\ 7 \\ 4 \end{bmatrix}$$

$I_1 = 3, I_2 = 7, I_3 = 4$ (amperes)

(C) $V_1 = 15$ $V_2 = 10$

$$\begin{bmatrix} I_1 \\ I_2 \\ I_3 \end{bmatrix} = \dfrac{1}{5}\begin{bmatrix} 2 & 3 & -1 \\ -2 & 2 & 1 \\ 1 & -1 & 2 \end{bmatrix}\begin{bmatrix} 0 \\ 15 \\ 10 \end{bmatrix} = \begin{bmatrix} 7 \\ 8 \\ 1 \end{bmatrix}$$

$I_1 = 7, I_2 = 8, I_3 = 1$ (amperes)

95. If the graph of $f(x) = ax^2 + bx + c$ passes through a point, the coordinates of the point must satisfy the equation of the graph. Hence

$k_1 = a(1)^2 + b(1) + c$

$k_2 = a(2)^2 + b(2) + c$

$k_3 = a(3)^2 + b(3) + c$

After simplification, we obtain:

$a + b + c = k_1$

$4a + 2b + c = k_2$

$9a + 3b + c = k_3$

We solve this system, for arbitrary k_1, k_2, k_3, by writing it as a matrix equation.

$$\begin{matrix} A & X & B \end{matrix}$$

$$\begin{bmatrix} 1 & 1 & 1 \\ 4 & 2 & 1 \\ 9 & 3 & 1 \end{bmatrix} \begin{bmatrix} a \\ b \\ c \end{bmatrix} = \begin{bmatrix} k_1 \\ k_2 \\ k_3 \end{bmatrix}$$

If A^{-1} exists, then $X = A^{-1}B$. To find A^{-1} we perform row operations on

$$\begin{bmatrix} 1 & 1 & 1 & | & 1 & 0 & 0 \\ 4 & 2 & 1 & | & 0 & 1 & 0 \\ 9 & 3 & 1 & | & 0 & 0 & 1 \end{bmatrix} \begin{matrix} \\ (-4)R_1 + R_2 \to R_2 \\ (-9)R_1 + R_3 \to R_3 \end{matrix} \sim \begin{bmatrix} 1 & 1 & 1 & | & 1 & 0 & 0 \\ 0 & -2 & -3 & | & -4 & 1 & 0 \\ 0 & -6 & -8 & | & -9 & 0 & 1 \end{bmatrix} -\tfrac{1}{2}R_2 \to R_2$$

$$\sim \begin{bmatrix} 1 & 1 & 1 & | & 1 & 0 & 0 \\ 0 & 1 & \tfrac{3}{2} & | & 2 & -\tfrac{1}{2} & 0 \\ 0 & -6 & -8 & | & -9 & 0 & 1 \end{bmatrix} \begin{matrix} (-1)R_2 + R_1 \to R_1 \\ \\ 6R_2 + R_3 \to R_3 \end{matrix} \sim \begin{bmatrix} 1 & 0 & -\tfrac{1}{2} & | & -1 & \tfrac{1}{2} & 0 \\ 0 & 1 & \tfrac{3}{2} & | & 2 & -\tfrac{1}{2} & 0 \\ 0 & 0 & 1 & | & 3 & -3 & 1 \end{bmatrix} \begin{matrix} \tfrac{1}{2}R_3 + R_1 \to R_1 \\ (-\tfrac{3}{2})R_3 + R_2 \to R_2 \end{matrix}$$

$$\sim \begin{bmatrix} 1 & 0 & 0 & | & \tfrac{1}{2} & -1 & \tfrac{1}{2} \\ 0 & 1 & 0 & | & -\tfrac{5}{2} & 4 & -\tfrac{3}{2} \\ 0 & 0 & 1 & | & 3 & -3 & 1 \end{bmatrix}$$

Hence $A^{-1} = \dfrac{1}{2} \begin{bmatrix} 1 & -2 & 1 \\ -5 & 8 & -3 \\ 6 & -6 & 2 \end{bmatrix}$

Check: $A^{-1}A = \dfrac{1}{2} \begin{bmatrix} 1 & -2 & 1 \\ -5 & 8 & -3 \\ 6 & -6 & 2 \end{bmatrix} \begin{bmatrix} 1 & 1 & 1 \\ 4 & 2 & 1 \\ 9 & 3 & 1 \end{bmatrix} = \begin{bmatrix} 1 & 0 & 0 \\ 0 & 1 & 0 \\ 0 & 0 & 1 \end{bmatrix}$

We can now solve the system as

$$\begin{matrix} X & A^{-1} & B \end{matrix}$$

$$\begin{bmatrix} a \\ b \\ c \end{bmatrix} = \dfrac{1}{2} \begin{bmatrix} 1 & -2 & 1 \\ -5 & 8 & -3 \\ 6 & -6 & 2 \end{bmatrix} \begin{bmatrix} k_1 \\ k_2 \\ k_3 \end{bmatrix}$$

(A) $\begin{bmatrix} a \\ b \\ c \end{bmatrix} = \dfrac{1}{2} \begin{bmatrix} 1 & -2 & 1 \\ -5 & 8 & -3 \\ 6 & -6 & 2 \end{bmatrix} \begin{bmatrix} -2 \\ 1 \\ 6 \end{bmatrix} = \begin{bmatrix} 1 \\ 0 \\ -3 \end{bmatrix}$ $a = 1, b = 0, c = -3$

(B) $\begin{bmatrix} a \\ b \\ c \end{bmatrix} = \dfrac{1}{2} \begin{bmatrix} 1 & -2 & 1 \\ -5 & 8 & -3 \\ 6 & -6 & 2 \end{bmatrix} \begin{bmatrix} 4 \\ 3 \\ -2 \end{bmatrix} = \begin{bmatrix} -2 \\ 5 \\ 1 \end{bmatrix}$ $a = -2, b = 5, c = 1$

(C) $\begin{bmatrix} a \\ b \\ c \end{bmatrix} = \dfrac{1}{2} \begin{bmatrix} 1 & -2 & 1 \\ -5 & 8 & -3 \\ 6 & -6 & 2 \end{bmatrix} \begin{bmatrix} 8 \\ -5 \\ 4 \end{bmatrix} = \begin{bmatrix} 11 \\ -46 \\ 43 \end{bmatrix}$ $a = 11, b = -46, c = 43$

97. The system to be solved, for an arbitrary diet, is derived as follows:

Let x_1 = amount of mix A

x_2 = amount of mix B

Then $0.20x_1 + 0.10x_2 = k_1$ (k_1 = amount of protein)

$0.02x_1 + 0.06x_2 = k_2$ (k_2 = amount of fat)

We solve the system by writing it as a matrix equation.

$$\begin{array}{ccc} A & X & B \end{array}$$

$$\begin{bmatrix} 0.20 & 0.10 \\ 0.02 & 0.06 \end{bmatrix} \begin{bmatrix} x_1 \\ x_2 \end{bmatrix} = \begin{bmatrix} k_1 \\ k_2 \end{bmatrix}$$

If A^{-1} exists, then $X = A^{-1}B$. To find A^{-1}, we perform row operations on

$$\begin{bmatrix} 0.20 & 0.10 & | & 1 & 0 \\ 0.02 & 0.06 & | & 0 & 1 \end{bmatrix} \begin{array}{c} 5R_1 \to R_1 \\ 50R_2 \to R_2 \end{array} \sim \begin{bmatrix} 1 & 0.5 & | & 5 & 0 \\ 1 & 3 & | & 0 & 50 \end{bmatrix} (-1)R_1 + R_2 \to R_2 \sim \begin{bmatrix} 1 & 0.5 & | & 5 & 0 \\ 0 & 2.5 & | & -5 & 50 \end{bmatrix} 0.4R_2 \to R_2$$

$$\sim \begin{bmatrix} 1 & 0.5 & | & 5 & 0 \\ 0 & 1 & | & -2 & 20 \end{bmatrix} (-0.5)R_2 + R_1 \to R_1 \sim \begin{bmatrix} 1 & 0 & | & 6 & -10 \\ 0 & 1 & | & -2 & 20 \end{bmatrix}$$

Hence $A^{-1} = \begin{bmatrix} 6 & -10 \\ -2 & 20 \end{bmatrix}$ Check: $A^{-1}A = \begin{bmatrix} 6 & -10 \\ -2 & 20 \end{bmatrix} \begin{bmatrix} 0.20 & 0.10 \\ 0.02 & 0.06 \end{bmatrix} = \begin{bmatrix} 1 & 0 \\ 0 & 1 \end{bmatrix}$

We can now solve the system as

$$\begin{array}{ccc} X & A^{-1} & B \end{array}$$

$$\begin{bmatrix} x_1 \\ x_2 \end{bmatrix} = \begin{bmatrix} 6 & -10 \\ -2 & 20 \end{bmatrix} \begin{bmatrix} k_1 \\ k_2 \end{bmatrix}$$

For Diet 1, $k_1 = 20$ and $k_2 = 6$

$$\begin{bmatrix} x_1 \\ x_2 \end{bmatrix} = \begin{bmatrix} 6 & -10 \\ -2 & 20 \end{bmatrix} \begin{bmatrix} 20 \\ 6 \end{bmatrix} = \begin{bmatrix} 60 \\ 80 \end{bmatrix}$$

Diet 1: 60 ounces Mix A and 80 ounces Mix B

For Diet 2, $k_1 = 10$ and $k_2 = 4$

$$\begin{bmatrix} x_1 \\ x_2 \end{bmatrix} = \begin{bmatrix} 6 & -10 \\ -2 & 20 \end{bmatrix} \begin{bmatrix} 10 \\ 4 \end{bmatrix} = \begin{bmatrix} 20 \\ 60 \end{bmatrix}$$

Diet 2: 20 ounces Mix A and 60 ounces Mix B

For Diet 3, $k_1 = 10$ and $k_2 = 6$

$$\begin{bmatrix} x_1 \\ x_2 \end{bmatrix} = \begin{bmatrix} 6 & -10 \\ -2 & 20 \end{bmatrix} \begin{bmatrix} 10 \\ 6 \end{bmatrix} = \begin{bmatrix} 0 \\ 100 \end{bmatrix}$$

Diet 3: 0 ounces Mix A and 100 ounces Mix B

SECTION 7–5

1. One is a matrix, the other is a determinant.

3. A minor is a determinant obtained by crossing out row i and column j of a larger determinant. A cofactor is $(-1)^{i+j}$ times the minor of the element in row i, column j.

5. The system does not have a unique solution; it is either inconsistent or dependent.

7. Yes, Cramer's method can be used, but doing it by hand is tedious.

9. $\begin{vmatrix} 5 & 4 \\ 2 & 3 \end{vmatrix} = 5 \cdot 3 - 2 \cdot 4 = 7$

11. $\begin{vmatrix} 3 & -7 \\ -5 & 6 \end{vmatrix} = 3 \cdot 6 - (-5)(-7) = -17$

13. $\begin{vmatrix} 4.3 & -1.2 \\ -5.1 & 3.7 \end{vmatrix} = (4.3)(3.7) - (-5.1)(-1.2) = 9.79$

15. $D = \begin{vmatrix} 1 & 2 \\ 1 & 3 \end{vmatrix} = 1; x = \dfrac{\begin{vmatrix} 1 & 2 \\ -1 & 3 \end{vmatrix}}{D} = \dfrac{5}{1} = 5; y = \dfrac{\begin{vmatrix} 1 & 1 \\ 1 & -1 \end{vmatrix}}{D} = \dfrac{-2}{1} = -2$

17. $D = \begin{vmatrix} 2 & 1 \\ 5 & 3 \end{vmatrix} = 1; x = \dfrac{\begin{vmatrix} 1 & 1 \\ 2 & 3 \end{vmatrix}}{D} = \dfrac{1}{1} = 1; y = \dfrac{\begin{vmatrix} 2 & 1 \\ 5 & 2 \end{vmatrix}}{D} = \dfrac{-1}{1} = -1$

19. $D = \begin{vmatrix} 2 & -1 \\ -1 & 3 \end{vmatrix} = 5; x = \dfrac{\begin{vmatrix} -3 & -1 \\ 3 & 3 \end{vmatrix}}{D} = \dfrac{-6}{5} = -\dfrac{6}{5}; y = \dfrac{\begin{vmatrix} 2 & -3 \\ -1 & 3 \end{vmatrix}}{D} = \dfrac{3}{5}$

21. $D = \begin{vmatrix} 4 & -3 \\ 3 & 2 \end{vmatrix} = 17; x = \dfrac{\begin{vmatrix} 4 & -3 \\ -2 & 2 \end{vmatrix}}{D} = \dfrac{2}{17}; y = \dfrac{\begin{vmatrix} 4 & 4 \\ 3 & -2 \end{vmatrix}}{D} = \dfrac{-20}{17} = -\dfrac{20}{17}$

23. $\begin{vmatrix} 5 & -1 & -3 \\ 3 & 4 & 6 \\ 0 & -2 & 8 \end{vmatrix} = \begin{vmatrix} 4 & 6 \\ -2 & 8 \end{vmatrix}$

25. $\begin{vmatrix} 5 & -1 & -3 \\ 3 & 4 & 6 \\ 0 & -2 & 8 \end{vmatrix} = \begin{vmatrix} 5 & -1 \\ 0 & -2 \end{vmatrix}$

27. $(-1)^{1+1} \begin{vmatrix} 4 & 6 \\ -2 & 8 \end{vmatrix} = (-1)^2[4 \cdot 8 - (-2)6] = 44$

29. $(-1)^{2+3} \begin{vmatrix} 5 & -1 \\ 0 & -2 \end{vmatrix} = (-1)^5[5(-2) - 0(-1)] = 10$

31. We expand by row 1

$\begin{vmatrix} 1 & 0 & 0 \\ -2 & 4 & 3 \\ 5 & -2 & 1 \end{vmatrix} = a_{11}(\text{cofactor of } a_{11}) + a_{12}(\text{cofactor of } a_{12}) + a_{13}(\text{cofactor of } a_{13})$

$= 1(-1)^{1+1} \begin{vmatrix} 4 & 3 \\ -2 & 1 \end{vmatrix} + 0(\;\diagup\;) + 0(\;\diagdown\;)$

It is unnecessary to evaluate these since they are multiplied by 0.

$= (-1)^2[4 \cdot 1 - (-2)3] = 10$

33. We expand by column 1

$\begin{vmatrix} 0 & 1 & 5 \\ 3 & -7 & 6 \\ 0 & -2 & -3 \end{vmatrix} = a_{11}(\text{cofactor of } a_{11}) + a_{21}(\text{cofactor of } a_{21}) + a_{31}(\text{cofactor of } a_{31})$

$= 0(\;\diagup\;) + 3(-1)^{2+1} \begin{vmatrix} 1 & 5 \\ -2 & -3 \end{vmatrix} + 0(\;\diagdown\;)$

It is unnecessary to evaluate these since they are multiplied by 0.

$= 3(-1)^3[1(-3) - (-2)5] = -21$

> **Common Error:** Neglecting the sign of the cofactor. The cofactor is often called the "signed" minor.

35. We expand by column 2

$\begin{vmatrix} -1 & 2 & -3 \\ -2 & 0 & -6 \\ 4 & -3 & 2 \end{vmatrix} = a_{12}(\text{cofactor of } a_{12}) + a_{22}(\text{cofactor of } a_{22}) + a_{32}(\text{cofactor of } a_{32})$

$= 2(-1)^{1+2} \begin{vmatrix} -2 & -6 \\ 4 & 2 \end{vmatrix} + 0(\;\diagup\;) + (-3)(-1)^{3+2} \begin{vmatrix} -1 & -3 \\ -2 & -6 \end{vmatrix}$

It is unnecessary to evaluate this since it's multiplied by zero.

$= 2(-1)^3[(-2)2 - 4(-6)] + (-3)(-1)^5[(-1)(-6) - (-2)(-3)] = (-2)(20) + 3(0) = -40$

37. We expand by the first row

$$\begin{vmatrix} 1 & 4 & 1 \\ 1 & 1 & -2 \\ 2 & 1 & -1 \end{vmatrix} = a_{11}(\text{cofactor of } a_{11}) + a_{12}(\text{cofactor of } a_{12}) + a_{13}(\text{cofactor of } a_{13})$$

$$= 1(-1)^{1+1}\begin{vmatrix} 1 & -2 \\ 1 & -1 \end{vmatrix} + 4(-1)^{1+2}\begin{vmatrix} 1 & -2 \\ 2 & -1 \end{vmatrix} + 1(-1)^{1+3}\begin{vmatrix} 1 & 1 \\ 2 & 1 \end{vmatrix}$$

$$= (-1)^2[1(-1) - 1(-2)] + 4(-1)^3[1(-1) - 2(-2)] + (-1)^4[1\cdot1 - 2\cdot1] = 1 + (-12) + (-1) = -12$$

39. We expand by the first row

$$\begin{vmatrix} 1 & 4 & 3 \\ 2 & 1 & 6 \\ 3 & -2 & 9 \end{vmatrix} = a_{11}(\text{cofactor of } a_{11}) + a_{12}(\text{cofactor of } a_{12}) + a_{13}(\text{cofactor of } a_{13})$$

$$= 1(-1)^{1+1}\begin{vmatrix} 1 & 6 \\ -2 & 9 \end{vmatrix} + 4(-1)^{1+2}\begin{vmatrix} 2 & 6 \\ 3 & 9 \end{vmatrix} + 3(-1)^{1+3}\begin{vmatrix} 2 & 1 \\ 3 & -2 \end{vmatrix}$$

$$= (-1)^2[1\cdot9 - (-2)6] + 4(-1)^3[2\cdot9 - 3\cdot6] + 3(-1)^4[2(-2) - 1\cdot3] = 21 + 0 - 21 = 0$$

41. $D = \begin{vmatrix} 0.9925 & -0.9659 \\ 0.1219 & 0.2588 \end{vmatrix} = 0.37460$

$$x = \frac{\begin{vmatrix} 0 & -0.9659 \\ 2,500 & 0.2588 \end{vmatrix}}{D} = \frac{2,414.75}{0.37460} = 6,400 \text{ to two significant digits}$$

$$y = \frac{\begin{vmatrix} 0.9925 & 0 \\ 0.1219 & 2,500 \end{vmatrix}}{D} = \frac{2,481.25}{0.37460} = 6,600 \text{ to two significant digits}$$

43. $D = \begin{vmatrix} 0.9954 & -0.9942 \\ 0.0958 & 0.1080 \end{vmatrix} = 0.20275$

$$x = \frac{\begin{vmatrix} 0 & -0.9942 \\ 155 & 0.1080 \end{vmatrix}}{D} = \frac{154.10}{0.20275} = 760 \text{ to two significant digits}$$

$$y = \frac{\begin{vmatrix} 0.9954 & 0 \\ 0.0958 & 155 \end{vmatrix}}{D} = \frac{154.29}{0.20275} = 760 \text{ to two significant digits}$$

45. $D = \begin{vmatrix} 1 & 1 & 0 \\ 0 & 2 & 1 \\ -1 & 0 & 1 \end{vmatrix} = 1; x = \dfrac{\begin{vmatrix} 0 & 1 & 0 \\ -5 & 2 & 1 \\ -3 & 0 & 1 \end{vmatrix}}{D} = \dfrac{2}{1} = 2; y = \dfrac{\begin{vmatrix} 1 & 0 & 0 \\ 0 & -5 & 1 \\ -1 & -3 & 1 \end{vmatrix}}{D} = \dfrac{-2}{1} = -2; z = \dfrac{\begin{vmatrix} 1 & 1 & 0 \\ 0 & 2 & -5 \\ -1 & 0 & -3 \end{vmatrix}}{D} = \dfrac{-1}{1} = -1$

47. $D = \begin{vmatrix} 1 & 1 & 0 \\ 0 & 2 & 1 \\ 0 & -1 & 1 \end{vmatrix} = 3; x = \dfrac{\begin{vmatrix} 1 & 1 & 0 \\ 0 & 2 & 1 \\ 1 & -1 & 1 \end{vmatrix}}{D} = \dfrac{4}{3}; y = \dfrac{\begin{vmatrix} 1 & 1 & 0 \\ 0 & 0 & 1 \\ 0 & 1 & 1 \end{vmatrix}}{D} = \dfrac{-1}{3} = -\dfrac{1}{3}; z = \dfrac{\begin{vmatrix} 1 & 1 & 0 \\ 0 & 2 & 0 \\ 0 & -1 & 1 \end{vmatrix}}{D} = \dfrac{2}{3}$

49. $D = \begin{vmatrix} 0 & 3 & 1 \\ 1 & 0 & 2 \\ 1 & -3 & 0 \end{vmatrix} = 3; \quad x = \dfrac{\begin{vmatrix} -1 & 3 & 1 \\ 3 & 0 & 2 \\ -2 & -3 & 0 \end{vmatrix}}{D} = \dfrac{-27}{3} = -9; \quad y = \dfrac{\begin{vmatrix} 0 & -1 & 1 \\ 1 & 3 & 2 \\ 1 & -2 & 0 \end{vmatrix}}{D} = \dfrac{-7}{3} = -\dfrac{7}{3};$

$$z = \dfrac{\begin{vmatrix} 0 & 3 & -1 \\ 1 & 0 & 3 \\ 1 & -3 & -2 \end{vmatrix}}{D} = \dfrac{18}{3} = 6$$

51. $D = \begin{vmatrix} 0 & 2 & -1 \\ 1 & -1 & -1 \\ 1 & -1 & 2 \end{vmatrix} = -6; \quad x = \dfrac{\begin{vmatrix} -3 & 2 & -1 \\ 2 & -1 & -1 \\ 4 & -1 & 2 \end{vmatrix}}{D} = \dfrac{-9}{-6} = \dfrac{3}{2}; \quad y = \dfrac{\begin{vmatrix} 0 & -3 & -1 \\ 1 & 2 & -1 \\ 1 & 4 & 2 \end{vmatrix}}{D} = \dfrac{7}{-6} = -\dfrac{7}{6};$

$$z = \dfrac{\begin{vmatrix} 0 & 2 & -3 \\ 1 & -1 & 2 \\ 1 & -1 & 4 \end{vmatrix}}{D} = \dfrac{-4}{-6} = \dfrac{2}{3}$$

53. Compute the coefficient determinant:

$$D = \begin{vmatrix} a & 3 \\ 2 & 4 \end{vmatrix} = 4a - 3(2) = 4a - 6$$

If $D \neq 0$, there is a unique solution: $4a - 6 = 0$

$$4a = 6$$

$$a = \dfrac{6}{4} = \dfrac{3}{2}$$

So if $a \neq \dfrac{3}{2}$ there is one solution. If $a = \dfrac{3}{2}$ we need to use Gauss–Jordan elimination to determine the nature

of the solutions after plugging in $\dfrac{3}{2}$ for a.

$$\begin{bmatrix} \frac{3}{2} & 3 & \Big| & b \\ 2 & 4 & \Big| & 5 \end{bmatrix} \frac{2}{3} R_1 \to R_1 \sim \begin{bmatrix} 1 & 2 & \Big| & \frac{2b}{3} \\ 2 & 4 & \Big| & 5 \end{bmatrix} -2R_1 + R_2 \to R_2 \sim \begin{bmatrix} 1 & 2 & \Big| & \frac{2b}{3} \\ 0 & 0 & \Big| & -\frac{4b}{3}+5 \end{bmatrix}$$

If the bottom row is all zeros, there are infinitely many solutions. If the bottom row has zero in the third

position, there is no solution. We need to know when $\dfrac{-4b}{3} + 5 = 0$.

$$\dfrac{-4b}{3} + 5 = 0 \qquad\qquad \text{So there are infinitely many solutions if } a = \dfrac{3}{2} \text{ and } b = \dfrac{15}{4} \text{, and no}$$

$$-4b + 15 = 0 \qquad\qquad \text{solutions if } a = \dfrac{3}{2} \text{ and } b \neq \dfrac{15}{4}.$$

$$-4b = -15$$

$$b = \dfrac{15}{4}$$

55. $x = \dfrac{\begin{vmatrix} -3 & -3 & 1 \\ -11 & 3 & 2 \\ 3 & -1 & -1 \end{vmatrix}}{\begin{vmatrix} 2 & -3 & 1 \\ -4 & 3 & 2 \\ 1 & -1 & -1 \end{vmatrix}} = \dfrac{20}{5} = 4$

57. $y = \dfrac{\begin{vmatrix} 12 & 5 & 11 \\ 15 & -13 & -9 \\ 5 & 0 & 2 \end{vmatrix}}{\begin{vmatrix} 12 & -14 & 11 \\ 15 & 7 & -9 \\ 5 & -3 & 2 \end{vmatrix}} = \dfrac{28}{14} = 2$

59. $z = \dfrac{\begin{vmatrix} 3 & -4 & 18 \\ -9 & 8 & -13 \\ 5 & -7 & 33 \end{vmatrix}}{\begin{vmatrix} 3 & -4 & 5 \\ -9 & 8 & 7 \\ 5 & -7 & 10 \end{vmatrix}} = \dfrac{5}{2}$

61.

$$\begin{vmatrix} 2 & 6 & -1 & 2 & 6 \\ 5 & 3 & -7 & 5 & 3 \\ -4 & -2 & 1 & -4 & -2 \end{vmatrix}$$

$$2 \cdot 3 \cdot 1 + 6(-7)(-4) + (-1)(5)(-2) - (-4)(3)(-1) - (-2)(-7)2 - 1 \cdot 5 \cdot 6 = 6 + 168 + 10 - 12 - 28 - 30 = 114$$

63. False. $\begin{vmatrix} 10 & 10 \\ 0 & 0 \end{vmatrix}$ is a counterexample.

65. True. Expanding $\begin{vmatrix} a_{11} & a_{12} & a_{13} & a_{14} \\ 0 & a_{22} & a_{23} & a_{24} \\ 0 & 0 & a_{33} & a_{34} \\ 0 & 0 & 0 & a_{44} \end{vmatrix}$ by the first column, we obtain successively

$$a_{11} \begin{vmatrix} a_{22} & a_{23} & a_{24} \\ 0 & a_{33} & a_{34} \\ 0 & 0 & a_{44} \end{vmatrix} = a_{11} a_{22} \begin{vmatrix} a_{33} & a_{34} \\ 0 & a_{44} \end{vmatrix} = a_{11} a_{22} a_{33} a_{44}.$$

Similarly for the determinant of an $n \times n$ upper triangular matrix, we would obtain $a_{11} a_{22} a_{33} \cdot \ldots \cdot a_{nn}$ as proposed.

67. Expanding by the first column

$$\begin{vmatrix} a_{11} & a_{12} & a_{13} \\ a_{21} & a_{22} & a_{23} \\ a_{31} & a_{32} & a_{33} \end{vmatrix}$$

$$= a_{11}(-1)^{1+1} \begin{vmatrix} a_{22} & a_{23} \\ a_{32} & a_{33} \end{vmatrix} + a_{21}(-1)^{2+1} \begin{vmatrix} a_{12} & a_{13} \\ a_{32} & a_{33} \end{vmatrix} + a_{31}(-1)^{3+1} \begin{vmatrix} a_{12} & a_{13} \\ a_{22} & a_{23} \end{vmatrix}$$

$$= a_{11} \begin{vmatrix} a_{22} & a_{23} \\ a_{32} & a_{33} \end{vmatrix} - a_{21} \begin{vmatrix} a_{12} & a_{13} \\ a_{32} & a_{33} \end{vmatrix} + a_{31} \begin{vmatrix} a_{12} & a_{13} \\ a_{22} & a_{23} \end{vmatrix}$$

$$= a_{11}(a_{22}a_{33} - a_{32}a_{23}) - a_{21}(a_{12}a_{33} - a_{32}a_{13}) + a_{31}(a_{12}a_{23} - a_{22}a_{13})$$

$$= a_{11}a_{22}a_{33} - a_{11}a_{32}a_{23} - a_{21}a_{12}a_{33} + a_{21}a_{32}a_{13} + a_{31}a_{12}a_{23} - a_{31}a_{22}a_{13}$$

$$ \quad ① \qquad\quad ② \qquad\quad ③ \qquad\quad ④ \qquad\quad ⑤ \qquad\quad ⑥$$

Expanding by the third row

$$\begin{vmatrix} a_{11} & a_{12} & a_{13} \\ a_{21} & a_{22} & a_{23} \\ a_{31} & a_{32} & a_{33} \end{vmatrix}$$

$$= a_{31}(-1)^{3+1} \begin{vmatrix} a_{12} & a_{13} \\ a_{22} & a_{23} \end{vmatrix} + a_{32}(-1)^{3+2} \begin{vmatrix} a_{11} & a_{13} \\ a_{21} & a_{23} \end{vmatrix} + a_{33}(-1)^{3+3} \begin{vmatrix} a_{11} & a_{12} \\ a_{21} & a_{22} \end{vmatrix}$$

$$= a_{31} \begin{vmatrix} a_{12} & a_{13} \\ a_{22} & a_{23} \end{vmatrix} - a_{32} \begin{vmatrix} a_{11} & a_{13} \\ a_{21} & a_{23} \end{vmatrix} + a_{33} \begin{vmatrix} a_{11} & a_{12} \\ a_{21} & a_{22} \end{vmatrix}$$

$$= a_{31}(a_{12}a_{23} - a_{13}a_{22}) - a_{32}(a_{11}a_{23} - a_{13}a_{21}) + a_{33}(a_{11}a_{22} - a_{12}a_{21})$$

$$= a_{31}a_{12}a_{23} - a_{31}a_{13}a_{22} - a_{32}a_{11}a_{23} + a_{32}a_{13}a_{21} + a_{33}a_{11}a_{22} - a_{33}a_{12}a_{21}$$

$$ \quad ⑤ \qquad\quad ⑥ \qquad\quad ② \qquad\quad ④ \qquad\quad ① \qquad\quad ③$$

Comparing the two expressions, with the aid of the numbers under the terms, shows that the expressions are the same.

69. $A = \begin{bmatrix} 2 & 3 \\ 1 & -2 \end{bmatrix}$ $B = \begin{bmatrix} -1 & 3 \\ 2 & 1 \end{bmatrix}$

We calculate $AB = \begin{bmatrix} 2 & 3 \\ 1 & -2 \end{bmatrix}\begin{bmatrix} -1 & 3 \\ 2 & 1 \end{bmatrix} = \begin{bmatrix} 2(-1)+3\cdot2 & 2\cdot3+3\cdot1 \\ 1(-1)+(-2)2 & 1\cdot3+(-2)\cdot1 \end{bmatrix} = \begin{bmatrix} 4 & 9 \\ -5 & 1 \end{bmatrix}$

$$\det(AB) = \begin{vmatrix} 4 & 9 \\ -5 & 1 \end{vmatrix} = 4 \cdot 1 - (-5)9 = 49$$

$$\det A = \begin{vmatrix} 2 & 3 \\ 1 & -2 \end{vmatrix} = 2(-2) - 1 \cdot 3 = -7$$

$$\det B = \begin{vmatrix} -1 & 3 \\ 2 & 1 \end{vmatrix} = (-1)1 - 2 \cdot 3 = -7$$

Thus, $\det A \det B = (-7)(-7) = 49 = \det(AB)$

71. (A) $D = \begin{vmatrix} 1 & -4 & 9 \\ 4 & -1 & 6 \\ 1 & -1 & 3 \end{vmatrix} = 1(-1)^{1+1}\begin{vmatrix} -1 & 6 \\ -1 & 3 \end{vmatrix} + 4(-1)^{2+1}\begin{vmatrix} -4 & 9 \\ -1 & 3 \end{vmatrix} + 1(-1)^{3+1}\begin{vmatrix} -4 & 9 \\ -1 & 6 \end{vmatrix}$

$= 1(-1)^2[(-1)3-(-1)6]+4(-1)^3[(-4)3-(-1)9]+1(-1)^4[(-4)6-(-1)9] = 3 + 12 - 15 = 0$

Since $D = 0$, the system either has no solution or infinitely many. Since $x = 0$, $y = 0$, $z = 0$ is a solution, the second case must hold.

(B) $D = \begin{vmatrix} 3 & -1 & 3 \\ 5 & 5 & -9 \\ -2 & 1 & -3 \end{vmatrix} = -6 \neq 0$; $x = 0$, $y = 0$, $z = 0$ is the only solution.

73. (A) $R = xp + yq = (200 - 6p + 4q)p + (300 + 2p - 3q)q = 200p - 6p^2 + 4pq + 300q + 2pq - 3q^2$
$$= 200p + 300q - 6p^2 + 6pq - 3q^2$$

(B) Rewrite the demand equations as
$6p - 4q = 200 - x$
$-2p + 3q = 300 - y$

Apply Cramer's rule: $D = \begin{vmatrix} 6 & -4 \\ -2 & 3 \end{vmatrix} = 10$

$$p = \frac{\begin{vmatrix} 200-x & -4 \\ 300-y & 3 \end{vmatrix}}{D} = \frac{1800-3x-4y}{10} = -0.3x - 0.4y + 180$$

$$q = \frac{\begin{vmatrix} 6 & 200-x \\ -2 & 300-y \end{vmatrix}}{D} = \frac{2200-2x-6y}{10} = -0.2x - 0.6y + 220$$

Then
$R = xp + yq = x(-0.3x - 0.4y + 180) + y(-0.2x - 0.6y + 220)$
$= -0.3x^2 - 0.4xy + 180x - 0.2xy - 0.6y^2 + 220y$
$= 180x + 220y - 0.3x^2 - 0.6xy - 0.6y^2$

Note: Sections 6, 7, 8 of this chapter are not printed in the text. They are available online. Solutions follow.

SECTION 7–6

1. Unless each equation is linear, that is, has the form $a_1x_1 + a_2x_2 + \ldots a_nx_n = b$, the system is non linear.
3. Substitution would be preferable. Solve the first equation for x in terms of y (or y in terms of x), substitute into the second equation, solve the single–variable equation that results, and plug any solutions into the first equation, to find the other variable.

5.
$$x^2 + y^2 = 169$$
$$x = -12$$
$$(-12)^2 + y^2 = 169$$
$$y^2 = 25$$
$$y = \pm 5$$

Solution: $(-12, 5)$, $(-12, -5)$

Check:
$$-12 \overset{\checkmark}{=} -12$$
$$(-12)^2 + (\pm 5)^2 \overset{\checkmark}{=} 169$$

7.
$$8x^2 - y^2 = 16$$
$$y = 2x$$

Substitute y from the second equation into the first equation.
$$8x^2 - (2x)^2 = 16$$
$$8x^2 - 4x^2 = 16$$
$$4x^2 = 16$$
$$x^2 = 4$$
$$x = \pm 2$$

For $x = 2$ For $x = -2$
$$y = 2(2) \qquad y = 2(-2)$$
$$y = 4 \qquad y = -4$$

Solutions: $(2, 4)$, $(-2, -4)$

Check:

For $(2, 4)$ For $(-2, -4)$
$$4 \overset{\checkmark}{=} 2 \cdot 2 \qquad -4 \overset{\checkmark}{=} 2(-2)$$
$$8(2)^2 - 4^2 \overset{\checkmark}{=} 16 \qquad 8(-2)^2 - (-4)^2 \overset{\checkmark}{=} 16$$

9.
$$3x^2 - 2y^2 = 25$$
$$x + y = 0$$

Solve for y in the first degree equation: $y = -x$
Substitute into the second degree equation.
$$3x^2 - 2(-x)^2 = 25$$
$$x^2 = 25$$
$$x = \pm 5$$

For $x = 5$ For $x = -5$
$$y = -5 \qquad\qquad y = 5$$

Solutions: $(5, -5)$, $(-5, 5)$

Check:

For $(5, -5)$ For $(-5, 5)$
$$5 + (-5) \overset{\checkmark}{=} 0 \qquad (-5) + 5 \overset{\checkmark}{=} 0$$
$$3(5)^2 - 2(-5)^2 \overset{\checkmark}{=} 25 \qquad 3(-5)^2 - 2(5)^2 \overset{\checkmark}{=} 25$$

From this point on we will not show the checking steps for lack of space. The student should perform these checking steps, however.

11.
$$y^2 = x$$
$$x - 2y = 2$$

Solve for x in the first degree equation.
$$x = 2y + 2$$

Substitute into the second degree equation.
$$y^2 = 2y + 2$$
$$y^2 - 2y - 2 = 0$$

$$y = \frac{-b \pm \sqrt{b^2 - 4ac}}{2a} \quad a = 1, b = -2, c = -2$$

$$y = \frac{-(-2) \pm \sqrt{(-2)^2 - 4(1)(-2)}}{2(1)}$$

$$y = \frac{2 \pm \sqrt{12}}{2}$$

$$y = 1 \pm \sqrt{3}$$

For $y = 1 + \sqrt{3}$ For $y = 1 - \sqrt{3}$
$$x = 2(1 + \sqrt{3}) + 2 \qquad x = 2(1 - \sqrt{3}) + 2$$
$$x = 4 + 2\sqrt{3} \qquad x = 4 - 2\sqrt{3}$$

Solutions: $(4 + 2\sqrt{3}, 1 + \sqrt{3})$, $(4 - 2\sqrt{3}, 1 - \sqrt{3})$

13.
$$2x^2 + y^2 = 24$$
$$x^2 - y^2 = -12$$

Solve using elimination by addition. Adding, we obtain:
$$3x^2 = 12$$
$$x^2 = 4$$
$$x = \pm 2$$

For $x = 2$ For $x = -2$
$$4 - y^2 = -12 \qquad 4 - y^2 = -12$$
$$-y^2 = -16 \quad \text{Similarly}$$
$$y^2 = 16 \qquad\qquad y = \pm 4$$
$$y = \pm 4$$

Solutions: $(2, 4)$, $(2, -4)$, $(-2, 4)$, $(-2, -4)$

15. $x^2 + y^2 = 10$
$16x^2 + y^2 = 25$
Solve using elimination by addition.
Multiply the top equation by -1 and add.

$$\begin{array}{rl} -x^2 - y^2 &= -10 \\ \underline{16x^2 + y^2} &= \underline{25} \\ 15x^2 &= 15 \\ x^2 &= 1 \\ x &= \pm 1 \end{array}$$

For $x = 1$

$1 + y^2 = 10$
$y^2 = 9$
$y = \pm 3$

For $x = -1$

$1 + y^2 = 10$
$y = \pm 3$

Solutions: $(1, 3), (1, -3), (-1, 3), (-1, -3)$

17. $xy - 4 = 0$
$x - y = 2$
Solve for x in the first degree equation.
$x = y + 2$
Substitute into the second degree equation

$$(y + 2)y - 4 = 0$$
$$y^2 + 2y - 4 = 0$$
$$y = \frac{-b \pm \sqrt{b^2 - 4ac}}{2a} \quad a = 1, b = 2, c = -4$$
$$y = \frac{-2 \pm \sqrt{(2)^2 - 4(1)(-4)}}{2(1)}$$
$$y = \frac{-2 \pm \sqrt{20}}{2}$$
$$y = -1 \pm \sqrt{5}$$

For $y = -1 + \sqrt{5}$

$x = -1 + \sqrt{5} + 2$
$x = 1 + \sqrt{5}$

For $y = -1 - \sqrt{5}$

$x = -1 - \sqrt{5} + 2$
$x = 1 - \sqrt{5}$

Solutions: $(1 + \sqrt{5}, -1 + \sqrt{5}), (1 - \sqrt{5}, -1 - \sqrt{5})$

19. $x^2 + 2y^2 = 6$
$xy = 2$
Solve for y in the second equation

$$y = \frac{2}{x}$$

Substitute into the first equation

$$x^2 + 2\left(\frac{2}{x}\right)^2 = 6$$
$$x^2 + \frac{8}{x^2} = 6 \quad x \neq 0$$
$$x^2 \cdot x^2 + x^2 \cdot \frac{8}{x^2} = 6x^2$$
$$x^4 + 8 = 6x^2$$
$$x^4 - 6x^2 + 8 = 0$$
$$(x^2 - 2)(x^2 - 4) = 0$$
$$(x - \sqrt{2})(x + \sqrt{2})(x - 2)(x + 2) = 0$$
$$x = \sqrt{2}, -\sqrt{2}, 2, -2$$

For $x = \sqrt{2}$

$y = \frac{2}{\sqrt{2}}$
$y = \sqrt{2}$

For $x = -\sqrt{2}$

$y = -\frac{2}{\sqrt{2}}$
$y = -\sqrt{2}$

For $x = 2$

$y = \frac{2}{2}$
$y = 1$

For $x = -2$

$y = \frac{2}{-2}$
$y = -1$

Solutions: $(\sqrt{2}, \sqrt{2}), (-\sqrt{2}, -\sqrt{2}), (2, 1), (-2, -1)$

21. $2x^2 + 3y^2 = -4$
$4x^2 + 2y^2 = 8$
Solve using elimination by addition.

Multiply the second equation by $-\dfrac{1}{2}$ and add.

$$\begin{array}{rl} 2x^2 + 3y^2 &= -4 \\ \underline{-2x^2 - y^2} &= \underline{-4} \\ 2y^2 &= -8 \\ y^2 &= -4 \\ y &= \pm 2i \end{array}$$

For $y = 2i$

$2x^2 + 3(2i)^2 = -4$
$2x^2 - 12 = -4$
$2x^2 = 8$
$x^2 = 4$
$x = \pm 2$

For $y = -2i$

$2x^2 + 3(-2i)^2 = -4$
$2x^2 - 12 = -4$
Similarly
$x = \pm 2$

Solutions: $(2, 2i), (-2, 2i), (2, -2i), (-2, -2i)$

23. $x^2 - y^2 = 2$
$y^2 = x$
Substitute y^2 from the second equation into the first equation.

$$x^2 - x = 2$$
$$x^2 - x - 2 = 0$$
$$(x - 2)(x + 1) = 0$$
$$x = 2, -1$$

For $x = 2$

$y^2 = 2$
$y = \pm \sqrt{2}$

For $x = -1$

$y^2 = -1$
$y = \pm i$

Solutions: $(2, \sqrt{2}), (2, -\sqrt{2}), (-1, i), (-1, -i)$

25.
$$x^2 + y^2 = 9$$
$$x^2 = 9 - 2y$$
Substitute x^2 from the second equation into the first equation.
$$9 - 2y + y^2 = 9$$
$$y^2 - 2y = 0$$
$$y(y - 2) = 0$$
$$y = 0, 2$$

For $y = 0$ 　　　 For $y = 2$
$$x^2 = 9 - 2(0) \qquad x^2 = 9 - 2(2)$$
$$x^2 = 9 \qquad\qquad x^2 = 5$$
$$x = \pm 3 \qquad\qquad x = \pm\sqrt{5}$$

Solutions: $(3, 0), (-3, 0), (\sqrt{5}, 2), (-\sqrt{5}, 2)$

27.
$$x^2 - y^2 = 3$$
$$xy = 2$$
Solve for y in the second equation.
$$y = \frac{2}{x}$$

Substitute into the first equation:
$$x^2 - \left(\frac{2}{x}\right)^2 = 3$$
$$x^2 - \frac{4}{x^2} = 3 \quad x \neq 0$$
$$x^4 - 4 = 3x^2$$
$$x^4 - 3x^2 - 4 = 0$$
$$(x^2 - 4)(x^2 + 1) = 0$$
$$x^2 - 4 = 0 \qquad\qquad x^2 + 1 = 0$$
$$x^2 = 4 \qquad\qquad\quad x^2 = -1$$
$$x = \pm 2 \qquad\qquad\quad x = \pm i$$

For $x = 2$ 　 For $x = -2$ 　 For $x = i$ 　 For $x = -i$
$$y = \frac{2}{2} \qquad y = \frac{2}{-2} \qquad y = \frac{2}{i} \qquad y = \frac{2}{-i}$$
$$y = 1 \qquad y = -1 \qquad y = -2i \qquad y = 2i$$

Solutions: $(2, 1), (-2, -1), (i, -2i), (-i, 2i)$

29.
$$y = 5 - x^2$$
$$y = 2 - 2x$$
Substitute y from the first equation into the second equation.
$$5 - x^2 = 2 - 2x$$
$$0 = x^2 - 2x - 3$$
$$0 = (x - 3)(x + 1)$$
$$x = 3, -1$$

For $x = 3$ 　　　 For $x = -1$
$$y = 2 - 2(3) \qquad y = 2 - 2(-1)$$
$$y = -4 \qquad\qquad y = 4$$

Solutions: $(3, -4), (-1, 4)$

31.
$$y = x^2 - x$$
$$y = 2x$$
Substitute y from the first equation into the second equation.
$$x^2 - x = 2x$$
$$x^2 - 3x = 0$$
$$x(x - 3) = 0$$
$$x = 0, 3$$

For $x = 0$ 　　　 For $x = 3$
$$y = 2(0) \qquad\qquad y = 2(3)$$
$$y = 0 \qquad\qquad\quad y = 6$$

Solutions: $(0, 0), (3, 6)$

33.
$$y = x^2 - 6x + 9$$
$$y = 5 - x$$
Substitute y from the first equation into the second equation.
$$x^2 - 6x + 9 = 5 - x$$
$$x^2 - 5x + 4 = 0$$
$$(x - 1)(x - 4) = 0$$
$$x = 1, 4$$

For $x = 1$ 　　　 For $x = 4$
$$y = 5 - 1 \qquad\qquad y = 5 - 4$$
$$y = 4 \qquad\qquad\quad y = 1$$

Solutions: $(1, 4), (4, 1)$

35.
$$y = 8 + 4x - x^2$$
$$y = x^2 - 2x$$
Substitute y from the first equation into the second equation.
$$8 + 4x - x^2 = x^2 - 2x$$
$$0 = 2x^2 - 6x - 8$$
$$0 = x^2 - 3x - 4$$
$$0 = (x - 4)(x + 1)$$
$$x = 4, -1$$

For $x = 4$ 　　　 For $x = -1$
$$y = 4^2 - 2(4) \qquad y = (-1)^2 - 2(-1)$$
$$y = 8 \qquad\qquad\quad y = 3$$

Solutions: $(4, 8), (-1, 3)$

37. (A)   The lines are tangent to the circle.

(B)   To find values of b such that
$$x^2 + y^2 = 5$$
$$2x - y = b$$
has exactly one solution, we solve the system for arbitrary b.
Solve for y in the second equation.
$$y = 2x - b$$
Substitute into the first equation:
$$x^2 + (2x - b)^2 = 5$$
$$x^2 + 4x^2 - 4bx + b^2 = 5$$
$$5x^2 - 4bx + b^2 - 5 = 0$$
This quadratic equation will have one solution if the discriminant
$B^2 - 4AC = (-4b)^2 - 4(5)(b^2 - 5)$ is equal to 0.
This will occur when
$$16b^2 - 20b^2 + 100 = 0$$
$$-4b^2 + 100 = 0$$
$$b^2 = 25$$
$$b = \pm 5$$

Consider $b = 5$
Then the solution of the system
$$x^2 + y^2 = 5$$
$$2x - y = 5$$
will be given by solving
$5x^2 - 4bx + b^2 - 5 = 0$
for $b = 5$.
$$5x^2 - 4 \cdot 5x + 5^2 - 5 = 0$$
$$5x^2 - 20x + 20 = 0$$
$$5(x - 2)^2 = 0$$
$$x - 2 = 0$$
$$x = 2$$
Since $2x - y = 5$
$2 \cdot 2 - y = 5$
$y = -1$
The intersection point is $(2, -1)$ for $b = 5$.

Consider $b = -5$
Then the solution of the system
$$x^2 + y^2 = 5$$
$$2x - y = -5$$
will be given by solving
$5x^2 - 4bx + b^2 - 5 = 0$
for $b = -5$.
$$5x^2 - 4(-5)x + (-5)^2 - 5 = 0$$
$$5x^2 + 20x + 20 = 0$$
$$5(x + 2)^2 = 0$$
$$x + 2 = 0$$
$$x = -2$$
Since $2x - y = -5$
$2(-2) - y = -5$
$y = 1$
The intersection point is $(-2, 1)$ for $b = -5$.

(C)   The line $x + 2y = 0$ is perpendicular to all the lines in the family and intersects the circle at the intersection points found in part B, since this line passes through the center of the circle and thus includes a diameter of the circle, which is perpendicular to the tangent line at their mutual point of intersection with the circle. Solving the system $x^2 + y^2 = 5$, $x + 2y = 0$ would determine the intersection points.

39. $2x + 5y + 7xy = 8$
$xy - 3 = 0$
Solve for y in the second equation.
$xy = 3$
$y = \dfrac{3}{x}$
Substitute into the first equation.
$$2x + 5\left(\dfrac{3}{x}\right) + 7x\left(\dfrac{3}{x}\right) = 8$$

$$2x + \dfrac{15}{x} + 21 = 8 \quad x \neq 0$$
$$2x^2 + 15 + 21x = 8x$$
$$2x^2 + 13x + 15 = 0$$
$$(2x + 3)(x + 5) = 0$$
$$x = -\dfrac{3}{2}, -5$$

For $x = -\dfrac{3}{2}$ For $x = -5$

$y = 3 \div \left(-\dfrac{3}{2}\right)$ $y = \dfrac{3}{-5}$

$y = -2$ $y = -\dfrac{3}{5}$

Solutions: $\left(-\dfrac{3}{2}, -2\right)$, $\left(-5, -\dfrac{3}{5}\right)$

41. $x^2 - 2xy + y^2 = 1$
$x - 2y = 2$
Solve for x in terms of y in the first–degree equation.
$x = 2y + 2$
Substitute into the second–degree equation.
$$(2y + 2)^2 - 2(2y + 2)y + y^2 = 1$$
$$4y^2 + 8y + 4 - 4y^2 - 4y + y^2 = 1$$
$$y^2 + 4y + 3 = 0$$
$$(y + 1)(y + 3) = 0$$
$$y = -1, -3$$

For $y = -1$ For $y = -3$
$x = 2(-1) + 2$ $x = 2(-3) + 2$
$= 0$ $= -4$

Solutions: $(0, -1)$, $(-4, -3)$

43. $2x^2 - xy + y^2 = 8$
$x^2 - y^2 = 0$
Factor the left side of the equation that has a zero constant term.
$(x - y)(x + y) = 0$

Common Error:
It is incorrect to replace $x^2 - y^2 = 0$ or $x^2 = y^2$ by $x = y$. This neglects the possibility $x = -y$.

$x = y$ or $x = -y$

Thus, the original system is equivalent to the two systems
$2x^2 - xy + y^2 = 8$ $2x^2 - xy + y^2 = 8$
$x = y$ $x = -y$
These systems are solved by substitution.

First system: Second system:
$2x^2 - xy + y^2 = 8$ $2x^2 - xy + y^2 = 8$
$x = y$ $x = -y$
$2y^2 - yy + y^2 = 8$ $2(-y)^2 - (-y)y + y^2 = 8$
$2y^2 = 8$ $2y^2 + y^2 + y^2 = 8$
$y^2 = 4$ $4y^2 = 8$
$y = \pm 2$ $y^2 = 2$
                        $y = \pm\sqrt{2}$

For $y = 2$ For $y = -2$ For $y = \sqrt{2}$ For $y = -\sqrt{2}$
$x = 2$ $x = -2$ $x = -\sqrt{2}$ $x = \sqrt{2}$

Solutions: $(2, 2)$, $(-2, -2)$, $(-\sqrt{2}, \sqrt{2})$, $(\sqrt{2}, -\sqrt{2})$

45.
$$x^2 + xy - 3y^2 = 3$$
$$x^2 + 4xy + 3y^2 = 0$$
Factor the left side of the equation that has a zero constant term.
$$(x + y)(x + 3y) = 0$$
$$x = -y \text{ or } x = -3y$$
Thus the original system is equivalent to the two systems

$$x^2 + xy - 3y^2 = 3 \qquad\qquad x^2 + xy - 3y^2 = 3$$
$$x = -y \qquad\qquad\qquad x = -3y$$

These systems are solved by substitution.

First system: Second system:
$$x^2 + xy - 3y^2 = 3 \qquad\qquad\qquad x^2 + xy - 3y^2 = 3$$
$$x = -y \qquad\qquad\qquad\qquad\qquad x = -3y$$
$$(-y)^2 + (-y)y - 3y^2 = 3 \qquad\qquad (-3y)^2 + (-3y)y - 3y^2 = 3$$
$$y^2 - y^2 - 3y^2 = 3 \qquad\qquad\qquad 9y^2 - 3y^2 - 3y^2 = 3$$
$$-3y^2 = 3 \qquad\qquad\qquad\qquad 3y^2 = 3$$
$$y^2 = -1 \qquad\qquad\qquad\qquad y^2 = 1$$
$$y = \pm i \qquad\qquad\qquad\qquad y = \pm 1$$

For $y = i$ For $y = -i$ For $y = 1$ For $y = -1$
$$x = -i \qquad\quad x = i \qquad\qquad\quad x = -3 \qquad\quad x = 3$$
Solutions: $(-i, i), (i, -i), (-3, 1), (3, -1)$

47. Before we can enter these equations in our graphing calculator, we must solve for y:
$$-x^2 + 2xy + y^2 = 1 \qquad\qquad 3x^2 - 4xy + y^2 = 2$$
$$y^2 + 2xy - 1 - x^2 = 0 \qquad\qquad y^2 - 4xy + 3x^2 - 2 = 0$$
Applying the quadratic formula to each equation, we have

$$y = \frac{-2x \pm \sqrt{4x^2 - 4(-1 - x^2)}}{2} \qquad\qquad y = \frac{4x \pm \sqrt{16x^2 - 4(3x^2 - 2)}}{2}$$

$$y = \frac{-2x \pm \sqrt{8x^2 + 4}}{2} \qquad\qquad\qquad y = \frac{4x \pm \sqrt{4x^2 + 8}}{2}$$

$$y = -x \pm \sqrt{2x^2 + 1} \qquad\qquad\qquad y = 2x \pm \sqrt{x^2 + 2}$$

Entering each of these four equations into a graphing
calculator produces the graph shown at the right.
Zooming in on the four intersection points, or using a built-in
intersection routine (details omitted), yields $(-1.41, -0.82)$,
$(-0.13, 1.15)$, $(0.13, -1.15)$, and $(1.41, 0.82)$ to two decimal
places.

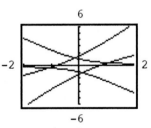

49. Before we can enter these equations in our graphing calculator, we must solve for y:
$$3x^2 - 4xy - y^2 = 2 \qquad\qquad 2x^2 + 2xy + y^2 = 9$$
$$y^2 + 4xy + 2 - 3x^2 = 0 \qquad\qquad y^2 + 2xy + 2x^2 - 9 = 0$$
Applying the quadratic formula to each equation, we have

$$y = \frac{-4x \pm \sqrt{16x^2 - 4(2 - 3x^2)}}{2} \qquad\qquad y = \frac{-2x \pm \sqrt{4x^2 - 4(2x^2 - 9)}}{2}$$

$$y = \frac{-4x \pm \sqrt{28x^2 - 8}}{2} \qquad\qquad\qquad y = \frac{-2x \pm \sqrt{36 - 4x^2}}{2}$$

$$y = -2x \pm \sqrt{7x^2 - 2} \qquad\qquad\qquad y = -x \pm \sqrt{9 - x^2}$$

Entering each of these four equations into a graphing calculator produces the graph shown at the right. Zooming in on the four intersection points, or using a built–in intersection routine (details omitted), yields $(-1.66, -0.84)$, $(-0.91, 3.77)$, $(0.91, -3.77)$, and $(1.66, 0.84)$ to two decimal places.

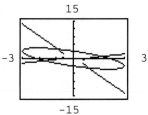

51. Before we can enter these equations in our graphing calculator, we must solve for y:

$$2x^2 - 2xy + y^2 = 9 \qquad\qquad 4x^2 - 4xy + y^2 + x = 3$$
$$y^2 - 2xy + 2x^2 - 9 = 0 \qquad\qquad y^2 - 4xy + 4x^2 + x - 3 = 0$$

Applying the quadratic formula to each equation, we have

$$y = \frac{2x \pm \sqrt{4x^2 - 4(2x^2 - 9)}}{2} \qquad\qquad y = \frac{4x \pm \sqrt{16x^2 - 4(4x^2 + x - 3)}}{2}$$

$$y = \frac{2x \pm \sqrt{36 - 4x^2}}{2} \qquad\qquad y = \frac{4x \pm \sqrt{12 - 4x}}{2}$$

$$y = x \pm \sqrt{9 - x^2} \qquad\qquad y = 2x \pm \sqrt{3 - x}$$

Entering each of these four equations into a graphing calculator produces the graph shown at the right. Zooming in on the four intersection points, or using a built–in intersection routine (details omitted), yields $(-2.96, -3.47)$, $(-0.89, -3.76)$, $(1.39, 4.05)$, and $(2.46, 4.18)$ to two decimal places.

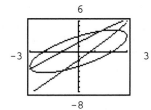

53. Let x and y equal the two numbers. We have the system

$$x + y = 3$$
$$xy = 1$$

Solve the first equation for y in terms of x, then substitute into the second degree equation.

$$y = 3 - x$$
$$x(3 - x) = 1$$
$$3x - x^2 = 1$$
$$-x^2 + 3x - 1 = 0$$
$$x^2 - 3x + 1 = 0$$

$$x = \frac{-b \pm \sqrt{b^2 - 4ac}}{2a} \quad a = 1, b = -3, c = 1$$

$$x = \frac{-(-3) \pm \sqrt{(-3)^2 - 4(1)(1)}}{2(1)} = \frac{3 \pm \sqrt{5}}{2}$$

For $x = \dfrac{3 + \sqrt{5}}{2}$ For $x = \dfrac{3 - \sqrt{5}}{2}$

$$y = 3 - x \qquad\qquad\qquad y = 3 - x$$

$$= 3 - \frac{3 + \sqrt{5}}{2} \qquad\qquad = 3 - \frac{3 - \sqrt{5}}{2}$$

$$= \frac{6 - 3 - \sqrt{5}}{2} \qquad\qquad = \frac{6 - 3 + \sqrt{5}}{2}$$

$$= \frac{3 - \sqrt{5}}{2} \qquad\qquad\quad = \frac{3 + \sqrt{5}}{2}$$

Thus the two numbers are $\dfrac{1}{2}(3 - \sqrt{5})$ and $\dfrac{1}{2}(3 + \sqrt{5})$.

55. Sketch a figure. Let x and y represent the lengths of the two legs.

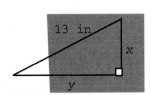

From the Pythagorean Theorem we have $x^2 + y^2 = 13^2$

From the formula for the area of a triangle we have $\frac{1}{2}xy = 30$

Thus the system of equations is $x^2 + y^2 = 169$

$$\frac{1}{2}xy = 30$$

Solve the second equation for y in terms of x, then substitute into the first equation.

$$xy = 60$$
$$y = \frac{60}{x}$$
$$x^2 + \left(\frac{60}{x}\right)^2 = 169$$
$$x^2 + \frac{3600}{x^2} = 169 \quad x \neq 0$$
$$x^4 + 3600 = 169x^2$$
$$x^4 - 169x^2 + 3600 = 0$$
$$(x^2 - 144)(x^2 - 25) = 0$$
$$(x - 12)(x + 12)(x - 5)(x + 5) = 0$$
$$x = \pm 12, \pm 5$$

Discarding the negative solutions, we have $x = 12$ or $x = 5$

For $x = 12$ For $x = 5$

$y = \frac{60}{x}$ $y = \frac{60}{x}$

$y = 5$ $y = 12$

The lengths of the legs are 5 inches and 12 inches.

57. Let x = width of screen.

y = height of screen.

From the Pythagorean Theorem, we have $x^2 + y^2 = (7.5)^2$

From the formula for the area of a rectangle we have $xy = 27$

Thus the system of equations is: $x^2 + y^2 = 56.25$

$$xy = 27$$

Solve the second equation for y in terms of x, then substitute into the first equation.

$$y = \frac{27}{x}$$
$$x^2 + \left(\frac{27}{x}\right)^2 = 56.25 \quad x \neq 0$$
$$x^2 + \frac{729}{x^2} = 56.25 \quad x \neq 0$$
$$x^4 + 729 = 56.25x^2$$
$$x^4 - 56.25x^2 + 729 = 0 \quad \text{quadratic in } x^2$$
$$x^2 = \frac{-b \pm \sqrt{b^2 - 4ac}}{2a} \quad a = 1, b = -56.25, c = 729$$
$$x^2 = \frac{-(-56.25) \pm \sqrt{(-56.25)^2 - 4(1)(729)}}{2(1)} = \frac{56.25 \pm 15.75}{2} = 36, 20.25$$
$$x = 6, 4.5 \text{ (discarding the negative solutions)}$$

For $x = 6$ For $x = 4.5$

$y = \frac{27}{6} = 4.5$ $y = \frac{27}{4.5} = 6$

The dimensions of the screen must be 6 inches by 4.5 inches.

59.

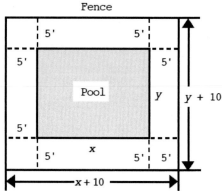

Redrawing and labeling the figure as shown, we have
Area of pool = 572
$$xy = 572$$
Area enclosed by fence = 1,152
$$(x + 10)(y + 10) = 1,152$$

We solve this system by solving for y in terms of x in the first equation, then substituting into the second equation.

$$y = \frac{572}{x}$$

$$(x + 10)\left(\frac{572}{x} + 10\right) = 1,152$$

$$572 + 10x + \frac{5,720}{x} + 100 = 1,152$$

$$10x + \frac{5,720}{x} - 480 = 0 \quad x \neq 0$$

$$10x^2 + 5,720 - 480x = 0$$

$$x^2 - 48x + 572 = 0$$

$$(x - 26)(x - 22) = 0$$

$$x = 26, 22$$

For $x = 26$

$$y = \frac{572}{26}$$

$$y = 22$$

For $x = 22$

$$y = \frac{572}{22}$$

$$y = 26$$

The dimensions of the pool are 22 feet by 26 feet.

61.   Let x = average speed of Boat B
Then $x + 5$ = average speed of Boat A

Let y = time of Boat B, then $y - \frac{1}{2}$ = time of Boat A

Using Distance = rate × time, we have
$$75 = xy$$

$$75 = (x + 5)\left(y - \frac{1}{2}\right)$$

Note: The *faster* boat, A, has the *shorter* time. It is a common error to confuse the signs here. Another common error: if rates are expressed in miles per hour, then $y - 30$ is not the correct time for boat A. Times must be expressed in hours.

Solve the first equation for y in terms of x, then substitute into the second equation.

$$y = \frac{75}{x}$$

$$75 = (x + 5)\left(\frac{75}{x} - \frac{1}{2}\right)$$

$$75 = 75 - \frac{1}{2}x + \frac{375}{x} - \frac{5}{2}$$

$$0 = -\frac{1}{2}x + \frac{375}{x} - \frac{5}{2} \quad x \neq 0$$

$$2x(0) = 2x\left(-\frac{1}{2}x\right) + 2x\left(\frac{375}{x}\right) - 2x\left(\frac{5}{2}\right)$$

$$0 = -x^2 + 750 - 5x$$

$$x^2 + 5x - 750 = 0$$

$$(x - 25)(x + 30) = 0$$

$$x = 25, -30$$

Discarding the negative solution,
we have $x = 25$ mph = average speed of Boat B
$x + 5 = 30$ mph = average speed of Boat A

SECTION 7–7

1. The graph of $y = mx + b$ is a straight line with slope m and y intercept b. The graph of $y < mx + b$ is a half-plane consisting of all points in the plane below the line. The graph of $y > mx + b$ is a half-plane consisting of all points in the plane above the line.

3. Variables representing numbers of real quantities (like tables or surfboards) cannot take on negative values. The graph of a linear inequality system with nonnegativity restrictions is in the first quadrant only.

5. Graph $2x - 3y = 6$ as a dashed line, since equality is not included in the original statement. The origin is a suitable test point.
    $$2x - 3y < 6$$
    $$2(0) - 3(0) = 0 < 6$$
    Hence $(0, 0)$ is in the solution set.
    The graph is the half–plane containing $(0, 0)$.

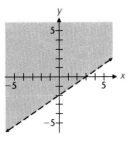

7. Graph $3x + 2y = 18$ as a solid line, since equality is included in the original statement. The origin is a suitable test point.
    $$3(0) + 2(0) = 0 \not\geq 18$$
    Hence $(0, 0)$ is not in the solution set.
    The graph is the line $3x + 2y = 18$ and the half–plane not containing the origin.

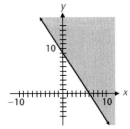

9. Graph $y = \dfrac{2}{3}x + 5$ as a solid line, since equality is included in

    the original statement. The origin is a suitable test point.
    $$0 \overset{?}{\leq} (0) + 5$$
    $$0 \leq 5$$
    Hence $(0, 0)$ is in the solution set. The graph is the line
    $= \dfrac{2}{3}x + 5$ and the half–plane containing the origin.

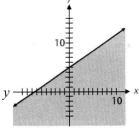

11. Graph $y = 8$ as a dashed line, since equality is not included in the original statement. Clearly the graph consists of all points whose y–coordinates are less than 8, that is, the lower half-plane.

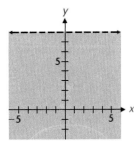

13. This system is equivalent to the system
    $$y \geq -3$$
    $$y < 2$$
    and its graph is the intersection of the graphs of these inequalities.

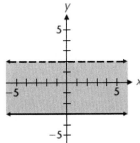

15. $x + 2y \leq 8$
$3x - 2y \geq 0$
Choose a suitable test point that lies on neither line, for example, (2, 0).
   $2 + 2(0) = 2 \leq 8$ Hence, the solution region is *below* the graph of $x + 2y = 8$.
   $3(2) - 2(0) = 6 \geq 0$ Hence, the solution region is *below* the graph of $3x - 2y = 0$.
Thus the solution region is region IV in the diagram.

17. $x + 2y \geq 8$
$3x - 2y \geq 0$
Choose a suitable test point that lies on neither line, for example, (2, 0).
   $2 + 2(0) = 2 \ngeq 8$ Hence, the solution region is *above* the graph of $x + 2y = 8$.
   $3(2) - 2(0) = 6 \geq 0$ Hence, the solution region is *below* the graph of $3x - 2y = 0$.
Thus the solution region is region I in the diagram.

19.   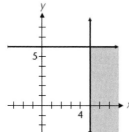   **21.**   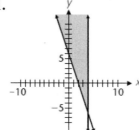   **23.**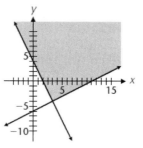

25.   Choose a suitable test point that lies on none of the lines, say (5, 1).
         $5 + 3(1) = 8 \leq 18$ Hence, the solution region is *below* the graph of $x + 3y = 18$.
         $2(5) + 1 = 11 \ngeq 16$ Hence, the solution region is *above* the graph of $2x + y = 16$.
            $5 \geq 0$
            $1 \geq 0$
Thus the solution region is region IV in the diagram.
The corner points are the labeled points (6, 4), (8, 0), and (18, 0).

27.   Choose a suitable test point that lies on none of the lines, say (5, 1).
         $5 + 3(1) = 8 \ngeq 18$ Hence, the solution region is *above* the graph of $x + 3y = 18$.
         $2(5) + 1 = 11 \ngeq 16$ Hence, the solution region is *above* the graph of $2x + y = 16$.
            $5 \geq 0$
            $1 \geq 0$
Thus the solution region is region I in the diagram.
The corner points are the labeled points (0, 16), (6, 4), and (18, 0).

29. The solution region is bounded (contained in, for
example, the circle $x^2 + y^2 = 16$).
The corner points are obvious from the graph:
(0, 0), (0, 2), (3, 0).

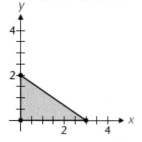

31. The solution region is unbounded. The corner points
are obvious from the graph: (0, 4) and (5, 0).

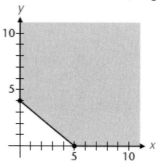

33. The solution region is bounded. Three corner points are obvious from the graph: $(0, 4)$, $(0, 0)$, $(4, 0)$. The fourth corner point is obtained by solving the system
$$x + 3y = 12$$
$$2x + y = 8 \text{ to obtain } \left(\frac{12}{5}, \frac{16}{5}\right).$$

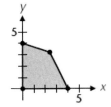

35. The solution region is unbounded. Two corner points are obvious from the graph: $(9, 0)$ and $(0, 8)$. The third corner point is obtained by solving the system
$$4x + 3y = 24$$
$$2x + 3y = 18 \text{ to obtain } (3, 4).$$

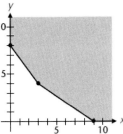

37. The solution region is bounded. Three corner points are obvious from the graph: $(6, 0)$, $(0, 0)$, and $(0, 5)$. The other corner points are obtained by solving:

$2x + y = 12$ and	$x + y = 7$
$x + y = 7$	$x + 2y = 10$
to obtain	to obtain
$(5, 2)$	$(4, 3)$

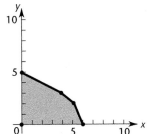

39. The solution region is unbounded. Two of the corner points are obvious from the graph: $(16, 0)$ and $(0, 14)$. The other corner points are obtained by solving:

$x + 2y = 16$ and	$x + y = 12$
$x + y = 12$	$2x + y = 14$
to obtain	to obtain
$(8, 4)$	$(2, 10)$

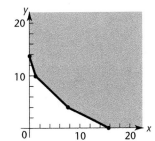

41. The solution region is bounded.
The corner points are obtained by solving:

$$\begin{cases} x + y = 11 \\ 5x + y = 15 \end{cases} \text{ to obtain } (1, 10)$$

$$\begin{cases} 5x + y = 15 \\ x + 2y = 12 \end{cases} \text{ to obtain } (2, 5), \text{ and}$$

$$\begin{cases} x + y = 11 \\ x + 2y = 12 \end{cases} \text{ to obtain } (10, 1)$$

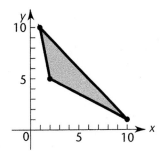

43. From the graph it should be clear that there is no point with x coordinate greater than 4 which satisfies both $3x + 2y \geq 24$ (arrows pointing, roughly, northeast) and $3x + y \leq 15$ (arrows pointing, roughly, southwest). The feasible region is empty.

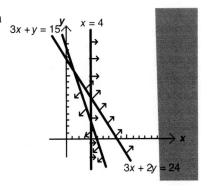

45. The feasible region is bounded.
The corner points are obtained by solving:

$$\begin{cases} x+y=10 \\ 3x-2y=15 \end{cases} \text{ to obtain } (7, 3)$$

$$\begin{cases} 3x-2y=15 \\ 3x+5y=15 \end{cases} \text{ to obtain } (5, 0),$$

$$\begin{cases} 3x+5y=15 \\ -5x+2y=6 \end{cases} \text{ to obtain } (0, 3), \text{ and}$$

$$\begin{cases} -5x+2y=6 \\ x+y=10 \end{cases} \text{ to obtain } (2, 8)$$

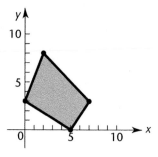

47. The feasible region is bounded.
The corner points are obtained by solving:

$$\begin{cases} 16x+13y=119 \\ 12x+16y=101 \end{cases} \text{ to obtain } (5.91, 1.88)$$

$$\begin{cases} 16x+13y=119 \\ -4x+3y=11 \end{cases} \text{ to obtain } (2.14, 6.53) \text{ and}$$

$$\begin{cases} 12x+16y=101 \\ -4x+3y=11 \end{cases} \text{ to obtain } (1.27, 5.36)$$

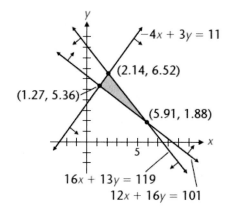

49. Let x = number of trick skis produced per day.
y = number of slalom skis produced per day
Clearly x and y must be non–negative.
Hence $x \geq 0$ (1)
$\quad\quad y \geq 0$ (2)
To fabricate x trick skis requires $6x$ hours. To fabricate y slalom skis requires $4y$ hours. 108 hours are available for fabricating; hence
$6x + 4y \leq 108$ (3)
To finish x trick skis requires $1x$ hours.
To finish y slalom skis requires $1y$ hours.
24 hours are available for finishing, hence
$x + y \leq 24$ (4)
Graphing the inequality system (1), (2), (3), (4), we have the diagram.

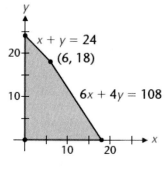

51. **(A)** All production schedules in the feasible region that are on the graph of $50x + 60y = 1,100$ will result in a profit of \$1,100.

(B) There are many possible choices. For example, producing 5 trick and 15 slalom skis will produce a profit of \$1,150. The graph of the line $50x + 60y = 1,150$ includes all the production schedules in the feasible region that result in a profit of \$1,150.

(C) A graphical approach would involve drawing other lines of the type $50x + 60y = A$. The graphs of these lines include all production schedules that will result in a profit of A. Increase A until the line either intersects the feasible region only in 1 corner point or contains an edge of the feasible region. This value of A will be the maximum profit possible.

53. Clearly x and y must be non–negative.
Hence $x \geq 0$ (1)
     $y \geq 0$ (2)
x cubic yards of mix A contains $20x$ pounds of phosphoric acid.
y cubic yards of mix B contains $10y$ pounds of phosphoric acid.
At least 460 pounds of phosphoric acid are required, hence
$20x + 10y \geq 460$ (3)
x cubic yards of mix A contains $30x$ pounds of nitrogen.
y cubic yards of mix B contains $30y$ pounds of nitrogen.
At least 960 pounds of nitrogen are required, hence
$30x + 30y \geq 960$ (4)
x cubic yards of mix A contains $5x$ pounds of potash. y cubic yards of mix B contains $10y$ pounds of potash.
At least 220 pounds of potash are required, hence
$5x + 10y \geq 220$ (5)
Graphing the inequality system (1), (2), (3), (4), (5), we
have the diagram:

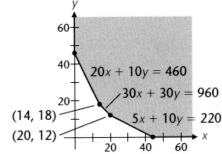

55. Clearly x and y must be non–negative.
Hence $x \geq 0$ (1)
     $y \geq 0$ (2)
Each sociologist will spend 10 hours collecting data: $10x$ hours.
Each research assistant will spend 30 hours collecting data: $30y$ hours.
At least 280 hours must be spent collecting data; hence
$10x + 30y \geq 280$ (3)
Each sociologist will spend 30 hours analyzing data: $30x$ hours.
Each research assistant will spend 10 hours analyzing data: $10y$ hours.
At least 360 hours must be spent analyzing data; hence
$30x + 10y \geq 360$ (4)
Graphing the inequality system (1), (2), (3), (4), we have the diagram.

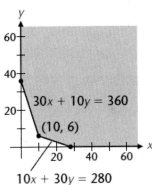

SECTION 7–8

1. The objective function is the quantity to be maximized or minimized.
3. The problem constraints are the limits imposed by reality.
5. The feasible region is the set of possible values of the variables under the constraints.
7. A corner point is a point where two boundaries of the feasible region intersect.

9.

Corner Point (x, y)	Objective Function $z = x + y$	
(0, 12)	12	
(7, 9)	16	Maximum value
(10, 0)	10	
(0, 0)	0	

The maximum value of z on S is 16 at (7, 9).

11.

Corner Point (x, y)	Objective Function $z = 3x + 7y$		
(0, 12)	84	Maximum value	
(7, 9)	84	Maximum value	Multiple optimal solutions
(10, 0)	30		
(0, 0)	0		

The maximum value of z on S is 84 at both (0, 12) and (7, 9).

13. Plugging in zero for x, we get $z = 2y$ or $y = \dfrac{z}{2}$. Plugging in zero for y,

we get $z = x$. So the intercepts of the line $z = x + 2y$ are $\left(0, \dfrac{z}{2}\right)$ and

$(z, 0)$. The feasible region is shown at the right with several constant z lines drawn in. Sliding a straight edge parallel to these constant z lines in the direction of increasing z, we can see that the point in the feasible region that will intersect the constant z line for largest possible z is (7, 9). When $x = 7$ and $y = 9$, $z = 25$.

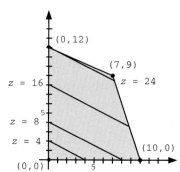

Check:

Corner Point (x, y)	Objective Function $z = x + 2y$	
(0, 12)	24	
(7, 9)	25	Maximum value
(10, 0)	10	
(0, 0)	0	

The maximum value of z on S is 25 at (7, 9).

15. Plugging in zero for x, we get $z = 2y$ or $y = \dfrac{z}{2}$. Plugging in zero for y,

we get $z = 7x$ or $x = \dfrac{z}{7}$. So the intercepts of the line $z = 7x + 2y$ are

$\left(0, \dfrac{z}{2}\right)$ and $\left(\dfrac{z}{7}, 0\right)$. The feasible region is shown at the right with

several constant z lines drawn in. If we slide a straight edge parallel to the constant z lines as z increases, the last point in S that will intersect our lines is (10, 0). When $x = 10$ and $y = 0$, $z = 70$.

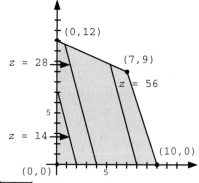

Check:

Corner Point (x, y)	Objective Function $z = 7x + 2y$	
(0, 12)	24	
(7, 9)	67	
(10, 0)	70	Maximum value
(0, 0)	0	

The maximum value of z on S is 70 at (10, 0).

17.

Corner Point (x, y)	Objective Function $z = 7x + 4y$	
(0, 12)	48	
(12, 0)	84	
(4, 3)	40	
(0, 8)	32	Minimum value

The minimum value of z on S is 32 at (0, 8).

19.

Corner Point (x, y)	Objective Function 3x + 8y	
(0,12)	96	
(12,0)	36	Minimum value ⎫ Multiple optimal solutions
(4,3)	36	Minimum value ⎭
(0,8)	64	

The minimum value of z on S is 36 at both (12, 0) and (4, 3).

21. If $x = 5$ and $y = 5$, $z = 5 + 2(5) = 15$, so the constant–value line we need is $x + 2y = 15$. The feasible region is shown at the right with the constant–value line. If we slide a straightedge parallel to this constant–value line in the direction of decreasing z (downward), the last point in T that will intersect our line is (4, 3). When $x = 4$ and $y = 3$, $z = 10$.

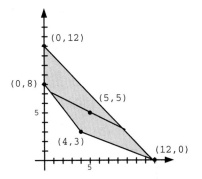

Check:

Corner Point (x, y)	Objective Function z = x + 2y	
(0, 12)	24	
(12, 0)	12	
(0, 8)	16	
(4, 3)	10	Minimum value

The minimum value of z on T is 10 at (4, 3).

23. If $x = 5$ and $y = 5$, $z = 5(5) + 4(5) = 45$, so the constant–value line we need is $5x + 4y = 45$. The feasible region is shown at the right with the constant–value line. The constant–value line appears to be parallel to the edge connecting (0, 8) and (4, 3). Thus the minimum could occur at either (0, 8) or (4, 3) when $x = 0$ and $y = 8$, $z = 32$. When $x = 4$ and $y = 3$, $z = 32$ also.

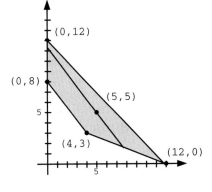

Check:

Corner Point (x, y)	Objective Function z = 5x + 4y	
(0, 12)	48	
(12, 0)	60	
(0, 8)	32	Minimum value
(4, 3)	32	Minimum value

The minimum value of 32 occurs at both (0, 8) and (4, 3).

25. The feasible region is graphed as follows:
The corner points (0, 5), (5, 0) and (0, 0) are obvious from the graph. The corner point (4, 3) is obtained by solving the system
$x + 2y = 10$
$3x + y = 15$
We now evaluate the objective function at each corner point.

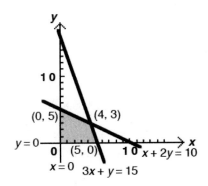

Corner Point (x, y)	Objective Function z = 3x + 2y	
(0, 5)	10	
(0, 0)	0	
(5, 0)	15	
(4, 3)	18	Maximum value

The maximum value of z on S is 18 at (4, 3).

27. The feasible region is graphed as follows:
The corner points $(4, 0)$ and $(10, 0)$ are obvious from the graph.
The corner point $(2, 4)$ is obtained by solving the system
$x + 2y = 10$
$2x + y = 8$
We now evaluate the objective function at each corner point.

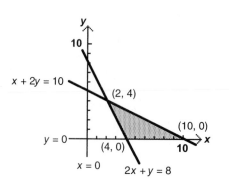

Corner Point (x, y)	Objective Function $z = 3x + 4y$	
$(4, 0)$	12	Minimum value
$(10, 0)$	30	
$(2, 4)$	22	

The minimum value of z on S is 12 at $(4, 0)$.

29. The feasible region is graphed below. The corner points $(0, 12)$, $(0, 0)$, and $(12, 0)$ are obvious from the graph. The other corner points are obtained by solving:
$x + 2y = 24$ and $x + y = 14$
 $x + y = 14$ to obtain $(4, 10)$ $2x + y = 24$ to obtain $(10, 4)$
We now evaluate the objective function at each corner point.

Corner Point (x, y)	Objective Function $z = 3x + 4y$	
$(0, 12)$	48	
$(0, 0)$	0	
$(12, 0)$	36	
$(10, 4)$	46	
$(4, 10)$	52	Maximum value

The maximum value of z on S is 52 at $(4, 10)$.

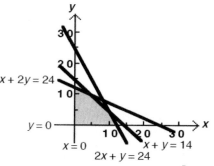

31. The feasible region is graphed as follows:
The corner points $(0, 20)$ and $(20, 0)$ are obvious from the graph.
The third corner point is obtained by solving:
$x + 4y = 20$
$4x + y = 20$ to obtain $(4, 4)$
We now evaluate the objective function at each corner point.

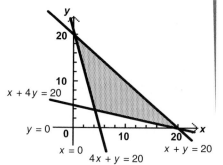

Corner Point (x, y)	Objective Function $z = 5x + 6y$	
$(0, 20)$	120	
$(20, 0)$	100	
$(4, 4)$	44	Minimum value

The minimum value of z on S is 44 at $(4, 4)$.

33. The feasible region is graphed as follows:
The corner points $(60, 0)$ and $(120, 0)$ are obvious from the graph.
The other corner points are obtained by solving:
  $x + y = 60$ and $x + 2y = 120$
$x - 2y = 0$ to obtain $(40, 20)$ $x - 2y = 0$ to obtain $(60, 30)$
We now evaluate the objective function at each corner point.

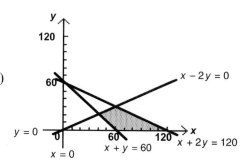

Corner Point (x, y)	Objective Function $25x + 50y$	
(60, 0)	1,500	Minimum value
(40, 20)	2,000	
(60, 30)	3,000	Maximum value ⎫ Multiple optimal solutions
(120, 0)	3,000	Maximum value ⎭

The minimum value of z on S is 1,500 at (60, 0).
The maximum value of z on S is 3,000 at (60, 30) and (120, 0).

35. The feasible region is graphed as follows:
The corner points (0, 45), (0, 20), (25, 0), and (60, 0) are obvious from the graph shown below.
The other corner points are obtained by solving:
$3x + 4y = 240$ and $3x + 4y = 240$
    $y = 45$ to obtain (20, 45) $x = 60$ to obtain (60, 15)
We now evaluate the objective function at each corner point.

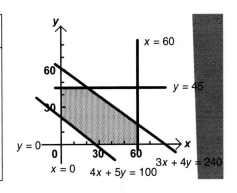

Corner Point (x, y)	Objective Function $25x + 15y$	
(0, 45)	675	
(0, 20)	300	Minimum Value
(25, 0)	625	
(60, 0)	1,500	
(60, 15)	1,725	Maximum Value
(20, 45)	1,175	

The minimum value of z on S is 300 at (0, 20).
The maximum value of z on S is 1,725 at (60, 15).

37. The feasible region is graphed as shown at the right.
The corner point (0, 0) is obvious from the graph. The other
corner points are obtained by solving:

$x_1 = 0$ $350x_1 + 340x_2 = 3762$
$275x_1 + 322x_2 = 3381$ $275x_1 + 322x_2 = 3381$
to obtain (0, 10.5)   to obtain (3.22, 7.75)

$350x_1 + 340x_2 = 3762$ $425x_1 + 306x_2 = 4114$
$425x_1 + 306x_2 = 4114$ $x_2 = 0$
to obtain (6.62, 4.25)   to obtain (9.68, 0)

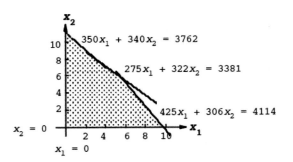

We now evaluate the objective function at each corner point.

Corner Point (x_1, x_2)	Objective Function $525x_1 + 478x_2$	
(0, 0)	0	Minimum value
(0, 10.5)	5019	
(3.22, 7.75)	5395	
(6.62, 4.25)	5507	Maximum value
(9.68, 0)	5082	

The maximum value of P is 5507 at the corner point (6.62, 4.25).

39. The feasible region is graphed as follows: (heavily outlined for clarity)
Consider the objective function $x + y$. It should be clear that it takes on
the value 2 along $x + y = 2$, the value 4 along $x + y = 4$, the value 7 along
$x + y = 7$, and so on. The maximum value of the objective function, then,
on S, is 7, which occurs at B. Graphically this occurs when the line
$x + y = c$ coincides with the boundary of S. Thus to answer questions
(A)-(E) we must determine values of a and b such that the appropriate
line $ax + by = c$ coincides with the boundary of S only at the specified
points.

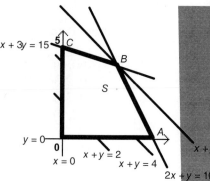

(A)   The line $ax + by = c$ must have slope negative, but greater in absolute value that that of line segment
AB, $2x + y = 10$. Therefore $a > 2b$.

(B)   The line $ax + by = c$ must have slope negative but between that of $x + 3y = 15$ and $2x + y = 10$.
Therefore $\frac{1}{3}b < a < 2b$.

(C)   The line $ax + by = c$ must have slope greater than that of line segment BC, $x + 3y = 15$.
Therefore $a < \frac{1}{3}b$ or $b > 3a$.

(D)   The line $ax + by = c$ must be parallel to line segment AB, therefore $a = 2b$.

(E)   The line $ax + by = c$ must be parallel to line segment BC, therefore $b = 3a$.

41.   We let $x =$ the number of trick skis
$y =$ the number of slalom skis
The problem constraints were
$6x + 4y \leq 108$
$x + y \leq 24$
The non–negative constraints were
$x \geq 0$
$y \geq 0$
The feasible region was graphed there.

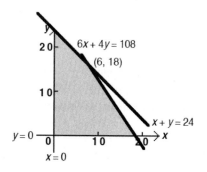

(A) We note now: the linear objective function $P = 40x + 30y$
represents the profit.
Three of the corner points are obvious from the graph: $(0, 24)$, $(0, 0)$, and $(18, 0)$. The fourth corner point is
obtained by solving: $6x + 4y = 108$
$x + y = 24$ to obtain $(6, 18)$.
Summarizing: the mathematical model for this problem is: Maximize $P = 40x + 30y$
subject to: $6x + 4y \leq 108$
$x + y \leq 24$
$x, y \geq 0$
We now evaluate the objective function $40x + 30y$ at each corner point.

Corner Point (x, y)	Objective Function $40x + 30y$	
$(0, 0)$	0	
$(18, 0)$	720	
$(6, 18)$	780	Maximum value
$(0, 24)$	720	

The optimal value is 780 at the corner point $(6, 18)$. Thus, 6 trick skis and 18 slalom skis should be
manufactured to obtain the maximum profit of \$780.

(B)   The objective function now becomes $40x + 25y$. We evaluate this at each corner point.

Corner Point (x, y)	Objective Function $40x + 25y$	
(0, 0)	0	
(18, 0)	720	Maximum value
(6, 18)	690	
(0, 24)	600	

The optimal value is now 720 at the corner point (18, 0). Thus, 18 trick skis and no slalom skis should be produced to obtain a maximum profit of $720.

(C)   The objective function now becomes $40x + 45y$. We evaluate this at each corner point.

Corner Point (x, y)	Objective Function $40x + 45y$	
(0, 0)	0	
(18, 0)	720	
(6, 18)	1,050	
(0, 24)	1,080	Maximum value

The optimal value is now 1,080 at the corner point (0, 24). Thus, no trick skis and 24 slalom skis should be produced to obtain a maximum profit of $1,080.

43.   Let x = number of model A trucks
y = number of model B trucks
We form the linear objective function $C = 15,000x + 24,000y$
We wish to minimize C, the cost of buying x trucks @ $15,000 and y trucks @ $24,000, subject to the constraints.
  $x + y \leq 15$ maximum number of trucks constraint
$2x + 3y \geq 36$ capacity constraint
  $x, y \geq 0$ non–negative constraints.
Solving the system of constraint inequalities graphically, we obtain the feasible region S shown in the diagram.

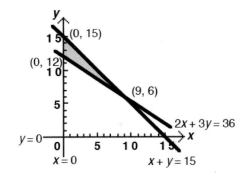

Next we evaluate the objective function at each corner point.

Corner Point (x, y)	Objective Function $C = 15,000x + 24,000y$	
(0, 12)	288,000	
(0, 15)	360,000	
(9, 6)	279,000	Minimum value

The optimal value is $279,000 at the corner point (9, 6). Thus, the company should purchase 9 model A trucks and 6 model B trucks to realize the minimum cost of $279,000.

45.   (A) Let x = number of tables
y = number of chairs
We form the linear objective function $P = 90x + 25y$
We wish to maximize P, the profit from x tables @ $90 and y chairs @ $25, subject to the constraints
$8x + 2y \leq 400$ assembly department constraint
  $2x + y \leq 120$ finishing department constraint
    $x, y \geq 0$ non–negative constraints
Solving the system of constraint inequalities graphically, we obtain the feasible region S' shown in the diagram.

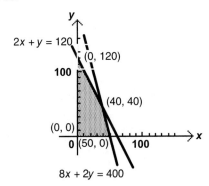

Next we evaluate the objective function at each corner point.

Corner Point (x, y)	Objective Function $P = 90x + 25y$	
(0, 0)	0	
(50, 0)	4,500	
(40, 40)	4,600	Maximum value
(0, 120)	3,000	

The optimal value is 4,600 at the corner point (40, 40). Thus, the company should manufacture 40 tables and 40 chairs for a maximum profit of $4,600.

(B) We are faced with the further condition that $y \geq 4x$.
We wish, then, to maximize $P = 90x + 25y$ under the constraints
$$8x + 2y \leq 400$$
$$2x + y \leq 120$$
$$y \geq 4x$$
$$x, y \geq 0$$
The feasible region is now S' as graphed.
Note that the new condition has the effect of excluding (40, 40) from the feasible region.
We now evaluate the objective function at the new corner points.

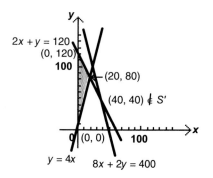

Corner Point (x, y)	Objective Function $P = 90x + 25y$	
(0, 120)	3,000	
(0, 0)	0	
(20, 80)	3,800	Maximum value

The optimal value is now 3,800 at the corner point (20, 80). Thus the company should manufacture 20 tables and 80 chairs for a maximum profit of $3,800.

47. Let x = number of gallons produced using the old process
y = number of gallons produced using the new process
We form the linear objective function $P = 0.6x + 0.2y$
(A)   We wish to maximize P, the profit from x gallons using the old process and y gallons using the new process, subject to the constraints
$$20x + 5y \leq 16,000 \qquad \text{sulfur dioxide constraint}$$
$$40x + 20y \leq 30,000 \qquad \text{particulate matter constraint}$$
$$x, y \geq 0 \qquad \text{non–negative constraints}$$
Solving the system of constraint inequalities graphically, we obtain the feasible region S shown in the diagram. Note that no corner points are determined by this (very weak) sulfur dioxide constraint.
We evaluate the objective function at each corner point.

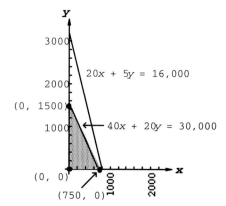

Corner Point (x, y)	Objective Function $P = 0.6x + 0.2y$	
(0, 0)	0	
(0, 1500)	300	
(750, 0)	450	Maximum value

The optimal value is 450 at the corner point (750, 0). Thus, the company should manufacture 750 gallons by the old process exclusively, for a profit of $450.

(B) The sulfur dioxide constraint is now
$20x + 5y \leq 11{,}500.$
We now wish to maximize P subject to the constraints
$$20x + 5y \leq 11{,}500$$
$$40x + 20y \leq 30{,}000$$
$$x, y \geq 0$$
The feasible region is now S_1 as shown.

We evaluate the objective function at the new corner points.

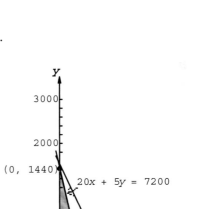

Corner Point (x, y)	Objective Function $P = 0.6x + 0.2y$	
(0, 0)	0	
(575, 0)	345	
(400, 700)	380	Maximum value
(0, 1500)	300	

The optimal value is now 380 at the corner point (400, 700).
Thus, the company should manufacture 400 gallons by the old
process and 700 gallons by the new process, for a profit of \$380.

(C) The sulfur dioxide constraint is now
$20x + 5y \leq 7{,}200.$
We now wish to maximize P subject to the constraints
$$20x + 5y \leq 7{,}200$$
$$40x + 20y \leq 30{,}000$$
$$x, y \geq 0$$
The feasible region is now S_2 as shown.

Note that now no corner points are determined by the
particulate matter constraint.
We evaluate the objective function at the new corner points.

Corner Point (x, y)	Objective Function $P = 0.6x + 0.2y$	
(0, 0)	0	
(360, 0)	216	
(0, 1440)	288	Maximum value

The optimal value is now 288 at the corner point (0, 1440). Thus, the company should manufacture 1,440
gallons by the new process exclusively, for a profit of \$288.

49. (A) Let x = number of bags of Brand A
    y = number of bags of Brand B
We form the objective function $N = 6x + 7y$
N represents the amount of nitrogen in x bags @ 6 pounds per bag and y bags @ 7 pounds per bag.
We wish to optimize N subject to the constraints
$2x + 4y \geq 480$ phosphoric acid constraint
$6x + 3y \geq 540$ potash constraint
$3x + 4y \leq 620$ chlorine constraint
    $x, y \geq 0$ non-negative constraints
Solving the system of constraint inequalities graphically, we
obtain the feasible region S shown in the diagram.
Next we evaluate the objective function at the corner points.

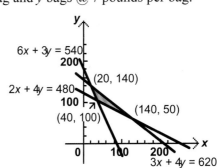

Corner Point (x, y)	Objective Function $N = 6x + 7y$	
(20,140)	1,100	
(40,100)	940	Minimum value
(140,50)	1,190	Maximum value

So the nitrogen will range from a minimum of 940 pounds when 40 bags of brand A and 100 bags of Brand B are used to a maximum of 1,190 pounds when 140 bags of brand A and 50 bags of brand B are used.

CHAPTER 7 REVIEW

1. $2x + y = 7$
$3x - 2y = 0$
We multiply the top equation by 2 and add.
$4x + 2y = 14$
$\underline{3x - 2y = \ 0}$
$7x \quad\quad = 14$
$\quad x = \ 2$
Substituting $x = 2$ in the top equation, we have
$2(2) + y = 7$
$\quad\quad y = 3$
Solution: (2, 3)   *(7–1)*

2. $3x - 6y = 5$
$-2x + 4y = 1$
We multiply the top equation by 2, the bottom by 3, and add.
$6x - 12y = 10$
$\underline{-6x + 12y = \ 3}$
$\quad\quad\quad 0 = 13$
No solution   *(7–1)*

3. $4x - 3y = -8$
$-2x + \dfrac{3}{2} y = 4$

We multiply the bottom equation by 2 and add.
$4x - 3y = -8$
$\underline{-4x + 3y = \ 8}$
$\quad\quad\quad 0 = 0$
There are infinitely many solutions. For any real number t, $4t - 3y = -8$, hence,
$-3y = -4t - 8$
$y = \dfrac{4t + 8}{3}$ Thus, $\left(t, \dfrac{4t + 8}{3} \right)$ is a solution for any real number t.   *(7–1)*

4. $x - 3y + z = 4 \qquad E_1$
$-x + 4y - 4z = \ 1 \qquad E_2$
$2x - y + 5z = -3 \qquad E_3$
Add E_1 to E_2 to eliminate x.
Also multiply E_1 by -2 and add to E_3 to eliminate x.
$\quad x - 3y + \ z = 4 \qquad E_1$
$\underline{-x + 4y - 4z = 1} \qquad E_2$
$\quad\quad\quad y - 3z = 5 \qquad E_4$
$-2x + 6y - 2z = \ -8 \qquad (-2)E_1$
$\underline{2x - \ y + 5z = \ -3} \qquad E_3$
$\quad\quad 5y + 3z = -11 \qquad E_5$
Equivalent system:
$x - 3y + \ z = \ \ 4 \qquad E_1$
$\quad\quad y - 3z = \ \ 5 \qquad E_4$
$\quad\quad 5y + 3z = -11 \qquad E_5$

5. $2x + y - z = 5 \qquad E_1$
$x - 2y - 2z = 4 \qquad E_2$
$3x + 4y + 3z = 3 \qquad E_3$
Multiply E_2 by -2 and add to E_1 to eliminate x.
Also multiply E_2 by -3 and add to E_3 to eliminate x.
$\quad 2x + \ y - \ z = \ \ 5 \qquad E_1$
$\underline{-2x + 4y + 4z = \ -8} \qquad (-2)E_2$
$\quad\quad 5y + 3z = \ -3 \qquad E_4$
$\quad 3x + 4y + 3z = \ \ 3 \qquad E_3$
$\underline{-3x + 6y + 6z = -12} \qquad (-3)E_2$
$\quad\quad 10y + 9z = \ -9 \qquad E_5$
Equivalent system:
$\quad x - 2y - 2z = \ \ 4 \qquad E_2$
$\quad\quad 5y + 3z = -3 \qquad E_4$
$\quad\quad 10y + 9z = -9 \qquad E_5$

Add E_4 to E_5 to eliminate z

$$\begin{array}{ll} y - 3z = 5 & E_4 \\ \underline{5y + 3z = -11} & E_5 \\ 6y \quad\;\; = -6 & \\ y = -1 & \end{array}$$

Substitute $y = -1$ into E_5 and solve for z.

$$\begin{array}{ll} 5y + 3z = -11 & E_5 \\ 5(-1) + 3z = -11 & \\ z = -2 & \end{array}$$

Substitute $y = -1$ and $z = -2$ into E_1 and solve for x.

$$\begin{array}{ll} x - 3y + z = 4 & E_1 \\ x - 3(-1) + (-2) = 4 & \\ x = 3 & \end{array}$$

$(3, -1, -2)$ $\hspace{3cm}$ *(7–1)*

Multiply E_4 by -2 and add to E_5 to eliminate y.

$$\begin{array}{ll} -10y - 6z = 6 & (-2)E_4 \\ \underline{10y + 9z = -9} & E_5 \\ 3z = -3 & \\ z = -1 & \end{array}$$

Substitute $z = -1$ into E_4 and solve for y.

$$\begin{array}{ll} 5y + 3z = -3 & E_4 \\ 5y + 3(-1) = -3 & \\ y = 0 & \end{array}$$

Substitute $y = 0$ and $z = -1$ into E_2 and solve for x.

$$\begin{array}{ll} x - 2y - 2z = 4 & E_2 \\ x - 2(0) - 2(-1) = 4 & \\ x = 2 & \end{array}$$

$(2, 0, -1)$ $\hspace{3cm}$ *(7–1)*

6.

(7–1)

7. $R_1 \leftrightarrow R_2$ means interchange Rows 1 and 2.

$$\begin{bmatrix} 3 & -6 & | & 12 \\ 1 & -4 & | & 5 \end{bmatrix}$$ $\hspace{2cm}$ *(7–2)*

8. $\frac{1}{3}R_2 \rightarrow R_2$ means multiply Row 2 by $\frac{1}{3}$.

$$\begin{bmatrix} 1 & -4 & | & 5 \\ 1 & -2 & | & 4 \end{bmatrix}$$ $\hspace{2cm}$ *(7–2)*

9. $(-3)R_1 + R_2 \rightarrow R_2$ means replace Row 2 by itself plus -3 times Row 1. $\begin{bmatrix} 1 & -4 & | & 5 \\ 0 & 6 & | & -3 \end{bmatrix}$ $\hspace{1cm}$ *(7–2)*

10. $x_1 = 4$
$x_2 = -7$
The solution is $(4, -7)$ $\hspace{1cm}$ *(7–2)*

11. $\begin{array}{l} x_1 - x_2 = 4 \\ \quad\quad 0 = 1 \end{array}$
No solution $\hspace{2cm}$ *(7–2)*

12. $\begin{array}{l} x_1 - x_2 = 4 \\ \quad\quad 0 = 0 \end{array}$
Solution: $x_2 = t$
$\hspace{1.5cm} x_1 = x_2 + 4 = t + 4$
Thus $x_1 = t + 4$, $x_2 = t$ is the solution, for t any real number. $\hspace{1cm}$ *(10–2)*

13. $AB = \begin{bmatrix} 4 & -2 \\ 0 & 3 \end{bmatrix}\begin{bmatrix} -1 & 5 \\ -4 & 6 \end{bmatrix} = \begin{bmatrix} 4(-1)+(-2)(-4) & 4\cdot 5+(-2)6 \\ 0(-1)+3(-4) & 0\cdot 5+3\cdot 6 \end{bmatrix} = \begin{bmatrix} 4 & 8 \\ -12 & 18 \end{bmatrix}$ $\hspace{1cm}$ *(7–3)*

14. $CD = \begin{bmatrix} -1 & 4 \end{bmatrix}\begin{bmatrix} 3 \\ -2 \end{bmatrix} = [(-1)3 + 4(-2)] = [-11]$ $\hspace{1cm}$ *(7–3)*

15. $CB = \begin{bmatrix} -1 & 4 \end{bmatrix}\begin{bmatrix} -1 & 5 \\ -4 & 6 \end{bmatrix} = [(-1)(-1) + 4(-4) \quad (-1)5 + 4\cdot 6] = [-15 \quad 19]$ $\hspace{1cm}$ *(7–3)*

16. $AD = \begin{bmatrix} 4 & -2 \\ 0 & 3 \end{bmatrix}\begin{bmatrix} 3 \\ -2 \end{bmatrix} = \begin{bmatrix} 4\cdot 3+(-2)(-2) \\ 0\cdot 3+3(-2) \end{bmatrix} = \begin{bmatrix} 16 \\ -6 \end{bmatrix}$ $\hspace{1cm}$ *(7–3)*

17. $A + B = \begin{bmatrix} 4 & -2 \\ 0 & 3 \end{bmatrix} + \begin{bmatrix} -1 & 5 \\ -4 & 6 \end{bmatrix} = \begin{bmatrix} 4+(-1) & (-2)+5 \\ 0+(-4) & 3+6 \end{bmatrix} = \begin{bmatrix} 3 & 3 \\ -4 & 9 \end{bmatrix}$ (7–3)

18. $C + D$ is not defined (7–3)   **19.** $A + C$ is not defined (7–3)

20. $2A - 5B = 2\begin{bmatrix} 4 & -2 \\ 0 & 3 \end{bmatrix} - 5\begin{bmatrix} -1 & 5 \\ -4 & 6 \end{bmatrix} = \begin{bmatrix} 8 & -4 \\ 0 & 6 \end{bmatrix} - \begin{bmatrix} -5 & 25 \\ -20 & 30 \end{bmatrix} = \begin{bmatrix} 13 & -29 \\ 20 & -24 \end{bmatrix}$ (7–3)

21. $CA + C = [-1 \ \ 4]\begin{bmatrix} 4 & -2 \\ 0 & 3 \end{bmatrix} + [-1 \ \ 4] = [(-1)4 + 4 \cdot 0 \ \ \ (-1)(-2) + 4 \cdot 3] + [-1 \ \ 4]$

$$= [-4 \ \ 14] + [-1 \ \ 4] = [-5 \ \ 18]$$ (7–3)

22. $\begin{bmatrix} 4 & 7 & | & 1 & 0 \\ -1 & -2 & | & 0 & 1 \end{bmatrix} R_1 \leftrightarrow R_2 \sim \begin{bmatrix} -1 & -2 & | & 0 & 1 \\ 4 & 7 & | & 1 & 0 \end{bmatrix} 4R_1 + R_2 \rightarrow R_2 \sim \begin{bmatrix} -1 & -2 & | & 0 & 1 \\ 0 & -1 & | & 1 & 4 \end{bmatrix} (-2)R_2 + R_1 \rightarrow R_1$

$\sim \begin{bmatrix} -1 & 0 & | & -2 & -7 \\ 0 & -1 & | & 1 & 4 \end{bmatrix} \begin{matrix} (-1)R_1 \rightarrow R_1 \\ (-1)R_2 \rightarrow R_2 \end{matrix} \sim \begin{bmatrix} 1 & 0 & | & 2 & 7 \\ 0 & 1 & | & -1 & -4 \end{bmatrix}$

Hence, $A^{-1} = \begin{bmatrix} 2 & 7 \\ -1 & -4 \end{bmatrix}$

$$A^{-1}A = \begin{bmatrix} 2 & 7 \\ -1 & -4 \end{bmatrix}\begin{bmatrix} 4 & 7 \\ -1 & -2 \end{bmatrix} = \begin{bmatrix} 2 \cdot 4 + 7(-1) & 2 \cdot 7 + 7(-2) \\ (-1)4 + (-4)(-1) & (-1)7 + (-4)(-2) \end{bmatrix} = \begin{bmatrix} 1 & 0 \\ 0 & 1 \end{bmatrix} = I$$

(7–4)

23. As a matrix equation the system becomes

$$\begin{matrix} A & X & B \end{matrix}$$
$$\begin{bmatrix} 3 & 2 \\ 4 & 3 \end{bmatrix}\begin{bmatrix} x_1 \\ x_2 \end{bmatrix} = \begin{bmatrix} k_1 \\ k_2 \end{bmatrix}$$

The solution of $AX = B$ is $X = A^{-1}B$.

Applying matrix methods, we obtain $A^{-1} = \begin{bmatrix} 3 & -2 \\ -4 & 3 \end{bmatrix}$ (details omitted). Applying this inverse, we have

$$X = \begin{bmatrix} 3 & -2 \\ -4 & 3 \end{bmatrix}\begin{bmatrix} k_1 \\ k_2 \end{bmatrix}$$

(A) $\begin{bmatrix} x_1 \\ x_2 \end{bmatrix} = \begin{bmatrix} 3 & -2 \\ -4 & 3 \end{bmatrix}\begin{bmatrix} 3 \\ 5 \end{bmatrix} = \begin{bmatrix} 3 \cdot 3 + (-2)5 \\ (-4)3 + 3 \cdot 5 \end{bmatrix} = \begin{bmatrix} -1 \\ 3 \end{bmatrix}$ $x_1 = -1, x_2 = 3$

(B) $\begin{bmatrix} x_1 \\ x_2 \end{bmatrix} = \begin{bmatrix} 3 & -2 \\ -4 & 3 \end{bmatrix}\begin{bmatrix} 7 \\ 10 \end{bmatrix} = \begin{bmatrix} 3 \cdot 7 + (-2)10 \\ (-4)7 + 3 \cdot 10 \end{bmatrix} = \begin{bmatrix} 1 \\ 2 \end{bmatrix}$ $x_1 = 1, x_2 = 2$

(C) $\begin{bmatrix} x_1 \\ x_2 \end{bmatrix} = \begin{bmatrix} 3 & -2 \\ -4 & 3 \end{bmatrix}\begin{bmatrix} 4 \\ 2 \end{bmatrix} = \begin{bmatrix} 3 \cdot 4 + (-2)2 \\ (-4)4 + 3 \cdot 2 \end{bmatrix} = \begin{bmatrix} 8 \\ -10 \end{bmatrix}$ $x_1 = 8, x_2 = -10$ (7–4)

24. $\begin{vmatrix} 2 & -3 \\ -5 & -1 \end{vmatrix} = 2(-1) - (-5)(-3) = -17$ (7–5)

25. $\begin{vmatrix} 2 & 3 & -4 \\ 0 & 5 & 0 \\ 1 & -4 & -2 \end{vmatrix} = 0 + 5(-1)^{2+2}\begin{vmatrix} 2 & -4 \\ 1 & -2 \end{vmatrix} + 0 = 5(-1)^4[2(-2) - 1(-4)] = 0$ (7–5)

26. $D = \begin{vmatrix} 3 & -2 \\ 1 & 3 \end{vmatrix} = 11$ $x = \dfrac{\begin{vmatrix} 8 & -2 \\ -1 & 3 \end{vmatrix}}{D} = \dfrac{22}{11} = 2$ $y = \dfrac{\begin{vmatrix} 3 & 8 \\ 1 & -1 \end{vmatrix}}{D} = \dfrac{-11}{11} = -1$ (7–5)

27. We write the augmented matrix:

$\begin{bmatrix} 1 & -1 & | & 4 \\ 2 & 1 & | & 2 \end{bmatrix}$ $(-2)R_1 + R_2 \rightarrow R_2$

$\begin{matrix} 1 & 2 & 3 \\ -2 & 2 & -8 \end{matrix}$

Need a 0 here

$\sim \begin{bmatrix} 1 & -1 & | & 4 \\ 0 & 3 & | & -6 \end{bmatrix}$ $\frac{1}{3}R_2 \rightarrow R_2$ corresponds to the linear system $\begin{cases} x_1 - x_2 = 4 \\ \quad\quad 3x_2 = -6 \end{cases}$

Need a 1 here
Need a 0 here
↓

$\sim \begin{bmatrix} 1 & -1 & | & 4 \\ 0 & 1 & | & -2 \end{bmatrix}$ $R_2 + R_1 \rightarrow R_1$ corresponds to the linear system $\begin{cases} x_1 - x_2 = 4 \\ \quad\quad x_2 = -2 \end{cases}$

$\sim \begin{bmatrix} 1 & 0 & | & 2 \\ 0 & 1 & | & -2 \end{bmatrix}$ corresponds to the linear system $\begin{cases} x_1 = 2 \\ x_2 = -2 \end{cases}$

The solution is $x_1 = 2$, $x_2 = -2$. Each pair of lines graphed has the same intersection point, $(2, -2)$.

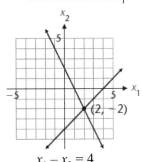

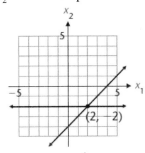

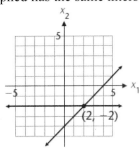

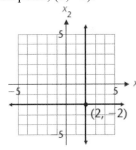

$x_1 - x_2 = 4$ $x_1 - x_2 = 4$ $x_1 - x_2 = 4$ $x_1 = 2$
$2x_1 + x_2 = 2$ $3x_2 = -6$ $x_2 = -2$ $x_2 = -2$ (7–1, 7–2)

28. Before we can enter these equations in our graphing calculator, we must solve for y:

$\begin{aligned} x + 3y &= 9 \\ 3y &= 9 - x \\ y &= \frac{9 - x}{3} \end{aligned}$ $\qquad \begin{aligned} -2x + 7y &= 10 \\ 7y &= 10 + 2x \\ y &= \frac{10 + 2x}{7} \end{aligned}$

Entering these equations into a graphing calculator and applying an intersection routine yields the solution $(2.54, 2.15)$ to two decimal places.

Intersection
X=2.5384615 Y=2.1538462

(7–1)

29. $\begin{bmatrix} 3 & 2 & | & 3 \\ 1 & 3 & | & 8 \end{bmatrix} R_1 \leftrightarrow R_2 \sim \begin{bmatrix} 1 & 3 & | & 8 \\ 3 & 2 & | & 3 \end{bmatrix} (-3)R_1 + R_2 \rightarrow R_2 \sim \begin{bmatrix} 1 & 3 & | & 8 \\ 0 & -7 & | & -21 \end{bmatrix} \left(-\frac{1}{7}\right)R_2 \rightarrow R_2 \sim \begin{bmatrix} 1 & 3 & | & 8 \\ 0 & 1 & | & 3 \end{bmatrix} (-3)R_2 + R_1 \rightarrow R_1$

$\qquad\qquad\qquad\qquad\qquad -3 \;\; -9 \;\; -24 \qquad\qquad\qquad\qquad\qquad\qquad\qquad\qquad\qquad\qquad 0 \; -3 \; -9$

$\sim \begin{bmatrix} 1 & 0 & | & -1 \\ 0 & 1 & | & 3 \end{bmatrix}$ Solution: $x_1 = -1, x_2 = 3$ $\qquad\qquad\qquad\qquad\qquad\qquad\qquad\qquad\qquad\qquad\qquad$ (7–2)

30. $\begin{bmatrix} 1 & 1 & 0 & | & 1 \\ 1 & 0 & -1 & | & -2 \\ 0 & 1 & 2 & | & 4 \end{bmatrix} (-1)R_1 + R_2 \rightarrow R_2$

$\sim \begin{bmatrix} 1 & 1 & 0 & | & 1 \\ 0 & -1 & -1 & | & -3 \\ 0 & 1 & 2 & | & 4 \end{bmatrix} (-1)R_2 \rightarrow R_2$

$\sim \begin{bmatrix} 1 & 1 & 0 & | & 1 \\ 0 & 1 & 1 & | & 3 \\ 0 & 1 & 2 & | & 4 \end{bmatrix} \begin{matrix} (-1)R_2 + R_1 \rightarrow R_1 \\ (-1)R_2 + R_3 \rightarrow R_3 \end{matrix}$

$\sim \begin{bmatrix} 1 & 0 & -1 & | & -2 \\ 0 & 1 & 1 & | & 3 \\ 0 & 0 & 1 & | & 1 \end{bmatrix} \begin{matrix} R_3 + R_1 \rightarrow R_1 \\ (-1)R_3 + R_2 \rightarrow R_2 \end{matrix}$

$\sim \begin{bmatrix} 1 & 0 & 0 & | & -1 \\ 0 & 1 & 0 & | & 2 \\ 0 & 0 & 1 & | & 1 \end{bmatrix}$

Solution: $x_1 = -1, x_2 = 2, x_3 = 1$ (7–2)

31. $\begin{bmatrix} 1 & 2 & 3 & | & 1 \\ 2 & 3 & 4 & | & 3 \\ 1 & 2 & 1 & | & 3 \end{bmatrix} \begin{matrix} (-2)R_1 + R_2 \rightarrow R_2 \\ (-1)R_1 + R_3 \rightarrow R_3 \end{matrix}$

$\sim \begin{bmatrix} 1 & 2 & 3 & | & 1 \\ 0 & -1 & -2 & | & 1 \\ 0 & 0 & -2 & | & 2 \end{bmatrix} \begin{matrix} (-1)R_2 \rightarrow R_2 \\ -\frac{1}{2}R_3 \rightarrow R_3 \end{matrix}$

$\sim \begin{bmatrix} 1 & 2 & 3 & | & 1 \\ 0 & 1 & 2 & | & -1 \\ 0 & 0 & 1 & | & -1 \end{bmatrix} (-2)R_2 + R_1 \rightarrow R_1$

$\sim \begin{bmatrix} 1 & 0 & -1 & | & 3 \\ 0 & 1 & 2 & | & -1 \\ 0 & 0 & 1 & | & -1 \end{bmatrix} \begin{matrix} R_3 + R_1 \rightarrow R_1 \\ (-2)R_3 + R_2 \rightarrow R_2 \end{matrix}$

$\sim \begin{bmatrix} 1 & 0 & 0 & | & 2 \\ 0 & 1 & 0 & | & 1 \\ 0 & 0 & 1 & | & -1 \end{bmatrix}$

Solution: $x_1 = 2, x_2 = 1, x_3 = -1$ (7–2)

32. $\begin{bmatrix} 1 & 2 & -1 & | & 2 \\ 2 & 3 & 1 & | & -3 \\ 3 & 5 & 0 & | & -1 \end{bmatrix} \begin{matrix} (-2)R_1 + R_2 \rightarrow R_2 \\ (-3)R_1 + R_3 \rightarrow R_3 \end{matrix}$

$\sim \begin{bmatrix} 1 & 2 & -1 & | & 2 \\ 0 & -1 & 3 & | & -7 \\ 0 & -1 & 3 & | & -7 \end{bmatrix} (-1)R_2 + R_3 \rightarrow R_3$

$\sim \begin{bmatrix} 1 & 2 & -1 & | & 2 \\ 0 & -1 & 3 & | & -7 \\ 0 & 0 & 0 & | & 0 \end{bmatrix} 2R_2 + R_1 \rightarrow R_1$

$\sim \begin{bmatrix} 1 & 0 & 5 & | & -12 \\ 0 & -1 & 3 & | & -7 \\ 0 & 0 & 0 & | & 0 \end{bmatrix} (-1)R_2 \rightarrow R_2$

$\sim \begin{bmatrix} 1 & 0 & 5 & | & -12 \\ 0 & 1 & -3 & | & 7 \\ 0 & 0 & 0 & | & 0 \end{bmatrix}$

This corresponds to the system

$$x_1 + \qquad 5x_3 = -12$$
$$x_2 - 3x_3 = 7$$

Let $\quad x_3 = t$

Then $\quad x_2 = 3x_3 + 7 = 3t + 7$
$$x_1 = -5x_3 - 12 = -5t - 12$$

Hence $x_1 = -5t - 12, x_2 = 3t + 7, x_3 = t$ is a solution for every real number t. There are infinitely many solutions.

$\qquad\qquad\qquad\qquad\qquad\qquad\qquad\qquad\qquad\qquad\qquad$ (7–2)

33. $\begin{bmatrix} 1 & -2 & | & 1 \\ 2 & -1 & | & 0 \\ 1 & -3 & | & -2 \end{bmatrix} \begin{matrix} (-2)R_1 + R_2 \rightarrow R_2 \\ (-1)R_1 + R_3 \rightarrow R_3 \end{matrix} \sim \begin{bmatrix} 1 & -2 & | & 1 \\ 0 & 3 & | & -2 \\ 0 & -1 & | & -3 \end{bmatrix} 3R_3 + R_2 \rightarrow R_2 \sim \begin{bmatrix} 1 & -2 & | & 1 \\ 0 & 0 & | & -11 \\ 0 & -1 & | & -3 \end{bmatrix}$

The second row corresponds to the equation $0x_1 + 0x_2 = -11$, hence there is no solution. $\qquad\qquad$ (7–2)

34.
$$\begin{bmatrix} 1 & 2 & -1 & | & 2 \\ 3 & -1 & 2 & | & -3 \end{bmatrix} (-3)R_1 + R_2 \to R_2$$

$$\sim \begin{bmatrix} 1 & 2 & -1 & | & 2 \\ 0 & -7 & 5 & | & -9 \end{bmatrix} -\tfrac{1}{7}R_2 \to R_2$$

$$\sim \begin{bmatrix} 1 & 2 & -1 & | & 2 \\ 0 & 1 & -\tfrac{5}{7} & | & \tfrac{9}{7} \end{bmatrix} (-2)R_2 + R_1 \to R_1$$

$$\sim \begin{bmatrix} 1 & 0 & \tfrac{3}{7} & | & -\tfrac{4}{7} \\ 0 & 1 & -\tfrac{5}{7} & | & \tfrac{9}{7} \end{bmatrix}$$

This corresponds to the system
$$x_1 + \tfrac{3}{7}x_3 = -\tfrac{4}{7}$$
$$x_2 - \tfrac{5}{7}x_3 = \tfrac{9}{7}$$

Let $x_3 = t$

Then $x_2 = \tfrac{5}{7}x_3 + \tfrac{9}{7} = \tfrac{5}{7}t + \tfrac{9}{7}$
$$x_1 = -\tfrac{3}{7}x_3 - \tfrac{4}{7} = -\tfrac{3}{7}t - \tfrac{4}{7}$$

Hence $x_1 = -\tfrac{3}{7}t - \tfrac{4}{7}$, $x_2 = \tfrac{5}{7}t + \tfrac{9}{7}$, $x_3 = t$ is a solution for every real number t. There are infinitely many solutions.

(7–2)

35. $AD = \begin{bmatrix} 1 & 2 \\ 4 & 5 \\ -3 & -1 \end{bmatrix}\begin{bmatrix} 7 & 0 & -5 \\ 0 & 8 & -2 \end{bmatrix} = \begin{bmatrix} 1\cdot7+2\cdot0 & 1\cdot0+2\cdot8 & 1(-5)+2(-2) \\ 4\cdot7+5\cdot0 & 4\cdot0+5\cdot8 & 4(-5)+5(-2) \\ (-3)7+(-1)0 & (-3)0+(-1)8 & (-3)(-5)+(-1)(-2) \end{bmatrix} = \begin{bmatrix} 7 & 16 & -9 \\ 28 & 40 & -30 \\ -21 & -8 & 17 \end{bmatrix}$ (7–3)

36. $DA = \begin{bmatrix} 7 & 0 & -5 \\ 0 & 8 & -2 \end{bmatrix}\begin{bmatrix} 1 & 2 \\ 4 & 5 \\ -3 & -1 \end{bmatrix} = \begin{bmatrix} 7\cdot1+0\cdot4+(-5)(-3) & 7\cdot2+0\cdot5+(-5)(-1) \\ 0\cdot1+8\cdot4+(-2)(-3) & 0\cdot2+8\cdot5+(-2)(-1) \end{bmatrix} = \begin{bmatrix} 22 & 19 \\ 38 & 42 \end{bmatrix}$ (7–3)

37. $BC = \begin{bmatrix} 6 \\ 0 \\ -4 \end{bmatrix}\begin{bmatrix} 2 & 4 & -1 \end{bmatrix} = \begin{bmatrix} 6\cdot2 & 6\cdot4 & 6(-1) \\ 0\cdot2 & 0\cdot4 & 0(-1) \\ (-4)2 & (-4)4 & (-4)(-1) \end{bmatrix} = \begin{bmatrix} 12 & 24 & -6 \\ 0 & 0 & 0 \\ -8 & -16 & 4 \end{bmatrix}$ (7–3)

38. $CB = \begin{bmatrix} 2 & 4 & -1 \end{bmatrix}\begin{bmatrix} 6 \\ 0 \\ -4 \end{bmatrix} = [2\cdot6 + 4\cdot0 + (-1)(-4)] = [16]$ (7–3)

39. Since D has 3 columns and E has 2 rows, DE is not defined. (7–3)

40. $ED = \begin{bmatrix} 9 & -3 \\ -6 & 2 \end{bmatrix}\begin{bmatrix} 7 & 0 & -5 \\ 0 & 8 & -2 \end{bmatrix} = \begin{bmatrix} 9\cdot7+(-3)0 & 9\cdot0+(-3)8 & 9(-5)+(-3)(-2) \\ (-6)7+2\cdot0 & (-6)0+2\cdot8 & (-6)(-5)+2(-2) \end{bmatrix} = \begin{bmatrix} 63 & -24 & -39 \\ -42 & 16 & 26 \end{bmatrix}$ (7–3)

41.
$$\begin{bmatrix} 1 & 0 & 4 & | & 1 & 0 & 0 \\ -2 & 1 & 0 & | & 0 & 1 & 0 \\ 4 & -1 & 4 & | & 0 & 0 & 1 \end{bmatrix} \begin{matrix} \\ 2R_1 + R_2 \to R_2 \\ (-4)R_1 + R_3 \to R_3 \end{matrix} \sim \begin{bmatrix} 1 & 0 & 4 & | & 1 & 0 & 0 \\ 0 & 1 & 8 & | & 2 & 1 & 0 \\ 0 & -1 & -12 & | & -4 & 0 & 1 \end{bmatrix} R_2 + R_3 \to R_3$$

$$\sim \begin{bmatrix} 1 & 0 & 4 & | & 1 & 0 & 0 \\ 0 & 1 & 8 & | & 2 & 1 & 0 \\ 0 & 0 & -4 & | & -2 & 1 & 1 \end{bmatrix} \begin{matrix} R_3 + R_1 \to R_1 \\ 2R_3 + R_2 \to R_2 \end{matrix} \sim \begin{bmatrix} 1 & 0 & 0 & | & -1 & 1 & 1 \\ 0 & 1 & 0 & | & -2 & 3 & 2 \\ 0 & 0 & -4 & | & -2 & 1 & 1 \end{bmatrix} (-\tfrac{1}{4})R_3 \to R_3$$

$$\begin{bmatrix} 1 & 0 & 0 & | & -1 & 1 & 1 \\ 0 & 1 & 0 & | & -2 & 3 & 2 \\ 0 & 0 & 1 & | & \tfrac{1}{2} & -\tfrac{1}{4} & -\tfrac{1}{4} \end{bmatrix} \quad \text{Hence } A^{-1} = \begin{bmatrix} -1 & 1 & 1 \\ -2 & 3 & 2 \\ \tfrac{1}{2} & -\tfrac{1}{4} & -\tfrac{1}{4} \end{bmatrix}$$

$$A^{-1}A = \begin{bmatrix} -1 & 1 & 1 \\ -2 & 3 & 2 \\ \frac{1}{2} & -\frac{1}{4} & -\frac{1}{4} \end{bmatrix} \begin{bmatrix} 1 & 0 & 4 \\ -2 & 1 & 0 \\ 4 & -1 & 4 \end{bmatrix} = \begin{bmatrix} (-1)1+1(-2)+1\cdot 4 & (-1)0+1\cdot 1+1(-1) & (-1)4+1\cdot 0+1\cdot 4 \\ (-2)1+3(-2)+2\cdot 4 & (-2)0+3\cdot 1+2(-1) & (-2)4+3\cdot 0+2\cdot 4 \\ \left(\frac{1}{2}\right)1+\left(-\frac{1}{4}\right)(-2)+\left(-\frac{1}{4}\right)4 & \left(\frac{1}{2}\right)0+\left(-\frac{1}{4}\right)1+\left(-\frac{1}{4}\right)(-1) & \left(\frac{1}{2}\right)4+\left(-\frac{1}{4}\right)0+\left(-\frac{1}{4}\right)4 \end{bmatrix}$$

$$= \begin{bmatrix} 1 & 0 & 0 \\ 0 & 1 & 0 \\ 0 & 0 & 1 \end{bmatrix} \qquad (7\text{–}4)$$

42.
$$\overset{A}{\begin{bmatrix} 1 & 2 & 3 \\ 2 & 3 & 4 \\ 1 & 2 & 1 \end{bmatrix}} \overset{X}{\begin{bmatrix} x_1 \\ x_2 \\ x_3 \end{bmatrix}} = \overset{B}{\begin{bmatrix} k_1 \\ k_2 \\ k_3 \end{bmatrix}}$$

The solution to $AX = B$ is $X = A^{-1}B$.

Applying matrix methods, we obtain $A^{-1} = \begin{bmatrix} -\frac{5}{2} & 2 & -\frac{1}{2} \\ 1 & -1 & 1 \\ \frac{1}{2} & 0 & -\frac{1}{2} \end{bmatrix}$ (details omitted).

Applying the inverse, we have

(A) $B = \begin{bmatrix} 1 \\ 3 \\ 3 \end{bmatrix}$ $X = \begin{bmatrix} x_1 \\ x_2 \\ x_3 \end{bmatrix} = \begin{bmatrix} -\frac{5}{2} & 2 & -\frac{1}{2} \\ 1 & -1 & 1 \\ \frac{1}{2} & 0 & -\frac{1}{2} \end{bmatrix} \begin{bmatrix} 1 \\ 3 \\ 3 \end{bmatrix} = \begin{bmatrix} 2 \\ 1 \\ -1 \end{bmatrix}$ $x_1 = 2,\ x_2 = 1,\ x_3 = -1$

(B) $B = \begin{bmatrix} 0 \\ 0 \\ -2 \end{bmatrix}$ $X = \begin{bmatrix} x_1 \\ x_2 \\ x_3 \end{bmatrix} = \begin{bmatrix} -\frac{5}{2} & 2 & -\frac{1}{2} \\ 1 & -1 & 1 \\ \frac{1}{2} & 0 & -\frac{1}{2} \end{bmatrix} \begin{bmatrix} 0 \\ 0 \\ -2 \end{bmatrix} = \begin{bmatrix} 1 \\ -2 \\ 1 \end{bmatrix}$ $x_1 = 1,\ x_2 = -2,\ x_3 = 1$

(C) $B = \begin{bmatrix} -3 \\ -4 \\ 1 \end{bmatrix}$ $X = \begin{bmatrix} x_1 \\ x_2 \\ x_3 \end{bmatrix} = \begin{bmatrix} -\frac{5}{2} & 2 & -\frac{1}{2} \\ 1 & -1 & 1 \\ \frac{1}{2} & 0 & -\frac{1}{2} \end{bmatrix} \begin{bmatrix} -3 \\ -4 \\ 1 \end{bmatrix} = \begin{bmatrix} -1 \\ 2 \\ -2 \end{bmatrix}$ $x_1 = -1, x_2 = 2, x_3 = -2$ $(7\text{–}4)$

43. $\begin{vmatrix} -\frac{1}{4} & \frac{3}{2} \\ \frac{1}{2} & \frac{2}{3} \end{vmatrix} = \left(-\frac{1}{4}\right)\left(\frac{2}{3}\right) - \left(\frac{1}{2}\right)\left(\frac{3}{2}\right) = -\frac{1}{6} - \frac{3}{4} = -\frac{11}{12}$ $(7\text{–}5)$

44. $\begin{vmatrix} 2 & -1 & 1 \\ -3 & 5 & 2 \\ 1 & -2 & 4 \end{vmatrix} = \begin{vmatrix} 0 & 0 & 1 \\ -7 & 7 & 2 \\ -7 & 2 & 4 \end{vmatrix} \begin{matrix} (-2)C_3 + C_1 \to C_1 \\ C_3 + C_2 \to C_2 \end{matrix} = 0 + 0 + 1(-1)^{1+3} \begin{vmatrix} -7 & 7 \\ -7 & 2 \end{vmatrix} = (-1)^4[(-7)2 - (-7)7] = 35$ $(7\text{–}5)$

45. $y = \dfrac{\begin{vmatrix} 1 & -6 & 1 \\ 0 & 4 & -1 \\ 2 & 2 & 1 \end{vmatrix}}{\begin{vmatrix} 1 & -2 & 1 \\ 0 & 1 & -1 \\ 2 & 2 & 1 \end{vmatrix}} = \dfrac{\begin{vmatrix} 1 & -6 & 1 \\ 0 & 4 & -1 \\ 0 & 14 & -1 \end{vmatrix}}{\begin{vmatrix} 1 & -2 & -1 \\ 0 & 1 & 0 \\ 2 & 2 & 3 \end{vmatrix}} = \dfrac{1(-1)^{1+1}\begin{vmatrix} 4 & -1 \\ 14 & -1 \end{vmatrix}}{1(-1)^{2+2}\begin{vmatrix} 1 & -1 \\ 2 & 3 \end{vmatrix}} = \dfrac{(-1)^2[4(-1)-14(-1)]}{(-1)^4[1\cdot 3 - 2(-1)]} = \dfrac{10}{5} = 2$ $(7\text{–}5)$

46.
$$\left[\begin{array}{ccc|c} 1 & 1 & 1 & 7000 \\ 0.04 & 0.05 & 0.06 & 360 \\ 0.04 & 0.05 & -0.06 & 120 \end{array}\right] \begin{array}{l} \\ (-0.04)R_1 + R_2 \to R_2 \\ (-0.04)R_1 + R_3 \to R_3 \end{array} \sim \left[\begin{array}{ccc|c} 1 & 1 & 1 & 7000 \\ 0 & 0.01 & 0.02 & 80 \\ 0 & 0.01 & -0.1 & -160 \end{array}\right] 100R_2 \to R_2$$

$$\sim \left[\begin{array}{ccc|c} 1 & 1 & 1 & 7000 \\ 0 & 1 & 2 & 8000 \\ 0 & 0.01 & -0.1 & -160 \end{array}\right] \begin{array}{l} (-1)R_2 + R_1 \to R_1 \\ \\ (-0.01)R_2 + R_3 \to R_3 \end{array} \sim \left[\begin{array}{ccc|c} 1 & 0 & -1 & -1000 \\ 0 & 1 & 2 & 8000 \\ 0 & 0 & -0.12 & -240 \end{array}\right] -\frac{25}{3}R_3 \to R_3$$

$$\sim \left[\begin{array}{ccc|c} 1 & 0 & -1 & -1000 \\ 0 & 1 & 2 & 8000 \\ 0 & 0 & 1 & 2000 \end{array}\right] \begin{array}{l} R_3 + R_1 \to R_1 \\ (-2)R_3 + R_2 \to R_2 \end{array} \sim \left[\begin{array}{ccc|c} 1 & 0 & 0 & 1000 \\ 0 & 1 & 0 & 4000 \\ 0 & 0 & 1 & 2000 \end{array}\right]$$

Solution: $x_1 = 1000$, $x_2 = 4000$, $x_3 = 2000$ (7–2)

47. $\begin{vmatrix} u+kv & v \\ w+kx & x \end{vmatrix} = (u+kv)x - (w+kx)v = ux + kvx - wv - kvx = ux - wv = \begin{vmatrix} u & v \\ w & x \end{vmatrix}$ (7–5)

48. (A) The system is independent. There is one solution.

(B) The matrix is in fact

$$\left[\begin{array}{ccc|c} 1 & 0 & -3 & 4 \\ 0 & 1 & 2 & 5 \\ 0 & 0 & 0 & n \end{array}\right]$$

The third row corresponds to the equation $0x_1 + 0x_2 + 0x_3 = n$. This is impossible. The system has no solution.

(C) The matrix is in fact

$$\left[\begin{array}{ccc|c} 1 & 0 & -3 & 4 \\ 0 & 1 & 2 & 5 \\ 0 & 0 & 0 & 0 \end{array}\right]$$

Thus, there are an infinite number of solutions ($x_3 = t$, $x_2 = 5 - 2t$, $x_1 = 4 + 3t$, for t any real number).

(7–2)

49. (A) If the coefficient matrix has an inverse, then the system can be written as $AX = B$ and its solution can be written $X = A^{-1}B$. Thus the system has one solution.

(B) If the coefficient matrix does not have an inverse, then the system can be solved by Gauss–Jordan elimination, but it will not have exactly one solution. The other possibilities are that the system has no solution or an infinite number of solutions, and either possibility may occur.   (7–4)

50. If we assume that A is a non–zero matrix with an inverse A^{-1}, then if $A^2 = 0$ we can write $A^{-1}A^2 = A^{-1}0$ or $A^{-1}AA = 0$ or $IA = 0$ or $A = 0$. But A was assumed non–zero, so there is a contradiction. Hence A^{-1} cannot exist for such a matrix.   (7–4)

51.
$$\begin{array}{rll} AX - B &= CX & \\ AX - B + B - CX &= CX - CX + B & \text{Addition property} \\ AX + 0 - CX &= 0 + B & M + (-M) = 0 \\ AX - CX &= B & M + 0 = M \\ (A - C)X &= B & \text{Right distributive property} \\ (A - C)^{-1}[(A - C)X] &= (A - C)^{-1}B & \text{Left multiplication property} \\ [(A - C)^{-1}(A - C)]X &= (A - C)^{-1}B & \text{Associative property} \\ IX &= (A - C)^{-1}B & A^{-1}A = I \\ X &= (A - C)^{-1}B & IX = X \end{array}$$

$\boxed{\begin{array}{l}\textbf{Common Errors:} \ (A - C)^{-1}B \neq B(A - C)^{-1} \\ \qquad\qquad\qquad (A - C)^{-1} \neq A^{-1} - C^{-1}\end{array}}$

(7–4)

52.
$$\left[\begin{array}{ccc|ccc} 4 & 5 & 6 & 1 & 0 & 0 \\ 4 & 5 & -6 & 0 & 1 & 0 \\ 1 & 1 & 1 & 0 & 0 & 1 \end{array}\right] (-1)R_1 + R_2 \to R_2 \sim \left[\begin{array}{ccc|ccc} 4 & 5 & 6 & 1 & 0 & 0 \\ 0 & 0 & -12 & -1 & 1 & 0 \\ 1 & 1 & 1 & 0 & 0 & 1 \end{array}\right] R_1 \leftrightarrow R_3$$

$$\sim \begin{bmatrix} 1 & 1 & 1 & 0 & 0 & 1 \\ 0 & 0 & -12 & -1 & 1 & 0 \\ 4 & 5 & 6 & 1 & 0 & 0 \end{bmatrix} (-4)R_1 + R_3 \rightarrow R_3 \qquad \sim \begin{bmatrix} 1 & 1 & 1 & 0 & 0 & 1 \\ 0 & 0 & -12 & -1 & 1 & 0 \\ 0 & 1 & 2 & 1 & 0 & -4 \end{bmatrix} R_2 \leftrightarrow R_3$$

$$\sim \begin{bmatrix} 1 & 1 & 1 & 0 & 0 & 1 \\ 0 & 1 & 2 & 1 & 0 & -4 \\ 0 & 0 & -12 & -1 & 1 & 0 \end{bmatrix} (-1)R_2 + R_1 \rightarrow R_1 \qquad \sim \begin{bmatrix} 1 & 0 & -1 & -1 & 0 & 5 \\ 0 & 1 & 2 & 1 & 0 & -4 \\ 0 & 0 & -12 & -1 & 1 & 0 \end{bmatrix} -\tfrac{1}{12}R_3 \rightarrow R_3$$

$$\sim \begin{bmatrix} 1 & 0 & -1 & -1 & 0 & 5 \\ 0 & 1 & 2 & 1 & 0 & -4 \\ 0 & 0 & 1 & \tfrac{1}{12} & -\tfrac{1}{12} & 0 \end{bmatrix} \begin{array}{l} R_3 + R_1 \rightarrow R_1 \\ (-2)R_3 + R_2 \rightarrow R_2 \end{array} \sim \begin{bmatrix} 1 & 0 & 0 & -\tfrac{11}{12} & -\tfrac{1}{12} & 5 \\ 0 & 1 & 0 & \tfrac{10}{12} & \tfrac{2}{12} & -4 \\ 0 & 0 & 1 & \tfrac{1}{12} & -\tfrac{1}{12} & 0 \end{bmatrix}$$

Hence $A^{-1} = \begin{bmatrix} -\tfrac{11}{12} & -\tfrac{1}{12} & 5 \\ \tfrac{10}{12} & \tfrac{2}{12} & -4 \\ \tfrac{1}{12} & -\tfrac{1}{12} & 0 \end{bmatrix}$ or $\tfrac{1}{12}\begin{bmatrix} -11 & -1 & 60 \\ 10 & 2 & -48 \\ 1 & -1 & 0 \end{bmatrix}$

$$A^{-1}A = \tfrac{1}{12}\begin{bmatrix} -11 & -1 & 60 \\ 10 & 2 & -48 \\ 1 & -1 & 0 \end{bmatrix}\begin{bmatrix} 4 & 5 & 6 \\ 4 & 5 & -6 \\ 1 & 1 & 1 \end{bmatrix}$$

$$= \tfrac{1}{12}\begin{bmatrix} (-11)4 + (-1)4 + 60\cdot1 & (-11)5 + (-1)5 + 60\cdot1 & (-11)6 + (-1)(-6) + 60\cdot1 \\ 10\cdot4 + 2\cdot4 + (-48)1 & 10\cdot5 + 2\cdot5 + (-48)1 & 10\cdot6 + 2(-6) + (-48)1 \\ 1\cdot4 + (-1)4 + 0\cdot1 & 1\cdot5 + (-1)5 + 0\cdot1 & 1\cdot6 + (-1)(-6) + 0\cdot1 \end{bmatrix}$$

$$= \tfrac{1}{12}\begin{bmatrix} 12 & 0 & 0 \\ 0 & 12 & 0 \\ 0 & 0 & 12 \end{bmatrix} = \begin{bmatrix} 1 & 0 & 0 \\ 0 & 1 & 0 \\ 0 & 0 & 1 \end{bmatrix} = I \qquad\qquad (7\text{--}4)$$

53. Multiplying the first two equations by 100, the system becomes

$4x_1 + 5x_2 + 6x_3 = 36{,}000$

$4x_1 + 5x_2 - 6x_3 = 12{,}000$

$x_1 + x_2 + x_3 = 7{,}000$

As a matrix equation, we have

$$\begin{array}{ccc} A & X & B \end{array}$$
$$\begin{bmatrix} 4 & 5 & 6 \\ 4 & 5 & -6 \\ 1 & 1 & 1 \end{bmatrix}\begin{bmatrix} x_1 \\ x_2 \\ x_3 \end{bmatrix} = \begin{bmatrix} 36{,}000 \\ 12{,}000 \\ 7{,}000 \end{bmatrix}$$

The solution to $AX = B$ is $X = A^{-1}B$. Using A^{-1} from problem 52, we have

$$X = \begin{bmatrix} x_1 \\ x_2 \\ x_3 \end{bmatrix} = \tfrac{1}{12}\begin{bmatrix} -11 & -1 & 60 \\ 10 & 2 & -48 \\ 1 & -1 & 0 \end{bmatrix}\begin{bmatrix} 36{,}000 \\ 12{,}000 \\ 7{,}000 \end{bmatrix} = \tfrac{1}{12}\begin{bmatrix} (-11)(36{,}000) + (-1)(12{,}000) + (60)(7{,}000) \\ (10)(36{,}000) + (2)(12{,}000) + (-48)(7{,}000) \\ 1(36{,}000) + (-1)(12{,}000) + (0)(7{,}000) \end{bmatrix}$$

$$= \tfrac{1}{12}\begin{bmatrix} 12{,}000 \\ 48{,}000 \\ 24{,}000 \end{bmatrix} = \begin{bmatrix} 1{,}000 \\ 4{,}000 \\ 2{,}000 \end{bmatrix} \qquad \text{Hence, } x_1 = 1{,}000,\ x_2 = 4{,}000,\ x_3 = 2{,}000 \qquad (7\text{--}4)$$

54. Let x = number of $\dfrac{1}{2}$ – pound packages

y = number of $\dfrac{1}{3}$ – pound packages

There are 120 packages. Hence

$$x + y = 120 \qquad (1)$$

Since x $\frac{1}{2}$ – pound packages weigh $\frac{1}{2}x$ pounds and y $\frac{1}{3}$ – pound packages weigh $\frac{1}{3}y$ pounds, we have

$$\frac{1}{2}x + \frac{1}{3}y = 48 \qquad (2)$$

We solve the system (1), (2) using elimination by addition. We multiply the second equation by –3 and add.

$$x + y = 120$$

$$-\frac{3}{2}x - y = -144$$

$$-\frac{1}{2}x = -24$$

$$x = 48$$

Substituting into equation (1), we have

$$48 + y = 120$$

$$y = 72$$

$48\,\frac{1}{2}$ –pound packages and $72\,\frac{1}{3}$ –pound packages. $\qquad\qquad$ (7–1, 7–2)

55. Let x_1 = number of grams of mix A

$\qquad x_2$ = number of grams of mix B

$\qquad x_3$ = number of grams of mix C

We have

$0.30x_1 + 0.20x_2 + 0.10x_3 = 27$ (protein)

$0.03x_1 + 0.05x_2 + 0.04x_3 = 5.4$ (fat)

$0.10x_1 + 0.20x_2 + 0.10x_3 = 19$ (moisture)

Clearing of decimals for convenience, we have

$3x_1 + 2x_2 + x_3 = 270$

$3x_1 + 5x_2 + 4x_3 = 540$

$\quad x_1 + 2x_2 + x_3 = 190$

Form the augmented matrix and solve by Gauss–Jordan elimination.

$$\begin{bmatrix} 3 & 2 & 1 & | & 270 \\ 3 & 5 & 4 & | & 540 \\ 1 & 2 & 1 & | & 190 \end{bmatrix} \begin{matrix} \\ \\ R_3 \leftrightarrow R_1 \end{matrix} \sim \begin{bmatrix} 1 & 2 & 1 & | & 190 \\ 3 & 5 & 4 & | & 540 \\ 3 & 2 & 1 & | & 270 \end{bmatrix} \begin{matrix} \\ (-3)R_1 + R_2 \rightarrow R_2 \\ (-3)R_1 + R_3 \rightarrow R_3 \end{matrix} \sim \begin{bmatrix} 1 & 2 & 1 & | & 190 \\ 0 & -1 & 1 & | & -30 \\ 0 & -4 & -2 & | & -300 \end{bmatrix} \begin{matrix} \\ (-1)R_2 \rightarrow R_2 \\ \\ \end{matrix}$$

$$\sim \begin{bmatrix} 1 & 2 & 1 & | & 190 \\ 0 & 1 & -1 & | & 30 \\ 0 & -4 & -2 & | & -300 \end{bmatrix} \begin{matrix} (-2)R_2 + R_1 \rightarrow R_1 \\ \\ 4R_2 + R_3 \rightarrow R_3 \end{matrix} \sim \begin{bmatrix} 1 & 0 & 3 & | & 130 \\ 0 & 1 & -1 & | & 30 \\ 0 & 0 & -6 & | & -180 \end{bmatrix} \begin{matrix} \\ \\ -\frac{1}{6}R_3 \rightarrow R_3 \end{matrix} \sim \begin{bmatrix} 1 & 0 & 3 & | & 130 \\ 0 & 1 & -1 & | & 30 \\ 0 & 0 & 1 & | & 30 \end{bmatrix} \begin{matrix} (-3)R_3 + R_1 \rightarrow R_1 \\ R_3 + R_2 \rightarrow R_2 \\ \\ \end{matrix}$$

$$\sim \begin{bmatrix} 1 & 0 & 0 & | & 40 \\ 0 & 1 & 0 & | & 60 \\ 0 & 0 & 1 & | & 30 \end{bmatrix}$$

Therefore

$x_1 = 40$ grams Mix A

$x_2 = 60$ grams Mix B

$x_3 = 30$ grams Mix C $\qquad\qquad$ (7–4)

56. Let x_1 = number of tons at Big Bend

$\qquad x_2$ = number of tons at Saw Pit

Then

$0.05x_1 + 0.03x_2$ = number of tons of nickel at both mines = k_1

$0.07x_1 + 0.04x_2$ = number of tons of copper at both mines = k_2

We solve

$0.05x_1 + 0.03x_2 = k_1$

$0.07x_1 + 0.04x_4 = k_2,$

for arbitrary k_1 and k_2, by writing the system as a matrix equation.

$$\begin{matrix} A & X & B \end{matrix}$$

$$\begin{bmatrix} 0.05 & 0.03 \\ 0.07 & 0.04 \end{bmatrix} \begin{bmatrix} x_1 \\ x_2 \end{bmatrix} = \begin{bmatrix} k_1 \\ k_2 \end{bmatrix}$$

If A^{-1} exists, then $X = A^{-1}B$. To find A^{-1}, we perform row operations on

$$\begin{bmatrix} 0.05 & 0.03 & | & 1 & 0 \\ 0.07 & 0.04 & | & 0 & 1 \end{bmatrix} \quad 20R_1 \to R_1 \sim \begin{bmatrix} 1 & 0.6 & | & 20 & 0 \\ 0.07 & 0.04 & | & 0 & 1 \end{bmatrix} (-0.07)R_1 + R_2 \to R_2$$

$$\sim \begin{bmatrix} 1 & 0.6 & | & 20 & 0 \\ 0 & -0.002 & | & -1.4 & 1 \end{bmatrix} -500R_2 \to R_2 \sim \begin{bmatrix} 1 & 0.6 & | & 20 & 0 \\ 0 & 1 & | & 700 & -500 \end{bmatrix} (-0.6)R_2 + R_1 \to R_1$$

$$\sim \begin{bmatrix} 1 & 0 & | & -400 & 300 \\ 0 & 1 & | & 700 & -500 \end{bmatrix} \quad \text{Hence } A^{-1} = \begin{bmatrix} -400 & 300 \\ 700 & -500 \end{bmatrix}$$

Check: $A^{-1}A = \begin{bmatrix} -400 & 300 \\ 700 & -500 \end{bmatrix} \begin{bmatrix} 0.05 & 0.03 \\ 0.07 & 0.04 \end{bmatrix} = \begin{bmatrix} 1 & 0 \\ 0 & 1 \end{bmatrix}$

We can now solve the system as:

$$\begin{matrix} X & A^{-1} & B \end{matrix}$$

$$\begin{bmatrix} x_1 \\ x_2 \end{bmatrix} = \begin{bmatrix} -400 & 300 \\ 700 & -500 \end{bmatrix} \begin{bmatrix} k_1 \\ k_2 \end{bmatrix}$$

(A)   If $k_1 = 3.6$, $k_2 = 5$,

$$\begin{bmatrix} x_1 \\ x_2 \end{bmatrix} = \begin{bmatrix} -400 & 300 \\ 700 & -500 \end{bmatrix} \begin{bmatrix} 3.6 \\ 5 \end{bmatrix} = \begin{bmatrix} 60 \\ 20 \end{bmatrix}$$

60 tons of ore must be produced at Big Bend, 20 tons of ore at Saw Pit.

(B)   If $k_1 = 3$, $k_2 = 4.1$,

$$\begin{bmatrix} x_1 \\ x_2 \end{bmatrix} = \begin{bmatrix} -400 & 300 \\ 700 & -500 \end{bmatrix} \begin{bmatrix} 3 \\ 4.1 \end{bmatrix} = \begin{bmatrix} 30 \\ 50 \end{bmatrix}$$

30 tons of ore must be produced at Big Bend, 50 tons of ore at Saw Pit.

(C)   If $k_1 = 3.2$, $k_2 = 4.4$,

$$\begin{bmatrix} x_1 \\ x_2 \end{bmatrix} = \begin{bmatrix} -400 & 300 \\ 700 & -500 \end{bmatrix} \begin{bmatrix} 3.2 \\ 4.4 \end{bmatrix} = \begin{bmatrix} 40 \\ 40 \end{bmatrix}$$

40 tons of ore must be produced at Big Bend, 40 tons of ore at Saw Pit.   (7–4)

57. (A)   The labor cost of producing one printer stand at the South Carolina plant is the product of the stand row of L with the South Carolina column of H.

$$[0.9 \quad 1.8 \quad 0.6] \begin{bmatrix} 10.00 \\ 8.50 \\ 4.50 \end{bmatrix} = 27 \text{ dollars}$$

(B)   The matrix HL has no obvious meaning, but the matrix LH represents the total labor costs for each item at each plant.

(C) $LH = \begin{bmatrix} 1.7 & 2.4 & 0.8 \\ 0.9 & 1.8 & 0.6 \end{bmatrix} \begin{bmatrix} 11.50 & 10.00 \\ 9.50 & 8.50 \\ 5.00 & 4.50 \end{bmatrix}$

$$= \begin{bmatrix} (1.7)(11.50)+(2.4)(9.50)+(0.8)(5.00) & (1.7)(10.00)+(2.4)(8.50)+(0.8)(4.50) \\ (0.9)(11.50)+(1.8)(9.50)+(0.6)(5.00) & (0.9)(10.00)+(1.8)(8.50)+(0.6)(4.50) \end{bmatrix}$$

$$\begin{array}{cc} \text{N.C.} & \text{S.C.} \end{array}$$

$$= \begin{bmatrix} \$46.35 & \$41.00 \\ \$30.45 & \$27.00 \end{bmatrix} \begin{array}{l} \text{Desk} \\ \text{Stands} \end{array}$$

$(7\text{–}3)$

58. (A) The average monthly production for the months of January and February is represented by the matrix $\frac{1}{2}(J+F)$

$$\begin{array}{cc} & \text{N.C.} \quad \text{S.C.} \end{array}$$

$$\frac{1}{2}(J+F) = \frac{1}{2}\left(\begin{bmatrix} 1,500 & 1,650 \\ 850 & 700 \end{bmatrix} + \begin{bmatrix} 1,700 & 1,810 \\ 930 & 740 \end{bmatrix}\right) = \frac{1}{2}\begin{bmatrix} 3,200 & 3,460 \\ 1,780 & 1,440 \end{bmatrix} = \begin{bmatrix} 1,600 & 1,730 \\ 890 & 720 \end{bmatrix} \begin{array}{l} \text{Desks} \\ \text{Stands} \end{array}$$

(B) The increase in production from January to February is represented by the matrix $F - J$.

$$\begin{array}{cc} & \text{N.C.} \quad \text{S.C.} \end{array}$$

$$F - J = \begin{bmatrix} 1,700 & 1,810 \\ 930 & 740 \end{bmatrix} - \begin{bmatrix} 1,500 & 1,650 \\ 850 & 700 \end{bmatrix} = \begin{bmatrix} 200 & 160 \\ 80 & 40 \end{bmatrix} \begin{array}{l} \text{Desks} \\ \text{Stands} \end{array}$$

(C) $\quad J\begin{bmatrix} 1 \\ 1 \end{bmatrix} = \begin{bmatrix} 1,500 & 1,650 \\ 850 & 700 \end{bmatrix}\begin{bmatrix} 1 \\ 1 \end{bmatrix} = \begin{bmatrix} 3,150 \\ 1,550 \end{bmatrix} \begin{array}{l} \text{Desks} \\ \text{Stands} \end{array}$

This matrix represents the total production of each item in January.

$(7\text{–}3)$

59. The inverse of matrix B is calculated to be

$$B^{-1} = \begin{bmatrix} 1 & 1 & -1 \\ 0 & -1 & 1 \\ -1 & 0 & 1 \end{bmatrix}$$

Putting the coded message into matrix form and multiplying by B^{-1} yields

$$\begin{bmatrix} 1 & 1 & -1 \\ 0 & -1 & 1 \\ -1 & 0 & 1 \end{bmatrix}\begin{bmatrix} 21 & 30 & 29 & 46 & 19 & 52 \\ 21 & 28 & 34 & 35 & 21 & 52 \\ 27 & 31 & 50 & 62 & 39 & 79 \end{bmatrix} = \begin{bmatrix} 15 & 27 & 13 & 19 & 1 & 25 \\ 6 & 3 & 16 & 27 & 18 & 27 \\ 6 & 1 & 21 & 16 & 20 & 27 \end{bmatrix}$$

This decodes to

15 6 6 27   3 1   13 16 21 19 27   16 1 18 20 25 27 27
 O F F   C A M P U S   P A R T Y

$(7\text{–}4)$

60. (A) Let x_1 = number of nickels, x_2 = number of dimes

Then $x_1 + x_2 = 30$ (total number of coins)

$5x_1 + 10x_2 = 190$ (total value of coins)

We form the augmented matrix and solve by Gauss–Jordan elimination.

$$\begin{bmatrix} 1 & 1 & | & 30 \\ 5 & 10 & | & 190 \end{bmatrix} (-5)R_1 + R_2 \rightarrow R_2 \sim \begin{bmatrix} 1 & 1 & | & 30 \\ 0 & 5 & | & 40 \end{bmatrix} \tfrac{1}{5}R_2 \rightarrow R_2 \sim \begin{bmatrix} 1 & 1 & | & 30 \\ 0 & 1 & | & 8 \end{bmatrix} (-1)R_2 + R_1 \rightarrow R_1$$

$$\sim \begin{bmatrix} 1 & 0 & | & 22 \\ 0 & 1 & | & 8 \end{bmatrix}$$

The augmented matrix is in reduced form. It corresponds to the system

$x_1 = 22$ nickels

$x_2 = 8$ dimes

(B) Let x_1 = number of nickels, x_2 = number of dimes, x_3 = number of quarters

Then $x_1 + x_2 + x_3 = 30$ (total number of coins)

$5x_1 + 10x_2 + 25x_3 = 190$ (total value of coins)

We form the augmented matrix and solve by Gauss–Jordan elimination

$$\begin{bmatrix} 1 & 1 & 1 & | & 30 \\ 5 & 10 & 25 & | & 190 \end{bmatrix} (-5)R_1 + R_2 \rightarrow R_2 \sim \begin{bmatrix} 1 & 1 & 1 & | & 30 \\ 0 & 5 & 20 & | & 40 \end{bmatrix} \tfrac{1}{5}R_2 \rightarrow R_2 \sim \begin{bmatrix} 1 & 1 & 1 & | & 30 \\ 0 & 1 & 4 & | & 8 \end{bmatrix} (-1)R_2 + R_1 \rightarrow R_1$$

$$\sim \begin{bmatrix} 1 & 0 & -3 & | & 22 \\ 0 & 1 & 4 & | & 8 \end{bmatrix}$$

The augmented matrix is in reduced form. It corresponds to the system:

$$x_1 - 3x_3 = 22$$
$$x_2 + 4x_3 = 8$$

Let $x_3 = t$. Then

$$x_2 = -4x_3 + 8 = -4t + 8$$
$$x_1 = 3x_3 + 22 = 3t + 22$$

A solution is achieved, not for every real value of t, but for integer values of t that give rise to non–negative x_1, x_2, x_3.

$x_1 \geq 0$ means $3t + 22 \geq 0$ or $t \geq -7\tfrac{1}{3}$

$x_2 \geq 0$ means $-4t + 8 \geq 0$ or $t \leq 2$

$x_3 \geq 0$ means $\qquad t \geq 0$

The only integer values of t that satisfy these conditions are 0, 1, 2. Thus we have the solutions

$x_1 = 3t + 22$ nickels

$x_2 = 8 - 4t$ dimes

$x_3 = t$ quarters   where $t = 0, 1,$ or 2

(7–1)

CHAPTER 8

Section 8-1

2. A recursion formula is a formula that defines each term of a sequence in terms of one or more preceding terms.

4. Answers will vary.

6. Since each term of the sequences is defined in terms of preceding terms there has to be a beginning somewhere – a first term must be given.

8. $a_n = n + 3$
$a_1 = 1 + 3 = 4$
$a_2 = 2 + 3 = 5$
$a_3 = 3 + 3 = 6$
$a_4 = 4 + 3 = 7$

10. $a_n = \left(1 + \dfrac{1}{n}\right)^n$
$a_1 = \left(1 + \dfrac{1}{1}\right)^1 = 2$
$a_2 = \left(1 + \dfrac{1}{2}\right)^2 = \left(\dfrac{3}{2}\right)^2 = \dfrac{9}{4}$
$a_3 = \left(1 + \dfrac{1}{3}\right)^3 = \left(\dfrac{4}{3}\right)^3 = \dfrac{64}{27}$
$a_4 = \left(1 + \dfrac{1}{4}\right)^4 = \left(\dfrac{5}{4}\right)^4 = \dfrac{625}{256}$

12. $a_n = \dfrac{(-1)^{n+1}}{n^2}$
$a_1 = \dfrac{(-1)^{1+1}}{1^2} = \dfrac{(-1)^2}{1} = 1$
$a_2 = \dfrac{(-1)^{2+1}}{2^2} = \dfrac{(-1)^3}{4} = -\dfrac{1}{4}$
$a_3 = \dfrac{(-1)^{3+1}}{3^2} = \dfrac{(-1)^4}{9} = \dfrac{1}{9}$
$a_4 = \dfrac{(-1)^{4+1}}{4^2} = \dfrac{(-1)^5}{16} = -\dfrac{1}{16}$

14. $a_n = n + 3$
$a_{10} = 10 + 3$
$a_{10} = 13$

16. $a_n = \left(1 + \dfrac{1}{n}\right)^n$
$a_{200} = \left(1 + \dfrac{1}{200}\right)^{200}$
$a_{200} = \left(\dfrac{201}{200}\right)^{200}$

18. $\displaystyle\sum_{k=1}^{4} k^2 = 1^2 + 2^2 + 3^2 + 4^2 = 1 + 4 + 9 + 16$

20. $\displaystyle\sum_{k=1}^{5} \left(\dfrac{1}{3}\right)^k = \left(\dfrac{1}{3}\right)^1 + \left(\dfrac{1}{3}\right)^2 + \left(\dfrac{1}{3}\right)^3 + \left(\dfrac{1}{3}\right)^4 + \left(\dfrac{1}{3}\right)^5 = \dfrac{1}{3} + \dfrac{1}{9} + \dfrac{1}{27} + \dfrac{1}{81} + \dfrac{1}{243}$

22. $\displaystyle\sum_{k=1}^{6} (-1)^{k+1} k = (-1)^{1+1}(1) + (-1)^{2+1}(2) + (-1)^{3+1}(3) + (-1)^{4+1}(4) + (-1)^{5+1}(5) + (-1)^{6+1}(6) = 1 - 2 + 3 - 4 + 5 - 6$

24. $a_n = (-1)^{n+1}\left(\dfrac{1}{2^n}\right)$
$a_1 = (-1)^{1+1}\left(\dfrac{1}{2^1}\right) = \dfrac{1}{2}$
$a_2 = (-1)^{2+1}\left(\dfrac{1}{2^2}\right) = -\dfrac{1}{4}$
$a_3 = (-1)^{3+1}\left(\dfrac{1}{2^3}\right) = \dfrac{1}{8}$
$a_4 = (-1)^{4+1}\left(\dfrac{1}{2^4}\right) = -\dfrac{1}{16}$
$a_5 = (-1)^{5+1}\left(\dfrac{1}{2^5}\right) = \dfrac{1}{32}$

26. $a_n = n[1 - (-1)^n]$
$a_1 = 1[1 - (-1)^1] = 2$
$a_2 = 2[1 - (-1)^2] = 0$
$a_3 = 3[1 - (-1)^3] = 6$
$a_4 = 4[1 - (-1)^4] = 0$
$a_5 = 5[1 - (-1)^5] = 10$

28. $a_n = \left(-\dfrac{3}{2}\right)^{n-1}$
$a_1 = \left(-\dfrac{3}{2}\right)^{1-1} = 1$
$a_2 = \left(-\dfrac{3}{2}\right)^{2-1} = -\dfrac{3}{2}$
$a_3 = \left(-\dfrac{3}{2}\right)^{3-1} = \dfrac{9}{4}$
$a_4 = \left(-\dfrac{3}{2}\right)^{4-1} = -\dfrac{27}{8}$
$a_5 = \left(-\dfrac{3}{2}\right)^{5-1} = \dfrac{81}{16}$

30. $a_n = a_{n-1} + 5$
$a_1 = 3$
$a_2 = 8$
$a_3 = 13$
$a_4 = 18$
$a_5 = 23$

32. $a_n = 2a_{n-1}, n \geq 2; a_1 = 2$
$a_1 = 2$
$a_2 = 2a_1 = 2(2) = 4$
$a_3 = 2a_2 = 2(4) = 8$
$a_4 = 2a_3 = 2(8) = 16$
$a_5 = 2a_4 = 2(16) = 32$

34. $a_1 = 1, a_2 = -1,$
$a_n = a_{n-2} - a_{n-1}, n \geq 2$
$a_1 = 1$
$a_2 = -1$
$a_3 = 2$
$a_4 = -3$
$a_5 = 5$
$a_6 = -8$
$a_7 = 13$

```
Pr9mRECUR
FIRST TERM? 1
COEF OF 1ST TERM
1
SECOND TERM? -1
COEF OF 2ND TERM
-1
NBR OF TERMS? 7
{1 -1 2 -3 5 -8 13}
                  Done
```

36. $a_1 = 2, a_2 = 1,$
$a_n = -a_{n-2} + a_{n-1}, n \geq 3$
$a_1 = 2$
$a_2 = 1$
$a_3 = -1$
$a_4 = -2$
$a_5 = -1$
$a_6 = 1$
$a_7 = 2$

```
Pr9mRECUR
FIRST TERM? 2
COEF OF 1ST TERM
-1
SECOND TERM? 1
COEF OF 2ND TERM
1
NBR OF TERMS? 7
{2 1 -1 -2 -1 1 2}
                  Done
```

38. a_n: 10, 11, 12, 13, ...
n: 1, 2, 3, 4, ...
Comparing a_n with n, we see that $a_n = n + 9$

40. a_n: 1, -1, -3, -5, ...
$a_n - 3$: -2, -4, -6, -8, ...
n: 1, 2, 3, 4, ...
Comparing $a_n - 3$ with n, we see that $a_n - 3 = -2n$, hence $a_n = 3 - 2n$

42. a_n: $1, -\dfrac{1}{2}, \dfrac{1}{3}, -\dfrac{1}{4}, ...$
n: 1, 2, 3, 4, ...
Comparing a_n with n, we see that $a_n = (-1)^{n+1}\dfrac{1}{n}$

44. a_n: $\dfrac{1}{3}, \dfrac{2}{4}, \dfrac{3}{5}, \dfrac{4}{6}, ...$
n: 1, 2, 3, 4, ...
Comparing a_n with n, we see that $a_n = \dfrac{n}{n+2}$

46. a_n: 5, 25, 125, 625, ...
n: 1, 2, 3, 4, ...
Comparing a_n with n, we see that a_n consists of successive nth powers of 5, $a_n = 5^n$

48. a_n: $x, -x^3, x^5, -x^7, ...$
n: 1, 2, 3, 4, ...
Comparing a_n with n, we see that x is raised to successive odd powers, and its coefficient is successive powers of -1. $a_n = (-1)^{n+1}x^{2n-1}$

50. (A) $a_1 = 9 \cdot 1^2 - 21 \cdot 1 + 14 = 2$; $a_2 = 9 \cdot 2^2 - 21 \cdot 2 + 14 = 8$; $a_3 = 9 \cdot 3^2 - 21 \cdot 3 + 14 = 32$; $a_4 = 9 \cdot 4^2 - 21 \cdot 4 + 14 = 74$

(B) A (simpler) sequence with the first three terms 2, 8, 32 would be $b_n = 2^{2n-1}$.

52. (A) $a_1 = 25 \cdot 1^2 - 60 \cdot 1 + 36 = 1$; $a_2 = 25 \cdot 2^2 - 60 \cdot 2 + 36 = 16$; $a_3 = 25 \cdot 3^2 - 60 \cdot 3 + 36 = 81$;
$a_4 = 25 \cdot 4^2 - 60 \cdot 4 + 36 = 196$

(B) A (simpler) sequence with the first three terms 1, 16, 81 would be $b_n = n^4$.

54. (A) $a_1 = -4 \cdot 1^2 + 15 \cdot 1 - 12 = -1$; $a_2 = -4 \cdot 2^2 + 15 \cdot 2 - 12 = 2$; $a_3 = -4 \cdot 3^2 + 15 \cdot 3 - 12 = -3$;
$a_4 = -4 \cdot 4^2 + 15 \cdot 4 - 12 = -16$

(B) A (simpler) sequence with the first three terms -1, 2, -3 would be $b_n = (-1)^n n$.

56.

WINDOW	WINDOW	Plot1 Plot2 Plot3	u=2+πη
nMin=1	↑PlotStep=1	nMin=1	
nMax=20	Xmin=0	\u(n)🔲2+πη	
PlotStart=1	Xmax=21	u(nMin)🔲	
PlotStep=1	Xscl=1	\v(n)=	
Xmin=0	Ymin=-20	v(nMin)=	
Xmax=21	Ymax=80	\w(n)=	n=20 Y=64.831853
↓Xscl=1■	Yscl=10■	w(nMin)=	X=20

58.

WINDOW	WINDOW	Plot1 Plot2 Plot3	u=(2/3)u(n-1)+1/2
nMin=1	↑PlotStep=1	nMin=1	
nMax=20	Xmin=0	\u(n)🔲(2/3)u(n-1	
PlotStart=1	Xmax=21	)+1/2	
PlotStep=1	Xscl=1	u(nMin)🔲{-1}	
Xmin=0	Ymin=-2	\v(n)=	
Xmax=21	Ymax=2	v(nMin)=	n=20 Y=1.4988723
↓Xscl=1■	Yscl=1■	\w(n)=	X=20

60. $\displaystyle\sum_{k=1}^{5} (-1)^{k+1}(2k-1)^2 = (-1)^{1+1}(2(1)-1)^2 + (-1)^{2+1}(2(2)-1)^2 + (-1)^{3+1}(2(3)-1)^2$

$$+ (-1)^{4+1}(2(4)-1)^2 + (-1)^{5+1}(2(5)-1)^2$$
$$= 1^2 - 3^2 + 5^2 - 7^2 + 9^2$$
$$\text{or}$$
$$= 1 - 9 + 25 - 49 + 81$$

62. $\displaystyle\sum_{k=1}^{5} x^{k-1} = x^{1-1} + x^{2-1} + x^{3-1} + x^{4-1} + x^{5-1} = 1 + x + x^2 + x^3 + x^4$

64. $\displaystyle\sum_{k=0}^{4} \frac{(-1)^k x^{2k+1}}{2k+1} = \frac{(-1)^0 x^{2(0)+1}}{2(0)+1} + \frac{(-1)^1 x^{2(1)+1}}{2(1)+1} + \frac{(-1)^2 x^{2(2)+1}}{2(2)+1} + \frac{(-1)^3 x^{2(3)+1}}{2(3)+1} + \frac{(-1)^4 x^{2(4)+1}}{2(4)+1}$

$$= x - \frac{x^3}{3} + \frac{x^5}{5} - \frac{x^7}{7} + \frac{x^9}{9}$$

66. $2 + 3 + 4 + 5 + 6 = \displaystyle\sum_{k=1}^{5} (k+1)$

68. $1 - \dfrac{1}{2} + \dfrac{1}{3} - \dfrac{1}{4} = \displaystyle\sum_{k=1}^{4} \frac{(-1)^{k+1}}{k}$

70. $2 + \dfrac{3}{2} + \dfrac{4}{3} + \ldots + \dfrac{n+1}{n} = \displaystyle\sum_{k=1}^{n} \frac{k+1}{k}$

72. $\dfrac{1}{2} - \dfrac{1}{4} + \dfrac{1}{8} - \ldots + \dfrac{(-1)^{n+1}}{2^n} = \displaystyle\sum_{k=1}^{n} \frac{(-1)^{k+1}}{2^k}$

74. (A) $a_n = \dfrac{(a_{n-1})^2 + 5}{2a_{n-1}}, n \geq 2; a_1 = 2$

$a_1 = 2$

$a_2 = \dfrac{2^2 + 5}{2(2)} = \dfrac{9}{4} = 2.25$

$a_3 = \dfrac{2.25^2 + 5}{2(2.25)} = 2.236\bar{1}$

$a_4 = \dfrac{2.236\bar{1}^2 + 5}{2(2.236\bar{1})} = 2.236067978$

(B) $\sqrt{5} = 2.2360679775$ which, to nine decimal places, $= a_4$ from (A)

(C) for

$a_1 = 3$

$a_2 = \dfrac{3^2 + 5}{2(3)} = 2.\bar{3}$

$a_3 = \dfrac{2.\bar{3}^2 + 5}{2(2.\bar{3})} = 2.238095238$

$a_4 = \dfrac{2.238095238^2 + 5}{2(2.238095238)} = 2.236068896$

$a_5 = \dfrac{2.236068896^2 + 5}{2(2.236068896)} = 2.2360679775$

$\sqrt{5} = 2.2360679775 = a_5$, to ten decimal places

76. $\{u_n\}: u_1 = 1, \ u_n = u_{n-1} + v_{n-1}$
$\{v_n\}: v_1 = 0, \ v_n = u_{n-1}, n \geq 2$

$u_1 = 1$	$v_1 = 0$
$u_2 = 1$	$v_2 = 1$
$u_3 = 2$	$v_3 = 1$
$u_4 = 3$	$v_4 = 2$
$u_5 = 5$	$v_5 = 3$
$u_6 = 8$	$v_6 = 5$
$u_7 = 13$	$v_7 = 8$
$u_8 = 21$	$v_8 = 13$
$u_9 = 34$	$v_9 = 21$
$u_{10} = 55$	$v_{10} = 34$

$\{u_n\}$ is the Fibonacci sequence
$\{v_n\}$ is the Fibonacci sequence preceded by 0.

78. $e^x = \sum_{k=0}^{\infty} \frac{x^k}{k!} \approx 1 + \frac{x}{1!} + \frac{x^2}{2!} + K + \frac{x^n}{n!}$

$e^{-0.5} \approx 1 + \frac{-0.5}{1} + \frac{(-0.5)^2}{2!} + \frac{(-0.5)^3}{3!} + \frac{(-0.5)^4}{4!}$

≈ 0.6067708333

$e^{-0.5} \approx 0.6065306597$, calculator

80. $\sum_{k=1}^{n} (a_k + b_k) = (a_1 + b_1) + (a_2 + b_2) + (a_3 + b_3) + .. + (a_n + b_n)$

$= (a_1 + a_2 + a_3 + .. + a_n) + (b_1 + b_2 + b_3 + .. + b_n)$

$= \sum_{k=1}^{n} a_k + \sum_{k=1}^{n} b_k$

82.   (A) $a_5 = 100 \left(\frac{1}{3}\right)^4 = \frac{100}{81} \approx 1.23$ feet; $a_{10} = 100 \left(\frac{1}{3}\right)^9 = \frac{100}{19,683} \approx 0.005$ feet

(B) $\sum_{n=1}^{10} 100 \left(\frac{1}{3}\right)^{n-1} = 100 \left(\frac{1}{3}\right)^{1-1} + 100 \left(\frac{1}{3}\right)^{2-1} + 100 \left(\frac{1}{3}\right)^{3-1} + 100 \left(\frac{1}{3}\right)^{4-1} + 100 \left(\frac{1}{3}\right)^{5-1} + 100 \left(\frac{1}{3}\right)^{6-1} + 100 \left(\frac{1}{3}\right)^{7-1}$

$+ 100 \left(\frac{1}{3}\right)^{8-1} + 100 \left(\frac{1}{3}\right)^{9-1} + 100 \left(\frac{1}{3}\right)^{10-1} = 100 + 33.33 + 11.11 + 3.704 + 1.235 + 0.4115$

$+ 0.1372 + 0.0457 + 0.0152 + 0.0051 \approx 150$ feet

This is the sum of the heights of all ten bounces.

84.   (A) First year: \$24,000 $= a_1$
Second year: \$24,000 + 0.03(\$24,000) = \$24,720 $= a_2$
Third year: \$24,720 + 0.03(\$24,720) = \$25,462 $= a_3$
Fourth year: \$25,462 + 0.03(\$25,462) = \$26,225 $= a_4$
Fifth year: \$26,225 + 0.03(\$26,225) = \$27,012 $= a_5$
Sixth year: \$27,012 + 0.03(\$27,012) = \$27,823 $= a_6$

(B) $a_n = 24,000(1.03)^{n-1}$

(C) $\sum_{n=1}^{6} a_n = 24,000 + 24,720 + 25,462 + 26,225 + 27,012 + 27,823 = \$155,242$

This is the total amount earned in the first six years.

Section 8–2

2. "P_1 is true" can be visualized as "the first domino can be pushed over". "If P_k is true, then P_{k+1} is also true" can be visualized as "if the kth domino falls, then so does the $(k+1)^{st}$ domino".

4. Although one counterexample can disprove a conjecture, no number of examples can prove a conjecture, including this one, which is false.

6. $n < 10$: 10 is the first positive integer which fails

8.

n	$n^3 + 11n$	$6n^2 + 6$
1	12	12
2	30	30
3	60	60
4	108	102 $\Rightarrow$ 4 is first positive integer which fails

10.

n	$4 + 8 + 12 + \ldots + 4n$	$2n(n + 1)$
1	4	$2(1)(1 + 1) = 4$
2	$4 + 8 = 12$	$2(2)(2 + 1) = 12$
3	$4 + 8 + 12 = 24$	$2(3)(3 + 1) = 24$

12.

n	$(a^5)^n$	a^{5n}
1	$(a^5)^1 = a^{5 \cdot 1} = a^5$	$a^{5 \cdot 1} = a^5$
2	$(a^5)^2 = a^{5 \cdot 2} = a^{10}$	$a^{5 \cdot 2} = a^{10}$
3	$(a^5)^3 = a^{5 \cdot 3} = a^{15}$	$a^{5 \cdot 3} = a^{15}$

14. $P_1: 4^1 - 1 = 3$ which is divisible by 3
$P_2: 4^2 - 1 = 15$ which is divisible by 3
$P_3: 4^3 - 1 = 63$ which is divisible by 3

16. $P_n: 4 + 8 + 12 + \cdots + 4n = 2n(n + 1)$
$P_k: 4 + 8 + 12 + \cdots + 4k = 2k(k + 1)$
$P_{k+1}: 4 + 8 + 12 + \cdots + 4k + 4(k + 1)$
$\qquad = 2(k + 1)((k + 1) + 1) = 2(k + 1)(k + 2)$

18. $P_n: (a^5)^n = a^{5n}$
$P_k: (a^5)^k = a^{5k}$
$P_{k+1}: (a^5)^{k+1} = a^{5(k+1)}$

20. $P_n: 4^n - 1 = 3r$, for some integer r
$P_k: 4^k - 1 = 3r$, for some integer r
$P_{k+1}: 4^{(k+1)} - 1 = 3s$, for some integer s

22. $P_n: 4 + 8 + 12 + \cdots + 4n = 2n(n + 1)$
Show P_1 is true.
$\qquad P_1: \ 4(1) = 2(1)(1 + 1)$
$\qquad\qquad 4 = 4$ Thus P_1 is true.
Show if P_k is true, then P_{k+1} is true.
$\qquad P_k: 4 + 8 + 12 + \cdots + 4k = 2k(k + 1)$
$\qquad P_{k+1}: \ 4 + 8 + 12 + \cdots + 4(k + 1) = 2(k + 1)(k + 2)$
Start with $\quad P_k: 4 + 8 + 12 + \ldots + 4k = 2k(k + 1)$
$\qquad P_{k+1}: \ 4 + 8 + 12 + \ldots + 4k + 4(k + 1) = 2k(k + 1) + 4(k + 1)$
$\qquad\qquad\qquad\qquad\qquad = (2k + 4)(k + 1)$
$\qquad\qquad\qquad\qquad\qquad = 2(k + 2)(k + 1)$
$\qquad\qquad\qquad\qquad\qquad = 2(k + 1)(k + 2) \Rightarrow P_{k+1}$ is true

24. $P_n: (a^5)^n = a^{5n}$
Show P_1 is true.
$\qquad P_1: (a^5)^1 \ = a^{5 \cdot 1}$
$\qquad\qquad a^5 \ = a^5$ Thus P_1 is true.
Show if P_k is true, then P_{k+1} is true.
$\qquad P_k: \quad (a^5)^k = a^{5k}$
$\qquad P_{k+1}: (a^5)^{k+1} = a^{5(k+1)}$
Start with $P_k:$ $\qquad\qquad (a^5)^k \ = a^{5k}$
$\qquad\qquad (a^5)^k \cdot a^5 \ = a^{5k} \cdot a^5$
$\qquad\qquad (a^{5k}) \cdot a^5 \ = a^{5k+5}$
$\qquad\qquad\quad a^{5k+5} \ = a^{5(k+1)}$
$\qquad\qquad (a^5)^{k+1} \ = a^{5(k+1)} \Rightarrow P_{k+1}$ is true

26. P_n: $4^n - 1 = 3r$ for some integer r

Show P_1 is true.

$\qquad P_1$: $4^1 - 1 = 4 - 1 = 3 = 3 \cdot 1$ Thus P_1 is true.

Show if P_k is true, then P_{k+1} is true.

$\qquad P_k$: $4^k - 1 = 3s$ for some integer s

$\qquad P_{k+1}$: $4^{k+1} - 1 = 3t$ for some integer t

Start with P_k: $\quad 4^k - 1 = 3s$ for some integer s

$$4(4^k - 1) = 4(3s)$$
$$4^{k+1} - 4 = 4(3s)$$
$$4^{k+1} - 1 = 4(3s) + 3$$
$$4^{k+1} - 1 = 3(4s + 1); \text{ let } t = 4s + 1$$
$$4^{k+1} - 1 = 3t \text{ for some integer } t \Rightarrow P_{k+1} \text{ is true.}$$

28.

n	n as the sum of 3 or fewer squares of positive integers	
8	$2^2 + 2^2 = 4 + 4 = 8$	
9	$3^2 = 9$	$1^2 = 1$
10	$1^2 + 3^2 = 1 + 9 = 10$	$2^2 = 4$
11	$1^2 + 1^2 + 3^2 = 1 + 1 + 9 = 11$	$3^2 = 9$
12	$2^2 + 2^2 + 2^2 = 4 + 4 + 4 = 12$	$4^2 = 16$
13	$2^2 + 3^2 = 4 + 9 = 13$	$5^2 = 25$
14	$1^2 + 2^2 + 3^2 = 1 + 4 + 9 = 14$	
15	fails	

30. Let $a = 1$, $b = 7$, $c = 5$, $d = 5$, then

$\qquad a^2 + b^2 = c^2 + d^2 \qquad$ becomes

$\qquad 1^2 + 7^2 = 5^2 + 5^2$

$\qquad 1 + 49 = 25 + 25$

$\qquad\qquad 50 = 50$ which is true but

$\qquad a = c$ or $a = d$ becomes

$\qquad 1 = 5$ or $1 = 5$ which is false.

32. P_n: $\dfrac{1}{2} + \dfrac{1}{4} + \dfrac{1}{8} + \cdots + \dfrac{1}{2^n} = 1 - \left(\dfrac{1}{2}\right)^n$

Show P_1 is true.

$\qquad P_1$: $\dfrac{1}{2^1} = 1 - \left(\dfrac{1}{2}\right)^1$

$\qquad\qquad \dfrac{1}{2} = \dfrac{1}{2}$ Thus P_1 is true.

Show if P_k is true, then P_{k+1} is true.

$\qquad P_k$: $\dfrac{1}{2} + \dfrac{1}{4} + \dfrac{1}{8} + \cdots + \dfrac{1}{2^k} = 1 - \left(\dfrac{1}{2}\right)^k$

$\qquad P_{k+1}$: $\dfrac{1}{2} + \dfrac{1}{4} + \dfrac{1}{8} + \cdots + \dfrac{1}{2^k} + \dfrac{1}{2^{k+1}} = 1 - \left(\dfrac{1}{2}\right)^{k+1}$

Start with P_k: $\dfrac{1}{2} + \dfrac{1}{4} + \dfrac{1}{8} + \cdots + \dfrac{1}{2^k} = 1 - \left(\dfrac{1}{2}\right)^k$

$$\dfrac{1}{2} + \dfrac{1}{4} + \dfrac{1}{8} + \cdots + \dfrac{1}{2^k} + \dfrac{1}{2^{k+1}} = 1 - \left(\dfrac{1}{2}\right)^k + \dfrac{1}{2^{k+1}} = 1 - \left(\dfrac{1}{2}\right)^k + \left(\dfrac{1}{2}\right)^{k+1}$$

$$= 1 - \left(\dfrac{1}{2}\right)^k + \left(\dfrac{1}{2}\right)^k \left(\dfrac{1}{2}\right) = 1 - \left(\dfrac{1}{2}\right)^k \left(1 - \dfrac{1}{2}\right)$$

$$= 1 - \left(\dfrac{1}{2}\right)^k \left(\dfrac{1}{2}\right) = 1 - \left(\dfrac{1}{2}\right)^{k+1} \Rightarrow P_{k+1} \text{ is true}$$

34. P_n: $1 + 8 + 16 + \cdots + 8(n - 1) = (2n - 1)^2$; $n > 1$

Show P_2 is true.

$$1 + 8(2 - 1) = (2(2) - 1)^2$$
$$9 = 9 \quad \text{Thus } P_2 \text{ is true.}$$

Show if P_k is true, then P_{k+1} is true.

$$P_k: \ 1 + 8 + 16 + \cdots + 8(k - 1) = (2k - 1)^2; \ k > 2$$
$$P_{k+1}: \ 1 + 8 + 16 + \cdots + 8(k - 1) + 8((k + 1) - 1) = (2(k + 1) - 1)^2; \ k > 2$$

Start with P_k: $1 + 8 + 16 + \cdots + 8(k - 1) = (2k - 1)^2$; $k > 2$

$$1 + 8 + 16 + \cdots + 8(k - 1) + 8((k + 1) - 1) = (2k - 1)^2 + 8((k + 1) - 1)$$
$$= 4k^2 - 4k + 1 + 8k = 4k^2 + 4k + 1$$
$$= (2k + 1)^2 = (2(k + 1) - 1)^2 \Rightarrow P_{k+1} \text{ is true}$$

36. P_n: $1 \cdot 2 + 2 \cdot 3 + 3 \cdot 4 + \cdots + n(n + 1) = \dfrac{n(n+1)(n+2)}{3}$

Show P_1 is true.

$$1 \cdot 2 = \frac{1(2)(3)}{3}$$
$$2 = 2 \quad \text{Thus } P_1 \text{ is true.}$$

Show if P_k is true, then P_{k+1} is true.

$$P_k: 1 \cdot 2 + 2 \cdot 3 + 3 \cdot 4 + \cdots + k(k + 1) = \frac{k(k+1)(k+2)}{3}$$

$$P_{k+1}: 1 \cdot 2 + 2 \cdot 3 + 3 \cdot 4 + \ldots + (k + 1)(k + 1 + 1) = \frac{(k+1)(k+1+1)(k+1+2)}{3}$$

Start with P_k: $\quad 1 \cdot 2 + 2 \cdot 3 + 3 \cdot 4 + \ldots + k(k + 1) = \dfrac{k(k+1)(k+2)}{3}$

$$1 \cdot 2 + 2 \cdot 3 + 3 \cdot 4 + \cdots + k(k + 1) + (k + 1)(k + 2) = \frac{k(k+1)(k+2)}{3} + (k + 1)(k + 2)$$

$$= \frac{k(k+1)(k+2)}{3} + \frac{3(k+1)(k+2)}{3} = \frac{(k+1)(k+2)(k+3)}{3}$$

$$= \frac{(k+1)(k+1+1)(k+1+2)}{3} \quad \text{Thus } P_{k+1} \text{ is true.}$$

38. P_n: $\dfrac{a^5}{a^n} = \dfrac{1}{a^{n-5}}$; $n > 5$

Show true for $n = 6$.

$$\frac{a^5}{a^6} = \frac{1}{a^{6-5}}$$
$$\frac{1}{a} = \frac{1}{a} \quad \text{Thus } P_6 \text{ is true.}$$

Show if P_k is true, then P_{k+1} is true; $n > 6$.

$$P_k: \ \frac{a^5}{a^k} = \frac{1}{a^{k-5}}$$

$$P_{k+1}: \ \frac{a^5}{a^{k+1}} = \frac{1}{a^{(k+1)-5}}$$

Start with P_k: $\qquad \dfrac{a^5}{a^k} = \dfrac{1}{a^{k-5}}$

$$\frac{a^5}{a^k} \cdot \frac{1}{a} = \frac{1}{a^{k-5}} \cdot \frac{1}{a}$$

$$\frac{a^5}{a^{k+1}} = \frac{1}{a^{k-4}}$$

$$\frac{a^5}{a^{k+1}} = \frac{1}{a^{(k+1)-5}} \Rightarrow P_{k+1} \text{ is true.}$$

40. P_n: $(a^n)^m = a^{mn}$; $m, n \in N$

Show true for P_1: $(a^1)^m = a^{m \cdot 1}$

$\qquad\qquad a^m = a^m$ Thus P_1 is true.

Show if P_k is true, then P_{k+1} is true.

$\qquad P_k$: $\qquad (a^k)^m = a^{mk}$

$\qquad P_{k+1}$: $(a^{k+1})^m = a^{m(k+1)}$

Start with P_k: $\qquad (a^k)^m = a^{mk}$

$\qquad\qquad (a^k)^m \cdot a^m = a^{mk} \cdot a^m$

$\qquad\qquad a^{km} \cdot a^m = a^{mk+m}$

$\qquad\qquad a^{km+m} = a^{m(k+1)}$

$\qquad\qquad a^{(k+1)m} = a^{m(k+1)}$

$\qquad\qquad (a^{k+1})^m = a^{m(k+1)} \Rightarrow P_{k+1}$ is true.

42. P_n: $x^n - y^n$ is divisible by $x - y$; $x \neq y$

Show true for P_1: $\dfrac{x^1 - y^1}{x - y} = 1$ Thus P_1 is true.

Show if P_k is true, then P_{k+1} is true.

$\qquad P_k$: $\quad x^k - y^k = (x - y)[Q_1(x, y)]$

$\qquad P_{k+1}$: $x^{k+1} - y^{k+1} = (x - y)[Q_2(x, y)]$

Start with P_k: $x^k - y^k = (x - y)[Q_1(x, y)]$

Then $x^{k+1} - y^{k+1} = x^{k+1} - x^k y + x^k y - y^{k+1}$

$\qquad\qquad = (x - y)x^k + y(x^k - y^k)$

$\qquad\qquad = (x - y)[x^k + y\, Q_1(x, y)]$

$\qquad\qquad = (x - y)x^k + y(x - y)[Q_1(x, y)]$

$\qquad\qquad = (x - y)[Q_2(x, y)]$

Thus P_{k+1} is true.

44. P_n: $x^{2n} - 1$ is divisible by $x + 1$, $x \neq -1$

Show true for P_1: $x^2 - 1 = (x - 1)(x + 1) = (x + 1)[Q(x)]$ Thus P_1 is true.

Show if P_k is true, then P_{k+1} is true.

$\qquad P_k$: $x^{2k} - 1 = (x + 1)[Q_1(x)]$

$\qquad P_{k+1}$: $x^{2(k+1)} - 1 = (x + 1)[Q_2(x)]$

$\quad$ Consider $x^{2(k+1)} - 1 = x^{2(k+1)} - x^2 + x^2 - 1$

$\qquad\qquad = x^{2k+2} - x^2 + x^2 - 1$

$\qquad\qquad = x^2(x^{2k} - 1) + (x - 1)(x + 1)$, using P_k

$\qquad\qquad = x^2[(x + 1)[Q_1(x)] + (x + 1)(x - 1)$

$\qquad\qquad = (x + 1)[x^2 Q_1(x) + x - 1]$

$\qquad\qquad = (x + 1)Q_2(x) \Rightarrow P_{k+1}$ is true.

46. P_n: $\dfrac{1}{1 \cdot 2 \cdot 3} + \dfrac{1}{2 \cdot 3 \cdot 4} + \dfrac{1}{3 \cdot 4 \cdot 5} + \cdots + \dfrac{1}{n(n+1)(n+2)} = \dfrac{n(n+3)}{4(n+1)(n+2)}$

Show P_1 is true.

$\dfrac{1(1+3)}{4(1+1)(1+2)} = \dfrac{1(4)}{4(2)(3)} = \dfrac{1}{1 \cdot 2 \cdot 3} \Rightarrow P_n$ is true for $n = 1$

Show if P_k is true, then P_{k+1} is true.

$\quad P_k$: $\dfrac{1}{1 \cdot 2 \cdot 3} + \dfrac{1}{2 \cdot 3 \cdot 4} + \dfrac{1}{3 \cdot 4 \cdot 5} + \cdots + \dfrac{1}{k(k+1)(k+2)} = \dfrac{k(k+3)}{4(k+1)(k+2)}$

$\quad P_{k+1}$: $\dfrac{1}{1 \cdot 2 \cdot 3} + \dfrac{1}{2 \cdot 3 \cdot 4} + \cdots + \dfrac{1}{k(k+1)(k+2)} + \dfrac{1}{(k+1)(k+2)(k+3)} = \dfrac{(k+1)(k+4)}{4(k+2)(k+3)}$

$\qquad \dfrac{1}{1 \cdot 2 \cdot 3} + \dfrac{1}{2 \cdot 3 \cdot 4} + \dfrac{1}{3 \cdot 4 \cdot 5} + \cdots + \dfrac{1}{k(k+1)(k+2)} + \dfrac{1}{(k+1)(k+2)(k+3)}$

$\qquad\qquad = \dfrac{k(k+3)}{4(k+1)(k+2)} + \dfrac{1}{(k+1)(k+2)(k+3)}$

$\qquad\qquad = \dfrac{1}{(k+1)(k+2)} \cdot \left[\dfrac{k(k+3)}{4} + \dfrac{1}{k+3} \right]$

$\qquad\qquad = \dfrac{1}{(k+1)(k+2)} \cdot \left[\dfrac{k(k+3)^2 + 4}{4(k+3)} \right]$

$$= \frac{1}{(k+1)(k+2)} \cdot \left[\frac{k(k^2+6k+9)+4}{4(k+3)} \right]$$

$$= \frac{1}{(k+1)(k+2)} \cdot \left[\frac{k^3+6k^2+9k+4}{4(k+3)} \right]$$

$$= \frac{1}{(k+1)(k+2)} \cdot \frac{(k+1)^2(k+4)}{4(k+3)}$$

$$= \frac{(k+1)(k+4)}{4(k+2)(k+3)} \implies P_{k+1} \text{ is true}$$

48. P_n: $\dfrac{1}{1\cdot 2} + \dfrac{1}{2\cdot 3} + \dfrac{1}{3\cdot 4} + \cdots + \dfrac{1}{n(n+1)} = \dfrac{n}{n+1}$

Show P_1 is true.

$$\frac{1}{1+1} = \frac{1}{2} = \frac{1}{1\cdot 2} \implies P_n \text{ is true for } n=1$$

Show if P_k is true, then P_{k+1} is true.

$$P_k: \frac{1}{1\cdot 2} + \frac{1}{2\cdot 3} + \frac{1}{3\cdot 4} + \cdots + \frac{1}{k(k+1)} = \frac{k}{k+1}$$

$$P_{k+1}: \frac{1}{1\cdot 2} + \frac{1}{2\cdot 3} + \cdots + \frac{1}{(k+1)(k+2)} = \frac{k+1}{k+2}$$

$$\frac{1}{1\cdot 2} + \frac{1}{2\cdot 3} + \frac{1}{3\cdot 4} + \cdots + \frac{1}{k(k+1)} + \frac{1}{(k+1)(k+2)} = \frac{k}{k+1} + \frac{1}{(k+1)(k+2)}$$

$$= \frac{1}{(k+1)} \cdot \left[k + \frac{1}{k+2} \right] = \frac{1}{(k+1)} \cdot \left[\frac{k(k+2)+1}{k+2} \right]$$

$$= \frac{1}{(k+1)} \cdot \frac{k^2+2k+1}{k+2} = \frac{1}{k+1} \cdot \frac{(k+1)^2}{k+2}$$

$$= \frac{k+1}{k+2} \implies P_{k+1} \text{ is true}$$

50. The number of diagonals in a polygon with n sides. P_n: $2+3+4+\cdots+(n-2) = \dfrac{n(n-3)}{2}$, $n>3$

Show P_4 is true.

$$\frac{4(4-3)}{2} = 2 \implies \text{true for } n=4$$

Show if P_k is true, then P_{k+1} is true.

$$P_k: 2+3+4+\cdots+(k-2) = \frac{k(k-3)}{2}, \; k>3$$

$$P_{k+1}: 2+3+4+\cdots+(k-2)+(k-1) = \frac{(k+1)(k-2)}{2}, \; k>3$$

$$2+3+4+\cdots+(k-2)+(k-1) = \frac{k(k-3)}{2}+k-1 = \frac{k(k-3)+2(k-1)}{2}$$

$$= \frac{k^2-3k+2k-2}{2} = \frac{k^2-k-2}{2} = \frac{(k+1)(k-2)}{2} \implies P_{k+1} \text{ is true}$$

52. Prove: $0 < a < 1 \Rightarrow 0 < a^n < 1 : P_n \quad (n \in N)$

Show P_1 is true.

$0 < a < 1 \Rightarrow 0 < a^1 < 1$, P_n is true for $n = 1$

Show if P_k is true, then P_{k+1} is true.

$P_k: \ 0 < a^k < 1$

$P_{k+1}: \ 0 < a^{k+1} < a < 1$

Start with $P_k: 0 < a^k < 1$

$0 < a^k \cdot a < 1 \cdot a$

$0 < a^{k+1} < a < 1 \Rightarrow P_{k+1}$ is true

54. $P_n: 2^n > n^2, n \geq 5$

Show P_5 is true.

$2^5 > 5^2$

$32 > 25 \Rightarrow P_5$ is true

Show if P_k is true, then P_{k+1} is true, $k \geq 5$.

$P_k: \ 2^k > k^2, \qquad k \geq 5$

$P_{k+1}: \ 2^{k+1} > (k+1)^2, \quad k \geq 5$

Start with

$P_k: \qquad 2^k > k^2 \qquad\qquad k \geq 5$

$2 \cdot 2^k > 2k^2 \qquad\qquad k^2 \geq 25 \text{ and } 2k \geq 10$

$2^{k+1} > k^2 + k^2 \qquad\qquad k^2 - 2k \geq 15$

$2^{k+1} > k^2 + 2k + 1 \qquad k^2 \geq 2k + 15 > 2k + 1$

$2^{k+1} > (k+1)^2 \ \Rightarrow P_{k+1}$ is true.

56. The statement is true. Proof by mathematical induction:

$P_n: 1^2 - 2^2 + 3^2 + \ldots (-1)^{n+1}n^2 = \dfrac{(-1)^{n+1}n(n+1)}{2}$

Show P_1 is true

$1^2 = 1 = \dfrac{(-1)^{1+1}1(1+1)}{2} \Rightarrow P_n$ is true for $n = 1$

Show if P_k is true, P_{k+1} is true.

$P_k: 1^2 - 2^2 + 3^2 + \ldots + (-1)^{k+1}k^2 = \dfrac{(-1)^{k+1}k(k+1)}{2}$

$P_{k+1}: 1^2 - 2^2 + 3^2 - \ldots + (-1)^{k+2}(k+1)^2 = \dfrac{(-1)^{k+2}(k+1)(k+2)}{2}$

$1^2 - 2^2 + 3^2 + \ldots + (-1)^{k+1}k^2 + (-1)^{k+2}(k+1)^2 = \dfrac{(-1)^{k+1}k(k+1)}{2} + (-1)^{k+2}(k+1)^2$

$= \dfrac{(-1)^{k+1}k(k+1) + (-1)^{k+2}2(k+1)^2}{2}$

$= \dfrac{(-1)^{k+2}(k+1)[(-1)k + 2(k+1)]}{2}$

$= \dfrac{(-1)^{k+2}(k+1)(k+2)}{2} \Rightarrow P_{k+1}$ is true

58. The statement is false. For example, if $n = 18$, $18^2 + 21 \cdot 18 + 1 = 703$. $703 = 19 \times 37$ is not a prime.

60. $a_1 = 2, a_n = a_{n-1} + 2; b_n = 2n$

Show P_1 is true: $a_1 = 2 = 2 \cdot 1 = b_1$: $\{a_n\} = \{b_n\}$ is true for $n = 1$

Assume $a_k = b_k$ and show $a_{k+1} = b_{k+1}$. $a_{k+1} = a_k + 2 = b_k + 2 = 2k + 2 = 2(k+1) = b_{k+1} \Rightarrow \{a_n\} = \{b_n\}$ for all n

62. $a_1 = 2, a_n = 3a_{n-1}; b_n = 2 \cdot 3^{n-1}$

Show P_1 is true: $a_1 = 2 = 2 \cdot 1 = 2 \cdot 3^0 = 2 \cdot 3^{1-1} = b_1 \Rightarrow \{a_n\} = \{b_n\}$ is true for $n = 1$.

Assume $a_k = b_k$ and show $a_{k+1} = b_{k+1}$. $a_{k+1} = 3a_k = 3b_k = 3 \cdot (2 \cdot 3^{k-1}) = 2 \cdot 3^k = b_{k+1} \Rightarrow \{a_n\} = \{b_n\}$ for all n.

Section 8-3

2. A geometric sequence is a sequence in which the ratio of any two successive terms is a constant, called the common ratio.

4. A repeating decimal consists of a block of n digits repeated. After any block, the next block is added on, but this block is 10^{-n} times the previous block. Thus the repeating decimal is a geometric series with common ratio 10^{-n}.

6. An infinite geometric sequence with common ratio r has a sum if and only if $|r| < 1$, that is, $-1 < r < 1$.

8. (A)   5, 20, 100, ...

Since $\begin{array}{c} 20 - 5 = 15 \\ 100 - 20 = 80 \end{array}$ and $\begin{array}{c} \dfrac{20}{5} = 4 \\ \dfrac{100}{20} = 5 \end{array}$ the sequence 5, 20, 100, ... is neither arithmetic nor geometric.

(B) $-5, -5, -5, ...$

Since $-5 - (-5) = 0$ and $\dfrac{-5}{-5} = 1$ the sequence $-5, -5, -5, ...$ is arithmetic with $d = 0$, and geometric with $r = 1$. The next two terms are $-5, -5$ in both cases.

(C)   7, 6.5, 6, ...

Since $6.5 - 7 = -0.5$ and $6 - 6.5 = -0.5$, the sequence is arithmetic with $d = -0.5$. The next two terms are 5.5, 5. Since $\dfrac{6.5}{7} = 0.92857...$ and $\dfrac{6}{6.5} = 0.92307...$ the sequence is not geometric.

(D)   512, 256, 128, ...

Since $256 - 512 = -256$ and $128 - 256 = -128$, the sequence is not arithmetic.

Since $\dfrac{256}{512} = \dfrac{1}{2}$ and $\dfrac{128}{256} = \dfrac{1}{2}$, the sequence is geometric with $r = \dfrac{1}{2}$. The next two terms are 64, 32.

10. $a_1 = -18, d = 3$
$a_2 = -18 + 3 = -15$
$a_3 = -15 + 3 = -12$
$a_4 = -12 + 3 = -9$

12. $a_1 = 3, d = 4$
$a_n = a_1 + d(n - 1)$
$a_{22} = 3 + 4(21) = 87$
$S_n = \dfrac{n}{2}[2a_1 + (n-1)d]$
$S_{21} = \dfrac{21}{2}(2(3) + 20(4)) = 903$

14. $a_1 = 5, a_2 = 11 \Rightarrow d = 6$
$S_n = \dfrac{n}{2}[2a_1 + (n-1)d]$
$S_{11} = \dfrac{11}{2}(2(5) + 10(6)) = 385$

16. $a_1 = -3, d = -4$
$a_n = a_1 + (n-1)d$
$a_{10} = -3 + (10 - 1)(-4) = -39$

18. $a_1 = 12, r = \dfrac{2}{3}$
$a_n = a_{n-1}r$
$a_2 = 12\left(\dfrac{2}{3}\right) = 8$
$a_3 = 8\left(\dfrac{2}{3}\right) = \dfrac{16}{3}$
$a_4 = \dfrac{16}{3} \cdot \dfrac{2}{3} = \dfrac{32}{9}$

20. $a_1 = 64, r = \dfrac{1}{2}$
$a_n = a_1 r^{n-1}$
$a_{13} = 64\left(\dfrac{1}{2}\right)^{12} = \dfrac{1}{64}$

22. $a_1 = 1, a_7 = 729, r = -3$

$$S_n = \frac{a_1 - a_1 r^n}{1 - r}$$

$$S_7 = \frac{1 - (1)(-3)^7}{1 - (-3)} = 547$$

24. $a_1 = 7, a_8 = 28$

$$a_n = a_1 + (n - 1)d$$

$$a_8 = a_1 + 7d$$

$$28 = 7 + 7d$$

$$21 = 7d$$

$$3 = d$$

$$a_{25} = 7 + 24(3) = 79$$

26. $a_1 = 24, \quad a_{24} = -28$

$$a_n = a_1 + (n - 1)d$$

$$a_{24} = -28 = 24 + (24 - 1)d$$

$$d = -\frac{52}{23}$$

$$S_n = \frac{n}{2}[2a_1 + (n - 1)d]$$

$$S_{24} = \frac{24}{2}\left[2(24) + (24 - 1)\left(-\frac{52}{23}\right)\right]$$

$$S_{24} = -48$$

28. $a_1 = \frac{1}{6}, \quad a_2 = \frac{1}{4}$

$$a_1 + d = a_2$$

$$\frac{1}{6} + d = \frac{1}{4}$$

$$d = \frac{1}{12}$$

$$a_n = a_1 + (n - 1)d$$

$$a_{19} = \frac{1}{6} + 18 \cdot \frac{1}{12} = \frac{5}{3}$$

$$S_n = \frac{n}{2}(a_1 + a_n)$$

$$S_{19} = \frac{19}{2}\left(\frac{1}{6} + \frac{5}{3}\right) = \frac{19}{2} \cdot \frac{11}{6} = \frac{209}{12}$$

30. $a_9 = -12, a_{13} = 3$

$$a_n = a_1 + (n - 1)d$$

$$a_9 = a_1 + 8d \Rightarrow (1): -12 = a_1 + 8d$$

$$a_{13} = a_1 + 12d \Rightarrow (2): 3 = a_1 + 12d$$

$$(1) - (2): -15 = -4d \Rightarrow d = \frac{15}{4} = 3.75$$

$$(1): -12 = a_1 + 8\left(\frac{15}{4}\right) \Rightarrow a_1 = -42$$

32. $a_1 = -6, a_2 = 2$

$$a_2 = a_1 r$$

$$2 = -6r$$

$$r = -\frac{1}{3}$$

34. $a_1 = \sqrt{2}, a_6 = 8$

$$a_n = a_1 r^{n-1}$$

$$a_6 = a_1 r^5$$

$$8 = \sqrt{2}\, r^5$$

$$r^5 = 4\sqrt{2}$$

$$r = \sqrt{2}$$

36. $S_n = \dfrac{a_1 - a_1 r^n}{1 - r}$ $S_9 = \dfrac{3 - 3(5)^9}{1 - 5} = \dfrac{-5,859,372}{-4} = 1,464,843$

38. First find r

$$a_n = a_1 r^{n-1}$$

$$a_{12} = a_1 r^{11}$$

$$1,024 = \frac{1}{2} r^{11}$$

$$2,048 = r^{11}$$

$r = 2$. Therefore

$$S_{12} = \frac{a_1 - a_1 r^{12}}{1 - r} = \frac{\frac{1}{2} - \frac{1}{2}(2)^{12}}{1 - 2}$$

$$= \frac{-4,095}{2} \div -1 = \frac{4,095}{2}$$

40. $a_4 = a_1 r^3, a_5 = a_1 r^4$

$$\frac{a_5}{a_4} = r$$

$$\frac{6}{8} = r$$

$$r = \frac{3}{4}. \text{ Therefore}$$

$$a_4 = a_1\left(\frac{3}{4}\right)^3$$

$$8 = a_1\left(\frac{3}{4}\right)^3$$

$$a_1 = 8\left(\frac{4}{3}\right)^3 = \frac{512}{27}$$

42.
$$a_8 = a_1 r^7$$
$$1 = (-1)r^7$$
$$-1 = r^7$$
$$r = -1$$
$$a_{99} = a_1 r^{98} = (-1)(-1)^{98} = -1$$

44. $S_{40} = \sum_{k=1}^{40} (2k - 3) \Rightarrow$ arithmetic seq: $a_1 = -1, d = 2$

$$S_n = \frac{n}{2}[2a_1 + (n-1)d]$$

$$S_{40} = \frac{40}{2}[2(-1) + 39(2)] = 1520$$

46. $S_7 = \sum_{k=1}^{7} 3k \Rightarrow$ geometric seq: $a_1 = 3, r = 3$

$$S_n = \frac{a_1 - a_1 r^n}{1 - r}$$

$$S_7 = \frac{3 - 3(3)^7}{1 - 3} = 3279$$

48. $S = 101 + 103 + 105 + \cdots + 499 \Rightarrow$ arithmetic seq:
$$a_1 = 101, d = 2$$

$$a_n = a_1 + (n-1)d$$
$$499 = 101 + (n-1)2$$
$$398 = 2n - 2$$
$$400 = 2n \Rightarrow n = 200$$

$$S_n = \frac{n}{2}[a_1 + a_n]$$

$$S_{200} = \frac{200}{2}[101 + 499] = 60{,}000$$

50. $2 + 4 + 6 + \cdots + 2n = n + n^2$; arithmetic seq:
$$a_1 = 2, d = 2$$

$$S_n = \frac{n}{2}[2a_1 + (n-1)d] = \frac{n}{2}[2(2) + (n-1)2]$$

$$= \frac{n}{2}[2n + 2] = n^2 + n = n + n^2$$

52. $r = \dfrac{a_2}{a_1} = \dfrac{2}{6} = \dfrac{1}{3}$

Since $|r| = \dfrac{1}{3} < 1$, the series has a sum.

$$S_\infty = \frac{a_1}{1-r} = \frac{6}{1 - \frac{1}{3}} = 9$$

54. $r = \dfrac{a_2}{a_1} = \dfrac{4}{3} \div 1 = \dfrac{4}{3}$

Since $|r| = \dfrac{4}{3} \geq 1$, the series has no sum.

56. $r = \dfrac{a_2}{a_1} = \dfrac{-2}{10} = \dfrac{-1}{5}$

Since $|r| = \left|\dfrac{-1}{5}\right| = \dfrac{1}{5} < 1$, the series has a sum.

$$S_\infty = \frac{a_1}{1-r} = \frac{10}{1 - \frac{-1}{5}} = \frac{25}{3}$$

58. $r = \dfrac{a_2}{a_1} = \dfrac{4}{-6} = -\dfrac{2}{3}$

Since $|r| = \left|-\dfrac{2}{3}\right| = \dfrac{2}{3} < 1$, the series has a sum.

$$S_\infty = \frac{a_1}{1-r} = \frac{-6}{1 - \left(\frac{-2}{3}\right)} = -\frac{18}{5}$$

60. $r = \dfrac{a_2}{a_1} = \dfrac{-80}{-100} = \dfrac{4}{5}$

Since $|r| = \dfrac{4}{5} < 1$, the series has a sum.

$$S_\infty = \frac{a_1}{1-r} = \frac{-100}{1 - \frac{4}{5}} = -500$$

62. $0.\overline{5} = 0.5 + 0.05 + 0.005 + \cdots$
$$a_1 = 0.5 \qquad r = 0.1$$

$$S_\infty = \frac{a_1}{1-r} = \frac{0.5}{1 - 0.1} = \frac{5}{9}$$

64. $0.\overline{27} = 0.27 + 0.0027 + 0.000027 + \cdots$
$$a_1 = 0.27 \qquad r = 0.01$$

$$S_\infty = \frac{a_1}{1-r} = \frac{0.27}{1 - 0.01} = \frac{3}{11}$$

66. $5.\overline{63} = 5 + 0.63 + 0.0063 + \cdots$
$$a_1 = 0.63 \quad r = 0.01$$

$$5 + S_\infty = 5 + \frac{a_1}{1-r} = 5 + \frac{0.63}{1 - 0.01} = 5 + \frac{7}{11} = \frac{62}{11}$$

68. $S_n = a_1 + (a_1 + d) + (a_1 + 2d) + \cdots + (a_1 + (n-1)d)$

$S_n = \dfrac{n}{2}[2a_1 + (n-1)d]$

Show S_1 is true.

$S_1 = \dfrac{1}{2}[2a_1 + (1-1)d] = a_1 \Rightarrow$ true for $n = 1$

Assume $S_k = \dfrac{k}{2}[2a_1 + (k-1)d]$ is true.

$S_{k+1} = S_k + a_{k+1} = S_k + a_1 + kd$

$= \dfrac{k}{2}[2a_1 + (k-1)d] + a_1 + kd$

$= ka_1 + \dfrac{k}{2}(k-1)d + a_1 + kd$

$= ka_1 + a_1 + \left(\dfrac{k}{2}(k-1) + k\right)d$

$= (k+1)a_1 + \left(\dfrac{k(k-1) + 2k}{2}\right)d$

$= (k+1)a_1 + \left(\dfrac{k^2 - k + 2k}{2}\right)d$

$= (k+1)a_1 + \left(\dfrac{k^2 + k}{2}\right)d$

$= (k+1)a_1 + \dfrac{k(k+1)}{2}d$

$= \dfrac{k+1}{2}[2a_1 + kd] \Rightarrow$ true for $k+1 \Rightarrow$ true for all n.

70. $a_1 = -2,\ a_n = -3a_{n-1},\ n > 1 \Rightarrow a_1 = -2,\ r = -3$

$S_n = \displaystyle\sum_{k=1}^{n} a_k = \dfrac{a_1 - a_1 r^n}{1-r} = \dfrac{-2 - (-2)(-3)^n}{1 - (-3)} = \dfrac{(-3)^n - 1}{2}$

72. S_n: $a_1 + a_1 r + a_1 r^2 + \cdots + a_1 r^{n-1} = \dfrac{a_1 - a_1 r^n}{1-r}$

Show true for S_1.

$S_1 = a_1 = a_1 \cdot \dfrac{1-r}{1-r} = \dfrac{a_1 - a_1 r^n}{1-r} \Rightarrow$ true for $n = 1$

Assume $S_k = a_1 + a_1 r + a_1 r^2 + \cdots + a_1 r^{k-1}$

$= \dfrac{a_1 - a_1 r^k}{1-r}$ is true.

$S_{k+1} = a_1 + a_1 r + a_1 r^2 + \cdots + a_1 r^{k-1} + a_1 r^k$

$= \dfrac{a_1 - a_1 r^k}{1-r} + a_1 r^k$

$= \dfrac{a_1 - a_1 r^k}{1-r} + \dfrac{a_1 r^k \cdot (1-r)}{1-r}$

$= \dfrac{a_1 - a_1 r^k + a_1 r^k - a_1 r^{k+1}}{1-r}$

$= \dfrac{a_1 - a_1 r^{k+1}}{1-r} \Rightarrow S_{k+1}$ is true

74. If $S_\infty = \dfrac{a_1}{1-r}$ so that $\dfrac{1}{2} = \dfrac{1}{1-r}$, then $1 - r = 2$ and $r = -1$. However, the sum of an infinite geometric sequence is not defined if $r = -1$. No, there is no such sequence.

76.

Firm A	Firm B
$a_1 = 25{,}000$	$a_1 = 28{,}000$
$d = 1200$	$d = 800$
$a_{10} = 25{,}000 + 9(1200)$	$a_{10} = 28{,}000 + 9(800)$
$a_{10} = \$35{,}800$	$a_{10} = \$35{,}200$

78. $S_\infty = \dfrac{a_1}{1-r}$

$600(0.7) + 600(0.7)^2 + \cdots = \dfrac{600(0.7)}{1 - 0.7} = \$1400$

80.

time	population
1	$A_0 + rA_0 = A_0(1+r)$
2	$A_0(1+r) + A_0(1+r)r = A_0(1+r)(1+r) = A_0(1+r)^2$
$\vdots$	
t	$A_0(1+r)^t$

If $r = 2\%$:

$A_0(1+r)^t = 2A_0$

$(1 + 0.02)^t = 2$

$t = \dfrac{\ln 2}{\ln 1.02} \approx 35$ years

82. (A) arithmetic sequence

(B) $T_n = 80 + (n)(-5)$

84. $10 + 10(0.9) + 10(0.9)^2 + \cdots$

$S_\infty = \dfrac{a_1}{1-r} = \dfrac{10}{1 - 0.9} = 100$ in

86. $\dfrac{600}{30} = 20$ generations

direct ancestors $= 2^{20} = 1{,}048{,}576$

88.

n	s	
1	$16 = 16 \cdot 1$	$1, 3, 5, \cdots, a_n, \cdots$
2	$48 = 16 \cdot 3$	$a_n = 1 + (n-1)2$
3	$80 = 16 \cdot 5$	

$\vdots$

20   (A) $d = 16 \cdot a_{20} = 16(1 + 19(2)) = 624$ feet

$\vdots$

t (B) $d = 16 \cdot a_t = 16(1 + (t-1)2) = 16(2t + 1 - 2) = 32t - 16$

90.

cells after t days $= 2^{2t} = 1,000,000,000$

$\ln 2^{2t} = \ln 1,000,000,000$

$2t \ln 2 = \ln 1,000,000,000$

$t = \dfrac{\ln 1,000,000,000}{2 \ln 2}$

$t \approx 14.95$ days

The mouse dies on the 15th day (discrete model; round up).

92. If $a_1 = 0.001, r = 2$, find a_{33}:

$a_n = a_1 r^{n-1}$

$a_{33} = 0.001(2)^{32}$ in $\times \dfrac{1\,\text{ft}}{12\,\text{in}} \times \dfrac{1\,\text{mi}}{5280\,\text{ft}} \approx 68$ miles

If $a_1 = 0.002, r = 2$, find a_{32}:

$a_n = a_1 r^{n-1}$

$a_{32} = 0.002(2)^{31}$ in $\times \dfrac{1\,\text{ft}}{12\,\text{in}} \times \dfrac{1\,\text{mi}}{5280\,\text{ft}} \approx 68$ miles

94.   (A) $a_1 = 400, a_{12} = 800$

$a_n = a_1 r^{n-1}$

$800 = 400 r^{11}$

$2 = r^{11}$

$r \approx 1.065$

(B) Find a_4: $a_4 = a_1 r^3$

$= 400(1.065)^3$

≈ 483 cps

96. $a_1 = \dfrac{220}{440}, a_2 = \dfrac{110}{440}, a_3 = \dfrac{55}{440}, \cdots \quad r = \dfrac{1}{2}$

$S_\infty = \dfrac{a_1}{1-r} = \dfrac{\frac{220}{440}}{1 - \frac{1}{2}} = \dfrac{\frac{1}{2}}{1 - \frac{1}{2}} \cdot \dfrac{2}{2} = \dfrac{1}{1} = 1$ min

98. shutter speeds: $1, \dfrac{1}{2}, \dfrac{1}{4}, \dfrac{1}{8}, \cdots \quad r = \dfrac{1}{2}$

f-stops: $1.4, 2, 2.8, 4, \cdots \quad r = 1.42857... \approx 1.4$

Section 8-4

2. A combination of a set of objects is a subset of the set.

4. Answers will vary.

6. Neither permutations nor combinations allow repetition of an object selected.

8. $10! = 10 \cdot 9 \cdot 8 \cdot \ \ldots \ \cdot 1 = 3,628,800$

10. $12! = 12 \cdot 11 \cdot 10 \cdot \ \ldots \ \cdot 1 = 479,001,600$

12. $\dfrac{14!}{12!} = \dfrac{14 \cdot 13 \cdot 12!}{12!}$

$= 182$

14. $\dfrac{6!}{4!2!} = \dfrac{6 \cdot 5 \cdot 4!}{2 \cdot 4!}$

$= 15$

16. $\dfrac{8!}{3!(8-3)!} = \dfrac{8!}{3!5!} = \dfrac{8 \cdot 7 \cdot 6 \cdot 5!}{6 \cdot 5!}$

$= 56$

18. Number 12: incorrect. "14 nPr 12" $= \dfrac{14!}{(14-12)!}$ Number 14: incorrect. "6!/4!2!" is interpreted as $\dfrac{6!}{4!} \cdot 2!$.

Number 16: correct.

20. $C_{20,10} = \dfrac{20!}{10!(20-10)!} = \dfrac{20!}{10!10!} = \dfrac{2.432902008 \times 10^{18}}{(3,628,800)^2} = 184,756$

22. $C_{20,4} = \dfrac{20!}{4!(20-4)!} = \dfrac{20!}{4!16!} = \dfrac{20 \cdot 19 \cdot 18 \cdot 17 \cdot 16!}{4 \cdot 3 \cdot 2 \cdot 1 \cdot 16!} = \dfrac{116,280}{24} = 4,845$

24. $P_{11,3} = \dfrac{11!}{(11-3)!} = \dfrac{11!}{8!} = \dfrac{11 \cdot 10 \cdot 9 \cdot 8!}{8!} = 990$ **26.** $P_{11,8} = \dfrac{11!}{(11-8)!} = \dfrac{11!}{3!} = \dfrac{39,916,800}{6} = 6,652,800$

28. (A) Renting 4 videos would be a combination since they are chosen in any order.
(B) Buying 4 videos for 4 different people would be a permutation since if you mix up how they are given out, the results differ.

30. $3 \cdot 5 \cdot 2 = 30$ **32.** $P_{50,5} = \dfrac{50!}{(50-5)!} = \dfrac{50 \cdot 49 \cdot 48 \cdot 47 \cdot 46 \cdot 45!}{45!} = 254,251,200$

34. (A) $P_{9,3} = \dfrac{9!}{6!} = 504$ (B) $C_{9,3} = \dfrac{9!}{3!6!} = 84$ **36.** $C_{7,2} = = \dfrac{7!}{2!5!} = 21$

38. $P_{7,5} = \dfrac{7!}{2!} = 2520$ with no digit repeated   **40.** $P_{10,3} = \dfrac{10!}{7!} = 720$ with no digit repeated

$7 \cdot 7 \cdot 7 \cdot 7 \cdot 7 = 7^5 = 16,807$ with repeated digits $10 \cdot 10 \cdot 10 = 10^3 = 1000$ with repeated digits

42. $C_{12,5} = \dfrac{12!}{5!7!} = 792$ with all face cards

$C_{8,5} = \dfrac{8!}{5!3!} = 56$ with only jacks and queens

44. $10 \cdot 10 \cdot 10 \cdot 10 \cdot 10 = 10^5 = 100,000$ possible 5 digit zip codes

$P_{10,5} = \dfrac{10!}{5!} = 30,240$ contain no repeated digits

46. $C_{13,2} \cdot C_{13,3} = \dfrac{13!}{2!11!} \cdot \dfrac{13!}{3!10!} = 22,308$ **48.** $P_{12,2} \cdot P_{15,2} \cdot P_{18,2} = \dfrac{12!}{10!} \cdot \dfrac{15!}{13!} \cdot \dfrac{18!}{16!} = 8,482,320$

50. (A) As the tables show, they are equal.

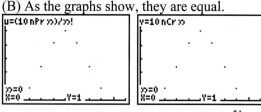

$\dfrac{P_{10,n}}{n!} = \dfrac{10!}{(10-n)!n!} = C_{10,n}$

(B) As the graphs show, they are equal.

52. $6 \cdot 5 = 30$ **54.** (A) $C_{5,2} = \dfrac{5!}{2!3!} = 10$ (B) $C_{5,3} = \dfrac{5!}{3!2!} = 10$ **56.** $2 \cdot 5!5! = 28,800$

58. (A) $C_{9,4} = \dfrac{9!}{4!5!} = 126$ (B) $C_{7,2} = \dfrac{7!}{2!5!} = 21$ (C) $2C_{7,3} = \dfrac{2 \cdot 7!}{3!4!} = 70$

60. There are $C_{26,10} = 5,311,735$ hands whose cards are all red and $C_{48,6} = 12,271,512$ hands containing all four aces, so the hand with four aces is more likely.

Section 8–5

2. Answers will vary.
4. An equally likely assumption is the assumption that each simple event is as likely to occur as any other.

6. A suitable sample space is $S = \{1, 2, 3, 4, 5, 6\}$. Assigning the probability of $\dfrac{1}{6}$ to each simple event in S,

we find that $E = \{4, 5, 6\}$ has probability $\dfrac{1}{6} + \dfrac{1}{6} + \dfrac{1}{6} = \dfrac{1}{2}$.

8. Since there are 52 equally likely cards and 13 of them are clubs, the event of drawing a club has probability

$\dfrac{13}{52} = \dfrac{1}{4}$.

10. A suitable sample space is $S = \{HH, HT, TH, TT\}$. Assigning the probability of $\dfrac{1}{4}$ to each simple event in

S, we find that $E = \{HT, TH\}$ has probability $\dfrac{1}{2}$.

12. A suitable sample space has the 36 elements shown in Example 2 of the text. Assigning the probability of

$\dfrac{1}{36}$ to each simple event in this space, we find that $E = \{(6,6)\}$ has probability $\dfrac{1}{36}$.

14. Since there are 52 equally likely cards and 4 twos, 4 threes, and so on, up to 4 10s, a total of 36 numbered

cards, the event of drawing a numbered card has probability $\dfrac{36}{52} = \dfrac{9}{13}$.

16. A suitable sample space is $S = \{HHH, HHT, HTH, HTT, THH, THT, TTH, TTT\}$. Assigning the

probability of $\dfrac{1}{8}$ to each simple event in S, we find that the probability of $E = \{TTT\}$ is $\dfrac{1}{8}$.

18. $P(E) = 0 \Rightarrow E$ is an impossible event, it cannot happen.

20.
$$\begin{aligned} P(\text{not Blue}) &= P(R) + P(G) + P(Y) \\ &= .26 + .14 + .30 \\ &= .7 \end{aligned}$$

22. $P(\text{not } R \text{ or not } Y) = P(G) + P(B) = .14 + .30 = .44$

24. $P(E) = \dfrac{f(E)}{n} = \dfrac{560}{4000} = .14$ **26.** $P(E) = \dfrac{f(E)}{n} = \dfrac{2400}{3000} = .8$

28. $\dfrac{1}{P_{10,5}} = \dfrac{1}{30,240} \approx .000033$ **30.** $\dfrac{C_{13,5}}{C_{52,5}} = \dfrac{1287}{2,598,960} \approx .000495$ **32.** $\dfrac{C_{40,5}}{C_{52,5}} = \dfrac{658,008}{2,598,960} \approx .25$

34. It is an acceptable sample space since these are all possible numbers of black cards in a 5−card hand. It is
not an equally likely sample space—it's far less likely to get five black cards than one or two.

36. $\dfrac{4^4}{6^4} = \dfrac{256}{1296} \approx .198$ **38.** $\dfrac{1}{P_{6,6}} = \dfrac{1}{6!} = \dfrac{1}{720} \approx .00139$

40. $E = $ sum of a and b is 5   **42.** $E = $ sum of a and b is less than 6
$E = \{(1, 4), (2, 3), (3, 2), (4, 1)\}$ $E = \{(1, 1), (2, 1), (3, 1), (4, 1), (1, 2), (2, 2), (3, 2), (1, 3), (2, 3), (1, 4)\}$
$n(E): 4$ $n(E): 10$
$P(E) = \dfrac{n(E)}{n(S)} = \dfrac{4}{36} = \dfrac{1}{9}$ $P(E) = \dfrac{n(E)}{n(S)} = \dfrac{10}{36} = \dfrac{5}{18}$

44. E = product of a and b is 6
$E = \{(1, 6), (2, 3), (3, 2), (6, 1)\}$
$n(E)$: 4

$$P(E) = \frac{n(E)}{n(S)} = \frac{4}{36} = \frac{1}{9}$$

46. E = product of a and b is greater than 15
$E = \{(6, 3), (4, 4), (5, 4), (6, 4), (4, 5), (5, 5), (6, 5), (3, 6), (4, 6), (5, 6), (6, 6)\}$
$n(E)$: 11

$$P(E) = \frac{n(E)}{n(S)} = \frac{11}{36}$$

48. E: $a \neq b$.
Since $n(\overline{E}) = 6$ (see problem 47),
$n(E) = 36 - 6 = 30$.

$$P(E) = \frac{n(E)}{n(S)} = \frac{30}{36} = \frac{5}{6}$$

50. E = exactly one of a or b is a 6
$E = \{(6, 1), (6, 2), (6, 3), (6, 4), (6, 5), (5, 6), (4, 6), (3, 6), (2, 6), (1, 6)\}$
$n(E)$: 10

$$P(E) = \frac{n(E)}{n(S)} = \frac{10}{36} = \frac{5}{18}$$

52. $S = \{C_1, C_2, C_3\}$ where C_i represents candidate i

$$P(C_1) = P(C_2) = \frac{2}{5}$$

$$P(C_3) = \frac{1}{5}$$

54. (A) $P(E) = \dfrac{f(E)}{n}$

$P(3 \text{ heads}) = \dfrac{58}{500} = .116$

$P(2 \text{ heads}) = \dfrac{198}{500} = .396$

$P(1 \text{ head}) = \dfrac{190}{500} = .38$

$P(0 \text{ heads}) = \dfrac{54}{500} = .108$

(B) $S = \{(H, H, H), (H, H, T), (H, T, T),$
$(H, T, H), (T, H, H), (T, H, T),$
$(T, T, H), (T, T, T)\}$

$P(3 \text{ heads}) = \dfrac{1}{8} = .125$

$P(2 \text{ heads}) = \dfrac{3}{8} = .375$

$P(1 \text{ head}) = \dfrac{3}{8} = .375$

$P(0 \text{ heads}) = \dfrac{1}{8} = .125$

(C) Expected frequencies: $n \cdot P(E)$

$E(3 \text{ heads}) = 500\left(\dfrac{1}{8}\right) = 62.5$

$E(2 \text{ heads}) = 500\left(\dfrac{3}{8}\right) = 187.5$

$E(1 \text{ head}) = 500\left(\dfrac{3}{8}\right) = 187.5$

$E(0 \text{ heads}) = 500\left(\dfrac{1}{8}\right) = 62.5$

(D) Let 0 represent tails and 1 represent heads, then a random sequence of 0's and 1's can be used to represent repeated tosses of one coin. Answers may vary. See the discussion following example 7.

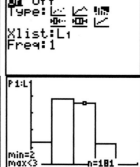

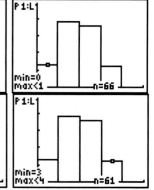

56.   (A) $P(E) = \dfrac{1}{36} \approx .028$; in 12 rolls, $P(E) = \dfrac{12}{432}$. In order to get 9 double sixes in 12 rolls, the probability would need to be $\dfrac{3}{4}$, so it is not very likely.

(B) $\dfrac{14}{40} = .35$ is far greater than .028. It would appear that the dice were loaded. The empirical probability

for $P(12) = \dfrac{14}{40} = .35$. (The expected frequency for non−loaded dice would be $\left(\dfrac{1}{36}\right)(40) = \dfrac{10}{9}$.)

Sample space for 58 − 62: {(H, H, H), (H, T, H), (T, T, H), (T, H, H)}

58. $P(E) = \dfrac{n(E)}{n(S)} = \dfrac{2}{4} = \dfrac{1}{2}$, $E = 2$ heads   **60.** $P(E) = \dfrac{n(E)}{n(S)} = \dfrac{0}{4} = 0$, $E = 0$ heads(there is always 1 H)

62. $P(E) = \dfrac{n(E)}{n(S)} = \dfrac{1}{4}$, $E = $ more than $1(= 2)$ tails

Sample space for 64 − 70: {(1, 1), (1, 1), (1, 2), (1, 2), (1, 3), (1, 3), (2, 1), (2, 1), (2, 2), (2, 2), (2, 3), (2, 3), (3, 1), (3, 1), (3, 2), (3, 2), (3, 3), (3, 3)}

64. $P(E) = \dfrac{n(E)}{n(S)} = \dfrac{4}{18} = \dfrac{2}{9}$, $E = $ sum of 3   **66.** $P(E) = \dfrac{n(E)}{n(S)} = \dfrac{4}{18} = \dfrac{2}{9}$, $E = $ sum of 5

68. $P(E) = \dfrac{n(E)}{n(S)} = \dfrac{0}{18} = 0$, $E = $ sum of 7   **70.** $P(E) = \dfrac{n(E)}{n(S)} = \dfrac{10}{18} = \dfrac{5}{9}$, $E = $ even sum

72. $\dfrac{C_{36,5}}{C_{52,5}} = \dfrac{376{,}992}{2{,}598{,}960} \approx .145$ **74.** $\dfrac{(13)(48)}{C_{52,5}} = \dfrac{624}{2{,}598{,}960} \approx .00024$

76. $\dfrac{4}{C_{52,5}} = \dfrac{4}{2{,}598{,}960} \approx .0000015$ **78.** $\dfrac{C_{4,2} \cdot C_{4,3}}{C_{52,5}} = \dfrac{(6)(4)}{2{,}598{,}960} \approx .000009$

80. (A) $\dfrac{10}{1000} = .01$

(B) $\dfrac{15 + 1 + 80 + 12}{1000} = \dfrac{108}{1000} = .108$

(C) $\dfrac{0 + 40 + 51 + 11 + 0 + 0 + 70 + 80 + 15 + 1 + 130 + 80 + 28}{1000} = \dfrac{506}{1000} = .506$

(D) $\dfrac{1000 - (1 + 12 + 21 + 20)}{1000} = \dfrac{946}{1000} = .946$

Section 8-6

2. Binomial coefficients are the values of the combination formula that form the coefficients in a binomial expansion.

4. Use the sixth row of Pascal's triangle as the coefficients and write
$(a + b)^5 = a^5 + 5a^4b + 10a^3b^2 + 10a^2b^3 + 5ab^4 + b^5$.

For Problems 6—12, the first ten lines of Pascal's triangle are as follows:

```
0            1
1           1  1
2          1  2  1
3         1  3  3  1
4        1  4  6  4  1
5       1  5 10 10  5  1
6      1  6 15 20 15  6  1
7    1  7 21 35 35 21  7  1
8  1  8 28 56 70 56 28  8  1
9 1  9 36 84 126 126 84 36  9  1
```

6. $\dbinom{8}{4}$ is the fifth entry in line 8 (start counting from 0) of the triangle. 70.

8. $\dbinom{9}{7}$ is the eighth entry in line 9 (start counting from 0) of the triangle. 36.

10. $C_{7,3}$ is the fourth entry in line 7 (start counting from 0) of the triangle. 35.

12. $C_{10,10}$ is the eleventh entry in line 10 (not shown) of the triangle. As the outside entry, it must be 1.

14. $\dbinom{13}{9} = \dfrac{13!}{9!(13-9)!} = \dfrac{13!}{9!4!} = \dfrac{13 \cdot 12 \cdot 11 \cdot 10 \cdot 9!}{9!4 \cdot 3 \cdot 2 \cdot 1} = \dfrac{17{,}160}{24} = 715$ **16.** $\dbinom{12}{11} = \dfrac{12!}{11!(12-11)!} = \dfrac{12!}{11!1!} = \dfrac{12 \cdot 11!}{11!} = 12$

18. $C_{52,4} = \dfrac{52!}{4!(52-4)!} = \dfrac{52!}{4!48!} = \dfrac{52 \cdot 51 \cdot 50 \cdot 49 \cdot 48!}{4 \cdot 3 \cdot 2 \cdot 1 \cdot 48!} = \dfrac{6{,}497{,}400}{24} = 270{,}725$ **20.** $C_{12,11} = \dbinom{12}{11} = 12$ from problem 16.

22. $(x+2)^3 = x^3 + \dfrac{3!}{2!1!} x^2 \cdot 2 + \dfrac{3!}{1!2!} x \cdot 2^2 + 2^3 = x^3 + 6x^2 + 12x + 8$

24. $(3u+2v)^3 = (3u)^3 + \dfrac{3!}{2!1!}(3u)^2(2v) + \dfrac{3!}{1!2!}(3u)(2v)^2 + (2v)^3 = 27u^3 + 54u^2v + 36uv^2 + 8v^3$

26. $(x-y)^4 = x^4 + \dfrac{4!}{3!1!}x^3(-y) + \dfrac{4!}{2!2!}x^2(-y)^2 + \dfrac{4!}{1!3!}x(-y)^3 + (-y)^4 = x^4 - 4x^3y + 6x^2y^2 - 4xy^3 + y^4$

28. $(3p-q)^4 = (3p)^4 + \dfrac{4!}{3!1!}(3p)^3(-q) + \dfrac{4!}{2!2!}(3p)^2(-q)^2 + \dfrac{4!}{1!3!}(3p)(-q)^3 + (-q)^4$

$\qquad = 81p^4 - 108p^3q + 54p^2q^2 - 12pq^3 + q^4$

30. $(2x-1)^5 = (2x)^5 + \dfrac{5!}{4!1!}(2x)^4(-1) + \dfrac{5!}{3!2!}(2x)^3(-1)^2 + \dfrac{5!}{2!3!}(2x)^2(-1)^3 + \dfrac{5!}{1!4!}(2x)(-1)^4 + (-1)^5$

$\qquad = 32x^5 - 80x^4 + 80x^3 - 40x^2 + 10x - 1$

32. $(2x-y)^6 = (2x)^6 + \dfrac{6!}{5!1!}(2x)^5(-y) + \dfrac{6!}{4!2!}(2x)^4(-y)^2 + \dfrac{6!}{3!3!}(2x)^3(-y)^3 + \dfrac{6!}{2!4!}(2x)^2(-y)^4 + \dfrac{6!}{1!5!}(2x)^1(-y)^5 + (-y)^6$

$\qquad = 64x^6 - 192x^5y + 240x^4y^2 - 160x^3y^3 + 60x^2y^4 - 12xy^5 + y^6$

34. $(x+1)^8$; x^5

In the expansion $(x+1)^8 = \displaystyle\sum_{k=0}^{8} \dbinom{8}{k} x^{8-k} \cdot 1^k$, the exponent of x is 5 when $k = 3$.

Thus, the term containing x^5 is $\dbinom{8}{3} x^5 \cdot 1^3 = 56x^5$

36. $(3x+1)^{12}$; x^7

In the expansion $(3x+1)^{12} = \displaystyle\sum_{k=0}^{12} \dbinom{12}{k}(3x)^{12-k} \cdot 1^k$ the exponent of x is 7 when $k = 5$.

Thus, the term containing x^7 is $\dbinom{12}{5}(3x)^7 \cdot 1^5 = 792 \cdot 2187x^7 = 1{,}732{,}104x^7$

38. $(3x-2)^{17}$; x^5

In the expansion $(3x-2)^{17} = \displaystyle\sum_{k=0}^{17} \dbinom{17}{k}(3x)^{17-k} \cdot (-2)^k$, the exponent of x is 5 when $k = 12$.

Thus, the term containing x^5 is $\dbinom{17}{12}(3x)^5(-2)^{12} = (6188)(243)(4096)x^5 = 6{,}159{,}089{,}664x^5$

40. $(x^2-1)^9$; x^7

Since all terms contain $(x^2)^n = x^{2n}$, the expansion cannot have a term with x^7.

42. $(x^2+1)^{10}$; x^{14}

In the expansion $(x^2+1)^{10} = \displaystyle\sum_{k=0}^{10} \dbinom{10}{k}(x^2)^{10-k}(1)^k$, the exponent of x is 14 when $(x^2)^7$, so $k = 3$.

Thus, the term containing x^{14} is $\dbinom{10}{3}(x^2)^7(1)^3 = 120x^{14}$

44. $(a+b)^{12}$: fifth term $= \dbinom{12}{4} a^8b^4 = 495a^8b^4$ **46.** $(x+2y)^{20}$: third term $= \dbinom{20}{2} x^{18}(2y)^2 = 760x^{18}y^2$

48. $(x-3)^{10}$: fourth term $= \begin{pmatrix} 10 \\ 3 \end{pmatrix}(x^7)(-3)^3 = -3240x^7$ **50.** $(2p-3q)^7$: fourth term $= \begin{pmatrix} 7 \\ 3 \end{pmatrix}(2p)^4(-3q)^3 = -15{,}120p^4q^3$

52. $f(x) = x^4$

$$\frac{f(x+h)-f(x)}{h} = \frac{(x+h)^4 - x^4}{h} = \frac{\left(x^4 + \binom{4}{1}x^3h + \binom{4}{2}x^2h^2 + \binom{4}{3}xh^3 + h^4\right) - x^4}{h}$$

$$= \frac{(x^4 + 4x^3h + 6x^2h^2 + 4xh^3 + h^4) - x^4}{h} = \frac{4x^3h + 6x^2h^2 + 4xh^3 + h^4}{h}$$

$$= 4x^3 + 6x^2h + 4xh^2 + h^3$$

As $h \to 0$, $4x^3 + 6x^2h + 4xh^2 + h^3 \to 4x^3$

54. $f(x) = x^6$

$$\frac{f(x+h)-f(x)}{h} = \frac{(x+h)^6 - x^6}{h} = \frac{\left(x^6 + \binom{6}{1}x^5h + \binom{6}{2}x^4h^2 + \binom{6}{3}x^3h^3 + \binom{6}{4}x^2h^4 + \binom{6}{5}xh^5 + h^6\right) - x^6}{h}$$

$$= \frac{(x^6 + 6x^5h + 15x^4h^2 + 20x^3h^3 + 15x^2h^4 + 6xh^5 + h^6) - x^6}{h}$$

$$= \frac{6x^5h + 15x^4h^2 + 20x^3h^3 + 15x^2h^4 + 6xh^5 + h^6}{h}$$

$$= 6x^5 + 15x^4h + 20x^3h^2 + 15x^2h^3 + 6xh^4 + h^5$$

As $h \to 0$, $6x^5 + 15x^4h + 20x^3h^2 + 15x^2h^3 + 6xh^4 + h^5 \to 6x^5$

56.

```
WINDOW
 nMin=1
 nMax=40
 PlotStart=1
 PlotStep=1
 Xmin=-1
 Xmax=40
↓Xscl=0▮
```

```
 n    │ u(n)
 17   │ 8.9E10
 18   │ 1.1E11
 19   │ 1.3E11
 20   │ 1.4E11
 21   │ 1.3E11
 22   │ 1.1E11
 23   │ 8.9E10
n=17
```

```
WINDOW
↑PlotStep=1
 Xmin=-1
 Xmax=40
 Xscl=0
 Ymin=-1
 Ymax=(1ᴇ12)/6
 Yscl=0
```

```
40 nCr 20
        1.378465288ᴇ11
Ans/2
        6.892326441ᴇ10
▮
```

```
Plot1 Plot2 Plot3
 nMin=0
\u(n)❚(40 nCr n)
 u(nMin)❚
\v(n)=▮
 v(nMin)=
\w(n)=
```

```
u=(40nCr n)
              ×
   n=20
   X=20         Y=1.3785E11
```

As both the graph and table show, $\begin{pmatrix} 40 \\ 20 \end{pmatrix} = 1.378465288 \times 10^{11}$ is the largest term and one half of this largest

term is $6.892326441 \times 10^{10}$. An examination of the table shows $\begin{pmatrix} 40 \\ 17 \end{pmatrix}$ through $\begin{pmatrix} 40 \\ 23 \end{pmatrix}$, a total of 7 terms, have

values larger than one half the largest term.

58. (A)

k	$\begin{pmatrix} 10 \\ k \end{pmatrix} \cdot (0.3)^{10-k} \cdot (0.7)^k$
0	5.9049×10^{-6}
1	1.37781×10^{-4}
2	0.0014467005
3	0.009001692
4	0.036756909
5	0.1029193452
6	0.200120949
7	0.266827932 ← largest
8	0.2334744405
9	0.121060821
10	0.0282475249
	1.000000000

```
                   0.4
u=(10nCr n)*.3^(10-n)*._
                   ×
-1                          12
  n=7
  X=7          Y=.26682793
                  -0.05
```

$a_7 \approx 0.267$

(B)   According to the binomial formula, the sum of $a_0 + a_1 + a_2 + \ldots + a_{10} = 1$.

60. $(0.99)^6 = (1 - 0.01)^6 = 1^6 + \dfrac{6!}{5!1!}(1)^5(-0.01) + \dfrac{6!}{4!2!}(1)^4(-0.01)^2 + \dfrac{6!}{3!3!}(1)^3(-0.01)^3$

$$+ \dfrac{6!}{2!4!}(1)^2(-0.01)^4 + \dfrac{6!}{1!5!}(1)(-0.01)^5 + (-0.01)^6$$

$$= 1 - 0.06 + 0.0015 - 0.00002 + 0.00000015 - 0.0000000006 + 0.000000000001$$

$$\approx 0.9414801494$$

$$= 0.9415 \text{ to four decimal places}$$

62. $\dbinom{n}{0} = \dfrac{n!}{0!(n-0)!} = \dfrac{n!}{n!} = 1$ **64.** $\dbinom{k}{0} = \dfrac{k!}{0!(k-0)!} = \dfrac{k!}{k!} = 1$

$\dbinom{n}{n} = \dfrac{n!}{n!(n-n)!} = \dfrac{n!}{n!0!} = 1$ $\dbinom{k+1}{0} = \dfrac{(k+1)!}{0!(k+1-0)!} = \dfrac{(k+1)!}{(k+1)!} = 1$

66. $\dfrac{n-r+1}{r}\dbinom{n}{r-1} = \dfrac{n-r+1}{r} \cdot \dfrac{n!}{(r-1)!(n-(r-1))!} = \dfrac{n-r+1}{r(r-1)!} \cdot \dfrac{n!}{(n-r+1)!}$

$$= \dfrac{n-r+1}{r!} \cdot \dfrac{n!}{(n-r+1)(n-r)!} = \dfrac{n!}{r!(n-r)!} = \dbinom{n}{r}$$

68. $0 = (1-1)^n = \displaystyle\sum_{k=0}^{n} \dbinom{n}{k}1^{n-k}(-1)^k = \dbinom{n}{0}1^n(-1)^0 + \dbinom{n}{1}1^{n-1}(-1)^1 + \dbinom{n}{2}1^{n-2}(-1)^2 + \ldots + \dbinom{n}{n}1^0(-1)^n$

$$= \dbinom{n}{0} - \dbinom{n}{1} + \dbinom{n}{2} - \ldots + (-1)^n\dbinom{n}{n}$$

Chapter 8 Group Activity

(A)   4, 14, 46, 146, 454, 1394   (B) $(-1)2^{100} + 2 \cdot 3^{100} \approx 1.031 \times 10^{48}$

(C)   Start with $5a_{n-1} - 6a_{n-2}$. This equals $5(u2^{n-1} + v3^{n-1}) - 6(u2^{n-2} + v3^{n-2})$

$$= u(5 \cdot 2^{n-1} - 6 \cdot 2^{n-2}) + v(5 \cdot 3^{n-1} - 6 \cdot 3^{n-2})$$

$$= u(4 \cdot 2^{n-2}) + v(9 \cdot 3^{n-2})$$

$$= u(2^2 \cdot 2^{n-2}) + v(3^2 \cdot 3^{n-2})$$

$$= u2^n + v3^n = a_n$$

(D)   If $\{r^n\}$ satisfies $b_n = 3b_{n-1} + 4b_{n-2}$, then

$$r^n = 3r^{n-1} + 4r^{n-2}$$

$$r^2 = 3r + 4$$

$$r^2 - 3r - 4 = 0$$

$$r = 4 \text{ or } r = -1$$

Therefore, $\{4^n\}$ and $\{-1\}^n$ satisfy the recursion formula, hence so does $\{u4^n + v(-1)^n\}$.
We now find u and v so that the first two terms of $\{u4^n + v(-1)^n\}$ are 5 and 55. Letting $n = 1$ and $n = 2$ yields

$$4u - v = 5$$

$$16u + v = 55$$

Solving yields $u = 3$, $v = 7$. Therefore, an nth term formula for the original sequence is $b_n = 3 \cdot 4^n + 7(-1)^n$.

(E)   If $\{r^n\}$ satisfies $a_n = a_{n-1} + a_{n-2}$ (Fibonacci sequence), then

$$r^n = r^{n-1} + r^{n-2}$$

$$r^2 = r + 1$$

$$r^2 - r - 1 = 0$$

$$r = \dfrac{1+\sqrt{5}}{2} \text{ or } r = \dfrac{1-\sqrt{5}}{2}$$

Therefore $\left\{\left(\dfrac{1+\sqrt{5}}{2}\right)^{n}\right\}$ and $\left\{\left(\dfrac{1-\sqrt{5}}{2}\right)^{n}\right\}$ satisfy the recursion formula, hence so does $\left\{u\left(\dfrac{1+\sqrt{5}}{2}\right)^{n}+v\left(\dfrac{1-\sqrt{5}}{2}\right)^{n}\right\}$.

We now find u and v so that the first two terms of $\left\{u\left(\dfrac{1+\sqrt{5}}{2}\right)^{n}+v\left(\dfrac{1-\sqrt{5}}{2}\right)^{n}\right\}$ are 1 and 1 (Fibonacci sequence).

Letting $n = 1$ and $n = 2$ yields

$$u\left(\frac{1+\sqrt{5}}{2}\right)+v\left(\frac{1-\sqrt{5}}{2}\right) = 1 \qquad E_1$$

$$u\left(\frac{1+\sqrt{5}}{2}\right)^{2}+v\left(\frac{1-\sqrt{5}}{2}\right)^{2} = 1 \qquad E_2$$

Solving (steps omitted) gives $u = \dfrac{1}{\sqrt{5}} \quad v = -\dfrac{1}{\sqrt{5}}$

Therefore, an nth term formula for the Fibonacci sequence is given by $\left\{\dfrac{1}{\sqrt{5}}\left(\dfrac{1+\sqrt{5}}{2}\right)^{n}-\dfrac{1}{\sqrt{5}}\left(\dfrac{1-\sqrt{5}}{2}\right)^{n}\right\}$

(F)   Outline of solution: The geometric sequence $\{r^n\}$ that satisfies
$c_n = 6c_{n-1} - 3c_{n-2} - 10c_{n-3}$ is given by
$r^3 = 6r^2 - 3r - 10$
$r^3 - 6r^2 + 3r + 10 = 0$
$r = -1$ or $r = 2$ or $r = 5$
Therefore, the required sequence is of form $\{u(-1)^n + v2^n + w5^n\}$.
u, v, w must satisfy
$u(-1) + v \cdot 2 + w \cdot 5 = -3$
$u(-1)^2 + v \cdot 2^2 + w \cdot 5^2 = 15$
$u(-1)^3 + v \cdot 2^3 + w \cdot 5^3 = 99$
Simplifying yields
$$-u + 2v + 5w = -3$$
$$u + 4v + 25w = 15$$
$$-u + 8v + 125w = 99$$
Solving yields $u = 2$, $v = -3$, $w = 1$. Hence the required sequence is $\{2(-1)^n - 3 \cdot 2^n + 5^n\}$.

APPENDIX A - CUMULATIVE REVIEWS

Chapters 1-3 Cumulative Review

1.

$$\frac{7x}{5} - \frac{3+2x}{2} = \frac{x-10}{3} + 2$$

$$30\frac{7x}{5} - 30\frac{(3+2x)}{2} = 30\frac{(x-10)}{3} + 2(30)$$

$$42x - 15(3+2x) = 10(x-10) + 60$$

$$42x - 45 - 30x = 10x - 100 + 60$$

$$12x - 45 = 10x - 40$$

$$2x = 5$$

$$x = \frac{5}{2} \qquad (1\text{--}1)$$

2.

$$2(3-y) + 4 \le 5 - y$$
$$6 - 2y + 4 \le 5 - y$$
$$-2y + 10 \le 5 - y$$
$$-y \le -5$$
$$y \ge 5$$

$[5, \infty)$

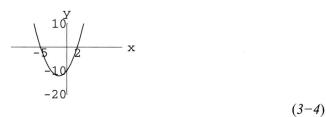

$(1\text{--}2)$

3. $|x-2| \quad < 7$

$$-7 < x - 2 < 7$$
$$-5 < x < 9$$

$(-5, 9)$

$(1\text{--}3)$

4. $x^3 + 3x \ge 10$

$f(x) = x^2 + 3x - 10 \ge 0$

$f(x) = (x+5)(x-2) \ge 0$

The zeros of f are -5 and 2.

Plotting the graph of $f(x)$, we see that $f(x) \ge 0$
for $x \le -5$ and $x \ge 2$, or $(-\infty, -5] \cup [2, \infty)$.

$(3\text{--}4)$

5. (A) $(2 - 3i) - (-5 + 7i) = 2 - 3i + 5 - 7i = 7 - 10i$

(B) $(1 + 4i)(3 - 5i) = 3 + 7i - 20i^2 = 3 + 7i + 20 = 23 + 7i$

(C) $\dfrac{5+i}{2+3i} = \dfrac{(5+i)}{(2+3i)}\dfrac{(2-3i)}{(2-3i)} = \dfrac{10-13i-3i^2}{4-9i^2} = \dfrac{10-13i+3}{4+9} = \dfrac{13-13i}{13} = 1 - i$

$(1\text{--}4)$

6.

$$3x^2 = -12x$$
$$3x^2 + 12x = 0$$
$$3x(x+4) = 0$$
$$3x = 0 \text{ or } x + 4 = 0$$
$$x = 0 \qquad x = -4 \qquad (1\text{--}5)$$

7.

$$4x^2 - 20 = 0$$
$$4x^2 = 20$$
$$x^2 = 5$$
$$x = \pm\sqrt{5} \qquad (1\text{--}5)$$

8.

$$x^2 - 6x + 2 = 0$$
$$x^2 - 6x = -2$$
$$x^2 - 6x + 9 = 7$$
$$(x-3)^2 = 7$$
$$x - 3 = \pm\sqrt{7}$$
$$x = 3 \pm \sqrt{7} \qquad (1\text{--}5)$$

9.

$$x - \sqrt{12-x} = 0$$
$$x = \sqrt{12-x}$$
$$x^2 = 12 - x$$
$$x^2 + x - 12 = 0$$
$$(x+4)(x-3) = 0$$
$$x = -4, 3$$

Check:

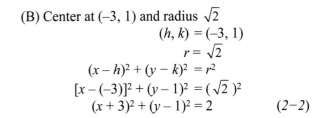

$$-4 - \sqrt{12-(-4)} \overset{?}{=} 0$$
$$-4 - 4 \overset{?}{=} 0$$
$$-8 \neq 0$$
$$3 - \sqrt{12-3} \overset{?}{=} 0$$
$$3 - 3 \overset{?}{=} 0$$
$$0 \overset{\checkmark}{=} 0$$

Solution: 3   (1–6)

10. (A) $d(A, B) = \sqrt{(5-3)^2 + (6-2)^2} = \sqrt{4+16} = \sqrt{20} = 2\sqrt{5}$

(B) $m = \dfrac{6-2}{5-3} = \dfrac{4}{2} = 2$

(C) The slope m_1 of a line perpendicular to AB must satisfy $m_1(2) = -1$. Therefore $m_1 = -\dfrac{1}{2}$ (2–2, 3–3)

11. (A) Center at $(0, 0)$ and radius $\sqrt{2}$

$$x^2 + y^2 = r^2$$
$$x^2 + y^2 = (\sqrt{2})^2$$
$$x^2 + y^2 = 2$$

(B) Center at $(-3, 1)$ and radius $\sqrt{2}$

$$(h, k) = (-3, 1)$$
$$r = \sqrt{2}$$
$$(x-h)^2 + (y-k)^2 = r^2$$
$$[x-(-3)]^2 + (y-1)^2 = (\sqrt{2})^2$$
$$(x+3)^2 + (y-1)^2 = 2$$ (2–2)

12.

$$2x - 3y = 6$$
$$-3y = -2x + 6$$
$$y = \frac{2}{3}x - 2$$

slope: $\dfrac{2}{3}$ y intercept: -2 x intercept: 3 (if $y = 0$, $2x = 6$, hence $x = 3$)

x	y
-3	-4
0	-2
3	0

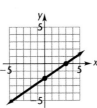

(2–3)

13. (A) A function; domain = $\{1, 2, 3\}$; range = $\{1\}$
(B) Not a function (three range values correspond to the only domain value)
(C) A function; domain = $\{-2, -1, 0, 1, 2\}$; range = $\{-1, 0, 2\}$ (3–1)

14. (A) $f(-2) = (-2)^2 - 2(-2) + 5 = 13$
    $g(3) = 3\cdot3 - 2 = 7$
    Therefore $f(-2) + g(3) = 13 + 7 = 20$
(B) $(f+g)(x) = f(x) + g(x) = x^2 - 2x + 5 + 3x - 2 = x^2 + x + 3$
(C) $(f \circ g)(x) = f[g(x)] = f(3x-2) = (3x-2)^2 - 2(3x-2) + 5 = 9x^2 - 12x + 4 - 6x + 4 + 5$
$$= 9x^2 - 18x + 13$$
(D) $\dfrac{f(a+h) - f(a)}{h} = \dfrac{[(a+h)^2 - 2(a+h) + 5] - (a^2 - 2a + 5)}{h} = \dfrac{a^2 + 2ah + h^2 - 2a - 2h + 5 - a^2 + 2a - 5}{h}$

$$= \frac{2ah + h^2 - 2h}{h} = \frac{h(2a+h-2)}{h} = 2a + h - 2$$ (3–1, 3–5)

15. (A) Stretched vertically by a factor of 2.   (B) Shifted right 2 units
(C) Shifted down 2 units   *(3–3)*

16. Domain: [–2, 3] Range: [–1, 2]   *(3–2)*

17. $f(2) = 2$, $f(-2) = -1$.
Therefore it is false to assert either that $f(x) = f(-x)$ for all x in the domain of f or that $-f(x) = f(-x)$ for all x in the domain of f. Thus f is neither even nor odd.   *(3–3)*

18. (A) The graph of $f(x)$ is shifted left one unit and   (B) The graph of $f(x)$ is stretched by a factor of two with
reflected across the x axis.   respect to the y axis and shifted down two units.

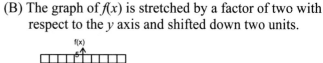

(3–3)

19.
$$\frac{x+3}{2x+2} + \frac{5x+2}{3x+3} = \frac{5}{6}$$

$$\frac{(x+3)}{2(x+1)} + \frac{(5x+2)}{3(x+1)} = \frac{5}{6} \quad \text{LCD: } 6(x+1) \quad \text{Excluded value: } x \neq -1$$

$$6(x+1)\frac{(x+3)}{2(x+1)} + 6(x+1)\frac{(5x+2)}{3(x+1)} = 6(x+1)\frac{5}{6}$$

$$3(x+3) + 2(5x+2) = 5(x+1)$$
$$3x + 9 + 10x + 4 = 5x + 5$$
$$13x + 13 = 5x + 5$$
$$8x = -8$$
$$x = -1$$

No solution: -1 is excluded   *(1–1)*

20.
$$\frac{3}{x} = \frac{6}{x+1} - \frac{1}{x-1} \text{ Excluded values: } x \neq 0, 1, -1$$

$$x(x+1)(x-1)\frac{3}{x} = x(x+1)(x-1)\frac{6}{x+1} - x(x+1)(x-1)\frac{1}{x-1}$$

$$3(x+1)(x-1) = 6x(x-1) - x(x+1)$$
$$3(x^2-1) = 6x^2 - 6x - x^2 - x$$
$$3x^2 - 3 = 5x^2 - 7x$$
$$0 = 2x^2 - 7x + 3$$
$$0 = (2x-1)(x-3)$$
$$2x - 1 = 0 \quad \text{or} \quad x - 3 = 0$$
$$2x = 1 \qquad\qquad x = 3$$
$$x = \frac{1}{2} \qquad\qquad\qquad\qquad (2–6)$$

21.
$$2x + 1 = 3\sqrt{2x-1}$$
$$(2x+1)^2 = 9(2x-1)$$
$$4x^2 + 4x + 1 = 18x - 9$$
$$4x^2 - 14x + 10 = 0$$
$$2x^2 - 7x + 5 = 0$$
$$(2x-5)(x-1) = 0$$
$$2x - 5 = 0 \quad \text{or} \quad\quad x - 1 = 0$$
$$x = \frac{5}{2} \qquad\qquad\qquad x = 1$$

Check: $2(\frac{5}{2}) + 1 \overset{?}{=} 3\sqrt{2(\frac{5}{2})-1}$

$$5 + 1 \overset{?}{=} 3\sqrt{5-1}$$
$$6 \overset{\checkmark}{=} 6$$
$$2\cdot1 + 1 \overset{?}{=} 3\sqrt{2\cdot1-1}$$
$$3 \overset{\checkmark}{=} 3$$

Solution: $1, \frac{5}{2}$ *(1–6)*

22. $|4x - 9| > 3$
$4x - 9 < -3$ or $4x - 9 > 3$
$4x < 6$ $4x > 12$
$x < \dfrac{3}{2}$ or $x > 3$

$\left(-\infty, \dfrac{3}{2}\right) \cup (3, \infty)$

$(1-3)$

23. $\sqrt{(3m - 4)^2} \leq 2$
$|3m - 4| \leq 2$
$-2 \leq 3m - 4 \leq 2$
$2 \leq 3m \leq 6$
$\dfrac{2}{3} \leq m \leq 2$

$\left[\dfrac{2}{3}, 2\right]$

$(1-3)$

24. $\dfrac{x+1}{2} > x - 2$
$x + 1 > 2x - 4$
$-x + 1 > -4$
$-x > -5$
$x < 5$
$(-\infty, 5)$

$(1-2)$

25. $\dfrac{\sqrt{x-2}}{x-4}$ represents a real number if $x - 2$ is positive or zero, except if $x = 4$. Thus, $x \geq 2$, $x \neq 4$, or $[2, 4) \cup (4, \infty)$.

$(1-2)$

26. (A) $(2 - 3i)^2 - (4 - 5i)(2 - 3i) - (2 + 10i)$
$= (2)^2 - 2(2)(3i) + (3i)^2 - (8 - 12i - 10i + 15i^2) - 2 - 10i = 4 - 12i + 9i^2 - (8 - 22i + 15i^2) - 2 - 10i$
$= 4 - 12i + 9i^2 - 8 + 22i - 15i^2 - 2 - 10i = 4 - 12i - 9 - 8 + 22i + 15 - 2 - 10i = 0 + 0i$ or 0

(B) $\dfrac{3}{5} + \dfrac{4}{5}i + \dfrac{1}{\frac{3}{5} + \frac{4}{5}i} = \dfrac{3}{5} + \dfrac{4}{5}i + \dfrac{1}{(\frac{3}{5} + \frac{4}{5}i)}\dfrac{(\frac{3}{5} - \frac{4}{5}i)}{(\frac{3}{5} - \frac{4}{5}i)} = \dfrac{3}{5} + \dfrac{4}{5}i + \dfrac{\frac{3}{5} - \frac{4}{5}i}{\frac{9}{25} - \frac{16}{25}i^2} = \dfrac{3}{5} + \dfrac{4}{5}i + \dfrac{\frac{3}{5} - \frac{4}{5}i}{\frac{9}{25} + \frac{16}{25}}$

$= \dfrac{3}{5} + \dfrac{4}{5}i + \dfrac{3}{5} - \dfrac{4}{5}i = \dfrac{6}{5}$

(C) $i^{35} = i^{32}i^3 = (i^4)^8(-i) = 1^8(-i) = -i$

$(1-4)$

27. (A) $(5 + 2\sqrt{-9}) - (2 - 3\sqrt{-16}) = (5 + 2i\sqrt{9}) - (2 - 3i\sqrt{16}) = (5 + 6i) - (2 - 12i) = 5 + 6i - 2 + 12i$
$= 3 + 18i$

(B) $\dfrac{2 + 7\sqrt{-25}}{3 - \sqrt{-1}} = \dfrac{2 + 7i\sqrt{25}}{3 - i} = \dfrac{2 + 35i}{3 - i} = \dfrac{(2 + 35i)}{(3 - i)}\dfrac{(3 + i)}{(3 + i)} = \dfrac{6 + 107i + 35i^2}{9 - i^2} = \dfrac{6 + 107i - 35}{9 + 1} = \dfrac{-29 + 107i}{10}$
$= -2.9 + 10.7i$

(C) $\dfrac{12 - \sqrt{-64}}{\sqrt{-4}} = \dfrac{12 - i\sqrt{64}}{i\sqrt{4}} = \dfrac{12 - 8i}{2i} = \dfrac{12 - 8i}{2i}\dfrac{i}{i} = \dfrac{12i - 8i^2}{2i^2} = \dfrac{12i + 8}{-2} = -4 - 6i$ $(1-4)$

28. $1 + \dfrac{14}{y^2} = \dfrac{6}{y}$ Excluded value: $y \neq 0$

$y^2(1) + y^2\dfrac{14}{y^2} = y^2\dfrac{6}{y}$

$y^2 + 14 = 6y$
$y^2 - 6y + 14 = 0$
$y^2 - 6y = -14$
$y^2 - 6y + 9 = -5$

$$(y-3)^2 = -5$$
$$y - 3 = \pm\sqrt{-5}$$
$$y = 3 \pm \sqrt{-5}$$
$$y = 3 \pm i\sqrt{5} \qquad (1\text{-}6)$$

29. $4x^{2/3} - 4x^{1/3} - 3 = 0$
Let $u = x^{1/3}$, then
$$4u^2 - 4u - 3 = 0$$
$$(2u - 3)(2u + 1) = 0$$
$$u = \frac{3}{2}, -\frac{1}{2}$$

$$x^{1/3} = \frac{3}{2} \qquad x^{1/3} = -\frac{1}{2}$$

$$x = \frac{27}{8} \qquad x = -\frac{1}{8} \qquad (1\text{-}6)$$

30. $u^4 + u^2 - 12 = 0$
Let $w = u^2$, then
$$w^2 + w - 12 = 0$$
$$(w + 4)(w - 3) = 0$$
$$w = -4, 3$$
$$u^2 = -4 \qquad u^2 = 3$$
$$u = \pm 2i \qquad u = \pm\sqrt{3} \qquad (1\text{-}6)$$

31.
$$\sqrt{8t-2} - 2\sqrt{t} = 1$$
$$\sqrt{8t-2} = 2\sqrt{t} + 1$$
$$8t - 2 = 4t + 4\sqrt{t} + 1$$
$$4t - 3 = 4\sqrt{t}$$
$$16t^2 - 24t + 9 = 16t$$
$$16t^2 - 40t + 9 = 0$$
$$(4t - 1)(4t - 9) = 0$$
$$t = \frac{1}{4}, \frac{9}{4}$$

Check: $\sqrt{8(\frac{1}{4})-2} - 2\sqrt{\frac{1}{4}} \overset{?}{=} 1$
$$0 - 2(\tfrac{1}{2}) \overset{?}{=} 1$$
$$-1 \neq 1$$
$$\sqrt{8(\tfrac{9}{4})-2} - 2\sqrt{\tfrac{9}{4}} \overset{?}{=} 1$$
$$\sqrt{16} - 2\sqrt{\tfrac{9}{4}} \overset{?}{=} 1$$
$$4 - 2(\tfrac{3}{2}) \overset{?}{=} 1$$
$$1 = 1 \; \sqrt{}$$

Solution: $\frac{9}{4}$ $\qquad (1\text{-}6)$

32. $-3.45 < 1.86 - 0.33x \leq 7.92$
$$-5.31 < -0.33x \leq 6.06$$
$$16.09 > x \geq -18.36$$
$$-18.36 \leq x < 16.09 \text{ or } [-18.36, 16.09) \qquad (1\text{-}2)$$

33. $2.35x^2 + 10.44x - 16.47 = 0$

$$x = \frac{-b \pm \sqrt{b^2 - 4ac}}{2a} \quad a = 2.35, b = 10.44, c = -16.47$$

$$x = \frac{-10.44 \pm \sqrt{(10.44)^2 - 4(2.35)(-16.47)}}{2(2.35)} = \frac{-10.44 \pm \sqrt{263.8116}}{4.70}$$

$$= \frac{-10.44 \pm 16.2423}{4.70} = -5.68, 1.23 \qquad (1\text{-}5)$$

34.
$$\frac{x-2}{x+1} = \frac{2y+1}{y-2}$$

$$(x + 1)(y - 2)\frac{x-2}{x+1} = (x + 1)(y - 2)\frac{2y+1}{y-2}$$

$$(y - 2)(x - 2) = (x + 1)(2y + 1)$$
$$xy - 2y - 2x + 4 = 2xy + x + 2y + 1$$
$$3 - 3x = xy + 4y$$
$$3 - 3x = y(x + 4)$$
$$y = \frac{3-3x}{x+4} \qquad (1\text{-}1)$$

35. (A) All real numbers $(-\infty, \infty)$
(B) From the graph, the possible function values include -2 (only) and all numbers greater than or equal to 1. In set and interval notation: $\{-2\} \cup [1, \infty)$.
(C) $f(-3) = 1$, $f(-2) = 2$ (not -2), $f(2) = -2$ (not 2). Thus, $f(-3) + f(-2) + f(2) = 1 + 2 + (-2) = 1$
(D) $[-3, -2]$ and $[2, \infty)$
(E) f is discontinuous at $x = -2$ and at $x = 2$.   *(3–1, 3–2)*

36. The line $3x + 2y = 12$, or

$$2y = -3x + 12, \text{ or } y = -\frac{3}{2}x + 6, \text{ has slope } -\frac{3}{2}.$$

(A) We require a line through $(-6, 1)$ with slope $-\frac{3}{2}$. Applying the point slope form, we have

$$y - 1 = -\frac{3}{2}(x + 6)$$

$$y - 1 = -\frac{3}{2}x - 9$$

$$y = -\frac{3}{2}x - 8$$

(B) We require a line with slope m satisfying $-\frac{3}{2}m = -1$, or $m = \frac{2}{3}$. Again applying the point slope form,

we have

$$y - 1 = \frac{2}{3}(x + 6)$$

$$y - 1 = \frac{2}{3}x + 4$$

$$y = \frac{2}{3}x + 5$$ *(2–3)*

37. $x + 4 \geq 0$ is equivalent to $x \geq -4$. Domain of $g(x) = \sqrt{x+4}$ is $[-4, \infty)$ *(3–1)*

38. $f(x) = x^2 - 2x - 8$. Complete the square.   Graph: Locate axis and vertex, then plot
  $f(x) = (x^2 - 2x + 1) - 1 - 8$ several points on either side of the axis.
  $\quad = (x - 1)^2 - 9$
Comparing with $f(x) = a(x - h)^2 + k$, $h = 1$ and $k = -9$. Thus, the vertex is $(1, -9)$, the axis of symmetry is $x = 1$, and the minimum value is -9. $y = f(x)$ can be any number greater than or equal to -9, so the range is $[-9, \infty)$.
y intercept: Set $x = 0$, then $f(0) = -8$ is the y intercept.
x intercepts: Set $f(x) = 0$, then
  $0 = x^2 - 2x - 8$
  $0 = (x - 4)(x + 2)$
  $x = 4$ or $x = -2$ are the x intercepts.

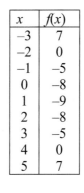

x	$f(x)$
-3	7
-2	0
-1	-5
0	-8
1	-9
2	-8
3	-5
4	0
5	7

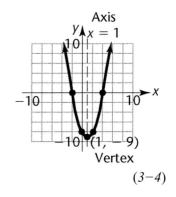

(3–4)

39. $(f \circ g)(x) = f[g(x)] = f\left(\dfrac{x+3}{x}\right) = \dfrac{1}{\frac{x+3}{3}-2} = \dfrac{x(1)}{x(\frac{x+3}{x}-2)} = \dfrac{x}{x+3-2x} = \dfrac{x}{3-x}$

The domain of f is all real numbers except 2.
The domain of g is all non-zero real numbers.
The domain of $f \circ g$ is the set of all non–zero real numbers for which $g(x) \neq 2$.

$g(x) = 2$ only if $\dfrac{x+3}{x} = 2$, that is $x + 3 = 2x$, or $x = 3$.

Thus the domain of $f \circ g$ is the set of all non–zero real numbers except 3, that is, $(-\infty, 0) \cup (0, 3) \cup (3, \infty)$.

> **Common Error:**
>
> The domain of $f \circ g$ cannot be found by looking at the final form $\dfrac{x}{3-x}$. It is not $\{x \mid x \ne 3\}$.

(3–5)

40. $f(x) = 2x + 5$

Assume $f(a) = f(b)$

$\qquad 2a + 5 = 2b + 5$

$\qquad\quad 2a = 2b$

$\qquad\quad\ \ a = b$

Thus, f is one-to-one.

Solve $y = f(x)$ for x:

$\qquad y = 2x + 5$

$\quad y - 5 = 2x$

$\qquad x = \dfrac{y-5}{2} = f^{-1}(y)$

Interchange x and y

$y = f^{-1}(x) = \dfrac{x-5}{2}$ or $\dfrac{1}{2}x - \dfrac{5}{2}$ Domain: $(-\infty, \infty)$

(3–6)

41.

x	$y = x - 1$	x	$y = x^2 + 1$
-1	-2	0	1
-2	-3	1	2
		2	5

Domain: all real numbers, $(-\infty, \infty)$

Range: $(-\infty, -1) \cup [1, \infty)$

Discontinuous at: $x = 0$

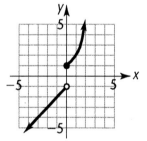

(3–2)

42. (A) This is the same as the graph of $y = \sqrt{x}$ stretched vertically by a factor of 2 and shifted up one unit.

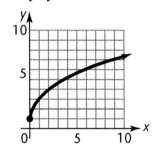

(B) This is the same as the graph of $y = \sqrt{x}$ shifted left 1 unit and reflected through the x axis.

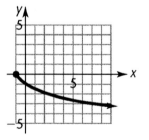

(3–3)

43. The graph of $y = |x|$ is shrunk by a factor of $\dfrac{1}{2}$, reflected through the x axis, shifted two units to the right and three units up; $y = -\dfrac{1}{2}|x - 2| + 3$.

(3–3)

44. $f(x) = \sqrt{x+4}$

Assume $f(a) = f(b)$
$$\sqrt{a+4} = \sqrt{b+4}$$
$$a+4 = b+4$$
$$a = b$$

Thus f is one–to–one.

(A) Solve $y = f(x)$ for x

$y = \sqrt{x+4}$
$y^2 = x+4 \quad y \geq 0$
$x = y^2 - 4 \quad y \geq 0 \quad f^{-1}(y) = y^2 - 4$

Interchange x and y:

$y = f^{-1}(x) = x^2 - 4$ Domain: $x \geq 0$

Check: $f^{-1}[f(x)] = (\sqrt{x+4})^2 - 4 = x + 4 - 4 = x$

$\qquad f[f^{-1}(x)] = \sqrt{x^2 - 4 + 4} = \sqrt{x^2} = x$ since $x \geq 0$ in the domain of f^{-1}.

(B) Domain of $f = [-4, \infty) = $ Range of f^{-1}
  Range of $f = [0, \infty) = $ Domain of f^{-1}

(C)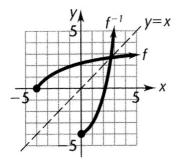

$(3-6)$

45.
$$x^2 - 6x + y^2 + 2y = 0$$
$$(x^2 - 6x + ?) + (y^2 + 2y + ?) = 0$$
$$(x^2 - 6x + 9) + (y^2 + 2y + 1) = 9 + 1$$
$$(x-3)^2 + (y+1)^2 = 10$$
$$(x-3)^2 + [y - (-1)]^2 = (\sqrt{10})^2$$

Center: $C(h, k) = (3, -1)$ Radius $r = \sqrt{10}$

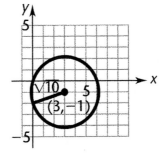

$(2-2)$

46. $xy + |xy| = 5$

Test y axis
Replace x with $-x$:
$(-x)y + |(-x)y| = 5$
$\quad -xy + |xy| = 5$

Test x axis
Replace y with $-y$:
$x(-y) + |x(-y)| = 5$
$\quad -xy + |xy| = 5$

Test origin
Replace x with $-x$ and y with $-y$:
$(-x)(-y) + |(-x)(-y)| = 5$
$\quad xy + |xy| = 5$
$\qquad (2-1)$

The graph has symmetry with respect to the origin.

47. Since the graph is a parabola opening up, $a = +1$. Since the vertex is at $(-2, -3) = (h, k)$, $h = -2$ and $k = -3$.
Thus, the equation is $y = (x+2)^2 - 3$.

$(3-4)$

48.

$$\frac{x+y}{y-\frac{x+y}{x-y}} = 1$$

$$\frac{(x+y)(x-y)}{y(x-y)-(x+y)} = 1$$

$$\frac{x^2-y^2}{xy-y^2-x-y} = 1$$

$$x^2 - y^2 = xy - y^2 - x - y$$
$$x^2 + x = xy - y$$
$$x^2 + x = y(x-1)$$
$$y = \frac{x^2+x}{x-1} \qquad (1-1)$$

49.

$$3x^2 = 2\sqrt{2}\,x - 1$$
$$3x^2 - 2\sqrt{2}\,x + 1 = 0$$

$$x = \frac{-b \pm \sqrt{b^2-4ac}}{2a} \qquad a = 3$$

$$b = -2\sqrt{2}$$
$$c = 1$$

$$x = \frac{-(-2\sqrt{2}) \pm \sqrt{(-2\sqrt{2})^2 - 4(3)(1)}}{2(3)}$$

$$x = \frac{2\sqrt{2} \pm \sqrt{8-12}}{6}$$

$$x = \frac{2\sqrt{2} \pm \sqrt{-4}}{6}$$

$$x = \frac{2\sqrt{2} \pm 2i}{6} = \frac{2(\sqrt{2} \pm i)}{6} = \frac{\sqrt{2} \pm i}{3}$$

$$(1-5)$$

50. In this problem, $a = 1$, $b = b$, $c = 1$. Thus, the discriminant $b^2 - 4ac = b^2 - 4 \cdot 1 \cdot 1 = b^2 - 4$.
Hence, the number and types of roots depend on the sign of $b^2 - 4 = (b+2)(b-2)$. The zeros of this polynomial are 2, –2.
Plotting the graph of $y = (b+2)(b-2)$, we see $b^2 - 4 > 0$
if $b < -2$ or $b > 2$, and $b^2 - 4 < 0$ if $-2 < b < 2$.

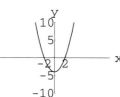

Hence,
if $b^2 - 4 > 0$, there are two distinct real roots. This occurs if $b < -2$ or $b > 2$.
if $b^2 - 4 = 0$, there is one real double root. This occurs if $b = -2$ or $b = 2$.
if $b^2 - 4 < 0$, there are two distinct imaginary roots. This occurs if $-2 < b < 2$. $\qquad (1-5)$

51.

$$\sqrt{3-2x} - \sqrt{x+7} = \sqrt{x+4}$$
$$3 - 2x - 2\sqrt{3-2x}\sqrt{x+7} + x + 7 = x + 4$$
$$-x + 10 - 2\sqrt{3-2x}\sqrt{x+7} = x + 4$$
$$-2\sqrt{3-2x}\sqrt{x+7} = 2x - 6$$
$$-\sqrt{3-2x}\sqrt{x+7} = x - 3$$
$$(3-2x)(x+7) = x^2 - 6x + 9$$
$$3x + 21 - 2x^2 - 14x = x^2 - 6x + 9$$
$$0 = 3x^2 + 5x - 12$$
$$3x^2 + 5x - 12 = 0$$
$$(3x - 4)(x + 3) = 0$$
$$3x - 4 = 0 \qquad x + 3 = 0$$
$$x = \frac{4}{3} \qquad x = -3$$

Check:

$x = \dfrac{4}{3}$:

$\sqrt{3-2(\frac{4}{3})} \; - \; \sqrt{\frac{4}{3}+7} \;\overset{?}{=}\; \sqrt{\frac{4}{3}+4}$

$\sqrt{\frac{9}{3}-\frac{8}{3}} \; - \; \sqrt{\frac{4}{3}+\frac{21}{3}} \;\overset{?}{=}\; \sqrt{\frac{4}{3}+\frac{12}{3}}$

$\sqrt{\frac{1}{3}} \; - \; \sqrt{\frac{25}{3}} \;\overset{?}{=}\; \sqrt{\frac{16}{3}}$

$\dfrac{1}{\sqrt{3}} - \dfrac{5}{\sqrt{3}} \neq \dfrac{4}{\sqrt{3}}$

Not a solution
Solution: –3

$x = -3$:

$\sqrt{3-2(-3)} \; - \; \sqrt{(-3)+7} \;\overset{?}{=}\; \sqrt{(-3)+4}$

$\sqrt{9} \; - \; \sqrt{4} \;\overset{?}{=}\; \sqrt{1}$

$3 - 2 \overset{\checkmark}{=} 1$

A solution

$(1-6)$

52. $\dfrac{a+bi}{a-bi} = \dfrac{(a+bi)}{(a-bi)}\dfrac{(a+bi)}{(a+bi)} = \dfrac{(a+bi)^2}{a^2-(bi)^2} = \dfrac{a^2+2abi+b^2i^2}{a^2-b^2i^2} = \dfrac{a^2+2abi-b^2}{a^2+b^2} = \dfrac{a^2-b^2+2abi}{a^2+b^2}$

$\qquad\qquad\qquad\qquad\qquad\qquad\qquad\qquad\qquad\qquad\qquad\qquad\quad = \dfrac{a^2-b^2}{a^2+b^2} + \dfrac{2ab}{a^2+b^2}\, i \qquad (1-4)$

53. (A) $g(x) = \sqrt{4-x^2}$
The domain of g is those values of x for which $4 - x^2 \geq 0$. Plotting
the graph of $y = 4 - x^2$, or $y = (2 - x)(2 + x)$, we see that the zeros
of y are –2 and 2, and $4 - x^2 \geq 0$ if $-2 \leq x \leq 2$.
The domain of g is $[-2, 2]$.

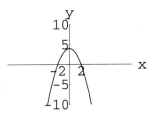

(B) $\left(\dfrac{f}{g}\right)(x) = \dfrac{f(x)}{g(x)} = \dfrac{x^2}{\sqrt{4-x^2}}$. The domain of $\dfrac{f}{g}$ is the intersection of the domains of f (all real numbers)
and $g([-2, 2])$ with the exclusion of those points (–2 and 2) where $g(x) = 0$. Thus, domain of $f/g = (-2, 2)$.

(C) $(f \circ g)(x) = f[g(x)] = f(\sqrt{4-x^2}) = (\sqrt{4-x^2})^2 = 4 - x^2$.
The domain of $f \circ g$ is the set of all real numbers in the domain of $g([-2, 2])$ for which $f(x)$ is real, that is,
all numbers in $[-2, 2]$. $(3-5)$

54. (A) $f(x) = x^2 - 2x - 3 \;\; x \geq 1$
f passes the horizontal line test (see graph below, in part C), hence f is one-to-one.
Solve $y = f(x)$ for x:

$$\begin{array}{ll} y = x^2 - 2x - 3 & x \geq 1 \\ x^2 - 2x = y + 3 & x \geq 1 \\ x^2 - 2x + 1 = y + 4 & x \geq 1 \\ (x-1)^2 = y + 4 & x \geq 1 \\ x - 1 = \sqrt{y+4} & x \geq 1 \end{array}$$

positive square root only because $x \geq 1$

$$x = 1 + \sqrt{y+4} = f^{-1}(y)$$

Interchange x and y: $y = f^{-1}(x) = 1 + \sqrt{x+4}$ Domain: $x \geq -4$ Check omitted for lack of space.

(B) Domain of $f^{-1} = [-4, \infty)$
Range of f^{-1} = Domain of $f = [1, \infty)$.

(C)

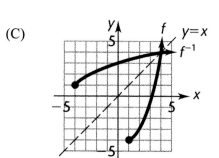

(3–6)

55. Let x = the number

$\dfrac{1}{x}$ = its reciprocal

Then

$$x - \frac{1}{x} = \frac{3}{2} \quad \text{Excl. value: } x \neq 0$$
$$2x^2 - 2 = 3x$$
$$2x^2 - 3x - 2 = 0$$
$$(2x + 1)(x - 2) = 0$$
$$2x + 1 = 0 \quad \text{or} \quad x - 2 = 0$$
$$x = -\frac{1}{2} \qquad x = 2 \quad (1-5)$$

56. Let x = the rate of the current
Then $15 - x$ = the rate of the boat upstream
$15 + x$ = the rate of the boat downstream

Solving $d = rt$ for t, we have $t = \dfrac{d}{r}$.

We use this formula, together with
time upstream + time downstream = 4.8.

time upstream $= \dfrac{\text{distance upstream}}{\text{rate upstream}} = \dfrac{35}{15 - x}$

time downstream $= \dfrac{\text{distance downstream}}{\text{rate downstream}} = \dfrac{35}{15 + x}$

So,

$$\frac{35}{15 - x} + \frac{35}{15 + x} = 4.8 \quad \text{Excluded values: } x \neq 15, -15$$
$$35(15 + x) + 35(15 - x) = 4.8(15 + x)(15 - x)$$
$$525 + 35x + 525 - 35x = 4.8(225 - x^2)$$
$$1050 = 1080 - 4.8x^2$$
$$-30 = -4.8x^2$$
$$6.25 = x^2$$
$$x = 2.5 \text{ miles per hour}$$
(discarding the negative answer)

(1–5)

57. Let x = amount of distilled water (0% acid)
24 = amount of 90% solution
Then $x + 24$ = amount of 60% solution

$$\begin{array}{ccccc} \text{acid in} & & \text{acid in} & & \text{acid in} \\ \text{distilled} & + & \text{90\% solution} & = & \text{60\% solution} \\ \text{water} & & & & \\ 0 & + & 0.9(24) & = & 0.6(x + 24) \end{array}$$
$$21.6 = 0.6x + 14.4$$
$$7.2 = 0.6x$$
$$x = 12 \text{ gallons} \qquad (1-1)$$

58. "Break even" means Cost = Revenue
Let x = number of books sold
Revenue = number of books sold × price per book = $x(9.65)$
Cost = Fixed Cost + Variable Cost = $41{,}800$ + number of books × cost per book = $41{,}800 + x(4.90)$
$$9.65x = 41{,}800 + 4.90x$$
$$4.75x = 41{,}800$$
$$x = \frac{41{,}800}{4.75} = 8{,}800 \text{ books} \qquad (1-1)$$

59. The distance of p from 200 must be no greater than 10. $|p - 200| \leq 10$ *(1-3)*

60. If x is linearly related to p, then we are looking for an equation whose graph passes through $(p_1, x_1) = (3.79, 1,160)$ and $(p_2, x_2) = (3.59, 1,340)$. We find the slope, and then we use the point slope form to find the equation.

$$m = \frac{x_2 - x_1}{p_2 - p_1} = \frac{1,340 - 1,160}{3.59 - 3.79} = \frac{180}{-0.2} = -900$$

$$x - x_1 = m(p - p_1)$$
$$x - 1,160 = -900(p - 3.79)$$
$$x - 1,160 = -900p + 3,411$$
$$x = -900p + 4,571$$

If the price is lowered to \$3.29, we are asked for x when $p = 3.29$

$x = -900(3.29) + 4,571 = 1,610$ bottles   *(2-4)*

61. If $0 \leq x \leq 60$, $C(x) = 0.06x$

If $60 < x \leq 60 + 90$,

that is, $\begin{pmatrix} \text{Cost of first} \\ \text{60 calls} \end{pmatrix}$ + $\begin{pmatrix} \text{Cost of next } x - 60 \\ \text{calls at 0.05 per call} \end{pmatrix}$

$60 < x \leq 150$, $\begin{aligned} C(x) &= 0.06(60) &+ 0.05(x - 60) \\ &= 3.60 + 0.05x - 3 \\ &= 0.05x + 0.6 \end{aligned}$

If $60 + 90 < x \leq 60 + 90 + 150$,

that is, $\begin{pmatrix} \text{Cost of first} \\ \text{150 calls} \end{pmatrix}$ + $\begin{pmatrix} \text{Cost of next } x - 150 \\ \text{calls at 0.04 per call} \end{pmatrix}$

$150 < x \leq 300$, $\begin{aligned} C(x) &= 0.05(150) + 0.6 &+ 0.04(x - 150) \\ &= 7.5 + 0.6 + 0.04x - 6 \\ &= 0.04x + 2.1 \end{aligned}$

Finally, if $x > 300$, $\begin{pmatrix} \text{Cost of first} \\ \text{300 calls} \end{pmatrix}$ + $\begin{pmatrix} \text{Cost of next } x - 300 \\ \text{calls at 0.03 per call} \end{pmatrix}$

$\begin{aligned} C(x) &= 0.04(300) + 2.1 &+ 0.03(x - 300) \\ &= 12 + 2.1 + 0.03x - 9 \\ &= 0.03x + 5.1 \end{aligned}$

Summarizing, $C(x) = \begin{cases} 0.06x & \text{if } 0 \leq x \leq 60 \\ 0.05x + 0.6 & \text{if } 60 < x \leq 150 \\ 0.04x + 2.1 & \text{if } 150 < x \leq 300 \\ 0.03x + 5.1 & \text{if } 300 < x \end{cases}$

x	$C(x) = 0.06x$	x	$C(x) = 0.05x + 0.6$	x	$C(x) = 0.04x + 2.1$	x	$C(x) = 0.03x + 5.1$
0	0	90	5.1	160	8.5	310	14.4
30	1.8	140	7.6	200	10.1	400	17.1
60	3.6						

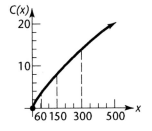

(3-2)

62. (A)   Let x = width of pen

Then $2x + \ell = 80$

So $\ell = 80 - 2x$ = length of pen

$A(x) = x\ell = x(80 - 2x) = 80x - 2x^2$

(B) Since all distances must be positive, $x > 0$ and $80 - 2x > 0$, hence $80 > 2x$ or $x < 40$.

Therefore $0 < x < 40$ or $(0, 40)$ is the domain of $A(x)$.

(C) Note: 0, 40 were excluded from the domain for geometrical reasons; but can be used to help draw the graph since the *polynomial* $80x - 2x^2$ has domain including these values.

x	$A(x)$
0	0
10	600
20	800
30	600
40	0

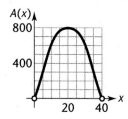

Since the function is quadratic, its maximum value occurs at the vertex of its parabola graph, which is given by the formula (h, k), where

$$h = -\frac{b}{2a} = -\frac{80}{2(-2)} = 20 \text{ and } k = c - \frac{b^2}{4a} = 0 - \frac{80^2}{4(-2)} = 800$$

Thus the maximum value of A occurs when $x = 20$ and $\ell = 80 - 2(20) = 40$;

the dimensions are 20 feet by 40 feet.   *(3–4)*

63. (A) $f(1) = 1 - 2[\![1/2]\!] = 1 - 2(0) = 1$

$f(2) = 2 - 2[\![2/2]\!] = 2 - 2(1) = 0$

$f(3) = 3 - 2[\![3/2]\!] = 3 - 2(1) = 1$

$f(4) = 4 - 2[\![4/2]\!] = 4 - 2(2) = 0$

(B) If n is an integer, n is either odd or even.

If n is even, it can be written as $2k$, where k is an integer.

Then $f(n) = f(2k) = 2k - 2[\![2k/2]\!] = 2k - 2[\![k]\!] = 2k - 2k = 0$.

Otherwise, n is odd, and n can be written as $2k + 1$, where k is an integer.

Then $f(n) = f(2k + 1) = 2k + 1 - 2[\![(2k + 1)/2]\!] = 2k + 1 - 2[\![k + \frac{1}{2}]\!] = 2k + 1 - 2k = 1$

Summarizing, if n is an integer, $f(n) = \begin{cases} 1 \text{ if } n \text{ is an odd integer} \\ 0 \text{ if } n \text{ is an even integer} \end{cases}$ *(3–2)*

64. (A) If v is linearly related to t, then we are looking for an equation whose graph passes through $(t_1, v_1) = (0, 20000)$ and $(t_2, v_2) = (8, 4000)$. We find the slope, m, and then we use the point slope form to find the equation.

$$m = \frac{v_2 - v_1}{t_2 - t_1} = \frac{4,000 - 20,000}{8 - 0} = -2,000$$

$$v - v_1 = m(t_2 - t_1)$$

$$v - 20,000 = -2,000(t - 0)$$

$$v - 20,000 = -2,000t$$

$$v = -2,000t + 20,000$$

(B) Solve for t

$$v = -2,000t + 20,000$$

$$v - 20,000 = -2,000t$$

$$t = \frac{v - 20,000}{-2,000}$$

$$t = -0.0005v + 10$$ *(3–6)*

65. (A) A profit will result if revenue is greater than cost; that is, if

$$R > C$$
$$15p - 2p^2 > 88 - 12p$$
$$-88 + 27p - 2p^2 > 0$$
$$2p^2 - 27p + 88 < 0$$
$$(2p - 11)(p - 8) < 0$$

Zeros: 5.5, 8

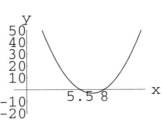

Graphing $f(p) = 2p^2 - 27p + 88$, we see that $2p^2 - 27p + 88 < 0$ and a profit will occur $(R > C)$
for $\$5.5 < p < \$8$ or ($\$5.5$, $\$8$).

(B) A loss will result if cost is greater than revenue, that is if

$$C > R$$
$$88 - 12p > 15p - 2p^2$$
$$2p^2 - 27p + 88 > 0$$

Referring to the graph in part (A), we see that $2p^2 - 27p + 88 > 0$, and a loss will occur $(C > R)$,
for $p < \$5.5$ or $p > \$8$. Since a negative price doesn't make sense, we delete any number to the left of 0.
Thus, a loss will occur for $\$0 \le p < \$5.5$ or $p > \$8$. [$\$0$, $\$5.5$) $\cup$ ($\$8$, ∞)   *(3-4)*

66.   Let x = the distance from port A to port B

Then $115 - x$ = the distance from port B to port C

Applying the Pythagorean theorem, we have

$$x^2 + (115 - x)^2 = 85^2$$
$$x^2 + 13,225 - 230x + x^2 = 7,225$$
$$2x^2 - 230x + 6,000 = 0$$
$$x^2 - 115x + 3,000 = 0$$
$$(x - 40)(x - 75) = 0$$
$$x = 40, 75$$
$$115 - x = 75, 40$$

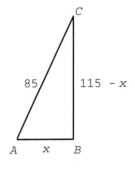

Based on the given information, there are two possible solutions:

40 miles from A to B and 75 miles from B to C *or*

75 miles from A to B and 40 miles from B to C *(1-5)*

67. $s = a + bt^2$

(A) We are given: When $t = 5$, $s = 2,100$

When $t = 10$, $s = 900$

Substituting these values into the given equation, we have

$2,100 = a + b(5)^2$

$900 = a + b(10)^2$ or

$2,100 = a + 25b$

$900 = a + 100b$

Solve the first equation for a in terms of b and substitute into the second equation to eliminate a.

$a = 2,100 - 25b$

$900 = 2,100 - 25b + 100b$

$-1,200 = 75b$

$b = -16$

$a = 2,100 - 25b = 2,100 - 25(-16) = 2,500$

(B) The height of the balloon is represented by s, the distance of the object above the ground, when $t = 0$.
Since we now know $s = 2,500 - 16t^2$ from part(A), when $t = 0$, $s = 2,500$ feet is the height of the balloon.
(C) The object falls until s, its distance above the ground, is zero. Since $s = 2,500 - 16t^2$
we substitute $s = 0$ and solve for t.

$$0 = 2{,}500 - 16t^2$$
$$16t^2 = 2{,}500$$
$$t^2 = \frac{2{,}500}{16}$$
$$t = \frac{50}{4} \text{ (discarding the negative solution)}$$
$$t = 12.5 \text{ seconds} \hspace{3cm} (3\text{--}4)$$

68. (A) 30,000 bushels
(B) The demand decreases by 10,000 bushels to 20,000 bushels.
(C) The demand increases by 10,000 bushels to 40,000 bushels.
(D) As the price varies from \$3.00 to \$3.50 per bushel, the demand varies from 15,000 to 50,000 bushels, increasing with decreasing price and decreasing with increasing price.
(E) From the graph, the following table is constructed:

q	20	25	30	35	40
P	340	332	325	320	315

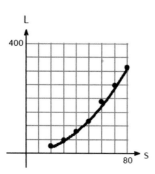

Enter the data

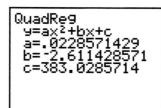

Compute the regression equation. $\hspace{2cm} (3\text{--}4)$

69. (A)

L

400

80 s

(B) $L = 0.05s^2 - 0.2s + 6.5$ domain $[20, \infty)$
From the graph, L is an increasing function on its domain. Hence the range of L consists of those values of L greater than or equal to
$L(20) = 0.05(20)^2 - 0.2(20) + 6.5 = 22.5$, or $[22.5, \infty)$.
Now solve for s.
First, complete the square.
$L = 0.05(s^2 - 4s + ?) + 6.5$
$L = 0.05(s^2 - 4s + 4) - 4(0.05) + 6.5$
$L = 0.05(s - 2)^2 + 6.3$
$L - 6.3 = 0.05(s - 2)^2$
$20L - 126 = (s - 2)^2$
$\sqrt{20L - 126} = s - 2$ (positive square root only, since $s \geq 20$)
$f^{-1}(L) = s = 2 + \sqrt{20L - 126}$, domain: $[22.5, \infty)$, range: $[20, \infty)$

(C) Substitute $L = 220$ to find
$$s = f^{-1}(220) = 2 + \sqrt{20(220) - 126} = 67 \text{ mph} \hspace{2cm} (3\text{--}4)$$

Chapters 4 & 5 Cumulative Review

1. (A) Since the graph has x intercepts -1, 1, and 2, and -1 is at least a double zero (the graph is tangent to the x axis at $x = -1$), the lowest degree equation would be $P(x) = (x + 1)^2(x - 1)(x - 2)$.
   (B) $P(x) \to \infty$ as $x \to \infty$ and as $x \to -\infty$.   *(4-1)*

2. (A) The graph of $y = \left(\dfrac{3}{4}\right)^x$ passes through $(0, 1)$ and $\left(1, \dfrac{3}{4}\right)$. This corresponds to graph m.

   (B) The graph of $y = \left(\dfrac{4}{3}\right)^x$ passes through $(0, 1)$ and $\left(1, \dfrac{4}{3}\right)$. This corresponds to graph g.

   (C) The graph of $y = \left(\dfrac{3}{4}\right)^x + \left(\dfrac{4}{3}\right)^x$ passes through $(0, 2)$. This corresponds to graph n.

   (D) The graph of $y = \left(\dfrac{4}{3}\right)^x - \left(\dfrac{3}{4}\right)^x$ passes through $(0, 0)$. This corresponds to graph f.   *(5-1)*

3.
$$\begin{array}{r} 3 \quad 5 \;\; -18 \;\; -3 \\ -9 \;\;\; 12 \;\;\; 18 \\ \hline -3\,\overline{)\,3 \;\; -4 \;\; -6 \;\;\; 15} \end{array}$$
   $3x^3 + 5x^2 - 18x - 3 = (x + 3)(3x^2 - 4x - 6) + 15$ *(4-1)*

4. $-2, 3, 5$ *(4-1)*

5. We investigate $P(1)$ and $P(2)$ by forming a synthetic division table.

	4	−5	−3	−1
1	4	−1	−4	−5
2	4	3	3	5

   Since $P(1)$ and $P(2)$ have opposite signs, there is at least one real zero between 1 and 2.   *(4-2)*

6. The possible rational zeros are $\pm 1, \pm 2, \pm 4, \pm 8$. We form a synthetic division table.

	1	1	−10	8	
1	1	2	−8	0	1 is a zero

   Thus $x^3 + x^2 - 10x + 8 = (x - 1)(x^2 + 2x - 8) = (x - 1)(x - 2)(x + 4)$. The rational zeros are $1, 2, -4$.   *(4-3)*

7. (A) $x = \log_{10} y$ or $x = \log y$ (B) $x = e^y$ *(5-3)*

8. (A) $(2e^x)^3 = 2^3(e^x)^3 = 8e^{3x}$ (B) $\dfrac{e^{3x}}{e^{-2x}} = e^{3x-(-2x)} = e^{5x}$ *(5-1)*

9. (A) $\log_3 x = 2$ (B) $\log_3 81 = x$ (C) $\log_x 4 = -2$
   $ x = 3^2 = 9$ $ \log_3 3^4 = x$ $ x^{-2} = 4$
    $ x = 4$ $ \dfrac{1}{x^2} = 4$
   $ 1 = 4x^2$
   $ x^2 = \dfrac{1}{4}$
   $ x = \dfrac{1}{2}$

   since bases are restricted positive   *(5-3)*

10. (A) $10^x = 2.35$ (B) $e^x = 87{,}500$
    $ x = \log 2.35$ $ x = \ln 87{,}500$
    $ x = 0.371$ $ x = 11.4$

(C) $\log x = -1.25$
$x = 10^{-1.25}$
$x = 0.0562$

(D) $\ln x = 2.75$
$x = e^{2.75}$
$x = 15.6$ (5–3)

11. $E = k\dfrac{P}{x^3}$ (4–5)   **12.** $F = k\dfrac{q_1 q_2}{r^2}$ (4–5)

13. The graph of a nonconstant polynomial cannot have a horizontal asymptote.   (4–1)

14. The graph of a rational function that has a horizontal asymptote has to approach the horizontal asymptote both as $x \to -\infty$ and $x \to \infty$.   (4–4)

15. $f(x) = 3 \ln x - \sqrt{x}$ (5–3)

16. The function f multiplies the base e raised to the power of one-half of the domain element by 100 and then subtracts 50.   (5–1)

17. $f(x) = \dfrac{2x+8}{x+2} = \dfrac{n(x)}{d(x)}$

(A) The domain of f is the set of all real numbers x such that $d(x) = x + 2 \neq 0$, that is $(-\infty, -2) \cup (-2, \infty)$ or $x \neq -2$. f has an x intercept where $n(x) = 2x + 8 = 0$, that is, $x = -4$. $f(0) = 4$, hence f has a y intercept at $y = 4$.

(B)*Vertical asymptote:* $x = -2$
Horizontal asymptote: Since $n(x)$ and $d(x)$ have the same degree, the line $y = 2$ is a horizontal asymptote.
Complete the sketch.
Plot a few more points.

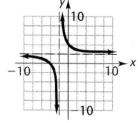

                   (4–4)

18. $P(x)$ can be factored further:
$P(x) = x(x^2 + 4)(x + 4)$
The zeros are 0, $2i$, $-2i$, and -4. Only 0 and -4 are x intercepts.   (4–1)

19. From the previous problem, the real zeros of $P(x) = (x^3 + 4x)(x + 4)$ are 0 and -4. They partition the x axis into the three intervals shown in the table. Choose a test number in each interval to determine the sign of P in that interval. The equality holds at the zeros.

Interval	$(-\infty, -4)$	$(-4, 0)$	$(0, \infty)$
Test number x	-5	-1	1
$P(x)$	145	-15	25
Sign of P	$+$	$-$	$+$

We conclude that the solution set of the inequality is $[-4, 0]$.   (4–2)

20.
$$\begin{array}{r} 2 \quad -5 \quad 3 \quad 2 \\ 1 \quad -2 \quad \tfrac{1}{2} \\ \hline \tfrac{1}{2}\Big|2 \quad -4 \quad 1 \quad \tfrac{5}{2} \end{array} \qquad P\!\left(\tfrac{1}{2}\right) = \tfrac{5}{2} \qquad (4\text{–}1)$$

21. $x - 1$ will be a factor of $P(x)$ if $P(1) = 0$
$P(1) = 1^{25} - 1^{20} + 1^{15} + 1^{10} - 1^5 + 1 = 1 - 1 + 1 + 1 - 1 + 1 = 2 \neq 0$,
so $x - 1$ is not a factor. $x + 1$ will be a factor of $P(x)$ if $P(-1) = 0$
$P(-1) = (-1)^{25} - (-1)^{20} + (-1)^{15} + (-1)^{10} - (-1)^5 + 1 = -1 - 1 - 1 + 1 + 1 + 1 = 0$, so $x + 1$ is a factor of $P(x)$.
$(4-1)$

22. (A) We form a synthetic division table:

	1	0	-8	0	3
-3	1	-3	1	-3	12 = P(-3)
-2	1	-2	-4	8	-13 = P(-2)
-1	1	-1	-7	7	-4 = P(-1)
0	1	0	-8	0	3 = P(0)
1	1	1	-7	-7	-4 = P(1)
2	1	2	-4	-8	-13 = P(2)
3	1	3	1	3	12 = P(3)

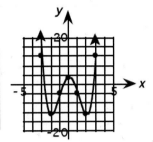

The graph of $P(x)$ has four x intercepts and three turning points; $P(x) \to \infty$ as $x \to \infty$ and as $x \to -\infty$
(B) There are real zeros in the intervals
$(-3, -2)$, $(-1, 0)$, $(0, 1)$, and $(2, 3)$ indicated in the table.
We search for the real zero in $(2, 3)$. Examining the graph of P
in a graphing utility we obtain the graph at the right.

The largest x intercept is 2.76.

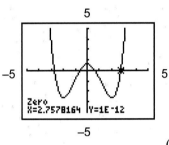

$(4-1)$

23. Examining the graph of $P(x)$, we see that there
may be a zero of even multiplicity between -1
and 0, a zero of odd multiplicity near 2, and a
zero of even multiplicity between 2 and 3.

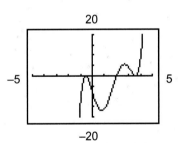

Applying a maximum routine between -1 and 0, a zero routine near 2, and a minimum routine between 2
and 3, we obtain

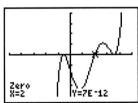
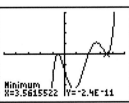

-0.56 is a zero of even multiplicity, 2 is a zero of odd multiplicity, and 3.56 is a zero of even multiplicity.
Since $P(x)$ is a fifth-degree polynomial, -0.56 and 3.56 must be double zeros and 2 must be a simple zero. $(4-2)$

24. (A) We form a synthetic division table:

	1	2	-20	0	-30
0	1	2	-20	0	-30
1	1	3	-17	-17	-47
2	1	4	-12	-24	-78
3	1	5	-5	-15	-75
4	1	6	4	16	34

−1	1	1	−21	21	−51
−2	1	0	−20	40	−110
−3	1	−1	−17	51	−183
−4	1	−2	−12	48	−222
−5	1	−3	−5	25	−155
−6	1	−4	4	−24	114

From the table, 4 is an upper bound and −6 is a lower bound.
(B) We search for the largest real zero in (3, 4). We organize our calculations in a table.

Sign Change Interval (a, b)	Midpoint m	Sign of P P(a)	P(m)	P(b)
(3, 4)	3.5	−	−	+
(3.5, 4)	3.75	−	−	+
(3.75, 4)	3.875	−	+	+
(3.75, 3.875)	3.8125	−	+	+
(3.75, 3.8125)	We stop here	−	−	+

Since each endpoint rounds to 3.8, a real zero lies on this last interval and is given by 3.8 to one decimal place accuracy. 4 further intervals were required.
(C) Examining the graph of $P(x)$, we obtain the graphs at the right. The real zeros are −5.68 and 3.80.

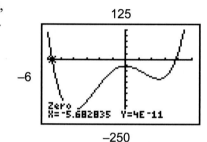
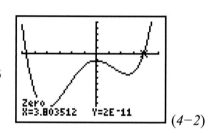

$(4\text{-}2)$

25. The possible rational zeros are $\pm 1, \pm 3, \pm 5, \pm 15, \pm\frac{1}{2}, \pm\frac{3}{2}, \pm\frac{5}{2}, \pm\frac{15}{2}, \pm\frac{1}{4}, \pm\frac{3}{4}, \pm\frac{5}{4}, \pm\frac{15}{4}$.

We form a synthetic division table.

	4	−20	29	−15
1	4	−16	13	−2
3	4	−8	5	0

3 is a zero

So $P(x) = (x - 3)(4x^2 - 8x + 5)$
To find the remaining zeros, we solve $4x^2 - 8x + 5 = 0$ by the quadratic formula.

$$4x^2 - 8x + 5 = 0$$

$$x = \frac{-b \pm \sqrt{b^2 - 4ac}}{2a} \quad a = 4, b = -8, c = 5$$

$$x = \frac{-(-8) \pm \sqrt{(-8)^2 - 4(4)(5)}}{2(4)} = \frac{8 \pm \sqrt{64 - 80}}{8} = \frac{8 \pm \sqrt{-16}}{8} = \frac{8 \pm 4i}{8} = 1 \pm \frac{1}{2}i$$

The zeros are $3, 1 \pm \frac{1}{2}i$

$(4\text{-}3)$

26. The possible rational zeros are $\pm 1, \pm 2, \pm 3, \pm 4, \pm 6, \pm 12$. We form a synthetic division table.

	1	5	1	−15	−12	
1	1	6	7	−8	−20	
2	1	7	15	15	18	a zero between 1 and 2; 2 is an upper bound
−1	1	4	−3	−12	0	−1 is a zero

We now examine $x^3 + 4x^2 - 3x - 12$. This factors by grouping into $(x + 4)(x^2 - 3)$, however, if we don't notice this, we find the remaining possible rational zeros to be −1, −2, −3, −4, −6, −12. We would then form a synthetic division table.
So $P(x) = (x + 1)(x + 4)(x^2 - 3) = (x + 1)(x + 4)(x - \sqrt{3})(x + \sqrt{3})$. The four zeros are $-1, -4, \pm\sqrt{3}$. $(4\text{-}3)$

27.
$$2^{x^2} = 4^{x+4}$$
$$2^{x^2} = (2^2)^{x+4}$$
$$2^{x^2} = 2^{2(x+4)}$$
$$x^2 = 2(x+4)$$
$$x^2 = 2x + 8$$
$$x^2 - 2x - 8 = 0$$
$$(x-4)(x+2) = 0$$
$$x - 4 = 0 \quad x + 2 = 0$$
$$x = 4 \qquad x = -2 \qquad (5\text{--}5)$$

28.
$$2x^2 e^{-x} + x e^{-x} = e^{-x}$$
$$2x^2 e^{-x} + x e^{-x} - e^{-x} = 0$$
$$e^{-x}(2x^2 + x - 1) = 0$$
$$e^{-x}(2x - 1)(x + 1) = 0$$
$$e^{-x} = 0 \quad 2x - 1 = 0 \quad x + 1 = 0$$
$$\text{never} \qquad x = \frac{1}{2} \qquad x = -1$$

Solutions: $\frac{1}{2}, -1$ $\qquad (5\text{--}5)$

29.
$$e^{\ln x} = 2.5$$
$$x = 2.5 \qquad (5\text{--}5)$$

30.
$$\log_x 10^4 = 4$$
$$x^4 = 10^4$$
$$x = 10 \qquad (5\text{--}5)$$

31.
$$\log_9 x = -\frac{3}{2}$$
$$9^{-3/2} = x$$
$$x = \frac{1}{27} \quad (5\text{--}5)$$

32. $\ln(x+4) - \ln(x-4) = 2 \ln 3$
$$\ln \frac{x+4}{x-4} = \ln 3^2$$
$$\frac{x+4}{x-4} = 3^2$$
$$\frac{x+4}{x-4} = 9 \quad x \neq 4$$
$$x + 4 = 9(x - 4)$$
$$x + 4 = 9x - 36$$
$$-8x = -40$$
$$x = 5$$

Check:
$$\ln(5+4) - \ln(5-4) \overset{?}{=} 2 \ln 3$$
$$\ln 9 - \ln 1 \overset{?}{=} 2 \ln 3$$
$$\ln 9 - 0 \overset{\checkmark}{=} \ln 9$$

Solution: $x = 5$ $\qquad (5\text{--}5)$

33.
$$\ln(2x^2 + 2) = 2 \ln(2x - 4)$$
$$\ln(2x^2 + 2) = \ln(2x - 4)^2$$
$$2x^2 + 2 = (2x - 4)^2$$
$$2x^2 + 2 = 4x^2 - 16x + 16$$
$$0 = 2x^2 - 16x + 14$$
$$0 = 2(x - 7)(x - 1)$$
$$x = 7, 1$$

Check: $x = 7$
$$\ln(2 \cdot 7^2 + 2) \overset{?}{=} 2 \ln(2 \cdot 7 - 4)$$
$$\ln 100 \overset{?}{=} 2 \ln 10$$
$$\ln 100 \overset{\checkmark}{=} \ln 100$$

$$x = 1$$
$$\ln(2 \cdot 1^2 + 2) \overset{?}{=} 2 \ln(2 \cdot 1 - 4)$$
$$\ln(4) \neq 2 \ln(-2)$$
Solution: $x = 7$ $\qquad (5\text{--}5)$

34.
$$\log x + \log(x + 15) = 2$$
$$\log[x(x + 15)] = 2$$
$$x(x + 15) = 10^2$$
$$x^2 + 15x = 100$$
$$x^2 + 15x - 100 = 0$$
$$(x - 5)(x + 20) = 0$$
$$x = 5, -20$$

Check: $x = 5$
$$\log 5 + \log(5 + 15) \overset{?}{=} 2$$
$$\log 5 + \log 20 \overset{?}{=} 2$$
$$\log 100 \overset{\checkmark}{=} 2$$
$$x = -20$$
$$\log(-20) + \log(-20 + 15) \neq 2$$
Solution: $x = 5$ $\qquad (5\text{--}5)$

35.
$$\log(\ln x) = -1$$
$$\ln x = 10^{-1}$$
$$\ln x = 0.1$$
$$x = e^{0.1} \qquad (5\text{--}5)$$

36.
$$4(\ln x)^2 = \ln x^2$$
$$4(\ln x)^2 = 2 \ln x$$
$$4(\ln x)^2 - 2 \ln x = 0$$
$$2 \ln x(2 \ln x - 1) = 0$$
$$2 \ln x = 0 \quad 2 \ln x - 1 = 0$$

$$\ln x = 0 \qquad \ln x = \frac{1}{2}$$

$$x = 1 \qquad x = e^{0.5}$$

Check:
$$x = 1$$
$$4(\ln 1)^2 \overset{?}{=} \ln 1^2$$
$$0 \overset{\surd}{=} 0$$
$$x = e^{0.5}$$
$$4(\ln e^{0.5})^2 \overset{?}{=} \ln(e^{0.5})^2$$
$$4(0.5)^2 \overset{?}{=} \ln (e^{2(0.5)})$$
$$4(0.25) \overset{?}{=} \ln e$$
$$1 \overset{\surd}{=} 1$$

Solution: $1, e^{0.5}$ *(5–5)*

37. $x = \log_3 41$

We use the change of base formula

$$x = \frac{\log 41}{\log 3} = 3.38 \qquad (5–5)$$

38. $\ln x = 1.45$
$$x = e^{1.45}$$
$$x = 4.26$$
(5–5)

39.
$$4(2^x) = 20$$
$$2^x = 5$$
$$x \log 2 = \log 5$$
$$x = \frac{\log 5}{\log 2} = 2.32 \quad (5–5)$$

40.
$$10e^{-0.5x} = 1.6$$
$$e^{-0.5x} = 0.16$$
$$-0.5x = \ln 0.16$$
$$x = \frac{\ln 0.16}{-0.5}$$
$$x = 3.67$$
(5–5)

41.
$$\frac{e^x - e^{-x}}{e^x + e^{-x}} = \frac{1}{2}$$

$$\frac{e^x - \frac{1}{e^x}}{e^x + \frac{1}{e^x}} = \frac{1}{2}$$

$$\frac{e^x \left(e^x - \frac{1}{e^x}\right)}{e^x \left(e^x + \frac{1}{e^x}\right)} = \frac{1}{2}$$

$$\frac{(e^x)^2 - 1}{(e^x)^2 + 1} = \frac{1}{2}$$

$$\frac{e^{2x} - 1}{e^{2x} + 1} = \frac{1}{2}$$

$$2(e^{2x} + 1)\,\frac{e^{2x} - 1}{e^{2x} + 1} = 2(e^{2x} + 1)\,\frac{1}{2}$$
$$2(e^{2x} - 1) = e^{2x} + 1$$
$$2e^{2x} - 2 = e^{2x} + 1$$
$$e^{2x} = 3$$
$$2x = \ln 3$$
$$x = \frac{1}{2} \ln 3$$
$$x = 0.549$$

(5–5)

42. Write $G = kx^2$. Substitute $G = 10$ and $x = 5$ and solve for k.
$$10 = k(5)^2$$
$$10 = 25k$$
$$k = 0.4$$
The equation of variation is $G = 0.4x^2$.
When $x = 7$
$$G = 0.4(7)^2 = 19.6 \qquad (4–5)$$

43. Write $H = \dfrac{k}{r^3}$. Substitute $H = 162$ and $r = 2$ and solve for k.

$$162 = \frac{k}{2^3}$$
$$k = 8(162)$$
$$k = 1296$$

The equation of variation is $H = \dfrac{1296}{r^3}$.

When $r = 3$
$$H = \frac{1296}{3^3} = 48 \qquad (4–5)$$

44. The graph of f is the same as the graph of the exponential function $g(x) = 2^x$ shifted upward 3 units. Therefore, f has domain all real numbers, range $(3, \infty)$, and horizontal asymptote $y = 3$.   *(5–1)*

45. The domain of f is the set of real numbers for which $x - 1 > 0$, that is, $x > 1$, or $(1, \infty)$. The graph of f is the same as the graph of the logarithmic function $g(x) = \log_3 x$ shifted right 1 unit, reflected through the x axis, and shifted up 2 units. Therefore, f has range all real numbers and vertical asymptote $x = 1$.   *(5–3)*

46. f is a polynomial function. Therefore, it has domain all real numbers and its graph has no asymptotes. Since $f(x) \to -\infty$ as $x \to \infty$ and $f(x) \to \infty$ as $x \to -\infty$, it has range all real numbers.   *(4–1)*

47. f is a polynomial function. Therefore it has domain all real numbers and its graph has no asymptotes. Since $x^4 \geq 0$ for all x, we can write

$$2x^4 \geq 0 \text{ all } x$$
$$3 + 2x^4 \geq 3 \text{ all } x$$

Hence the range of f is $[3, \infty)$ *(4–1)*

48. $f(x) = \dfrac{5}{x+3} = \dfrac{n(x)}{d(x)}$

Domain: $d(x) = x + 3$ zero: -3

  domain: $(-\infty, -3) \cup (-3, \infty)$

Range: If we set $y = \dfrac{5}{x+3}$ then $x + 3 = \dfrac{5}{y}$, $x = 3 - \dfrac{5}{y}$. Hence, y can take on any value except 0.

  range: $(-\infty, 0) \cup (0, \infty)$

Vertical asymptote: $x = -3$

Horizontal asymptote: Since the degree of $n(x) <$ the degree of $d(x)$ the x axis, $y = 0$ is a horizontal asymptote.   *(4–4)*

49. The graph of f is the same as the graph of the exponential function $g(x) = e^x$ reflected through the y axis, stretched vertically by a factor of 20, and shifted downward 15 units. Therefore, f has domain all real numbers, range $(-15, \infty)$, and horizontal asymptote $y = -15$.   *(5–1)*

50. The domain of f is the set of real numbers for which $x + 2 > 0$, that is, $x > -2$ or $(-2, \infty)$. The graph of f is the same as the graph of the logarithmic function $g(x) = \ln x$ shifted left 2 units and upward 8 units. Therefore, f has range all real numbers and vertical asymptote $x = -2$.   *(5–3)*

51. If the graph of $y = \ln x$ is reflected in the x axis, y is replaced by $-y$ and the graph becomes the graph of $-y = \ln x$ or $y = -\ln x$.

  If the graph of $y = \ln x$ is reflected in the y axis, x is replaced by $-x$ and the graph becomes the graph of $y = \ln(-x)$.   *(5–3)*

52. (A) For $x > 0$, $y = e^{-x}$ decreases from 1 to 0 while $\ln x$ increases from $-\infty$ to ∞. Consequently, the graphs can intersect at exactly one point.

(B) Graphing $y_1 = e^{-x}$ and $y_2 = \ln x$, we obtain

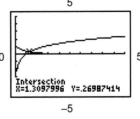

The solution is 1.31.   *(5–3)*

53. (A) Let $u = x^2$. Then

$$P(x) = x^4 + 9x^2 + 18$$
$$P(x) = u^2 + 9u + 18$$
$$P(x) = (u + 6)(u + 3)$$
$$P(x) = (x^2 + 6)(x^2 + 3)$$

(B) $x^2 + 6$ has $i\sqrt{6}$ and $-i\sqrt{6}$ as zeros, so it factors as

$x^2 + 6 = (x + i\sqrt{6})(x - i\sqrt{6})$. $x^2 + 3$ has $i\sqrt{3}$ and $-i\sqrt{3}$ as zeros, so it factors as

$x^2 + 3 = (x + i\sqrt{3})(x - i\sqrt{3})$.

$P(x) = (x + i\sqrt{6})(x - i\sqrt{6})(x + i\sqrt{3})(x - i\sqrt{3})$ *(4–3)*

54. (A) Let $u = x^2$. Then

$P(x) = x^4 - 23x^2 - 50$

$P(x) = u^2 - 23u - 50$

$P(x) = (u - 25)(u + 2)$

$P(x) = (x^2 - 25)(x^2 + 2)$

$P(x) = (x + 5)(x - 5)(x^2 + 2)$

(B) $x^2 + 2$ has zeros $i\sqrt{2}$ and $-i\sqrt{2}$ so it factors as $x^2 + 2 = (x + i\sqrt{2})(x - i\sqrt{2})$.

$P(x) = (x + 5)(x - 5)(x + i\sqrt{2})(x - i\sqrt{2})$ *(4–3)*

55. $f(x) = \dfrac{x^2 + 4x + 8}{x + 2} = \dfrac{n(x)}{d(x)}$

Intercepts. There are no real zeros of $n(x) = x^2 + 4x + 8$. No x intercept

$f(0) = 4$ y intercept

Vertical asymptotes. Real zeros of $d(x) = x + 2$. $x = -2$

Horizontal asymptote. Since the degree of $n(x)$ is greater than the degree of $d(x)$, there is no horizontal asymptote.

Oblique asymptote.

$$
\begin{array}{r}
x + 2 \\
x + 2 \overline{)\; x^2 + 4x + 8} \\
\underline{x^2 + 2x} \\
2x + 8 \\
\underline{2x + 4} \\
4
\end{array}
$$

Thus, $f(x) = x + 2 + \dfrac{4}{x + 2}$

Hence, the line $y = x + 2$ is an oblique asymptote.

Complete the sketch.
Graphing utility:

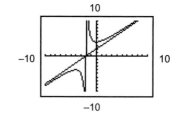

Hand sketch:

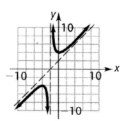

56. A preliminary graph of $y = P(x)$ is shown at the right.

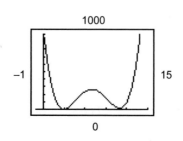

Examining the behavior near the maxima and minima, we obtain

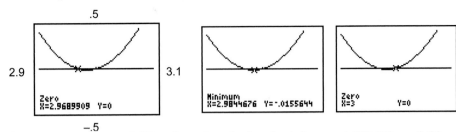

There are zeros at $x = 2.97$ and $x = 3$ and a local minimum at $P(2.98) \approx -0.02$.

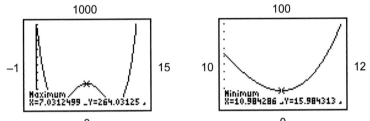

There is also a local maximum at $P(7.03) \approx 264.03$ and a local minimum at $P(10.98) \approx 15.98$.　　　　(4–2)

57.　$[x - (-1)]^2(x - 0)^3[x - (3 + 5i)][x - (3 - 5i)] = (x + 1)^2x^3(x - 3 - 5i)(x - 3 + 5i)$
　　degree 7　　　　　　　　　　　　　　　　　　　　　　　　　　　　　　　(4–3)

58.　Yes, for example:
　　$P(x) = (x + i)(x - i)(x + \sqrt{2})(x - \sqrt{2}) = x^4 - x^2 - 2$ has irrational zeros $\sqrt{2}$ and $-\sqrt{2}$.　　(4–3)

59.　(A) We form a synthetic division table:

	1	9	−500	0	20,000
0	1	9	−500	0	20,000
10	1	19	−310	−3,100	−11,000
20	1	29	80	1,600	52,000
−10	1	−1	−490	4,900	−29,000
−20	1	−11	−280	5,600	−92,000
−30	1	−21	130	−3,900	137,000

From the table, 20 is an upper bound and −30 is a lower bound.

(B) Examining the graph of $y = P(x)$, we obtain

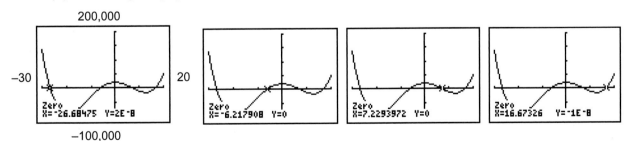

The zeros of $P(x)$ are −26.68, −6.22, 7.23, and 16.67.　　　　　　　　　　　(4–2)

60. The possible rational zeros of $P(x)$ are $\pm1, \pm2, \pm3, \pm4, \pm6, \pm12$. Examining the graph of $y = P(x)$, we obtain the graph at the right. It appears that there may be a zero of even multiplicity near -1 and a zero of odd multiplicity near 2. We test the likely candidates and find

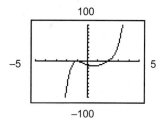

$$
\begin{array}{r}
1 \;\; -4 \;\;\;\; 3 \;\; 10 -10 -12 \\
 \;\;\;\;\; 2 \;\; -4 \;\; -2 \;\; 16 \;\; 12 \\
\hline
2\,|1 \;\; -2 \;\; -1 \;\;\;\; 8 \;\;\;\; 6 \;\;\;\; 0
\end{array}
$$

2 is a zero. $P(x) = (x - 2)(x^4 - 2x^3 - x^2 + 8x + 6) = (x - 2)\ Q(x)$. Testing -1 in $Q(x)$ we obtain

$$
\begin{array}{r}
1 \;\; -2 \;\; -1 \;\;\;\; 8 \;\;\;\; 6 \\
 \;\;\;\; -1 \;\;\;\; 3 \;\; -2 \;\; -6 \\
\hline
-1\,|1 \;\; -3 \;\;\;\; 2 \;\;\;\; 6 \;\;\;\; 0
\end{array}
$$

-1 is a zero. $Q(x) = (x + 1)(x^3 - 3x^2 + 2x + 6) = (x + 1)\ R(x)$. Testing -1 again in $R(x)$ we obtain

$$
\begin{array}{r}
1 \;\; -3 \;\;\;\; 2 \;\;\;\; 6 \\
 \;\;\;\; -1 \;\;\;\; 4 \;\; -6 \\
\hline
-1\,|1 \;\; -4 \;\;\;\; 6 \;\;\;\; 0
\end{array}
$$

-1 is a double zero of $Q(x)$. $P(x) = (x - 2)(x + 1)^2(x^2 - 4x + 6)$.
We complete the solution by solving $x^2 - 4x + 6 = 0$ by completing the square.

$$x^2 - 4x = -6$$
$$x^2 - 4x + 4 = -2$$
$$(x - 2)^2 = -2$$
$$x - 2 = \pm i\sqrt{2}$$
$$x = 2 \pm i\sqrt{2}$$

Thus the zeros of $P(x)$ are 2, -1 (double), and $2 \pm i\sqrt{2}$.

$$P(x) = (x - 2)(x + 1)^2[x - (2 + i\sqrt{2})][x - (2 - i\sqrt{2})] = (x - 2)(x + 1)^2(x - 2 - i\sqrt{2})(x - 2 + i\sqrt{2}) \qquad (4\text{--}3)$$

61. The possible rational zeros of $P(x)$ are $\pm1, \pm2, \pm4$. Examining the graph of $y = P(x)$, we obtain the graph at the right.
It appears that there may be zeros of unclear multiplicity near -2, as well as zeros between 1 and 2. The only possible rational zero allowed by the graph from the above list is -2. Testing it, we obtain

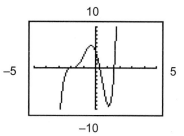

$$
\begin{array}{r}
1 \;\;\;\; 4 \;\;\;\; 1 \;\; -11 \;\; -8 \;\;\;\; 4 \\
 \;\;\;\; -2 \;\; -4 \;\;\;\; 6 \;\;\;\; 10 \;\; -4 \\
\hline
-2\,|1 \;\;\;\; 2 \;\; -3 \;\; -5 \;\;\;\; 2 \;\;\;\; 0
\end{array}
$$

-2 is a zero. Testing whether it is a double zero, we obtain

$$
\begin{array}{r}
1 \;\;\;\; 2 \;\; -3 \;\; -5 \;\;\;\; 2 \\
 \;\;\;\; -2 \;\;\;\; 0 \;\;\;\; 6 \;\; -2 \\
\hline
-2\,|1 \;\;\;\; 0 \;\; -3 \;\;\;\; 1 \;\;\;\; 0
\end{array}
$$

Thus $P(x) = (x + 2)^2(x^3 - 3x + 1) = (x + 2)^2 Q(x)$. Examining the graph of $Q(x)$, we obtain

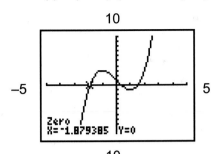
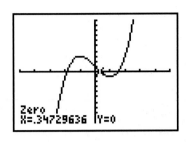
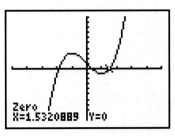

Thus, the zeros of $P(x)$ are -2 (double), -1.88, 0.35, and 1.53.   *(4-3)*

62. Since the real zeros are 5 and 8, we should have factors of $x - 5$ and $x - 8$ in the numerator. A factor of $x - 1$ in the denominator provides vertical asymptote 1, but we need the degree of the numerator and denominator to be equal in order to have a non-zero horizontal asymptote. So we'll make the denominator $(x - 1)^2$. Finally, a factor of 3 in the numerator makes $y = 3$ the horizontal asymptote:

$$f(x) = \frac{3(x-8)(x-5)}{(x-1)^2}.$$ *(4-4)*

63.
$$A = P\frac{(1+i)^n - 1}{i}$$

$$Ai = P[(1 + i)^n - 1]$$

$$\frac{Ai}{P} = (1 + i)^n - 1$$

$$1 + \frac{Ai}{P} = (1 + i)^n$$

$$\ln\left(1 + \frac{Ai}{P}\right) = n \ln(1 + i)$$

$$n = \frac{\ln\left(1 + \frac{Ai}{P}\right)}{\ln(1+i)}$$ *(5-5)*

64.
$$\ln y = 5x + \ln A$$
$$\ln y - \ln A = 5x$$
$$\ln\left(\frac{y}{A}\right) = 5x$$
$$\frac{y}{A} = e^{5x}$$
$$y = Ae^{5x}$$ *(5-5)*

65.
$$y = \frac{e^x - 2e^{-x}}{2}$$

$$2y = e^x - 2e^{-x}$$

$$2y = e^x - \frac{2}{e^x}$$

$$2ye^x = e^x e^x - e^x\left(\frac{2}{e^x}\right)$$

$$2ye^x = (e^x)^2 - 2$$
$$0 = (e^x)^2 - 2ye^x - 2$$

This equation is quadratic in e^x

$$e^x = \frac{-b \pm \sqrt{b^2 - 4ac}}{2a} \quad a = 1, b = -2y, c = -2$$

$$e^x = \frac{-(-2y) \pm \sqrt{(-2y)^2 - 4(1)(-2)}}{2(1)}$$

$$e^x = \frac{2y \pm \sqrt{4y^2 + 8}}{2}$$

$$e^x = y \pm \sqrt{y^2 + 2}$$

Note: Since $0 < 2$, $y^2 < y^2 + 2$, $\sqrt{y^2} < \sqrt{y^2 + 2}$ and $y < \sqrt{y^2 + 2}$ for all real y.

Hence $y - \sqrt{y^2 + 2}$ is always negative. Also, $y + \sqrt{y^2 + 2}$ is always positive. $x = \ln(y + \sqrt{y^2 + 2})$ $(5-5)$

66. $\dfrac{x^3 - x}{x^3 - 8} \geq 0$

Let $f(x) = \dfrac{p(x)}{q(x)} = \dfrac{x^3 - x}{x^3 - 8}$

The zeros of $p(x) = x^3 - x = x(x - 1)(x + 1)$ are -1, 0, and 1.
The real zero of $q(x) = x^3 - 8 = (x - 2)(x^2 + 2x + 4)$ is 2. These four zeros partition the x axis into the five intervals shown in the table. A test number is chosen from each interval to determine the sign of $f(x)$.

Interval	Test number x	$f(x)$	Sign of f
$(-\infty, -1)$	-2	0.375	$+$
$(-1, 0)$	$-\dfrac{1}{2}$	-0.05	$-$
$(0, 1)$	$\dfrac{1}{2}$	0.05	$+$
$(1, 2)$	$\dfrac{3}{2}$	-0.4	$-$
$(2, \infty)$	3	1.3	$+$

The equality holds at -1, 0, and 1, but not at 2.
We conclude that the solution set is $(-\infty, -1] \cup [0, 1] \cup (2, \infty)$. $(4-4)$

67. Algebraic solution:

$$\frac{4x}{x^2 - 1} - 3 < 0$$

$$\frac{4x}{x^2 - 1} - \frac{3(x^2 - 1)}{x^2 - 1} < 0$$

$$\frac{4x - 3x^2 + 3}{x^2 - 1} < 0$$

$$\frac{-3x^2 + 4x + 3}{x^2 - 1} < 0$$

zeros of the numerator: $a = -3$, $b = 4$, $c = 3$

$$x = \frac{-4 \pm \sqrt{16 - 4(-3)(3)}}{2(-3)} = \frac{-4 \pm \sqrt{52}}{-6} = -0.535, \ 1.869$$

zeros of the denominator:

$$x^2 - 1 = 0$$
$$x^2 = 1$$
$$x = \pm 1$$

These four zeros divide the real line into the five intervals shown below.

Interval	$(-\infty, -1)$	$(-1, -0.535)$	$(-0.535, 1)$	$(1, 1.869)$	$(1.869, \infty)$
Test number x	-2	-0.8	0.8	$\dfrac{3}{2}$	3
$f(x)$	-5.9	5.9	-11.9	1.8	-1.5
Sign of f	$-$	$+$	$-$	$+$	$-$

The expression is negative on $(-\infty, -1) \cup (-0.535, 1) \cup (1.869, \infty)$.

Graphical solution:

Graph $y_1 = \dfrac{4x}{x^2 - 1}$, $y_2 = 3$ and find where the graph of y_1 is below the graph of y_2.

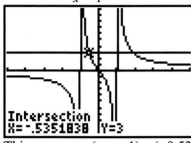 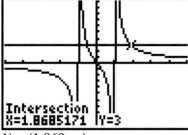 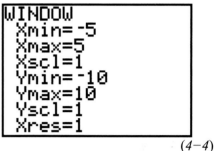

This occurs on $(-\infty, -1) \cup (-0.535, 1) \cup (1.869, \infty)$.   (4–4)

68. We are given y = length of container
x = width of one end
Hence $4x$ = girth of container
Length + girth = $y + 4x = 10$
So $y = 10 - 4x$
Since   Volume = $8 = x^2 y$, we have
$$8 = x^2(10 - 4x)$$
$$8 = 10x^2 - 4x^3$$
$$4x^3 - 10x^2 + 8 = 0$$
$$2x^3 - 5x^2 + 4 = 0$$
The possible rational solutions of this equation are

$\pm 1, \pm 2, \pm 4, \pm \dfrac{1}{2}$.

Examining the graph of $y = 2x^3 - 5x^2 + 4$, we obtain the
graph at the right.

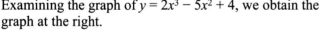

It appears that there may be an integer zero at 2, a zero between -1 and 0, and a zero between 1 and 2.
Testing 2, we obtain

$$
\begin{array}{r}
\;\;2 \;\; -5 \;\;\;\; 0 \;\;\;\; 4 \\
\;\;\;\;\;\;\;\;\; 4 \;\; -2 \;\; -4 \\
\hline
2|\;\;2 \;\; -1 \;\; -2 \;\;\;\; 0
\end{array}
$$

2 is a zero.
Thus, the equation can be factored $(x - 2)(2x^2 - x - 2) = 0$
To find the remaining zeros, we solve $2x^2 - x - 2 = 0$ by the quadratic formula.
$$2x^2 - x - 2 = 0$$

$$x = \frac{-b \pm \sqrt{b^2 - 4ac}}{2a} \quad a = 2, b = -1, c = -2$$

$$x = \frac{-(-1) \pm \sqrt{(-1)^2 - 4(2)(-2)}}{2(2)} = \frac{1 + \sqrt{17}}{4} \text{ (discarding the negative solution)}$$

Thus, the possible side lengths of the end are $x = 2$ feet and $x = \dfrac{1 + \sqrt{17}}{4} \approx 1.28$ feet.   (4–2)

69.

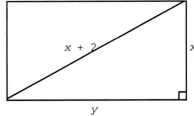

Labeling the rectangle as in the diagram, we have

$$\text{Area} = xy = 6$$

Hence $y = \dfrac{6}{x}$

Applying the Pythagorean theorem, we have

$$(x + 2)^2 = x^2 + y^2$$

$$(x + 2)^2 = x^2 + \left(\dfrac{6}{x}\right)^2$$

$$x^2 + 4x + 4 = x^2 + \dfrac{36}{x^2}$$

$$4x + 4 = \dfrac{36}{x^2}$$

$$4x^3 + 4x^2 = 36$$

$$4x^3 + 4x^2 - 36 = 0$$

$$x^3 + x^2 - 9 = 0$$

There are no rational zeros of $P(x) = x^3 + x^2 - 9$. Examining the graph of $y = P(x)$, we obtain the graph at the right. The only real zero is $x = 1.79$.

Then $y = \dfrac{6}{1.79} = 3.35$. The dimensions of the

rectangle are 1.79 feet by 3.35 feet.

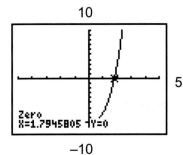

$(4-2)$

70. We use the Doubling Time Growth Model:

$P = P_0 2^{t/d}$

Substituting $P_0 = 60$ million and $d = 23$, we have

$P = 60(2^{t/23})$ million

(A) $t = 5$, hence $P = 60(2^{5/23})$ million = 69.8 million

(B) $t = 30$, hence $P = 60(2^{30/23})$ million = 148 million

$(5-2)$

71. We solve $P = P_0(1.07)^t$ for t, using $P = 2P_0$

$$2P_0 = P_0(1.07)^t$$

$$2 = (1.07)^t$$

$$\ln 2 = t \ln 1.07$$

$$\dfrac{\ln 2}{\ln 1.07} = t$$

$$t = 10.2 \text{ years}$$

$(5-1)$

72. We solve $P = P_0 e^{0.07t}$ for t, using $P = 2P_0$

$$2P_0 = P_0 e^{0.07t}$$

$$2 = e^{0.07t}$$

$$\ln 2 = 0.07t$$

$$t = \dfrac{\ln 2}{0.07}$$

$$t = 9.90 \text{ years}$$

$(5-1)$

73. First, we solve $M = \frac{2}{3} \log\left(\frac{E}{E_0}\right)$ for E.

$$M = \frac{2}{3} \log\left(\frac{E}{E_0}\right)$$

$$\frac{3M}{2} = \log\frac{E}{E_0}$$

$$\frac{E}{E_0} = 10^{3M/2}$$

$$E = E_0(10^{3M/2})$$

We now compare E_1 for $M = 8.3$ with E_2 for $M = 7.1$.

$$E_1 = E_0(10^{3\cdot8.3/2}) \qquad\qquad E_2 = E_0(10^{3\cdot7.1/2})$$

$$E_1 = E_0(10^{12.45}) \qquad\qquad E_2 = E_0(10^{10.65})$$

Hence $\dfrac{E_1}{E_2} = \dfrac{E_0(10^{12.45})}{E_0(10^{10.65})} = 10^{12.45-10.65} = 10^{1.8}$

$$E_1 = 10^{1.8}E_2 \text{ or } 63.1E_2.$$

The 1906 earthquake was 63.1 times as powerful.   (5–4)

74. We solve $D = 10 \log\dfrac{I}{I_0}$ for I, with $D = 88$, $I_0 = 10^{-12}$

$$88 = 10 \log\frac{I}{10^{-12}}$$

$$8.8 = \log\frac{I}{10^{-12}}$$

$$10^{8.8} = \frac{I}{10^{-12}}$$

$$I = 10^{8.8}\cdot10^{-12} = 10^{-3.2} = 6.31 \times 10^{-4}\, w/m^2 \qquad (5\text{–}4)$$

75. $t^2 = kd^3$ (4–5)

76. Write $v = \dfrac{k}{\sqrt{w}}$. Substitute $v = 0.3$ and $w = w_1$ and solve for k.

$$0.3 = \frac{k}{\sqrt{w_1}}$$

$$k = 0.3\sqrt{w_1} \text{ where } w_1 = \text{weight of oxygen molecule.}$$

The equation of variation is

$$v = \frac{0.3\sqrt{w_1}}{\sqrt{w_2}}$$

If $w_2 = \dfrac{w_1}{16}$ (weight of hydrogen molecule) then

$$v = \frac{0.3\sqrt{w_1}}{\sqrt{w_1/16}} = \frac{0.3\sqrt{w_1}}{\sqrt{w_1}/4} = 4(0.3) = 1.2 \text{ mile/second} \qquad (4\text{–}5)$$

77. Enter the data (note that the whole list is not visible in this window):

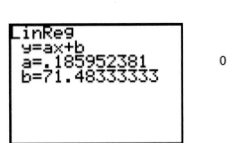

(A) Compute the linear regression equation, graph, and compute the value of the life expectancy that corresponds to $x = 40$ (year 2010).

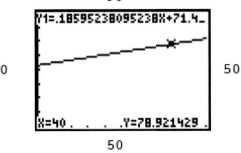

The model predicts a life expectancy of 78.9 years in 2010.

(B) Compute the quadratic regression equation, graph, and compute the value of the life expectancy that corresponds to $x = 40$.

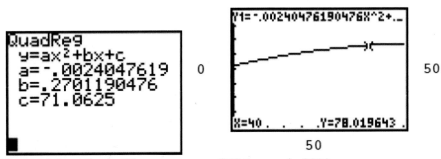

The model predicts a life expectancy of 78.0 years in 2010.

(C) Compute the cubic regression equation, graph, and compute the value of the life expectancy that corresponds to $x = 40$.

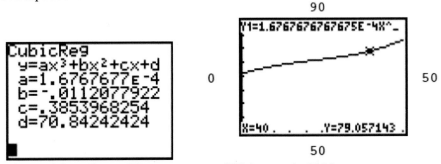

The model predicts a life expectancy of 79.1 years in 2010.

(D) Compute the exponential regression equation, graph, and compute the value of the life expectancy that corresponds to $x = 40$

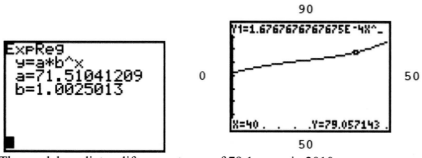

The model predicts a life expectancy of 79.1 years in 2010.   (4–1, 5–2)

78.   The quadratic model (78.0 years) is closest to the Census Bureau projection.

(4–1, 5–2)

Chapters 6, 7, & 8 Cumulative Review

1. We choose elimination by addition.
We multiply the top equation by 3, the bottom by 5, and add.

$$9x - 15y = 33$$
$$\underline{10x + 15y = 5}$$
$$19x \quad\quad = 38$$
$$x = 2$$

Substituting $x = 2$ in the bottom equation, we have

$$2(2) + 3y = 1$$
$$4 + 3y = 1$$
$$3y = -3$$
$$y = -1$$

Solution: $(2, -1)$ $(7-1)$

3. $-6x + 3y = 2$
        $2x - y = 1$

Solve the second equation for y and substitute into the first.

$$2x - y = 1$$
$$2x - 1 = y$$
$$-6x + 3(2x - 1) = 2$$
$$-6x + 6x - 3 = 2$$
$$-3 = 2$$

This is a contradiction so the system has no solution. $(7-1)$

2.

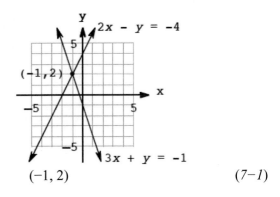

$(-1, 2)$ $(7-1)$

4.

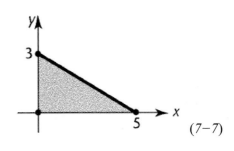

$(7-7)$

5.   (A)   Since $15 - 20 = 10 - 15 = -5$, this could start an arithmetic sequence.

(B)   Since $\dfrac{25}{5} = \dfrac{125}{25} = 5$, this could start a geometric sequence.

(C)   Since $\dfrac{25}{5} \neq \dfrac{50}{25}$ and $25 - 5 \neq 50 - 25$, this could start neither an arithmetic nor a geometric sequence.

(D)   Since $\dfrac{-9}{27} = \dfrac{3}{-9} = -\dfrac{1}{3}$, this could start a geometric sequence.

(E)   Since $(-6) - (-9) = (-3) - (-6) = 3$, this could start an arithmetic sequence. $(8-3)$

6. $a_n = 2 \cdot 5^n$

(A) $a_1 = 2 \cdot 5^1 = 10$
        $a_2 = 2 \cdot 5^2 = 50$
        $a_3 = 2 \cdot 5^3 = 250$
        $a_4 = 2 \cdot 5^4 = 1{,}250$

(B) This is a geometric sequence with $r = 5$.
        Hence,
$$a_n = a_1 r^{\,n-1}$$
$$a_8 = 10(5)^{8-1} = 781{,}250$$

(C) $S_n = \dfrac{a_1 - r a_n}{1 - r}$

$$S_8 = \dfrac{10 - 5(781{,}250)}{1 - 5} = 976{,}560 \quad (8-3)$$

7. $a_n = 3n - 1$

(A) $a_1 = 3 \cdot 1 - 1 = 2$
        $a_2 = 3 \cdot 2 - 1 = 5$
        $a_3 = 3 \cdot 3 - 1 = 8$
        $a_4 = 3 \cdot 4 - 1 = 11$

(B)   This is an arithmetic sequence with $d = 3$.
        Hence,
$$a_n = a_1 + (n - 1)d$$
$$a_8 = 2 + (8 - 1)3 = 23$$

(C) $S_n = \dfrac{n}{2}(a_1 + a_n)$

$$S_8 = \dfrac{8}{2}(2 + 23) = 100 \quad (8-3)$$

8. $a_1 = 100$ $a_n = a_{n-1} - 6$ $n \geq 2$

(A) $a_1 = 100$

$a_2 = a_1 - 6 = 94$

$a_3 = a_2 - 6 = 88$

$a_4 = a_3 - 6 = 82$

(B) This is an arithmetic sequence with
$d = -6$. Hence,

$a_n = a_1 + (n-1)d$

$a_8 = 100 + (8-1)(-6) = 58$

(C) $S_n = \dfrac{n}{2}(a_1 + a_n)$

$S_8 = \dfrac{8}{2}(100 + 58) = 632$ $(8-3)$

9. (A) $8! = 8 \cdot 7 \cdot 6 \cdot 5 \cdot 4 \cdot 3 \cdot 2 \cdot 1 = 40{,}320.$

(B) $\dfrac{32!}{30!} = \dfrac{32 \cdot 31 \cdot 30!}{30!} = 992$

(C) $\dfrac{9!}{3!(9-3)!} = \dfrac{9!}{3!6!} = \dfrac{9 \cdot 8 \cdot 7 \cdot 6!}{3 \cdot 2 \cdot 1 \cdot 6!} = 84$

$(8-4)$

10. (A) $\dbinom{7}{2} = \dfrac{7!}{2!(7-2)!} = \dfrac{7!}{2!5!} = \dfrac{7 \cdot 6 \cdot 5!}{2 \cdot 1 \cdot 5!} = 21$ (B) $C_{7,2} = \dfrac{7!}{2!(7-2)!} = 21$

(C) $P_{7,2} = \dfrac{7!}{(7-2)!} = \dfrac{7!}{5!} = \dfrac{7 \cdot 6 \cdot 5!}{5!} = 42$ $(8-4, 8-5)$

11. First, write the equation in standard form by dividing both sides by 900.

$25x^2 - 36y^2 = 900$

$\dfrac{x^2}{36} - \dfrac{y^2}{25} = 1$

In this form the equation is identifiable as that of a hyperbola.

When $x = 0$, $-\dfrac{y^2}{25} = 1$. There are no y intercepts, but $b = 5$.

When $y = 0$, $\dfrac{x^2}{36} = 1$. x intercepts: ± 6.

Sketch the asymptotes using the asymptote rectangle, then sketch in the hyperbola.

Foci: $c^2 = 5^2 + 6^2$

$c^2 = 61$

$c = \sqrt{61}$

Foci: $F' = (-\sqrt{61}, 0), F = (\sqrt{61}, 0)$

Transverse axis length $= 2(6) = 12$

Conjugate axis length $= 2(5) = 10$

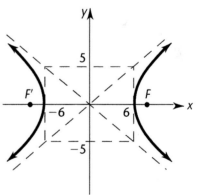

$(6-3)$

12. First, write the equation in standard form by dividing both sides by 900.

$$25x^2 + 36y^2 = 900$$

$$\frac{x^2}{36} + \frac{y^2}{25} = 1$$

In this form the equation is identifiable as that of an ellipse. Locate the intercepts:

When $y = 0$, $\dfrac{x^2}{36} = 1$. x intercepts: ± 6.

When $x = 0$, $\dfrac{y^2}{25} = 1$. y intercepts: ± 5

Thus, $a = 6$, $b = 5$, and the major axis is on the x axis.

Foci: $c^2 = a^2 - b^2$

$\qquad c^2 = 36 - 25$

$\qquad c^2 = 11$

$\qquad c = \sqrt{11}$

Foci: $F' = (-\sqrt{11}, 0)$, $F = (\sqrt{11}, 0)$

Major axis length = $2(6) = 12$; Minor axis length = $2(5) = 10$

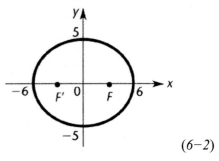

$(6-2)$

13. $25x^2 - 36y = 0$ is the equation of a parabola. For convenience, we rewrite this as $25x^2 = 36y$. To graph, assign y values that make $25x^2$ a perfect square (y must be positive or zero for x to be real) and solve for x. Since the coefficient of x is positive, a must be positive, and the parabola opens up.

x	0	$\pm\frac{6}{5}$	$\pm\frac{12}{5}$
y	0	1	4

To find the focus and directrix, solve

$$4a = \frac{36}{25}$$

$$a = \frac{9}{25}$$

Focus: $\left(0, \dfrac{9}{25}\right)$. Directrix: $y = -\dfrac{9}{25}$

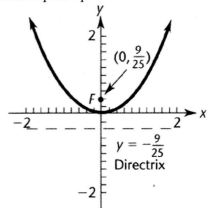

$(6-1)$

14. (A) $\begin{vmatrix} -3 & 5 \\ 2 & -2 \end{vmatrix} = (-3)(-2) - 2 \cdot 5 = -4$

(B) $\begin{vmatrix} 5 & 3 \\ -5 & -3 \end{vmatrix} = 5(-3) - (-5)3 = 0$

$(7-5)$

15. $x^2 + y^2 = 2$
$2x - y = 1$

We choose substitution, solving the first-degree equation for y in terms of x, then substituting into the second-degree equation.

$$2x - y = 1$$
$$-y = 1 - 2x$$
$$y = 2x - 1$$
$$x^2 + (2x - 1)^2 = 2$$
$$x^2 + 4x^2 - 4x + 1 = 2$$
$$5x^2 - 4x - 1 = 0$$
$$(5x + 1)(x - 1) = 0$$
$$x = -\tfrac{1}{5}, 1$$

For $x = -\tfrac{1}{5}$ For $x = 1$

$$y = 2\left(-\tfrac{1}{5}\right) - 1 \qquad y = 2(1) - 1$$
$$= -\tfrac{7}{5} \qquad\qquad = 1$$

Solutions: $\left(-\tfrac{1}{5}, -\tfrac{7}{5}\right), (1, 1)$

The checking steps are omitted for lack of space.

(7–6)

16.

Corner Point (x, y)	Objective Function $z = 2x + 3y$	
(0, 4)	12	
(5, 0)	10	Minimum value
(6, 7)	33	Maximum value
(0, 10)	30	

The minimum value of z on S is 10 at (5, 0).
The maximum value of z on S is 33 at (6, 7).

(7–8)

17.   (A) $M - 2N = \begin{bmatrix} 2 & 1 \\ 1 & -3 \end{bmatrix} - 2\begin{bmatrix} 1 & 2 \\ -1 & 3 \end{bmatrix} = \begin{bmatrix} 2 & 1 \\ 1 & -3 \end{bmatrix} - \begin{bmatrix} 2 & 4 \\ -2 & 6 \end{bmatrix} = \begin{bmatrix} 0 & -3 \\ 3 & -9 \end{bmatrix}$

(B) $P + Q$ is not defined

(C) $PQ = \begin{bmatrix} 1 & 2 \end{bmatrix}\begin{bmatrix} -1 \\ 2 \end{bmatrix} = [1(-1) + 2\cdot 2] = [3]$

(D) $MN = \begin{bmatrix} 2 & 1 \\ 1 & -3 \end{bmatrix}\begin{bmatrix} 1 & 2 \\ -1 & 3 \end{bmatrix} = \begin{bmatrix} 2\cdot 1 + 1(-1) & 2\cdot 2 + 1\cdot 3 \\ 1\cdot 1 + (-3)(-1) & 1\cdot 2 + (-3)3 \end{bmatrix} = \begin{bmatrix} 1 & 7 \\ 4 & -7 \end{bmatrix}$

(E) $PN = \begin{bmatrix} 1 & 2 \end{bmatrix}\begin{bmatrix} 1 & 2 \\ -1 & 3 \end{bmatrix} = [1\cdot 1 + 2(-1) \quad 1\cdot 2 + 2\cdot 3] = [-1 \quad 8]$

(F) QM is not defined

(7-3)

18.   (A) The outcomes can be displayed in a tree diagram as follows:

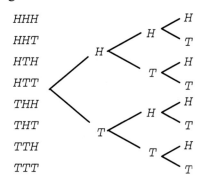

HHH
HHT
HTH
HTT
THH
THT
TTH
TTT

(B) O_1: First flip of the coin
N_1: 2 outcomes
O_2: Second flip of the coin
N_2: 2 outcomes
O_3: Third flip of the coin
N_3: 2 outcomes

Applying the multiplication principle, there are $2\cdot 2\cdot 2 = 8$ possible outcomes.

(8–5)

19. **(A)** O_1: Place first book N_1: 4 ways
O_2: Place second book N_2: 3 ways
O_3: Place third book N_3: 2 ways
O_4: Place fourth book N_4: 1 way

Applying the multiplication principle, there are $4 \cdot 3 \cdot 2 \cdot 1$, or 24, arrangements.

(B) Order is important here. We use permutations to determine the number of arrangements of 4 objects.
$P_{4,4} = 4! = 24.$ *(8−5)*

20. The sample space S is the set of all possible 3-card hands, chosen from a deck of 52 cards. $n(S) = C_{52,3}$.
The event E is the set of all possible 3-card hands that are all diamonds, thus, are chosen from the 13 diamonds. $n(E) = C_{13,3}$

$$P(E) = \frac{n(E)}{n(S)} = \frac{C_{13,3}}{C_{52,3}} = \frac{13!}{3!(13-3)!} \div \frac{52!}{3!(52-3)!} \approx .0129 \qquad \textit{(8−5)}$$

21. In the first case, order is important. The sample space is the set of all possible arrangements of four objects, drawn from a set of 10 objects.
$n(S) = P_{10,4}.$
The event E is one of these arrangements. $n(E) = 1.$

$$P(E) = \frac{n(E)}{n(S)} = \frac{1}{P_{10,4}} = \frac{1}{10 \cdot 9 \cdot 8 \cdot 7} \approx .0002$$

In the second case, order is not important. The sample space is the set of all possible ways of drawing four objects from a set of 10 objects $n(S) = C_{10,4}.$
The event E is one of these ways. $n(E) = 1.$

$$P(E) = \frac{n(E)}{n(S)} = \frac{1}{C_{10,4}} = 1 \div \frac{10!}{4!(10-4)!} \approx .0048 \qquad \textit{(8−5)}$$

22. $P(E) \approx \dfrac{f(E)}{n} = \dfrac{100-38}{100} = .62$ *(8−5)*

23. **(A)** $x_1 = 3$
$x_2 = -4$

(B) $x_1 - 2x_2 = 3$
Let $x_2 = t$
Then $x_1 = 2x_2 + 3 = 2t + 3$
Hence, $x_1 = 2t + 3$, $x_2 = t$ is a solution for every real number t.

(C) $x_1 - 2x_2 = 3$
$0x_1 + 0x_2 = 1$
No solution.   *(8−2)*

24. **(A)** $\begin{bmatrix} 1 & 1 & | & 3 \\ -1 & 1 & | & 5 \end{bmatrix}$

(B) $\begin{bmatrix} 1 & 1 & | & 3 \\ -1 & 1 & | & 5 \end{bmatrix} R_1 + R_2 \rightarrow R_2$

$\sim \begin{bmatrix} 1 & 1 & | & 3 \\ 0 & 2 & | & 8 \end{bmatrix} \frac{1}{2}R_2 \rightarrow R_2$

$\sim \begin{bmatrix} 1 & 1 & | & 3 \\ 0 & 1 & | & 4 \end{bmatrix} (-1)R_2 + R_1 \rightarrow R_1$

$\sim \begin{bmatrix} 1 & 0 & | & -1 \\ 0 & 1 & | & 4 \end{bmatrix}$

(C) Solution: $x_1 = -1$, $x_2 = 4$

                                (8−2)

25. (A)   As a matrix equation the system becomes

$$\underset{A}{\begin{bmatrix} 1 & -3 \\ 2 & -5 \end{bmatrix}} \underset{X}{\begin{bmatrix} x_1 \\ x_2 \end{bmatrix}} = \underset{B}{\begin{bmatrix} k_1 \\ k_2 \end{bmatrix}}$$

(B)   To find A^{-1}, we perform row operations on

$$\begin{bmatrix} 1 & -3 & | & 1 & 0 \\ 2 & -5 & | & 0 & 1 \end{bmatrix} \underset{(-2)R_1 + R_2 \to R_2}{\sim} \begin{bmatrix} 1 & -3 & | & 1 & 0 \\ 0 & 1 & | & -2 & 1 \end{bmatrix} \underset{3R_2 + R_1 \to R_1}{\sim} \begin{bmatrix} 1 & 0 & | & -5 & 3 \\ 0 & 1 & | & -2 & 1 \end{bmatrix}$$

Hence $A^{-1} = \begin{bmatrix} -5 & 3 \\ -2 & 1 \end{bmatrix}$

Check: $A^{-1}A = \begin{bmatrix} -5 & 3 \\ -2 & 1 \end{bmatrix}\begin{bmatrix} 1 & -3 \\ 2 & -5 \end{bmatrix} = \begin{bmatrix} (-5)1+3\cdot 2 & (-5)(-3)+3(-5) \\ (-2)1+1\cdot 2 & (-2)(-3)+1(-5) \end{bmatrix} = \begin{bmatrix} 1 & 0 \\ 0 & 1 \end{bmatrix}$

(C)   The solution of $AX = B$ is $X = A^{-1}B$. Using the result of (B), we have

$$X = \begin{bmatrix} -5 & 3 \\ -2 & 1 \end{bmatrix}\begin{bmatrix} k_1 \\ k_2 \end{bmatrix}$$

If $k_1 = -2$, $k_2 = 1$, we have

$$\begin{bmatrix} x_1 \\ x_2 \end{bmatrix} = \begin{bmatrix} -5 & 3 \\ -2 & 1 \end{bmatrix}\begin{bmatrix} -2 \\ 1 \end{bmatrix} = \begin{bmatrix} (-5)(-2)+3\cdot 1 \\ (-2)(-2)+1\cdot 1 \end{bmatrix} = \begin{bmatrix} 13 \\ 5 \end{bmatrix} \quad x_1 = 13, x_2 = 5$$

(D)   If $k_1 = 1$, $k_2 = -2$, reasoning as in (C) we have

$$\begin{bmatrix} x_1 \\ x_2 \end{bmatrix} = \begin{bmatrix} -5 & 3 \\ -2 & 1 \end{bmatrix}\begin{bmatrix} 1 \\ -2 \end{bmatrix} = \begin{bmatrix} (-5)1+3(-2) \\ (-2)1+1(-2) \end{bmatrix} = \begin{bmatrix} -11 \\ -4 \end{bmatrix} \quad x_1 = -11, x_2 = -4 \qquad\qquad (7-4)$$

26.   We write the augmented matrix:

$$\begin{bmatrix} 1 & 3 & | & 10 \\ 2 & -1 & | & -1 \end{bmatrix} \underbrace{(-2)R_1 + R_2 \to R_2}$$
$$-2 \quad -6 \quad -20$$
$$\uparrow$$
Need a 0 here

$$\sim \begin{bmatrix} 1 & 3 & | & 10 \\ 0 & -7 & | & -21 \end{bmatrix} -\tfrac{1}{7}R_2 \to R_2 \quad \text{corresponds to the linear system} \quad \begin{aligned} x_1 + 3x_2 &= 10 \\ -7x_2 &= -21 \end{aligned}$$
$$\uparrow$$
Need a 1 here
Need a 0 here
$$\downarrow$$

$$\begin{bmatrix} 1 & 3 & | & 10 \\ 0 & 1 & | & 3 \end{bmatrix} \underbrace{(-3)R_2 + R_1 \to R_1} \quad \text{corresponds to the linear system} \quad \begin{aligned} x_1 + 3x_2 &= 10 \\ x_2 &= 3 \end{aligned}$$
$$0 \quad -3 \quad -9$$

$$\sim \begin{bmatrix} 1 & 0 & | & 1 \\ 0 & 1 & | & 3 \end{bmatrix} \quad \text{corresponds to the linear system} \quad \begin{aligned} x_1 &= 1 \\ x_2 &= 3 \end{aligned}$$

The solution is $x_1 = 1$, $x_2 = 3$. Each pair of lines graphed below has the same intersection point, $(1, 3)$.

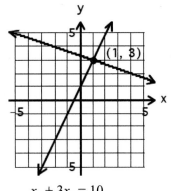

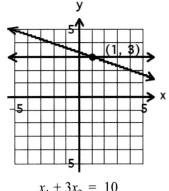

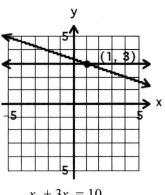

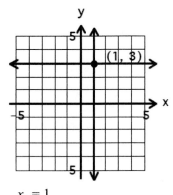

$$x_1 + 3x_2 = 10$$
$$2x_1 - x_2 = -1$$

$$x_1 + 3x_2 = 10$$
$$-7x_2 = -21$$

$$x_1 + 3x_2 = 10$$
$$x_2 = 3$$

$$x_1 = 1$$
$$x_2 = 3$$

$(7-1, 7-2)$

27. Here is a computer-generated graph of the system, entered as

$$y = \frac{7+2x}{3}$$

$$y = \frac{18-3x}{4}$$

After zooming in (graph not shown) the intersection point is located at (1.53, 3.35) to two decimal places.

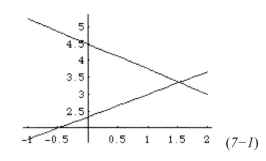

$(7-1)$

28. P_1: $1 = 1(2 \cdot 1 - 1) = 1 \cdot 1 = 1$
P_2: $1 + 5 = 2(2 \cdot 2 - 1)$
          $6 = 6$
P_3: $1 + 5 + 9 = 3(2 \cdot 3 - 1)$
          $15 = 15$ $(8-2)$

29. P_1: $1^2 + 1 + 2$ is divisible by 2
          $4 = 2 \cdot 2$ true
      P_2: $2^2 + 2 + 2$ is divisible by 2
          $8 = 2 \cdot 4$ true
      P_3: $3^2 + 3 + 2$ is divisible by 2
          $14 = 2 \cdot 7$ true $(8-2)$

30. P_k: $1 + 5 + 9 + \cdots + (4k - 3) = k(2k - 1)$
P_{k+1}: $1 + 5 + 9 + \cdots + (4k - 3) + (4k + 1) = (k + 1)(2k + 1)$ $(8-2)$

31. P_k: $k^2 + k + 2 = 2r$ for some integer r
P_{k+1}: $(k + 1)^2 + (k + 1) + 2 = 2s$ for some integer s $(8-2)$

32. The parabola is opening either up or down and has an equation of the form $x^2 = 4ay$. Since $(2, -8)$ is on the graph, we have:

$$2^2 = 4a(-8)$$
$$4 = -32a$$
$$a = -\frac{1}{8}$$

Thus, the equation of the parabola is

$$x^2 = 4\left(-\frac{1}{8}\right)y$$

$$x^2 = -\frac{1}{2}y$$

$$y = -2x^2$$

$(6-1)$

33. Make a rough sketch of the ellipse, locate focus and x intercepts, then determine y intercepts using the special triangle relationship.

$$\frac{x^2}{a^2} + \frac{y^2}{b^2} = 1$$

$$a = \frac{10}{2} = 5$$

$$b^2 = a^2 - c^2 = 5^2 - 3^2 = 25 - 9 = 16$$

$$b = 4$$

$$\frac{x^2}{25} + \frac{y^2}{16} = 1$$

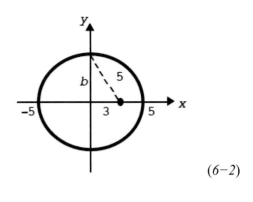

$(6-2)$

34. Start with $\dfrac{x^2}{a^2} - \dfrac{y^2}{b^2} = 1$ and find a and b.

$$a = \frac{16}{2} = 8$$

To find b, sketch the asymptote rectangle, label known parts, and use the Pythagorean Theorem.

$$b^2 = (\sqrt{89})^2 - 8^2 = 89 - 64$$

$$b^2 = 25$$

$$b = 5$$

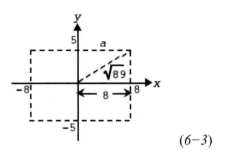

$(6-3)$

Thus, the equation is $\dfrac{x^2}{64} - \dfrac{y^2}{25} = 1$

35.
$$\begin{bmatrix} 1 & 2 & -1 & | & 3 \\ 0 & 1 & 1 & | & -2 \\ 2 & 3 & 1 & | & 0 \end{bmatrix} (-2)R_1 + R_3 \to R_3$$

$$\sim \begin{bmatrix} 1 & 2 & -1 & | & 3 \\ 0 & 1 & 1 & | & -2 \\ 0 & -1 & 3 & | & -6 \end{bmatrix} \begin{array}{l}(-2)R_2 + R_1 \to R_1 \\ \\ R_2 + R_3 \to R_3\end{array}$$

$$\sim \begin{bmatrix} 1 & 0 & -3 & | & 7 \\ 0 & 1 & 1 & | & -2 \\ 0 & 0 & 4 & | & -8 \end{bmatrix} \tfrac{1}{4}R_3 \to R_3$$

$$\sim \begin{bmatrix} 1 & 0 & -3 & | & 7 \\ 0 & 1 & 1 & | & -2 \\ 0 & 0 & 1 & | & -2 \end{bmatrix} \begin{array}{l}3R_3 + R_1 \to R_1 \\ (-1)R_3 + R_2 \to R_2\end{array}$$

$$\sim \begin{bmatrix} 1 & 0 & 0 & | & 1 \\ 0 & 1 & 0 & | & 0 \\ 0 & 0 & 1 & | & -2 \end{bmatrix}$$

Solution: $x_1 = 1,\ x_2 = 0,\ x_3 = -2$ $(7-2)$

36.
$$\begin{bmatrix} 1 & 1 & -1 & | & 2 \\ 0 & 4 & 6 & | & -1 \\ 0 & 6 & 9 & | & 0 \end{bmatrix} (-\tfrac{3}{2})R_2 + R_3 \to R_3$$

$$\sim \begin{bmatrix} 1 & 1 & -1 & | & 2 \\ 0 & 4 & 6 & | & -1 \\ 0 & 0 & 0 & | & \tfrac{3}{2} \end{bmatrix}$$

The last row corresponds to the equation

$0x_1 + 0x_2 + 0x_3 = \dfrac{3}{2}$, hence there is no solution.

$(7-2)$

37.
$$\begin{bmatrix} 1 & -2 & 1 & | & 1 \\ 3 & -2 & -1 & | & -5 \end{bmatrix} (-3)R_1 + R_2 \to R_2 \sim \begin{bmatrix} 1 & -2 & 1 & | & 1 \\ 0 & 4 & -4 & | & -8 \end{bmatrix} \tfrac{1}{4}R_2 \to R_2 \sim \begin{bmatrix} 1 & -2 & 1 & | & 1 \\ 0 & 1 & -1 & | & -2 \end{bmatrix} 2R_2 + R_1 \to R_1$$

$$\sim \begin{bmatrix} 1 & 0 & -1 & | & -3 \\ 0 & 1 & -1 & | & -2 \end{bmatrix}$$

This corresponds to the system

$$x_1 \quad - x_3 = -3$$
$$x_2 - x_3 = -2$$

Let $x_3 = t$

Then $x_2 = x_3 - 2 = t - 2$
$$x_1 = x_3 - 3 = t - 3$$

Hence $x_1 = t - 3$, $x_2 = t - 2$, $x_3 = t$ is a solution for every real number t.   (7–2)

38. (A) $MN = [1 \quad 2 \quad -1]\begin{bmatrix} 1 \\ -1 \\ 2 \end{bmatrix} = [1 \cdot 1 + 2(-1) + (-1)2] = [-3]$

(B) $NM = \begin{bmatrix} 1 \\ -1 \\ 2 \end{bmatrix}[1 \quad 2 \quad -1] = \begin{bmatrix} 1 \cdot 1 & 1 \cdot 2 & 1(-1) \\ (-1)1 & (-1)2 & (-1)(-1) \\ 2 \cdot 1 & 2 \cdot 2 & 2(-1) \end{bmatrix} = \begin{bmatrix} 1 & 2 & -1 \\ -1 & -2 & 1 \\ 2 & 4 & -2 \end{bmatrix}$ (7–3)

39. (A) $LM = \begin{bmatrix} 2 & -1 & 0 \\ 1 & 2 & 1 \end{bmatrix}\begin{bmatrix} 1 & 2 \\ -1 & 0 \\ 1 & 1 \end{bmatrix} = \begin{bmatrix} 2 \cdot 1 + (-1)(-1) + 0 \cdot 1 & 2 \cdot 2 + (-1)0 + 0 \cdot 1 \\ 1 \cdot 1 + 2(-1) + 1 \cdot 1 & 1 \cdot 2 + 2 \cdot 0 + 1 \cdot 1 \end{bmatrix}$

$LM - 2N = \begin{bmatrix} 3 & 4 \\ 0 & 3 \end{bmatrix} - 2\begin{bmatrix} 2 & 1 \\ -1 & 0 \end{bmatrix} = \begin{bmatrix} 3 & 4 \\ 0 & 3 \end{bmatrix} - \begin{bmatrix} 4 & 2 \\ -2 & 0 \end{bmatrix} = \begin{bmatrix} -1 & 2 \\ 2 & 3 \end{bmatrix}$

(B) Since ML is a 3×3 matrix and N is a 2×2 matrix, $ML + N$ is not defined.

(7–3)

40. $x^2 - 3xy + 3y^2 = 1$
$$xy = 1$$

Solve for y in the second equation.

$$y = \frac{1}{x}$$

$$x^2 - 3x\left(\frac{1}{x}\right) + 3\left(\frac{1}{x}\right)^2 = 1$$

$$x^2 - 3 + \frac{3}{x^2} = 1 \quad x \neq 0$$

$$x^4 - 3x^2 + 3 = x^2$$
$$x^4 - 4x^2 + 3 = 0$$
$$(x^2 - 1)(x^2 - 3) = 0$$

$$x^2 - 1 = 0 \qquad\qquad x^2 - 3 = 0$$
$$x^2 = 1 \qquad\qquad\quad x^2 = 3$$
$$x = \pm 1 \qquad\qquad\quad x = \pm\sqrt{3}$$

For $x = 1$ For $x = -1$ For $x = \sqrt{3}$ For $x = -\sqrt{3}$

$y = \dfrac{1}{1}$ $y = \dfrac{1}{-1}$ $y = \dfrac{1}{\sqrt{3}}$ $y = \dfrac{1}{-\sqrt{3}}$

$y = 1$ $y = -1$ $y = \dfrac{\sqrt{3}}{3}$ $y = -\dfrac{\sqrt{3}}{3}$

Solutions: $(1, 1)$, $(-1, -1)$, $\left(\sqrt{3}, \dfrac{\sqrt{3}}{3}\right)$, $\left(-\sqrt{3}, -\dfrac{\sqrt{3}}{3}\right)$ (7–6)

41.
$$x^2 - 3xy + y^2 = -1$$
$$x^2 - xy = 0$$

Factor the left side of the equation that has a zero constant term.

$x(x - y) = 0$

$x = 0$ or $x = y$

Thus the original system is equivalent to the two systems

$x^2 - 3xy + y^2 = -1$	$x^2 - 3xy + y^2 = -1$
$x = 0$	$x = y$

These systems are solved by substitution.

First system:

$$x^2 - 3xy + y^2 = -1$$
$$x = 0$$
$$0^2 - 3(0)y + y^2 = -1$$
$$y^2 = -1$$
$$y = \pm i$$
$$x = 0$$

Second system:

$$x^2 - 3xy + y^2 = -1$$
$$x = y$$
$$y^2 - 3yy + y^2 = -1$$
$$-y^2 = -1$$
$$y^2 = 1$$
$$y = \pm 1$$

For $y = 1$ For $y = -1$
$x = 1$ $x = -1$

Solutions: $(1, 1), (-1, -1), (0, i), (0, -i)$ (7–6)

42. We expand by column 2

$$\begin{vmatrix} 1 & 0 & 4 \\ 2 & 5 & -1 \\ 3 & 0 & -6 \end{vmatrix} = a_{12}(\text{cofactor of } a_{12}) + a_{22}(\text{cofactor of } a_{22}) + a_{32}(\text{cofactor of } a_{32})$$

$$= 0(\quad) + 5(-1)^{2+2}\begin{vmatrix} 1 & 4 \\ 3 & -6 \end{vmatrix} + 0(\quad)$$

$\uparrow$ $\uparrow$

It is unnecessary to evaluate these since they are multiplied by 0.

$$= 5(-1)^4[1(-6) - 3\cdot4]$$
$$= -90$$ (7–5)

43. We expand by row 1

$$\begin{vmatrix} -4 & 5 & -6 \\ 3 & -2 & -1 \\ 2 & 4 & 6 \end{vmatrix} = a_{11}(\text{cofactor of } a_{11}) + a_{12}(\text{cofactor of } a_{12}) + a_{13}(\text{cofactor of } a_{13})$$

$$= (-4)(-1)^{1+1}\begin{vmatrix} -2 & -1 \\ 4 & 6 \end{vmatrix} + 5(-1)^{1+2}\begin{vmatrix} 3 & -1 \\ 2 & 6 \end{vmatrix} + (-6)(-1)^{1+3}\begin{vmatrix} 3 & -2 \\ 2 & 4 \end{vmatrix}$$

$$= (-4)(-1)^2[(-2)6 - 4(-1)] + 5(-1)^3[3\cdot6 - 2(-1)] + (-6)(-1)^4[3\cdot4 - 2(-2)]$$
$$= 32 - 100 - 96 = -164$$ (7–5)

44. Before we can enter these equations in our graphing utility, we must solve for y:

$$x^2 + 2xy - y^2 = 1 \qquad\qquad 9x^2 + 4xy + y^2 = 15$$
$$y^2 - 2xy - x^2 + 1 = 0 \qquad\qquad y^2 + 4xy + 9x^2 - 15 = 0$$

Applying the quadratic formula to each equation, we have

$$y = \frac{2x \pm \sqrt{4x^2 - 4(-x^2 + 1)}}{2} \qquad\qquad y = \frac{-4x \pm \sqrt{16x^2 - 4(9x^2 - 15)}}{2}$$

$$y = \frac{2x \pm \sqrt{8x^2 - 4}}{2} \qquad\qquad y = \frac{-4x \pm \sqrt{60 - 20x^2}}{2}$$

$$y = x \pm \sqrt{2x^2 - 1} \qquad\qquad y = -2x \pm \sqrt{15 - 5x^2}$$

Entering each of these four equations into a graphing utility produces the graph shown at the right. Zooming in on the four intersection points, or using a built-in intersection routine (details omitted), yields $(-1.35, 0.28)$, $(-0.87, -1.60)$, $(0.87, 1.60)$, and $(1.35, -0.28)$ to two decimal places.

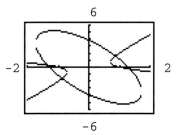

(7–6)

45. $\displaystyle\sum_{k=1}^{5} k^k = 1^1 + 2^2 + 3^3 + 4^4 + 5^5 = 1 + 4 + 27 + 256 + 3{,}125 = 3{,}413$ *(8–1)*

46. $\displaystyle S_6 = \frac{2}{2!} - \frac{2^2}{3!} + \frac{2^3}{4!} - \frac{2^4}{5!} + \frac{2^5}{6!} - \frac{2^6}{7!}$

$k = 1, 2, 3, 4, 5, 6$

Noting that the terms alternate in sign, we can rewrite as follows:

$$S_6 = (-1)^2\frac{2}{2!} + (-1)^3\frac{2^2}{3!} + (-1)^4\frac{2^3}{4!} + (-1)^5\frac{2^4}{5!} + (-1)^6\frac{2^5}{6!} + (-1)^7\frac{2^6}{7!}$$

Clearly, $a_k = (-1)^{k+1}\dfrac{2^k}{(k+1)!}$

$$S_6 = \sum_{k=1}^{6} (-1)^{k+1}\frac{2^k}{(k+1)!}$$ *(8–1)*

47. $\dfrac{a_2}{a_1} = \dfrac{-36}{108} = -\dfrac{1}{3} = r.\ |r| < 1.$

Therefore, this infinite geometric series has a sum.

$$S_\infty = \frac{a_1}{1-r} = \frac{108}{1-\left(-\frac{1}{3}\right)} = 81$$ *(8–3)*

48. The solution region is unbounded. Two corner points are obvious from the graph: $(0, 6)$ and $(8, 0)$. The third corner point is obtained by solving the system
$3x + 2y = 12$
$x + 2y = 8$ to obtain $(2, 3)$.

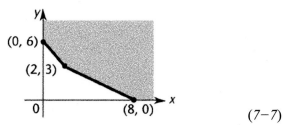

(7–7)

49. The feasible region is graphed as follows:
The corner points $(0, 7)$, $(0, 0)$ and $(8, 0)$ are obvious from the graph. The corner point $(6, 4)$ is obtained by solving the system
$$x + 2y = 14$$
$$2x + y = 16$$
We now evaluate the objective function at each corner point.

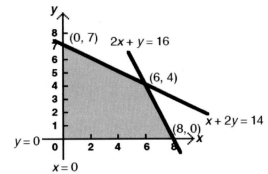

Corner Point (x, y)	Objective Function $z = 4x + 9y$	
$(0, 7)$	63	Maximum value
$(0, 0)$	0	
$(8, 0)$	32	
$(6, 4)$	60	

$(7-8)$

50. **(A)** As a matrix equation the system becomes

$$\underset{A}{\begin{bmatrix} 1 & 4 & 2 \\ 2 & 6 & 3 \\ 2 & 5 & 2 \end{bmatrix}} \underset{X}{\begin{bmatrix} x_1 \\ x_2 \\ x_3 \end{bmatrix}} = \underset{B}{\begin{bmatrix} k_1 \\ k_2 \\ k_3 \end{bmatrix}}$$

(B) To find A^{-1}, we perform row operations on

$$\begin{bmatrix} 1 & 4 & 2 & | & 1 & 0 & 0 \\ 2 & 6 & 3 & | & 0 & 1 & 0 \\ 2 & 5 & 2 & | & 0 & 0 & 1 \end{bmatrix} \begin{matrix} \\ (-2)R_1 + R_2 \to R_2 \\ (-2)R_1 + R_3 \to R_3 \end{matrix} \sim \begin{bmatrix} 1 & 4 & 2 & | & 1 & 0 & 0 \\ 0 & -2 & -1 & | & -2 & 1 & 0 \\ 0 & -3 & -2 & | & -2 & 0 & 1 \end{bmatrix} -\tfrac{1}{2}R_2 \to R_2$$

$$\sim \begin{bmatrix} 1 & 4 & 2 & | & 1 & 0 & 0 \\ 0 & 1 & \tfrac{1}{2} & | & 1 & -\tfrac{1}{2} & 0 \\ 0 & -3 & -2 & | & -2 & 0 & 1 \end{bmatrix} \begin{matrix} (-4)R_2 + R_1 \to R_1 \\ \\ 3R_2 + R_3 \to R_3 \end{matrix} \sim \begin{bmatrix} 1 & 0 & 0 & | & -3 & 2 & 0 \\ 0 & 1 & \tfrac{1}{2} & | & 1 & -\tfrac{1}{2} & 0 \\ 0 & 0 & -\tfrac{1}{2} & | & 1 & -\tfrac{3}{2} & 1 \end{bmatrix} R_3 + R_2 \to R_2$$

$$\sim \begin{bmatrix} 1 & 0 & 0 & | & -3 & 2 & 0 \\ 0 & 1 & 0 & | & 2 & -2 & 1 \\ 0 & 0 & -\tfrac{1}{2} & | & 1 & -\tfrac{3}{2} & 1 \end{bmatrix} -2R_3 \to R_3 \sim \begin{bmatrix} 1 & 0 & 0 & | & -3 & 2 & 0 \\ 0 & 1 & 0 & | & 2 & -2 & 1 \\ 0 & 0 & 1 & | & -2 & 3 & -2 \end{bmatrix}$$

Hence $A^{-1} = \begin{bmatrix} -3 & 2 & 0 \\ 2 & -2 & 1 \\ -2 & 3 & -2 \end{bmatrix}$

Check: $A^{-1}A = \begin{bmatrix} -3 & 2 & 0 \\ 2 & -2 & 1 \\ -2 & 3 & -2 \end{bmatrix} \begin{bmatrix} 1 & 4 & 2 \\ 2 & 6 & 3 \\ 2 & 5 & 2 \end{bmatrix} = \begin{bmatrix} (-3)1 + 2\cdot2 + 0\cdot2 & (-3)4 + 2\cdot6 + 0\cdot5 & -3\cdot2 + 2\cdot3 + 0\cdot2 \\ 2\cdot1 + (-2)2 + 1\cdot2 & 2\cdot4 + (-2)6 + 1\cdot5 & 2\cdot2 + (-2)3 + 1\cdot2 \\ (-2)1 + 3\cdot2 + (-2)2 & (-2)4 + 3\cdot6 + (-2)5 & (-2)2 + 3\cdot3 + (-2)2 \end{bmatrix}$

$= \begin{bmatrix} 1 & 0 & 0 \\ 0 & 1 & 0 \\ 0 & 0 & 1 \end{bmatrix}$

(C)   The solution of $AX = B$ is $X = A^{-1}B$. Using the result of (B), we have

$$X = \begin{bmatrix} -3 & 2 & 0 \\ 2 & -2 & 1 \\ -2 & 3 & -2 \end{bmatrix} \begin{bmatrix} k_1 \\ k_2 \\ k_3 \end{bmatrix}$$

If $k_1 = -1$, $k_2 = 2$, $k_3 = 1$, we have

$$\begin{bmatrix} x_1 \\ x_2 \\ x_3 \end{bmatrix} = \begin{bmatrix} -3 & 2 & 0 \\ 2 & -2 & 1 \\ -2 & 3 & -2 \end{bmatrix} \begin{bmatrix} -1 \\ 2 \\ 1 \end{bmatrix} = \begin{bmatrix} 7 \\ -5 \\ 6 \end{bmatrix} \quad x_1 = 7, x_2 = -5, x_3 = 6$$

(D)   If $k_1 = 2$, $k_2 = 0$, $k_3 = -1$, reasoning as in (C) we have

$$\begin{bmatrix} x_1 \\ x_2 \\ x_3 \end{bmatrix} = \begin{bmatrix} -3 & 2 & 0 \\ 2 & -2 & 1 \\ -2 & 3 & -2 \end{bmatrix} \begin{bmatrix} 2 \\ 0 \\ -1 \end{bmatrix} = \begin{bmatrix} -6 \\ 3 \\ -2 \end{bmatrix} \quad x_1 = -6, x_2 = 3, x_3 = -2 \qquad (7\text{-}4)$$

51.

	Case 1	Case 2	Case 3
O_1: Select the first letter	N_1: 6 ways	6 ways	6 ways
O_2: Select the second letter	N_2: 5 ways	6 ways	5 ways (exclude first letter)
O_3: Select the third letter	N_3: 4 ways	6 ways	5 ways (exclude second letter)
O_4: Select the fourth letter	N_4: 3 ways	6 ways	5 ways (exclude third letter)
	$6 \cdot 5 \cdot 4 \cdot 3 =$	$6 \cdot 6 \cdot 6 \cdot 6 =$	$6 \cdot 5 \cdot 5 \cdot 5 = 750$ words
	360 words	1,296 words	$(8\text{-}4)$

52.   The sample space is the set of all possible ways to choose 5 players out of 12. $n(S) = C_{12,5}$

The event E is the set of all those choices that include 2 particular people, thus

O_1: Choose the two centers N_1: 1

O_2: Choose 3 more people out of the 10 remaining N_2: $C_{10,3}$

Applying the multiplication principle, $n(E) = N_1 \cdot N_2 = 1 \cdot C_{10,3} = C_{10,3}$

$$P(E) = \frac{n(E)}{n(S)} = \frac{C_{10,3}}{C_{12,5}} = \frac{\dfrac{10!}{3!(10-3)!}}{\dfrac{12!}{5!(12-5)!}} = 120 \div 792 = \frac{5}{33} = .\overline{15} \qquad (8\text{-}5)$$

53.   (A) P (this event) $= \dfrac{195 + 170}{1000} = .365$

(B) A sample space of equally likely events is: $S = \{1, 2, 3, 4, 5, 6\}$. $n(S) = 6$

The event E is the set of those outcomes that are divisible by 3. $E = \{3, 6\}$. $n(E) = 2$

Then $P(E) = \dfrac{n(E)}{n(S)} = \dfrac{2}{6} = \dfrac{1}{3}$ $\qquad (8\text{-}5)$

54.

| Enter the sequences in the sequence editor. | Graph the sequences. | Display the points in a table. |

From the graph, 22 is the least positive integer n such that $a_n < b_n$.

The table confirms this. $\qquad (8\text{-}3)$

55. (A) $\quad P_{25,5} = 25 \cdot 24 \cdot 23 \cdot 22 \cdot 21 = 6,375,600$

(B) $\quad C_{25,5} = \dfrac{25!}{5!(25-5)!} = \dfrac{25!}{5!20!} = \dfrac{25 \cdot 24 \cdot 23 \cdot 22 \cdot 21 \cdot 20!}{5 \cdot 4 \cdot 3 \cdot 2 \cdot 1 \cdot 20!} = 53,130$

(C) $\quad \dbinom{25}{5} = \dfrac{25!}{5!(25-5)!} = 53,130$ $\hfill$ (8–4, 8–6)

56. $\quad \left(a + \dfrac{1}{2}b\right)^6 = \sum_{k=0}^{6} \dbinom{6}{k} a^{6-k}\left(\dfrac{1}{2}b\right)^k$

$= \dbinom{6}{0}a^6 + \dbinom{6}{1}a^5\left(\dfrac{1}{2}b\right)^1 + \dbinom{6}{2}a^4\left(\dfrac{1}{2}b\right)^2 + \dbinom{6}{3}a^3\left(\dfrac{1}{2}b\right)^3 + \dbinom{6}{4}a^2\left(\dfrac{1}{2}b\right)^4$

$+ \dbinom{6}{5}a\left(\dfrac{1}{2}b\right)^5 + \dbinom{6}{6}\left(\dfrac{1}{2}b\right)^6$

$= a^6 + 3a^5b + \dfrac{15}{4}a^4b^2 + \dfrac{5}{2}a^3b^3 + \dfrac{15}{16}a^2b^4 + \dfrac{3}{16}ab^5 + \dfrac{1}{64}b^6$ $\hfill$ (8–6)

57. In the expansion of $(a + b)^n$, the exponent of b in the rth term is $r - 1$ and the exponent of a is $n - (r - 1)$. Here, in the first case, $r = 5$, $n = 10$.

$\quad$ Fifth term $= \dbinom{10}{4}(3x)^6(-y)^4 = 153,090x^6y^4$

In the second case, $r = 8$, n is still 10.

$\quad$ Eighth term $= \dbinom{10}{7}(3x)^3(-y)^7 = -3,240x^3y^7$ $\hfill$ (8–6)

58. $\quad P_n: 1 + 5 + 9 + \cdots + (4n - 3) = n(2n - 1)$

Part 1: Show that P_1 is true.

$P_1: 1 = 1(2 \cdot 1 - 1) = 1$ True

Part 2: Show that if P_k is true, then P_{k+1} is true.

Write out P_k and P_{k+1}.

$\quad P_k: 1 + 5 + 9 + \cdots + (4k - 3) = k(2k - 1)$

$\quad P_{k+1}: 1 + 5 + 9 + \cdots + (4k - 3) + (4k + 1) = (k + 1)(2k + 1)$

We start with P_k:

$\quad 1 + 5 + 9 + \cdots + (4k - 3) = k(2k - 1)$

Adding $4k + 1$ to both sides:

$\quad 1 + 5 + 9 + \cdots + (4k - 3) + (4k + 1) = k(2k - 1) + 4k + 1 = 2k^2 - k + 4k + 1$

$\quad\quad\quad\quad\quad\quad\quad\quad\quad\quad\quad\quad\quad = 2k^2 + 3k + 1 = (k + 1)(2k + 1)$

We have shown that if P_k is true, then P_{k+1} is true.

Conclusion: P_n is true for all positive integers n. $\hfill$ (8–2)

59. P_n: $n^2 + n + 2 = 2p$ for some integer p.

Part 1: Show that P_1 is true.

P_1: $1^2 + 1 + 2 = 4 = 2 \cdot 2$ is true.

Part 2: Show that if P_k is true, then P_{k+1} is true.

Write out P_k and P_{k+1}.

P_k: $k^2 + k + 2 = 2r$ for some integer r

P_{k+1}: $(k+1)^2 + (k+1) + 2 = 2s$ for some integer s

We start with P_k:

$k^2 + k + 2 = 2r$ for some integer r

Now, $(k+1)^2 + (k+1) + 2 = k^2 + 2k + 1 + k + 1 + 2 = k^2 + k + 2 + 2k + 2 = 2r + 2k + 2 = 2(r + k + 1)$

Therefore,

$(k+1)^2 + (k+1) + 2 = 2s$ for some integer s $(= r + k + 1)$

$(k+1)^2 + (k+1) + 2$ is divisible by 2.

We have shown that if P_k is true, then P_{k+1} is true.

Conclusion: P_n is true for all positive integers n. $(8-2)$

60. We are to find $51 + 53 + \cdots + 499$.

This is the sum of an arithmetic sequence, S_n, with $d = 2$.

First, find n:

$a_n = a_1 + (n-1)d$

$499 = 51 + (n-1)2$

$n = 225$

Now, find S_{225}

$S_n = \dfrac{n}{2}(a_1 + a_n)$

$S_{225} = \dfrac{225}{2}(51 + 499) = 61{,}875$ $(8-3)$

61. $2.\overline{45} = 2.454545\ldots = 2 + 0.454545\ldots$

$0.454545\ldots = 0.45 + 0.0045 + 0.000045 + \cdots$

This is an infinite geometric series with $a_1 = 0.45$ and $r = 0.01$.

Thus $S_\infty = \dfrac{a_1}{1-r} = \dfrac{0.45}{1-0.01} = \dfrac{0.45}{0.99} = \dfrac{5}{11}$

Hence, $2.\overline{45} = 2 + \dfrac{5}{11} = \dfrac{27}{11}$ $(8-3)$

62. Graphing the sequence, we obtain the graph at the right. The solid line indicates 0.01. The largest term of the sequence is a_{27}. From the table display,

$a_{27} = \dbinom{30}{27}(0.1)^{30-27}(0.9)^{27} = 0.236088$

There are 8 terms larger than 0.01, as can be seen from the graph or the table display (details omitted).

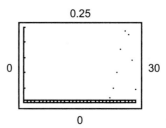

$(8-6)$

63. $D = \begin{vmatrix} -2 & 0 & 3 \\ 1 & -6 & 5 \\ -1 & 2 & 0 \end{vmatrix} = 8$ $\qquad x = \dfrac{\begin{vmatrix} -13 & 0 & 3 \\ -16 & -6 & 5 \\ -1 & 2 & 0 \end{vmatrix}}{D} = \dfrac{16}{8} = 2$ $(7-5)$

64. From problem 63, $D = 8$

$$y = \dfrac{\begin{vmatrix} -2 & -13 & 3 \\ 1 & -16 & 5 \\ -1 & -1 & 0 \end{vmatrix}}{D} = \dfrac{4}{8} = \dfrac{1}{2}$$ *(7–5)*

65. From problem 63, $D = 8$

$$z = \dfrac{\begin{vmatrix} -2 & 0 & -13 \\ 1 & -6 & -16 \\ -1 & 2 & -1 \end{vmatrix}}{D} = \dfrac{-24}{8} = -3$$ *(7–5)*

66.

	Allowing digits to repeat	No digit can be repeated
O_1: Selecting first digit	N_1: 10 ways	N_1: 10 ways
O_2: Selecting second digit	N_2: 10 ways	N_2: 9 ways
$\vdots$	$\vdots$	$\vdots$
O_9: Selecting ninth digit	N_9: 10 ways	N_9: 2 ways

$$10 \cdot 10 \cdot 10 \cdot 10 \cdot 10 \cdot 10 \cdot 10 \cdot 10 \cdot 10$$
$$= 10^9 \text{ zip codes}$$

$$P_{10,9} = 10 \cdot 9 \cdot 8 \cdot 7 \cdot 6 \cdot 5 \cdot 4 \cdot 3 \cdot 2$$
$$= 3{,}628{,}800 \text{ zip codes}$$

(8–1)

67. Prove P_n: $\dfrac{1}{1\cdot 3} + \dfrac{1}{3\cdot 5} + \dfrac{1}{5\cdot 7} + \cdots + \dfrac{1}{(2n-1)(2n+1)} = \dfrac{n}{2n+1}$

Part 1: Show that P_1 is true.

P_1: $\dfrac{1}{1\cdot 3} = \dfrac{1}{2\cdot 1 + 1}$

$\dfrac{1}{3} = \dfrac{1}{3}$ P_1 is true

Part 2: Show that if P_k is true, then P_{k+1} is true.

Write out P_k and P_{k+1}:

P_k: $\dfrac{1}{1\cdot 3} + \dfrac{1}{3\cdot 5} + \dfrac{1}{5\cdot 7} + \cdots + \dfrac{1}{(2k-1)(2k+1)} = \dfrac{k}{2k+1}$

P_{k+1}: $\dfrac{1}{1\cdot 3} + \dfrac{1}{3\cdot 5} + \dfrac{1}{5\cdot 7} + \cdots + \dfrac{1}{(2k-1)(2k+1)} + \dfrac{1}{(2k+1)(2k+3)} = \dfrac{k+1}{2k+3}$

We start with P_k:

$$\dfrac{1}{1\cdot 3} + \dfrac{1}{3\cdot 5} + \dfrac{1}{5\cdot 7} + \cdots + \dfrac{1}{(2k-1)(2k+1)} = \dfrac{k}{2k+1}$$

Adding $\dfrac{1}{(2k+1)(2k+3)}$ to both sides, we get

$$\dfrac{1}{1\cdot 3} + \dfrac{1}{3\cdot 5} + \dfrac{1}{5\cdot 7} + \cdots + \dfrac{1}{(2k-1)(2k+1)} + \dfrac{1}{(2k+1)(2k+3)}$$

$$= \dfrac{k}{2k+1} + \dfrac{1}{(2k+1)(2k+3)} = \dfrac{k(2k+3)}{(2k+1)(2k+3)} + \dfrac{1}{(2k+1)(2k+3)} = \dfrac{k(2k+3)+1}{(2k+1)(2k+3)}$$

$$= \dfrac{2k^2+3k+1}{(2k+1)(2k+3)} = \dfrac{(2k+1)(k+1)}{(2k+1)(2k+3)} = \dfrac{k+1}{2k+3}$$

We have shown that if P_k is true, then P_{k+1} is true.

Conclusion: P_n is true for positive integers n.

(8–2)

68. Case 1: No repetition.

The sample space S is the set of all possible sequences of three digits, chosen from $\{1, 2, 3, 4, 5\}$ with no repeats.

$n(S) = P_{5,3} = 5 \cdot 4 \cdot 3 = 60$

The event E is the set of those sequences that end in 2 or 4.

$n(E) = N_1 \cdot N_2 \cdot N_3$

where

$N_1 = 2$ (digits 2 or 4 only for the last digit)

$N_2 = 4$ (digits remaining for middle digit after last digit is chosen)

$N_3 = 3$ (digits remaining for first digit after others are chosen)

$n(E) = 2 \cdot 4 \cdot 3 = 24$

$P(E) = \dfrac{n(E)}{n(S)} = \dfrac{24}{60} = \dfrac{2}{5}$

Case 2: Allowing repetition

The sample space S is the set of all possible three digit numbers chosen from $\{1, 2, 3, 4, 5\}$.

$n(S) = 5 \cdot 5 \cdot 5 = 125$

The event E is the set of those numbers that end in 2 or 4.

$n(E) = 5 \cdot 5 \cdot 2 = 50$

$P(E) = \dfrac{n(E)}{n(S)} = \dfrac{50}{125} = \dfrac{2}{5}$ $\hfill (8-5)$

69. (A) The matrix is in fact

$$\begin{bmatrix} 1 & 0 & -5 & | & 2 \\ 0 & 1 & 3 & | & 6 \\ 0 & 0 & 0 & | & 0 \end{bmatrix}$$

Thus there are an infinite number of solutions ($x_3 = t$, $x_2 = 6 - 3t$, $x_1 = 2 + 5t$, for t any real number.)

(B) The matrix is in fact

$$\begin{bmatrix} 1 & 0 & -5 & | & 2 \\ 0 & 1 & 3 & | & 6 \\ 0 & 0 & 0 & | & n \end{bmatrix}$$

The third row corresponds to the equation $0x_1 + 0x_2 + 0x_3 = n$. This is impossible. The system has no solution.

(C) The system is independent. There is one solution. $\hfill (7-2)$

70. If $A^2 = A$ and A^{-1} exists, then $A^{-1}A^2 = A^{-1}A$ or $A^{-1}AA = I$ or $IA = I$. Thus, $A = I$, the $n \times n$ identity matrix. $(7-4)$

71. L, M, and P are in reduced form.

N is not in reduced form; it violates condition 1 of the definition of reduced matrix, Section 10-2: there is a row of 0's above rows having non-zero elements.

$\hfill (7-2)$

72. True. For example,

$$\begin{bmatrix} a_{11} & a_{12} & a_{13} \\ 0 & a_{22} & a_{23} \\ 0 & 0 & a_{33} \end{bmatrix} + \begin{bmatrix} b_{11} & b_{12} & b_{13} \\ 0 & b_{22} & b_{23} \\ 0 & 0 & b_{33} \end{bmatrix} = \begin{bmatrix} a_{11}+b_{11} & a_{12}+b_{12} & a_{13}+b_{13} \\ 0 & a_{22}+b_{22} & a_{23}+b_{23} \\ 0 & 0 & a_{33}+b_{33} \end{bmatrix}$$

proves the statement for 3×3 matrices. A similar proof can be given for any order matrix. $\hfill (7-3)$

73. True. For example, $\begin{bmatrix} a_{11} & 0 \\ a_{21} & a_{22} \end{bmatrix}\begin{bmatrix} b_{11} & 0 \\ b_{21} & b_{22} \end{bmatrix} = \begin{bmatrix} a_{11}b_{11} & 0 \\ a_{21}b_{11}+a_{22}b_{21} & a_{22}b_{22} \end{bmatrix}$ proves the statement for 2×2 matrices. A similar proof can be given for any order matrix. $(7-3)$

74. False. For example, $\begin{bmatrix} 1 & 1 \\ 0 & 1 \end{bmatrix} + \begin{bmatrix} 1 & 0 \\ 1 & 1 \end{bmatrix} = \begin{bmatrix} 2 & 1 \\ 1 & 2 \end{bmatrix}$ which is not a diagonal matrix. $(7-3)$

75. False. For example, $\begin{bmatrix} 1 & 1 \\ 0 & 1 \end{bmatrix}\begin{bmatrix} 1 & 0 \\ 1 & 1 \end{bmatrix} = \begin{bmatrix} 2 & 1 \\ 1 & 1 \end{bmatrix}$ which is not a diagonal matrix. $(7-3)$

76. True. If all elements above and all elements below the principal diagonal are zero, then all elements not on the principal diagonal are zero. $(7-4)$

77. True. For example, the inverse of $\begin{bmatrix} a_{11} & 0 & 0 \\ 0 & a_{22} & 0 \\ 0 & 0 & a_{33} \end{bmatrix}$ is $\begin{bmatrix} \frac{1}{a_{11}} & 0 & 0 \\ 0 & \frac{1}{a_{22}} & 0 \\ 0 & 0 & \frac{1}{a_{33}} \end{bmatrix}$.

This is defined if none of elements on the principal diagonal are zero.
A similar situation holds for any order matrix. $(7-4)$

78. $(x - 2i)^6 = [x + (-2i)]^6 = \displaystyle\sum_{k=0}^{6} \binom{6}{k} x^{6-k}(-2i)^k = \binom{6}{0}x^6 + \binom{6}{1}x^5(-2i)^1 + \binom{6}{2}x^4(-2i)^2 + \binom{6}{3}x^3(-2i)^3$

$$+ \binom{6}{4}x^2(-2i)^4 + \binom{6}{5}x(-2i)^5 + \binom{6}{6}(-2i)^6$$

$$= x^6 - 12ix^5 - 60x^4 + 160ix^3 + 240x^2 - 192ix - 64$$

$(8-6)$

79. Let $P(x, y)$ be a point on the parabola.

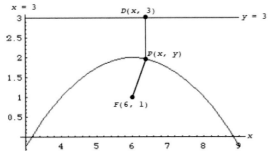

Then by the definition of the parabola, the distance from $P(x, y)$ to the focus $F(6, 1)$ must equal the perpendicular distance from P to the directrix at $D(x, 3)$. Applying the distance formula, we have

$$d(P, F) = d(P, D)$$

$$\sqrt{(x-6)^2 + (y-1)^2} = \sqrt{(x-x)^2 + (y-3)^2}$$

$$(x-6)^2 + (y-1)^2 = (x-x)^2 + (y-3)^2$$

$$x^2 - 12x + 36 + y^2 - 2y + 1 = 0 + y^2 - 6y + 9$$

$$x^2 - 12x + 4y + 28 = 0$$

$(6-1)$

80. Make a rough sketch of the ellipse, locate focus and x intercepts, then determine y intercepts using the special triangle relationship.

$a = 4$

$b^2 = a^2 - c^2 = 4^2 - 2^2 = 12$

$b = \sqrt{12} = 2\sqrt{3}$

y intercepts: $\pm 2\sqrt{3}$

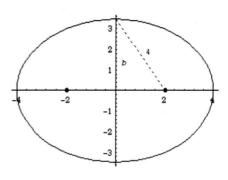

(6–2)

81. Sketch the asymptote rectangle, label known parts, and use the Pythagorean Theorem.

$a = 3 \quad c = 5$

$b^2 = c^2 - a^2$

$\quad = 5^2 - 3^2$

$\quad = 16$

$b = 4$

Thus, the length of the conjugate axis is $2b = 8$.

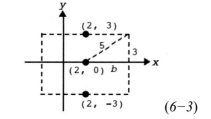

(6–3)

82. We can select any three of the seven points to use as vertices of the triangle. Order is not important.

$C_{7,3} = \dfrac{7!}{3!(7-3)!} = 35$ triangles

(8–4)

83. P_n: $2^n < n!$ $n \ge 4$ (for n an integer, this is identical with the condition $n > 3$)

Part 1: Show that P_4 is true

P_4: $\quad 2^4 < 4!$

$\quad\quad 16 < 24$ True.

Part 2: Show that if P_k is true, then P_{k+1} is true.

Write out P_k and P_{k+1}:

$\quad P_k$: $\quad 2^k < k!$

$\quad P_{k+1}$: $2^{k+1} < (k+1)!$

We start with P_k:

$\quad 2^k < k!$

Multiplying both sides by 2: $2 \cdot 2^k < 2 \cdot k!$

Now, $k > 3$, thus $1 < k$, $2 < k + 1$, hence $2 \cdot k! < (k+1)k!$

Therefore, $\quad 2^{k+1} = 2 \cdot 2^k < 2 \cdot k! < (k+1)k! = (k+1)!$

$\quad\quad\quad\quad\quad 2^{k+1} < (k+1)!$

Thus, if P_k is true, then P_{k+1} is true.

Conclusion: P_n is true for all $n \ge 4$. $\quad\quad$ (8–2)

84. To prove $a_n = b_n$ for all positive integers n, write:

P_n: $a_n = b_n$

Proof: Part 1: Show P_1 is true.

P_1: $a_1 = b_1$. $a_1 = 3$. $b_1 = 2^1 + 1 = 3$.

Thus, $a_1 = b_1$

Part 2: Show that if P_k is true, then P_{k+1} is true.

Write out P_k and P_{k+1}.

$\qquad P_k$: $a_k = b_k$

$\qquad P_{k+1}$: $a_{k+1} = b_{k+1}$

We start with P_k:

$\qquad a_k = b_k$

Now, $a_{k+1} = 2a_{k+1-1} - 1 = 2a_k - 1 = 2b_k - 1 = 2(2^k + 1) - 1 = 2 \cdot 2^k + 2 - 1 = 2^1 \cdot 2^k + 1 = 2^{k+1} + 1 = b_{k+1}$

Therefore, $a_{k+1} = b_{k+1}$

Thus, if P_k is true, then P_{k+1} is true.

Conclusion: P_n is true for all positive integers n. Hence, $\{a_n\} = \{b_n\}$. $\qquad$ *(8-2)*

85. Make a rough sketch of the situation.

We are given $d(P, A) = 3d(P, B)$. Applying the distance formula, we have

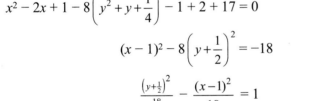

$$\sqrt{(x-1)^2 + (y-4)^2} = 3\sqrt{(x-x)^2 + (y-0)^2}$$
$$(x-1)^2 + (y-4)^2 = 9[(x-x)^2 + (y-0)^2]$$
$$x^2 - 2x + 1 + y^2 - 8y + 16 = 9y^2$$
$$x^2 - 2x - 8y^2 - 8y + 17 = 0$$

is the equation of the curve. Completing the square relative to x and y, we have

$$x^2 - 2x + 1 - 8\left(y^2 + y + \frac{1}{4}\right) - 1 + 2 + 17 = 0$$

$$(x-1)^2 - 8\left(y + \frac{1}{2}\right)^2 = -18$$

$$\frac{\left(y + \frac{1}{2}\right)^2}{\frac{18}{8}} - \frac{(x-1)^2}{18} = 1$$

This is the equation of a hyperbola. $\qquad$ *(6-3)*

86. The sample space S is the set of all possible ways of selecting 3 bulbs out of 12.

$n(S) = C_{12,3}$

P(at least one defective bulb) $= 1 - P$(no defective bulbs chosen)

The event, no defective bulbs chosen, is the set of all possible 3-bulb subsets of the 8 acceptable bulbs.

$n(E) = C_{8,3}$

Then P(at least one defective bulb) $= 1 - \dfrac{n(E)}{n(S)} = 1 - \dfrac{C_{8,3}}{C_{12,3}} = 1 - \dfrac{56}{220} = \dfrac{41}{55} = .7\overline{45}$ $\qquad$ *(8-5)*

87. We are asked for the sum of an infinite geometric series.

$a = \$2,000,000(0.75)$

$r = 0.75$ $|r| \leq 1$, so the series has a sum,

$S_\infty = \dfrac{a_1}{1-r} = \dfrac{\$2,000,000(0.75)}{1-0.75} = \dfrac{\$2,000,000(0.75)}{0.25} = \$6,000,000$ $\qquad$ *(8-3)*

88. Let x = the length and y = the width.
The perimeter is $2x + 2y$ so $2x + 2y = 24$.
The area is xy so $xy = 32$.
We solve the second equation for y and substitute into the first:

$$xy = 32 \qquad\qquad 2x + 2\left(\frac{32}{x}\right) = 24$$

$$y = \frac{32}{x} \qquad\qquad 2x + \frac{64}{x} = 24 \quad \text{(Multiply both sides by } x.)$$

$$2x^2 + 64 = 24x$$
$$2x^2 - 24x + 64 = 0$$
$$2(x^2 - 12x + 32) = 0$$
$$2(x - 8)(x - 4) = 0$$
$$x = 8 \quad \text{or} \quad x = 4$$

If $x = 8$, $y = \dfrac{32}{8} = 4$. If $x = 4$, $y = \dfrac{32}{4} = 8$. The dimensions are 4m × 8m. $(7-6)$

89.

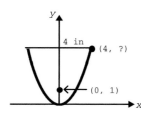

From the figure, we see that the parabola can be positioned so that it is opening up with axis the y axis, hence it has an equation of the form $x^2 = 4ay$. Since the focus is at $(0, a) = (0, 1)$, $a = 1$ and the equation of the parabola is $x^2 = 4y$.

Since the depth represents the y coordinate y_1 of a point on the parabola with $x = 4$, we have

$$4^2 = 4y_1$$
$$y_1 = \text{depth} = 4 \text{ in.}$$ $(6-1)$

90.

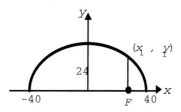

From the figure, we see that the x and y intercepts of the ellipse must be 40 and 24 respectively. Hence the equation of the ellipse must be

$$\frac{x^2}{(40)^2} + \frac{y^2}{(24)^2} = 1 \quad \text{or} \quad \frac{x^2}{1,600} + \frac{y^2}{576} = 1$$

To find the distance c of each focus from the center of the arch, we use the special triangle relationship.
$a = 40$, $b = 24$
$$c^2 = a^2 - b^2 = 40^2 - 24^2 = 1024$$
$$c = 32 \text{ ft.}$$

To find the height of the arch above each focus, we need the y coordinate y_1 of the point P whose x coordinate is 32. Since P is on the ellipse, we have

$$\frac{32^2}{1,600} + \frac{y_1^2}{576} = 1$$

$$\frac{1,024}{1,600} + \frac{y_1^2}{576} = 1$$

$$0.64 + \frac{y_1^2}{576} = 1$$

$$\frac{y_1^2}{576} = 0.36$$

$$y_1^2 = 576(0.36)$$

$$y_1^2 = 207.36$$

$$y_1 = 14.4 \text{ ft.}$$ $(6-2)$

91. Let x = amount invested at 8%
$\qquad y$ = amount invested at 14%
Then $x + y = 12,000$ (total amount invested) $\qquad\qquad\qquad$ (1)
$0.08x + 0.14y = 0.10(12,000)$ (total yield on investment) $\qquad$ (2)
We solve the system of equations (1), (2) using elimination by addition.
$-0.08x - 0.08y = -0.08(12,000)$ $\quad -0.08$[equation (1)]
$\underline{0.08x + 0.14y = 0.10(12,000)} \qquad$ equation (2)
$\qquad\qquad 0.06y = -0.08(12,000) + 0.10(12,000)$
$\qquad\qquad 0.06y = 240$
$\qquad\qquad\quad y = 4,000$
$\qquad x + y = 12,000$
$\qquad\qquad\quad x = 8,000$
$8,000 at 8% and $4,000 at 14%. $\qquad\qquad\qquad\qquad\qquad\qquad\qquad$ *(7−1)*

92. Let x_1 = number of ounces of mix A.
$\qquad x_2$ = number of ounces of mix B.
$\qquad x_3$ = number of ounces of mix C.
Then
$\qquad 0.2x_1 + 0.1x_2 + 0.15x_3 = 23$ (protein)
$\qquad 0.02x_1 + 0.06x_2 + 0.05x_3 = 6.2$ (fat)
$\qquad 0.15x_1 + 0.1x_2 + 0.05x_3 = 16$ (moisture)
or
$\qquad 4x_1 + 2x_2 + 3x_3 = 460$
$\qquad 2x_1 + 6x_2 + 5x_3 = 620$
$\qquad 3x_1 + 2x_2 + x_3 = 320$
is the system to be solved. We form the augmented matrix and solve by Gauss-Jordan elimination.

$$\begin{bmatrix} 4 & 2 & 3 & | & 460 \\ 2 & 6 & 5 & | & 620 \\ 3 & 2 & 1 & | & 320 \end{bmatrix} \begin{matrix} \frac{1}{4}R_1 \to R_1 \\ \\ \end{matrix} \sim \begin{bmatrix} 1 & \frac{1}{2} & \frac{3}{4} & | & 115 \\ 2 & 6 & 5 & | & 620 \\ 3 & 2 & 1 & | & 320 \end{bmatrix} \begin{matrix} \\ (-2)R_1 + R_2 \to R_2 \\ (-3)R_1 + R_3 \to R_3 \end{matrix}$$

$$\sim \begin{bmatrix} 1 & \frac{1}{2} & \frac{3}{4} & | & 115 \\ 0 & 5 & \frac{7}{2} & | & 390 \\ 0 & \frac{1}{2} & -\frac{5}{4} & | & -25 \end{bmatrix} R_2 \leftrightarrow R_3 \sim \begin{bmatrix} 1 & \frac{1}{2} & \frac{3}{4} & | & 115 \\ 0 & \frac{1}{2} & -\frac{5}{4} & | & -25 \\ 0 & 5 & \frac{7}{2} & | & 390 \end{bmatrix} \begin{matrix} (-1)R_2 + R_1 \to R_1 \\ \\ (-10)R_2 + R_3 \to R_3 \end{matrix}$$

$$\sim \begin{bmatrix} 1 & 0 & 2 & | & 140 \\ 0 & \frac{1}{2} & -\frac{5}{4} & | & -25 \\ 0 & 0 & 16 & | & 640 \end{bmatrix} \begin{matrix} \\ 2R_2 \to R_2 \\ \frac{1}{16}R_3 \to R_3 \end{matrix} \sim \begin{bmatrix} 1 & 0 & 2 & | & 140 \\ 0 & 1 & -\frac{5}{2} & | & -50 \\ 0 & 0 & 1 & | & 40 \end{bmatrix} \begin{matrix} (-2)R_3 + R_1 \to R_1 \\ (\frac{5}{2})R_3 + R_2 \to R_2 \\ \end{matrix}$$

$$\sim \begin{bmatrix} 1 & 0 & 0 & | & 60 \\ 0 & 1 & 0 & | & 50 \\ 0 & 0 & 1 & | & 40 \end{bmatrix}$$

Thus, $x_1 = 60$g Mix A, $x_2 = 50$g Mix B, $x_3 = 40$g Mix C $\qquad\qquad\qquad$ *(7−2)*

93. Let x_1 = number of model A trucks
$\qquad x_2$ = number of model B trucks
$\qquad x_3$ = number of model C trucks
Then $x_1 + x_2 + x_3 = 12$ (total number of trucks)
$\qquad 18,000x_1 + 22,000x_2 + 30,000x_3 = 300,000$ (total funds needed)

We form the augmented matrix and solve by Gauss-Jordan elimination.

$$\begin{bmatrix} 1 & 1 & 1 & | & 12 \\ 18{,}000 & 22{,}000 & 30{,}000 & | & 300{,}000 \end{bmatrix} \xrightarrow{\frac{1}{2{,}000}R_2 \to R_2} \begin{bmatrix} 1 & 1 & 1 & | & 12 \\ 9 & 11 & 15 & | & 150 \end{bmatrix} (-9)R_1 + R_2 \to R_2$$

$$\sim \begin{bmatrix} 1 & 1 & 1 & | & 12 \\ 0 & 2 & 6 & | & 42 \end{bmatrix} \left(-\tfrac{1}{2}\right)R_2 + R_1 \to R_1 \sim \begin{bmatrix} 1 & 0 & -2 & | & -9 \\ 0 & 2 & 6 & | & 42 \end{bmatrix} \tfrac{1}{2}R_2 \to R_2 \sim \begin{bmatrix} 1 & 0 & -2 & | & -9 \\ 0 & 1 & 3 & | & 21 \end{bmatrix}$$

Let $x_3 = t$. Then
$$x_2 = -3x_3 + 21 = -3t + 21$$
$$x_1 = 2x_3 - 9 = 2t - 9$$

A solution is achieved, not for every value of t, but for integer values of t that give rise to non-negative x_1, x_2, x_3.

$x_1 \geq 0$ means $\quad 2t - 9 \geq 0 \;$ or $\; t \geq 4\tfrac{1}{2}$

$x_2 \geq 0$ means $\quad -3t + 21 \geq 0 \;$ or $\; t \leq 7$

The only integer values of t that satisfy these conditions are 5, 6, 7. Thus we have the solutions

$x_1 = 2t - 9 \quad$ model A trucks

$x_2 = -3t + 21 \quad$ model B trucks

$x_3 = t \quad\quad\quad$ model C trucks

where $t = 5, 6,$ or 7. Thus the distributor can purchase

1 model A truck, 6 model B trucks, and 5 model C trucks, or

3 model A trucks, 3 model B trucks, and 6 model C trucks, or

5 model A trucks and 7 model C trucks.   (7–2)

94.   Let x = number of standard day packs

y = number of deluxe day packs

(A)   We form the linear objective function

$P = 8x + 12y$

We wish to maximize P, the profit from x standard packs @ \$8 and y deluxe packs @ \$12, subject to the constraints

$0.5x + 0.5y \leq 300 \;$ fabricating constraint

$0.3x + 0.6y \leq 240 \;$ sewing constraint

$\quad\quad x, y \geq 0 \quad$ non-negative constraints

Solving the system of constraint inequalities graphically, we obtain the feasible region S shown in the diagram. The three corner points (0, 400), (0, 0), and (600, 0) are obvious from the diagram. The corner point (400, 200) is found by solving the system

$0.5x + 0.5y = 300$

$0.3x + 0.6y = 240$

Next we evaluate the objective function at each corner point.

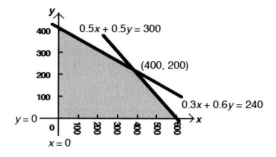

Corner Point (x, y)	Objective Function $P = 5x + 15y$	
(0, 0)	0	
(600, 0)	4,800	
(400, 200)	5,600	Maximum value
(0, 400)	4,800	

The optimal value is 5,600 at the corner point (400, 200). Thus, the company should manufacture 400 standard packs and 200 deluxe packs for a maximum profit of \$5,600.

(B)   The objective function now becomes $5x + 15y$. We evaluate this at each corner point.

Corner Point (x, y)	Objective Function $P = 5x + 15y$

(0, 0)	0	
(600, 0)	3,000	
(400, 200)	5,000	
(0, 400)	6,000	Maximum value

The optimal value is now 6,000 at the corner point (0, 400). Thus, the company should manufacture no standard packs and 400 deluxe packs for a maximum profit of $6,000.

(C) The objective function now becomes $11x + 9y$. We evaluate this at each corner point.

Corner Point (x, y)	Objective Function $P = 5x + 15y$	
(0, 0)	0	
(600, 0)	6,600	Maximum value
(400, 200)	6,200	
(0, 400)	3,600	

The optimal value is now 6,600 at the corner point (600, 0). Thus, the company should manufacture 600 standard packs and no deluxe packs for a maximum profit of $6,600.   *(7–8)*

95. (A) $M\begin{bmatrix} 0.25 \\ 0.25 \\ 0.25 \\ 0.25 \\ 0.25 \end{bmatrix} = \begin{bmatrix} 78 & 84 & 81 & 86 \\ 91 & 65 & 84 & 92 \\ 95 & 90 & 92 & 91 \\ 75 & 82 & 87 & 91 \\ 83 & 88 & 81 & 76 \end{bmatrix}\begin{bmatrix} 0.25 \\ 0.25 \\ 0.25 \\ 0.25 \end{bmatrix} = \begin{bmatrix} 0.25(78+84+81+86) \\ 0.25(91+65+84+92) \\ 0.25(95+90+92+91) \\ 0.25(75+82+87+91) \\ 0.25(83+88+81+76) \end{bmatrix} = \begin{bmatrix} 82.25 \\ 83 \\ 92 \\ 83.75 \\ 82 \end{bmatrix}\begin{matrix} \text{Ann} \\ \text{Bob} \\ \text{Carol} \\ \text{Dan} \\ \text{Eric} \end{matrix}$

(B) $M\begin{bmatrix} 0.2 \\ 0.2 \\ 0.2 \\ 0.2 \\ 0.4 \end{bmatrix} = \begin{bmatrix} 78 & 84 & 81 & 86 \\ 91 & 65 & 84 & 92 \\ 95 & 90 & 92 & 91 \\ 75 & 82 & 87 & 91 \\ 83 & 88 & 81 & 76 \end{bmatrix}\begin{bmatrix} 0.2 \\ 0.2 \\ 0.2 \\ 0.4 \end{bmatrix} = \begin{bmatrix} 0.2(78+84+81)+0.4\cdot 86 \\ 0.2(91+65+84)+0.4\cdot 92 \\ 0.2(95+90+92)+0.4\cdot 91 \\ 0.2(75+82+87)+0.4\cdot 91 \\ 0.2(83+88+81)+0.4\cdot 76 \end{bmatrix} = \begin{bmatrix} 83 \\ 84.8 \\ 91.8 \\ 85.2 \\ 80.8 \end{bmatrix}\begin{matrix} \text{Ann} \\ \text{Bob} \\ \text{Carol} \\ \text{Dan} \\ \text{Eric} \end{matrix}$

(C) $[0.2\ 0.2\ 0.2\ 0.2\ 0.2]M = [0.2\ 0.2\ 0.2\ 0.2\ 0.2]\begin{bmatrix} 78 & 84 & 81 & 86 \\ 91 & 65 & 84 & 92 \\ 95 & 90 & 92 & 91 \\ 75 & 82 & 87 & 91 \\ 83 & 88 & 81 & 76 \end{bmatrix}$

$= [0.2(78 + 91 + 95 + 75 + 83)\ \ 0.2(84 + 65 + 90 + 82 + 88)\ \ 0.2(81 + 84 + 92 + 87 + 81)\ \ 0.2(86 + 92 + 91 + 91 + 76)]$

Test 1 Test 2 Test 3 Test 4
$= [84.4 \quad\ 81.8 \quad\ 85 \quad\quad 87.2]$ *(7–3)*

96. (A) P (this event) $= \dfrac{130}{1,000} = .13$

(B) P (this event) $= \dfrac{80+90}{1,000} = .17$

(C) P (this event) $= P$ (being an independent) $+ P$ (being over 59) $- P$ (being both)
$$= \frac{120}{1,000} + \frac{230}{1,000} - \frac{30}{1,000} = .32$$ *(8–5)*

APPENDIX B

Section B–1

1. <u>123,005</u> **3.** <u>20,040</u> **5.** <u>6.0</u> **7.** <u>80.000</u> **9.** 0.0<u>12</u> **11.** 0.000 <u>960</u> **13.** 3.08 **15.** 924,000

17. 23.7 **19.** 2.82×10^3 **21.** 6.78×10^{-4}

23.

Using the Pythagorean Theorem,
$$25^2 + 20^2 = d^2$$
$$625 + 400 = d^2$$
$$1{,}025 = d^2$$
$$32.0156 = d$$
Rounded to 1 significant digit, which is the smallest number of significant digits in the original measurements, the diagonal is 30 ft.

Section B–2

1. $\dfrac{7x-14}{(x-4)(x+3)} = \dfrac{A}{x-4} + \dfrac{B}{x+3} = \dfrac{A(x+3)+B(x-4)}{(x-4)(x+3)}$

Thus, for all x
$7x - 14 = A(x + 3) + B(x - 4)$

<u>Graphical Solution:</u>
$7x - 14 = A(x + 3) + B(x - 4) \Rightarrow 7x - 14 = (A + B)x + 3A - 4B$

$\begin{matrix} A+B=7 \\ 3A-4B=-14 \end{matrix} \Rightarrow \begin{matrix} B=7-A \\ B=\dfrac{14+3A}{4} \end{matrix}$

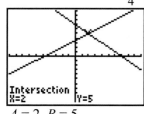

$A = 2, B = 5$

<u>Algebraic Solution:</u>
If $x = -3$, then
$-35 = -7B$
$B = 5$
If $x = 4$, then
$14 = 7A$
$A = 2$
$A = 2, B = 5$

3. $\dfrac{17x-1}{(2x-3)(3x-1)} = \dfrac{A}{2x-3} + \dfrac{B}{3x-1} = \dfrac{A(3x-1)+B(2x-3)}{(2x-3)(3x-1)}$

Thus, for all x
$17x - 1 = A(3x - 1) + B(2x - 3)$

<u>Graphical Solution:</u>
$17x - 1 = A(3x - 1) + B(2x - 3) \Rightarrow 17x - 1 = (3A + 2B)x - A - 3B$

$\begin{matrix} 3A+2B=17 \\ -A-3B=-1 \end{matrix} \Rightarrow \begin{matrix} B=\dfrac{17-3A}{2} \\ B=\dfrac{1-A}{3} \end{matrix}$

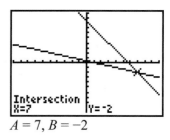

$A = 7, B = -2$

Algebraic Solution: If $x = \dfrac{1}{3}$, then

$17\left(\dfrac{1}{3}\right) - 1 = B\left[2\left(\dfrac{1}{3}\right) - 3\right]$

$\dfrac{14}{3} = -\dfrac{7}{3}B$

$B = -2$

If $x = \dfrac{3}{2}$, then

$17\left(\dfrac{3}{2}\right) - 1 = A\left[3\left(\dfrac{3}{2}\right) - 1\right]$

$\dfrac{49}{2} = \dfrac{7}{2}A$

$A = 7$

$A = 7, B = -2$

5. $\dfrac{3x^2+7x+1}{x(x+1)^2} = \dfrac{A}{x} + \dfrac{B}{x+1} + \dfrac{C}{(x+1)^2} = \dfrac{A(x+1)^2+Bx(x+1)+Cx}{x(x+1)^2}$

$3x^2 + 7x + 1 = A(x + 1)^2 + Bx(x + 1) + Cx$

$3x^2 + 7x + 1 = A(x^2 + 2x + 1) + Bx^2 + Bx + Cx$

$3x^2 + 7x + 1 = Ax^2 + 2Ax + A + Bx^2 + Bx + Cx$

$3x^2 + 7x + 1 = (A + B)x^2 + (2A + B + C)x + A$

Equating coefficients, we know $A = 1$. Also, $A + B = 3$, so $1 + B = 3$ and $B = 2$.

Finally, $2A + B + C = 7$, so $2 + 2 + C = 7$ and $C = 3$.

Check by addition:

$\dfrac{1}{x} + \dfrac{2}{x+1} + \dfrac{3}{(x+1)^2} = \dfrac{(x+1)^2}{x(x+1)^2} + \dfrac{2x(x+1)}{x(x+1)^2} + \dfrac{3x}{x(x+1)^2} = \dfrac{x^2+2x+1+2x^2+2x+3x}{x(x+1)^2} = \dfrac{3x^2+7x+1}{x(x+1)^2}$

Check with graphing calculator:

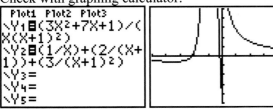

The graphs appear to be identical and the tables are the same.

7. $\dfrac{3x^2+x}{(x-2)(x^2+3)} = \dfrac{A}{x-2} + \dfrac{Bx+C}{x^2+3} = \dfrac{A(x^2+3)+(Bx+C)(x-2)}{(x-2)(x^2+3)}$

$3x^2 + x = A(x^2 + 3) + (Bx + C)(x - 2)$

First, plug in $x = 2$:

$\qquad 3(2)^2 + 2 = A(4 + 3) + 0$

$\qquad\qquad\quad 14 = 7A$

$\qquad\qquad\quad\ A = 2$

$\qquad 3x^2 + x = 2(x^2 + 3) + (Bx + C)(x - 2)$

$\qquad\quad 3x^2 + x = 2x^2 + 6 + Bx^2 - 2Bx + Cx - 2C$

$\qquad\quad 3x^2 + x = (2 + B)x^2 + (C - 2B)x + 6 - 2C$

Equating coefficients,

$\ 2 + B = 3$, so $B = 1$

$6 - 2C = 0$, so $6 = 2C$ and $C = 3$.

Check by addition:

$\dfrac{x}{x-2} + \dfrac{x+3}{x^2+3} = \dfrac{2(x^2+3)+(x+3)(x-2)}{(x-2)(x^2+3)} = \dfrac{2x^2+6+x^2+x-6}{(x-2)(x^2+3)} = \dfrac{3x^2+x}{(x-2)(x^2+3)}$

Check with graphing calculator:

The graphs appear to be identical and the tables are the same.

9. $\dfrac{2x^2+4x-1}{(x^2+x+1)^2} = \dfrac{Ax+B}{x^2+x+1} + \dfrac{Cx+D}{(x^2+x+1)^2} = \dfrac{(Ax+B)(x^2+x+1)+(Cx+D)}{(x^2+x+1)^2}$

$2x^2 + 4x - 1 = (Ax + B)(x^2 + x + 1) + Cx + D$

$2x^2 + 4x - 1 = Ax^3 + Ax^2 + Ax + Bx^2 + Bx + B + Cx + D$

$2x^2 + 4x - 1 = Ax^3 + (A + B)x^2 + (A + B + C)x + B + D$

Equating coefficients,

$\quad A = 0$

$\quad A + B = 2$, so $B = 2$

$\quad A + B + C = 4$, so $0 + 2 + C = 4$, and $C = 2$

$\quad B + D = -1$, so $2 + D = -1$, and $D = -3$

Check by addition:

$\dfrac{2}{x^2+x+1} + \dfrac{2x-3}{(x^2+x+1)^2} = \dfrac{2(x^2+x+1)}{(x^2+x+1)^2} + \dfrac{2x-3}{(x^2+x+1)^2} = \dfrac{2x^2+2x+2+2x-3}{(x^2+x+1)^2} = \dfrac{2x^2+4x-1}{(x^2+x+1)^2}$

Check with graphing calculator:

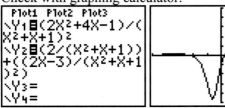

The graphs appear to be identical and the tables are the same.

11. Since $x^2 - 2x - 8 = (x + 2)(x - 4)$, we write

$\dfrac{-x+22}{x^2-2x-8} = \dfrac{A}{x+2} + \dfrac{B}{x-4} = \dfrac{A(x-4)+B(x+2)}{(x+2)(x-4)}$

Thus, for all x

$-x + 22 = A(x - 4) + B(x + 2)$

$\quad$ If $x = 4 \qquad\quad$ If $x = -2$

$\quad\quad 18 = 6B \qquad\quad 24 = -6A$

$\quad\quad B = 3 \qquad\qquad A = -4$

So $\dfrac{-x+22}{x^2-2x-8} = \dfrac{-4}{x+2} + \dfrac{3}{x-4}$.

13. Since $6x^2 - x - 12 = (3x + 4)(2x - 3)$, we write

$\dfrac{3x-13}{6x^2-x-12} = \dfrac{A}{3x+4} + \dfrac{B}{2x-3} = \dfrac{A(2x-3)+B(3x+4)}{(3x+4)(2x-3)}$

Thus, for all x

$3x - 13 = A(2x - 3) + B(3x + 4)$

$\quad$ If $x = \dfrac{3}{2} \qquad\qquad\qquad$ If $x = -\dfrac{4}{3}$

$3\left(\dfrac{3}{2}\right) - 13 = B\left[3\left(\dfrac{3}{2}\right)+4\right] \qquad 3\left(-\dfrac{4}{3}\right) - 13 = \left[2\left(-\dfrac{4}{3}\right)-3\right]$

$\quad -\dfrac{17}{2} = \dfrac{17}{2}B \qquad\qquad\qquad -17 = -\dfrac{17}{3}A$

$\quad\quad B = -1 \qquad\qquad\qquad\qquad A = 3$

So $\dfrac{3x-13}{6x^2-x-12} = \dfrac{3}{3x+4} - \dfrac{1}{2x-3}$

15. Since $x^3 - 6x^2 + 9x = x(x^2 - 6x + 9) = x(x - 3)^2$, we write

$\dfrac{x^2-12x+18}{x^3-6x^2+9x} = \dfrac{A}{x} + \dfrac{B}{x-3} + \dfrac{C}{(x-3)^2} = \dfrac{A(x-3)^2+Bx(x-3)+Cx}{x(x-3)^2}$

Thus, for all x

$x^2 - 12x + 18 = A(x - 3)^2 + Bx(x - 3) + Cx$

$\quad$ If $x = 3 \qquad$ If $x = 0 \qquad$ If $x = 2$

$\quad -9 = 3C \qquad 18 = 9A \qquad -2 = A - 2B + 2C$

$\quad C = -3 \qquad\ A = 2 \qquad\ -2 = 2 - 2B - 6$ using $A = 2$ and $C = -3$

$\qquad\qquad\qquad\qquad\qquad\qquad 2 = -2B$

$\qquad\qquad\qquad\qquad\qquad\qquad B = -1$

So $\dfrac{x^2-12x+18}{x^3-6x^2+9x} = \dfrac{2}{x} - \dfrac{1}{x-3} - \dfrac{3}{(x-3)^2}$

17. Since $x^3 + 2x^2 + 3x = x(x^2 + 2x + 3)$, we write

$$\frac{5x^2 + 3x + 6}{x^3 + 2x^2 + 3x} = \frac{A}{x} + \frac{Bx + C}{x^2 + 2x + 3} = \frac{A(x^2 + 2x + 3) + (Bx + C)x}{x(x^2 + 2x + 3)}$$

Common Error: Writing $\frac{B}{x^2 + 2x + 3}$. Since $x^2 + 2x + 3$ is quadratic, the numerator must be first degree.

Thus, for all x
$$5x^2 + 3x + 6 = A(x^2 + 2x + 3) + (Bx + C)x = (A + B)x^2 + (2A + C)x + 3A$$
Equating coefficients of like terms, we have
$$5 = A + B$$
$$3 = 2A + C$$
$$3A = 6$$
Hence $A = 2$, $C = -1$, $B = 3$

So $\dfrac{5x^2 + 3x + 6}{x^3 + 2x^2 + 3x} = \dfrac{2}{x} + \dfrac{3x - 1}{x^2 + 2x + 3}$

19. Since $x^4 + 4x^2 + 4 = (x^2 + 2)^2$, we write

$$\frac{2x^3 + 7x + 5}{x^4 + 4x^2 + 4} = \frac{Ax + B}{x^2 + 2} + \frac{Cx + D}{(x^2 + 2)^2} = \frac{(Ax + B)(x^2 + 2) + Cx + D}{(x^2 + 2)^2}$$

Thus, for all x
$$2x^3 + 7x + 5 = (Ax + B)(x^2 + 2) + Cx + D = Ax^3 + Bx^2 + (2A + C)x + 2B + D$$
Equating coefficients of like terms, we have
$$2 = A$$
$$0 = B$$
$$7 = 2A + C$$
$$5 = 2B + D$$
Hence $A = 2$, $B = 0$, $C = 3$, $D = 5$

$$\frac{2x^3 + 7x + 5}{x^4 + 4x^2 + 4} = \frac{2x}{x^2 + 2} + \frac{3x + 5}{(x^2 + 2)^2}$$

21. First we divide to obtain a polynomial plus a proper fraction.

$$
\begin{array}{r}
x - 2 \\
x^2 - 5x + 6 \,\overline{\big)\, x^3 - 7x^2 + 17x - 17} \\
\underline{x^3 - 5x^2 + 6x} \\
-2x^2 + 11x - 17 \\
\underline{-2x^2 + 10x - 12} \\
x - 5
\end{array}
$$

So, $\dfrac{x^3 - 7x^2 + 17x - 17}{x^2 - 5x + 6} = x - 2 + \dfrac{x - 5}{x^2 - 5x + 6}$

To decompose the proper fraction, we note $x^2 - 5x + 6 = (x - 2)(x - 3)$ and we write:

$$\frac{x - 5}{x^2 - 5x + 6} = \frac{A}{x - 2} + \frac{B}{x - 3} = \frac{A(x - 3) + B(x - 2)}{(x - 2)(x - 3)}$$

Thus for all x
$$x - 5 = A(x - 3) + B(x - 2)$$

If $x = 3$ If $x = 2$
$$-2 = B \qquad -3 = -A$$
$$A = 3$$

So $\dfrac{x^3 - 7x^2 + 17x - 17}{x^2 - 5x + 6} = x - 2 + \dfrac{3}{x - 2} - \dfrac{2}{x - 3}$

23. First, we must factor $x^3 - 6x - 9$. Possible rational zeros of this polynomial are $\pm 1, \pm 3, \pm 9$. Forming a synthetic division table, we see

	1	0	−6	−9
1	1	1	−5	−14
3	1	3	3	0

Thus $x^3 - 6x - 9 = (x-3)(x^2 + 3x + 3)$

$x^2 + 3x + 3$ cannot be factored further in the real numbers.

So $\dfrac{4x^2 + 5x - 9}{x^3 - 6x - 9} = \dfrac{A}{x-3} + \dfrac{Bx+C}{x^2+3x+3} = \dfrac{A(x^2+3x+3) + (Bx+C)(x-3)}{(x-3)(x^2+3x+3)}$

Thus, for all x

$$4x^2 + 5x - 9 = A(x^2 + 3x + 3) + (Bx + C)(x - 3)$$
$$= Ax^2 + 3Ax + 3A + Bx^2 - 3Bx + Cx - 3C$$
$$= (A + B)x^2 + (3A - 3B + C)x + 3A - 3C$$

Before equating coefficients of like terms, we note that if $x = 3$

$$4(3)^2 + 5(3) - 9 = A(3^2 + 3\cdot 3 + 3)$$
$$\text{So } 42 = 21A$$
$$A = 2$$
$$\text{Since } 4 = A + B, B = 2$$
$$5 = 3A - 3B + C = 6 - 6 + C, \text{ so } C = 5$$

We have $A = 2, B = 2, C = 5$

So $\dfrac{4x^2 + 5x - 9}{x^3 - 6x - 9} = \dfrac{2}{x-3} + \dfrac{2x+5}{x^2+3x+3}$

25. First, we must factor $x^3 + 2x^2 - 15x - 36$. The possible rational zeros are $\pm 1, \pm 2, \pm 3, \pm 4, \pm 6, \pm 9, \pm 12, \pm 18, \pm 36$. Forming a synthetic division table, we see

	1	2	−15	−36
1	1	3	−12	−48
2	1	4	−7	−50
3	1	5	0	−36
4	1	6	9	0

Hence $x^3 + 2x^2 - 15x - 36 = (x - 4)(x^2 + 6x + 9) = (x - 4)(x + 3)^2$.

So $\dfrac{x^2 + 16x + 18}{x^3 + 2x^2 - 15x - 36} = \dfrac{A}{x-4} + \dfrac{B}{x+3} + \dfrac{C}{(x+3)^2} = \dfrac{A(x+3)^2 + B(x-4)(x+3) + C(x-4)}{(x-4)(x+3)^2}$

Thus, for all x

$x^2 + 16x + 18 = A(x + 3)^2 + B(x - 4)(x + 3) + C(x - 4)$

If $x = -3$	If $x = 4$	If $x = 5$
$-21 = -7C$	$98 = 49A$	$123 = 64A + 8B + C$
$C = 3$	$A = 2$	$= 128 + 8B + 3$ using $A = 2$ and $C = 3$
		$-8 = 8B$
		$B = -1$

So $\dfrac{x^2 + 16x + 18}{x^3 + 2x^2 - 15x - 36} = \dfrac{2}{x-4} - \dfrac{1}{x+3} + \dfrac{3}{(x+3)^2}$

27. First, we must factor $x^4 - 5x^3 + 9x^2 - 8x + 4$. The possible rational zeros are $\pm 1, \pm 2, \pm 4$. We form a synthetic division table:

	1	−5	9	−8	4
1	1	−4	5	−3	1
2	1	−3	3	−2	0

We examine $x^3 - 3x^2 + 3x - 2$ to see if 2 is a double zero.

	1	−3	3	−2
2	1	−1	1	0

Thus $x^4 - 5x^3 + 9x^2 - 8x + 4 = (x-2)^2(x^2 - x + 1)$. $x^2 - x + 1$ cannot be factored further in the real numbers, so

$$\frac{-x^2+x-7}{x^4-5x^3+9x^2-8x+4} = \frac{A}{x-2} + \frac{B}{(x-2)^2} + \frac{Cx+D}{x^2-x+1} = \frac{A(x-2)(x^2-x+1)+B(x^2-x+1)+(Cx+D)(x-2)^2}{(x-2)^2(x^2-x+1)}$$

Thus, for all x

$-x^2 + x - 7 = A(x-2)(x^2 - x + 1) + B(x^2 - x + 1) + (Cx + D)(x-2)^2$

If $x = 2$

$-9 = 3B$

$B = -3$

$-x^2 + x - 7 = A(x^3 - 3x^2 + 3x - 2) + B(x^2 - x + 1) + (Cx + D)(x^2 - 4x + 4)$
$\qquad = (A + C)x^3 + (-3A + B - 4C + D)x^2 + (3A - B + 4C - 4D)x - 2A + B + 4D$

We have already $B = -3$, so equating coefficients of like terms,

$0 = A + C$

$-1 = -3A - 3 - 4C + D$

$1 = 3A + 3 + 4C - 4D$

$-7 = -2A - 3 + 4D$

Since $C = -A$, we can write

$-1 = -3A - 3 + 4A + 4D$

$1 = 3A + 3 - 4A - 4D$

$-7 = -2A - 3 + 4D$

So $D = 0$ (adding the first equations), $A = 2$, $C = -2$.

Hence $\dfrac{-x^2+x-7}{x^4-5x^3+9x^2-8x+4} = \dfrac{2}{x-2} - \dfrac{3}{(x-2)^2} - \dfrac{2x}{x^2-x+1}$

29.   First we divide to obtain a polynomial plus a proper fraction.

$$
\begin{array}{r}
x + 2 \\
4x^4 + 4x^3 - 5x^2 + 5x - 2 \overline{\smash{\big)}\, 4x^5 + 12x^4 - x^3 + 7x^2 - 4x + 2} \\
\underline{4x^5 + 4x^4 - 5x^3 + 5x^2 - 2x} \\
8x^4 + 4x^3 + 2x^2 - 2x + 2 \\
\underline{8x^4 + 8x^3 - 10x^2 + 10x - 4} \\
-4x^3 + 12x^2 - 12x + 6
\end{array}
$$

Now we must decompose $\dfrac{-4x^3+12x^2-12x+6}{4x^4+4x^3-5x^2+5x-2}$, starting by factoring $4x^4 + 4x^3 - 5x^2 + 5x - 2$.

Possible rational zeros are $\pm 1, \pm 2, \pm\dfrac{1}{2}, \pm\dfrac{1}{4}$. We form a synthetic division table:

	4	4	−5	5	−2	
1	4	8	3	8	6	1 is an upper bound, eliminating 2
−1	4	0	−5	10	−12	
−2	4	−4	3	−1	0	−2 is a zero

We investigate $4x^3 - 4x^2 + 3x - 1$; the only remaining rational zeros are $\pm\dfrac{1}{2}, \pm\dfrac{1}{4}$. We form a synthetic division table:

	4	−4	3	−1
$\frac{1}{2}$	4	−2	2	0

So $4x^4 + 4x^3 - 5x^2 + 5x - 2 = (x+2)\left(x-\dfrac{1}{2}\right)(4x^2 - 2x + 2) = (x+2)\left(x-\dfrac{1}{2}\right)2(2x^2 - x + 1)$

$\qquad\qquad = (x+2)(2x-1)(2x^2 - x + 1)$

$2x^2 - x + 1$ cannot be factored further in the real numbers, so we write:

$$\frac{-4x^3+12x^2-12x+6}{4x^4+4x^3-5x^2+5x-2} = \frac{A}{x+2} + \frac{B}{2x-1} + \frac{Cx+D}{2x^2-x+1}$$

$$= \frac{A(2x-1)(2x^2-x+1)+B(x+2)(2x^2-x+1)+(Cx+D)(x+2)(2x-1)}{(x+2)(2x-1)(2x^2-x+1)}$$

Thus, for all x

$-4x^3 + 12x^2 - 12x + 6 = A(2x-1)(2x^2-x+1) + B(x+2)(2x^2-x+1) + (Cx+D)(x+2)(2x-1)$

If $x = -2$

$$-4(-2)^3 + 12(-2)^2 - 12(-2) + 6 = A(-5)[2(-2)^2 - (-2) + 1]$$
$$32 + 48 + 24 + 6 = -55A$$
$$110 = -55A$$
$$A = -2$$

If $x = \dfrac{1}{2}$

$$-4\left(\frac{1}{2}\right)^3 + 12\left(\frac{1}{2}\right)^2 - 12\left(\frac{1}{2}\right) + 6 = B\left(\frac{5}{2}\right)\left[2\left(\frac{1}{2}\right)^2 - \frac{1}{2} + 1\right]$$

$$-\frac{1}{2} + 3 - 6 + 6 = B\left(\frac{5}{2}\right)(1)$$

$$B = 1$$

If $x = 0$
$$6 = A(-1)(1) + B(2)(1) + D(2)(-1)$$
$$6 = -A + 2B - 2D$$
$$6 = 2 + 2 - 2D$$
$$D = -1$$

If $x = 1$ $-4 + 12 - 12 + 6 = A(1)(2) + B(3)(2) + (C+D)(3)(1)$
$$2 = 2A + 6B + 3C + 3D = -4 + 6 + 3C - 3$$
$$C = 1$$

So $\dfrac{4x^5 + 12x^4 - x^3 + 7x^2 - 4x + 2}{4x^4 + 4x^3 - 5x^2 + 5x - 2} = x + 2 - \dfrac{2}{x+2} + \dfrac{1}{2x-1} + \dfrac{x-1}{2x^2-x+1}$.

Section B-3

1. Note that if you eliminate the parameter from the parametric equations by substituting x for t^2 in $y = t^2 - 2$, the result is the equation $y = x - 2$. Since $x = t^2$, x must be non-negative. Thus, the graph of the parametric equations will consist only of a ray, the portion of the line $y = x - 2$ for $x \geq 0$.

3. Construct a table and graph.

t	0	1	2	3	−1	−2	−3
x	0	−1	−2	−3	1	2	3
y	−2	0	2	4	−4	−6	−8

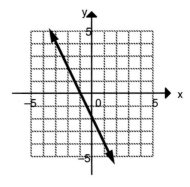

To eliminate the parameter t we solve
$x = -t$ for t to obtain $t = -x$
Then we substitute the expression for t into
$y = 2t - 2$ to obtain
$y = 2(-x) - 2$
$y = -2x - 2$
This is the equation of a straight line.

5. Construct a table and graph.

t	0	1	2	3	−2	−3	
x	0	−1	−4	−9	−4	−9	Note: $x \le 0$
y	−2	0	6	16	6	16	

To eliminate the parameter t we solve
$x = -t^2$ for t^2 (we do not need t) to obtain $t^2 = -x$
Then we substitute the expression for t^2 into
$y = 2t^2 - 2$ to obtain
$y = 2(-x) - 2$
$y = -2x - 2$
This is the equation of a straight line. However, since $x = -t^2$, x is restricted so that $x \le 0$. Therefore the equation of the curve is actually $y = -2x - 2$, $x \le 0$
This is the equation of a ray (part of a straight line).

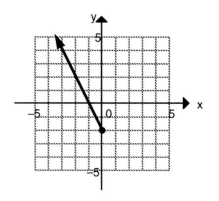

7. Construct a table and graph.

t	0	1	2	3	−1	−2	−3
x	0	3	6	9	−3	−6	−9
y	0	−2	−4	−6	2	4	6

To eliminate the parameter t we solve

$x = 3t$ for t to obtain $t = \dfrac{x}{3}$

Then we substitute the expression for t into
$y = -2t$ to obtain

$$y = -2\left(\frac{x}{3}\right)$$

$$y = -\frac{2}{3}x$$

This is the equation of a straight line.

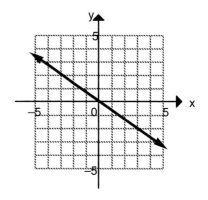

9. Construct a table of values and graph.

t	0	1	2	3	−1	−2	−3
x	0	$\dfrac{1}{4}$	1	$\dfrac{9}{4}$	$\dfrac{1}{4}$	1	$\dfrac{9}{4}$
y	0	1	2	3	−1	−2	−3

To eliminate the parameter t we substitute $t = y$ (from $y = t$) into the expression for x to obtain

$$x = \frac{1}{4}y^2$$
$$y^2 = 4x$$

This is the equation of a parabola.

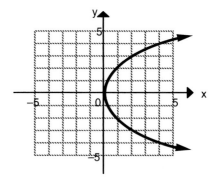

11. Construct a table of values and graph.

t	0	1	2	3	-1	-2	-3
x	0	$\dfrac{1}{4}$	4	$\dfrac{81}{4}$	$\dfrac{1}{4}$	4	$\dfrac{81}{4}$
y	0	1	4	9	1	4	9

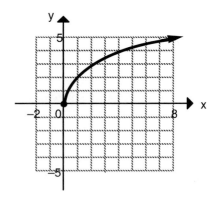

To eliminate the parameter we substitute $t^2 = y$ (from $y = t^2$) into the expression for x to obtain

$$x = \frac{1}{4} t^4$$

$$x = \frac{1}{4} (t^2)^2$$

$$x = \frac{1}{4} y^2$$

$$y^2 = 4x$$

This is the equation of a parabola. However, since $y = t^2$, y is restricted to nonnegative values only. Hence the equation of the curve is actually $y^2 = 4x$, $y \geq 0$
This is the equation of the upper half of a parabola.

13. We eliminate the parameter t as follows:

$$x = t - 2$$
$$x + 2 = t$$

Substituting this expression for t into the expression for y, we obtain
$$y = 4 - 2t$$
$$y = 4 - 2(x + 2)$$
$$y = 4 - 2x - 4$$
$$y = -2x$$
This is the equation of a line.

15. We eliminate the parameter t as follows:

Solve $x = t - 1$ for t to obtain $t = x + 1$. Substitute the expression for t into $y = \sqrt{t}$ to obtain $y = \sqrt{x+1}$ or $y^2 = x + 1$, $y \geq 0$. Since t is restricted so that $t \geq 0$, we also have $x + 1 \geq 0$ or $x \geq -1$. This graph is a parabola with vertex at $(-1, 0)$, opening right. Since $y \geq 0$ only the upper half of the parabola is traced out.

17. We eliminate the parameter t as follows: Solve $x = \sqrt{t}$ for t to obtain $t = x^2$.

Substitute the expression for t into $y = 2\sqrt{16-t}$ to obtain

$$y = 2\sqrt{16-x^2} \quad \text{or}$$
$$y^2 = 4(16 - x^2)$$
$$y^2 = 64 - 4x^2$$
$$4x^2 + y^2 = 64$$
$$\frac{x^2}{16} + \frac{y^2}{64} = 1 \quad \text{(ellipse in standard form)}$$

Since $0 \leq t \leq 16$ and $x = \sqrt{t}$, it follows that $0 \leq x \leq 4$.
Since $0 \leq t \leq 16$ and $t = x^2$, it follows that $0 \leq x^2 \leq 16$, $0 \leq 16 - x^2 \leq 16$,
$0 \leq \sqrt{16-x^2} \leq 4$, and $0 \leq 2\sqrt{16-x^2} \leq 8$. Thus $0 \leq y \leq 8$.

The graph of $\dfrac{x^2}{16} + \dfrac{y^2}{64} = 1$, $0 \leq x \leq 4$ and $0 \leq y \leq 8$, is the portion of an ellipse lying in the first quadrant.

19. We eliminate the parameter t as follows:
Solve $x = -\sqrt{t+1}$ for t to obtain

$$x^2 = t + 1$$
$$t = x^2 - 1$$

Substitute the expression for t into $y = -\sqrt{t-1}$ to obtain

$$y = -\sqrt{x^2 - 1 - 1}$$
$$y = -\sqrt{x^2 - 2}$$
$$y^2 = x^2 - 2$$
$$x^2 - y^2 = 2 \text{ (hyperbola)}$$

Since $t \geq 1$ it follows that $t + 1 \geq 2$, $\sqrt{t+1} \geq \sqrt{2}$ and $x = -\sqrt{t+1} \leq -\sqrt{2}$.

Also it follows that $t - 1 \geq 0$, $\sqrt{t-1} \geq 0$, and $y = -\sqrt{t-1} \leq 0$.

The graph of $x^2 - y^2 = 2$, $x \leq -\sqrt{2}$ and $y \leq 0$, is the portion of a hyperbola lying in the third quadrant.

21. If $A \neq 0$, $C = 0$, and $E \neq 0$, write $Ax^2 + Dx + Ey + F = 0$

There are many possible parametric equations for this curve. A simple approach is to set $x = t$ and solve for y in terms of t.

$$At^2 + Dt + Ey + F = 0$$
$$At^2 + Dt + F = -Ey$$
$$\frac{At^2 + Dt + F}{-E} = y$$

Then $x = t$, $y = \dfrac{At^2 + Dt + F}{-E}$, $-\infty < t < \infty$, are parametric equations for this curve. The curve is a parabola.

23. We eliminate the parameter t as follows:

Square the expressions for x and y.

$$x^2 = t^2 + 1 \quad y^2 = t^2 + 9$$

Solve the first equation for t^2 and substitute the result into the second equation.

$$t^2 = x^2 - 1$$
$$y^2 = x^2 - 1 + 9$$
$$y^2 = x^2 + 8$$
$$y^2 - x^2 = 8$$

This is the equation of a hyperbola.

Since $t^2 \geq 0$, $t^2 + 1 \geq 1$, $\sqrt{t^2 + 1} \geq 1$. It follows that $x \geq 1$.

Since $t^2 \geq 0$, $t^2 + 9 \geq 9$, $\sqrt{t^2 + 9} \geq 3$. It follows that $y \geq 3$.

The curve is the part of the hyperbola $y^2 - x^2 = 8$ for $x \geq 1$ and $y \geq 3$.

25. We eliminate the parameter t as follows:

Square the expressions for x and y.

$$x^2 = \frac{4}{t^2 + 1} \qquad y^2 = \frac{4t^2}{t^2 + 1}$$

$$x^2 + y^2 = \frac{4}{t^2 + 1} + \frac{4t^2}{t^2 + 1} = \frac{4 + 4t^2}{t^2 + 1} = \frac{4(1 + t^2)}{t^2 + 1}$$

$$x^2 + y^2 = 4$$

This is the equation of a circle.

Since $t^2 \geq 0$, $t^2 + 1 \geq 1$, $\sqrt{t^2 + 1} \geq 1$, $0 < \dfrac{1}{\sqrt{t^2 + 1}} \leq 1$, $0 < \dfrac{2}{\sqrt{t^2 + 1}} \leq 2$.

It follows that $0 < x \leq 2$. Therefore $0 < x^2 \leq 4$, $0 > -x^2 \geq -4$, $4 > 4 - x^2 \geq 0$,

$2 > \sqrt{4 - x^2} \geq 0$, $-2 < -\sqrt{4 - x^2} \leq 0$. Since $y = \pm\sqrt{4 - x^2}$ on the circle $x^2 + y^2 = 4$, it follows that $-2 < y < 2$

(since $x \neq 0$). Thus the curve is the portion of the circle $x^2 + y^2 = 4$ for which $0 < x \leq 2$, $-2 < y < 2$. This is the right-hand semicircle, excluding the points $(0, \pm 2)$.

27. We eliminate the parameter t as follows: First note that since $x = \dfrac{8}{t^2 + 4}$,

$(t^2 + 4)x = 8$ or $t^2 + 4 = \dfrac{8}{x}$. Therefore x cannot be 0. Now square the expressions for x and y.

$$x^2 = \frac{64}{(t^2 + 4)^2}$$

$$y^2 = \frac{16t^2}{(t^2 + 4)^2}$$

$$x^2 + y^2 = \frac{64}{(t^2 + 4)^2} + \frac{16t^2}{(t^2 + 4)^2} = \frac{64 + 16t^2}{(t^2 + 4)^2} = \frac{16(4 + t^2)}{(t^2 + 4)^2} = \frac{16}{t^2 + 4}$$

Since $x = \dfrac{8}{t^2 + 4}$, $2x = \dfrac{16}{t^2 + 4}$, so $x^2 + y^2 = 2x$ $x \neq 0$

This is the equation of a circle. Completing the square we see
$$x^2 - 2x + y^2 = 0$$
$$x^2 - 2x + 1 + y^2 = 1$$
$$(x - 1)^2 + y^2 = 1, x \neq 0$$
Hence the circle has center $(1, 0)$ and radius 1. The origin is not part of the curve since x cannot equal zero, hence there is a hole in the graph there.

29. Here are the graphs in a squared viewing window (shown together with the line $y = x$).
(A) The graphs are reflections of each other in the line $y = x$.
(B) Since $t = x_1, y_1 = e^{x_1}$.

Since $t = y_2, x_2 = e^{y_2}, y_2 = \ln x_2$.

The functions are inverse functions of each other.

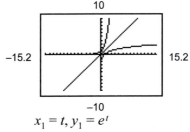

$$x_1 = t, y_1 = e^t$$
$$x_2 = e^t, y_2 = t$$

31. At the instant the supplies are dropped, the vertical speed is 0, the horizontal speed is 125 meters per second, and the altitude is 1,000 meters. Substitute these values into
$$x = h_0 t$$
$$y = a_0 + v_0 t - 4.9t^2$$
to obtain
$$x = 125t$$
$$y = 1000 - 4.9t^2$$
The supplies strike the ground when $y = 0$. Solving, we have
$$y = 0 = 1{,}000 - 4.9t^2$$
$$4.9t^2 = 1{,}000$$
$$t = \sqrt{\frac{1{,}000}{4.9}} \approx \frac{100}{7} \text{ sec.}$$

Substituting, we have $x = 125 \times \dfrac{100}{7} \approx 1{,}786$ meters.